White Zombie

CONTRIBUTIONS TO ZOMBIE STUDIES

White Zombie: Anatomy of a Horror Film. Gary D. Rhodes. 2001

The Zombie Movie Encyclopedia. Peter Dendle. 2001

*American Zombie Gothic: The Rise and Fall (and Rise)
of the Walking Dead in Popular Culture.* Kyle William Bishop. 2010

*Back from the Dead: Remakes of the Romero
Zombie Films as Markers of Their Times.* Kevin J. Wetmore, Jr. 2011

*Generation Zombie: Essays on the Living Dead
in Modern Culture.* Edited by Stephanie Boluk and Wylie Lenz. 2011

*Race, Oppression and the Zombie: Essays on Cross-Cultural Appropriations
of the Caribbean Tradition.* Edited by Christopher M. Moreman
and Cory James Rushton. 2011

Zombies Are Us: Essays on the Humanity of the Walking Dead.
Edited by Christopher M. Moreman and Cory James Rushton. 2011

The Zombie Movie Encyclopedia, Volume 2: 2000–2010. Peter Dendle. 2012

Great Zombies in History. Edited by Joe Sergi. 2013 (graphic novel)

Unraveling Resident Evil*: Essays on the Complex Universe
of the Games and Films.* Edited by Nadine Farghaly. 2014

"We're All Infected": Essays on AMC's The Walking Dead
and the Fate of the Human. Edited by Dawn Keetley. 2014

Zombies and Sexuality: Essays on Desire and the Walking Dead.
Edited by Shaka McGlotten and Steve Jones. 2014

White Zombie
Anatomy of a Horror Film

GARY D. RHODES

FOREWORD BY GEORGE E. TURNER

CONTRIBUTIONS TO ZOMBIE STUDIES

McFarland & Company, Inc., Publishers
Jefferson, North Carolina

"I hope this book by Gary Rhodes serves to enhance the memory of my dear husband Victor Hugo Halperin and increase the gratitude film fans feel for his many talents. I am very thankful that Gary has spent so much time researching and writing such a splendid book."—Venita H. Halperin, the director's second wife.

ALSO BY GARY D. RHODES

Lugosi: His Life in Films, on Stage, and in the Hearts of Horror Lovers (McFarland, 1997)

Frontispiece: **Zombie Chauvin (Frederick Peters) carries the young heroine Madeline (Madge Bellamy) through the Castle of theLiving Dead—*White Zombie* (courtesy of Leonard J. Kohl).**

The present work is a reprint of the library bound edition of White Zombie: Anatomy of a Horror Film, *first published in 2001 by McFarland.*

LIBRARY OF CONGRESS CATALOGUING-IN-PUBLICATION DATA

Rhodes, Gary D.
   White zombie : anatomy of a horror film / Gary D. Rhodes ;
foreword by George E. Turner.
     p. cm. — (Contributions to Zombie Studies)
    Includes index.

    ISBN-13: 978-0-7864-2762-8
    softcover : 50# alkaline paper ∞

    1. White zombie (Motion picture)   I. Title.
PN1997.W5339R49 2006
791.43'72—dc21   2001031255

BRITISH LIBRARY CATALOGUING DATA ARE AVAILABLE

Printed in the United States of America

On the cover: Color poster for the film *White Zombie*

McFarland & Company, Inc., Publishers
  Box 611, Jefferson, North Carolina 28640
   www.mcfarlandpub.com

For Richard Sheffield,
my godfather, my friend, my inspiration

Table of Contents

Foreword

by George E. Turner

White Zombie is an old friend. As a cornfed kid I saw it during its initial release, in 1932, at the Rex Theatre in Amarillo, Texas. I had already seen *Frankenstein* and *Dr. Jekyll and Mr. Hyde* a short time earlier and felt that the zombie picture was almost as good as these classics and at least as scary. One difference was that *White Zombie*, despite its daringly different theme, looked and sounded old fashioned by comparison. It seemed even more so during the next few months as I watched several sophisticated horror yarns made by RKO-Radio: *Thirteen Women*, *The Most Dangerous Game*, and *Secrets of the French Police*. In truth, the acting in *White Zombie* is in a definite silent picture mode. This fact is intensified by the musical score, which was assembled in large part from silent picture cue sheets. Naturally, the critics tore it apart. I thought they were nuts.

My next look at *White Zombie* was in 1938, when it reappeared at Los Angeles' lamented Regina Theatre, whose manager had introduced periodic "Triple Spook Shows" which were heavily attended by college and high school students. It was a crisp nitrate print on Eastman's Aquagreen Colortone stock (following the lead of Universal's successful reissues of *Frankenstein* and *Dracula*) and was teamed with *Secrets of the French Police* and a green-tinted print of *The Most Dangerous Game* (temporarily retitled *Skull Island*), an all–1932 retrospective.

Film acting had become more naturalistic in style during the ensuing six years, although the difference was only slightly noticeable in the two RKO pictures, which had the further advantage of being scored in a romantic-modern style by Max Steiner. The capacity audience watched these two in respectful attention. In this company, *White Zombie*—with its declamatory speeches and ancient music cues—seemed as outmoded as Madge Bellamy's cupid's-bow lip makeup and rococo underthings.

Every line of dialogue drew howls and hoots from the rowdier members of the audience. Before long they were repeating Lugosi's lines loudly, exaggerating his Hungarian accent. It was a ghastly experience for a guy who loved the show. A later trip to the Regina proved futile; the same rubes were back, but by this time they had memorized Lugosi's lines and were reciting them in synch with the actor! The same thing happened the following year when *White Zombie* returned with Columbia's *The Black Room* and *Behind the Mask*.

One thing is certain about *White Zombie*; it will always be a subject for controversy. Many lovers of classic movies agree with what many critics said in the beginning, that this is a silly, badly played example of penny-dreadful filmmaking. Others of us take an opposing view, finding in it romantic and poetic qualities seldom encountered in motion pictures.

Any attempt to find favorable contemporary reviews in the national media would be an exercise in futility. *Time*, for example, commented that Lugosi resembled "a comic imbecile," called Johnny Harron "slack jawed," and cracked that the acting of everybody involved suggested there may be good reason to believe in zombies. The major critics had been kind to *Dracula*, *Frankenstein*, and *Dr. Jekyll and Mr. Hyde* during the 1931-32 season, but by the summer of 1932 the honeymoon had ended and they tended to toss "horror" pictures into the same garbage bin into which they had already dumped westerns, slapstick comedies, and gangster films.

Now the worm has turned, so to speak. The picture that was greeted so scornfully (read that *snottily*) by the intelligentsia of the thirties is regarded highly by many (but not all) of their successors. This evolution began about forty years ago when several hardy film historians including William K. Everson, Edward Connor, and

1

Though this image is of an advertisement in Hobbs, New Mexico, circa 1938, it is reminiscent of ads in Amarillo, Texas, that first caught George E. Turner's eye. (Courtesy of Lynn Naron.)

Carlos Clarens championed the picture in print. I remember it well because one critic referred to several writers (including this one) as idiots for venturing to suggest that *White Zombie* possessed some merit. The *White Zombie* chapter in Everson's 1974 book, *Classics of the Horror*

Film, is a landmark of insightful reporting. Forrest Ackerman, Arthur Lennig, and others added their support. Mike Price and I explored the film in some depth in our 1979 tome *Forgotten Horrors* and plunged a bit deeper in *The Cinema of Mystery, Romance and Terror* (1989).

White Zombie *"will always be a subject for controversy,"* writes George E. Turner.

The truth is that we see these films differently now. The acting in *all* early talkies is sufficiently remote from the near-realism of today's movies as to minimize whatever differences might have been noticeable in the thirties. In fact, one reason why *White Zombie* is so charming is that Garnett Weston's fairy-tale storyline is served perfectly by dialogue, histrionics, and musical treatment of a bygone day.

There are so many things about *White Zombie* to cherish. Two players in particular are magnificent: Bela Lugosi and Robert Frazer. Lugosi appears leaner and more wolfish than in any of his other pictures, including *Dracula*. His performance, admittedly over the top, is tailored to the character of "a man called Murder" and is perfectly within context. His delivery, with its distinctive phrasings and stage-trained sonority, is almost as hypnotic as the close-ups of his eyes. He offers no leavening of sympathy in his portrayal of a thoroughly amoral, hundred percent villain who offers zombie-in-the-making Frazer a toast, "To the future, monsieur," and later snorts

derisively as his half-paralyzed victim fumbles a glass of wine. Frazer's sensitive features and body English eloquently reflect the Byronic image of Gothic fiction. His reaction of revulsion verging on panic is unforgettable in a scene wherein a zombie touches his arm, and again as Lugosi offers him a suggestion so unholy that it can only be whispered.

The rented sets, most of them redecorated artifacts from *The Cat and the Canary, Dracula, Frankenstein, The Hunchback of Notre Dame, My Pal, the King,* and other past Universal epics, in no way reflect the small budget art director Ralph Berger had to work with. By moving the set elements around and filling in some spaces with Conrad Tritschler's fine glass paintings, Berger gave a low-budget picture epic scope. The cinematography of Arthur Martinelli, ASC makes the most of the cavernous spaces of the Castle of the Living Dead, as well as the Lugosi grimaces and Madge Bellamy's wonderful eyes. Director Victor Halperin, although he seemed incapable of adjusting his direction of actors to the demands of the new age of talking pictures, shows in this—his one masterpiece—a surer instinct than any of his contemporaries for dramatically marrying images to sound. Not until the advent of Val Lewton in the mid-forties do we encounter his equal at using sound to create audience suspense and terror.

I felt good about being one of the writers who tried to tell others that the critically despised *White Zombie* was actually an unjustly denigrated piece of truly distinctive—even great—cinema. I doubt, however, that any of us suspected we would one day hold in our hands this tasteful book devoted entirely to the Poverty Row stepchild of United Artists' otherwise high-toned 1932 programme. How sweet it is!

George E. Turner†
Hollywood, 1996

---

†*My friend George died during the summer of 1999. Those involved in film studies will mourn his loss for years to come.* —*G.D.R.*

Introduction

The Kingdom of the Dead is the only one safe from all invasion. Those who enter are humble and obedient. There are no coups or Palace Revolutions in the Kingdom of the Dead.
   —Garnett Weston, screenwriter of *White Zombie*

If Garnett Weston believed in obedient and humble entrances to the Kingdom of the Dead, he would hardly have ascribed the same comment to those critics of the 1932 horror film *White Zombie*, critics who have over the decades entered the cinematic land of the living dead with skepticism, truculence, and at times even disgust. Even among horror films, *White Zombie* has been regularly berated by many film reviewers and some of the few scholars who have passed judgment on it. In short, its kingdom has suffered many vituperative invasions.

A very small vanguard of horror film enthusiasts and scholars (including my friend, the late film historian William K. Everson) did attempt to promote *White Zombie*'s artistic merits during the 1960s and 1970s, but those who heard their praise were generally horror film fans already eager to enjoy any Bela Lugosi film of the 1930s. I happily admit being in that category even years before actually seeing *White Zombie*.

My first viewing of the film quickly led to innumerable repeats. As I have moved into more academic pursuits of film studies, my respect for *White Zombie* has continued to grow. Aside from an initial excitement over Lugosi's performance and the film's very moody, atmospheric treatment of zombies, I have come to respect *White Zombie*'s aesthetic worth on many other levels. In addition to its pictorial design and imagery, I have developed an appreciation of the film's highly innovative cinematic technique. Indeed, as this text will argue, *White Zombie* works in such unique ways as to be an anomaly among horror movies and indeed Hollywood cinema in general.

Despite my praise, however, I equally acknowledge *White Zombie*'s many faults, and hardly make a request for its apotheosis. But I do suggest the film be studied and canonized as an important work of 1930s cinema, of independent filmmaking, and of the horror film genre. To that end, some discussions herein offer highly detailed theoretical observations of the film, while others pursue historical data with enthusiasm. Indeed, I spent several weeks trying to determine which actress (Annette Stone or Velma Gresham) played which maid in the film; innumerable phone calls finally determined which actress's name went with which face on the screen. This book's goal is to pursue an exhaustive historical account of the film within a theoretical framework which decodes meaning from the empirical data gathered; I believe this to be the most worthwhile goal of modern film studies.

Yet this goal creates a conundrum for my work with *White Zombie*. The topics of theoretical discourse are usually of little interest to most aficionados of the horror film, who often view such perspectives as overly polemical in their findings and overly academic in their language and form; indeed, the very word "academic" carries pejorative connotations for some such readers. Instead, their drive is usually towards empirical data: how much a film cost to make, how much a given actor was paid, how many anecdotes exist regarding a film's production, how many rarely seen photographs are discovered and published. Worthwhile pursuits I readily encourage and embrace—as the level of detail in this book will all too readily show—but pursuits which taken alone obfuscate the more important large questions to be asked and answered.

At the same time, those scholars who study film in the academy have generally devoted little attention to the horror genre, and certainly almost none to *White Zombie*. Given its film director's virtual anonymity among scholars, its actors' theatrical histrionics, its rather bizarre subject matter, and of course its connection to horror—all of these become reasons why the film has been overlooked by academics. The rubric of academic film studies has often been to discard lesser-known films and less-respectable genres (into which horror seemingly falls) with ease. The result might well suggest that, however much this text will illustrate why *White Zombie* deserves at least a level of recognition among scholars, many of them will likely not examine the present study for the same reasons they would not examine the film itself.

Ultimately, therefore, this book may well be in a situation not dissimilar to *White Zombie*'s tenuous critical history. And that is where I feel a deep kinship with my chosen film. Much of my own work in film studies seems to exist in a borderland between academic acceptance (partially given my topics of choice) and the anecdotal kind of historical commentary which satiates most horror movie buffs. As a result, this text taken as a whole may please few readers of standard horror film history and may be overlooked automatically by those film scholars who offer little respect for horror films. Nonetheless, the anatomy of the horror film must be seen to be analyzed.

However, despite screenwriter Garnett Weston's comment that no revolutions occur in the palace of the Kingdom of the Dead, I have hope that my re-examination of *White Zombie* will cause just that: a revolution in which both camps of previously described readers merge to create a new historical-theoretical territory while clinging to the old, thus overcoming the seemingly unstoppable inertia of film studies. The debacle of *White Zombie* may well open the floodgates to a new understanding of an old film; to thoughtful exegesis rather than mindless excoriation.

More generally, we can consider the word "anatomy" in this book's title as an important reason why this text needs to exist. Many books and many essay collections have been published on the topic of a single film, but I do not think most of them flesh out their subjects with the level of detail needed to prove their claims. Though it would be possible to charge that this book is overly detailed, I believe that the level of thorough and credible data offers necessary and critical evidence. Conclusions are *reached*; they are not based on hasty generalizations and speculations. And they are reached through an inquiry not based on the template of any prior text. To me, that distinguishes this book from many others of its kind and allows it to truly be an anatomy of its subject. As a result, perhaps the current text on *White Zombie* can serve as a model of one way to study the life of a film.

Though it is important to appreciate the anatomy of

White Zombie in a gestalt fashion, I think it is critical to study the parts that contribute to the whole. Chapter One presents an exhaustive reading of *White Zombie*, examining it as a fairy tale, a horror film, and an example of the fantastic. The reading also traces the pantextual origins of *White Zombie*'s narrative, drawing on fiction (e.g., *Faust, Trilby*), folklore and science (e.g., evil eye mythology, mesmerism, somnambulism), prior films (e.g., *Der müde Tod, Svengali*), nonfiction literature (e.g., *The Magic Island*), and U.S. culture (e.g., race relations, labor concerns). By reconstructing these sources and analogues, Chapter One also reveals narrative and thematic devices regarding the characters in *White Zombie* and their motivations, many of which are sexually transgressive.

Chapter One also offers a lengthy analysis of the film's pictorial imagery, its acting styles, its use of sound, music, and silence, as well as its cinematic technique. The latter opens the door to an extensive exploration of spectatorship as constructed by *White Zombie*'s unique, albeit subtle, inclusion of what I have termed the *spectator-as-character*. In addition to surveying the film as a whole, this section makes a shot-by-shot analysis of one of *White Zombie*'s key scenes, thus amplifying the construction and the affects/effects of the *spectator-as-character*.

Subsequent chapters attempt to cover *White Zombie* chronologically, surveying its origins, preproduction, production, postproduction, and later influences. Chapter Two discusses the relevant history of Haiti, voodoo, and zombies, beginning with a brief description of U.S.-Haitian relations prior to *White Zombie*'s 1932 production. In addition, it surveys the vast array of nonfiction books and essays on voodoo printed in the English language prior to 1932, as well as the equally expansive vistas of fiction on the same subject—ranging from novels and short stories to poems and plays. Chapter Two also details the early life and work of William B. Seabrook, author of *The Magic Island*, a 1929 book from which *White Zombie* drew its title creature. That book will be shown as a line of demarcation between prior sources on voodoo and zombies and those which would follow, specifically *White Zombie*. The discussion then concludes with an examination of the 1932 play *Zombie*, the most immediate textual descendant of *The Magic Island* and a major precursor to *White Zombie*. Taken as a whole, Chapter Two presents an intellectual history, a chain of successive texts with sometimes repeated, sometimes re-evaluated information and arguments, leading up to the construction of *White Zombie* and responsible for sculpting the mind-set of the film's 1932 viewers.

To offer an in-depth exploration of *White Zombie*'s production, Chapter Three includes a cross-section of information, such as interviews with its stars and director Victor Halperin, relevant facts from 1932 film indus-

From the first time I saw images of White Zombie *in a book on horror films, I became forever fascinated with it.*

try trade publications, and an overview of the film's original preview and its many distribution troubles. In order to focus the chapter's content, *White Zombie* is contextualized within the independent film industry of the 1930s, a category in which it belongs.

Continuing in a chronological mode of analysis, Chapter Four inquires into the next stage of *White Zombie*'s history, its first theatrical release. The chapter helps to determine not just the film's box-office success, but also specific audience responses to the picture. Along with comparing *White Zombie*'s success to that of prior films in the 1930s horror cycle, the chapter investigates various publicity materials and exploitation techniques used to promote the film. In addition, the chapter differentiates and analyzes the plethora of viewer responses to the film. Religion, age, ethnicity, and gender are all discussed, but the most exhaustive aspect of the study is a

geographical one. *White Zombie*'s theatrical run in many major U.S. cities is explored at length, including specific examples of its audience reception. The result of the investigation, as well as the chapter as a whole, suggests *White Zombie* elicited a wide range of responses from critics and especially moviegoers. Some laughed, some shuddered, some shrugged their shoulders. Audiences hardly gave block responses of any kind, let alone the sort of group fear that might be expected from a horror film.

In addition to acting as an autonomous study, Chapter Four also works in tandem with Section II of Chapter One in building an analysis of *White Zombie*'s spectatorship, particularly an analysis of the theoretical subject (Chapter One), the historical viewer (Chapter Four), and—if the two chapters are considered together—the spectator who emerges when the subject and viewer meet.

Chapter Five gauges *White Zombie*'s influence on the U.S. culture of the 1930s, specifically its impact on subsequent voodoo and zombie-related books, articles, films, and plays. In addition, it describes the film's immediate effect on the career of director Victor Halperin and his brother, producer Edward Halperin. After a brief stay at a major studio, they returned to independent filmmaking, and eventually to the subject of zombies. However much their *White Zombie* influenced the 1930s, its financiers attempted to make a legal claim on the very word "zombie" and block the Halperins from releasing another film on that topic. Zombies had become marketable, and as a result those same financiers tried to wrest them back from U.S. culture, to control them as something akin to a trademark.

Similarly, Chapter Six illustrates *White Zombie*'s cultural impact, examining how the film resonates in popular expression decades after the 1930s. The discussion ranges from *White Zombie* references in other, more recent films, to more extended tributes paid to the movie in noncinematic forums. The latter part of the discussion details model kits, comic books, and rock bands—all of which show an appreciation of the film and illustrate its effect on more modern moviegoers.

Yet in addition to surveying models and comics of recent years, it is equally important to ask, "Which *White Zombie* should we view in the modern era?" Chapter Seven examines the two major attempts to restore *White Zombie*, a film which has suffered visually and aurally through editing, duping, and poor handling. These stories yield not only steps toward an answer to the aforementioned question, but they also open an important discussion on the ethical and aesthetic concerns behind film restoration.

Chapter Eight includes critiques of *White Zombie* from numerous reviewers and film historians; some have been in print before, while others were penned especially for this book. Together, they show that—while a rising tide of voices favor the film—its position critically is still tenuous. However much *White Zombie*'s modern reception is different from its reception in 1932, in one way it is still the same: the film is controversial. In many respects, the lack of critical analysis quoted from academic sources in this chapter is itself important; the absence of scholarly work on the subject points to its marginalization among academics.

In addition to the many reviews collected in Chapter Eight, a few print sources on the film offer necessary insight, analysis, and information. Chapter Nine gives an annotated bibliography of those books and articles which provide important readings of *White Zombie*. While most are mentioned elsewhere within this text, they should be read *in toto* to best appreciate the insight they bring to the subject.

Lastly (aside from voluminous appendices), Chapter Ten offers the first printed biography of director Victor Halperin, featuring an in-depth discussion of his life and career. Until this volume, he was a particularly shadowy figure, having blazed an important trail of independent filmmaking in the 1930s and then, seemingly, disappeared from Hollywood in the 1940s. Such esteemed reference books as Ephraim Katz's *The Film Encyclopedia* have been unable to publish even his date of death, let alone paint a picture of his life. Thanks to his widow, Venita Halperin, Victor's own papers were made available and used in this chapter to flesh out an in-depth biography.

Chapter Ten also includes a critique of Halperin's filmmaking style, which attempts to reconcile the moments of genius that coexist in his films with lengthy segments of visual plainness, poor acting, and narrative lapses. A major question readers might raise, especially after reading Chapter One, is whether I claim Victor Halperin was responsible (consciously or otherwise) for the many levels of meaning and many background sources that I discern in *White Zombie*. Overall, I would answer no. But what aesthetic and intellectual choices can we attribute to Halperin in *White Zombie* and in his body of work in general? My discussion in Chapter Ten addresses this question through the lens of auteurism, and will act in the end hopefully as an assessment of both Halperin's work and notions of auteurism.

As the breadth of knowledge in the aforementioned chapters probably suggest, *White Zombie* for me has almost reached the proportions of an obsession. For years, I saw photos from the film in magazines like *Famous Monsters* and books like *The Films of Bela Lugosi*, and was fascinated by the Lugosi makeup. I was finally able to see excerpts from *White Zombie* in an oft-repeated PBS horror film documentary called *The Horror of It All*. Just to see the *White Zombie* clips repeatedly, I tried to catch every one of the documentary's broadcasts. After seeing the full-length film on Christmas Day of 1985, I began a regimen of repeat screenings to the degree I almost memorized its dialogue. My extreme fascination meant that my own Lugosi newsletter—*The World of Bela Lugosi*—devoted an entire issue to *White Zombie* in December 1988.

Fortunately, my past history with *White Zombie* also allowed me to help on the 1994 Roan Group restoration of the film by providing historical information and liner notes for its laser disc release, later even recording an audio commentary for their 1999 DVD of the film. In addition to helping on documentary films like *Rivals* (Discovery Channel, on Karloff and Lugosi) and *Mysteries and Scandals* (E! Channel, on Lugosi) by providing commentary, and providing images and footage to *Biography*

(Arts and Entertainment, on Lugosi), I have been fortunate enough to produce and direct my own documentary film on the subject: *Lugosi: Hollywood's Dracula* (Cut to the Chase Productions, 1999). The opportunity gave me the chance to spotlight restored *White Zombie* footage within a discussion of the film between film historian George E. Turner and Lugosi friend F. Richard Sheffield. Even earlier, I was able to include a quick snippet of the film in a PBS documentary film of mine called *Majestic Dreams: The Coleman Theatre Beautiful* (Cut to the Chase, 1994). But while all these productions afforded tribute to *White Zombie*, none afforded a tribute in depth: another reason for this volume.

A large number of very kind and helpful people contributed toward the desired depth through various information and ideas which they shared. My deepest thanks to the following persons: Forrest J Ackerman, Ron Adams, Jason Asenap, Buddy Barnett, Joan Barney, Richard Bojarski, Tom Brannan, Bart Bush, Bill Chase, George Chastain, Peter Cheard, Spencer Christian, Jim Clatterbaugh, Michael Copner, Lee and Tracy Cox, Patrick Crain, Kristin Dewey, Jack Dowler, the late William K. Everson, Phillip Fortune, Fritz Frising/Vampires Unlimited, Richard Gordon, JoAnne Graham, Ollie Gray, Eugene C. Gresham, Gordon Guy, William N. Harrison, David H. Hogan, Roger Hurlburt, Paul Jensen, John Paul Jones, Eugene Kirschenbaum, Steve Kronenberg, Lana and Nicholas Krueger, "Larry the Wolf" of the Manimals, Frank Liquori, Wendy Lohman, Bela G. Lugosi, Bob Madison, Peter Michaels, Jean-Claude Michel, Mark A. Miller, Ted Newsom, Dick Norstorb, Jim Nye, Ted Okuda, Father Mike Paraniuk, Michael F. Price, Dr. Joanna Rapf, Robert Rees, Cary Roan, Toby Roan, Joe "Sorko" Schovitz, Bryan Senn, Sideshow Toys, David J. Skal, Anthony Slide, Stephen D. Smith, John Stell, Gary and Sue Svehla, Mathew Swanson, Brian Taves, Maurice Terenzio, the late Chris Todd, Mario Toland, John Ulakovic, Chris Veinof, Jon Wang, Aaron White, Glenn P. White, Devin Williams, John Wooley, and Rob Zombie.

Also, let me acknowledge the institutions and businesses that were instrumental in the completion of this work: Bizzell Library at the University of Oklahoma, Cinema Collectors, *Cult Movies* magazine, Dallas Public Library, *Filmfax* magazine, Janus Models, Lincoln Center for the Performing Arts, Lugosi Enterprises and the Bela Lugosi Estate, Margaret Herrick Library, *Monsterscene* magazine, *Monsters from the Vault* magazine, New Bedford Free Public Library, North Texas University, Tulsa City-County Library, the library at Texas Christian University, the University of Arkansas Library, the University of Central Oklahoma Library, and the film archive at the University of Wisconsin–Madison.

A round of applause must also be given for a number of film collectors who actively supported this project, freely offering items from their personal archives. Film collectors in general have a mixed reputation among film historians. Nonetheless, thanks to the efforts of early collectors, amazingly so many archival materials—posters, pressbooks, scripts, photos, 16mm and 35mm film, personal items belonging to stars and directors—still exist. Certainly these kinds of sources help inform history and those who learn from it—us, all of us.

But modern collectors of film memorabilia tend to drift into one of two categories, resulting in their being either the scourge or savior of history. Some believe, by the sheer fact that they physically possess certain historical items, that a part of history may be selfishly hidden from the world. They apparently believe such physical materials are a conduit, a spiritual medium, to the past. But in reality, by intentionally shielding materials from the purview of historians, this particular class of collector commits crimes against history and the historical process.

For example, for this book I contacted (through an intermediary) the owner of a Bela Lugosi scrapbook containing those clippings Lugosi himself saved from the press regarding *White Zombie*. Those articles and reviews would have given insight into what Lugosi thought of the film's press response (for instance, by an examination of those he intentionally kept and those he did not) and I hoped to include that information within these pages. I did not request copies of the scrapbook or the specific clippings; I did not want to borrow anything; I did not wish to infringe anyone's property rights. Rather, I just simply wanted a list—even if read over the phone or scratched down on a postcard or grocery sack—of the names of the articles and reviews, as the actual text of such materials I would have already uncovered anyway. The selfish, unwavering answer from this collector: "No." Very sad, not because this book could not be finished or because it will sell any more or fewer copies or because it will make any more or less money. The concealment of these clippings is sad because this book may well be the only work of any real length ever written and published on *White Zombie*, and that information cannot be included for the benefit of history—a true disservice to the future.

The paradigm shifts, though, to collectors who realize that there is an obligation to history and the historical process. It is with extreme gratitude then that, in complete contrast to the story described above, I can thank generous people like Lynn Naron and Dennis Phelps—two Bela Lugosi and horror film collectors of note and both gentlemen of the highest caliber—for offering reproductions of rare items from their personal archives.

Despite my praise, I equally acknowledge White Zombie's *many faults, and hardly make a request for its apotheosis. But I do suggest the film be studied and canonized as an important work of 1930s cinema, of independent filmmaking, and of the horror film genre.*

Similarly, I want to offer Larry Ellig, another major collector in the horror genre, my tremendous thanks for use of images in the complete *White Zombie Exhibitors* [*sic*] *Campaign Book* in his possession, as well as of several *White Zombie* lobby cards. Ellig's collection is superb—a perfect match for his kindness towards this project.

Other collectors in this category to whom I am forever indebted are Kevin Gardner and Bill Pirola. Both hold collections of Lugosiana which have few rivals, and both have bestowed a tremendous kindness on this work by jointly offering a color reproduction of the single sheet to the film. In addition, Pirola provided a color reproduction of a *White Zombie* window card—one far different from that shown in the 1932 pressbook. True carriers of the Lugosi torch, they deserve our thanks.

Another bearer of the same flame is my friend and colleague Frank J. Dello Stritto, who kindly delved into British archives to find reviews, clippings, and images from the London screenings of both *White Zombie* and *Revolt of the Zombies*. His skill as a dedicated researcher in the world of Bela Lugosi is unmatched.

Also, let me raise a glass of ale, quote the Marx Brothers in *Animal Crackers* and say "Three Chairs" for Michael T. Wilson—or perhaps that's three cheers and one chair, sans termite damage. Many thanks for preserving history, at whatever the cost, casualty, or insult. A person I knew once didn't have much of a past or a future, but he said one thing that was important, even if he didn't understand it himself: "Truth, integrity, and honesty matter in this life." I'm so happy that's what you *do* understand, and what you *do* represent.

I would offer great thanks to Bob Stovall and Vision Digital, who helped for hour after hour to carefully and intricately restore many of the images printed in this book, some of which have not been seen for decades. Bob's dedication has helped transform this work into a visual feast for those interested in *White Zombie*.

My gratitude must also go to James F. Cain and Gregory W. Mank. The former has long been a trusted and valued friend, and the latter an inspiration in the practice of horror film historiography. Along with Tom Weaver and David J. Skal, Mank is at the forefront of preserving history in both a credible and exciting manner.

Many thanks also to Jeffrey Roberts and Michael Ferguson, both of key importance in gathering research materials for this text. Roberts kindly gave his time to undertake a study of the legal history of *White Zombie* and also the biography of Kenneth Webb, and Ferguson greatly helped in providing historical materials on Victor Halperin's life and education in Chicago.

Tom Weaver, certainly the pre-eminent interviewer in horror film studies and also one of its best writers, offered hour after hour in a search for clippings from *The Film Daily*, *The Hollywood Reporter*, and the New York *Morning Telegraph*. Few people on the planet could make a better friend than Tom, few writers can match his wit, and few historians can claim to have preserved as much information for horror film history. He's been an inspiration of mine for many years, and his work deserves all of our applause.

For innumerable suggestions of extreme value and endless examinations of rough drafts, I also extend appreciation to Dr. Robert Con Davis, Dr. Michael Morrison, and Dr. John Parris Springer. To all I owe a great debt for their proofreading efforts and important suggestions. John Springer has indeed proven a valued friend and a source of encouragement and help in my attempts to reconcile academic theory with popular enthusiasm.

Undying gratitude on this particular project must also go to Victor Pierce, esquire. This would have been an impossible task without your fortitude, your resourcefulness, and your confidence in the project. Somehow you always seem to take the buggy whip and ride the horses over the opposition.

Another important friend and researcher is Galen Wilkes, who offered immeasurable help at the last minute on some of Victor Halperin's post–*White Zombie* films. His efforts greatly enhanced the Halperin biography in Chapter Ten, and his friendship has been very important to me.

A very special thanks to Leonard J. Kohl, who offered help on every possible level. Making phone calls to Halperins across the country in search of family members, searching for and finding a living costar from the 1932 *Zombie*, providing a huge number of still photographs, scouring microfilms of Chicago newspapers, and—most importantly—being a true friend and continually offering help for a book he believed in.

Deep thanks to Karola, who spent untold hours proofreading copy, making invaluable suggestions, and generally encouraging me to move ever forward, ever onward with this project. My brief words here cannot understate the enormous impact you had on this text. My undying appreciation to you always.

Heartfelt gratitude must go to the late George E. Turner, a friend of mine, but also someone I deeply respected and admired. His work on film history will remain forever important, but his fortitude and integrity also deserve mention. More than anyone else, he and my dear friend Leonard Kohl believed in the film *White Zombie* and in this book. Unfortunately, George—who was so kind as to proofread chapters, and contribute illustrations, and write a foreword for this text—died only a few weeks before I delivered the final manuscript to the publisher. Only two weeks or so before his passing, George mailed me a few rare images for inclusion in this book; as an unfortunate procrastinator, I did not get around to thanking him for them in time. I deeply regret he did not live to see this book to fruition. I feel his loss, as I'm sure I'll continue to do for many years.

My extreme thanks go to the family that ensued from Victor Halperin's first marriage. His granddaughter Linda Ortiz contacted shortly before this text went to press with much needed information on Victor's personal life and first marriage, as well as a smattering of breathtaking photographs that can be seen in the "Family Scrapbook" appendix. Though Linda became involved at the very end of the work on this text, her additions are of profound importance.

Similarly, this book would have been impossible without the help and enthusiasm of Mrs. Venita Halperin, widow of director Victor Halperin. She is a gem of a person, one of Victor's biggest fans, and the source of many of the photographs and paperwork belonging to Victor used for this study. She is someone I am proud to number among my acquaintances.

As always, I must also offer a word on F. Richard Sheffield, though even a smattering of sentences cannot do justice to a friend of so many years, who has helped and encouraged me in so many ways. When I met him at age twelve, he treated me like a princely son, and not a day goes by that I don't think about him and the kindness he has bestowed upon me. Dick's assistance was also of critical importance in both my book *Lugosi* (McFarland, 1996) and my documentary film *Lugosi: Hollywood's Dracula* (Cut to the Chase, 1997). His last remaining Lugosi autograph—one of the greatest gifts I've ever received from anyone—now proudly hangs above my office desk. Again, I offer cheers—but that's hardly an adequate compliment for one of the most special, fascinating, and unique persons walking this planet. His faith in me time after time has meant more than I can ever say, and his approval is key to my happiness.

My love always to Melissa Sue Smith, who helped me battle out the last year of work on this book. Along with helping examine proof pages and offer last minute suggestions, she has become the answer to a prayer. My affection for her knows no bounds.

Lastly, enormous thanks to Mom and Pop. They gave me a Christmas gift in 1985—that first video copy of *White Zombie*, which was quickly worn out after repeat viewings. Thanks to their gift, and their constant encouragement and support, this book was born.

Gary D. Rhodes
Norman, Oklahoma
Summer 2001

Chapter One

Analyzing the Text and Contexts: *White Zombie* Under Scrutiny

Extended Analysis

White Zombie, the first feature-length zombie film in cinema history and an early entry in the 1930s horror movie cycle, remains one of the most worthwhile efforts in the history of the horror genre. While its often poor critical reception and its association with the horror film genre has limited the attention given it in academic circles, *White Zombie*'s unique narrative, cinematic technique, and positioning of the spectator may have also contributed to its marginalization within film history. For example, film theorist Winston Wheeler Dixon believes:

> Films that operate against the grain of the dominant mode of discourse within any given era run a substantially higher risk of being marginalized than do works that belong to a specific cinematic set or subset.[1]

However, regardless of the causes of *White Zombie*'s previously limited appeal to theorists and historians, the film—given its somewhat anomalous status among 1930s horror films and indeed the cinema in general—is eminently deserving of scholarly study.

The narrative of *White Zombie* presents the characters Neil Parker (actor John Harron) and Madeline Short (actress Madge Bellamy) as a young couple engaged to be married. A middle-aged aristocrat in Haiti named Beaumont (actor Robert Frazer) has recently met and fallen in love with Madeline. To lure her to Haiti, he offers his mansion for the site of Madeline and Neil's wedding ceremony and reception; in addition, he promises Neil a job.

The film begins with a burial in the middle of a Haitian road; Neil and Madeline are in a carriage traveling to Beaumont's estate. They learn from the carriage driver (actor Clarence Muse) that natives bury their loved ones in roads because the regular passage of carriages keeps bodysnatchers from unearthing the corpses and transforming them into zombies. Shortly thereafter, the carriage driver stops to ask directions from a man accompanied by several zombies; the film later reveals him to be a mysterious zombie master named Murder Legendre (actor Bela Lugosi).

The young couple arrives safely at Beaumont's home, where they meet Dr. Bruner (actor Joseph Cawthorn), the missionary who will marry them. Beaumont quickly leaves his guests, and consults with Murder about how best to possess Madeline for himself. The voodoo master whispers that the only method is to turn her into a zombie by use of a voodoo powder. Beaumont reluctantly follows his advice, and offers Madeline a flower tainted by the powder. This gift, as well as the burning of a wax effigy of Madeline by Murder, causes her to appear medically dead by the end of the wedding reception. Unknown to her new husband, vivisepulture occurs at a nearby cemetery.

Beaumont, Legendre, and a group of zombies then excavate her body, and the entire group retreats to Legendre's castle. Soon after their arrival, Murder transforms Beaumont into a zombie as well, hoping to keep Madeline for himself. At the same time, Neil—in a drunken state of misery—visits Madeline's grave and discovers her body has been stolen. With Dr. Bruner's help, Neil travels to Legendre's castle to rescue Madeline.

Neil quickly discovers Madeline and manages to escape a group of zombies meant to kill him. Reunification with Madeline only allows him to be physically near her, as she remains in a zombified state from which he cannot awaken her. Dr. Bruner knocks Legendre unconscious, but the villain soon regains his faculties. It is only when a half-zombified Beaumont—in an apparent act of remorse—hurls Murder off the cliff of his castle that Madeline returns to normal. Beaumont falls over the same cliff, leaving Madeline and Neil together at last.[2]

While on first inspection a simple story, *White Zombie*'s narrative, as well as its cinematic presentation, is a complex text worthy of attention both as a single work and as an amalgamation of various filmic and cultural texts. By disinterring the various layers of *White Zombie*, we can better understand the many contexts which spurred its formation. In addition to identifying appropriations from well-known literature, we can also explore the film's dependence on lesser-known sources. Many of these sources have rested entombed among forgotten books and essays; alternatively, many draw on U.S. culture of the period. Unearthing these analogues will yield a better understanding of *White Zombie*'s plot and thematic structure. In conjunction with such historical archeology, we can further understand *White Zombie* by examining its unique, often anomalous status among horror films. Its pictorial imagery, its acting, its cinematic technique, and in particular its construction of a theoretical spectator are not just noteworthy, but at times present a singular and highly stylized form of filmmaking.

CARL DREYER, DREAMS, AND NIGHTMARES

Many critics of the film since the 1960s have noticed a dreamlike quality to *White Zombie*, perhaps due to its pictorial imagery, relatively simplistic plotline, essentially cardboard characters, and farrago of acting styles. This has in turn spawned many comparisons to Carl Dreyer's very nightmarish Danish film *Vampyr* (1931). Director Victor Halperin and screenwriter Garnett Weston were probably not familiar with *Vampyr* due to its limited screenings and publicity in the U.S.; more importantly, however, the two films bear only surface similarities.

For example, both *White Zombie* and *Vampyr* do feature subjective point-of-view shots, with *Vampyr* forcing the viewer to assume the position of its character David Gray in numerous instances, to the degree that the audience is placed in his coffin and sees through his eyes. However, as will be discussed in detail in Section II of this chapter, *White Zombie* works much differently from the Dreyer film (and any other horror movie of the era) in the way it constructs a position for the spectator; rather than extended sequences in which the spectator assumes the point-of-view of a major character, *White Zombie* allows the spectator to become a minor character in the text.

Other surface similarities occur as well. *Vampyr* and *White Zombie* both make interesting uses of shadows. The former offers shadowy dancers shown against a wall,

just as Scene 14 in *White Zombie* features Neil surrounded by shadows of happy couples dancing and laughing.[3] A visual similarity perhaps, but still a textual difference. In *Vampyr*, the shadows are apparently disembodied spirits; in *White Zombie*, they are merely darkened reflections of living persons, shown by their shadows to heighten Neil's isolation and mourning for the deceased Madeline.

The two films also feature characters who are keenly aware of their death in progress, which is perhaps their strongest point of similarity. David Gray in *Vampyr* is a witness to his own coffin lid being screwed down onto the coffin and to himself as if a corpse; Beaumont in *White Zombie* becomes the first of Legendre's victims to—as the zombie master says—"know what is happening" in that he too will be corpselike as a result of zombification. But any other similarities between the two characters (the former a "hero," the latter an "anti-hero") do not exist.

Under scrutiny, *White Zombie* then illustrates very much a different style than *Vampyr*. The latter becomes through its vague and disjointed narrative a cinematic simulacrum of a nightmare, a dream. *White Zombie*, on the other hand, generally shows clear and undeniable causality for its unfolding events, even if they are admittedly illogical events; such causality is generally absent from *Vampyr*'s narrative. Perhaps the only sequence in the Halperin film lacking explanation is Scene 17, in which we are never told why Beaumont and his butler have relocated to Legendre's estate. However, this single instance represents more a narrative lapse than the intentionally distorted architecture of Dreyer's dreamwork.

Vampyr visually suggests the mistlike quality of a dream by the intentional and heavy use of greys, rather than stark blacks and high-contrast lighting. Dreyer achieved his effects by a minor, intentional light leak during exposure of the film, as well as by using a limited amount of gauze over the lens. *White Zombie* appears with a vaguely similar grey cast only in the badly duped (but often circulated) prints of the film that have lost sharpness and clarity in the process. While some critics have no doubt viewed such prints of the film and have thus perhaps found a minor visual similarity to Dreyer, the comparison is false; a restored version, as well as existing 35mm prints of the film, reveal *White Zombie* to be a generally high-contrast black-and-white movie—certainly divergent from the oneiric results of *Vampyr*'s low-contrast dreamscape.

Why then the repeated comparisons? Given that the scholarship of the horror film genre overall is quite poor, we can explain some of the repetition by realizing the intense degree of derivation which occurs from horror film book and article to horror film book and article. Mindlessly, many authors who write on horror films for

Neil (John Harron) and Madeline (Madge Bellamy) gaze at the approaching Murder Legendre on their way to Beaumont's estate. (Courtesy of Leonard J. Kohl.)

nonacademic audiences plagiarize ideas and facts from other texts as easily as Legendre exhumes and galvanizes zombies from the graveyard. As a result, the tactics of these author-historians generally precludes either original or extended analyses. Wrongly then, horror film histories occasionally continue to draw the same comparison between Dreyer and Halperin.

WHITE ZOMBIE AND FAIRY TALES

We can better understand *White Zombie* by noting that a strong similarity inherently exists between the film and fairy tales, the latter in a way being oft-repeated, albeit much more accurate, descriptions of *White Zombie*. An analysis of this kind brings to bear only one of many needed perspectives on the film, but it does lead to an exploration of which is far more fruitful than invoking Dreyer and *Vampyr*.

For example, Freud recognized that—given their correspondence to one another—fairy tales can be interpreted in the same manner as dreams. In his *Interpretation of Dreams* (as well as in his shorter, more accessible *On Dreams*) he offered the very ideas that we can apply to the fairy tale structure which exists in *White Zombie*. Freud believed that dream interpretations must uncover the wish fulfillment attempted by the tale. Even within the realm of fantasy, instinctual wishes appear disguised. They always appear encoded in condensed, shifted, or symbolic forms. In this way, fairy tale figures can be seen as representations of instinctual drives.

Freud's explanation suggests that Neil, Beaumont,

In White Zombie, *Beaumont (Robert Frazer, pictured on right) realizes he is descending into the world of the living dead.*

and Legendre are not as different as they might at first seem. Perhaps one can suggest that Neil's desire to possess Madeline is legitimate and moral because of marriage vows, and that Legendre's lascivious hopes for a master-slave scenario are sadomasochistic in nature. However, at heart *all three* men wish to own her sexually. The wish fulfillment then revolves around sexual drives, suggesting a male-engendered quality to the tale of *White Zombie.*

But to invoke dream and fairy tale analysis leads us at least briefly to Jungian myth criticism, as Jung himself held an apparently deep interest in fairy tales. A Jungian perspective of *White Zombie* would show a greater differentiation between characters, as his methods are concerned with more than merely wish fulfillment. In discussing the "anatomy" of the psyche, Jung refers to archetypes, which are "...by definition, factors and motifs that arrange the psychic elements into certain images, characterized as archetypal, but in such a way that they can be recognized only from the effects they produce."

The grief and turmoil caused by a Legendre would thus represent an evil archetype, in contrast with, for example, the kindly effects of the good Dr. Bruner.

Such a perspective would also suggest that Legendre is essentially Neil's shadow. Jung wrote:

> ...the shadow can by the conscious mind of the individual contain the hidden, repressed, and unfavorable (or nefarious) aspects of the personality. But this darkness is not just the simple converse of the conscious ego. Just as the ego contains unfavorable and destructive attitudes, so the shadow has good qualities—normal instincts and creative impulses. Ego and shadow, indeed, although separate, are inextricably linked together in much the same way that thought and feeling are related to each other.[4]

Drawing from these comments, we might not only see the relationship between the young hero and the ageless villain, but we can explain the inner conflict of Beaumont, who exemplifies both the shadowlike repression that surfaces to control his actions at times, as well as the "normal"

HP 31-z-103

From a Jungian perspective, we might view Murder Legendre (Bela Lugosi, left) as the shadow of Neil (John Harron, right).

instincts which lead him to destroy Legendre at the end of the film. But however much Jung's contributions yield a level of insight, they also limit an understanding of the sexual tension which works amongst *White Zombie*'s male characters on other levels, and of the important battle between good and evil present in the fairy tale aspects of the storyline.

As invoking Freud and Jung suggests, the fairy tale is often an outward expression of inward struggles. Scholar Bruno Bettelheim has said, "…The unrealistic nature of these tales … is an important device, because it makes obvious that the fairy tales' concern is not useful information about the external world, but the inner processes taking place in an individual."[5] But while Bettelheim's explanation addresses the world of Jungian shadows and Freudian wish fulfillment, other elements of the fairy tale inform *White Zombie*'s narrative structure.

Given their simplistic struggles between good and evil, fairy tales are generally timeless in their retellings. And they also often lack a clear time period in the setting of their stories. Much the same can be said of *White Zombie*, as we never learn a date or time period in which the story is taking place. One might assume it is contemporary with its 1932 production, simply because the clothing (and actress Madge Bellamy's hairstyle) signify that period. But these signs are indistinct markers. No other clues are present, as the dialogue offers no particularized 1920s or 1930s slang and the narrative itself includes no automobiles, airplanes, phones, or technology of any type to root the film to any epoch.

Indeed, the only mention of anything similar to technology is Madeline's mention of a journey to Haiti by ship, but—rather than anchoring the film to a time—this serves only to seize upon a common metaphor for a journey to the underworld. In Greek myths of the River Styx and boat rides with ferryman Charon, in historical ship burial sites unearthed by archeologists in England, and even in the plots of films like *Outward Bound* (1930), the association between seafaring vessels and the travel to the underworld is common.[6] In Madeline's case, she has been carried by a ship to the "Land of the Living Dead," as the native witch doctor character Pierre calls it. The use of a ship, though somewhat nebulous in *White Zombie* since it is never seen, reinforces the film's lack of a clear time frame and helps create its resulting time-lessness.[7]

White Zombie also presents characters who are in some ways emblematic of their fairy tale counterparts. Legendre, like most fairy tale villains, casts spells and abducts an innocent victim; even his ordering the murder of Silver, the butler, is a device common in fairy tales. His appearances in the film also echo scholar Vladimir Propp's description of fairy tale villains:

> First he makes a sudden appearance from outside (flies to the scene, sneaks up on someone, etc.), and then disappears. His second appearance in the tale is as a person *who has been sought out*, usually as the result of guidance.[8]

In his first appearance, Legendre unexpectedly appears on the road and in a sense "sneaks up" on Madeline. He is then sought out by Beaumont in his second appearance. Subsequently, Neil—who receives guidance from Dr. Bruner—seeks out Legendre as well.

Neil's journey to Legendre's castle represents a quest, another key aspect of many fairy tale plots, which generally leads to a happy ending. In *White Zombie*, the journey is not unlike the Greek myth of Orpheus and Eurydice, in which the former undertook a quest to the underworld to return the latter to the land of the living. Similarities to the underworld in *White Zombie* have already been discussed, but—unlike Orpheus—Neil fails to be a viable savior. As a result, the film represents in many ways what theorist Verena Kast has termed the "second structure" of fairy tales. It:

> begins with a situation of deficiency, and ... there is a confrontation with obstructing powers. However, ... this does not lead to a process of development and maturation; rather, all means must be engaged in order to escape a nasty situation. The heroes and heroines are happy just to be able to save their own skin.[9]

Kast continues by relating, "I also count as having the second structure those tales in which the hero does not fulfill his task."[10] These fairy tale heroes often reflect the everyman who incorporates many weaknesses inherent in readers and filmgoers. Neil in *White Zombie*, for example, lacks both wisdom and even the physical stamina needed to complete the quest. It is not he, the "hero," who possesses these features, but instead it is Dr. Bruner. The second structure, then, precludes what Rosemary Haughton has said of hero and heroine in many such fairy tales: "Even when her role is passive, the fairy-tale princess releases powers in the hero which would otherwise remain unused...."[11]

Just as Haughton's comments about fairy tale heroes do not apply to Neil, many other aspects of common fairy tale structures also do not inform *White Zombie*'s plot. For example, Legendre does not disguise himself to achieve his ends, even if he does wish—as villains in fairy tales often do—to take possession of a victim. The film does adopt some thematic and narrative devices from fairy tales, including the journeylike quest, certain character traits, and an unclear time frame. But the film is not a fairy tale. *White Zombie* merely borrows particular codes of that form, codes which are only a part of both the film's textual and contextual matrix.

WHITE ZOMBIE AND THE HORROR FILM

Cinema scholarship has yet to determine definitively when the burning flames of the U.S. horror film cooled and coalesced into a codified genre. Many histories cite the 1930s, suggesting the U.S. horror film genre began with *Dracula* (1931); others find important roots in the silent film era. Reconsidering the question of genre-fication helps us to understand *White Zombie*'s lineage and placement in horror film history. It also allows us to comprehend the film's uniqueness. In other words, if the horror film genre had not yet fully formed by the time of *White Zombie*'s production, we can see the ways in which the film differs from its predecessors as a kind of experimentation which does usually occur in the early stages of a genre's evolution.

Certainly the early days of film in the United States included movies whose stories would generally be classified as horror; these include *Frankenstein* (1910), *Dr. Jekyll and Mr. Hyde* (1911 and 1913), and—based on the tales of Poe—*The Avenging Conscious* (1914). By the twenties, Hollywood was producing innumerable films that both intended to and succeeded in scaring viewers. Some of these, like *The Phantom of the Opera* (1925), revolved around the makeup and pantomime of Lon Chaney; others emphasized the old dark house, such as *The Cat and the Canary* (1927). Some, like *London After Midnight* (1927), denied the existence of the supernatural even while invoking it as a topic; others, like *Dante's Inferno* (1924), made quite the opposite statement.

Despite the success of such films, conventional wisdom in horror film studies has suggested that *Dracula* began the classical period of the genre's formation through the financial success of the movie and its textual introduction of the supernatural to the U.S. horror film. Under scrutiny, we may dispense with the latter notion. Ghosts and the supernatural walked in the U.S. cinema prior to *Dracula*, even if popular storylines during the twenties most often revolved instead around deformities and partially comedic old dark houses. We might quickly attribute the predominance of tales in the 1920s involving deformities to the box-office success of actor Lon Chaney and his makeup techniques which were uniquely suited to creating deformities. Stage successes informed a stream of old dark house films in the 1920s, just as finally the 1927 stage success of *Dracula* would lead the way to *Dracula* on film. At the same time, however, films like *One Glorious Day* (1922) and *Outward Bound* (1930) clearly addressed the supernatural before *Dracula* (1931).

Though it wasn't the first U.S. film to invoke the supernatural, we can talk extensively about the uniqueness of *Dracula*. Its plot of a singular supernatural villain was quite unusual in terms of the newly born talking picture, but that same supernaturalness cannot act as a defining quality of what would become the 1930s horror genre. After all, the bulk of horror films from that decade consist not of the supernatural, but of themes like science versus religion.[12] A definition of "horror film" would help us better understand when the horror film cycle of 1931–32 became a genre. But any definition leads to contention among scholars; after all, what really makes a horror film of any era a horror film? For example, is a movie like *The Most Dangerous Game* (1932) too tangential to include in a list of horror films?

Answers to the problem of genrefication usually attempt to build lists of characteristics of horror films, though they are of little help in answering our concerns. Descriptions of old dark houses or of a film's mention of vampires might just as well make a 19th century novel like *Jane Eyre* a horror film. Themes regarding male fears and male fantasies also prove to be of little worth as criteria for what makes a film a horror film, as these characteristics might just as easily apply to a film like *All Quiet on the Western Front* (1930) as to *Dracula* (1931). Some theorists suggest fear, or at least an attempt to inspire fear, is a quality of the horror film. However, dozens of movies from the Hollywood of the 1920s did just that, as did the German Expressionist silent films like *The Cabinet of Dr. Caligari* (1919) and *Nosferatu* (1922).

Difficulties abound in formulating answers to these questions of genrefication and the horror film. At a minimum, however, we can see growth and evolution from, say, the 1910 *Frankenstein* or the 1925 *Phantom of the Opera* to the 1931 *Frankenstein*, in the same way the genre has evolved in the decades after the 1930s. Some of this stems from technical advances and changes in the cinema itself, but some of it occurs from changes in the cultural tastes of audiences.

What we can do with some level of success is to consider recurrent cultural themes in the horror film cycle during the period immediately prior to *White Zombie*. The result can yield insight into plot characteristics that may have influenced *White Zombie*, as well as more readily allowing us to see it at least in part as a horror film and part of horror film history.

For one, films like *Dracula* often begin with travel to a foreign land, a journey made by Americans or, even if the particular role deems it otherwise, American actors. After all, hatred brewed against immigrants in the 1920s, with Sacco and Vanzetti's wrongful execution boiling in the same cauldron as the Red Scare. To some, Europeans were the most to blame, for U.S. involvement in World War I, for strain on the world economic structure resulting from the lack of payment of war reparations, and for causing the Great Depression itself. If perceived villains in real life were foreigners (and often European), so were those in the horror film of the thirties. Even by the time of *White Zombie*'s production, Bela Lugosi and Boris Karloff wore the faces that caused fear. And as with U.S. involvement in World War I, the horror film saw fit to place Americans in Europe or some other unfamiliar locale to confront trouble outside the U.S. Troubles are faced by Renfield in *Dracula* on his journey (for, even if character Renfield travels from England, actor Dwight Frye was clearly an American), just as they are faced by Neil and Madeline in *White Zombie*. "Turn back before it is too late," we hear Pierre warn Dr. Bruner and Neil as they travel to Legendre's castle. For thirties' horror films like *Dracula*, *White Zombie*, and *The Black Cat* (1934), the plot device of travel to a foreign land subtly revealed U.S. xenophobia.

Gender also plays an important part in the 1930s horror cycle. The female in the horror film—whether in such silent fare as *Nosferatu* (1922) and *The Cat and the Canary* (1927) or in *White Zombie*'s talkie predecessors like *Dracula* (1931)—becomes the hunted, the quarry. She has little to do, and so the question becomes "What will be done *with* her?" The heroines are young and beautiful, but represent more a prize to be possessed—whether "stolen" by a villain or "owned" by a young hero at the films' conclusions. Those in early talkies like *Dracula* (1931) show no essential differences from heroines of earlier years like actress Mary Philbin in *Phantom of the Opera* (1925) and actress Laura La Plante in *The Cat and the Canary* (1927).

By contrast, the heroes in the thirties' horror film differ in some ways from their silent screen counterparts. While almost all are handsome, young, polite, well-mannered, yet inexperienced, those of the twenties often wore the cloak of comedic relief as well; for example, Creighton Hale in *The Cat and the Canary* (1927) shudders under his bed to provide impetus for giggles. By the talkies, other, lesser characters became responsible for the humor: Charles Gerrard in *Dracula* (1931), for example, or Dr. Bruner with his repeated request for a match in *White Zombie*.[13] The result provides the heroes at least a chance to be taken seriously, though their purpose in the thirties horror films was to act as a "doubter" of the supernatural.

David Manners, the actor who portrayed Jonathan Harker in *Dracula* (1931), spoke of his character's purpose even before the vampire film was released. He claimed, "...I'm the only sane one of the lot, though I don't think I will be long ... all I do is wander about and say 'Things like that don't happen today.' And then they do to show me, so after all I'm pretty useless."[14] His comment proved not only an astute analysis, but a fair indicator of the dialogue he spouts in the film. As the supernatural becomes a stronger force, Harker pronounces, "I don't mean to be rude, but that's the sort of thing I'd expect one of the patients [in Dr. Seward's mental institute] to say."

Director Victor Halperin and producer Edward Halperin believed much the same. The *New York Times* once described the brothers' hypothesis of "audience reciprocality." They believed audiences' lives were "monotonized," and as a consequence they sought vicarious pleasures in the cinema. As a result, the two always had "one character who represents the audience. He is the doubter, the scoffer, the man from Missouri.... As this character is won over in the film, so also, Mr. [Edward] Halperin thinks, is the audience."[15]

The Halperins position Neil as the doubter in *White Zombie*, with Scene 16 being devoted to his consultation with Dr. Bruner and his immediate doubts of voodooism and zombiism. The scene begins with Neil speaking of Madeline's missing body; the composition shows Dr. Bruner framed through the armpit of Neil, who is leaning on Bruner's desk. Director Victor Halperin visually allows the audience the basic vantage point of Neil, and—assuming his basic point of view—they can thus associate with his doubts. Dr. Bruner explains his thoughts on what could possibly have happened to Madeline and suggests a plan. If he has certainly not dispelled Neil's doubts by the end of the scene, he has at least begun to persuade the young man. The lengthy tracking shot returns to its original composition, with Bruner again seated and Neil's arm—he is once again leaning on the desk—framing the composition. The audience, at least according to the Halperins, is being "won over" at the same time as Neil, the "Man from Missouri."

In addition to doubting the existence of zombies, Neil must also rely on a wise male elder for assistance, just as Jonathan Harker must depend on Dr. van Helsing in *Dracula* (1931) and just as many other horror film

"heroes" subsequent to *White Zombie* would be dependent on an older figure—usually male—for advice and guidance.[16] It is Dr. Bruner who understands that, even if some superstitions are false, voodoo and zombies cannot be entirely discounted.

The inability to grasp key events and to respond properly to them leads the hero to be ineffectual against the villain who takes an interest in the heroine. In both *Dracula* (1931) and *Frankenstein* (1931), the villain—whether the undead count or the Monster—threatens the heroine near the moment of their wedding, an event that presumably will be followed by the heroine's physical consummation with the hero. Essentially the same plot device occurs in *White Zombie*, as Madeline falls ill and seemingly dies at her wedding reception.

The villains—Dracula, the Monster, and Legendre—cause a coitus interruptus, which the heroes—Harker, Dr. Frankenstein (even if he is a hero only to a certain degree), and Neil—are unable to overcome by themselves. They are, at least compared to the villains, impotent. Conversely, the villains are usually older than the young male heroes, and thus are powerful and wise; certainly this is true of *Dracula* (1931). Even when the villain is vanquished, it is usually not the virile young hero who wins out; it is the wise elder. Dr. van Helsing, for example, removes the sexual threat of Dracula by penetrating the fiend with a stake; in *White Zombie*, Dr. Bruner knocks Legendre unconscious, while Neil merely watches.[17] A happy ending occurs, but not due to the inexperienced and impotent young hero.

The happy ending of the fairy tale becomes for the horror film of the twenties and thirties a kind conservative social dogma. If Freud's wish fulfillment means that characters in horror films of the period run rampant, destroying property and lives (*Frankenstein* of 1931) or essentially raping or controlling women (*Dracula* of 1931, as well as *White Zombie*), we must consider that the conclusion to such films is diametrically the opposite of the repressed behavior which has so dramatically surfaced. The continual use of happy endings dispels the evil, with horror film villains destroyed or imprisoned. Similar narrative climaxes are seen in silent horror films like *Nosferatu* (1922), *The Phantom of the Opera* (1925), and *The Cat and the Canary* (1927). Dominant patriarchal, sociosexual norms are, in these films—as well as in *Dracula* (1931), *Frankenstein* (1931), and *Murders in the Rue Morgue* (1932)—completely restored.

Morality and the status quo (as it existed prior to the disruption caused by the villain) are held as an example of how people and society should work; after all, the film is a stage where everyone is happy. Hero and heroine are reunited, and normal life for all resumes. However fond we may be of such climaxes, their strict adherence to the

The inability to grasp key events and to respond properly to them leads Neil (played by John Harron, pictured) to be generally ineffectual against the obstacles he faces. (Courtesy of Leonard J. Kohl.)

norm implicity argues against the subversive pleasures enjoyed while villains wreak havoc. Nonetheless, all things religious often hold sway, especially when they come into conflict with science and technology, and this in general denies the validity of radical change.

During the Great Depression, a plot endorsing the status quo would have resonated with the views and position of President Hoover. Roosevelt represented change, but still not the vast and sweeping change desired by supporters of Huey Long, Father Coughlin, and other such political figures. Many U.S. citizens looked to the past stability with fondness, while realizing their lives had changed radically; many—whether by moving or by supporting leftist political causes or by joining unions in greater numbers than ever before—sought to restore stability through what they saw as crucially needed disruption. The horror film of the 1930s allowed such subversive disruption to occur for the bulk of their running times, only to prescribe conservatism at their climaxes to cure the ill effects of that subversion.

Like earlier horror films, *White Zombie* follows the same blueprint. Those causing disruption—Beaumont and Legendre—die, but in an even larger sense, no indication exists that major changes will follow. Voodooism and zombiism will presumably continue to flourish, as they live on even if Legendre does not; as a result, many poor Haitians will continue to be the "living dead." The present debacle's intrusion must end, but the status quo is protected at all costs, even if it means leaving the good with the bad.

In these respects, *White Zombie*'s plot—its use of travel to a foreign land, its treatment of the hero and heroine, its inclusion of a wise elder—follows from its 1930s predecessors like *Dracula*. *White Zombie* was impacted by the horror film cycle as it existed at that stage. At the same time, *White Zombie* represents narrative distinctions that differ from other, prior 1930s horror films.

Like Dracula *(1931) and other horror films,* White Zombie's *plot dispels all evil and ends with a return to the conservative status quo. Here Madeline (Madge Bellamy, left) can be seen shortly before her soul is restored and she returns to the arms of her husband, Neil (John Harron, middle). The wise elder Dr. Bruner (Joseph Cawthorn, right) stands nearby. (Courtesy of Leonard J. Kohl.)*

TODOROV AND THE FANTASTIC

While we have placed *White Zombie* in the horror film category as it existed in the early 1930s, we can define the film with more depth and better examine some of its differences from prior cinematic horrors by considering the work of scholar Tzvetan Todorov.

In his landmark study *The Fantastic: A Structural Approach to a Literary Genre,* Todorov defines what he considers to be the fantastic in a particularized way. To him:

> ...the text must oblige the reader to consider the world of the characters as a world of living persons and to hesitate between a natural and a supernatural explanation of the events described.[18]

In Todorov's schema, then, the reader/viewer must question whether the supernatural is at work, or a character or characters within the work must be puzzled by the same inquiry, or perhaps all are plagued by the issue.

More specifically, Todorov suggests that: "The fantastic occupies the duration of this uncertainty. The concept of the fantastic is therefore to be defined in relation to those of the real and the imaginary."[19] Thus, the sheer use of "hesitation" as a qualifier suggests that most works would possess the fantastic for perhaps only part of their length.

To apply his ideas to filmic texts previously discussed, *Dracula* and *Nosferatu* would hardly qualify as representative of the fantastic. Both evince the supernatural as reality early in their respective narratives, and—whatever the audience makes of it—no "hesitation" occurs in the interpretation of the supernatural. *Franken-stein* certainly would not qualify as the fantastic either. Hesitation never occurs, as science alone galvanizes the Monster into life. On the other hand, moments exist in films like *The Phantom of the Opera* (1925) and *The Cat and the Canary* (1927) which suggest—however briefly—that the supernatural *may* be at play, even if we do quickly learn that is not the case, and even if the familiarity of the tales mean that devices attempting to create the hesitation are hardly effective for some modern viewers.

By contrast to such examples, *White Zombie*—intentionally or not—ably sustains the fantastic throughout the entire film. It's impossible to know finally the degree to which, if any, a world beyond the natural exists in the tale it offers. This places the film in a unique and relatively small group of cinematic works that brilliantly keep complete understandability at bay, not—as in *Vampyr*—by a lack of causal relationships, but rather through sometimes conflicting or vague information about Legendre and zombies.

Legendre, for example, has no known history, no known origin, and no name by which he is ever discussed—except when witch doctor Pierre suggests he is "called Murder"; after all, "Legendre" as a character name is printed in promotional materials, but never actually heard in the film. Pierre also further blurs Legendre's history by dubbing him a "spirit man," who lives in the "land of the living dead." Legendre also seems little dependent on standard human physiological needs; he is never shown to eat or sleep or to possess signifiers of such acts (e.g., food or a bedroom). He certainly breathes; his breath fogs eerily into the cold, night air. He also controls the minds of others from afar, though it is unclear if that represents supernatural control or a kind of mesmerism to be discussed later in this chapter. Legendre at times seems all-powerful and all-knowing, and his house features doors that open by themselves on two separate occasions.[20] At other times, he is surprised from behind with ease by Beaumont, and is dependent on a simplistic smoke bomb for an escape from Dr. Bruner. Are the opening doors in his home then a trick or the workings of otherworldliness? Whether he is a supernatural demon or a successful charlatan dependent on voodoo tricks and mesmerism is never revealed.

The zombies cause an equally ambiguous hesitation. Breath can be seen emanating from their lips, but whether that suggests life is in question; for example, bullets do not at all slow their pace. But if bullets have no effect on zombies, a fall from the cliff of Legendre's castle to the waters below immediately stops their advances. Why? We do not know. We do know that Legendre creates zombies by use of a powder, and that—with his death—Madeline is released from what seems to be a hypnotic spell. But the same cannot be said of Legendre's other zombies, who are not released from zombiism in like fashion; they are not even released for a moment when Legendre is hit from behind by Dr. Bruner. Instead, they seem to be truly dead, prompted back to life by Legendre. "In life they were my enemies," he says of them, implying that life is what they no longer possess. Legendre speaks their introductions to Beaumont not in his sugar mill, when we first see some of them, but rather in the graveyard during Scene 15; the tombstones seem to act as signs of their condition. Legendre suggests their souls are also no longer owned by them, that they would have to "regain" them to become conscious. Audience members are thus unsure whether the zombies are merely drugged persons or supernatural creatures.

More than any other U.S. horror film of the 1930s, *White Zombie* skews its narrative to a degree that a Todorovian hesitation is successfully sustained even through its climax for characters like Neil and audience members alike. It is impossible to determine with certainty the presence or the lack of the supernatural. To a degree this theme occurs from a narrative built on actual Haitian superstitions which have at their core a scientific basis. But it is also made more complex due to screenwriter Weston's use of plot devices appropriated from Goethe's most famous work.

FAUST AND MEPHISTOPHELES

While *White Zombie* exemplifies at least some aspects of the horror film and fairy tale, it has a specific narrative which—unlike *Dracula* (1931) and *Frankenstein* (1931)—was not based on any single novel or short story. Rather, the story it tells developed out of numerous influences that we can decode from analyzing the film. One of these is Goethe's *Faust*, from which *White Zombie* appropriates several narrative constructs.

The major plot device *White Zombie* adopts is the contractual bargain with a devilish figure and the tense relationship between Faust and Mephistopheles. With regard to the latter, we might wish to return to the earlier discussion of *White Zombie* as a Freudian dreamwork-fairy tale. Freud analyzed Goethe's *Faust* at length, believing that Mephistopheles represented the return of the repressed within Faust; in the tale, the repressed instincts are of an eroticized destruction. In general, Freud believed Faust's repression, "proliferates in the dark, and takes on extreme forms of expression."[21]

Mephistopheles represents repressed forms of expression, applying pressure to the rational Faust. Little pressure is needed, however, as Faust's desires outweigh his caution. For example, Faust's excitement can be seen in these lines he speaks to Mephistopheles:

Dr. Bruner (Joseph Cawthorn, center) tries to sneak up on Murder Legendre (Bela Lugosi, right). A zombie approaches from the rear.

Fetch me something the angel wears!
Take me to her place of rest!
Fetch me a garter as a token—
Fetch me the kerchief from her breast![22]

Spirit of Evil, what do you wish from me?
Brass, marble, parchment, paper—which shall I use?
Shall I write with a chisel or a quill? Come, choose!
Or perhaps a style? Decide—your choice is free.[23]

In *White Zombie*, Legendre pulls from inside the breast of his shirt a scarf belonging to Madeline. In Scene 2, he approaches the carriage holding her and Neil, and pulls the scarf from her neck as the driver prods the horses into motion. The scarf is so strong a signifier of Madeline that she tells Neil, "It felt like hands clutching me." In Scene 9, the signifier proves understandable to the degree that, even though Beaumont has presumably never seen the scarf itself, he immediately recognizes its relationship to Madeline.

As with his desire for "something the angel wears," the bargain Faust makes with Mephistopheles is struck with a measure of glee. Faust happily suggests a signing a contract:

The parallel in *White Zombie* is unmistakable. Beaumont is equally willing to make a pact with Legendre, speaking the lines "You give me what I want, and you may ask anything."

Additionally, though she is not the topic of his contract, Faust later says to Margarete: "One glance, one word from you appeals far more/Than wisdom and all wordly lore!"[24] Beaumont echoes those lines to Madeline when he proclaims his love: "I love you Madeline, more than anything else in this whole world, dear.... You could raise me up to paradise, or blast my world into nothingness." And like Faust's oscillation between lust and love for Margarete, the same seems to be case with Beaumont's desires for Madeline.

Beaumont (Robert Frazer, left) and Murder Legendre (Bela Lugosi, right) agree on a bargain that borrows heavily from Goethe's Faust. *Note the cigar in Legendre's mouth, which is not seen in the film.*

In his meeting with Legendre in Scene 9 to discuss her, Beaumont suggests he can transfer Madeline's affections to himself if only he can get a month alone with her. "Not in a month, nor even a year," Legendre replies. "I have looked at her eyes. She is deep in love, but not with you." Perhaps he believes what he says, or perhaps he is simply setting the stage for the next exchange:

BEAUMONT: "There must be a way."
LEGENDRE [who stands]: "There ... is ... a way.... The cost ... the cost is heavy."

After Beaumont stands, Legendre quickly places a hand on his shoulder and whispers a suggestion of zombiism. Despite his initial reluctance, Beaumont does proceed to cause Madeline's zombification; the bargain is complete and Beaumont's fate is sealed in the manner of Faust's.

Though Mephisto must act as Faust's slave for a time, roles eventually switch.[25] Similarly, Legendre is a slave only for a brief time in *White Zombie*; he serves Beaumont only to the degree of creating a zombie from Madeline. It is Beaumont, like Faust, who will be the true slave; indeed, the tilt shot of zombie Chauvin in Shot 140 from Beaumont's point of view foreshadows his fate.

Like Mephistopheles, Legendre seems quite certain in the bargain he makes as to who will profit, and he seems equally positive that he already has Beaumont in his grasp. For example, when Beaumont refuses a vial of zombie powder, Legendre urges him to keep it. Beaumont reflects on the idea, with Legendre—prompted by his certainty of Beaumont's desire for Madeline—stating the confident, imperative: "Send me word when you use it."

Legendre positions himself in order to achieve total

An illustration by Harry Clarke of Mephistopheles that appeared in a 19th century U.S. edition of Goethe's Faust.

control over Beaumont and the others around him by converting them to zombies, whether they are prior enemies or new acquaintances like Madeline. Legendre denies Beaumont the life and possessions for which the latter hopes, and—in doing so—he makes himself the major character in the film, much in the same way as Mephistopheles does in *Faust*. He has not forgotten that, at the outset of their bargain, Beaumont tells Legendre that the voodoo master may ask "anything" of him in exchange for Madeline.

Inner conflict plagues both Beaumont and Faust. The two realize the folly of their desires, but too late to change their fates. The latter speaks the lines:

Alas! two souls within my breast abide,
And each from the other strives to seprate.
The one, with love and healthy lust,

The world with clutching tentacles holds fast;
The other soars with power above this dust
Into the domain of our ancestral past.[26]

But Beaumont and Faust attempt to escape the rule of their masters, who both have premature assumptions of victory. As D.J. Enright claims in his *Commentary on Goethe's Faust*, "…it is Mephisto, in his complacent assurance of victory—'You are lost in every way—the elements are sworn to us, and all will end in annihilation'—who is the target for irony."[27] Goethe's Mephistopheles, much like Legendre at the climax of *White Zombie*, has overextended himself; both certainly incur misfortune thanks to their lusts for females.

Carl Jung once wrote of Goethe's tale that, "…Faust had failed to live out to the full an important part of his early life. He was, accordingly, an unreal or incomplete person who lost himself in a fruitless quest for metaphysical goals that failed to materialize."[28] While Beaumont's attempt at wish fulfillment in *White Zombie* could hardly be termed "metaphysical," he does undertake a quest as fruitless as Faust's. Despite their individual follies, however, both men attain something akin to redemption at the conclusion of the respective tales.[29] More and more Faust's mind conquers Mephistopheles'. For Beaumont, who is never driven by as noble an aspiration as Faust is, redemption means regrouping himself mentally to the degree that he pushes Legendre over a cliff, killing his tormentor even though he himself must die.

But if *Faust* clearly provided Weston and Halperin a narrative from which they could successfully plunder, their purpose was not to adapt Goethe to the screen. Rather, their purpose was to construct a horror film around zombies, with Legendre—however much he resembles Mephistopheles—a zombie master. Though Legendre makes a satanic bargain with Beaumont, other major aspects of the narrative bear no commonality with Goethe's tale. For example, Legendre controls zombies and, eventually, Madeline by a means not dissimilar to those of the villain in another literary analogue, *Trilby*.

SVENGALI AND TRILBY

George Du Maurier's 1894 novel *Trilby* and its film adaptation *Svengali* (1931) are other sources from which *White Zombie* screenwriter Weston and director Halperin apparently adopted various ideas. Weston was certainly familiar with *Trilby*; he even refers to it in a 1933 novel: "Anyone who had heard *Trilby* could imitate Svengali with sufficient fearsomeness."[30] And given the box-office success of the film *Svengali* in 1931, both Weston and Halperin probably viewed it.

It is likely that Weston appropriated both the novel

Artwork of Svengali from the first edition of Du Maurier's novel Trilby.

and film's use of Svengali's health p r o b l e m s, which—when they erupt—cause Trilby's individuality and memory to return to her. Much the same happens in Scene 23 of *White Zombie*, as Madeline briefly seems to return to consciousness when Legendre is struck by Dr. Bruner, only to drift back to her zombified state when Legendre regains mental control. *White Zombie* also echoes *Trilby* in that Du Maurier's title character feigns ignorance of her time as a famed singer with Svengali after he dies. In *White Zombie*, Madeline awakes from her entrancement simply claiming she "dreamed" and showing no leftover fear from her travails.

More than any other narrative element, however, *White Zombie* borrows the idea of Svengali's control over Trilby to fulfill his sexual greed. Legendre's relationship with Madeline resonates with many ideas from both Du Maurier's novel and its film adaptations. Along with the basic idea of sexual domination, *White Zombie* adopts the use of eyes as a method of control. For example, in the 1931 film version, Svengali (John Barrymore) tells Trilby (Marian Marsh), "...you do not look at Svengali!—Svengali, who looks at you with all his eyes...."[31] Svengali looks directly into the camera, his eyes open but no pupils are visible. He first hypnotizes Trilby to remove her headache, but quickly realizes his power over her. During the evening hours, he stares into the camera again, with the camera starting on an extreme closeup of his pupilless eyes, pulling out of his window, tracking across a very Expressionistic town, and entering Trilby's upstairs bedroom window. Svengali beckons and controls her from afar with his gaze.

"Look me in the eyes," he tells Trilby on a later occasion. The film cuts back and forth from each of their stares; when the focus stays on Svengali, the lighting fades to black with the exception of two lights pinpointed on his eyes. Trilby realizes their power, as she pleads: "No ... no ... please take your eyes off of me ... let me go ... let me go." Given the film's financial and artistic success—as well as its release in 1931 shortly before *White Zombie*'s 1932 production—it is very possible that the image of Svengali's eyes was the most direct inspiration for the extreme closeups of Legendre's eyes surrounded by darkness in *White Zombie*.

During the film *Svengali*, the young lover Billie thinks Trilby has died, a plot device not dissimilar to Neil believing Madeline dead in *White Zombie*. When Billie realizes she is alive, Trilby suggests she is not who he thinks she is; she is under the mind control of Svengali, which is only broken when the latter suffers briefly from health problems. Svengali's spell is only broken completely when he dies. The same happens in *White Zombie* at the end of Scene 23; when Legendre's body is pushed off a cliff and crashes into the waters below, Madeline's consciousness returns.

The 1931 film version of *Svengali* with John Barrymore was not the first adaptation of Du Maurier's novel; an earlier version in 1917 starred Wilton Lackey, who appeared in a long-running stage version of the same. The 1917 film, titled *Trilby*, is more dependent on the novel, but offers some curious additions.[32] The silent film's title cards refer to Svengali as "the vulture" and later as "that bird of evil omen." Legendre in *White Zombie* is also identified by a vulture, in his case an actual bird that acts as a signifier of him.

But the 1917 film version does not include a concentration on Svengali's control over Trilby by the use of his eyes. Nor in fact does Du Maurier's novel, in which Svengali is actually less of a hypnotist than he is a mesmerist. His initial mesmerism of Trilby comes when he tells her "to sit down on the divan, and sat opposite to her, and bade her look him well in the white of the eyes."[33] But if that is the beginning of the entrancement, it is certainly not the whole of it. Subsequently, Svengali, "made little passes and counterpasses on her forehead and temples and down her cheek and neck. Soon her eyes closed and her face grew placid." She is then "spellbound" and in his power. Du Maurier writes that Trilby has:

> ...a singularly impressionable nature, as was shown by her quick and ready susceptibility to Svengali's hypnotic influence. And all that day, ... she was haunted by the memory of Svengali's big eyes and the touch of his soft, dirty finger-tips on her face; and her fear and her repulsion grew together.[34]

As this passage indicates, Svengali's "influence" is not limited to his eyes. And *despite* Du Maurier's adjective "hypnotic"—(hypnosis was a word introduced by Dr. James Baird in the 19th century and it became a generic term for prior systems like mesmerism) Svengali in the novel is not a true hypnotist. The passes he makes on Trilby's forehead, the touch of his fingertips on her face—these are much more representative of mesmerism, not hypnotism.

Trilby (Marian Marsh) and Svengali (John Barrymore) in the 1931 film Svengali.

Mesmerism was one of many movements that led toward modern hypnosis, but in the strictest sense the two are not the same. To learned individuals in the 1890s, hypnosis as a concept would have been viewed as different from mesmerism. Indeed, in Du Maurier's novel, the Laird describes Svengali's first attempt to gain control of Trilby as mesmerism. He excitedly claims:

> He's a bad fellow, Svengali—I'm sure of it! He's mesmerized you; that's what it is—mesmerism! I've often heard of it, but never seen it done before. They get you into their power, and just make you do any blessed thing they please—lie, murder, steal—anything! and kill yourself into the bargain when they've done with you! It's just too terrible to think of![35]

The fact that Svengali is a mesmerist in the novel means that he does not rely on his eyes alone to control another person; instead, it is Trilby's eyes that are normally on *him*, not necessarily the other way around. Her singing talent, in fact, depends on her intently gazing at him.[36]

The distinction between mesmerism and hypnotism, especially considering the sometimes generic application of the latter term, may seem at first unimportant, especially to *White Zombie*. But it becomes important in gauging the influence of the novel *Trilby* versus the film *Svengali* on *White Zombie*. In the 1931 film version, Svengali's eyes are generally a singular, all-powerful tool of control.[37] It is this element—something more akin to a hypnotist's eyes—which *White Zombie* adopts at times in its narrative. In other words, Legendre in *White Zombie* exerts power over others on *some* occasions by his gaze alone, as does Svengali in the 1931 film.

We can see the immediate influence of the 1931 film *Svengali* and a limited transformation of the novel's Svengali-Trilby relationship into that of Legendre-Madeline, specifically in the theme of sexual greed. However, with regard to the idea of mental control over another human, we should realize that, while *Trilby* was the most direct influence on *White Zombie*, the 1894 Du Maurier novel was itself symptomatic of a popular 19th century fascination with mesmerism, somnabulism, and hypnotism. Many literary talents—Poe, Hoffmann, Balzac, Dickens Melville, and others—worked with these same themes in their texts; Nathaniel Hawthorne often employed such phenomena to create master-slave relationships within his stories. Furthermore, it would be difficult to catalogue the sheer number of nonfiction texts on mesmerism and the like from the 19th century. As scholar Fredrik Björnström wrote in 1889, "Suffice it to say that the literature on the subject of the past two decades is almost alarmingly voluminous in its extent, and most cosmopolitan in its extent."[38]

Because *White Zombie* probably borrowed devices such as the emphasis on the power of eyes from intellectual history prior to and after the publication of Du Maurier's novel, it is appropriate to make an even deeper inquiry into the film's sources.

HYPNOTISM, MESMERISM, AND THE EVIL EYE

Aspects of hypnotism and mesmerism external to Du Maurier's novel also affected *White Zombie*'s inception. Even earlier in Western civilization there was a lengthy tradition of "evil eye" folklore, the belief that eyes could cause sinister, baleful, and even injurious effects; their power was supernatural rather than scientific. By the end of the 19th century, the whirlpool of such superstitions twisted in the same vortex as hypnotism, mesmerism, and somnabulism. The everyday person in Western civilization at the time often held suspicions of systems like hypnotism in the same way others in prior epochs had feared the evil eye. Elements of these methods of control appear in *White Zombie*—partially because they had roots in Lugosi's performance as Dracula, and partially because information about hypnotism, mesmerism, and the evil eye may have been known to screenwriter Garnett Weston.

For example, neither Stoker's character Dracula or Du Maurier's Svengali depend solely on their eyes for control over another. As suggested earlier, systems like mesmerism often relied on accompanying touches or passes of the hand. Though sometimes Legendre uses his eyes alone as a method of control, he at times uses other means to exert his will; hand gestures and thought processes (as enunciated by his intentful facial expression) are also key to his control over zombies. Björnström, in his text on hypnosis and related schools, covers cults like the fanatics of Auxanne, who allegedly "obeyed involuntarily orders that had been thought but not uttered."[39] Their supposed use of mental suggestion seems strikingly similar to Legendre's power:

> ...we refer to the effects of the so-called *mental suggestion*, which might be defined as *transmission of thought*, and which from a certain point of view, also embraces mind-reading. For, by *'suggestion mentale,'* the French mean the operation by which sensation, will, or any psychical force affects the brain of another directly, in what may be called an immaterial matter, without manifesting itself by anything perceptible to the external senses....[40]

In his 1897 book on hypnosis, Ralph Harry Vincent would echo these possibilities: "In very many ways, by a look or a movement, the hypnotist is often able to convey a suggestion to his subject which will be quite as potent as if made by means of speech."[41] Hence Legendre controls Madeline and other zombies by his gaze, his look, as well as by the clasp of his hands. But the zombies do not even have to see Legendre's eyes or hands; they seemingly understand his mental suggestion, his thoughts transmitted through his eyes and hands.

In general, the very employment of mesmerism, hypnotism, or somnambulism carried mysterious connotations to many laypersons in the 19th and early 20th centuries. Scholar Nathan Oppenheim wrote in 1913:

> Commonly we are apt to think of hypnotism ... as if it were some occult and mysterious thing which had a close connection with the evil powers of darkness. In reality its only element of mystery lies in our imperfect acquaintance with all of its possible phases and manifestations.[42]

But at the same time Oppenheim realized, "The fanciful doctrines, which Mesmer [prime mover of mesmerism] revived, originated in medieval mysticism and superstition...."[43] The ties to superstitions help explain why topics like hypnotism seemed mysterious enough to Weston to incorporate into *White Zombie*.

As Roswell Park wrote in the 1912 essay "The Evil Eye Thanatology," it was indeed the evil eye that acted, at least in the minds of some, as the nexus between the science of hypnotism-mesmerism and the superstitions of folklore:

> Those familar with the history of so-called animal magnetism, mesmerism or hypnotism, will see a close connection between those beliefs and the practice of this peculiar form of influence [i.e., the evil eye].[44]

The invocation of the evil eye in *White Zombie* draws less on any elements in Du Maurier's *Trilby* than on literary sources like Bram Stoker's 1897 novel *Dracula*, which places great emphasis on the count's eyes. Much of that emphasis draws close parallels to prior descriptions of evil eyes.

William Carleton, in his 1912 book *The Evil Eye; Or,*

the Black Spectre, writes of the predominance of the superstition: "There is not a country on the face of the earth where a belief in the influence of the Evil Eye does not prevail."[45] Some five decades later, Helmut Shoeck would write, "Fear of the Evil Eye is man's oldest and most universal superstition. It is probably our most destructive one too...."[46] It was this "destructive" set of beliefs that acted as a palimpsest of sorts, with its text still visible under writings about hypnotism and mesmerism. Evil eye folklore acted as a quite mysterious and ominous antecedent of more scientific schools of thought like hypnotism. Lugosi's eyes in *White Zombie* thus embodied the foreboding world of evil eye folklore, as well as having connections to mesmerism and hypnotism.

Even years before his live and cinematic portrayals of Dracula, actor Bela Lugosi (consciously or not) invoked both evil eye folklore and hypnotism. The use of his eyes to heighten the villainy of his screen characters stems from his work in Weimar cinema; for example, he appeared as a Svengaliesque hypnotist in the 1919 film *Sklaven fremdes Willens*. Only a few years later, Lugosi's first U.S. film, *The Silent Command* (1923), used extreme closeups of his eyes as a signifier of his character's evil plans.[47] The *New York Times* review commented on his role, "There is a great deal of acting by turning the pupils of the eyes back and forth. The villain, of course, at times turns his eyes into mere slits.[48] The same could be said of certain shots in *The Midnight Girl* (1925), a melodrama in which Lugosi portrayed an opera impresario.

His eyes also proved particularly important in his stage role of Dracula on Broadway in 1927. Both makeup and stage lighting attempted to emphasize his eyes, with which his character could exercise a level of hypnotic control over other characters. Critics in New York noted the emphasis on Lugosi's eyes, as did those in California when the play toured in 1928 and 1929. Period movie fan magazines spoke often of his eyes, as well as of the eyes of alleged vampires that haunted him in real life.[49] The 1931 film *Dracula* even used spot lighting to highlight his eyes and eye makeup. Lugosi's performance brokered Bram Stoker's accent on Dracula's gaze in the 1897 novel into a powerful cultural image.

White Zombie knowingly built on Lugosi's Dracula characterization in terms of his own eyes and the character's ability to hypnotize, but at the same time it chose to follow a new path. For one, differences occur in aesthetic presentation, with *White Zombie* including extreme closeups of Lugosi's eyes surrounded by darkness and gazing directly into the camera, constituting shots of a type not seen in *Dracula*. And rather than gazing at his victims and using moving hand motions to control them hypnotically as he did portraying Dracula, Lugosi's Legendre uses a distinctive clasp of his hands and often stares not at his victims but away from them, usually into the camera. At times his gaze into the camera may be attributable to Legendre's victims being in different locations than he is; however, as Scene 15 shows on two separate occasions, even when Legendre is within a few feet of those he wishes to control he still generally gazes away from them and into the camera. In other words, Lugosi's portrayal of Dracula was a direct (and certainly economically wise) influence on Legendre, but it was only one of several influences; Legendre is a unique character with a unique presentation and use of his powers and eyes.[50]

The emphasis on his malignant glance was noted by various persons in 1932 as well. One of the advertising "Catchlines" in the *White Zombie* pressbook suggested for theaters to use made clear its warning: "Watch out for those eyes. They will cast a spell over you, turning you into a slave, making you do his every bidding." Critics would also notice much the same in *White Zombie*, with the New Orleans *Times-Picayune* writing in their review, "Through it all, Lugosi's eyes shine with uncanny fascination."[51]

A commingling of various sources brought about Legendre's eyes playing an important role in *White Zombie*. If direct appropriations were made from *Trilby* and the 1931 film *Svengali*, the history of hypnotism and mesmerism further informed *White Zombie*, particularly in the controlling power of Legendre's eyes. Traditions of evil eye folklore intensified the supernatural and mysterious qualities of the eyes. And the addition of Bela Lugosi to *White Zombie* extended the narrative's emphasis on eyes, given that he had already developed fame with his eyes in *Dracula*.

WILLIAM B. SEABROOK AND *THE MAGIC ISLAND*

If the fairy tale and emerging horror film helped shape *White Zombie* and if *Faust* and *Trilby* helped provide it with specific narrative instruction, the knowledge of zombies the film drew on can be most directly traced to William B. Seabrook's 1929 travelogue *The Magic Island*. As Chapter Two will explore, a lengthy intellectual history precedes Seabrook and *White Zombie*, sculpting U.S. attitudes toward Haiti, constructing a knowledge base of voodooism, and slowly introducing the idea of zombiism.

However, it was Seabrook who confronted zombies for the first time in an overt way in an English-language text. It was also Seabrook whose work was used by screenwriter Garnett Weston and director Victor Halperin in their attempt to build a narrative around a creature other than a vampire, ghost, or Frankensteinian monster. And it would be Seabrook's shadow that hovered over the production, with uncredited quotations from *The Magic Island* appearing even in *White Zombie*'s pressbook.[52]

Though Chapter Two will cover the history of Seabrook in detail, the most specific appropriations that *White Zombie* made from his book need to be considered here. Certainly Garnett Weston probably used additional texts explored in Chapter Two as well, and thus it becomes difficult to know where, for example, the film's use of voodoo drums and chants originates. However, we can see the direct reflection of *The Magic Island* in *White Zombie* in many ways. For example:

> "Why, so often, do you see a tomb or grave set close beside a busy road or footpath where people are always passing? It is to assure the poor unhappy dead such protection as we can."[53]

Those words, spoken by a Haitian with whom Seabrook became acquainted, form the basis of Scene 1 in *White Zombie*. As a carriage moves down a rural Haitian road, Neil and Madeline hear chants and see natives in the road. They quickly learn a burial is taking place. To some 1932 audiences, the opening might at first have seemed similar to *Frankenstein* (1931), which also begins with a funeral; however, the purpose in *White Zombie* is the same as in *The Magic Island*: to build an understanding of Haitian zombiism.

After witnessing the burial, Neil and Madeline soon see the "living dead" on a hillside, led by their master, Murder Legendre. His black plantation outfit and hat borrow directly from two of Alexander King's pen-and-ink illustrations in *The Magic Island*.[54] The film also duplicates the blank stares of the Haitian zombies in King's artwork. In addition, in *White Zombie* zombies are repeatedly seen on hillsides—an effective technique which prefigures similar shots of the dead characters in Ingmar Bergman's *The Seventh Seal* (1957), and which again draws on King's artwork as a reference.

Artwork from the first edition of William B. Seabrook's book The Magic Island *(1929). The original caption read, "Here are deep matters, not easily to be dismissed by crying blasphemy." The swaying zombies shown on the hillside seem to have influenced similar shots in* White Zombie.

After stopping briefly and seeing Legendre, Neil and Madeline's carriage driver moves with the speed Renfield's carriage driver gallops into the Borgo Pass in *Dracula* (1931). When he finally stops, Neil asks him about his reckless driving. In response, the driver claims that the trio might have been caught by zombies, and proceeds to offer the definition of such creatures, pivotal in an era when the word "zombie" was little known: "They are not men, Monsieur. They are dead bodies.... Zombies, the living dead. Corpses taken from their graves who are made to work in sugar mills in the fields at night."

Certainly the idea of zombiism was the most important appropriation that Weston and Halperin made from *The Magic Island,* and—as the following excerpt shows—even the definition of such creatures as used in *White Zombie* closely echoes Seabrook's book:

> The zombie, they say, is a soulless human corpse, still dead, but taken from the grave and endowed by sorcery with a mechanical semblance of life—it is a dead body which is made to walk and act and move as if it were alive. People who have the power to do this go to a fresh grave, dig up the body before it has had time to rot, galvanize it into movement, and then make of it a servant or slave, occasionally for the commission of some crime, more often simply as a drudge around the habitation or the farm, setting it dull heavy tasks, and beating it like a dumb beast if it slackens.[55]

The mention of zombies used for "dull heavy tasks" introduces also the idea of sugar mills, which stems most certainly from the title of the chapter in *The Magic Island* that covers zombiism: "...Dead Men Working in the Cane Fields."

The connection of cane fields and sugar mills to Haiti would also have been supported by the common knowledge of that crop being one of Haiti's best known and most important exports. For example, *A Guide to Hayti* (Haytian Bureau of Emigration, 1861) details "sugarcane," a "native of the plains, where the traveller often sees, with astonishment, gigantic specimens of it, varying from 18 to 24 feet in height.... Once planted this staple requires no further care, excepting to be cut down when it reaches maturity." And of course the latter chore is attended by Legendre's zombies, who carry the sugar

Artwork from the first edition of William B. Seabrook's book The Magic Island *(1929). The image of the zombie leader on horseback seems to have been one of the myriad of influences for Murder Legendre, especially in his all-black dress and plantation hat.*

cane in baskets on their heads and turn the millstone by hand.

After arriving at Beaumont's plantation, Neil and Madeline meet Dr. Bruner, who—when Neil questions the notion of zombies—responds that while, "Haiti is full of nonsense and superstition," he does not know what to make of talk of zombies.

As previously mentioned, in Scene 16 Bruner lectures Neil at more length on the issue of zombiism. His dialogue stems from the following passage in *The Magic Island*:

"My dear sir, I do not believe in miracles nor in supernatural events, and I do not want to shock your Anglo-Saxon intelligence, but this Polynice of yours, with all his superstition, may have been closer to the partial truth than you were. Understand me. I do not believe that anyone has ever been raised literally from the dead—neither Lazarus, nor the daughter of Jairus, nor Jesus Christ himself—yet I am not sure, paradoxical as it may sound, that there is not something frightful, something in the nature of criminal sorcery if you like, in some cases at least, in this matter of zombies. I am by no means sure that some of them who now toil in the fields were not dragged from the actual graves in which they lay in their coffins, buried by the mourning families."[56]

These words, spoken by one Dr. Antoine Villiers to Seabrook in Haiti, exemplify the cautious but serious consideration given Haitian superstitions by Dr. Bruner in *White Zombie*.

Villiers' comments to Seabrook also helped Weston and Halperin to invoke Article 249 of the Haitian Penal Code in Scene 16 . For example:

"I will show you [Villiers said to Seabrook] a thing which may supply the key to what you are seeking," and standing on a chair, he pulled down a paper bound book from a top shelf. It was nothing mysterious or esoteric. It was the current official *Code Pénal* (Criminal Code) of the Republic of Haiti. He thumbed through it and pointed to a paragraph which read:

"Article 249. Also shall be qualified as attempted murder the employment which may be made against any person of substances which, without causing actual death, produce a lethargic coma more or less prolonged. If, after the administering of such substances, the person has been buried, the act shall be considered murder no matter what result follows."[57]

"Why, so often, do you see a tomb or grave set close beside a busy road or footpath where people are always passing? It is to assure the poor unhappy dead such protection as we can." Those words from William B. Seabrook's The Magic Island *helped shape the* White Zombie *scene shown in this publicity still. (Courtesy of Leonard J. Kohl.)*

In this publicity still, Dr. Bruner (Joseph Cawthorn, left) can be seen wearing both the black exterior disguise that is reminiscent of Legendre's appearance, as well as his white clothes underneath. (Courtesy of Leonard J. Kohl.)

Dr. Bruner tells Neil: "The use of drugs or other practices which produce lethargic coma or lifeless sleep shall be considered attempted murder.... If the person has been buried alive, the act will be considered murder, no matter what result follows." Article 249 not only helped develop Scene 16 of *White Zombie*, but—as will be shown in Chapter Four—also became a part of the United Artists' pressbook for the film.

In addition to *The Magic Island*, however, other texts may well have helped Weston and director Victor Halperin. For example, the ox cart visible in Scene 18 probably stems from its appearance in King's illustrations for *The Magic Island*, and photographs of peasants in H.P. Davis' *Black Democracy: The Story of Haiti* (Dodge, 1928) are strikingly similar in appearance to the Haitian witch doctor Pierre with whom Dr. Bruner speaks in Scene 18. But whatever other books may have assisted in the writ-

ing of the script and planning of the film, *The Magic Island* was a major source alongside *Trilby* and *Faust*. It was with these texts in mind that individual characters were fleshed out.[58]

LEGENDRE AND DR. BRUNER

By examining characters like Legendre and Dr. Bruner, we can better understand a key duality that exists in *White Zombie*. Actor John Carradine once said:

> In the early days of Hollywood, pictures were black and white, black and white in more than one way. Not only in the character of the film material, but in the plotlines. Everything was either black or white; there were no greys. The villains were steeped in villainy, and the heroes were just too good to be true.[59]

An 1888 literary study of Goethe's *Faust* suggests much the same: "If we delve to the bottom of the Faust legend, we shall find that it strikes its deepest root into the ultimate great dualism of the world, usually known as good and evil."[60] *White Zombie* highlights that very conflict.

In particular, Dr. Bruner and Legendre reflect that duality, being on one level signifiers of a religious dichotomy. The former is a missionary; given his apparent identification with the U.S., he represents a Christian tradition. Legendre is—at least in some respects—a Mephistopheleslike character, a "devil" as Beaumont calls him in Shot 274.

If not Satan incarnate, Legendre does possess numerous facets that suggest an association with or direct similarity to the Christian archfiend. He dresses in black in each scene, a readily acknowledged signifier of dark forces. Legendre's makeup design clearly resembles prior visual conceptions of Satan and Mephistopheles; for example, actor Lugosi's makeup and hair closely mimic those of Russian opera star Chaliapin in his famed appearances as Mephistopheles in stage adaptations of Goethe, as well as to a lesser degree those of Emil Jannings in his portrayal of the same in F.W. Murnau's 1926 film version of *Faust*.[61] His extravagant palace is itself a signifier of ill-gotten gains: sources of worldly pleasures attained through sin. And, though we may later question its exact narrative purpose, Legendre's talisman is the almost ever-present vulture, the bird of death which feeds on decay.[62]

However, we can also consider Legendre's actions and abilities. He is, for example, very much like Satan in his role as a tempter and trickster of mortals; in fact, he is not too different from Satan in the Garden of Eden. Legendre tempts Beaumont with knowledge, without making clear the price it carries. He uses language to trick; for example, he beguiles Beaumont by arguing there is "no other way" to possess Madeline except through completing the devil's bargain. Later, he deceives Beaumont again, when in Scene 17 he transforms a toast between friends into an opportunity to claim Beaumont's soul. That act represents the role which both Satan and Legendre play: they tempt, and then they take souls from their rightful owners.

Similarly, Dr. Bruner's alignment with righteous, Christian forces is also reinforced by various signifiers. For one, in Scenes 16, 18, 19, and 23, he wears white clothes, a clear indicator of decency and morality. Additionally, he offers not trickery to those around him, but truthful knowledge upon request. Rather than a palacial estate, Bruner has a modest office, with bookcases and innumerable texts serving as signs of his wisdom. Artifacts of life, including life masks on the wall and a sculpture on his desk, also serve to differentiate him from Legendre.

A 1923 pencil portrait of Russian opera star Feodor Chaliapin as Mephistopheles, a role he performed on numerous occasions.

Overall, Bruner is kindly and good. He is the only male in the film (outside of the carriage driver and the zombies) who does not show an interest in Madeline on any level other than fatherly concern, which is in stark contrast to Legendre's lust for her. Bruner is also quite deferential to the wishes of others; without even a verbal request, he quits smoking prior to entering Beaumont's home in Scene 3. Also, Bruner's consistent requests to light his pipe are always made of Neil or Neil and Madeline as a pair. Bruner's striking of matches brings light into the dark; he thus wields one of the most common signifiers of Christianity: light, whether from a fire, a candle, or a modern, blinking Christmas tree bulb. It is Bruner who will, in a metaphorical sense, provide light for Neil, whereas Legendre provides darkness for Beaumont.

Problematic, though, is that Bruner is not actually the giver of light; he relies on the matches of those who have traveled to Haiti. While the focus on matches is a minor point, the film offers numerous moments which blur the lines between Bruner and Legendre, between good and evil. For example, if anyone bears greater knowledge, it is not the representative of Christianity but instead Legendre. His eyes hovering over the countryside in Shots 17–18 suggest it is he that is the more omnipotent. Some of this may be that Haiti, especially the region dubbed the "Land of the Living Dead," bears similarity to the underworld—a quality previously discussed with regard to the film's fairy tale–like structure. Regardless, though, Legendre seems the more all-knowing of the two.

More unusual is that Dr. Bruner on occasion is mistaken for Legendre, with his clothes in Scene 3 acting as a deceptive signifier. In the former case, Neil and Madeline have just completed a harrowing carriage ride in which they saw Legendre; at the conclusion of their trip, the carriage driver explains zombiism to them. A shadowy figure who appears similar to Legendre (mainly because of his large-brim hat) approaches Neil and Madeline in Shot 57. The tension mounts in Shot 58 as the young couple embrace. The figure continues to approach in Shot 59, with Shot 60 depicting a huddled Neil and Madeline who watch as the shadowy figure grows closer.

Shot 61 cuts to Neil and Madeline alone; finally, Shot 62 gives a closeup of Dr. Bruner, who has been mistaken for his antithesis. He requests a match from the young couple, which provides intended comic relief.

An even more interesting case of mistaken identity between Bruner and Legendre occurs in Scene 22. Madeline, under Legendre's control, attempts to stab Neil. In Shot 394, a mysterious hand extends from screen left to knock the knife out of Madeline's grasp. The cloak on the hand's arm is black; it immediately begs

A portrait of opera star Maurice Renaud as Mephistopheles published in the May 1921 issue of Theatre Magazine. *Such images influenced the creation of Murder Legendre.*

comparison to Shots 119 and 120, in which Legendre's objectified hand is the first image seen in his meeting with Beaumont. But in Scene 22, despite the black cloak, the hand belongs to Dr. Bruner.[63] It is the first we see of him inside Legendre's castle.[64]

While a parallel can be drawn between the objectified hands of both men in the aforementioned shots, a repetitive use of stylized hand gestures belongs only to Legendre. Throughout the film, emphasis is placed on his hands; they are seen in closeups as he uses a particular hand clasp to control zombies.[65] Legendre's hand motions in general do not stem from Seabrook's *The Magic Island*, and have seemingly no connection with any other writings on zombiism. Perhaps screenwriter Weston or director Halperin read about palmistry in texts on voodoo in Louisiana; perhaps it is only a deliberate variation on the hand gestures actor Lugosi used in the film *Dracula* (1931). Regardless, they become a repeated motif in the film. At times they mark the dialogue; at other times, they obviate the dialogue.

Legendre's hands, however, are not necessary to providing mental orders to his minions, as Scene 15 shows. Indeed, his use of the hand clasp does not occur in Shot 228 either, though in this case—whatever the original intention—actor Lugosi flubbed in a minor way. After an odd and unclear hesitation, he finally offers a brief stare and a hand motion toward screen left; its use perhaps suggests Halperin's eventual need for a less-than-perfect take.

In addition to his overtones of Mephistopheles/ Satan and his parallels and contrasts to Dr. Bruner, Murder Legendre becomes an even more vague entity given his occasional similarity to Death incarnate. Garnett Weston and Victor Halperin's idea for Legendre to work on this level as well may have been spurred by Alexander King's pen-and-ink illustration of the zombie overseer in *The Magic Island*; costumed in the black plantation outfit that would become actor Lugosi's costume, the overseer's is a deathlike skull.

The vulture, which we have previ-

Yet another of the innumerable Satan/ Mephistopheles/Devil images that preceded and collectively influenced the appearance of Murder Legendre. This artwork was published in February 1931 national advertisements for Peek Frean's AllWheat Crispbread.

ously viewed as Legendre's talisman, may be better described as a metaphor for Legendre himself. If the vulture is an acknowledged symbol of death, its tie to Legendre is irrevocable. Dr. Bruner learns that a "cloud of vultures always hovers over the house of the living dead"; in Scene 18, he even throws a rock at one that is screeching above the temporary campsite he has erected. By the time of Legendre's death, the connection between him and the vulture has been established repeatedly in Scenes 12 and 16. After the zombie master is thrown off the castle cliff, the bird flies off the castle as well. A 1932 critical review of *White Zombie* even referred to the vulture as "Murder's spirit."[66]

Perhaps the strongest link between Legendre, the vulture, and death occurs in Scene 16. Legendre deceives Beaumont into drinking the zombie powder, and in Shot 294 the latter sees a vulture squawking at the castle window. Beaumont realizes at that moment that Legendre has brought him death. In Shot 295, he comprehends the reciprocity between the vulture and the zombie master; with a fearful expression covering his face, he stammers out, "The vulture! You!" Shot 296 again shows the vulture, with 297 returning to a medium long shot of Legendre and Beaumont. The latter knows death, at least of a sort, is at hand; he again speaks, crying out, "No ... not that ... not that!" Shot 298 brings a medium shot of the two characters, with a fade to black ending the scene and acting as a mournful, cinematic shroud over Beaumont's existence.

From the perspective of Legendre as Death, his commentary regarding zombies and Madeline in Scene 15 seems even more pointed: "I took them, just as we will take [pause] this one." He seems at this moment little different from images of Death in prior texts in which he appears to take those whose earthly time is over. Echoes of this idea can also be heard when he answers Neil's question, "What are they?" in reference to the cadre of zombies: "For you, my friend, they are the angels of death."

Even the repeated use of Legendre's eyes reinforces Legendre's role as Death. For example, in his book *The Evil Eye in the Bible and in Rabbinic Literature*, Rivka Ulmer writes that:

> According to the Talmud, the Angel of Death is perceived as having eyes everywhere. ... The Angel of Death [has also been] depicted as full of eyes, wich means that he cannot avoid looking at people, and that nothing can escape him.[67]

Augmenting *White Zombie*'s use of evil eye folklore, the film may well be using—as Ulmer's text suggests—the inescapable vision of Death, which helps explain Legendre's eyes in Shots 17–18, hovering as they do over the entire countryside.

We should also now invoke the similarities between *White Zombie* and Fritz Lang's film *Der müde Tod* (1921), the latter being a tale in which Death (actor Bernhard Goetzke) takes one of a pair of lovers (actors Walter Janssen and Lil Dagover) to the underworld. In it, Death appears dressed essentially the same as Legendre—completely in black, with a large hat. His first meeting with the young couple closely echoes Legendre's visual introduction with Madeline in Scene 2. The youthful lovers in *Der müde Tod* ride in a carriage, with the female peering out one of its windows when it stops. It is then she sees the cold, silent figure of Death.

However, we should not believe that Legendre is simply Death embodied, given the former's many similarities to Mephistopheles and his dissimilarities to Death—not the least of which is that Legendre presumably dies at the climax of the film. Rather, the resemblance to Death adds to the mystery of who and what Legendre is.

Given Legendre's mysterious qualities, we should also examine his very name. In the film, he is referred to by name only once, when in Scene 18 witch doctor Pierre speaks of "an evil spirit man that is called Murder"—worded almost is if to suggest it's not certain whether that really is his name or merely an appellation by which Haitian natives refer to him; and worded as if to leave a question as to whether he is a man or a human incarnation of a spirit. Later, in Scene 23, Neil directly asks Legendre, "Who are you, and what are they [the zombies];" Legendre avoids the first question, while answering the second with a metaphor.

Other direct references to the character come during a discussion in Scene 5 between Beaumont and Silver. The former asks, "Has that *other* person sent word yet? ... [pause] he's 24 hours late." Silver replies, "I wish you'd keep away from *that* man, sir." Later, in Scene 19, one maid warns another, "*He* might hear you," audibly placing the stress on the pronoun, and not providing the antecedent noun. The emphasis on being vague with his name increases Legendre's mysterious qualities, as well as further suggesting his connection with Satan or the possibility he is, in one sense at least, Mephistopheles.

It would seem that the name Legendre was in the script (as it definitely appeared in the *Complete Exhibitors* [*sic*] *Campaign Book*), though director Halperin must have deleted it during filming. It is true that footage was cut between the June 1932 preview and the July premiere, but such material seems not to have included a dialogue sequence.[68] Rather, especially given the manner in which the aforementioned characters present their dialogue with an emphasis on the vague, it seems no use was made of the name Legendre during the production. Given that the name remained in the U.S. pressbook's credits, newspapers in 1932 occasionally mentioned the character as "Legendre." In the *Los Angeles Times*, the name was even mangled into "Lengendre."[69]

Why Weston decided to use Legendre as the villain's name is itself difficult to determine. Certainly the most famous figure in history bearing that unusual name was Adrien Marie Legendre (1752–1833), a well-respected and influential French mathematician whose texts were well read in the 19th century.[70] More likely, though, Weston read the name Legendre in relation to New Orleans voodoo. While it is difficult to find examples of the name in easily accessible texts printed prior to 1932, Legendre was a person of some importance in the recorded stories of voodoo queen Marie Laveau. Many tales claim Laveau's daughter was one Madame Legendre, who incidentally bore the reputation of being quite a religious woman who abhorred voodoo and attempted to rehabilitate the family name. In response to articles in the mid–1880s by journalist George W. Cable regarding Laveau's voodoo activities, Legendre protested and even threatened libel suits. When a New Orleans *Times-Picayune* reporter read one of Cable's accounts to her in her home, Legendre cried out, "It's a lie. It's a lie."[71]

Though it is difficult to pinpoint the precise origins of the character's name, Legendre definitely acts as a counterpoint and occasional reflection of Bruner. In general, *White Zombie* positions the two as opposing forces, as the embodiments of evil and good. But however much the Mephistopheles-like Legendre is different from the Christian missionary Bruner, the latter is occasionally mistaken for the former. That element in *White Zombie* subtly suggests an unnerving possibility: that good and evil are not as clearly defined as we might think.

NEIL, BEAUMONT, AND MADELINE

If we have already seen how in some ways Neil echoes the typical "hero" of the horror film as it existed in 1932, we can now examine his role—especially as it relates to Beaumont and Madeline—as being unique in many respects. For example, however much heroes of horror films often experienced conflict with a villain over a female, Neil fights this battle on two fronts, as Madeline is desired not just by Legendre but also of course by Beaumont. Legendre's very appearance suggests his evil nature, but Beaumont's motives seem unbeknownst to Neil until after Madeline's funeral.

For example, Neil never questions the speed with which Beaumont ingratiates himself with Madeline on the journey to Haiti from New York, nor does he find it unusual that Beaumont agrees to hire him as his financial agent before he ever even meets him. When the two finally are introduced, Neil completely misses the irony

of Beaumont's remark that, "We have something very special prepared for this occasion." That "something very special" becomes Madeline's descent into zombification.

The film makes Madeline's endangered situation known to spectators, however, in Scene 6. Neil is dressed in the heroic and righteous color white, while Beaumont appears in black. The latter confesses to Madeline that, however much he has tried to make the upcoming wedding special, he wanted to do more. The film cuts to Shot 89, a solitary view of Neil, displaced from Madeline and the lecherous Beaumont. As Beaumont continues to fawn over Madeline, Shot 91 cuts back to Neil when his name is mentioned. Neil's arms are folded, as they were in Shot 89, and his face appears worried. Until Madeline speaks her fiancé's name, Beaumont has momentarily even forgotten Neil's existence. In addition then to Neil and Beaumont's clothes coding their respective morals, the scene visually illustrates Neil as the one from whom Madeline will be taken.

At first, Beaumont seems to be stronger than Neil. Signifiers of sexual prowess and physical power—such as swords and weapons hanging on his wall and a length of chain in his hand—are seen in Scene 5. In his first on-screen sequence, we find him sporting hunting clothes, happy at the arrival of Madeline, his female quarry. However, he does bear some similarities to Neil. If we have just seen Neil's importance and power minimized in Scene 6, Beaumont will eventually suffer isolation as well. Immediately before and during his meeting with Legendre in Scenes 7–9 he appears visibly worried. During the wedding in Scene 11, Beaumont is shown in Shot 172 separate from Neil and Madeline, again appearing visibly concerned. He is cinematically depicted much as Neil was in Scene 6, momentarily displaced from Madeline as she weds another.

A further example of Beaumont's isolation can be found in Scene 17, in which he approaches Madeline. "I was mad to do this...," he cries out, his words unheard by her deaf, zombified ears. In Shots 244 and 246, Beaumont is framed behind the prop of the piano lid, which visibly shows the division within him. After Legendre enters the great hall of the palace, Shots 256 to 261 alternate between images of Legendre and Madeline together and solitary medium shots of Beaumont. Visually, we realize he has definitely lost Madeline to Legendre.

Also like Neil, Beaumont seems unable to grasp the implications of unfolding events. Early in the film, for example, Shot 102 pans from a closeup of Beaumont's worried profile to the blank stare of a zombie carriage driver. The cinematic technique has visually linked the two, prophesying Beaumont's fate. Later, during his first meeting with Legendre, Beaumont overlooks Legendre's

Tension between Neil (John Harron, right) and Beaumont (Robert Frazer, center) over Madeline (Madge Bellamy): Neil seems much more aware of Beaumont's intentions for Madeline in this publicity still than in the film itself. (Courtesy of Leonard J. Kohl.)

comment that the zombification of Madeline will bring heavy costs.

In Scene 11, Beaumont reveals to Madeline his love for her: "You can raise me up to paradise, or you can blast my world into nothingness." She rebukes him, and then he gives her the flower his loyal butler, Silver, has laced with the zombie powder. "One last gift before I lose you forever," he tells her, without knowing that—in his attempt to own her through zombification—he really is ensuring his loss of her.

Madeline, as we have already suggested, does little to impact the film's narrative, but rather is acted upon. She is generally featured in white clothing, for it is indeed she who becomes the "white zombie." The color suggests her innocence and virginal qualities, symbolism with deep roots in literature and poetry. Exemplars of this symbolism would be too voluminous to list, but S. Bar-ing-Gould's 1896 book *Curiosities of Olden Times* employs it with a flourish Garnett Weston would have appreciated: "White has been supposed to denote purity; and to this day white gloves and hat-band and scarves are employed at the funeral of a young girl, as in the old ballad of 'The Bride's Burial':—"

> A garland fresh and fair
> Of lilies there was made
> In signs of her virginity,
> And on her coffin laid.
> Six pretty maidens, all in white,
> Did bear her to the ground
> The bells did ring in solemn swing
> And made a doleful sound.[72]

Madeline's first appearance is in white attire; her wedding dress and funeral gown continue the imagery.

After her revivification, Madeline does little other than play Liszt's "Liebestraum" on Legendre's piano—one of the four major examples of diegetic music used in the film.[73] Weston and Halperin would have been aware from tales included in *The Magic Island* that zombies can perform rote execution of physical tasks. It is possible they were further aware of the kinds of repeated actions undertaken by those under hypnosis, such as the piano playing discussed in the following passage from George Romanes' 1897 essay on hypnotism:

> …we know from daily experience that the most complicated neuro-muscular actions—such as those required for piano-playing—become by frequent repetition "mechanical," or performed without consciousness of the processes by which the result is achieved. So it is in the case of hypnosis. Actions which have long been previously rendered mechanical by long habit are, in the state of hypnosis, performed automatically in response to their appropriate stimuli.[74]

The appropriate stimuli in Madeline's case is provided by Legendre, who apparently keeps her performing repetitive tasks just as his zombies at the sugar mill do.

She is also generally oblivious to the presence of others around her. For example, Beaumont speaks at length to her in Scene 17 to no avail. Working in tandem with her character name, her entombment, her pale visage, her lack of dialogue while a zombie, and her white clothing, Madeline's behavior in part echoes Poe's short story "The Fall of the House of Usher." The narrator in the Poe story speaks of Madeline Usher, who passes "through a remote portion of the apartment, and, without having noticed my presence, disappeared."

More importantly, though, Madeline is repeatedly referred to in the dialogue as a flower. As early as Scene 1, she appears in a hat with floral designs. Later, the first verbalization of the metaphor comes in Scene 9, when Legendre instructs Beaumont on the use of the zombie powder: "Only a pinpoint, Monsieur Beaumont, in a flower … or perhaps a glass of wine." As previously mentioned, Beaumont chooses the former, which continues a motif repeated throughout the film. Similar to the color white, the use of flowers as a symbol for femininity has deep roots in literature and poetry. Among the multitude of examples is Du Maurier's *Trilby*, in which the title character is likened to a flower.[75]

Madeline's own connection to the image is repeated visually at Legendre's castle. She wears a dress with a floral, clover-like imprint, and is even framed in Shot 368 through an almost identical design in the staircase of the castle. Even more directly, Legendre speaks to Beaumont of her, suggesting: "It would be a pity to destroy such a lovely flower. Let's drink to the future of this lovely flower."

Screenwriter Garnett Weston apparently enjoyed use of the symbolism, as he would incorporate it in his future writings. For example, in the *Poldrate Street*, flowers—and their signification of a female character—again played an important role in the narrative: "Considering her very real love of flowers and the fact she had so much ground at her disposal, one would have thought Sarah Reckon would grow her own blooms."[76] Apparently pleased with the metaphor, Weston played off a similar symbol again in a novel called *The Man with the Monocle*: "The flowers would flame in tropic beauty. But tropic sun and tropic flowers grew pale beside the glory of what was burning their hearts."[77]

Hearts burn in *White Zombie* as well, with the innocent flower named Madeline causing flames of passion. Neil and Beaumont, who are very different characters in many ways, are similar in that they both desire Madeline. But their interests in her represent only two of the various sexual appetites embedded in the narrative.

SEXUAL GREED AND NECROPHILIA

In many ways, *White Zombie* is a sexually charged tale of greed for Madeline, the innocent flower. Immediately we might cite Shot 10, in which Madeline for no apparent narrative reason is shown in her undergarments in preparation for the wedding. Much more important than such fleeting images, though, is the detail through which the sexual is woven into the tale, ranging from love-lust triangles to issues of necrophilia and homosexuality.

Flowers help signify the feminine sexual qualities which the males in the narrative seek. If we have already seen numerous examples of the floral metaphor, we can extend the discussion by noting the symbolic relationship between flowers and female genitalia. For example, in Shot 361 we see Madeline walking past a table on which a floral arrangement rests. The visual composition is such that, when she strides past the table, the flowers cover the region of her genitals. At that stage, she is metaphorically in the grip of the villain. Legendre—who has apparently sinister "plans for Mademoiselle"[78]—is framed through the flowerlike design in the castle staircase in Shot 251; visually, he intrudes upon her genitalia, penetrating her as a result.

Legendre attempts complete sexual possession of Madeline, foreshadowed by taking her scarf which he keeps in the breast of his shirt. His plans of ownership again recall Du Maurier. Svengali talks to Trilby in the novel while playing Chopin on the piano; he wickedly claims that he will come to "look at you in your mahogany glass case!"[79] Trilby is a possession to be displayed, much as Madeline is for a time in Legendre's castle.

Neil (John Harron) and Madeline (Madge Bellamy) are reunited at the film's conclusion.

Eyes are also employed as a sexual sign, much as they are in both the 1931 film *Dracula* and the 1897 Bram Stoker novel. They represent the phallic, and Legendre penetrates Madeline with them from the first time he sees her. Later, for example, she lies in his castle, awaiting his command. In Shot 358, Legendre's superimposed eyes dissolve into an image of Madeline lying on a bed. Penetration is suggested, though far more implicitly than in some 1932 advertisements, one of which has rays from Legendre's eyes beaming onto the unclothed genitals of a pen-and-ink female.

Whatever the symbol of their lust, Neil, Legendre, and Beaumont oscillate between successions of conflicting triangulations with Madeline. First, Neil and Beaumont compete for her. Then, Beaumont and Legendre form a sexual triangle with Madeline. Finally, after Beaumont becomes incapacitated, a triangulation occurs between Legendre, Neil, and Madeline.

Of the three males, Neil shows the greatest fear of Madeline becoming sexually tainted. In Scene 16, he expresses a belief that Madeline is "better dead" than in the hands of sex-crazed natives. And when Neil finds Madeline in the castle, he immediately asks a knowing, "What have they done to you?" Despite his fears, though, Neil engages in a minor way in necrophilia with Madeline, just as his male competitors do. To Dr. Bruner, Neil admits: "I kissed her as she lay there in the coffin ... and her lips were cold." His dialogue brings to mind the gothic romanticism with which screenwriter Weston and director Halperin were acquainted. For example, Shelley's 1818 "Invocation to Misery" suggests the combination of death and romance:

> Kiss me;—oh! thy lips are cold:
> Round my neck thine arms enfold—
> They are soft, but chill and dead;

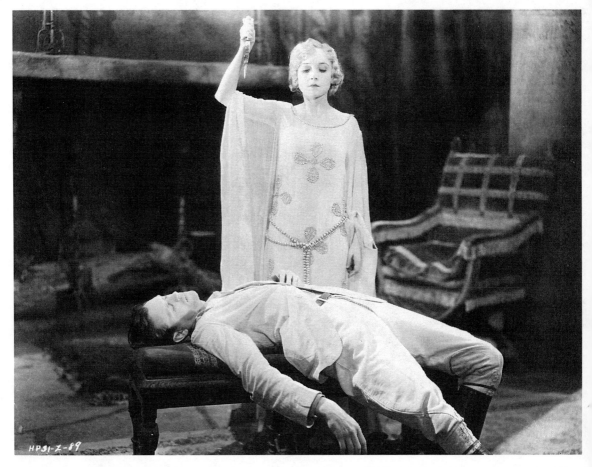

Madeline (Madge Bellamy), wearing a dress with a floral design, prepares to stab Neil (John Harron). (Courtesy of Leonard J. Kohl.)

And thy tears upon my head
Burn like points of frozen lead.

Hasten to the bridal bed—
Underneath the grave 'tis spread:
In darkness may our love be hid,
Oblivion be our coverlid—
We may rest, and none forbid.

If Neil chose to kiss his deceased bride, Beaumont and certainly Legendre—who is "afraid [Beaumont] might not agree" with his devious intentions—have more sexualized desires for Madeline.

The film implicitly suggests necrophilia, as Madeline is the "living dead." One of the themes of *Dracula* is then inverted, as now it is the victim who is deceased, rather than the antagonist. For the bulk of the film, Beaumont and Legendre yearn for more than the kiss Neil steals from a corpse.

As film theorist Harry Benshoff has noted, homoeroticism is also present in *White Zombie*, particularly in Scene 21.[80] Beaumont's eroded mind slips deeper into zombiism; Legendre sits at a table with him, carving a voodoo doll with his knife, a phallic signifier seen once earlier when he helps transform Madeline into a zombie. Legendre sits the partially completed doll on the table; it is suggestive of Beaumont—a plaything, a toy.

Beaumont then shakes Legendre's hand, and the latter says: "You refused to shake hands one, I remember.... Very well, we understand each other better now." The homoerotic qualities are heightened when we recall Legendre's gleeful dialogue from Scene 17, in which he begins Beaumont's zombification: "I have taken a fancy to you, Monsieur!"

Even more complex, though, are the sexual implications of Scene 22. Legendre, aware of Neil's presence in his castle, uses his control over Madeline to force her to stab her husband, her rightful lover.

She takes the knife and approaches his unconscious body in a manner not dissimilar to the way somnambulist Cesare (actor Conrad Veidt) approaches Joan (Lil Dagover) in Wiene's film *The Cabinet of Dr. Caligari* (1919). Both are under mind control, but both hesitate.

Madeline is about to penetrate Neil, but cannot. The hesitation in those moments prior to Dr. Bruner knocking the knife from her hand proves uncomfortable to audiences as it suggests two transgressive possibilities: a gender inversion, as Madeline holds the knife and Neil is to be emasculated, or an indirectly homoerotic encounter, as she is under the control of Legendre.

White Zombie overall then proves to be a sexually charged tale, with lust and sexual greed surfacing as perhaps its most consistent and overt themes. Sexuality erupts as heterosexual and homosexual, between living and dead.

Sex binds the major characters into triads built around the character of Madeline. Sex hovers over the entire narrative and all in it, with the exception of the unfortunate zombies housed in Legendre's sugar mill.

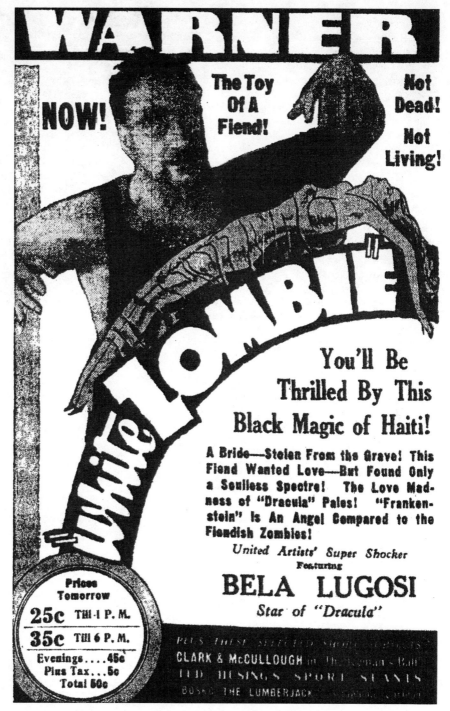

Printed on September 17, 1932, in the Pittsburgh Post-Gazette, *this ad pictures Frederick Peters as zombie Chauvin. The text heavily suggests the theme of necrophilia.*

Zombies and Laborers

If Legendre's zombies, with the exception of Madeline and Beaumont, are not kept for sexual purposes, then we need identify their situation and purpose in the narrative. We must decode the zombies' relevance in *White Zombie*, searching beyond their shock value to 1932 audiences to reveal important connections with aspects of the U.S. culture of the early 1930s. Furthermore, in this exercise we can gain insight into how screenwriter Garnett Weston and director Victor Halperin created and added to existing zombie lore to construct their narrative.

The Magic Island and other pre–1932 texts provide no definite account of the process of zombification; that is to say, no stories are told of the physical reactions of a person becoming a zombie. As a result, Weston and Halperin had to draw on other sources to devise scenes like Beaumont's transformation into a zombie. Perhaps, given the film's debt in other narrative respects to hypnotism and mesmerism, Weston and Halperin were aware of the physical results of such mental states and used them in *White Zombie*. In 1897, for example, George Romanes wrote that during some hypnotic trances:

> ...the rate at which a reflex excitation is propagated through the central nerve-organs is very slow, as compared with the rapidity with which such propagation takes place in ordinary circumstances. ... Moreover, the muscles are prone to go into tonic contraction, rather than respond to a stimulus in the ordinary way. The whole condition thus so strongly resembles catalepsy that [it] is nothing other than the latter artificially induced.[81]

Beaumont's mental slippage and inability to control his muscular functions bears similarity to descriptions like those Romanes provides.

Charcot also spoke of a cataleptic state induced by hypnotism, with behavior described in his discussion bearing great resemblance to that of the zombies in *White Zombie*: "the eyes are open, the gaze is fixed, the eyelids do not quiver...." He too discussed the absence of neuromuscular hyperexcitability and the "complete insensitivity to pain."[82] Beliefs like the latter may have influenced Scene 23, in which zombie Chauvin does not slacken or even show emotion when Neil's bullets hit him in the chest.[83]

The literary world also produced numerous fictional accounts of catalepsy-like trances which may have influenced *White Zombie*. For example, in Sheridan Le Fanu's short story collection *Through a Glass Darkly* (1872), the tale of "The Room in the Dragon Volant" features an Englishman who enters such a trance:

> I was, indeed, a spirit in prison; and unspeakable was my dumb and unmoving agony.

Beaumont (Robert Frazer) on his descent into zombiism. (Courtesy of Venita Halperin.)

> The power of thought remained clear and active. Dull terror filled my mind. How would this end? Was it actual death?
>
> You will understand that my faculty of observing was unimpaired. I could hear and see anything as distinctly as ever I did in my life. It was simply that my will had, as it were, lost its hold of my body.

While Madeline's entrance into zombiism appears onscreen as a swift death, Beaumont's physical degradation in Scene 21 is not at all dissimilar to descriptions such as Le Fanu's.

However much the influenza epidemics of the late teens are forgotten now, they could certainly have been the partial basis for the way in which Beaumont loses physical control during Scene 21. Over 50 million people died worldwide from the flu epidemic during some 18 months. In the United States, more than 550,000 adults died in 1918—more than the combined total of American battle deaths in World War I, World War II, Korea, and Vietnam.[84] Among the problems aggravated by the epidemic was an outbreak of encephalitis lethargica, symptoms of which very much resemble the kind of deprivation of motor control Beaumont experiences.[85]

Like vampires, zombies are resurrected bodies, corpses (or drugged, corpselike bodies) which are no longer in their graves. However, zombies are not in control of their own wills; they do the bidding of another, silently carrying out orders. For example, the zombies approach Neil at the climax, closely echoing a similar scene in Fritz Lang's *Der müde Tod* when dead spirits advance on the young female lead. Legendre's zombies are workers who do not—and presumably cannot—question his dictates.

However, the zombies are represented in a more complex manner than as mere slaves; *White Zombie* portrays them as laborers in a capitalist regime. The literary influences we have already encountered may have helped shape this subtle political commentary within *White Zombie*. For example, Goethe's Mephistopheles, Du Maurier's Svengali, and Stoker's Dracula all participate, albeit differently, in capitalist franchises. Much the same could be said of Legendre, who attempts to gain power, control, and financial gain through the use of his workers. Scene 8 shows them at work in the sugar mill, carrying baskets of sugar cane on their heads and manually operating the millstone.

The zombies' work is one of repetitive labor, and their blank stares reveal their listless lives devoid of meaning. They are numb to their own hardships and to the hardships of others that they witness. In Scene 19, R. Nathaniel Dett's "Listen to the Lambs" plays in the background as we visually see a zombified Madeline. But the lambs—whether a lower class Haitian, a middle class Madeline, or an upperclass Beaumont—make clear that labor troubles do not discriminate, much as the Great Depression destroyed those involved in the capitalist enterprise across the financial spectrum.

At the same time, most of the slaughtered lambs during the Depression were of the lower classes, just as the predominant number of zombies in *White Zombie* seem to be. And when Legendre introduces them, we realize that while at one point they were individuals, zombiism has erased their individuality. Zombification—their work in Legendre's capitalist endeavor—has destroyed their lives. Indeed, in Scene 8, the zombies are numb to the fact that one of their own has fallen into the sugar mill, certain to be dismembered. Mindlessly, the zombies continue at their tasks.

"They work faithfully, and they are not worried about long hours," Legendre tells Beaumont. The reference to U.S. labor problems and unionization (which in the early 1930s, among other demands, called for regulated work hours and overtime pay) is quite pointed. For example, the roaring twenties saw a U.S. government

Rare portrait of the zombie (unknown actor) who drives the carriage that delivers Beaumont to Murder Legendre's sugar mill.

quite eager to retard basically all movements toward employee unionization. During the early thirties, economic unrest made many employees more bold in seeking their rights through interdependence. For example, coal miners mobilized to a degree that major strikes occurred in the time immediately prior to *White Zombie* being scripted.[86] Indeed, some 324,210 laborers in 1932 participated in strikes.[87] Even within the film industry of 1931–32, various union-related strikes occurred, especially of projectionists in a number cities.[88]

Allusions in *White Zombie* to then current labor troubles in the U.S. did not go unnoticed in 1932. The New Orleans *Times-Picayune* suggested, "the zombie system is the kind of thing that increases unemployment…,"[89] while the *St. Louis Post* noted that zombiism can "provide employment for a vast army [of 'laboring classes'] which has already passed beyond the need of work."[90]

If we can trace the physical reactions of zombie transformation to historical and literary roots, the remaining question is more difficult to answer. Does *White*

A phalanx of Murder Legendre's zombies prepare to throw Silver (Brandon Hurst) into the rocky waters below.

Zombie engage in a criticism of capitalism? The answer is yes, as the plight of the zombies strikes too similar a chord with the U.S. worker, especially those harmed by the Great Depression, to be otherwise. At the same time, it is very much a subordinate theme to issues like sexual greed, and it is not—as James B. Twitchell suggests in his book *Dreadful Pleasures*[91]—framed as a particularly "Marxist" criticism. Indeed, the theme never surfaces to the degree that the zombies rise up against Legendre or are freed upon his death.

AFRICAN-AMERICANS AND *WHITE ZOMBIE*

One of the *White Zombie* "Catchlines" suggested by United Artists for theater use in 1932 was, "They knew that this was taking place among the blacks, but when this fiend practiced it on a white girl ... all hell broke loose."[92] However, the bulk of all studio materials and publicity did not invoke racism. The title may well have caused at least a few viewers and critics to consider ethnicity, but it seems quite clear in the film's narrative that the intended meaning of *White Zombie* was Madeline's innocence, virginity, and most particularly her status as a bride. Still, the multifaceted possibilities of the title—intentional or not—highlight the need to investigate the film's treatment of blacks and whites and to develop an understanding of how closely it adopts then dominant U.S. views tainted by discrimination and racism.

As in almost every major Hollywood film of the twenties and thirties, blacks are not given lead roles in *White Zombie*; instead, most central parts are portrayed by white actors. This extends in part to the zombies, many of whom are whites in blackface; some, like both the witch doctor-turned-zombie and the witch doctor Pierre, present ethnic caricatures. The use of blackface alone generally smacks of racism, but it follows in the unfortunate path of many Hollywood films of the era. Discriminatory and racist, but regrettably not unusual.

One of Murder Legendre's many zombies prepares to take Beaumont (Robert Frazer, right) to the sugar mill.

On the other hand, it needs to be said that the film is not a racist document. In fact, it is far less racist than its storyline might have permitted, which is an outcome that would easily have been allowed in the early 1930s and, in some quarters, even encouraged. But to its credit, no black voodoo cults or characters play major roles in the film, as they do in texts like *The Magic Island*. The villain is not black, even though the sheer ethnicity of Haiti might have suggested it. Additionally, Madeline's pall-bearers, who visibly seem to be black actors rather than whites in blackface, are very nicely dressed and do not suggest racial caricatures. And we might mention too that one background musical selection, R. Nathaniel Dett's "Listen to the Lambs," credibly and seriously presents the music of this famed African-American composer.

Most importantly, African-American actor-composer Clarence Muse's role as the carriage driver acts as an important barometer of the film's view toward blacks in general. While he admittedly appears as a laborer, nothing about him or the circumstances he is in suggest anything demeaning. Indeed, he is well dressed and is well spoken in terms of the script's dialogue. He is not a source of humor, and does not appear part of any "Uncle Tom" tradition.

Rather, Muse appears knowledgeable and credible, and offers through his dialogue a crucial piece of information on which the credibility (and even understandability) of the entire film rests: a definition of zombies.[93] As later chapters will explore in further detail, almost all audience members in 1932 would have been unaware of what a zombie was. If Muse's performance had been less than believable, *White Zombie* would have been a failure dramatically. His description offers concern for the nearby creatures, but never humor. All depends on his credibility, especially as he conveys the meaning of zombiism.

As will also be explored in subsequent chapters,

Muse's credibility as a serious actor and composer would have helped render his character trustworthy to 1932 audiences. Perhaps when he later wrote of the African-American actor's situation in a discriminatory and racist performing arts world, he had favorable memories of his role in *White Zombie*:

> ...what of this new character which cries for self-expression? The Negro actor is willing to depict him. The black audience, comparatively small in number, applauds loudly for him, but with no avail. When the white audience sees him, it smiles and seems to say, "That is good, but when will he sing and dance? That is what we want to see and hear." The Negro actor is truly perplexed. What will he do?[94]

Some might see Muse's limited screen time as an indicator of the African-American's plight in Hollywood and indeed the U.S. at large. Regardless, though, Muse's carriage driver did not leave most viewers in 1932 (or later) expecting humor or song or dance. If anything, his role suggests the production's modicum of sympathy to the situation of serious black actors.

For a film set in a predominantly black country and built around superstitions and religious beliefs stemming from that ethnic group, *White Zombie* certainly does not pursue a racist argument, even if it does possess discriminatory undercurrents that can be felt in the Hollywood films—and indeed in almost every aspect of U.S. society—of the twenties and early thirties. Instead, it seems to skirt easy opportunities for racist diatribes, whether visual or verbal, and even offers a credible, nondemeaning role to an established African-American performer.

PICTORIAL DESIGN, ACTING EXPRESSIONS, AND CINEMATIC STYLE

White Zombie's aesthetic excellence stems from a confluence of talented planning and execution and of happy accidents. The film creates a visual work generally outside the purview of German Expressionism and pre–1932 Hollywood horror films. Its vision is one of moving camera shots, of optically printed transitions, and of a methodical and at times glacially slow pace. Its use of music, sound effects, and silence is highly sophisticated for its time. And though the film's on-screen talent often overacts, the overacting at certain moments contributes to the otherwordly aspects of the story.

Both the sets and lighting help create an original and nightmarish vision, but one less dependent on German Expressionism than *Dracula* (1931), *Frankenstein* (1931), or *Murders in the Rue Morgue* (1932)—three of the major contributions to the 1930s horror film cycle before *White Zombie*'s production. Darkness and lightness are important throughout in the lighting schema, but—even remembering our discussion of fairy tales and their tendency to externalize inner feelings—they still exhibit a less overarching, enunciative capacity than in the other films. Even the interior of Legendre's cliffside castle—a leftover set from Universal's *Dracula*—looks less ominous than in its vampiric predecessor thanks to a more high key lighting style. Dark and light are visually important to *White Zombie*'s opposition of good and evil to be sure, but while shadows are cast, it is hero Neil in Shots 345–346 who casts the longest shadow. Nowhere can be found the overt and Expressionistic use of shadows for the sake of horror as in *Frankenstein* or *Murders in the Rue Morgue*; the latter even used painted shadows on the set to achieve the desired effect.

In addition to less reliance on shadows and high key lighting, *White Zombie* does not use the expressionist sets seen in films like *The Cabinet of Dr. Caligari* (1919) and the initial trio of 1930s horror cycle films, as well as in other Hollywood films like *Svengali* (1931). For example, however ominous Legendre's castle exterior appears, it appears more like a fairy tale setting than an Expressionistic painting or woodcut; it is mysterious, but features none of the distorted angles structures bear in films like *Caligari*. And the exterior of Beaumont's estate is more visually adumbrative of Henri Christophe's historic Sans-Souci palace in Haiti than anything seen in German Expressionism.

The film's artful composition, lighting, and atmosphere—presumably an amalgamation of director Victor Halperin and cinematographer Arthur Martinelli's visions—are closer to the art of Romanticism. In particular, Shots 229–231 in Scene 15—which show the zombies carrying Madeline's corpse through the cemetery—are among the most haunting seen in the 1930s horror film. Eerie trees, dark lighting, and the stoic zombie figures fuse into a nightmarish vision very evocative of the work of Caspar David Friedrich, the 19th-century German Romanticist. Friedrich's paintings *Winter* (1807–1808), *Abbey in the Oak Forest* (1809–1810), *Winter Landscape* (1811), *Monastery Graveyard in the Snow* (1817–1819), *Two Men Contemplating the Moon* (1819), *The Raven Tree* (1822), and the unfinished *Cemetery Entrance* (1825) visually appear to inform the film's *mise en scène* in Scene 15 far more than any other artistic movement or style.

If any major aspect of *White Zombie* borrows from German Expressionism, it is its constructed world, which places extreme importance on the gesture. Legendre in particular uses hand movements, hand clasps, and facial expressions that emphasize what German film historian-theorist Lotte Eisner once termed the "Expressionist gesture."[95] Legendre's very introduction in Scene 9 at Shot 119 and 120 occurs only as an objectified hand; only in

Henri Christophe's Palace of "Sans-Souci" in Haiti.

Shot 121 are his face and body revealed. But these elements borrow only indirectly from Expressionism, with the most immediate source being Lugosi's similar array of gestures and expressions in *Dracula* on stage and in the 1931 film.

Some of the film's acting is also reminiscent of a style popular in 1920s German cinema. In Expressionism, what on the surface might appear to be overacting is instead an intentional attempt to outwardly show the inward emotions of a character. But of the actors only Lugosi had been part of the Expressionist movement in German cinema, and even his role in it had been brief and inconsequential.[96] Certainly *no* evidence of any kind can support an argument that acting styles in *White Zombie* were intentionally evocative of Expressionistic acting, or intentional at all for that matter; indeed, the visual evidence suggests otherwise. But even if not intentional, the acting overall does instill an ethereal quality; the unbelievable performances merge well with other elements of the film and appear so stylized and incredible as to be suitable for the story at hand. Lugosi's Legendre offers malevolent histrionics, Bellamy's Madeline seems sedated even before her zombification, and Harron's Neil is acted so poorly as to be—at least at times—strangely appropriate for the frustrated, ineffectual, and impotent hero he portrays.

However, *White Zombie* is not merely a cinematic simulacrum of earlier painting styles and a collection of less than realistic acting styles. The film presents highly original visuals and cinematic technique. Segments like Scene 14, in which a drunken Neil mourns his deceased bride, seem wholly original in design and execution. Shot 205 introduces the scene, showing Neil at a table in a bar while a Spanish *jota* plays in the background; shadows of people enjoying themselves are thrown on a wall behind him. Neil is framed between two bottles of liquor. In Shot 206, he sees a transparent vision of Madeline's upper torso, superimposed in the lower righthand corner of the screen. It disappears when he reaches for it. In Shot 208, yet another image of Madeline appears to torment him, this time over the shadow of a woman in the tavern. The image of Madeline calls his name in Shot 209, but again disappears when he attempts to embrace it. In Shot 210, Neil is left against the wall, surrounded by nothing but the shadows of those enjoying themselves. He is disoriented and alone.

Augmenting the artful composition and shot sequencing, *White Zombie* features some advanced camera movements. The most noteworthy is in Scene 16, Shot 236, which comprises a discussion between Neil and Dr. Bruner on Haitian superstitions and the potential whereabouts

Caspar David Friedrich's haunting painting Abbey in the Oak Forest *(1809–1810).*

of Madeline's stolen corpse. The mobility of the shot is a highly creative achievement. It begins with an extreme closeup of Neil's back; his body moves to the right to reveal Dr. Bruner through an arch made by his arm resting on a desk. The camera tracks back to reveal both men seated at a desk in a medium long shot; the camera pans slightly to catch their movements as they stand, then tracks in as the two speak behind the desk. The camera then briefly pans to the right to keep Dr. Bruner in frame as he sits at the desk. Next, the camera pans right to follow Bruner as he stands and makes his way to a bookcase; then, it pans left as he returns to the desk and sits. The camera tracks back and pans left as Bruner moves to the front of the desk and sits on its corner. The camera then pans right and tracks in as Bruner returns to his seat behind the desk. It then pans right again to match the earlier composition of Bruner shown through the arch made by Neil's arm on the desk. Finally, the camera pans further right for Neil's back to fill the screen with black. The shot (and thus the scene) has reached its teleological and artistic end.

Scene 16 lasts just over five minutes, and represents a remarkable achievement in independent filmmaking style. Wholly original and intelligently planned, the movements are executed so seamlessly as to almost hide its cinematic beauty. Yet under scrutiny the scene reveals intense planning and a story within a story. Neil's dialogue begins with his doubts of Haitian superstitions and ends with his being more inclined to defer to Bruner's judgment. At all times Neil bows to the missionary's knowledge, and the shot itself signifies that, in its circular pattern and ending with the exact composition with which it began. As well as offering one of the highlights of cinematic technique in the 1930s Hollywood independent film, Shot 236 prefigures the kind of roving camera movements in a confined geographic area which would be explored at much greater length in Hitchcock's *Rope* (1948).

Less pivotal but still worthy of discussion is the film's use of optical printing in both its titles and in transitional wipes between shots. *White Zombie* as a title appears at the film's opening in a very angular, art deco font. The word "*White*" appears, then the word "*Zombie*" Each letter of the second word beats up one at a time in

Actors (from left to right) John Harron, Madge Bellamy, and Robert Frazer constitute part of the farrago of acting styles in White Zombie.

rhythm to the diegetic voodoo drums heard in the opening musical theme. A beam of light from the bottom of the screen accompanies the appearance of each new letter, as if the aurora of a new day is the source of each letter. Once the entire title is spelled, the rays of light disappear, as if day has become twilight and then, finally, the darkened night that begins Scene 1.

White Zombie's use of optically printed transitions is even more interesting as they visually echo the characters' entry into Legendre's world.[97] Most transitions from shot to shot during the film are straight cuts, but the introductions of danger and death are often made by dissolves. For example, a dissolve occurs between Shots 40 and 41; at that moment, the carriage driver is about to deliver his definition of the term zombie. A dissolve also occurs between Shots 96 and 97; the latter shot begins Scene 7, in which Beaumont leaves his estate to meet Legendre and seal his fate in a bargain. A dissolve into

Scene 11 at Shot 162 prefaces the tainted flower being passed from Beaumont to Madeline. A subsequent dissolve introduces Scene 12 at Shot 174, which begins with Legendre carving the voodoo doll which induces Madeline's deathlike, prezombie state. Later, several dissolves occur within Scene 17, which is set at Legendre's castle.

Subsequently, wipe transitions further illustrate the possibly supernatural, potentially magical geography of the "land of the living dead." Unusual passages between shots reflect Dr. Bruner and Neil's passage to an unusual place.[98] The first, a diagonal wipe, occurs at the beginning of Scene 19 at Shot 310. The second at Shot 322 includes two diagonal wipes that merge at screen center to become a split screen image of the zombified Madeline and her weak and ineffective hero Neil. A horizontal wipe reveals Shot 323, an elaborate curtain wipe introduces Shot 324, and a diagonal wipe presents Shot 325. While artful, the wipes—which occur as all characters finally converge at Legendre's castle—illustrate an overtly cinematic style that both calls attention to itself and the potentially supernatural aspects of Murder, his castle, and his zombies. The wipes also represent a conscious divergence from the editing norms established by prior films of the 1930s horror cycle; none of them use wipes in this way, and none create as thoughtful a progression through any kind of optical transition.[99]

White Zombie is also very evocative of a silent film, not only because of the lengthy nondialogue moments of action, but also due to a number of other reasons. For one, the selection of nondiegetic music in segments like Scene 12 offers overly dramatic moods, quite reminiscent of the aural accompaniment given to silent cinema serials. In addition, the lengths of individual shots and their editing create a slow pace that strikes a brooding, methodical tempo. Even the cadences of the actors' speech, their deliberate reactions to the unfolding drama, and their physical movements in general sustain a lethargical rhythm.

Unlike a silent movie, however, the film is punctuated with a well-calculated and extended use of sound effects and at times an intentional lack of background music, representing in both regards a greater sophistication than can be heard in the soundtracks of most early talkies. And, while some silent films employed sound effects, *White Zombie* does so in a particularly developed manner; the sounds are not merely accompaniments to on-screen visuals, but an integral aspect of the constructed mood. Indeed, sometimes they are even an index of offscreen action. For example, following the musical composition "Chant" heard in the opening title sequence, no music—diegetic or otherwise—is heard during the first seven scenes of the film. By Scene 8, Beaumont arrives at Legendre's sugar mill. The grind of the wooden mill is heard as an offscreen sound effect as Beaumont approaches the building. No dialogue is exchanged between him and the zombie who leads him inside, where the sound of the mill becomes louder. It continues even as one zombie topples from a second floor and falls within the millstone. Its blades presumably mangle the zombie as the sound effect continues. Even as Beaumont and Legendre meet for the first time in the film, the sound of the mill persists as a signifier of the latter's zombie enterprise.

Similarly, no music is heard at the beginning of Scene 15, in which Legendre introduces his favored phalanx of zombies to Beaumont. In Shot 211, a left to right pan is made, from a graveyard hillside to Legendre's collection of the living dead. As the pan begins, the cries of unseen wolves are heard in the distance. Later in the same scene, crickets are heard in the background as the zombies carry Madeline's body. The vulture which hovers ever near Legendre performs a similar function. At times its screeches are heard before the ominous bird is visually seen, with the initial sounds acting as an aural transition to the subsequent shot.

Together, *White Zombie*'s pictorial imagery, acting, editing, and aural effects help pinpoint the less traditional aspects of its cinematic style. While often reminiscent of a silent film, it employs a highly sophisticated use of sound. Though similar in some ways to the hallmarks of German Expressionism, a visual style so key to the 1930s horror film cycle, *White Zombie* relies more often on imagery evocative of fairy tales and pre–Expressionist paintings. While employing far less consistent and restrained performances from actors than its predecessors in the horror cycle, the film's acting at times actually helps reinforce the ethereal storyline and setting. *White Zombie*'s camera movements and use of optical printing also help place it in a category apart from prior horror films. But more than any of these qualities, it is *White Zombie*'s positioning of the spectator which establishes its anomalous place in horror film history.

Constructed Spectatorship

White Zombie is particularly singular in its construction of a place within its text for the spectator, the audience member.[100] The film was the first attempt in horror film history at constructing what I have termed the *spectator-as-character*, a device by which *White Zombie* allows the spectator to become—albeit in a very limited fashion—a character in the narrative. Specifically, spectators engage with character Murder Legendre, his eyes inviting them into the filmic text. To understand best how *White Zombie* works in this respect, we must consider major theoretical perspectives in the study of cinematic spectatorship, and then closely scrutinize the film. Though the following pursuit is necessarily rigorous, painstaking, and "academic" (a term which I certainly do not apply pejoratively, even if some readers of horror film texts do), it yields rich results about one of horror film history's most unique moments.

Throughout the history of film scholarship, cinema spectatorship has generally been divided into studies of how film creates positions for subjects who are swayed by a medium which causes them to react in specific ways, and studies of actual responses given by historically situated viewers. As film theorist Judith Mayne suggests, film studies have oscillated between theories regarding the positioning of a cinema *subject*, a theoretical construct, and reactions of *viewers*, the real persons who watch films. Academics have had difficulties reconciling both approaches, often choosing to concentrate on one or

When Murder Legendre's sugar mill is shown, the film is punctuated with a well-calculated and extended use of sound effects and an intentional lack of background music, representing in both regards a greater sophistication than most early talkies.

the other. Such a singular path is in direct opposition to the need to historicize theory and to develop a theoretical framework for historical study. Mayne argues that spectatorship itself cannot be examined in terms of only subjects or viewers; indeed, she believes that spectatorship itself "occurs at precisely those spaces where 'subjects' and 'viewers' rub against each other."[101]

Despite these arguments, the history of spectatorship studies since the 1970s has generally concentrated on theoretical constructs of subjects.[102] This trend has occurred at least partially because of the importance of English studies and psychoanalytic criticism to film theory in general; as a result, empirically and historically based studies have been less frequently explored. However, even those analyses concentrating solely on subjects causes extensive debate among theorists, much of which concerns the degree to which a film positions a subject, and thus the level of the subject's free will in responding.

Often the dispute centers on whether the subject is merely a passive repository for images they see, or whether they engage films in a more active manner. For example, theorist Richard Allen observes that:

> Contemporary film theorists construe the film spectator as a passive observer of the image who is duped into believing it is real. In fact, ... the film spectator knows it is only a film and actively participates in the experience of illusion that the cinema affords.[103]

Various other film theorists have argued against the belief that the filmic text unilaterally determines the subject's reading of it.[104] Film theorist Harriet E. Margolis, for example, views the spectator as "a free agent, but one whose freedom is quickly restricted" by the presentation of the narrative to the spectator, including the plot itself, point-of-view cinematography, and film editing styles.[105] In his text *Narration in the Fiction Film*, David Bordwell

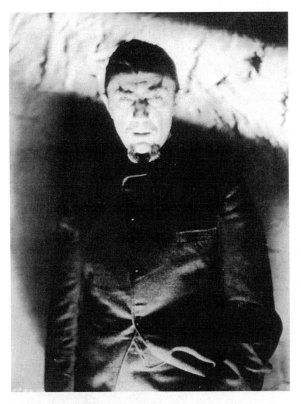

A rare publicity portrait of Bela Lugosi as Murder Legendre. (Courtesy of Venita Halperin.)

In addition to such questions surrounding the passive or active position of spectators, arguments persist over the origin of the gaze that occurs during a film. In other words, do spectators gaze at the screen with freedom, or does the film hold the power of the gaze? Film theorist Wheeler Winston Dixon believes:

> Since the very act of seeing a film is an act of submission—and the darkened theater, our mostly unidentified companions, the secrecy and individuality of our responses, the enormous size of the screen, the rapidly shifting (for the most part) image sizings all contribute to this willing subservience to the "gaze that controls"—it seems odd that most reception theory continues to center upon the viewer as giver of the gaze, and the screen the bearer of the viewer's look. The viewer, it seems to me, is instead the subject/object of the gaze of the cinematic image.[108]

Dixon's argument presents an extreme view, in opposition to the equally extreme views held by the reception theory to which it responds. We can easily, however, meld both extremes into a viewpoint not unlike Branigan's regarding subject positions. The "gaze" may well be given both by the film to the spectator, as well as by the spectator to the film. The latter idea becomes further informed by a discussion of actual viewers, who bring with them knowledge beyond that of a single film.

Despite the usefulness of studying actual viewers, theorist Judith Mayne understands the resistance of empirical inquiry in some areas of film studies.[109] She writes:

> It has been an observation of long standing in film studies that the cinematic subject refers not to real people who attend movies and who may respond in a number of complex and compelling ways to the spectacle on screen ... film theorists have insisted that the subject should not be confused with the individual.[110]

also argues for the free will of the spectator, even if it is limited by the film's presentation: "A film ... does not 'position' anybody. A film cues the spectator to execute a definable variety of *operations* [author's emphasis]."[106]

Analyzing spectators and cinematic point of view, theorist Edward Branigan refers to the cinema subject as a "reader" and suggests that "the reader will at all times be present as a co-producer of the text along with the narrator." Branigan also believes that:

> The film is a discourse which itself creates a set of subject positions for the viewer, just as the viewer is able to frame and reframe the film and create subject positions for the presumed "author" of the film.[107]

Indeed, in Branigan's schema, terms like "subject" and "spectator" do not adequately convey the active nature of the filmic "reader." From Branigan—as well as Margolis and Bordwell—we can build an image of a spectator who does have free will in interpreting, judging, and responding to a film, but who works in tandem with a film which limits free will through various cinematic and narrative processes.

Yet, in reality the two modes of analysis (actual viewers and cinema subjects) connect and at times overlap, each informing questions raised by the other. For example, when theorists question the passivity of a subject and propose that the subject hold a more active position, historical and empirical inquiries into viewers can reinforce that argument. However, many film theorists still resist empirical examinations of viewers. The purpose of spectatorship in modern film studies should be to consider both real viewers' responses and the factors that inform them, as well as theoretical constructs of subjects as created by films. We must use this approach to examine *White Zombie*'s spectatorship, and perhaps reconcile its subjects and viewers.

The emphasis on Lugosi's eyes in the film—Murder Legendre's malignant stare—suggests exactly the way in which *White Zombie*'s "subjects" and "viewers," in Mayne's words, "rub against each other."[111] In the film, the eyes of Lugosi/Murder repeatedly stare directly at the subject, a gaze which is sometimes connected to other characters in the film, but which is often meant for the subject alone. The result is a highly unique aspect of *White Zombie* and horror film history.[112]

Nick Browne's seminal essay "The Spectator-in-the-Text" describes what he calls the "position of the spectator"; he suggests that cinematic techniques can constitute a connection between a given character or characters and the theoretical spectator, and thus the cinema does position the spectator.[113] In his schema, this connection solidifies less through narrative techniques like plot or dialogue, than through purely cinematic means such as cinematography. The composition of a shot can allow the subject to see over the shoulder of a given character, thus positioning the spectator in the character's approximate point of view; likewise, action or dialogue from another character can be shown from the approximate field of vision of the character who is linked with the spectator. As a result, Browne believes the subject becomes positioned within the text itself through links to the text's character or characters, rather than being a passive entity who only watches an unfolding cinematic drama.

White Zombie not only places the spectator in the position of some of its characters through its use of cinematography, but also creates something Browne does not discuss, a spatial closeness to the narrative that, as already mentioned, allows the subject to become a character in the film itself.[114] This occurs centrally through the use of the character Murder looking directly into the camera eye. At times the recipients of this gaze are characters within the film; at other moments, these shots are not logically linked to such characters, but rather to the audience member alone. This cinematic device moves the viewer from a more traditional and perhaps more passive role as spectator to a more active role as participant/character.

White Zombie then proves to be distinct from other, prior horror films. *Dracula* (1931), *Frankenstein* (1931), *Murders in the Rue Morgue* (1932), and *Dr. Jekyll and Mr. Hyde* (1932) represent the four major U.S. horror films of the talkie era that preceded *White Zombie*.[115] None of these four films construct a position for the *spectator-as-character* in the same way as *White Zombie*; indeed, no major silent horror films do either.[116] It is true that films like *Nosferatu* (1922), *Dracula* (1931), and *Svengali* (1931) feature characters who gaze briefly into the lens, but these films do not feature repeated uses of it, nor do they incorporate the spectator into the text as a character. For example, one gaze by Svengali looking directing into camera in *Svengali* is clearly linked to Trilby, another

character offscreen; in *Dracula*, the title character stares into the camera, presumably at the subject, but *not* repeatedly. *White Zombie* is different from these examples and is certainly not representative of the horror film cycle as it existed in or before 1932; at least in the manner it constructs a position for its subject, *White Zombie* is an anomaly among the 1930s horror cycle.

Though other kinds of films (e.g., comedies) prior to *White Zombie* feature characters gazing into the camera lens and interacting with the audience, they generally cause nondiegesis, an action apart from the story and the characters in the story. Perhaps one of the most famous practitioners of this technique is Oliver Hardy in the films of Laurel and Hardy. He looks into the camera at the audience, usually after growing disgusted with Laurel and thus seeking sympathy. In a way, the film's story stops momentarily for this action, with the narrative continuing after Hardy begins interacting with Laurel again. *White Zombie* does not use the gaze into the camera in the same way; as this analysis will show, its use of the technique *is* diegetic, as the subject becomes a limited character within a narrative rather than a disruption of it.

Despite its innovative use of the spectator-as-character, *White Zombie* does indeed ground itself *overall* in the tradition of the classical Hollywood paradigm. In other words, however differently the film may work at given moments, it does not forego the conventions of Hollywood studio filmmaking and aims for a major audience. Examining specific shots reveals the less innovative components of the film. For example, Shot 103 in Scene 7 is a high angle long shot of character Beaumont leaving his home in a carriage with a zombie carriage driver.[117] Shot 104 becomes a medium shot of Neil on a second story terrace of Beaumont's home, looking to an off-camera space understood by the spectator to be the carriage just seen. The high angle composition of Shot 103 has thus approximated the field of vision available to Neil. Indeed, these more traditional aspects of the film help cause its more radical moments of constructing the spectator-as-character to seem all the more unusual.

These connections between characters and their point of view as represented by cinematographic composition are always approximate, but understood by spectators due to the tradition developed by Hollywood. For example, Shot 139 in Scene 9 shows a medium shot of Beaumont and Legendre. Beaumont stands, his head tilting from the ground to eye level to examine a zombie that has entered the room. Shot 140 becomes a tilt from the feet of the zombie to his head at the eye level of the camera. The spatial difference between Beaumont to the zombie and the camera to the zombie in the two shots is apparent; but in essence, the shots work no differently than 103 and 104 (Neil looking out the window) in representing the given character's point of view. However, Shots 139 and 140 do represent a much more approximate temporal connection. Beaumont's head in 139 has already tilted to eye level; in 140, the camera repeats a field of vision linked to Beaumont, but one that has already been shown to have taken place. Rather than deviations from the norm of Hollywood cinema or prior horror films, these examples actually support traditional elements of spectatorship in filmic texts.

Not unlike in other prior horror films, the camera's point-of-view shots in *White Zombie* are often linked to the characters that could be classified as victims. The result attempts to make the audience develop certain feelings for those characters. Browne suggests:

> The spectator's place, the locus around which the spatiotemporal structures of presentation are organized, is a construction of the text which is ultimately the product of the narrator's disposition toward the tale.[118]

Browne presumably chooses the term "narrator"—rather than, say, "director"—to avoid addressing more specific questions of authorship.

Browne's discussion of the "narrator's disposition" means that the spectator's connection to characters through point-of-view shots should cue certain emotional responses. In *White Zombie*, the narrator seems to imply that Madeline and Neil should receive sympathy (or similar emotions) from the spectator, as should the more complex character Beaumont. Beaumont becomes a counterpoint of point-of-view shots throughout the film; though he sets the narrative conflict in motion and is hardly a hero, he does slowly erode into zombiism, and ends up destroying both Legendre and himself. Thus, Beaumont's depiction fits into a pattern of the narrator attempting to shape the audience's reaction toward victims in the plot in a certain way; the association is one in which the audience is often placed, through the visual composition, in the role of victim.

Theorist Judith Mayne believes that "identification understood as a position—and more properly as a series of shifting positions—assumes that cinematic identification is as fragile and unstable as identity itself."[119] Mayne makes clear that such tension is the result of a spectator's role in a "complex and difficult negotiation of a series of determinations."[120] In addition to these shifting positions, other theorists have noted that problems of identification result from the active ability of spectators to make judgments regarding the characters whose positions might be linked to them. Nick Browne argues:

> Because our feelings as spectators are not "analogous" to the interest and feelings of the characters, we are not

bound to accept their views either of themselves or of others. Our "position" as spectator then is very different from the previous senses of "position"; it is defined neither in terms of orientation within the constructed geography of the fiction nor in terms of social position of the viewing character. On the contrary, our point of view on the sequence is tied more closely to our attitude of approval or disapproval and is very different from any literal viewing angle or character's point of view.[121]

Outside the composition and cinematic techniques of *White Zombie*, then, an active and participating spectator can make his or her own judgments regarding the characters, rather than passively being forced to consider the "narrator's disposition" as Browne terms it. Thus, even if the spectator is positioned to feel sympathy for characters, an individual viewer—a free and active agent—might choose other responses. Audience members of *White Zombie* might not necessarily feel sympathetic emotions toward Neil, whose character throughout the narrative proves ineffectual in battling evil. A spectator could also reject the pleas for sympathy for Madeline, preferring instead that she remain in the clutches of the villain. These might be rare responses, but they are possible, and indeed the poor acting on the parts of both cast members prompted a variety of responses to their characters in 1932 amongst critics and audiences.[122] A spectator may have greater difficulty accepting the "narrator's disposition" towards Beaumont, a character who possesses shades of extreme villainy and yet makes extreme sacrifice.

All of these examples highlight the traditional cinematic aspects of *White Zombie*. However, discussing Legendre's repeated gazes directly into the camera highlights the film's more radical positioning of the spectator. Scene 15 presents one example of this, with Shot 216 showing Legendre and Beaumont in the medium distance. Legendre steps toward the camera away from his companion to exert his power over zombies that are located behind and to screen right of him; as he does, the camera pans to screen right to center Legendre in the visual composition. He looks directly into the camera, with Shot 217 showing an extreme closeup of his hands clasped in the manner necessary to motivate zombies into action. His gaze is definitely in the direction of the zombies in 216, but the spectator is now positioned as a victim under Legendre's control, similar to but distinct from the zombies shown in Shots 214, 215, and 218. Legendre's gaze briefly but overtly acknowledges the spectator as a character within the narrative. That the audience is constituted as victim exposes the narrator's disposition; at this stage, the spectator shares a commonality with Neil and Madeline, whether accepting it or not.

As a sequence of four shots in Scene 17 reveals, the

use of Legendre staring into the lens and thus at the audience seems to place the subject in the role of victim. For example, Shot 280 shows a closeup of Legendre turning from the side to gaze directly at the audience. Shot 281 is a medium shot of Silver the butler clasping a tray and looking to screen right; Silver appears frightened, but also ready to use the tray as a weapon. The two shots already suggest a spatial disconnect, as Legendre should be gazing screen left toward the geographical placement of Silver. Instead, Legendre again looks directly toward the camera in Shot 282. His extended stare remains unbroken except for a gradual blurring of focus by the camera lens; cinematic technique has duplicated the effects of Legendre's hypnotic stare. Shot 283 is a medium shot of Silver, who now appears hypnotized and drops the metal tray that he held in 281.

The four shots at first imply that Legendre's gaze has greatly affected Silver, and that the blurred focus Shot 282 has momentarily positioned the subject in the butler's place. Yet, the geographical differential between Silver's location and the direction in which Legendre stares suggests instead that Legendre's eyes are affecting not just Silver, with whom the audience is supposed to empathize, but rather Silver and a second character, the audience member whose geographical placement—unlike Silver's—is directly in line with the focus of Legendre's gaze.

Scene 21 offers yet a third example of the spatial discontinuity between the focus of Legendre's eyes and the direction in which Legendre is actually looking. Shot 354 is a medium long shot of Legendre approaching Neil, which is followed in 355 by a closeup of Neil. Shot 356 is a medium closeup of Legendre looking directly into the camera and smiling; the visual composition of the scene makes clear that this is not toward the vicinity of Neil. After a closeup of Legendre's hands in 357, Legendre again leers at the audience in Shot 358, staring into the camera as it tracks in to compose an extreme closeup of his face.[123]

Arguments can be made that shots of this kind are still representative of a narrative open to viewing by spectators but closed to their inclusion in the storyline. Theorists like Edward Branigan would suggest that—despite the spatial difference between the vision represented in the shot and the location of a given character—the composition is still likely linked to a given character. He believes:

> The act of "telling" or representing is first of all a creation of space, a display of the visual through acts of vision. ... Subjectivity in film depends on linking the framing of space at a given moment to a *character* [author's emphasis] as origin. The link may be direct or indirect. In the POV structure it is direct, because the character

is shown and then the camera occupies his or her (approximate!) position, thus framing a spatial field derived from him or her as origin. In character "projection," however, ... there is no coincidence of space, rather space is joined to a character by other logical or metaphorical, means. What is important, therefore, in determining subjectivity is to examine the logic which links the framing of space to a character as origin of that space.[124]

Branigan refers to indirect, "character projection" structures as "deviant"[125] point-of-view shots, with character origin made clear through "secondary cues [that] reinforce spatial orientation."[126] But in many cases within *White Zombie*, no secondary cues (e.g., dialogue) are present, and spatial orientation between, say, Legendre and other characters is so awry geographically that little exists to "reinforce." As Browne suggests:

> ...film [tries] not just to direct the attention but to place the eye of the spectator inside the fictional space, to make his presence integral and constitutive of the structure of views.[127]

White Zombie takes the enterprise addressed by Browne to an extreme, making Branigan's point of view not applicable for sections of the film. Character projection and indirect POV do not explain what occurs; it is the spectator-as-character that does.

Indeed, at times the film allows Legendre's gaze to strike the audience without it being linked to other characters in any plausible way. In Scene 2, for example, Legendre briefly stares into the camera in Shot 35. He has just placed Madeline's scarf inside his vest, and the carriage in which Madeline rides would not only be in a different direction spatially than his glance, but temporally would be out of his field of vision. Rather, his glance at the audience seems purposeful, a attempt to acknowledge the spectator and offer a sense of glee at his forthcoming evil deeds.

A more overt example occurs even earlier in the narrative. Scene 2 offers the first occasion in which Legendre gazes into the camera and at the audience, establishing within the first 20 shots of the entire film the kind of spectatorial positioning to take place throughout. Shot 17 is a long shot of a carriage approaching the camera; an extreme closeup of Legendre's eyes—fixed on the audience—is quickly superimposed over the carriage. The camera tracks back to make the superimposed eyes appear smaller, and they remain superimposed throughout most of Shot 18. In that shot, his eyes drift into the upper left corner of the screen and dissolve away; however, they are visible on-screen while the figure of Legendre is seen approaching the carriage. While his character in the narrative may well be looking at those in the carriage he

approaches, his gaze—his eyes as superimposed—exist in a second and detached manner, looking at the subject to prepare them for the role of a participating character in the filmic text.[128]

To understand best how *White Zombie* works on these various levels of spectatorship— whether allowing the audience to empathize with a character, share a scene with a character, or be the only central character at a given moment—examining an entire scene becomes necessary. For this purpose, Scene 12 proves a worthwhile vehicle. At first the sequence of shots seems to focus on Madeline.[129] By the end of the scene, however, the audience has been included as a character to various degrees. The narrative

Top: *A publicity photo of the wedding reception in Scene 12. Though Silver (Brandon Hurst) is second from the left in this photo, he does not appear in Scene 12.* Bottom: *Shot 174. Legendre approaches Beaumont's estate.*

covers Neil and Madeline's wedding reception. The scene crosscuts to Legendre, who carves a wax voodoo effigy of Madeline outside the Beaumont home. In the space of some 28 shots, the wedding reception culminates in Madeline's zombification.

Scene 12 begins on a dissolve from Shot 173, a medium long shot of the wedding ceremony. The transition to Scene 12 proves a stark one, as the white clothes and decor of the marriage ritual contrast sharply with Shot 174, a long shot of the dark back of Legendre, who is standing in front of Beaumont's home. His figure is recognizable, but it is made clear through a jarring cut to Shot 175, which crosses the 180° line. Legendre is now seen from a frontal view in long shot, standing between two candlelit lamps. The sequence illustrates the narrator's disposition to Legendre, an evil figure not only clad in black and shown geographically apart from the other characters, but one that is represented through a disconcerting style of editing.

Shot 176, a medium long shot, shows Legendre blowing out and removing a candle from the lamp on screen right; he is preparing to carve a wax effigy of Madeline. The shot itself is longer in length than the three shots prior to it, which causes it to command the attention of the subject. In an even greater way, however, the film attempts to gain the subject's attention by having Legendre noticeably and purposefully look directly into the camera. No secondary cues exist to attach the gaze to another character. Indeed, no other characters have been shown since Scene 11, and—at least to the spectator's knowledge—no other character is outside Beaumont's home in the vicinity of Legendre. He must, therefore, be looking at the audience, staring in a wickedly gleeful fashion. The invitation on his part for the audience to become an even more active participant reinforces the belief that the spectator need not accept the narrator's negative disposition toward Legendre, even if the spectator is well aware of it. A multiplicity of active responses could occur here, not the least of which could be a spectator associating with Legendre's antics, rather than spurning them. At any rate, the audience's participation becomes potentially more charged at this moment as Legendre's gaze reminds the spectator of their involvement in the unfolding narrative, and indeed places them in it.

Shot 176. Legendre unfurls Madeline's scarf and carves a voodoo doll from a candle.

In continuing his work on the wax effigy, Legendre, in a medium closeup of his hands in Shot 177, wraps Madeline's scarf around the candle. The camera tilts upward in the same shot to reveal his face; Shot 178 then shows a long shot of the exterior of Beaumont's home. The connection between the two shots suggests that the view in 178 belongs to Legendre; the subject is able to understand this by being placed by the camera position in his approximate geographical location. This allows again the potential of an audience member to associate or empathize with Legendre, even though the narrator's disposition toward the character throughout the text at large suggests that a subject should not approve of the character. Indeed, this is a subtle but crucial moment, as the eyes that dominate the film, as they do only two shots prior to 178, belong briefly to the audience, which goes from being gazed at by Legendre to gazing. This change of position is akin to the effects of the cross of the 180° line between Shots 174 and 175, and as such causes, intentionally or not, a further identification with Legendre.

Legendre and the lamp are shown again in Shot 179 in a medium closeup. The camera tilts upward to reveal

visually what has already been introduced aurally earlier in the shot: a vulture. The tilt within 179, rather than, say, a cut between two shots, helps link the two beings metaphorically. Again the narrator's negative disposition toward Legendre is clear, whatever response a spectator may make, as the vulture becomes a signifier not just of death, but of Legendre.[130] The two are again linked in Shots 180 and 181. The former is a closeup of Legendre's smiling face, looking upward at the vulture in an approving way; the latter is a closeup of the vulture's face. The similarity in composition in the two shots, as well as Legendre's expression, solidify the connection between the two.

The emphasis on Legendre at this point in the scene continues for a trio of shots that illustrate his progress on the wax effigy. A closeup in Shot 182 shows Legendre's glance shifting away from the offscreen vulture above him to his offscreen hands. A closeup in 183 shows the wax effigy and a closeup of Legendre's hands. The subject has prior knowledge of events transpiring in the plot, as Beaumont has asked Legendre for help in securing Madeline's affections for himself. Shot 177 has helped

Shot 181. Legendre's talisman, the vulture.

Shot 184. As he continues working on the voodoo doll, Legendre stares at the spectator-as-character.

make clear that the effigy is indeed one of Madeline, as it is her scarf that enshrouds it. But it is in 183 that the subject understands that it will be Legendre that possesses Madeline, not Beaumont. The shot places emphasis on Legendre's hands, and it is his hands when clasped that allow him to control his zombies. The closeup dissolves into Shot 184, acting as a cue to the audience of the passage of time. Legendre now stands in long shot carving an almost finished wax doll; he moves across the frame and, as he does, he again noticeably and purposefully looks directly at the camera. He engages with the spectator-as-character, presumably to gloat over the power he holds over all of the characters. Again, the subject identifies with Legendre, though the spectator's resulting judgments or discourse are still unfixed.

After engaging in a mutual gaze with Legendre in Shot 184, the subject then sees what Legendre presumably cannot: the wedding reception taking place inside Beaumont's mansion, as depicted in a long shot in 185. Again the film attempts to position the subject to give a certain reaction, much in same manner as the cut from Shot 173 to 174. In other words, the darkness of night and

the black regalia of Legendre, set up as signs of evil, collide with the high key lighting of Beaumont's home and the white wedding gown of Madeline, the narrator's indicators of innocence and goodness. The arrangement is more complex than a simple duality, however, as Beaumont is present at the wedding reception. Audience association and reaction to his character offer many possibilities, as his character is at times evil and at times good. Shot 186, a medium shot of Beaumont, does differentiate him from Madeline and Neil. The camera tilts upward to keep him in frame as he stands; the movement recalls the camera tilts on Legendre in 177 and 179. This offers a comparison between the two men, both of whom wish to possess Madeline through the process of zombification.

Shot 186 continues, and a pan to screen right reveals a medium shot of Neil. Though not introduced by an upward tilt, the narrator introduces Neil into the same group as Beaumont and Legendre to the degree that all three desire Madeline's attentions. The camera then pans to screen left past Beaumont to reveal a medium shot of Madeline; the final pan links her to Neil, who has just

Shot 185. The wedding reception begins.

spoken to her. Their glances are fixed on one another; in terms of the narrative, they have just been married in Scene 11. The tension at work between the characters present at the reception becomes more clear when Shot 187 depicts all three in a medium long shot. Madeline is on screen left, and Neil, the good hero, is positioned, literally and figuratively, on the right side of the visual composition. Beaumont's position in the center indicates his crucial role in the narrative events; he has geographically and textually come between the married couple.

The narrative emphasis on Madeline, the woman whom all three men in the plot desire, becomes the focus of Shot 188. She peers into a glass of wine held in her hands; Neil has just requested that Madeline, the "fair gypsy" in his words, read his fortune. As it is a medium shot of just Madeline, the shot does belong to her. The spectator may associate with her in this displacement or dispossession of her from the other characters that results from her being framed alone. In a narrative sense, Madeline is about to be removed from her present condition and social situation; with regard to spectatorship, Shot 188 causes what Browne refers to as the "double structure

of the viewer/viewed."[131] The audience is "with" the depicted person in the sense of identification, but the audience is also viewing her from the geography constructed by the camera placement. For Browne, this kind of cinematic technique is a "powerful emotional process" that "throws into question any account of the spectator as centered at a single point or at the center of any simply optical system."[132]

In the case of *White Zombie*, Shot 188 embodies Browne's description, but Shot 189 creates a more complex set of positions. An extreme closeup of the wine glass from the top view places the subject in the approximate geographical position of Madeline, who had just been peering into the glass. The audience now must associate with Madeline on at least one level, seeing through her eyes; at the same time, the spectator still of course exists apart from her. Indeed, that the direct overhead angle of the glass is slightly different from the angle available to Madeline in Shot 188 can remind the audience of their position as witnesses to the action. The shot then shows a superimposition of Legendre's face in the wine; his gaze is directly at the camera. The result means that the

Shot 186. Neil hands a glass of wine to Madeline at the wedding reception.

audience now occupies three positions. The subject is witness to the action, a "stand-in" of sorts for Madeline, on whose face Legendre's gaze is fixed, as well as the character that the audience portrays throughout the film. In other words, Legendre's gaze is one that reaches both Madeline and the "spectator-as-character" in the fashion of Shots 176 and 184.

Shot 190 returns to the composition of Shot 188, and removes the spectator from sharing Madeline's approximate field of vision to witness from a distance the fear that blankets her expression. Shot 191 links her again to Neil and Beaumont, as all three characters appear in a long shot. At the same time, Shot 191 does not reinforce her existence in the social dynamic of the two male characters. Rather, her continued fear and Legendre's actions juxtaposed with Beaumont and Neil's apparent good health suggest what is to follow: her removal from them by becoming a zombie. Earlier narrative content in Scene 9 (when Murder first suggests turning Madeline into a zombie) has already indicated this fate might occur to her. Foreshadowing is heightened when Shot 192 shows a medium two shot of her and Neil, the man that she has just married and from whom she will be taken.

Scene 12 grows more complex as Shot 193 begins a series of crosscutting between the three characters at the reception and Legendre, who has remained outside the Beaumont mansion. The first in the sequence is a medium long shot of Legendre, standing beside the candle lamp on screen left, in which he is burning the wax effigy of Madeline carved during earlier shots in the scene. Shot 194 is a closeup of Legendre's hand holding the effigy in the flame; his hand gripping the wax doll reiterates that it will be he that is united with a zombified Madeline.

The gravity of the unfolding drama heightens in Shot 195, a medium two shot of Madeline and Neil. Her pain is clear from her cries and facial expressions; she quickly faints into Neil's arms. The married couple are still together, but now merely in terms of their momentary geography. The camera pans to screen right to frame a worried Beaumont. The movement to him and his solitary status in the composition reinforces that it is he who has caused the transpiring events. As a character in the narrative, Beaumont is apart from both the innocent and good married couple and the thoroughly evil Legendre. If figuratively and literally (in terms of their dress) the

Shot 187. Madeline, pretending to be a gypsy, begins to tell Neil his fortune.

married couple and Legendre represent "white" and "black," Beaumont possesses shades of both. He is in many ways the most realistic character present in Scene 12 and the film as a whole. As a result of his more human qualities, some spectators might more easily identify with him than the other characters in the film. Shot 195 embodies this possibility; it shows Beaumont, who is responsible for Madeline's condition, but who already displays a worried and perhaps regretful expression. Beaumont's emotional dilemma in this shot allows the subject to choose from an array of potential responses, from disgust to sympathy.

The next four shots in the scene show the subtle battle over Madeline's condition and eventual possessor. Shot 196 is a medium shot of Neil holding Madeline in his arms, and is followed by a medium closeup of smiling Legendre in profile still holding the wax doll in the flame of the candle. Shot 198 continues this image, but as a closeup of Legendre's hand clasping the burning effigy. He is in effect holding Madeline, as the effigy is obviously of her. Both males, Neil and Legendre, then are attempting to hold her for their own. Shot 199 makes

clear the only difference at this moment between Legendre and Neil's attempts. Neil holds Madeline in his arms in a two shot, but his cries and visible expression reveal the little to no power that he possesses. By contrast, Legendre's actions and expressions in Shot 197

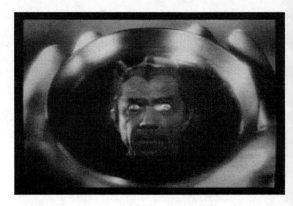

Shot 189. Legendre's face appears in Madeline's glass of wine, revealing her fate.

Shot 194. Legendre's hand holds the voodoo doll of Madeline into the flame of the lamp.

show that the voodoo master is in control of Madeline's fate; he holds the power.

Legendre's authority extends even further in Shot 200, an extreme closeup of his eyes looking directly into the camera and surrounded by blackness. They are separated and detached from his face; their gaze is similar to that in Madeline's wine glass in Shot 189. Legendre stares at the spectator as a participating character, but the almost floating eyes suggest their dual purpose: he is aware of the spectator-as-character and also privy to the actions unfolding in the Beaumont home. Shot 201 makes this clear in a closeup of Madeline, her eyes closing as she enters the deathlike state necessary to becoming zombified. Legendre's dominant and staring eyes in the former shot contrast sharply with Madeline's lifeless stare that is quickly covered by her eyelids. It is as if she has seen, just prior to her death, Legendre's eyes.

The focus on his eyes continues in Shot 202, a medium shot of Legendre looking directly into the camera, acknowledging again the presence of the spectator-as-character. The voodoo master is still outside the Beaumont mansion. As he so often has before, he gazes at the audience. Madeline is now a zombie; his gaze is obviously not meant for her, nor are there any secondary cues to suggest his gaze is connected with Neil or Beaumont. He looks now only at the spectator, smiling and raising his eyebrows; he walks forward into the camera lens, with his face filling the screen and eventually covering the spectator's vision in darkness. Legendre's geography might at

Shot 195. Neil in Madeline's arms.

Shot 195. Camera has panned to Beaumont.

first suggest he is walking toward the Beaumont home, yet that analysis must be discarded, as in no subsequent shot or scene does that take place. Instead, just as he has gazed upon the character that the audience plays, so does

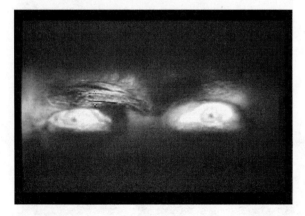

Shot 200. The quintessential image of Legendre's eyes staring into the camera lens.

he walk toward the spectator in 202. In terms of the narrative, his movement, culminating as it does in a black screen, allows a temporal transition to Scene 13, Madeline's funeral.

From the standpoint of spectatorship, Legendre has engaged yet again with the spectator-as-character. He illustrates for the audience his pride in the zombification of Madeline; his smile, as well as his gaze of which the spectator has often been the recipient, suggests that he can exert his power over the audience just as he has over Madeline. His movement toward the camera and thus the spectator-as-character is another example of his power over the audience; the composition, before fading to blackness, has become an extreme closeup of his face moving ever closer to the spectator. Legendre's power is clear—his spatial closeness to the audience can even potentially allow the spectator to identify more strongly with him than before. Indeed, just as images of Legendre opened Scene 12, so do they now close it. Rather than be left with an image of, say, Madeline's lifeless body yearning for audience sympathy, it is Legendre's staring eyes with which the spectator-as-character engages.

Top: *Shot 201. Madeline's eyes close slowly as she seemingly dies.* Bottom: *Shot 202. Legendre stares gleefully at the spectator-as-charac-ter as he begins to walk directly into the camera to end the scene.*

Scene 12 has thus acted as a microcosm of the entire film in the manner in which it positions the spectator. In general, the examined scene makes clear that it is Madeline and Neil with whom the spectator should identify strongly, at least according to the narrator; it is the young married couple who are the embodiment of good. By contrast, Legendre is, as his vulture signifier suggests, the very symbol of death and decay; he is evil, and thus the spectator should dislike and perhaps fear him. The placement of Beaumont in Scene 12 indicates the narrator's mixed feelings toward him: he possesses qualities of both good and evil. Perhaps he should be punished for his role in Madeline's zombification, but he does visibly show a modicum of regret for his actions. But if these are the apparent dispositions of the narrator toward the characters, it is important to consider that the spectator, as an active participant in the process of the film's narrative, need not accept the judgments and beliefs of the narrator. A spectator might associate more strongly with Legendre, for example, and feel less than sympathetic to Neil and Madeline's plight.

To expand on the latter point, Legendre's prominence in the scene needs further elaboration. In Scene 12 and indeed throughout the entire film, Legendre engages with the spectator; no other characters in the film interact with the spectator-as-character. As examinations of individual shots have revealed, the narrator's disposition toward Legendre is a negative one. Thus, Legendre's acknowledgment of the audience attempts to place the subject in the role of victim. Such a positioning might hold much power, as the spectator-as-character may as a result associate and identify further with other victims present in the narrative (e.g., Neil and Madeline). At the same time, however, a subject might identify and associate with Legendre as a result of engaging with him while being closed off to direct contact with other characters. Legendre's gaze might thereby subvert the narrator's disposition, with the subject considering themselves more of a henchman or lackey approving Legendre's actions rather than being frightened by them.

Similarly, the durations of shots in Scene 12 have a possible impact on the spectator's judgments and opinions. Theorist Nick Browne's schema considers only the composition of a shot, its potential effects, and its relationship to other shots in the same scene; he does not ponder the potential impacts of the length of a given shot. But the durations of shots must also be considered, as the longer a spectator is exposed to a certain shot or shots, very possibly the greater is their impact. It is true that in certain cases the brevity or even extreme brevity of a shot juxtaposed with more lengthy shots might cause it to stand out and perhaps move up the hierarchy of importance in a spectator's mind.[133] But barring such contrast, a spectator exposed to one image for a greater length of time than another image may well place more importance on it. In Scene 12, it is important to consider that Legendre is on-screen for some 117 seconds; all of the other characters *combined* are onscreen for only 111 seconds during the same scene.[134] The degree of prominence given to Legendre by his lengthy footage on-screen may well cause a spectator to identify with him to a greater extent than with other characters. Indeed, Legendre's screen time could work in tandem with his ability to interact with the audience and cause a spectator's attentions, interests, and empathies to be placed with him rather than with Neil, Madeline, or Beaumont.[135]

Along with revealing Legendre's potential impact on the spectator, Scene 12 helps in our understanding of the sheer variety of positions the spectator occupies during the film. To begin with, the spectator is always a witness, albeit an active one capable of constructing opinions regarding the narrative, even to the extent of not accepting the validity or plausibility of what is seen. At times, as in Shot 189, the spectator assumes a particular character's field of vision, or an approximation of that same point of view. This limited appropriation of one character's position can of course be shifted to another character, allowing the spectator to take on the identities of different and perhaps opposing characters. In addition, Scene 12 offers multiple examples of what I have termed the spectator-as-character, in which the audience might still be an active witness to the transpiring events and might associate or identify with particular characters, but has also become a member of the narrative events and whose presence is acknowledged by Legendre.

These many point-of-view shots allow the spectator of *White Zombie* to readjust their position rapidly, at least if they want to do so. The shots also cause the spectator to assume an active position at all times, making judgments and forming opinions from one shot to the next. Indeed, at times, as Scene 12 has shown, the spectator may assume multiple positions at once in a complex stratification of spectatorship. The spectator is then a discriminating witness to events, with an active capability to engage intellectually with the narrative and visual images. At the same time, the spectator is governed to a degree by the fixed narrative in the film, as well as the rigid and unchanging images and visuals that compose it.

White Zombie therefore clearly illustrates the fluidity and instability of a constructed subject position. Legendre's direct gaze into the camera, whether connected to a character in the narrative or not, suggests the spectator should fear him. The audience member is in danger of becoming a zombie themselves, and they are imperiled further by witnessing what happens to the "good" characters, the "heroes." But the possibility of a spectator vicariously enjoying Legendre's activities would subvert the narrator's disposition toward the unfolding story; the subject, the spectator-as-character, would become Legendre's lackey, and receive a voyeuristic pleasure from watching his villainy. Similarly, a subject could retaliate against the narrator's disposition as a result of, say, rendering unfavorable judgments on less than believable characters and the stilted acting in their portrayal. The subject's resulting response could be to take the film less than seriously, and, for example, have little desire to see the "heroes" escape the villain's clutches. The potential variety of extremely different responses suggests that the subject position, if we should even refer to it in the singular, is a tenuous one constructed as much by the subject's free will as by the cinematic techniques of a given film.

At the same time, however, *White Zombie* attempts to involve the audience on a more intimate level than a more strictly diegetic film experience, meaning one that draws a sharper line between film and subject. In these terms, *White Zombie* has minor echoes in future horror films which have also attempted to blur the line between the film on the screen and the subject watching it. For example, horror films constituted some of Hollywood's first major releases in 3-D. *The House of Wax* (1953) and *The Creature from the Black Lagoon* (1955) used the 3-D device to a similar end as *White Zombie*'s spectator-as-character, sometimes producing as varied an audience response. Much the same could be said of producer William Castle's various attempts at greater audience involvement in his horror films, whether by having a fake skeleton descend from the theater ceiling at showings of *The House on Haunted Hill* (1958) or by wiring some theater seats to take electrical shocks for screenings of *The Tingler* (1959).[136] By the 1970s and 1980s, horror filmmakers still groped for ways of involving the audience to a greater degree. For example, in addition to the brief and unsuccessful return of 3-D in horror films like *Friday the 13th Part 3* (1982) and *Jaws 3-D* (1983), more and more use was made of handheld camera shots simulating the point of view of both killers and victims. John Carpenter's *Halloween* (1978) popularized the technique with subsequent horror filmmakers, but he later admitted that—like 3-D and William Castle's gimmicks—audience reactions to such involvement in the narrative are at best varied and at worst negative.[137]

Many horror films subsequent to *White Zombie* would also feature characters staring into the camera lens. But their gazes would usually be clearly tied to the point of view of another character in the film (see, for example, Hershell Gordon Lewis' 1963 *Blood Feast*), or would occur as nondiegetic comedic asides to the audience in the same tradition as Laurel and Hardy (e.g., Gene Wilder, Marty Feldman et al. in Mel Brooks' 1974 *Young Frankenstein*). But even though the aforementioned kinds of horror films try to situate their subjects in more active roles, they do so in different ways than *White Zombie*, ways not too different to those of *Dracula* (1931) and *Nosferatu* (1922) before it. Among horror films, *White Zombie* remains unique in its subtle creation of the spectator-as-character, a repetitive device by which the spectator takes an active role as a character within the film.

Throughout this analysis of the spectatorship created by *White Zombie* and its spectator, the subject referred to is merely a theoretical construct. Mayne notes that, in the past, "spectatorship was identified as purely a function of the individual film text, and presumably the critical spectatorship thus embodied would be identical whether you were in Paris or Buffalo or Leningrad."[138] In other words, the spectator as positioned by the filmic text—and as considered by many film theorists in the past—is an ahistorical and acultural one. Film historian Miriam Hansen, however, has highlighted that:

> There is no doubt that theoretical concepts of spectators need to be historicized so as to include empirical formations of reception. By the same token, however, a reception-oriented film history cannot be written without a theoretical framework that conceptualizes the possible relations between films and viewers.[139]

Her comments, as well as our goal of finding that place where subjects and viewers "rub" against one another, suggest the need for an investigation of *White Zombie*'s historical reception. If the eyes of actor Bela Lugosi as Legendre engage with the theoretical subject, they certainly engaged with historical viewers in 1932 movie posters, theater ballyhoos, and aesthetic and critical responses. His eyes invite and frame the spectator-as-character; they gazed with equal invitation at 1932 viewers. Chapter Four then becomes a *crucial* counterpart to the present argument, chronicling as it does viewer reactions during the film's original 1932 release. Together, the two discussions paint a comprehensive portrait of *White Zombie*'s spectatorship.

Chapter Two

Casting the Mold: The Pre-Halperin World of Voodoo and Zombies

Prior to the scripting of *White Zombie*, numerous texts and articles were written on the subject of voodoo in Haiti and the U.S. Many of these contained elements similar to those that would surface in the Halperins' 1932 film. In particular, author William B. Seabrook's book *The Magic Island* (Harcourt, 1929) is an important predecessor to *White Zombie*, specifically in its coverage of the zombie image. Its popularity spawned playwright Kenneth Webb's stage play *Zombie*, that—while a box-office failure on Broadway—also proved significant at the dawn of *White Zombie*'s production. Beyond the specific appropriations made by the Halperins' film examined in Chapter One, an investigation of the following books, articles, and films is necessary to establish the background of voodoo and zombiism that indirectly influenced both *White Zombie* and the opinions of Americans toward Haiti in 1932.

Such depictions of Haiti and voodoo both echoed and inspired dominant U.S. prejudices that have existed through the 19th and into the 21st centuries. Just as some writers and scholars painted Africa as the "dark" continent, so did they similarly condemn Haiti to unfair and often unsubstantiated stereotypes and criticisms. These ranged from charges of Haitians' inferiority and inability to rule themselves to allegations of child sacrifice and cannibalism.

Generally, those English authors who wrote of Haiti were not in the least concerned about the negative repercussions of their work. In an 1873 book on Santo Domingo and Haiti, for example, the author makes clear that "it is possible that the notes on Hayti may give offense to some; but the author does not see that anything is to be gained by glossing over the present utterly hopeless condition of this part of the island."[1]

Comments of this kind overlooked the hope of Haiti while highlighting its alleged hopelessness. For example, aside from the United States, Haiti has had independence longer than any other nation in the Western Hemisphere. A lengthy slave revolt led by Toussaint Louverture and Jean Jacques Dessalines achieved independence from the French commanded by General Leclerc, the brother-in-law of Napoleon. Though white supremacy had basically been at an end since 1796, the new nation of Haiti (meaning "land of mountains") formally began of January 1, 1804. Louverture became the country's leader, later writing an autobiography and even becoming the subject of a Wordsworth poem. He and Dessalines (who has usually been considered a military genius by historians) were heroes in Haiti.

As Robert Lawless suggests in his 1992 text *Haiti's Bad Press*, the Haitian revolution had a profound effect on nineteenth century America, especially the South. Louverture became a hero to those American slaves that were aware of him, while white slaveowners obviously feared the potential spread of revolt. This in turn made many whites particularly suspicious of slave gatherings and their practice of superstitious rituals. Many whites, informed by their newspapers and by accounts such as those chronicled in this chapter, viewed Haiti with disdain rather than admiration.[2]

Even after the Civil War, these negative sentiments continued. Parallel to them were attempts to paint a slanderous portrait of Haitians, thus devaluing their role in hemispheric politics. This cacophony of anti–Haitian voices helped the United States in the late 19th and early 20th centuries move toward goals of geographical expansionism and militant imperialism in competition with European countries; supporting such endeavors were Theodore Roosevelt and Henry Cabot Lodge, among many other notables. The occupation of Haiti by the

U.S., which began in 1915, is an example of a closed-door, sphere of influence control, typified by the U.S. military's systematic deportation of German businessmen from Haiti in the early twenties. The Haitian experiment allowed the U.S. to become the premier power in the Caribbean under the guise of installing a liberal democracy for the first time in Haiti. A multitude of difficulties hampered the mission, not the least of which were the imperialist aims of the United States, but U.S. officials maintained the goal was a noble one in the best interests of the Haitians.

Whatever the problems and mixed priorities, the occupation's desire to "civilize" Haiti included efforts at building roads, hospitals, and modernizing the country to whatever degree possible. However, marines used forced labor for much of the construction, as well as suppressing Haitian revolts against the occupation. Hans Schmidt's text *The United States Occupation of Haiti, 1915–1934*, notes that "the materialistic approach fit the methods and priorities dictated by selfish American purposes and also conformed to American prejudices, which held that Haitians were incapable of political and intellectual achievements."[3] Schmidt also makes clear that:

> The Haitian-American Treaty of 1915, in effect a unilateral document executed by the [U.S.] State Department, was frequently cited as justification for continuing the occupation, a binding commitment by which the United States was morally and legally obligated to continue the occupation until 1936. That the treaty could have been abrogated at any time in exactly the same way that it was originally imposed, with the enthusiastic approval of Haitian nationalists, was ignored until after the 1929 uprisings, when the United States decided on early termination of the occupation as best serving American ends.[4]

Insults against Haitians, which had their basis in many biased, nonfiction texts, had helped justify the larger goals of the U.S. during the years prior to termination of the experiment.

Many Haitians buckled under the occupation, rose up against the U.S. intervention in 1929, and voted in large numbers against candidates sympathetic to the U.S. when free elections were held the same year. Though the dependency had begun in 1915, it was from 1922 to the 1929 elections that Haiti was in a particularly subordinate position to the United States' intervention.[5]

Indeed, it's the American presence in and growing frustrations toward Haiti that become important to this study. The situation there shaped more negative feelings into a growing brew of suspicions and—in many quarters—a strong dislike of the "Black Republic." Along with racist sentiments, some of this disdain centered around a fear and hatred of the voodoo religion. As Patrick Belle-

garde-Smith wrote, "The phobia against Vodun [voodoo] … culminated in nationwide persecutions. These were led by the Haitian bourgeoisie, the Roman Catholic establishment, and the United States military authorities in the 1920s…."[6]

During the 1920s, most Americans seemed ready for an end to U.S. military intervention, but only a small number of voices cried out for fairness towards the Haitian people. For example, James Weldon Johnson, the eminent African-American thinker and former U.S. consul in Nicaragua and Venezuela, wrote a four-part article in *The Nation* in 1920 which helped kindle the flames of criticism against the U.S. occupation.[7] Seven years later, Senator Paul Douglas wrote a stinging criticism of American abuses and imperialist aims in the Haitian experiment.[8]

Still, impatience with occupation and accusatory comments aimed at the U.S., however justified they were, could not transmute decades of widespread American abhorrence of the Haitian citizenry. As a supposedly impartial period study suggested, Americans believed Haitians to be 95 percent illiterate and "unmoral," with "wants … for the bare necessities of tropical and primitive existence—a thatch-roofed hut, a modicum of clothes, food naturally grown and easily obtained, crude and sensual social, and sexual satisfaction. To an American they appeared indolent and poverty-stricken."[9] Though certainly harmed by the occupation, Haitians hardly met this condescending description.

Historically, William Seabrook's 1929 book *The Magic Island* acts as a textual line of demarcation in adding to U.S. sentiments toward Haiti and Haitian voodoo. The U.S. was moving away from forcing diplomacy on nations, as it had in the twenties, to the Good Neighbor policy of the thirties. In a way, the shift in tactics had begun with U.S. difficulties in Haiti in 1929. That same year also marked the introduction of most English-speaking audiences to "living dead" zombies thanks to *The Magic Island*. Along with discussing Haiti's living dead, Seabrook's text also ignited a new awareness and popularity of Haitian superstitions in general. Though in many ways he was sympathetic to Haiti, Seabrook was not as radical a shift in literature as the Good Neighbor policy became in a governmental manner; in some ways, he was a mere extension of what had come before. The sensational style of writing he employed—not to mention the grotesque and racist caricatures of Haitians seen in the book's illustrations—reflects the influence of his predecessors. But *The Magic Island* proved to be less a culmination of Haitian or voodoo texts than a well-read link in a chain which led to other popular-audience works like author Kenneth Webb's 1932 play *Zombie*.

The rocky history of U.S.–Haitian relations from

the 19th century to the 1920s became an important background against which both fictional and nonfictional works were digested by the American public or debated in U.S. academic circles. These texts both reflected and influenced popular thought on the subject, as well as subsequent works that borrowed and repeated earlier ideas. The ideas presented by more academic works, even if they themselves did not draw mass readership, often proved the basis of more popular, sometimes fictional works. The end result meant most works resonated with echoes of prior prejudices, both informing and reinforcing U.S. views on Haiti and voodooism. *White Zombie* as a text mainly drew on the ideas of zombiism, with Haiti used as an exotic setting. Even so, the very choice of zombiism as a film subject invoked preformed opinions and ideas about Haiti in the minds of many U.S. moviegoers. In sum, the works chronicled in this chapter are illustrative of a long shadow cast over the American public, under which *White Zombie* would fall during its first theatrical release in 1932.

Nonfiction Works Prior to The Magic Island

By the early 19th century, several English-language texts were published on the subject of Haiti. Most likely the revolution, tales of its brutal bloodshed, and the uniqueness of black self-rule spawned interest in writers from the U.S. and Great Britain. At the same time, such literary efforts spoke almost without exception about the superstitions of Haiti, often devoting page after page to graphic descriptions of voodoo ceremonies, human sacrifice, and cannibalism.

W. W. Harvey's *Sketches of Hayti* [sic]: *From the Expulsion of the French to the Death of Christophe* (published by L. B. Seeley, 1827), was more optimistic towards the Haitians' self-government than most other printed matter of the time. Harvey believed that any "savagery" exhibited by Haitians during their rebellion in 1804 was in reaction to slavery. However, he still felt the need to expound upon the Haitians' bent toward superstition and supernatural events:

> These superstitious fears, however, did arise not wholly from their ignorance. ... But to attempt to shake their belief in such supernatural appearances, or to convince them of the folly of entertaining such groundless fears, was utterly vain. Every argument that could be proposed for this purpose, would be answered by a long history of extraordinary noises and fearful appearances, sufficiently appalling in the recital, and so generally did the belief in them prevail, that there were sufficiently resolute to their possibility, or to doubt their truth.

Harvey's comments form a hasty generalization about the entire populace, and are built on his own limited experience.

Most U.S. writers were not so kind as Harvey, however. Spenser St. John's 1884 account of voodooism and Haitian cannibalism—*Hayti, or the Black Republic*—became a much read text in the 19th century, and was far reaching in its influence on American thought. The author himself lived in Haiti some 12 years between 1863 and 1884, acting as a minister resident and consul-general. Though he admits that he never actually attended a voodoo ceremony, St. John does describe a court trial regarding cannibalism. The story includes references to "congo stew," a dish made of beans and human flesh allegedly eaten by some Haitians. The widespread distribution and multiple printings of St. John's book meant that it perhaps had a greater impact than any other 19th century text on the subject.

Though editions of his book varied, the chapter on voodoo ("vaudoux" in his spelling) was always extensive. In the 1889 edition, for example, it runs 44 pages. To him, it was crucial for an understanding of the Haitian people to explore the topic in detail:

> There is no subject of which it is more difficult to treat than Vaudoux-worship and the cannibalism which too often accompanies its rites. Few living out of the Black Republic are aware of the extent to which it is carried, and if I insist at length upon the subject it is in order to endeavor to fix attention on this frightful blot, and thus induce enlightened Haytians to take measures for its extirpation, if that be possible.[10]

He then poses and answers the question, "'Who is tainted by Vaudoux-worship?' I fear the answer must be, 'Who is not?'"[11] Despite his lengthy investigation, St. John does not mention zombies. He does briefly talk of bodies "dug from their graves," but suggests their primary purpose is food.[12] And when corpses are not used, the "goat without horns"—a human sacrifice—is.[13] He even goes so far as to intimate that the voodoo problem worsened after Haiti's independence. Rather than a political leader or Christian god, St. John proclaims, "Vaudoux reigns triumphant" in Haiti.[14]

In addition to its overall tainting with racism, the fault in Spencer's text which can be most readily condemned is a lack of any sources or citations for his often outrageous claims. Only in subtle language, such as the brief phrase "my friend learnt"[15] buried within a lengthy voodoo story, does St. John indicate some of his knowledge is from secondhand hearsay. His zeal for lambasting Haiti allowed him to set a low bar of credibility for the alleged facts that he includes.

Regardless of its factual shortcomings, the St. John

text was well known to academics and popular-audience readers. Few questioned its accounts of voodooism, probably because of St. John's apparent believability. If he makes sparse mention of his lack of firsthand knowledge of voodoo, his years of service in Haiti allow him to seem on the surface quite credible. Beyond his apparent veracity, St. John proved a good storyteller. Readers enjoyed his tales, whose popularity spawned a plethora of literary projects following his lead. Some would be more academic in nature; others were targeted to popular audiences. Occasionally, the writers' investment in the work of St. John would make them seem more like his apostles than independent voices speaking from independent research.

One such acolyte was James Anthony Froude. In his 1888 book *The English in the West Indies*, Froude speaks with St. John's confident tone and inadequate research:

> Behind the immorality, behind the religiosity, there lies active and alive the horrible revival of the West African superstitions: the serpent worship, the child sacrifice, and the cannibalism. There is no room to doubt it.[16]

More than merely briefly repeating St. John's thesis, Froude inserts his own belief that the U.S. government should become involved to stop the "cannibalism and devil worship" at work in the sovereign country of Haiti.

Public and scholarly interest in voodoo spurred a number of magazines to run various pieces on voodoo in the late 19th century.[17] During 1888 and 1889, *The Journal of American Folk-lore* published two essays regarding the generally unfair and inaccurate nature of literature on Haitian voodoo. Both were written by William W. Newell. His "Myths of Voodoo Worship and Child Sacrifice in Hayti" became an explicit rebuttal of St. John, Froude, and the like.[18] In particular, he questioned the rumors of cannibalism and child sacrifice offered by his predecessors, stating that the "accusations against ... the Vaudoux ... are imaginary."

The next year, Newell's follow-up article—"Reports of Voodoo Worship in Hayti and Louisiana"—attempted again to prove the excesses of 19th century texts on voodoo and Haiti, this time drawing on the U.S. minister to Haiti's disbelief in cannibalistic practices among voodoo cults.[19] But Newell's results, perhaps due to continued and even growing U.S. frustrations toward Haiti, did not capture the attention of the public or future writers. St. John's version of Haitian life was more exciting to read, even though far less accurate.

Perhaps the major nonfiction work created in St. John's image is Hesketh Pritchard's *Where Black Rules White: A Journey Across and About Hayti*, first published in 1900. In his chapter "Vaudoux Worship and Sacrifice,"

Pritchard claims he "made it a special point while in the island to learn as much of the sect as possible, to get at the truth concerning them by personal experience, and to glean actual facts at firsthand."[20] Despite the fact that he never saw cannibalism, Pritchard is so confident following St. John's lead that he declares that "there is no doubt that the child sacrificed in the worst Vaudoux rites is afterwards dismembered, cooked, and eaten...."[21] Faith in the picture of Haiti that St. John had sketched allows Pritchard to agree with him on more general concerns as well. For example, he suggests, "...Vaudoux is so inextricably woven in with every side of the Haytian's life, his politics, his religion, his outlook upon the world, his social and family relations, his prejudices and peculiarities that [it] cannot be judged apart from it."[22] Such influences will remain in place, he believes, "as long as Hayti retains an entirely negro Government [*sic*]."[23] These arguments helped set the stage for U.S. claims of Haiti's inability to continue self-rule in an age of imperialism.[24]

During the early 20th century, the U.S. press continued to claim voodooism ran rampant in Haiti. In 1908, the allegedly academic *National Geographic* warned: "It is well to consider whether we too may not expect some such acts of savagery [seen in Haitian voodooism] to break out in our own country if our own colored people are not educated for better things."[25] By 1920, the same publication offered the following analysis of Haitians: "Here, in the elemental wilderness, the natives rapidly forgot their thin veneer of Christian civilization and reverted to utter, unthinking animalism, swayed only by fear of local bandit chiefs and the black magic of voodoo witch doctors."[26] Comments like these, which had historical precedence thanks to the literature of St. John and others, allowed the U.S. to justify military intervention.

Many other magazines and newspapers followed with more verbal condemnations. The *New England Magazine* of March-April 1921 reinforced beliefs that voodoo cults existed in Haiti, even as the U.S. military tightened its stranglehold on the country. Along with a Naval Board of Inquiry report during 1921, the U.S. Marines told of allegedly flourishing and evil voodoo activities. News of the latter hit the New Orleans *Times-Picayune* on May 14, 1922, in the article "Voodoo Still has its Worshippers in 'Black Republic.'" In such instances, the popular press helped suggest a larger goal: it was almost a moral imperative for the U.S. to be involved in Haiti, even if "moral" is hardly an apt description of the government's imperialistic greed.

In the February 13, 1921, issue of the *New York American*, an article titled "Why the Black Cannibals of Hayti Mutilated Our Soldiers" discussed a "High Priest of Voodooism named Cadeus Bellegarde." Bellegarde held

A photograph of Haiti which appeared in the revised edition of Hesketh Pritchard's book Where Blacks Rule Whites: A Journey Across and About Hayti *(1910).*

voodoo ceremonies and supposedly authored a "code of rules for the ceremonial eating of white people." Similar to fears of the fictitious character Legendre in *White Zombie*, Haitian natives held a tremendous fear of Bellegarde, to the degree that it was difficult for a U.S. Naval Board of Inquiry to mount a broad charge of cannibalism against him. He claimed that, if sentenced to death, he would return to life in the form of a "crocodile, or in the shape of a swarm of mosquitoes, and devour his judges!" With Bellegarde, journalists found a narrative with a villain that seemingly embodied all that was wrong with Haiti. He despised the U.S. and attempted to harm the U.S. military, but was brought to justice by those same enemies. The story proved an almost perfect one to bolster the American public's support for continued intervention in Haiti.

However, mass-audience newspapers and magazines were not the only literary forum for discussions of voodooism in Haiti in the early 20th century. A major academic study during the 1920s was J. B. Hollis Tegarden's *Voodooism*, a dissertation submitted to the University of Chicago in candidacy for a Master of Arts degree. His efforts included an examination of the various spellings of the word voodoo, such as "vodoo," "vodoun," "hoodoo," the African "vodu," and the French "vaudoux." Moreover, he included a discussion of voodoo songs used as parts of rituals, and transcribed lyrics from them. Though he devotes much time to the history and psychology of snake worship, the term "zombi" is not discussed. Despite

its grounding in academia and a seemingly sincere attempt at objectivity, the dissertation still follows the tradition of St. John, trusting all too well the words of Haiti's detractors. Thus, the dissertation's credibility does not seem stronger than most nonfiction on the subject written for mass audiences. In general, both camps of readership—the scholarly and the popular—seemed all too willing to support U.S. involvement and to believe most if not all of the alleged activities in which voodoo cults engaged.

In the period immediately before and during U.S. intervention, the texts that were sympathetic to Haiti and voodooism were few. One notable example was J. N. Léger's *Haiti: Her History and Her Detractors* (published by Neale, 1907), which examined the country and the perspectives of others in the world in a relatively objective light. Rather than create an exposé, Léger attempted to diffuse the influence of Spencer St. John.[27] From another standpoint, Emily Greene Balch's *Occupied Haiti* (Writers Publishing Co., 1927) justifies voodoo as an old African ceremony, "deliberately employed in the closing days of slavery [in Haiti] by those who were planning ... insurrection as a means of bringing people together." For instance, the night of August 14, 1791, found a voodoo ceremony that was allegedly a veiled meeting of black leaders that planned an uprising against whites. And Robert P. Parsons' *History of Haitian Medicine* (Paul B. Hoeber, 1930) discussed voodoo less as religion, cult or political force, than in terms of its medicinal capacities.[28] In general, these voices were quieted by the excitement generated by the more sensational voodoo texts.

Most texts of the early 20th century oscillate between the ongoing belief and acceptance of St. John's work and a kind of paternalistic feeling extended to "primitives." They are also symptomatic of the growing frustrations against U.S. intervention in Haiti, as well as dying attempts to bolster support for the same. Whether academic, governmental, or popular, these works illustrate little movement from the kind of descriptions and beliefs that Spenser St. John had outlined in the prior century.

Fascination with voodoo was strong enough that

discussions of it were not limited to Haiti, however. Throughout the years prior to *White Zombie* various articles on the topic of domestic voodoo appeared in U.S. newspapers, particularly those in Louisiana. Voodoo had made its way to America, authors declared, but their descriptions of it were somewhat different than those of its Haitian counterpart. Rather than cannibalism, tales of love powders and voodoo magic that frequently appeared in the New Orleans press.[29] In addition, talk of deities revolved less around human sacrifices than often erotic ceremonies and "discussions" with "Zombi," the name of a voodoo snake god in the Louisiana voodoo tradition. For example, "Mammy Zoe Appeases Gran' Zombi and Saves Brides [*sic*] Wedding Gown," printed in the *New Orleans Item* on March 30, 1919, described an incident regarding the voodoo god blessing a wedding dress. The article included a lengthy chant that began, "Ya! Yi! Gran Zombi, qui courri a l'écola avec viex [*sic*] diable!"[30]

Articles like "Mammy Zoe" invoke another important area of inquiry, perhaps that to which *White Zombie* owes its greatest debt: the use of the very word "zombie." In its meaning as a synonym for "living dead" or for the medical condition caused by powders or potions in Haiti, the term did appear in print earlier than one might expect: 1792, in Moreau de Saint-Méry's text on the last years of white colonial rule in Haiti. He separately defines *revenants* (spirits), *loupgaroux* (vampires), and *zombis*, which he says is a "Creole word that means spirit, revenant." Given that his book was rarely seen or read— it was also published only in French—it held little if any influence in the history of English-speaking texts on the subject of voodoo and zombies.[31]

It would be safe to assume that some volumes published in the early 19th century in France or at Port-au-Prince discussed the historical figure of Jean Zombi, who was instrumental during Haiti's fight for independence and in the period immediately thereafter. A slave turned rebel, Zombi was known for his brutal savagery during Dessalines's 1804 massacre of whites. According to one source, Zombi would stop a white on the road, strip him, then—after leading him to the steps of the government palace—stab him to death.[32] Zombi would make a final transformation, becoming an Iwa in the voodoo pantheon of gods.[33] As with Moreau de Saint-Méry's text, information regarding Jean Zombi was not well circulated in the United States. Indeed, he does not seem to appear in English-language texts on Haiti or Haitian independence in the 19th or early 20th century.

Perhaps the earliest mention of the word "zombie" in a U.S. publication came in an 1889 essay on Louisiana voodoo by George W. Cable printed in *Century* magazine. He spoke of "an imaginary being of vast supernatural powers residing in the form of a harmless snake.

This spiritual influence or potentate is the recognized antagonist or opposite of Obi, the great African manitou or deity, or him whom the Congoes vaguely generalize as Zombi."[34] Though the term may have stemmed from Jean Zombi, he is not mentioned in Cable's essay, nor is the term's use as a synonym for the living dead. The term instead acts as the name for a voodoo snake god, as it would in many subsequent texts.

Henry C. Castellanos' 1905 text *New Orleans As It Was: Episodes of Louisiana Life* also mentioned the term, but in the quite different context of "philters, drugs, and poisonous substances" called "*gris-gris*":

> One of the favorite ingredients used is a decoction of the "*concombre zombi*,"—Jamestown weed—which they mix in coffee. It is the plant from which that rank toxicant, known as *stramonium*, is extracted.

The text added that dirt unearthed from cemeteries provided another ingredient for those same *gris-gris* packets.[35]

One of the first allusions in the English language to zombies as the living dead, though the actual term "zombie" was not used, came in an essay by Judge Henry Austin in a 1912 *New England Magazine*. He speaks of a:

> ...concoction of strange draughts from the native herbs of Hayti. Aside from poisons that kill at once, they are reputed to distill potions that kill by a long, slow process, the time being regulated by the strength of the dose to meet the exigencies of the case. Most uncanny, however, is the poison which will cause the victim to pass into an unconscious condition, so profound that it might be easily mistaken for death. This last-mentioned trance-producing potion might seem to be a creation of the imagination, if it were not for the fact that many observers of Hayti have vouched for the evidence of its use.[36]

Austin follows these comments with a surprising description of the purpose of such zombie-producing potions. Rather than claiming that the poor unconscious souls are made to work as slaves on plantations, he suggests that the reason is to sedate those planned for cannibalistic sacrifice.

Stephen Bonsal, author of *The American Mediterranean* (published by Moffat, Yard, and Co., 1912) offered another early description in the English language of a zombified person. The incident allegedly occurred in 1908. Though the description does not use the term "zombie," the victim's state clearly echoes that condition:

> A man of the working-class in Port-au-Prince fell ill. He had at intervals a high fever which physicians could not reduce. He had joined a foreign mission church and the head of the mission visited him. On his second visit this clergyman saw the patient die and at the invitation of the

dead man's wife and his physician, he helped dress the dead man in his grave-clothes. The next day he assisted at the funeral, closed the coffin lid, and saw the dead man buried. The mail rider to Jacmel found some days later a man dressed in grave-clothes, tied to a tree, moaning. He freed the poor wretch, who soon recovered his voice but not his mind. He was subsequently identified by his wife, by the physician who had pronounced him dead, and by the clergyman. The recognition was not mutual, however. The victim recognized no one, and his days and nights were spent moaning inarticulate words no one could understand. President [of Haiti] Nord Alexis placed him on a government farm, near Gonaives, where he was cared for.

Bonsal's description was the closest to defining the characteristics of a zombie as the living dead until William Seabrook's *The Magic Island* (1929).

In 1921, an article in the *New York American* did relate a tale that speaks of a deathlike sleep, but does not use any terminology to identify it. Don Mariano Alfarez, the source of the story and a chargé d'affaires at Port-au-Prince, claimed:

> A young woman died suddenly and was buried on the day following. At night several individuals of both sexes went to the cemetery, took up the coffin and opened it. What they actually did is not known; but what is positive is that the woman who was supposed to have been dead was heard to shriek and shout for help. The guard near the cemetery, composed of Jamaica [*sic*] and Louisiana blacks, approached and saw the woman sitting up in the coffin. Various persons were standing around her, chanting loudly words they did not understand.[37]

Alfarez concluded the story by telling readers that the guard ran away, returning later with help. The woman in the grave had been killed by a knife wound, however, and her heart and lungs had been torn from her body.

Texts like this *New York American* article meant that some readers in the U.S. by the end of the 1920s would have encountered either the term or (in this case) the concept of zombiism prior to William B. Seabrook's book *The Magic Island*. Those that read articles using the word zombie, however, would not have yet associated it with the concept of the living dead. *The Magic Island* synthesized both that concept and the term zombie for mass audiences in the U.S.

In general, the English-language nonfiction works on voodoo and Haiti prior to *The Magic Island* are, with some exceptions, emblematic of the general U.S. views on the subjects. Texts like Spenser St. John's reflect American suspicions and overt dislike of Haiti that grew throughout the first half of the 19th century, heightened with the Civil War, and continued during Reconstruction. St. John channeled racism into so powerful a work

that it strongly influenced those who followed him. It hardly seemed contradictory to U.S. citizens during the military intervention that they could offer sympathy to "primitives" who needed their help, and at the same time despise them for their evil and cannibalistic rituals. Imperialist gains and racist sentiment painted the picture of Haiti for most Americans. Indeed, literature on the subject echoed popular sentiment while shaping it. These texts then form links in a chain that helped educate the American populace about voodooism in only a sketchy and skewed way, while reinforcing their unfavorable perspectives of Haiti.

Fictional Works Prior to The Magic Island

While it is easiest to catalogue and examine texts on Haiti and voodoo by separating them into nonfiction and fiction, the poor scholarship and intentional fallacies regarding both in nonfiction blur the lines between the two. The bulk of fictional texts acknowledged that they were heavily influenced by their nonfiction counterparts, with the shadow of Spenser St. John cast over all their efforts. The following texts helped promote prevalent American and Western European views and disseminated them to a popular audience who may well not have read nonfiction, allegedly "academic" works of the 19th and early 20th centuries.

Voodoo and zombies proved popular fare for novels and short stories in the 19th century.[38] One of the earliest works of fiction in English on the subject depicts a Jamaican sugar plantation, love spells, and the powers that can restore life. Captain Mayne Reid, an adventurer and acquaintance of Edgar Allan Poe, penned the novel *The Maroon: A Tale of Voodoo and Obeah* in 1883. Chapter XXII, entitled "The Resurrection," offers not the word "zombie" itself, but rather the concept of the living dead, as a voodoo practitioner causes his own corpse to return to life.[39] In the following excerpt, the sorcerer Chakra describes how he brought himself back from beyond the grave:

> De folk 'peek da troof. My 'keleton it was, jess as dey say. ... Dem same old bones—de 'kull, de ribs, de jeints, drum-ticks, an' all. Golly, gal Cynthy! dat ere 'pears 'stonish you. Wha fo'? Nuffin' in daat. You sabby old Chakra? ... Be shoo Chakra no die hisself, so long he knows how bring dead body to de life. ... Dey did try kill 'im, you know. Dey 'tarve him till he die ob hunger and thuss. De John Crow pick out him eyes and tear de flesh from de old nigga's body; leab nuffin' but de bare bones. Ha! Chakra 'lib yet; he hab new bones, new flesh! Golly! you him see? he 'trong, he fat as ebber he wa'! Ha! Ha! Ha!

Mayne Reid's tale is unique not in that voodoo is the background of the story, but in that it combines a tale of the living dead with voodooism.[40] Not dissimilar to Seabrook's *The Magic Island* in this regard, *The Maroon* featured poor ethnic caricatures in both artwork and dialogue.

Henry Francis Downing's play *Voodoo*, published in London in 1914, offered the topic of voodoo and similar caricatures to theatergoers.[41] Set in Barbados and England in 1688–89, the four-act drama included characters ranging from "James II, King of England" to a group of generic "Voodoo Hags." Regrettably the play is informed by the word choice of its era, but the following excerpt does illustrate the use of a voodoo chant:

> First Negress *(stirs* [contents of a pot] *with spoon, in a sing-song and weirdly).*
>   Boonee, boonee, boo-oo-oo!
>   Soonee, soonee, soo-oo-oo!
>
> Others [additional elderly women] *(circling).*
>   Oo-oo-oo-oo-oo!
>
> First Negress *(still stirring).*
>   Boonee, boonee, boo-oo-oo!
>   Soonee, soonee, soo-oo-oo!
>
> Others *(still circling).*
>   Oo-oo-oo-oo-oo!

Chants of this type are important in the picture they helped develop of voodooism for those in the U.S. They were eventually echoed in Scene 1 of *White Zombie*.

Voodoo chants appear again in Annie Calland's "Voodoo"; the poem appeared in a 1926 volume of her work under the same name. Calland's creation revolves around voodoo drums and rhythms mixed with images of passion (in the dance and flames of the fire). There is a (possibly unintentional) acknowledgment of the author's lack of familiarity with the subject matter in her mention of the God Pan, who is not a part of the voodoo tradition. The following is her opening verse:

> Ho, the pan-pipes call to Bassin Bleu
> To dance the dance of the great voodoo;
> The big drums boom, the conch shells blare,
> The signal fires flame and flare;
> Oh-o-ay-o-eyah, the strange songs sound
> While the dancers gather at the singing ground
> The tympani louder and louder boom,
> Echoing far their song of doom;
> Oh-o-ay-o-eyah, the wild songs seem
> The echo of the conchs' scream.
> Ho, the panpipes call to Bassin Bleu
> To dance the dance of the great voodoo!
>
> *And ever the great drum beat, and beat,*
> *And ever the woman sang.*[42]

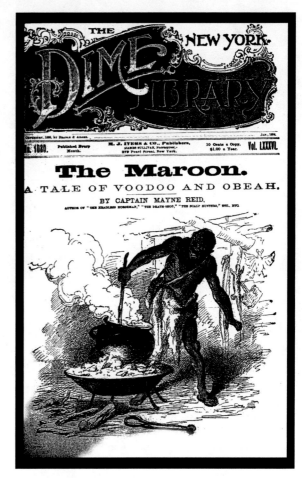

Artwork for Captain Mayne Reid's 1883 story "The Maroon: A Tale of Voodoo and Obeah."

A few years later, Natalie Vivian Scott's play *Zombi* also detailed voodoo in Louisiana. Set in New Orleans, the major players included Marie Laveau (a "young Quadroon girl, known as the Voodoo Queen"), Mammy ("her mother"), Buck (a young African-American), and M'so Henri (a "young Creole beau"). In January 1929, *Theatre Arts Monthly* printed one act, set as follows:

> A fire is burning in a small, rough chimney-place in the corner. There are low stools and blocks of wood around, with various utensils containing the viscera of chickens. On the walls are nailed knots of horse-hair, feathers of turkeys and buzzards, dried snake-skins, rabbits' feet, and other charms. A large cage made of four strong uprights stands on the floor at the back. Before it is spread a square of gaily colored rug on which are laid out numbers of knotted string, crude wax figures, finger bones of children, mounds of meal, bunches of gaily colored feathers.

A heap of dead chickens is piled directly in front of the cage.

Scott's *Zombi* thus finds inspiration in New Orleans voodoo and its most infamous voodoo queen, Marie Laveau, rather than anything to do with Haiti. The scene excerpted in *Theatre Arts Monthly* ends with Laveau screaming "Gran' Zombi! Devil!" The word "zombi" itself is a signifier of Louisiana voodoo, and suggests a voodoo god instead of the Haitian conception of the living dead.[43]

Before the curtain even goes up for Scott's play, there is a "primitive music of stringed instruments and drums, a hushed ecstatic moaning through which sounds a voice chanting a voodoo song, at first loud, then sinking to a low wail." The song carries this vocal:

> Zombie there is a voodoo
> Zombie there is a voodoo
> I see you here
> I say to you
> I feel you near
> You've come, you're here
> Zombie...!!

In addition to poetry and the theater, voodoo became a subject for popular music in the teens and especially the twenties.[44] For example, Al Jolson sang Sigmund Romberg's "Voodoo Maiden" at New York's Winter Garden in 1916, Jazzman Tiny Parham recorded the foxtrot "Voodoo" for Victor in 1929, and Obdulio Morales recorded "Voodoo Moon" for Decca in 1930. Each used the topic of voodoo exotically but without depth. More interesting is David W. Guion's 1929 piece "Voodoo," which explored voodoo in a vocal with a built-in dialect.[45] The opening lyrics are as follows:

> De air am full o' tings Wid wings
> m-m-m
> De eyes ob snakes an' bats An' rats
> m-m-m
> Am some po' sinner's soul turned col'
> Chained t'de Debble in de Debble's hole,
> Longin'-in'fo' t'git out an' shout.

Guion's notations on the sheet music describe the "*m-m-m*" as a "sort of weird humming sound," an apparent attempt to echo the voodoo cries that Calland penned as "Oh-o-ay-o-eyah." The rest of the piece is marked by the particularly fascinating lines, "Now when de moon am bright, At night ... *m-m-m* ... From out de graves come hosts Ob ghosts! ... *m-m-m*." Again repeated chants form an impression of a facet of voodooism for those in the U.S.

While perpetuating prevailing U.S. attitudes toward Haiti and voodooism, some of these fictional works utilized the swamps of Louisiana as their setting. Given the believed prevalence of voodoo in Louisiana, the Haitian ancestry of some members of that state, and the long-standing fears that African-Americans would adopt the ways of Haitians, the conflation of the two geographical places in voodoo lore is not difficult to understand.[46] The most consistent description in these poems and plays, regardless of setting, is in the voodoo chants and the relationship drawn between the religion of voodoo and the rhythm of music. The connection of voodoo to music itself is not all that odd, as it would have emphasized both the exotic and erotic elements most in the U.S. would have seen in the topic.[47] After all, even as sophisticated as Duke Ellington's music is, promoters in the 1920s sometimes advertised it as "jungle music." By 1931, voodoo drumming could be heard on the radio.[48] Indeed, in the case of music with voodoo themes, it was rhythm that gave white Americans a sense of what they believed voodoo to be. The emphasis on drum beats would be repeated in the cinema.

Filmmakers used voodooism as a movie topic long before either *The Magic Island* or *White Zombie.* "Haven't you ever seen it in the movies?" a devout believer in voodooism asked the author of a 1927 *American Mercury* article on the subject.[49] Contemporary descriptions of Joe Brandt and Frank Whitman's *Voodoo Fires* (1913) and Sidney Olcott's *Ghost of the Twisted Oak* (Lubin, 1915) make clear that voodooism is depicted. Later, Paramount's five-reeler *Unconquered* (1917), starring Mabel Van Buren and Tully Marshall, featured a voodoo-inspired savage seeking humans for use in sacrifices. Earnest Stern's screenplay for *The Witching Eyes* (1929), which is apparently set in Haiti, features a lustful witch doctor who puts a voodoo curse on a poet in order to seize his lover for himself. These few fictional films echo printed literature on the subject, reinforcing the dominant and unfavorable opinions in U.S. culture about both Haiti and voodooism.

The Zombies of William B. Seabrook

More than any prior texts or films, William B. Seabrook's *The Magic Island* brought fanciful, allegedly nonfiction tales of voodoo and zombies to a mass audience. As stated previously, his text adopted some prior prejudices while attempting to reframe the discussion of Haitians and voodooism in a more "objective" light. The book reads less like a standard travelogue of Haiti than an incredibly descriptive piece of fiction, which may not be surprising since Seabrook was more of an adventurer and raconteur than a historian or journalist. Indeed, his sensationalized writing style helped make the book successful. The result heightened the American public's interest in voodoo and educated readers about a specific result of voodooism: zombiism. The word zombie and its definition as the living dead converged for mass audiences. As a result, *The Magic Island* conveyed the very superstitions which *White Zombie* would soon appropriate.

William Buehler Seabrook was born on February 22, 1886, in Westminster, Maryland. After graduating from Mercersburg Academy in Pennsylvania in 1901, he attended Newberry College in South Carolina. As a journalist, Seabrook lived in Europe during 1907–08 and then began a graduate program in philosophy in 1908 at the University of Geneva in Switzerland. Following that, he returned to the U.S. and Georgia, becoming a partner in an advertising agency. It was in Atlanta in 1912 that he married his first wife, Katherine Pauline Edmondson.

He made his way back to Europe when World War I began, enlisting in the French Army and fighting at Verdun. Yet, by 1917, Seabrook had returned to New York. At the encouragement of H. L. Mencken of *The American Mercury*, he concentrated his time on writing. Seven years of feature stories for newspaper syndicates led to a 1924 trip to Arabia. Seabrook's experiences translated into his first book, *Adventures in Arabia* (1927).

As a follow-up, Seabrook decided to pursue his interests in Haitian voodoo. Friends like Hal Smith attempted to dissuade him, however, telling him: "Look Willie, I can show you from eighty to a hundred books on voodoo, some more or less recent. Not a one of them has ever sold over four thousand copies. No white man can write a book that's any good about voodoo." After Seabrook detailed his plans and hopes to actually become a part of the voodoo culture, Smith changed his mind. "Hal looked at me, gave me sort of a hug, and said, 'Hell,

Photographed by Eric Shaal, this portrait of William Seabrook was taken in 1943.

Willie, if that's the way you feel, maybe you *can* do it. Maybe it's an idea.'"[50]

To embark on his quest, Seabrook "learned Haitian creole, which was easy since I already had French, and went down to Haiti, and went back into the mountains and stayed there a year ... and it wasn't enough ... and returned there a second year and was at home with Maman Célie [a sorceress] and her family and her village."[51]

His stay with Célie was pivotal in his gaining access to various voodoo ceremonies and sacrifices; his bond with the woman even extended to his becoming her "adopted son." As well as dedicating the book to her, Seabrook believed:

> It was as if Maman Célie and I had known each other always, had been at some past time united by the mystical equivalent of an umbilical cord; as if I had suckled in infancy at her dark breasts, had wandered far and was now returning home. And it was because I was at home there, in Maman Célie's thatched house on the mountainside, with her other black sons and daughters, now my brothers and sisters, that it all came about naturally without my urging.[52]

Seabrook's integration into the Célie household allowed him to claim deeper insight into the actualities of Haitian life and voodoo than his predecessors in the 19th century.

Of the whole experience, he wrote "It was a blazing revelation to me—as if another dream had come true, and I came home to America, and wrote it excitedly because I was excited. I had a hard time writing it, but hard in a new and different way."[53] The text became an examination of Haitian cults, voodoo practices, and zombiism.

One chapter, "The *Ouanga* Charm," finds Seabrook discussing Maman Célie's role as "sorceress, as well as a priestess of voodoo." To help her grandson attract the attention of an indifferent "damsel," Célie went about designing an *ouanga* to act as a love packet. Dried powder of a humming bird and the pollen of jungle flowers, mixed with a few dried drops of the grandson's blood and semen, formed the ingredients.[54] Seabrook also became aware of other kinds of *ouanga* packets. Into these went "aromatic leaves and powders," as well as other ingredients that apparently depended upon its intended use. For example, Célie designed one for the author himself that was "bright-colored, friendly and protective...." He also learned of "certain other *ouanga* packets in this voodoo sorcery, horridly devised, [which] were sometimes as definitely deadly as the murderer's knife or poison."[55]

"The Altar of Skulls," another chapter, explains various kinds of voodoo ceremonies, including one that

Seabrook allegedly witnessed. He describes the chief sorcerers of one cult—"Papa Nebo, "Gouédo Mazacca," and "Gouédé Oussou"—as well as the activities that took place at one voodoo meeting. The cult's oracle "spoke with the dead, in the subhuman vernacular of death itself," with sorcerer Mazacca then translating its message to those who had come for answers to questions. In exchange, participants left gifts at the altar as a sign of thanks to the voodoo gods.[56]

Another of the stories covers an occurrence during the night in a small cemetery. Three women arrive and pray to Baron Samedi, ruler of the cemetery, for permission to desecrate graves. After spouting phrases like *"Mortoo tomboo miyi!"* (a "jargonized creole" for "Dead in the tomb, to me!"), they dig up a body for multiple "necromantic uses." Grease from the brains would be used on the heads of tools, making them more accurate; the heart would be dried and given to those who lacked courage; other parts of the body went into *ouangas* and charms. Bones and the skulls, however, would be made a part of the specific cult's altar.[57]

Lengthy notes at the end of the text cover recipes for *ouangas* and music used at voodoo ceremonies. Seabrook devotes part of this section to a lengthy investigation of the three kinds of voodoo drums: the *maman*, *papa*, and *boula* (also known as *cata*). Such drums would undergo a consecration and baptism after being crafted, even to the extent of being given individual names. His discussion highlights the voodoo rhythms and beat that were often incorporated in subsequent texts and entertainment depictions, just as they had been previously in the works of Calland, Guion, and others.[58]

Most relevant to the subject of *White Zombie*, however, is the chapter "...Dead Men Walking in the Cane Fields." In it, Seabrook speaks of a conversation he had with one of his Haitian friends, Polynice:

> "It seems to me that these werewolves and vampires [in Haiti] are first cousins to those we have at home, but I have never, except in Haiti, heard of anything like *zombies* [author's emphasis]. Let us talk of them for a little while. I wonder if you can tell me something of this *zombie* superstition." My rational friend Polynice was deeply astonished. He leaned over and put his hand on my knee. "Superstition? But I assure you that this of which you now speak is not a matter of superstition. Alas, these things—and other evil practices connected with the dead—exist. They exist to an extent that you whites do not dream of, even though evidences are everywhere under your eyes."[59]

Polynice also told Seabrook of the four nights he guarded his dead brother's grave with shotguns, watching it until he was certain the body had begun to rot. To explain further, he added:

"At this very moment, in the moonlight, there are *zombies* working on this island, less than two hours' ride from my own habitation. We know about them, but we do not dare interfere so long as our own dead are left unmolested. If you will ride with me tomorrow night, yes, I will show you dead men working in the cane fields. Close even to the cities, there are sometimes *zombies*."[60]

By way of description, Polynice related that zombies in a group look like "a band of ragged creatures who [shuffle] along ... staring dumbly, like people walking in a daze. [They are] vacant-eyed like cattle, [and make] no reply when asked to give their names."[61] He added that "zombies must never be permitted to taste salt or meat," as that would make them understand they were dead.[62] One of Polynice's stories describes an incident where the zombies did eat salt, which caused them to make "a dreadful outcry. ... No one dared stop them, for they were corpses walking in the sunlight, and they themselves and all the people knew that they were corpses. And they disappeared toward the mountain."[63]

Original artwork from the first edition of William B. Seabrook's book, The Magic Island *(1929). The blank stares and lumbering quality of the zombies in* White Zombie *definitely borrow from images such as this one.*

Other zombies walked through the marketplace of their own village, though they did not recognize any of their relatives. Seabrook writes what he was told of the incident:

> ...a woman whose daughter was in the procession of the dead threw herself screaming before the girl's shuffling feet, and begged her to stay; but the grave cold feet of the daughter and the feet of the other dead shuffled over her and onward; and as they approached the graveyard, they began to shuffle faster and rushed among the graves, and each before his own empty grave began clawing at the stones and earth to enter it again; and as their cold hands touched the earth of their own graves, they fell and lay there, rotting carrion.[64]

Before leaving his friend Polynice, Seabrook finally saw the creatures for himself:

> three supposed *zombies*, who continued dumbly at work ... there was something about them unnatural and strange. They were plodding like brutes, automatons. Without stooping down, I could not fully see their faces, which were bent expressionless over their work. ... The eyes were the worst. It was not my imagination. They were in truth like the eyes of a dead man, not blind, but staring, unfocused, unseeing. The whole face, for that matter, was bad enough. It was vacant, as if there was nothing behind it. It seemed not only expressionless, but incapable of expression.[65]

He continues by describing physical contact with one of them. "I reached out for one of the dangling hands. It was callused, solid, human." The zombie did not respond when Seabrook held his hand and said "Bonjour, com-pére." The keeper of the trio grew impatient and pushed Seabrook away, telling him it was none of his affair.[66]

Seabrook ends his chapter convinced zombies exist, but far less certain of their supernatural qualities. He would later write about his experiences in his autobiography, as well as about the word zombie and concept of zombiism:

> Zombie is one of the African words. I didn't invent the word zombie, nor the concept of zombies. But I brought the word and concept to America from Haiti and gave it in print to the American public—for the first time. The word is now a part of the American language. ... The word had never appeared in English print before I wrote *The Magic Island*.

As this chapter has already shown, however, the word zombie/zombi had appeared in English print before *The Magic Island*, but as a term for other voodoo concepts, such as the snake god. The concept of zombies as the living dead had also appeared in English print prior to *The Magic Island*, but Seabrook was the first major English-language author to publish the word zombie as the term for the living dead. Seabrook would also claim that:

> The attempted rational explanation I gave of how the zombie may actually exist without being supernatural is recognized in the Haitian code and accepted by ethnologists as probably correct.[67]

On this point, Seabrook is apparently accurate, as no prior texts seem to suggest the nonsupernatural explanations that he does.

To strengthen the credibility of all his claims regarding zombies, Seabrook cites Article 249 of the Haitian Penal Code in *The Magic Island*. It was quoted in Chapter One of this volume, but it is worth doing so again. It reads:

> Also shall be qualified as attempted murder the employment which may be made against any person of substances which, without causing actual death, produce a lethargic coma more or less prolonged. If, after the administering of such substances, the person has been buried, the act shall be considered murder no matter what result follows.[68]

Seabrook is correct in his citation of the penal code, which actually did contain this article in the 1920s.

When finished at the end of the 1920s, *The Magic Island* caused a level of excitement among publishers, with one magazine offering $15,000 for the serialization rights. Ecstatic over the amount, Seabrook had a lengthy meeting with the editor regarding a few "simple and trivial changes." After an hour had passed, he realized the sum total of such small alterations were significantly changing the book, even to the degree of eliminating references to Maman Célie. Seabrook turned the magazine down, opting instead for a hardback printing with Harcourt in 1929.[69]

Literary reviews of the book were favorable overall, with most critics remarking on the particularly unique experiences Seabrook had. The *Outlook and Independent* believed his writing to have "imagination and sympathy," and the "material ... he secured is remarkable and valuable."[70] The *New York Post* even called it "the best and most thrilling book of exploration that we have ever read."[71] Such critics rarely questioned Seabrook's credibility or the validity of his often outlandish findings.

Concern over Seabrook's accuracy and credibility were voiced, but usually by academic journals. For example, *The Yale Review* believed "He spoils much of his material by his exaggerated style and his dubious psychology," and the *American Journal of Sociology* passed the judgment: "He has written as an artist, not an ethnologist."[72] These criticisms constituted both a minority and scholarly view that, while certainly accurate, did not compare in frequency with the favorable reactions of popular publications and everyday readers.

The Magic Island became a bestselling travel book in the U.S. after being honored as a Literary Guild choice for 1929. As a result, its author made far more than the initial $15,000 he had been offered in serial rights. In addition to its great success in the United States, a translation was published in French in 1932.[73] The project helped educate many U.S. citizens in the voodoo practices and zombies of Haiti, but—despite Seabrook's fascinating tales and firsthand experiences—it is still in some ways a culmination of the many works on Haiti and voodoo that preceded it. Seabrook's penchant for the sensational is much in line with Spenser St. John's exploration of Haiti in the previous century. Furthermore, his introduction of zombies helped pave the way for the depictions of Haitian superstition in the theater and film of the 1930s.

Post-Seabrook, Pre-Halperin Voodoo Literature

The Magic Island's success helped steer the attentions of many authors working in both fiction and nonfiction toward voodoo and zombies. Some of these show little if any influence of the Seabrook text; however, it seems nearly impossible to imagine others having been written without guidance from *The Magic Island*. In any event, these books and articles constitute *White Zombie*'s immediate past. Even if *White Zombie* screenwriter Garnett Weston did not read or otherwise become aware of these, such texts helped further construct the knowledge and impressions of voodooism and zombiism for many citizens in the U.S.

Hilda Phelps Hammond's "Beware the Veil of Voodooism in America," printed in the October 5, 1930 New Orleans *Times-Picayune*, was a major investigation of the issue. Though centering on New Orleans voodoo and its various "queens" (e.g., Marie Laveau and Malvina Latour), Hammond does speak briefly of the "African god Zombi."[74] Rather than *The Magic Island*, Hammond's article helped blaze the trail of discussing snake gods bearing the same name as Haiti's living dead.

From a fictional standpoint, John Esteven's novel *Voodoo: A Murder Mystery* (Doubleday, 1930) discussed voodoo from a Cuban character's point of view. He says:

> Belonging to no race, I chose the race your white law thrust on me. I found its essence in the voodoo cult, and sought to make of this a weapon and a flame. Hatred has its gods. I served them. Filled with their power, I was able to quicken and restore old practices and rites.

At its heart, the story discusses the problems of ethnic identity, highlighted as a result the tension between races. Questions of race would become a 1932 interpretation of the title *White Zombie*.[75]

Closest in chronology to *White Zombie*'s production was probably H. Bedford-Jones' *Drums of Damballa* (Covici-Friede, 1932). Identified by the author as historical fiction, the book details the alleged atrocities of voodoo. Its source was a series of documents and letters brought from Haiti to the U.S. in 1803, as well as the Navy Chroncile and Annual Registers. Among those materials from 1803 were documents on zombies, marking probably the first time the word arrived on American soil, even though these documents were not published.

Bedford-Jones' book hit U.S. bookstores in February and March of 1932, to favorable critical reviews. *The Outlook and Independent* of April 1932 made a strong recommendation of it to readers, while the *New York Herald Tribune* "Books" of February 28 called it a "thrilling yarn." Among the book's more exciting passages is one that details a zombie encounter:

> O'Donnell stretched out. He was entirely reassured by this reception, so far as personal safety was concerned. He had some dim memory of hearing nursery tales about a *zombi*, a resurrected corpse that obeyed the orders of the vaudou priest, but understood little about the fable. He could not at all understand, for that matter, why or how his brother could be here in the mountains. Surely if Alexandre were alive, he must have sent messages![76]

In a later passage, Bedford-Jones' text describes a zombie character in a manner reminiscent of *The Magic Island*:

> O'Donnell looked through the opening. There in the gathering dusk of evening, not ten feet outside the hut, he saw a figure led by a black. It was the figure of an old man, gray-faced, with matted gray hair about face and head, eyes blank and staring, body cloaked with rags. "Alexandre!," cried O'Donnell, starting to his feet. "No, no-impossible—" The blank eyes looked at him and passed him by. He halted in the doorway. Horrified realization burst upon him. Where was the handsome, soldierly, laughing man he had known two years ago? Vanished utterly. Here stood an idiot, it seemed, a man stricken, old, unkempt, a dream caught roaming through daylight hours....[77]

The book's discussion of "zombis"—in an era before the spelling of the word met conformity—is the most detailed and, in terms of Haitian folklore, the most accurate in any fictional text appearing prior to *White Zombie*'s release.

Post-Seabrook, Pre-Halperin Zombie Cinema

Following the release of Seabrook's *The Magic Island*, filmmakers seized on the subject of voodoo and zombies. The first major producer to draw on such topics was Walter Futter. Walter and his brother Fred were known in the early 1930s as the "junk-men of filmdom" because of their successful stock footage library. The two started buying negatives of bankrupt firms and amateur cameramen in 1926, calling their firm "Wafilms." By 1928, the duo started a sideline business purchasing "short ends," unexposed footage at the end of used film reels. After buying the footage, the brothers Futter spliced it together and sold it for large profits.[78]

Walter Futter ad published on October 30, 1931, in The Film Daily.

Walter Futter's time was also devoted to producing short subject films for theatrical release, most of which were distributed by Columbia Studios. His first film to broach the subject of voodoo was part of a short subject series titled *Curiosities.*[79] In August 1931, *The Film Daily* described it as a "weird yarn of the 'Zombies,' who, [Futter] avers, are the dead brought back to life by the powers of voodooism." Futter showed "the corpses being taken from the graves and prodded into life," and "the rice fields where they [were] working." His short apparently ended with shots of the zombies being put "back to sleep in their graves to be ready for another hard day of toil."[80]

Motion Picture Daily reviewed a subsequent *Curiosities* short in December 1931. Their critic wrote that the short featured "the Zombies [*sic*]," as well as a "junk dealer who collects airplane parts, the richest and poorest church in the world at Columbia, Washington, and a number of varieties of fish and their peculiar habits."[81] All of these topics were covered in a scant eight minutes. Though some of the zombie footage may have been similar to or even the same as that in the earlier *Curiosities*, this is a different short subject than the one *The Film Daily* had reviewed in August. Perhaps Futter believed zombies had been a successful topic, or perhaps he simply had an abundance of footage on the subject; it is difficult to determine given the little information available on these projects.

In December of 1931, Futter announced he would produce six three-reel travelogues, all to be patterned after his popular film *Africa Speaks* and meant to play at the bottom of double bills. The proposed films included *Tiger Tales* (on India), *Vale of Kashmir* (on Punjab), *Jade* (on Tibet), and *Dreams of Empire*. The last project was planned as an examination of Haitian voodoo, though Futter released no further details and critical reviews of the period seem not to exist. It is possible he never completed the project, as no copyright form was filed.

The following year, audiences did see Futter's short subject *Voodoo Land*, which appeared at theaters in late February and early March of 1932.[82] The 12-minute motion picture featured veteran humorist and journalist John P. Medbury as what *The Film Daily* called a "wisecracking off-stage lecturer."[83] The early section of *Voodoo Land* showed the various "native occupations and primitive methods" used in Haiti, as well as scenes of "voodoo ceremonies." Supposedly "real" and filmed in the heart of Haiti, the scenes were deemed by *The Film Daily* as "nothing very special, just a little hip shaking and drinking, but the comedy comments by Medbury make it quite amusing."[84]

Futter wasn't alone in his attempt to capitalize on voodooism. RKO Pathé released the short subject *The Song of the Voodoo* in October 1931. Subtitled *Vagabond Adventure*, the nine-minute short presented a travelogue of scenes shot by "Van Bueren's adventure men" throughout the Caribbean and on Haiti.[85] After showing various shots of Haitian life, the film divulges allegedly "real" footage of a voodoo dance and ceremony.[86]

Kenneth Webb's 1932 Zombie

The major venue in which Haiti and zombies were translated into entertainment after Seabrook's *The Magic Island* was Kenneth Webb's play *Zombie*. George Sherwood, a producer and director, became intrigued by the production, presumably envisioning financial success on the crest of plays like _Dracula_ and the burgeoning 1930s horror film cycle. The subject matter, of course, stemmed less from pre–1929 sources than it did from Seabrook.

Kenneth Webb was a native New Yorker, forever enamored of Greenwich Village. As a youth he attended the Collegiate School in the Upper West Side, then entered Columbia University. While there, he wrote and directed four or five varsity shows. With brother Roy,[87] Webb collaborated in scripting and directing various productions for clubs, churches, and other organizations in New York.[88]

After writing numerous vaudeville sketches, Webb went to work for the film industry in New York. Just after World War I, for instance, he directed various projects for the Vitagraph Company; in 1922, he was associated with the Yonkers studio of C. C. Burr and Whitman Bennett.[89] Webb gave up the movies when he sold his first play. Though it received mixed notices, _One of the_

Publicity still of Kenneth Webb, circa 1920s.

Family ran some 230 performances after opening on December 21, 1925.[90] The successful farce led Webb to collaborate with John E. Hazzard on the storyline for _The Houseboat on the Styx_, an operetta about a meeting of several famous persons (Shakespeare, Sappho and Salome among them) in Hades. Following that came work on the 1930 Broadway revue _Who Cares?_

"I am writing new plays all the time," he said in 1926. "My trouble is that they get half way through and I then become disgusted, put the play away, and then bring it out again six months later."[91] It's unclear when he first began work on _Zombie_, though it was seemingly after the printing of Seabrook's book in 1929; its narrative clearly shows the influence of _The Magic Island_.

Zombie's plot features Sylvia and Jack Clayton, American plantation owners on the edge of the Haitian jungles. Clayton dies, but Pedro—a huge and ominous overseer—causes his body to return to life as a zombie as a way to get at the family fortune. The young Dr. Thurlow, with whom Sylvia has flirtations, and an elder scholar named Professor Wallace begin tracking down clues to lead them to the zombie masters. At one point, an entire band of zombies lumber across the stage in a half-live, half-dead fashion. Thanks to a twist ending, the zombie master turns out to be not the suspicious Pedro, but kindly old Professor Wallace himself.

As for the cast, Pauline Starke offered the most marquee value. A silent film siren, her cinematic star dimmed sharply when talkies arrived. Hailing originally from Joplin, Missouri, she was signed to a contract by D. W. Griffith before she even finished school. Her screen debut came as a bit player in his _The Birth of a Nation_ (1915). Along with such other early films as Frank Borzage's _Until They Get Me_ (1917), she appeared in the well-remembered _A Connecticut Yankee in King Arthur's Court_ (1921) and _Dante's Inferno_ (1924).[92]

Her screen career declined as the decade progressed, so much so that she was replaced by Betty Compson in James Cruze's _The Great Gabbo_ (1929). Compson appeared opposite Erich von Stroheim in that film at Cruze's request, as she was his wife at the time. By November 10, 1932, however, the Los Angeles Superior Court awarded Starke full payment of her lost salary on the film.

Yet, her career continued to slide. In April 1931, _Photoplay_ claimed Starke was "recovering from a serious nervous breakdown which sent her to a California sanitarium for over a month." The following month, on May 11, she finalized a divorce from film producer Jack White, reaping $750 a month in alimony.

During 1931, she made a cross-country vaudeville tour that according to contemporary accounts was moderately successful. Though she had appeared in some

The Zombies Will Get You If—

PAULINE STARKE IN "ZOMBIE."

Artwork of Pauline Stark and cohorts in Zombie, *published in the* Chicago Sunday Tribune *of March 27, 1932.*

stage productions, Starke probably received the lead of Sylvia Clayton in *Zombie* thanks to its producer George Sherwood, to whom she was wed in 1932.[93] "It was a comeback play for her," costar Etta Moten recalled. "The play was very much like her life, because she was trying to make a comeback through the play, as was [her character in] the play."[94] But Starke received generally unenthusiastic reviews for her work in *Zombie*. For example, *The Billboard* flatly mentioned to its readers she "is possessed of ... no great acting ability."[95]

The cast also included Hunter Gardner as Dr. Paul Thurlow. He had been a leading man and director of the Jessie Bonstelle Repertoire Company of Detroit for two seasons prior to *Zombie*, and before that had been associated with various stock companies. Rose Tapley also appeared; her career prior to the play had been spent between the stage and screen. In the former, she had appeared opposite such legends as Chauncey Olcott; in the latter, Tapley acted alongside stars like Norma Talmadge and Maurice Costello.[96]

Particularly intriguing is George Regas, who took fourth billing in the *Zombie* program as the ominous overseer Pedro. Born in Sparta, Greece and educated in Athens, he left school for a life on the stage. Regas had toured the U.S. on various occasions in Greek plays, as well as appearing on-screen in such U.S. films as *The Love Light* (1921) with Mary Pickford. At the time of *Zombie*'s

staging, he was married to Reine Davies, sister of Hollywood film star Marion Davies.[97]

Actress Etta Moten [neé Burnett], who would later work in Hollywood films and on the Broadway stage, appeared as a maid. Years later, she could recall little of *Zombie*'s history. "All I remember," Moten said in an interview with film historian Leonard J. Kohl, "was that I spoke a patois, a French patois, and I had to *scream*. Everybody said they remembered the fact that I screamed in it."[98]

With cast ready, Sherwood and Webb opened the play at New York's Biltmore Theater on February 10, 1932. Ads and promotional materials made the play's intentions at least seem to be serious; the repetitive tag line "A Play of the Tropics" appeared on most such publicity. Additionally, Article 249 of the Haitian Penal Code made its way into both the script and some press releases. Despite Sherwood and Webb's hopes, however, the critics weren't impressed.

The *New York Evening Post* believed *Zombie* to be "written and acted half as well as its subject matter deserves," and the *Herald Tribune* noted that "Happily, Mr. Webb hasn't the skill to make himself be taken seriously by the ingenuous judges of book-of-the-month clubs...." Even the more kind reviews—such as the *Brooklyn Eagle*'s notice—suggested, "...some elimination of the repetition and a little better acting...." [99]

Most patrons were not convinced either. As the *New York American* review told readers, "Last night's audience, a rather irreverent one, seemed to think them things more humorous than strange. Corpses walked about and opened safes and strangled the living and fell away again into corrupt dust ... but I fear there was laughter in the morgue and hilarity among the dead-heads."[100]

Industry trades were also unimpressed. For example, *The Billboard* believed "[Webb] multiplied his zombies endlessly and then set them parading around the stage, a veritable army of the dead. Where one zombie might have been fearfully effective, a long lean line of them became merely funny."[101]

After its failure in New York closed the show after 20 performances, Webb quickly arranged for the production to move West. On March 13, 1932, the play opened at Chicago's Adelphi Theater with its major New York players intact. Ads that afternoon dubbed it "the sensational South Sea mystery," with subsequent promotional materials adding such adjectives as "Different!" "Excitement!" "Thrills!" and "Laughs!" Mention of the last marked a change in advertising, obviously to capitalize on the giggles that met some scenes in New York. The more lighthearted approach even extended to March 27 ads with Pauline Starke in an artistic Easter egg.

Webb's press releases overstated it, claiming the play

Borden, *Times*), "How the audience screamed" (Frederick McQuigg, *American*), and "*Zombie* rivals *Dracula* as terror drama, with hysterical laughs" (C. J. Bulliet, *Post*).[104]

Charles Collins himself gave a follow-up treatise in the March 20, 1932 *Chicago Daily Tribune*, remaking "'Another *Dracula*' would be a good trademark for it. [*Zombie*] deals with the supernatural and draws its material out of folklore. … Meanwhile, a cablegram from London brings word that the Christian council of the African Gold Coast, the ancestral home of voodooism, is preparing to beat the jungles of that region for the devil and his disciples. They have an idea that witchcraft must be challenged and they are hanging up prizes for any black wizard who can do his stuff as advertised, before

A striking advertisement for Zombie's *appearance at the Adelphi Theatre, published in the* Chicago Tribune *on March 13, 1932.*

"received favorable press comment" in New York. Such publicity also promised that "several native Haitians" would be in the cast. Reviews, however, remained skeptical. For Charles Collins at the *Chicago Daily Tribune*, it "might have been a truly bloodcurdling affair" if recent mystery plays like *The Bat* had not "blunted and twisted" horror with comedic elements, thus decreasing the impact of serious efforts like Webb's play.[102] He added that: "It is much better than the average 'mystery' not only because it celebrates the Great God Voodoo but also because it contains a certain amount of persuasiveness and a folklore background."[103]

The papers continued to offer *Zombie* space in their columns, with the overall response stronger than in New York. Capitalizing on this, Webb printed quotations from some critiques in the company's newspaper ads. Such excerpts included: "No cheating and a real thrill in a different mystery 'mello'" (Ashton Stevens, *Herald-Examiner*), "Sure-fire stuff will give you the jitters (Gail

witnesses with clear, scientific minds."[105] After describing tests that would be put to the sorcerers, Collins noted that "if the Gold Coast magicians can do these things, the Christian clergy thereabouts will undoubtedly be flabbergasted, but will strive zealously to exorcise the devils of black magic."[106]

Though they may have been less flabbergasted than the aforementioned Christian clergy, audiences in Chicago must have seen something in *Zombie*, as it remained in the city until early May. It did, however, switch venues on two occasions. After closing at the Adelphi, *Zombie* moved to the Oriental. The theater heralded its opening night on April 29 as a landmark in theatrical history, claiming it was the first time a complete stage mystery of three acts had been performed in a "new" movie theater. Ads played up the admission, which—rather than the $3 usual at the Adelphi—was the same price as a standard movie. However, only a handful of performances were played before *Zombie* moved once again, this time

This rather bizarre ad combines Easter sentiment with Zombie
publicity. Published in the Chicago Tribune *on March 27, 1932.*

to the Tivoli Theatre at Cottage Grove and 63rd. Its
opening on May 5, 1932, at the venue brought much less
attention, and the play closed down after a mere week.

Advertisements and programs for *Zombie*'s life after
Chicago seem lost to history, but Etta Moten claimed
that she acted in "one night stands" of the play "all the
way across the country to get it to Hollywood."[107] Thorough examination of newspapers in the Los Angeles area
do not reveal promotion for any West Coast appearance
of *Zombie*, but certainly it is possible that the play was
staged in numerous cities between Chicago and Hollywood. Indeed, *Zombie*'s lengthy run in the Windy City
may have given it the economic boost needed to keep it
running as a roadshow.

Even though the bulk of Americans would not have

seen or even been aware of the short-lived play, *Zombie*
provided a few theatergoers with a better understanding
of zombiism. For example, the often hypercritical J.
Brooks Atkinson of the *New York Times* ended his review
not with any stinging comments about the play, but
rather an observation based on a zombie metaphor. "If
zombies are those who work without knowing and see
without understanding, one begins to look around among
one's fellow countrymen with a new apprehension. Perhaps those native drums are sounding the national an-
them." Atkinson's comment about Depression-era citizens, while hardly funny and certainly arrogant, once
again highlights the importance of drums to the image
many in the U.S. had of voodoo and zombies.

If nothing else, however, *Zombie* implied that voodoo and zombies were fertile ground for continued experiments in the entertainment world. The play then became a building block towards *White Zombie*'s production
(although not necessarily its narrative), suggesting the
potential of zombie stories and prophesying the critical
distaste for such topics.

Conclusion

For some 130 years prior to the production of *White
Zombie* in 1932, sentiment in the U.S. towards Haiti grew
from prejudices against and disbelief in the possibility of
black self-rule, and suspicions that such nationalism and
independence would have an influence on slaves in the
South. Later, imperialist motivations and military intervention resulted in massive frustrations. Feeding on these
views and feelings and simultaneously informing them
were the various books and essays published throughout
the 19th and early 20th centuries. In particular, Spenser
St. John's opinions in *Hayti, or the Black Republic* illustrated the predominant racism and ethnocentrism at
work, as well as sculpting views on Haitian voodoo which
helped reinforce existing hatreds.

Strong and unfavorable opinions flowered in the
American cultural landscape with the many subsequent
books and essays that relied on St. John's text, books that
helped convey often unfounded and inaccurate opinions
on Haiti and voodooism to a mass audience. Unfair as-
sessments and erroneous information found its way into
poetry, stage plays, novels, short stories, and later the cinema. The American public, however much it would be
frustrated by Haiti politically, developed an insatiable
appetite for tales of voodoo. Indeed, from the mid–19th
century onward the hunger for information on voodooism led to a repetitive exploration of the religion as it existed in Louisiana.

The intellectual and cultural history of voodoo and

Haiti reaches a culmination of sorts in William Sea-brook's *The Magic Island*, a work that strived for objectivity while still irrevocably traveling down the trail blazed by St. John. The paradigm that emerged in the 19th century remained intact, with Seabrook offering more friendly semantics but still ethnocentric beliefs to describe Haiti and voodoo. If anything, he popularized knowledge of many voodoo concepts that were seldom discussed, and even overlooked, in the past, including zombiism. Such information captivated readers and quickly spawned works like Kenneth Webb's play *Zombie*.

Together, such works present threads in a lengthy tapestry that is the history of expression on Haiti, voodoo, and zombies in the many years prior to *White Zombie*'s production. While the writer and director of the film examined only Seabrook and possibly a handful of others discussed in this chapter, reverberations of those prior years were still heard in *White Zombie*. The opinions of authors and filmmakers mentioned in this chapter represent not only the research materials from which *White Zombie* emerged, but also the available background knowledge informing U.S. citizens who would view the film.

Chapter Three

Bringing an Independent Film to Life: *White Zombie* in Production

Out of the cultural background of voodoo and zombies (as discussed in Chapter Two), *White Zombie* evolved into a film project in early 1932. Its production offers insight into the larger issue of independent filmmaking in the early 1930s. While *White Zombie* would have a higher budget than many "indie" films of the period and it would also prove unique in terms of its immense box-office success, the film does bear much in common with many of its cinematic colleagues. For example, hopes for success were built around a popular "cycle" (in this case horror), and a popular star agreeing to appear in a low-budget film (in this case Bela Lugosi). Like most other independent films, the making of the film (preproduction, production, and postproduction) was very rapidly paced with no room for mistakes of any magnitude. Additionally, distribution problems followed the production, as the very nature of indie films meant they were not anchored to a major studio.

These factors mean that it is usually very difficult to reconstruct an independent film's production history with any degree of detail. After all, no studio production files exist to exhume. Moreover, indie films generally received less attention in trade publications than their higher-budgeted, studio-produced counterparts. With films from the distant past, often few if any cast or crewmembers are alive to interview. By the time of this writing, that certainly became the case with *White Zombie*.

Quotations from those interviewed in years past prove paradoxically helpful and infuriating, as no clarification can be made of the points interviewees discussed years ago. At the same time these memories fill in the gaps, they generate new questions, either by unknowingly contradicting other interviewees or by attempting—intentionally or not—to construct a history that they *want* the world to know. Even if interviewees

were still alive, they might either contradict themselves in a subsequent interview or take umbrage if their earlier word is questioned. As author Garnett Weston, screenwriter of *White Zombie*, once said: "Hell hath no fury like an old-timer contradicted in his memories."[1]

Historians should always consider the problems of oral history, though all too often those who write on films (especially for popular audiences) readily believe every word spoken by cast and crew involved in the production of a given movie. These problems are compounded further with independent films of the thirties, as generally no internal memos, contracts, or paperwork of any kind exists decades later. Indeed, this specific production history of *White Zombie* exemplifies the problems inherent for film historians in reconstructing the making of an independent film.

Making Independent Films in the Early 1930s

To understand the process of *White Zombie*'s creation, it becomes necessary to paint a picture of independent film production itself at the time of and immediately prior to the Halperin film's inception.[2] Indie filmmakers had indeed been the earliest movie producers, and independent filmmaking continued to be prevalent during the 1910s and 1920s. *White Zombie* director Victor Halperin had himself been involved in independent filmmaking for over a decade prior to involving himself with zombies. Though the transition to talking pictures in the late twenties caused many independent producers to lag behind major studios in terms of technology, by 1931 a more level playing field existed.

Portrait of Victor Halperin, circa 1920s.

For many months prior to *White Zombie*'s production, the industry trades spoke of the growing possibilities for independent producers, who by 1931 were taking advantage of certain factors, including the exorbitant budgets of major studios, the curtailment of some production during the Great Depression, and lessening theater grosses. By the summer of 1931, the majors were even more closely watching indie filmmaking, hoping to distribute some of the productions themselves.[3] For this reason, as well as the demand for films by independently owned theaters and cuts in admission prices, *The Film Daily* claimed that 1931 marked "the start of the greatest opportunity independent producers have ever had."[4] Opportunities aside, industry trades also noted a higher quality in independent film stories and cinematic technique in releases of mid– to late 1931.[5]

Aesthetic successes and growing economic viability spawned increased numbers of production companies and productions during 1931 as well. *The Film Daily* noted that "more independent producers sprung up during the past few months than have started during any one previous year. Every independent producing company has increased its schedule and many are daily adding to their original lineup."[6] *Motion Picture Herald* added that most indie producers believed that "there never [had] been a more favorable time" for their product than late 1931.[7] Successes with some films provided finances for others to be made, with one trade publication claiming that many independents were "firmly and substantially established."[8] The result of all these factors meant that, of 622 U.S. film releases in 1931, some 104 were independently produced.[9]

The following year began with continued forecasts of optimism for indie producers. To strengthen their bonds, an "Indies Club" began on the West Coast, with its members, according to one film trade, "going about their cooperative work with real enthusiasm."[10] Thirty-five indie producers came together in January 1931 to form a protection body called the Independent Motion Picture Producer's Association. By early February 1932, their president, M. H. Hoffman, promised that in that year the understanding and association between indie producers and exhibitors would be strengthened, thus empowering the overall independent film experience.[11] Predictions in industry trades about the number of independent films to be made in the 1932-33 season suggested a figure of more than 200 movies, doubling the output produced in the prior season.[12] And to assist in the production of those films, much available and experienced personnel existed due to layoffs at major studios caused by the Great Depression.[13]

"Will or Must Pictures Go Independent?" asked a *Variety* editorial in February 1932. They believed that "the condition of the picture industry [in 1932] seems to suggest that perhaps the business is headed back toward the independents; the independent film producer and the independent theater operator. They pioneered the industry; the indies brought it forward."[14] By the following month, *The Hollywood Reporter* underscored the viability of indie films. Author W. Scott Darling wrote that, "[t]aking into consideration the budget involved in each case, many [persons] have gone even further and said that the independents are making the best pictures."[15]

Darling echoed the earlier *Variety* editorial, which had claimed that "the independent producer won't find it required to spend a highly profitless figure for a program picture; he will gamble on turning out a good picture. A good picture nowadays in the theatres, relatively, will do just as well, perhaps better for the producer and theatre owner than the higher cost 'class' production."[16] In early 1932, these "good pictures" generally cost indies $20,000 to $60,000 to produce, with less than $5,000 of that amount allotted for the cost of the story.[17]

Variety and other trades spoke about stories and specifically about the evils of film cycles, the repetition of like ideas based upon a successful theme in a highly original film, cinema genres in embryo. The editorial apparently saw independent films as more free of that problem than the Hollywood studio system:

> ...a "cycle" in the picture business is a rush of producers to hog what some daring, speculative, or inventive producer has gambled with, with that producer perhaps receiving as his benefit the returns from only his first picture instead of having his novelty field to himself for a year, by which time the idea would doubtlessly have died away. The copy or cycle thing merely ruins initiative in any ... studio, it being so much easier to borrow than to create in the show business. How many producers would have dared *Dracula*? How many producers since *Dracula* have turned out a thriller or are thinking of making one or more?

The speaker of these words in March 1932, was apparently unaware that director Victor Halperin and his brother, producer Edward Halperin, dared to venture down the same path as director Tod Browning had with *Dracula*.

Regardless of topic choice, though, most independent filmmakers were beset with difficulties on all fronts. A 1932 *Hollywood Reporter* detailed the general order and manner of events:

> The average indie producer, having no contract stars on his payroll, has to pick up his stars when and where he can get them. An agent comes to a producer and tells him he can get Miss Felicia Fewclothes for ten days in the middle of April for a certain figure. Now Miss Fewclothes is a good bet in the eyes of his releasing organization, as he speedily finds out by wiring, and a deal is made for the services of Miss Fewclothes for the said ten days in the middle of April. It is only about ten days or two weeks to the middle of April so Mr. Producer has to get a story and get one quick.
> The news travels fast and far among the free lance writers catering to the independents and, within twenty-four hours. He does not waste too much time coming to a decision for the simple reason that if he does dilly-dally, the script will not be ready in time. Similarly, his director does not insist on the interminable story conferences common in the major studios. The story is judged, first of all on its merit as the possible basis for a motion picture, and second, as to its possibilities in view of the limited budget involved. It if is satisfactory from these standpoints, the writer is told to go home and get a script out and be dam' quick about it!
> And thus the producing organization gets a story. It gets a story, with an idea which so intrigued and enthused the writer that he was willing to sit down in his spare time and work it out on speculation in the hope that he might sell it to one of the major studios. ... To this extent, Poverty Row is profiting by its own hasty method of production.

The description "hasty" would apply well to the *White Zombie* preproduction and production periods, for it was out of this fast-paced and financially strapped milieu that the Halperins' film would erupt. And—despite a May 1931 editorial in *Motion Picture Daily* that claimed "[i]ndependents won't get to first base if they figure on big theatre revenue"[18]—the Halperins' created one of the box-office winners of 1932.

Unearthing Specific Origins of White Zombie[19]

The earliest press mention of *White Zombie* was likely the January 6, 1932, *Hollywood Reporter* comment that the Halperins had leased office space at Universal Studios to get their film "*Zombie*" underway. Whether they were aware of the preproduction of the Broadway play *Zombie* is unknown, but many readily thought the play was a natural for the screen. The "Picture Possibilities" column in a February 16, 1932, *Variety* had pegged *Zombie* with a "favorable" nod, though the review of the play in *Vogue* was a bit closer to the mark: "One constantly longs for a fuller development.... From such material should have come a contemporary *Trilby* of the Tropics."[21] By February 20, *Motion Picture Herald* claimed that "*Zombie* ... will soon find its way into celluloid. Representatives ... are ... negotiating for screen rights."[22] Whatever the actual influence of Webb's *Zombie* on the decision to produce a zombie film in general, the play's preproduction hype may have helped the Halperins justify audience interest in cinematic zombies to themselves or potential investors.

In both a March 8, 1932, *Los Angeles Times* and an April production survey in *Variety*, *White Zombie* was still referred to simply as *Zombie*. It was mentioned as a project of "Halperin prods."[23] The rumored budget was $62,500, but $50,000 was also once mentioned as the amount. Some of that money may have come from the Halperins, who had recently divested themselves of their financial interest in Liberty Productions and may well have used some or all of the proceeds from that sale.[24] Regardless, the other key financial figure in *White Zombie*'s earliest stages was Phil Goldstone, who in the 1920s was head of Phil Goldstone Productions. He had produced such films as *Deserted at the Altar* (1922), *The Verdict* (1925), *Lost at Sea* (1926), and a number of westerns starring Franklyn Farnum.[25] Even as early as 1923, *Exhibitors Herald* proclaimed that "there is no liver 'independent' in Hollywood" than Goldstone.[26]

Still well known in the Hollywood of the early 1930s, Goldstone was highly adept at securing production funds.[27] In December 1931, only a few months before *White Zombie*'s production began, *Motion Picture Daily* wrote that he was "a leader in the [present independent film] movement."[28] That same year and in early 1932, Goldstone had produced a number of films for Tiffany Productions, and had financial interests in a plethora of other film projects.[29] Along with his financial support, Goldstone would become important in hiring Madge Bellamy, *White Zombie*'s female lead, and possibly in choosing sets to rent. Additionally, Goldstone was the exclusive licensee for RCA Photophone sound usage in independent films; *White Zombie* would utilize Photophone for its audio, presumably at their standard flat rate of $2,400.[30]

Apparently neither Goldstone nor the Halperins contacted Kenneth Webb or George Sherwood or attempted to buy any rights to the play *Zombie*. As a *Chicago Tribune* article that spring made clear, "Cinema Rights to Plays Bring Pretty Prices."[31] The press seemingly did not suggest the Halperins stole or appropriated the idea of zombies from Webb's play. Perhaps the only question to have arisen was one posed by *The Hollywood Reporter*. Immediately after discussing *White Zombie*, the trade asked, "What producer, strapped for a suitable title on a finished film, appropriated one from a play which had been submitted and then found out he would have to pay a century for its use—and is it worth it?"[32] The comment seems to point to *White Zombie*, but if so the answer to the question "Is it worth it?" would have to be a resounding "no." After all, the word "zombie" had appeared both in Seabrook's book *The Magic Island* and as the title of 1929's unproduced play *Zombi* [*sic*].

Decades later, actress Pauline Starke and producer George Sherwood would comment on the *White Zombie* debacle. Sherwood claimed the Halperins stole his idea of zombies being the topic of a horror melodrama, while Starke lamented that the brothers did not consider her for a role in the film.[33] Why the regret? For one, given that the part went to another silent screen actress, Starke possibly viewed the film as a lost opportunity for a potential screen comeback. In addition, Starke may have believed the situation a slap in the face not only to her husband given the topic of the film, but also to herself in terms of Victor Halperin's allegiance. After all, he had directed her in the 1927 film *Dance Magic*.

Starke, however, was encumbered with myriad personal problems immediately prior to and during the *White Zombie* shoot. During the spring of 1931, the press acknowledged she was recovering from a nervous breakdown.[34] By May of that year, her plea for alimony from husband Jack White was heard in a Los Angeles court. Their bitter stories of cruelty helped secure the divorce they both desired, and soon Starke was hoping to regain

stardom on the stage.[35] Enter Sherwood and *Zombie*. In addition to her recent personal problems, the Halperins would most likely not have wanted to draw additional comparisons to the play *Zombie* by hiring Starke—not merely because it would have meant dealing with Sherwood legally, but also because she was a definite signifier of a failed play: hardly an omen for a successful film.

Such frustrations of Starke, Sherwood, and presumably playwright Kenneth Webb have led many film historians to write of a lawsuit by these parties (or Webb alone)

Actress Pauline Starke as she appeared in the 1923 film In the Palace of the King.

against the Halperins. While it is entirely possible that Sherwood or Webb or both contacted the Halperins, no evidence exists of a lawsuit. Not only did no mention of legal action appear in the movie trade publications or theater magazines, absolutely no pertinent legal documents exist in the New York City area. This is key, because any lawsuit actually heard before a court with regard to Amusement Securities (ASC, partial financiers of *White Zombie*) or Halperin Productions as defendants would have had to have occurred in New York City; a later, 1936 court case made that fact quite clear. Secondarily, the same 1936 case covered in detail the legal history of *White Zombie*, as well as any trademarks or rights to the word "zombie"; it makes no mention of any legal encounter between ASC and the Halperins and Webb and Sherwood.[36]

The complete lack of evidence and the historical details recorded in the 1936 court case, certainly suggest that no case actually went to court in 1932, and—given the extensive legal history of the word "zombie" as explored by a 1936 judge[37]—no case was even ended by dismissal or summary judgment. Furthermore, the production, sale, and distribution of *White Zombie* was itself not hindered in any way, as it almost certainly would have been by such a legal encounter.

However, this would not exclude the possibility that either Webb or Sherwood (or both) contacted the Halperins or ASC and made an out-of-court settlement, or that Sherwood or Webb threatened legal action but—given the failure of their play—could not financially pursue a lawsuit. It is even possible that such talks could have been the decisive factor in the Halperins changing the title of their film from its originally announced *Zombie* to *White Zombie*.

The larger question, though, is the degree to which audiences would have been familiar with either the book *The Magic Island* or the play *Zombie*. Certainly a few reviewers would eventually compare those texts with *White Zombie*. For example, Clark Rodenbach at the *Chicago Daily News* wrote tongue in cheek that, "Through the efforts of the book and the play, any blond you may encounter on the street may be a zombie. And probably is." His acquaintance with *Zombie* probably came largely from the play's lengthy run in Chicago that spring, and from the fact that his own newspaper had reviewed it. Furthermore, the play had spawned a good deal of talk regarding Seabrook's *The Magic Island* in the Chicago media. Thus, Rodenbach's quotation could be taken as an exception rather than the rule. Most of America would not have seen *Zombie* or even heard of it, given its abysmally short run on Broadway. In addition, even though *The Magic Island* was written for a popular audience, zombiism comprised only one chapter of it, and the book had been published three years prior to *White Zombie*'s production.

Even if most audiences had not read the book, however, period speculation on the origin of the film's idea generally cited *The Magic Island*.[38] The film's pressbook would hint at Seabrook's importance even to the degree of briefly quoting from his book without actually naming him as a direct source of inspiration, probably as much for legal reasons as anything else.[39] The pressbook also mentioned that "[r]umors have been reaching the United States for years of these sinister practices [of zombiism], and now, for the first time, light is thrown upon them by a screen presentation. *White Zombie* is based upon personal observation in Haiti by American writers and research workers, and, fantastic as it sounds, its entire substance is based upon fact."

Oddly, some publicity would hint at yet another source, even if the film and the pressbook did not. For example, a brief article in the *Los Angeles Times* claimed the tale of "Lengendre [*sic*]" was "an adaptation of the novel *Black Magic*."[40] This seems to be a falsehood, however, as a cursory glance at all texts printed under that name prior to 1932 does not reveal any stories about voodoo, zombies, or anything similar to the subject matter of *White Zombie*.

Arthur Edward Waite's *The Book of Black Magic and of Facts (Including the Rites and Mysteries of Goëtic Theurgy, Sorcery, and Infernal Necromancy)*, published in 1898 and 1910, covers only what its lengthy subtitle suggests. Investigations of Edward Harry William Mererstein's *Black and White Magic* (Blackwell, 1917), Kenneth Lewis

Roberts' *Black Magic: An Account of Its Beneficial Use in Italy, of Its Perversion in Bavaria, and of Certain Tendencies Which Might Necessitate Study in America* (Bobbs-Merrill, 1924), and J. Godfrey Raupert's *The New Black Magic and the Truth About the Ouija Board* (Devin-Adair, 1924) all reveal little to nothing in common with the Halperins' film.

Fictional works with that title include Robert Melville Baker's *Black Magic: A Burlesque Negro Sketch* (Walter Baker, 1900), Jack Kahane's play *Black Magic* (published in 1912 by Sherratt and Hughes in the book *Two Plays*), and Harman Howland's play *Black Magic* (published by Wells Gardner, Darton in 1923 in the book *Black Magic and Other Plays*). None chronicle voodoo or zombies.

To a regular U.S. reader of the early 20th century, the title *Black Magic* would most likely have brought to mind Marjorie Bowen's novel of that same name, which sometimes carried the subtitle *A Tale of the Rise and Fall of the AntiChrist*.[41] Published in 1909 by Sphere, 1912 by Hodder and Stoughton, and in 1926 by John Lane, The Bodley Head Limited, the book was a well-known tale about witchcraft and magic in Western Europe during the early Middle Ages. Written while Bowen was still a teenager, it had become a popular and financially successful novel. Despite its exploration of the supernatural, it is no closer to *White Zombie* than any of the aforementioned plays and nonfiction books.

Perhaps the closest in chronology and thought to *White Zombie* is Paul Morand's *Black Magic* (Viking, 1929), which does include a chapter on the West Indies and some mysterious pen-and-ink artwork evoking the mood of that region. Morand's book, outside of its discussion of Haiti, has nothing in common with *White Zombie*. Thus, mention of a "novel" named *Black Magic* seems to be in error, another of the many dead ends in the journey towards reconstructing the history of *White Zombie*'s production.

Director Victor Halperin, in his own reminiscences of the story and script, did not mention any specific play or book as inspiration. In the 1970s, he recalled its origin:

> Well, I had heard stories of zombies in Haiti and the practices of voodooism and they fascinated me. And I concocted an idea with the assistance of a writer, Garnett Weston, who worked with me on the script and we developed the story. And we got the approval of the commandant of the United States marines who had been stationed in Haiti for background and general verification of the things we mentioned in our script. In fact, while I was in his office in San Diego, he called his wife and asked her if she had seen any zombies wandering around. She said she had as far as she knew had never seen any loose zombies, but she felt the voodoo practices were

such that they could make people subject to their will, that is, the so-called sorcerers.[42]

No independent record exists of Halperin consulting with the marines. Indeed, it seems unusual that—if true—mention of it did not appear in the 1932 press. Also lost to history is the origin of Halperin's association with writer Garnett Weston, who would be credited with both the script and story of *White Zombie*. Whatever influences were at work, credit for the end story rests with him.

Writing White Zombie

Born in Toronto, Ontario, on June 27, 1890, Garnett Weston would eventually describe the night of his birth as a mysterious snowstorm in which almost conscious "shadows from the trees leaped in and out."[43] As a young man, he attended Toronto University before heading to the Royal Naval Academy in Greenwich, London. He spent nine years as a newspaper journalist and four years at sea.[44] During that period, Weston wrote poems and wise sayings, many of which were not published until decades later, in 1970.

His dream was to be an important author, and in his later years honestly posed the rhetorical question: "What writer—or artist—or musician, God Willing,—would be anything less than great?"[45] Weston was definitely well read, as his poems and later novels are judiciously sprinkled with references to everything from *Don Quixote* to *Trilby*. The final verse of his 1915 poem *Futility* reads like an already frustrated young man still years away from encountering the cinema:

> The years descend like snow
> On all that I have wrought.
> God's promise to set my youth aglow
> With heavenly fire,—then He forgot.

Many of Weston's early poems steam with romanticism. *Lonely Man's Lament*, for example, finds him ending with the words:

> It seems to me 'twould be no sin,
> If she just up and bundled in [my bed],
> And wrapped her arms around my neck,
> To keep the beastly cold in check.
> I'd be a happy man, by heck!
> And warm in bed.
>
> Oh, darling dark or darling fair,
> With chestnut, blonde or auburn hair.

When it is not replete with despondent angst, his poetry from the pre–1920 period often exudes this kind of youthful vigor and interest in females.

Portrait of Garnett Weston taken in Vancouver during the author's last years of life.

Weston also had a plentiful supply of comments on show business. He wrote of *The Actor*, claiming: "Like all show people, when he suffered it was the greatest suffering ever experienced by a member of the human race and it was right out in the open where everyone could see it and feel the awful tragedy of it all."[46] Of *Show Business*, Weston quipped, "if you have to tell them who you are—you ain't!"[47]

His description of the entertainment industry would have generally applied to Weston himself in the early spring of 1932. By that time, he had invested some two years in the Paramount publicity department before spending approximately the same amount of time supervising films like *Lord Jim* (1925), *Son of His Father* (1925), *Not So Long Ago* (1925), *Golden Princess* (1925), and *Behind the Front* (1926). As a writer, his poems were essentially unpublished, and his plays had found little success.[48] His only produced screenplay at the time was *The Viking*, filmed in 1931 by producer Varick Frissell and director George Melford. The story idea came from Frissell, and the screenplay itself was cowritten with T. Bell Sweeney.

The Viking starred a then unknown Charles Starrett, but the major news of the production was a real-life tragedy. Varick Frissell and approximately 20 crew members all died when attempting to get a shot of an iceberg turning over. Their ship—the vessel named in the film's title—exploded and sank, killing all aboard.[49]

Despite the tragedy, *The Viking* was completed and released in 1931. Reviews varied, and the story was generally berated. The *New York Times* (June 17, 1931) called it "sketchy," while *Theatre Guild Magazine* (August 1931) dubbed it "melodramatic" and believed the screenplay uninteresting by comparison to its cinematography of seal hunters in the Arctic. *The Film Daily* said much the same, noting "weakness" in the story.[50] These kinds of notices would hardly have caused producers to gravitate towards Weston as a writer, but indie filmmakers like the Halperins may have had economic considerations in mind more than aesthetics.

As his biographies would generally read post–1932, Weston not only developed the story for *White Zombie* after his work on *The Viking*, but he also penned the screenplay and dialogue. In terms of the latter, it seems difficult to know whether the limited use of character dialogue was Weston's idea or Victor Halperin's. The pressbook revealed that:

> ...the producers decided that the public is tired unto death of 100 per cent dialogue in pictures. In fact, it is their firm contention that the public is tired of even 20 or 30 per cent dialogue. The result is that only fifteen per cent of the length of *White Zombie* is accompanied by dialogue. This was permitted because the story is all action, and stirring action at that.[51]

Their decision would not go unnoticed by the press in 1932, either. *The San Francisco Examiner*, using *White Zombie* as an example, noted an "interesting commentary on motion pictures in general that the average amount of dialogue to be found in the more up-to-date films is diminishing, and the silent portions increasing. ... now, after five or six years, Hollywood realizes that its greatest powers lie mainly in its own art of the camera."[52]

By the spring of 1932, Victor Halperin and Garnett Weston were not the only ones who had decided less dialogue was needed in talkies. They may have been swayed in that direction by numerous articles of 1931 and 1932 which suggested that filmmakers minimize unnecessary dialogue.[53] In March 1932, for example, *The Hollywood Reporter* claimed:

> ...of one thing [talking pictures have] too much—talk. Too much to hear—too little to see. ... Words always fail

to portray action as well as action portrays itself. ... The camera, having found its tongue, is losing its eyesight. ... Because the characters on the screen are now able to talk, the tendency is to make them talk whether they have anything to say or not. Nothing is more tiresome than just talk—on the screen or off. ... Instead of more and then more dialogue, we should have less. ... That was the strength of the silent pictures. They didn't just say something—they did something. They still should."[54]

Weston's script for *White Zombie* understood the mantra of *The Hollywood Reporter*, and allowed as much room for the actors to act as to speak.[55]

Assembling the Cast of White Zombie

In terms of the on-screen talent, it was not unusual on an independent film set of the time for an actor to get involved in other ways, aesthetic or not. For example, one trade in the spring of 1932 claimed:

Bela Lugosi in a publicity pose as Murder Legendre. (Courtesy of Leonard J. Kohl.)

Bela Lugosi, Madge Bellamy, and Robert Frazer were three of the key actors contracted for White Zombie.

A good actor, to some of the indie producers having their first fling at picture making, is one who can write dialog, direct a tough scene, ad lib for missing sequences, and isn't unwilling to help move props. Acting ability isn't of much importance. ... Filming started, and also the overhead, [indie producers] become panicky and cry for help and advice. Even the electricians are asked for hints on picture making. Result is there are sometimes as many as ten directors trying to manage the company while the perspiring producer hangs on the ropes. ... When things blow up, [the] producer turns to the actor first, knowing he has had past experience. [The] actor is usually obliging, even thrilled when he has that long desired chance to direct a scene.[56]

Being experienced in the movie industry and having a higher budget than many indie films, the Halperin brothers would have probably been less reliant on actors for writing scenes or moving props than many of their indie colleagues. Regardless, they were highly dependent on the name value of their on-screen talent.

For their cast, the Halperins attempted to put together a number of talented actors with name recognition among moviegoers. The star of the film, Bela Lugosi, was an ideal choice; the role of Murder Legendre—evil incarnate—was a logical extension of his work in *Dracula*. Though no notes or files still exist, it is easy to assume that—in order to capitalize best on the burgeoning horror film cycle—the Halperins desired an actor already familiar to movie audiences for malevolent performances.

Boris Karloff was also a renowned performer, with his portrayal of the Frankenstein monster a hit during late 1931. *Frankenstein* was still playing theaters in early 1932, and Universal Studios quickly formulated plans to build the actor into a star. From a financial standpoint, he would have been far outside the Halperins' budget. Much the same would have been the case with Fredric March, who had in late 1931 and early 1932 scored with audiences in *Dr. Jekyll and Mr. Hyde*, a film for which he would win an Oscar for Best Actor. Beyond their immediate successes, both actors—even if welcome additions because of their name value—would have been less suited to portray Murder Legendre than Lugosi; neither possessed the dark personality he embodied on the screen.

Other choices would possibly have been John Barrymore and Chester Morris. The latter proved his worth as a heavy in mysteries in *The Bat Whispers* (1930), though—in addition to the salary he would have expected—Morris had made a decision to avoid mystery and horror films in his immediate future, so much so that he had even intentionally excluded himself from the pool of talent slated for the title role of *Dracula* (1931). As for Barrymore, he would have been an excellent choice, having been for years a matinee idol and having just achieved notoriety for his dark portrayals in *Svengali* and *The Mad Genius* (both 1931). However, he would also have probably been unfeasible financially, and probably of a mind to avoid independent films, as so many actors were—they sometimes considered them beneath their status.

Indeed, almost any actor of star status would have presented a financial burden to the Halperins' budget. But Bela Lugosi did not. It is still uncertain what salary he commanded for the film, as apparently no contract exists. Rumors abound, with Lugosi himself claiming at times $500, at other times $800–900. Other unsubstantiated tales insist it was $900. Another memory comes from the actor's friend, Richard Sheffield. After befriending Lugosi as a teenager in the 1950s, Sheffield became a trusted and close companion. Fascinated by the actor's films, Sheffield was allowed to examine all manner of personal movie mementos from the Lugosi career. He distinctly remembers seeing $5,000 on a copy of Lugosi's 1932 tax returns as the *White Zombie* salary, but at the same time he readily acknowledges how many decades have passed since looking through those already yellowed pages.[57] At any rate, whether for $500 or $5000, Lugosi was well within the range of money the Halperins could afford.

It becomes quite important to ask why that would have been the case. In the winter of 1932, Lugosi was a famed performer, at that moment similar to a Chester Morris or a Fredric March; indeed, he was certainly better established at that moment than the rising star named Boris Karloff. It was only a year before that he had dazzled audiences in Universal's film adaptation of *Dracula* (1931). Reprising his vampire role from the 1927 Broadway stage success, Lugosi's performance and the film's success ushered in the 1930s horror cycle. Having played the heavy (or at least perceived heavy) in the Charlie Chan mystery *The Black Camel* (1931) and now headlining Universal's adaptation of Poe's *Murders in the Rue Morgue* (1932), which was playing theaters as *White Zombie* was in production, Lugosi was at that moment one

Artwork publicizing Bela Lugosi and Murders in the Rue Morgue, *published in February 15, 1932*, New York Evening Post.

of—if not the—greatest purveyor of evil and horror in Hollywood.

Horror film history has oft repeated the tale of Lugosi refusing the heavy makeup and nonspeaking role of the Frankenstein Monster, thus opening the door for an unknown Boris Karloff to inspire chills in moviegoers in the released film. Karloff immediately rose to fame, and Lugosi then—whether prompted by an agent or of his own accord—began taking every role offered him, apparently out of fear that yet another horror star would be created and infringe on his hegemony.

This theory is in need of revision for obvious reasons. An intelligent man, Lugosi—had he given any thought to potential competition—would have realized even at the time of *Frankenstein*'s success that it would be impossible to keep other horror films and stars from emerging. For example, *Dr. Jekyll and Mr. Hyde* was already on the horizon for a late 1931 or early 1932 release. The very manner by which the studio system worked in the thirties would not have allowed one to skip from studio to studio with ease to take *every* horror film role. Additionally, the production of more than one horror film at one time would have made it logistically impossible for any individual to corner the market.

Yet another question is what market there was to corner. In 1932, when Lugosi signed the *White Zombie* contract, the horror film genre was less a genre than a nascent cycle, one in its infancy. In retrospect, it is easy to forget the lengthy debates in 1932 about the horror film's long-term possibilities, the many essays warning about audiences' growing boredom with such movies, and the trade publication articles that spoke of studios moving away from horror projects and even the term "horror" itself.[58] An intelligent person reading these signs in 1932 would have probably tried to diversify rather than wholeheartedly embrace—indeed, dominate without peer—a cycle of films that could have quickly become unpopular and been halted.

If Lugosi did not try to keep competition at bay by appearing in every horror film, he did take many low-budget projects in the early thirties when his star was burning as bright as it ever would. However, this seems far less unusual if it is compared to the decisions of many of his cinematic colleagues. Being loaned to other studios and making quick deals to star in low-budget films was not unusual. Though the upper echelon of stars—Greta Garbo, for example—would not dabble in those realms, some popular and prominent actors did. Boris Karloff would himself become an examplar of this practice.

Thus, one still must ask, why did Lugosi sign for an independent film for apparently so little money? Rather than an attempt to lock Karloff or other potential rivals out of horror parts, it may have been an attempt to garner as much money as possible within a given span of time. Articles like "Lugosi Broke, with Furniture Main Asset" appeared in print during the early autumn of 1932[59]; he even filed bankruptcy papers in a Los Angeles court on October 17 of that year.[60] While these legal problems mounted months after his portrayal of Legendre, the debts themselves dated as far back as 1926; most were from the period 1931 to early 1932. Lugosi's need for money may well have driven him to accept lesser roles, lesser billing, and lesser budgeted films in the period immediately prior to declaring bankruptcy, as well as in the period immediately following. Debts more than new Frankensteins probably drove Lugosi to *White Zombie* and some of his other film work of the period.

It's almost impossible to say for certain, but Lugosi may also have accepted the role because he enjoyed the script, because he found the tale a logical extension of the kind of hypnotic qualities he brought to the role of Dracula, because he appreciated the sheer amount of screen time his role would have, because he had somehow befriended some person or persons involved in bringing the film before the cameras,[61] or many other possible reasons. It could easily have been a combination of reasons in addition to financial woes that led him to join the *White Zombie* cast. Whatever the case, it is clear that the simplistic idea that he was out to seize the lead roles in every horror film must be discarded. Regardless, the Halperins were fortunate when Lugosi's hand scrawled a signature on their contract.

Despite the eerie image of Lugosi that 1930s studio publicity machines attempted to construct, not all that came into contact with him on the *White Zombie* set believed him to be a real vampire or a man of mystery. "The great mystery to me working with Bela Lugosi was his avid desire of closeups. He never got tired of closeups," Victor Halperin would laughingly recall some decades later.

Actress Madge Bellamy found him "very pleasant" during the *White Zombie* shoot, adding that "Universal [one location that the Halperins used] was always the most agreeable studio in which to work."[62] On another occasion, she even more flatteringly proclaimed him "...by far the most exciting actor I ever worked with—he was fascinating—there was something very unusual about him—he even frightened me a little." Bellamy also added, "I remember Bela Lugosi used to kiss my hand in the morning when we'd come on the set ... very courtly mannered."[63]

Not all on the set would find Lugosi so kind, however. Assistant cameraman Enzo Martinelli recalled that: "Lugosi wasn't really a friendly type. In those days, of course, most of the stars were a little aloof in order to preserve their mystique. Only a few would fraternize much with the help or be chummy with the guy who fixed the coffee. I thought he looked ill, as though he was in pain. Later, I learned he *was* [Martinelli's emphasis] ill during the whole production."[64]

As for *White Zombie*'s female lead, *Photoplay* reminded readers in June 1931 that ten years prior a roto picture of the then seventeen-year-old Madge Bellamy had appeared in their publication. "Where are you, Madge?" the fan magazine asked in the present tense. *Los Angeles Times* columnist Grace Kingsley had bumped into her in May 1931, when the actress was out from her Venice seaside home to shop for traveling bags. Kingsley wrote:

> Miss Bellamy and her mother are to buy a place in Switzerland as their headquarters in Europe, and expect to remain there some time. ... Madge is to become a writer when she reaches Europe, having contracted for a series of articles on art. [She] will probably be persuaded to do some picture work when she reaches London and Paris. She is [also] to study music, following up a course which she took here with Felix Hughes, who, by the way, tells us that Madge has a real grand opera voice.[65]

She did not, however, find a permanent place in Europe or European moviemaking. Columnist Rosalind Shaffer

Madge Bellamy as she appeared in the film Summer Bachelors. *Printed in the October 1926 issue of* Theatre Magazine.

instead judged her real destination to be "oblivion."[66] In the Hollywood of 1932, Madge was spoken of as "the young woman who once was a star."[67] A decade before, *The Silver Sheet* dubbed her "America's Sweetheart," mentioning she had been selected by critics as "one of the fourteen most beautiful women in America...."[68]

A newspaper column written at the dawn of *White Zombie*'s production mentioned that "they use the name of Madge Bellamy in past tense." Along with reassuring movie fans that "she still is pretty," the journalist spoke of her recent and "protracted fling on the speaking stage, principally in stock."[69]

Even if the film world had moved into the 1930s without her, Bellamy's "pretty" face still enticed admirers. Jay Hormel, head of the famed meat company, pleaded with her to run away with him—despite the fact that he was married. Another wealthy suitor, Sidney Spiegel, offered flowers and his affection as well. Though she was intimate with Spiegel, Bellamy did not marry him or Hormel.[70]

Her film career was basically stalled from 1930 to 1932. Universal Studios released *Tonight at Twelve* in September 1929; no more film roles materialized, except

for a series of low-budget film shorts.[71] Attempting to find work in the theater, she rushed to New York in early 1932 to speak with Preston Sturges about appearing in a new play. As a result of their talks, she went to Philadelphia where his hit *Strictly Dishonorable* was still running. Sturges never met her in New York a second time; the lure of a Hollywood contract had taken him west.

As for the *White Zombie* offer, Bellamy later mentioned that she needed the work, and accepted the role after receiving a telegram from Phil Goldstone. Along with many other films, Goldstone had earlier produced the Bellamy's *The Reckless Sex* (1925), which is probably the reason that he, rather than the Halperins, contacted her about *White Zombie*. Bellamy later mentioned in her autobiography that Goldstone promised and soon delivered a $5,000 salary to her for the horror film. The money was much needed; Bellamy's financial situation was dire. Venita Halperin later remembered, "She was having such a struggle financially when she started working for Victor, she had her father pretend to be her chauffeur. She tried to make everybody think she was still way up there in society."[72]

Bellamy's memories of the shoot itself always featured compliments for director Halperin. She went so far as to say "I learned to love and respect him very much."[73] On another occasion, she discussed the screen tests she had to take. "Well, I had just arrived from a personal appearance tour doing the three songs from *Mother Knows Best*, you know, the songs I sang in that picture. [Phil Goldstone] told me he had this United Artists release and so as soon as I came he wanted me for it.[74] He did make some tests of me, and that's how I got into it." Of director Halperin, she said, "I had admired and known of him before."[75]

Bellamy's personal life during the shoot was far less sedate, with admirer Sidney Spiegel wrongly developing the belief that she and producer Goldstone were romantically involved. In her autobiography, she wrote:

> I had been home only a few days, already at work on *White Zombie*, when Sidney Spiegel arrived from Chicago. He proposed to me in the garden of the Miramar Hotel at Santa Monica. "I know that you are sleeping with that black Jew," he said, meaning Phil Goldstone. (How could Spiegel, himself a Jew, say such a thing?) "I hurried here as soon as I heard. I can't stand the thought. I want us to be married at once."

Her response to him was less love than repulsion. Despite some prior money problems, Bellamy had an easy time turning down Spiegel's proposal. With *White Zombie* in production, she believed her career was "in the groove again."[76] After all, as the *New York Daily Mirror* would soon comment, "...it is not her work [in a horror film that is of note], but that she works at all, that occasions this comment [about her career]."[77]

Despite such skeptical press notices and the less than praiseworthy critical reviews to come, director Victor Halperin definitely considered her an asset in terms of name value and talent. In later years, he would remember: "I think she was a real lady ... very sweet and very plastic, [meaning that she was] very amenable to direction."[78] Regardless, she was a name, a name still familiar to many movie fans, even if seldom on their lips due to her disappearance from the screen. That alone may have also made her attractive to the Halperins: the "comeback" story of a well-known silent screen actress would have meant potential publicity.

To supplement the two leads, the Halperins searched for both talent and name value. For example, Joseph Cawthorn played Dr. Bruner, both the strong voice of reason and—in the mold he was most known to audiences for—the source of comic relief. As the San Francisco Chronicle told readers in the early thirties, "nobody need tell you who Joe Cawthorn is," the implication being he was well known enough to movie fans that he needed no introduction.[79] A New Yorker, he had made his stage debut at age four in a children's revue called the Picaninny Minstrels. A year later he was with Harvey's Minstrels. By age nine, Cawthorn sailed for England, where he would achieve great success in music halls for some four years. His return to the U.S. meant writing and appearing in vaudeville skits, composing songs, and working in "legit" stage productions, with a concentration on musical comedies. Some of his better-known stage productions include Half-Moon (1920), Bunch and Judy (1922), and Sunny (1925).[80]

His film career began in 1927, and over the next few years he appeared in such well-known movies as Taming of the Shrew (1929) and Dixiana (1930). Throughout 1930 and 1931, he had been a popular star in such RKO films as The Old Accordion Man (1930) and Peach O' Reno (1931). In late December 1931, Cawthorn re-signed with RKO Pictures, with whom he was still involved when casting for White Zombie occurred. It would not be the first time RKO loaned him to another company's project. For instance, in October 1930, he was allowed to appear in United Artists' Kiki with Mary Pickford.[81]

Cawthorn was long known as a favorite comedian of various famous persons, including President Woodrow Wilson.[82] After a few years in Hollywood, Cawthorn and his wife—the former musical comedy star Queenie Vassar—were the toast of the town. The Los Angeles Times, for example, deemed the Cawthorns' New Year's party the best that ushered in 1931.[83] He would go fishing with John Barrymore; she would entertain the brightest stars in Tinseltown.[84] They vacationed often in New York;

they took holidays in Europe. In short, the Cawthorns were a major fixture in Hollywood society between 1930 and 1932, and his name would have meant much to those in the industry, as well as a large number of movie fans.

Robert Frazer was chosen to portray Beaumont, certainly the most complex character in the tale. Born in Worcester, Massachusetts, in 1891, Frazer as a young man enjoyed a degree of success on Broadway, appearing in such plays as Ben Hur and The Wanderer before making his way to Hollywood. He scored the title roles in Robin Hood (1912) and Rob Roy (1913), but the bulk of his screen credits in the teens and twenties came from supporting roles.[85] By the 1930s, his career had slowed down dramatically; he appeared in just one film in 1930 and one in 1931. To help offset his lack of screen time, Frazer—who possessed a quite striking voice—occasionally appeared again onstage, in Los Angeles–area productions like Remote Control (1929).[86]

Though certainly less remembered than Bellamy and less notable in 1932 than Joseph Cawthorn, Frazer was one of the best-cast and most talented actors in White Zombie. He would appear in only one other 1932 film, The Rainbow Trail.

By contrast, John Harron, who essayed the role of Neil, was probably the least skilled member of White Zombie's cast. The younger brother of famed actor Bobby Harron, John—known to friends as Jack—entered films with a bit part in D. W. Griffith's Hearts of the World (1920). That same year, Bobby died from an allegedly accidental gunshot.[87] Johnny's 1920 film appearance led to a relatively successful career in the early to mid-twenties in which he was known for playing young romantic leads. By the latter part of the decade, his work in films had dwindled. Harron was briefly considered for the lead in All Quiet on the Western Front (1930), though Lew Ayres would be Universal's final choice for the role. As with so many silent screen stars, the advent of sound curtailed his career.

In short, White Zombie would almost certainly have been a lift to his frame of mind; it was his only film in 1932, and he had made only four films over the prior four years. He was only 29 in 1932 and his career was essentially over. At the same time, the Halperins probably saw in him a bit of what they saw in Madge Bellamy: a silent film actor who still possessed a modicum of name value, but one that could be signed for a relatively cheap price. Since his star had never burned as bright as Bellamy's, it is safe to assume he was probably hired by the Halperins for a much smaller salary than she was.

He in White Zombie embodies what the Halperins believed a necessary component of a horror film: "audience reciprocality." The New York Times once discussed this issue with producer Edward Halperin:

Sheet music printed in 1919 picturing screen actors Corinne Griffith and Robert Frazer. Note the incorrect spelling of Frazer's name.

That character in *White Zombie* is John Harron's very inadequate and stiff Neil, Madeline's fiancé turned husband.

Clarence Muse, who would play the pivotal if brief role as carriage driver, was born in Baltimore in 1889. While studying for a degree in International Law at Dickerson University, he worked various odd jobs to help pay the mounting tuition bills. Among many other labors, Muse began singing for money. This led to a summer job as an entertainer on Hudson River excursion boats, and then—after graduation—a successful vaudeville career. His break, however, came when he joined the Lafayette Players at Harlem's high-profile Lafayette Theater. His most popular role for them was the lead in a stage adaptation of *Dr. Jekyll and Mr. Hyde*. Muse soon went to Chicago, and then further west to Hollywood.[89]

His first film performance came in *Hearts in Dixie* (1929); William Fox had invited him to Hollywood especially for the role.[90] Along with stage and screen successes, Muse's musical talents were also well known by 1932. The year before, he impressed Hollywood with his singing role as Porgy in a Los Angeles Music Box performance of *Porgy and Bess*.[91] Along with his outstanding vocals, Muse also gained fame as a songwriter, penning the lyrics to *When It's Sleepy Time Down South*—a jazz favorite that served for years as trumpeter Louis Armstrong's theme song after it was first heard in the film *Safe in Hell* (1931).[92]

Audiences' lives are "monotonized," he says, and as a consequence they seek escape in vicarious participation in situations outside their own lives. Under the Halperin hypothesis the audience writes its own continuity, in theory anyway, for in Halperin pictures there is always one character who represents the audience. He is the doubter, the scoffer, the man from Missouri. ... As this character is won over in the course of the film, so also, Mr. Halperin thinks, is the audience.[88]

Muse, a recognized talent in white America, found himself almost at the epicenter of the longstanding racial divide within the performing arts. In a manifesto entitled *The Dilemma of the Negro Actor*, Muse would state:

> There are two audiences in America to confront—the white audience with a definite desire for buffoonery and song, and the Negro audience with a desire to see the real elements of Negro life portrayed. [The African-American

actor] would love, for the sake of race pride, to satisfy and entertain his colored admirers, but the call of the mighty dollar of the white race compels his attention. White America controls the destiny of the Negro actor. The call of the blood controls his hidden ambitions.[93]

Muse was not only an important talent, but he was an important thinker and promoter of African-American artists.

Muse may have been thinking of Victor Halperin and similar directors when he would say in 1934, "I am indeed glad we have organs powerful enough to stop the desire of most white producers to poke fun."[94] Certainly Muse was an important and dignified figure; his addition to the *White Zombie* cast added a credible dimension to the character who would define for audiences the very meaning of the word "zombie."

Brandon Hurst, a favorite character actor, played the

JOHN T. PRINCE
44 years Stage and Screen in April

"Just a kid, tryin', etc."
Talkies or Silent; also Radio
Dialects: Negro, Irish, French Canuck and others
Courtesy to Agents

HE mpstd 5846   HO lly 4102

From the Standard Casting Directory *of March 1931. (Courtesy of George E. Turner.)*

role of Silver, Beaumont's butler. Born in London in 1866, he was almost certainly the oldest member of the cast. After studying philology, Hurst began a somewhat successful stage career. In films since approximately 1915, he proved very memorable as Sir George Carewe in the Barrymore version of *Dr. Jekyll and Mr. Hyde* (1920), Jehan in *The Hunchback of Notre Dame* (1923), and the villainous caliph in *The Thief of Bagdad* (1924).[95] He also appeared in *The King of Kings* (1927), *The Man Who Laughs* (1928), and *Murders in the Rue Morgue* (1932) with Bela Lugosi. Though his name may well not have been known to most cinemagoers, Hurst's appearance would have been instantly recognizable.

As for the cadre of zombies, the 250-pound, six-foot-six Frederick Peters became the ominous Chauvin.[96] George Burr MacAnnan played Von Gelder. John T. Prince—incorrectly referred to as "John Printz" in the pressbook—played Latour. Born in Boston in 1891, Prince had been successful on the stage and a well-versed actor in silent films since first appearing in *Mission Bells* (1913). His most noticed role until that time was probably as "Thaddeus" in *The King of Kings* (1927).[97] Other zombies included John Fergusson and Claude Morgan; not only is *White Zombie* apparently their first film, it seems to have been their only one.[98]

On the other hand, Dan Crimmins—portraying not a zombie, but the native sage Pierre—had earlier appeared in *The Midnight Express* (1924) and *Not So Long Ago* (1925). He had started in films at Pathé in 1912 in a duo with his wife, actress Rosa Gore; prior to that, the two had been in vaudeville. As with some of the other zombies, Crimmins was a white actor—British, born in Liverpool—appearing in black face in the film.[99]

Seen only briefly as one of the two maids, the now long-forgotten actress Velma Gresham was somewhat unique in her unsuccessful attempt at stardom. After limited success in films like *White Zombie*, she decided to start a corporation called "Miss Velma, Inc." Memphis, Tennessee investors put some $20,000 into the company whose sole asset was Gresham's acting career.. Their stock would allow them dividends if Velma made it. She never did.[100] The same lack of stardom could be attributed to Annette Stone, who played the other maid; *White Zombie* was seemingly her only credit.

Enlisting Crew Members for the Production

If the on-screen talent was comprised mainly of thespians whose fame had dimmed prior to 1932, some of the technical team, generally well versed in their crafts,

DAN CRIMMINS

of Crimmins and Gore

Character Comedian

Height 5 ft. 3 in.

Latest Engagements

Several talking characters for First Nat'l Prods.

The Irishman in a James Cruze Talking Comedy

Phone FAber 0434 or ALL AGENTS

From the Standard Casting Directory *of May 1929. (Courtesy of George E. Turner.)*

had also shifted from major film work to fewer projects at lesser studios or for indie producers. Arthur Martinelli, pioneer cameraman whose work as a lead cinematographer stems back to at least 1918, had worked on the films of John Barrymore and Mary Pickford; he headed up the cinematography team. Among his more noteworthy 1920s films are *A Message from Mars* (1921) and *Ella Cinders* (1926).[101] But—while prolific in the early twenties—he hardly worked during the second half of that decade. It seems that *White Zombie* was his first film in the thirties. Second cameraman was J. Arthur "Jockey" Feindel, and assistant cameramen included Charles Bohny and Enzo Martinelli, Arthur's nephew.

Howard Anderson, founder of the Howard Anderson Company, created the film's special photographic effects.[102] The company had been formed in 1927 and was located in 1932 at Metropolitan Studios in Hollywood, which would become General Service Studios and even later Zoetrope Studios. For *White Zombie*, Ander-

son's company produced glass shots and optical photography. The opticals, however impressive, bore the rough quality inherent in most such work of the era; poor duping capabilities meant most opticals contained jumps and were grainy in image.

Working for Anderson was Conrad Tritschler, who was responsible for *White Zombie*'s glass paintings, such as the exterior and upper interior of Legendre's castle. In an interview, Victor Halperin once described the combined technical processes of Anderson and Tritschler:

> We had sets built up to a certain height … maybe 25–30 feet high, and they worked in and fitted in paintings to finish the rest of the interior of the castle where much of the main action took place. You couldn't tell one part from another. It looked like all interior stone. Individuals walked in the front when they were searching for the castle, and they'd see the castle off in the distance on top of a huge rock, and that was all painted. We saw the individuals move and the waves of the sea in the foreground, so we could combine them in the same camera shot.[103]

A key element in the amalgam of images was the physical sets, handled by Ralph Berger. Though *White Zombie* was his first film credit, Berger proved an expert at adapting existing materials to the needs of the Halperin film. In addition to the rented Universal Studios set for Castle Dracula's great hall and stairway, Berger utilized pillars, a hanging balcony, and other items from *The Hunchback of Notre Dame* (1923), as well as dark corridors seen in *Frankenstein* (1931) and *My Pal, the King* (1932).[104] The impressive chairs at Legendre's table had earlier been seen in *The Cat and the Canary* (1927). Some of the rooms in Beaumont's palatial estate had been seen the year before in *Dracula*, constituting part of Dr. Seward's home.[105]

As with Ralph Berger, it seems *White Zombie* was the first film (or at least the first credited film work) for a number of other technical participants, including assistant director Herbert Glazer and assistant to the producer Sidney Marcus. The film was also apparently the first credit for both assistant director William Cody and sound engineer L. E. "Pete" Clark.

By contrast, some talent behind the scenes was already well known to those in the Hollywood system. Dialogue director Herbert Farjeon had been a stage director when he first met the Halperins, then worked on numerous of their films in the 1920s. Victor and Edward had made Farjeon an important part of their Liberty Productions by 1930, having hired him to try out stage plays as potential stories for screen adaptation.[106]

Also, makeup man Jack Pierce had not only worked with Bela Lugosi on *Dracula* (1931) and *Murders in the Rue Morgue* (1932), but had created the Frankenstein's Monster makeup for Boris Karloff in 1931. It was Pierce

HP31-2-170.

After exhaustive research, it is now possible to identify the actresses who portrayed maids in White Zombie. *From left to right are Velma Gresham and Annette Stone, with Madge Bellamy.*

who applied Lugosi's makeup for *White Zombie*. Fellow makeup artist Carl Axcelle had spent some 15 years providing makeup for Broadway shows and had also worked on such films as *The Awakening* (1928) and *The Singapore Mutiny* (1928).[107] In addition, Harold McLernon—who had earlier edited *Viennese Nights* (1930, which included Bela Lugosi in a bit role), *Children of Dreams, Gold Dust Gertie*, and *Star Witness* (all 1931)—acted as editor. He may well have been the one who suggested some of the fascinating wipes and transitions used in *White Zombie*.

Shooting White Zombie

Jack Pierce and Harold McLernon's s prior experience probably meant that they noticed the difference between the film's budget and studio-based projects in a more heightened way than some others in the crew. *White*

Zombie's production certainly featured the standard financial limitations of the 1930s independent film. Enzo Martinelli once claimed, "It was just two weeks' work, a short budget picture. After all, we were on Poverty Row. I was lucky to get on the show. I think it was my only picture that year. I really needed that $30 or $40 a week; needed it badly."[108]

Martinelli is right except on only one minor point. As the April 12, 1932, *Variety* indicated, the *White Zombie* shoot lasted *less* than two weeks. Eleven March days is all it took to complete the filming, though no record seems to exist regarding exactly which eleven days those were.[109] The first day on the set had to have been after March 8, given that that was the date the Halperins announced having "just engaged" Cawthorn.[110] That seems to place the shoot's first day in mid–March.

As for the locations involved, Enzo Martinelli remembered their whereabouts and the chosen lighting schemes:

White Zombie used sets and artifacts from many prior films, including Dracula *(1931).*

We were never off the Universal lot. Even the night exteriors on the backwoods roads were shot there. All the night shots were night for night. My uncle always made sure it was possible to recognize the source of the light in those scenes. In so many shows today, they just ignore the light sources. When working on the indoor sets, he always gave them a little scope ... a little depth. He kept the actors well *into* the set, not back against the walls. The sets were nicely lit for depth and mood.[111]

On this topic, the *White Zombie* pressbook proclaimed the "settings and photography" to be "among the best ever done for the screen. They include, for example, a castle in the Haitian mountains which is one of the largest of its kind in the history of motion pictures. This, with the tropical scenery of Haiti, makes an unusually striking background for the weird story."

While certainly *White Zombie* was not shot in Haiti (as some newspapers would later print, probably because of pressbook quotations like the aforementioned one), it seems that—despite Enzo Martinelli's statement of no shooting off the Universal lot—other sets and locations *were* used. Indeed, it is possible that such shots were filmed by a separate unit without the younger Martinelli's involvement. For example, some of the verandah at the film's climax seems to be that used in *The King of Kings* (1927), and it was on the Pathé lot in Culver City. In addition, the cliff at which Neil and Dr. Bruner camp is actually one at Bronson Canyon, California, and the stone steps that Neil climbs to reach the Legendre castle are near Malibu.[112]

Actor Clarence Muse once recalled to film historian Robert Cremer a drastically different vision of the production:

It was shot on the backlot of United Artists in the dead of night. Bela made a lot changes in the script and directed some of the scenes himself. Those guys on the set cut out a lot of lights they needed and they only used reflectors. I was driving the carriage with two wild horses, and they just had the road marked out with reflectors. It was tough keeping those horses going in the right direction, but Bela knew what atmosphere he wanted to create and never settled for anything less.[113]

In this quotation, however, two aspects of Muse's memory are either skewed or mentioned so briefly that they inaccurately reflect the production. For one, the film was not shot on the backlot of United Artists. Secondly, while Muse may have attempted to drive the horses in a brief rehearsal, a stand-in actually handles them in the film of *White Zombie*. Thus, the paragraph already possesses two falsehoods, even if they were made unintentionally. However, another, more recently debated point surfaces in the same reminiscence. Robert Cremer takes these comments to mean that "Lugosi's peerless sense of the macabre caused him to become disgruntled at such carelessness, and he went about reordering scenes, restaging some completely, rewriting others, and finally taking the director's baton in hand to mold the film to his personal specifications."[114]

In reality, no one else actually on the set can corroborate the story. Both Madge Bellamy and Enzo Martinelli's stories of the set, limited in scope though they are, do not include any mention of Lugosi's directing the film to any degree at all. By contrast, Bellamy's discussion of the film highly praised Halperin's methods and directions. On one occasion, she claimed:

> I just worked with the greatest directors. Jack Ford, Frank Borzage, Lewis Milestone, and I would say that Victor Halperin directed you in such a gentle, such a respectful, and such an intimate way, that he didn't intrude on the actor. He just kind of helped bring you out. In other words, I think he was a great, great director.[115]

Muse's memory about Lugosi directing the film is then very much in question.

The following Muse quotation suggests a relationship between him and Lugosi of more length than the day or two he was on the *White Zombie* set. Though he gave the story to Cremer in an interview on *White Zombie*, it may in reality be based more on Muse's relationship with Lugosi on the set of *The Invisible Ghost* (1941), a film in which both actors appeared and in which Muse had a much more prominent role and shared many more scenes with Lugosi than he did in *White Zombie*:

> We talked a great deal about social issues, and he said "Your people certainly did have a hard time of it, especially in the beginning." It was your people this and your people that, but it was no time before we would get to talking and he dropped that your people thing and it became us. ... Those were times when a black man couldn't talk to another guy, because, hell, you didn't know what he was going to tell the boss! But there was something strange about Bela, because you never felt that way about him.[116]

So, if these words more accurately reflect his memory of Lugosi on the later film, it is possible that Muse meant that Lugosi took over the artistic reins from Joseph H.

Lewis, the veteran director of *Invisible Ghost*. However, Lewis was a veteran professional and it is difficult to imagine him yielding control of his picture to anyone.

How else can Muse's comments on Lugosi's directing—assuming that they were not a blatant lie or the result of a misquotation by Cremer—be reconciled with the memories of others? It is true that Lugosi at times was known to offer suggestions to coactors and directors. Stories of this type have surfaced regarding projects as early as the stage version of *Arabesque* (1925) and as late as *Abbott and Costello Meet Frankenstein* (1948) and *Bride of the Monster* (1955). Secondly, it is possible that Lugosi might have offered others on the set some suggestions on the day or two that Muse worked, though Muse himself did not see the entire production to understand that Halperin was the real director. This seems all the more possible if one reconsiders Bellamy's own comments about Halperin's minimal suggestions to actors, as he was apparently happy letting actors enjoy the freedom to let their characters (hopefully) grow while he himself became consumed with matters like the sets, lighting, camerawork, and other issues.

At any rate, Lugosi was probably not the one who decided to emphasize his eyes via extreme closeups, nor was he the one who determined how to capture the desired effect. But a minor controversy surrounds exactly who developed the scheme by which his eyes would be lit so effectively. Venita Halperin, the director's widow, maintains that—while Lugosi didn't seem to care that the lights might hurt his eyes if the resulting shots benefited the film—it was her husband, Victor, the director. Enzo Martinelli suggested that it was his uncle, Arthur, the cinematographer, and told film historian George E. Turner:

> I learned how that was done on the first day. Arthur just took a cardboard and cut two holes in it about as wide apart as Lugosi's eyes, placed it in front of Lugosi's face and put a light through it. It put two little spots right on his eyeballs when he started to become dangerous.[117]

Victor himself was only once recorded talking about the topic of the use of Lugosi's eyes, and said that:

> I had to emphasize his eyes. The light on his eyes was very, very intense and it was quite trying. It would be for anybody, but—though it burned him up—he felt it was the thing that would do the most good for the picture and himself too.[118]

The quotation suggests that Victor may have decided to "emphasize" Lugosi's eyes in the movie, but that he and Lugosi mutually decided how best to proceed.

Except for such contradictory recollections, few anecdotes have surfaced regarding the production. The

The cast take a break in the shooting of White Zombie.

pressbook does offer a fun but almost certainly invented Madge Bellamy story called "Actress Collapses After Seeing Own Death Role." It claims: "Miss Bellamy went through [the interment/disinterment] scenes one morning, and later that day she and other members of the company went into the projection room to look at the result. That part of the sequence in which she is seen lying in a coffin was flashed upon the screen, and, after taking one look, Miss Bellamy let out one piercing scream and bolted for the door. And nothing could prevail upon her to return. Now Miss Bellamy is a convert to cremation."

Another pressbook yarn claimed, "A director of a motion picture, if he is a good one, is able at all times to undertake jobs which do not usually come under his attention. Take, for instance, ... Victor Halperin. In the picture, Madge Bellamy is supposed to appear in an undressed state in her boudoir, and for the scene she purchased a long slip.

But when the director saw the slip he said 'No.' He thereupon procured scissors and made the slip into two other garments, a brassiere and a pair of knickerbockers. And a bit of lace from the prop department completed the job."[119] Less than accurate, especially if one believes one of Madge Bellamy's own memories. In 1970, she recalled "...I made all my own clothes that I wore in *White Zombie*, including the dress in the [opening scene]."[120]

More tales about the production were seldom heard from her. When once asked about *White Zombie*, she merely claimed, "I have no anecdotes about it. ... I wish I could write how Lugosi took me to lunch and bit me, but alas I cannot."[121] On another occasion, she quipped, "I can't think of a single catastrophe or strange thing happening [on the set]. I feel like making up something—like telling how Bela invited me to take a nap in his coffin! [O]r how his false teeth got caught in my neck!"[122]

However, she did make one brief claim about the film's production that seems impossible to substantiate. In a 1970 letter to *Classic Film Collector*, she reminisced: "...here is a secret I will tell you that nobody ever knew other than the people connected with the picture. My voice was not used during filming. I caught a cold the second day of filming and lost my voice completely—did my lines as we made the film, but later, they hired another actress and dubbed in her voice."[123]

The pressbook, while hardly a fact forum given its tendency to spin fiction, does speak about her voice. In its brief article "Madge Bellamy Comes Back After Absence of Two Years," readers are told that "[s]he has devoted [two years] to the spoken stage with a view to obtaining vocal training for the talkies, and it will be seen in a glance in *White Zombie* that she has succeeded in her mission. In fact, the young woman now displays a vocal poise which is bound to stand her in very good stead."

Aural evidence of Bellamy's voice in the serial *Gordon of Ghost City* (1933) and in the film *Charlie Chan in London* (1935) proves that it is indeed her voice heard in *White Zombie*. In addition, simply watching *White Zombie* and carefully listening substantiates that her voice was not dubbed. Why then the anecdote, which she would not repeat in her later, book-length autobiography? The answer is unclear. Perhaps she intended to use the false story of a substitute voice as the reason for her inability to make a comeback in the talkies, only to have the story questioned by film historians. On the other hand, perhaps she remembered the Halperins suggesting her voice be dubbed without finally doing so. Regardless of whether her attempt was to deceive or was the result of forgetfulness, the remembrance is certainly false.

Choosing White Zombie's Music

In addition to using Madge Bellamy's actual voice, the *White Zombie* soundtrack features a cornucopia of music. The decision to emphasize the role of music was quite a departure from prior horror films of the cycle. *Dracula* (1931), after all, featured only a snippet of Wagner during an opera house scene and brief strains of Tchaikovsky during the opening and closing titles. The extended use of music in *White Zombie* was a logical choice based on the film's limited dialogue, and was an answer to calls for more film music. "Without music pictures are dead," one film exhibitor declared in a June 1932 issue of *Motion Picture Herald*.[124]

Subsequently, a column in *The Film Daily* claimed that:

Though Madge Bellamy (pictured) once suggested the voice of her character in White Zombie *was dubbed, no evidence can substantiate her claim. (Courtesy of Leonard J. Kohl.)*

[Film music will be] designed to interpret the mood and action of the story, rather than ... the plot ... [being a] medium for "plugging" songs. Music will become more and more an integral part of the motion picture in the future. ... The work of the composer and scenario writer must be blended carefully. ... The successful song number must be able to stand the same test as dialogue. It must be indispensable. ... Nothing is so delightful as an appropriate musical setting that flows along with the tempo and trend of the story without exerting its influence too strongly.[125]

By the end of 1933, *The Film Daily* continued to report on music's growing importance. Warner Brothers, it was said, would use an increased amount of "special musical arrangements as supplementary aids to the dramatic and comedy action in features.... Writers have been instructed to create scenes particularly suitable for use of music that will aid in stimulating audience reaction."[126] *White Zombie* heard the early calls for music in talkies and anticipated those that came in 1933.

Voodoo was inseparable from music, at least in the eyes of some. The New Orleans *Times-Picayune* would write in its August 21, 1932, review of *White Zombie* that the theme of voodooism "runs through much of the still famous music composed here by Louis Moreau Gott-schalk, his *Danse Negre*, *Calinda*, and *Bamboula*." The subject had also entered popular music of the 1920s as well, including David W. Guion's 1929 composition *Voodoo*.

To supervise the music recorded for the film, either the Halperins or Phil Goldstone contacted Abe Meyer.[127] Even by 1932, Meyer, head of the independent Meyer Synchronizing Service, was known as a friend to independent filmmakers. That very year, for example, he realized that only 200 or so union musicians of the L.A. local were being used by studios due to their high recording scale. Meyer went to the union with a plan to help everyone. He tried to convince them that a lower scale for independent producers would encourage the use of more music in indie productions, as well as allowing those on limited budgets to hire larger orchestras. In turn, the musicians would benefit by increased opportunities for work.[128]

It was Meyer who brought *White Zombie*'s music to life. Rather than already-recorded music from a library, Meyer hired orchestras to play and record new versions of compositions specifically for any film he was involved in. He would also suggest compositions and, when necessary for reasons of copyright, would acquire the needed rights. In 1932 alone, his company provided music for such films as *Honeymoon Lane*, *Police Court*, *Texas Pioneers*, *Trailing the Killer*, and *Unholy Love*.

For *White Zombie*, he supervised a particularly curious collection of little-known works. For example, in Scene 12 when Legendre transforms Bellamy into a zombie, the music is a bizarre pastiche of passages from the *Limoges* section of Mussorgsky's *Pictures at an Exhibition*, Gaston Borch's *Incidental Symphonies*, and—when Legendre's face appears in Bellamy's wine glass—Hugo Riesenfeld's *Death of the Great Chief*, which had originally been written for James Cruze's *The Covered Wagon* (1923). The scene ends with moments from Borch's *Agitato*.

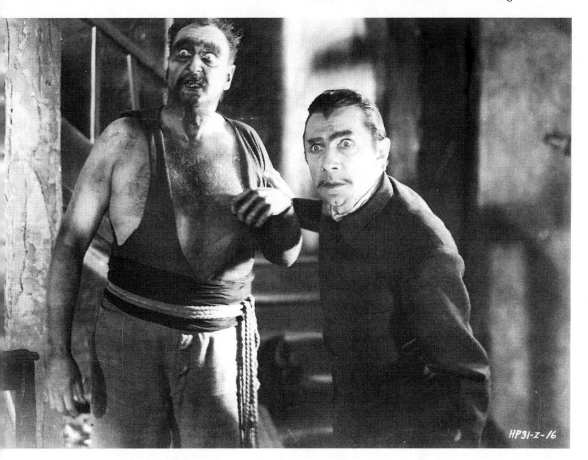

Music became a pivotal aspect of White Zombie. *(Courtesy of Leonard J. Kohl.)*

The appearance of Riesenfeld's music in the film is not surprising, as he and Meyer were longtime friends. Their association arose in part from Riesenfeld's tenure as music director of the Rialto and Rivoli theaters.[129] During the silent film era, Riesenfeld himself had built up a library of some 6,000 orchestral scores and thousands of piano compositions.[130] Furthermore, he was well known for his background scores of silent films like Fritz Lang's *Siegfried* (1924).[131] Riesenfeld had also been involved in scoring music and effects for talking pictures beginning in 1928.[132] *Moving Picture World* had even dubbed him, "... one of the best composers of motion picture scores."[133] In the summer of 1932 as *White Zombie* neared release, Riesenfeld was conducting the orchestra at the Roxy Theatre in New York City.[134]

On the other hand, the reason for using so many of Borch's compositions in *White Zombie* is difficult to determine, although they do possess an aesthetic ability to generate mood. Given that all of his included works were published in Germany, perhaps Meyer received an inexpensive rate or even nothing for their use. Regardless, Borch's *Agitato Pathetique* is heard in Scene 17 when Legendre asks Beaumont if he would take Madeline back to the grave; the selection lasts until the zombies seize the butler Silver. At that point, yet another Borch *Agitato* is used, lasting until the zombies hurl Silver into the waters running through the castle. Meyer also used the composer's work in Scene 22, when Madeline vacillates about murdering Neil, and Legendre strains to impose his will on her. When Dr. Bruner knocks the knife from her hands, the music shifts to Riesenfeld's *Death of the Great Chief*, then returns again to Borch. Even the music heard when Neil and Madeline are reunited at the film's conclusion is yet another Borch composition.

Other composers heard in *White Zombie* include Wagner and Liszt. The former's *Lohengrin* is used in a brief organ solo during the wedding march in Scene 11, while a zombified Madeline performs a piano solo of the latter's *Liebestraum* in Scene 17. More unexpected is the work of Xavier Cugat, who would become popular with music fans for his Latin, rumba-style orchestra. He wrote a Spanish *jota* heard in the barroom during Scene 14. Unfortunately, Cugat did not reflect upon the film in his autobiography, but his composition was written expressly for *White Zombie*.[135]

In addition, a few other 20th century composers' work can be heard in the film. H. Maurice Jacquet's work is used in Scene 17, heard after Silver's death. A selection by Leo Kempenski is played in Scene 22, when Madeline is first sent to kill Neil. And two selections by Hen Herkan constitute much of the music at the film's climax in Scene 23. Near the end of Scene 22, when Madeline rushes away from Neil after the knife has been knocked from her hand, Herkan's *S-O-S* is used.[136]

Perhaps the most striking selection of all is *Chant*; made up of native drumming and a wordless vocal, it generates a more ominous mood than any other composition on the soundtrack.[137] Heard during the roadside burial in Scene 1, the piece was written by Guy Bevier Williams. Though some texts—like the *AFI Catalog of Motion Pictures Produced in the United States*[138]—refer to *White Zombie* as his only credit of the 1930s, Williams was actually a Universal Studios employee specializing in ethnic music during the period. No doubt his work can be heard in numerous other contemporary films, even if it was not credited.

Outside of the work of Liszt, Wagner, and Mussorgsky, the most famous piece heard in *White Zombie* is used during Scene 19: R. Nathaniel Dett's 1914 hymn *Listen to the Lambs*. The original music features lyrics, taken from the Bible in a passage where Jesus tells Simon Peter to "feed the lambs" and "tend the sheep" of the Christian flock.[139] For the film, these lyrics are supplanted with a wordless vocal not dissimilar to that of Adelaide Hall on the 78 rpm recording of *Creole Love Song* with Duke Ellington made in the late 1920s. *White Zombie*'s version also features alternating male and female choruses. A 20th century American spiritual, *Listen to the Lambs* is certainly out of place on the lips of Haitian natives in *White Zombie*, even if Dett had hoped it would appeal to a variety of people. He once said of the composition:

> I recall that I wrote *Listen to the Lambs* out of a feeling that Negro people, especially the students of Hampton Institute, where I was then teaching, should have something musically which would be peculiarly their own and yet which would bear comparison with the nationalistic utterances of other people's work in art forms.[140]

At any rate, *Listen to the Lambs* was still quite popular in the U.S. during the mid–1920s; its sheet music outsold all of Dett's other published compositions. The tune also received reviews from many well-known commentators of that decade. H. L. Mencken of the *American Mercury* magazine called it "the only really good Negro composition," while Will Marion Cook—an African-American orchestra leader and composer—dubbed it "third rate."[141] Regardless, criticisms like these, as well as Dett's continued presence on the national music scene, suggest the spiritual would have been familiar to at least some 1932 audiences.[142] Moreover, since *Listen to the Lambs* was still under copyright at the time, it is possible Victor Halperin (perhaps at Meyer's urging) specifically wanted to use it, as the film could have relied solely on public domain classical works.

These composers and Meyer's hired musicians generally bore little resemblance to those described in the

"Weird Music in *White Zombie*" types of articles that appeared in 1932 newspapers.[143] One claimed that the "special musical arrangement by Abraham Meyer" included "the chants of the native Haitians, the beating of tom-toms, and, strange as it may seem, some piano playing by Madge Bellamy…." Despite the article's claim, no native Haitians are heard on the film's soundtrack; the discussion probably refers to Williams' *Chant*, but that recording certainly did not use talent from Haiti. Similarly, while one review spoke of "a musical score that reminds us where jazz had its real beginnings,"[144] the score evokes something closer to Hollywood's poorly researched conception of Haitian music (Williams), Americanized and jazz-influenced Cuban music (Cugat), and a beautiful example of a 20th century African-American spiritual (Dett).

Finding More Money

Though music would be crucially important to *White Zombie* aesthetically, financial concerns were at times the Halperins' paramount concern. At some point, they became financially involved with the Amusement Securities Corporation (ASC) of New York City. ASC's connection to *White Zombie* is usually mentioned in film histories in such a spotlight that it makes it appear as if the company was involved in the film from its inception or at least during its production phase. However, given the date of ASC's formation (in late May 1932, some two months after *White Zombie* was shot), it seems clear that ASC did not get involved until late May or early June of 1932.

Also important to consider is the fact that ASC was not a studio or even an independent production firm. On May 25, 1932, *Motion Picture Daily* described the true functions of Amusement Securities:

> The company will advance capital on completed negatives, and will buy notes, trade acceptances and accounts of recognized state right exchanges. Amusement Securities Corp. has been incorporated with a capital of $100,000 and it is announced that additional funds will be available if the response of independent producers warrants an increase. …[ASC] will enable producers to maintain a constant flow of product, which is often impossible when they must await returns on one picture before starting another.[145]

The trade publication added that, along with its other roles, ASC would provide "banking facilities" for independent films.

It doesn't seem as if Amusement Securities became aesthetically involved in editing *White Zombie*, even though Sherman S. "Sam" Krellberg, General Manager

Advertisement for Amusement Securities Corporation published in the 1935–36 International Motion Picture Almanac.

of ASC, would later produce serials like *The Lost City* (1935). In general, Krellberg seemed more interested in financial matters and distribution concerns. The same year as *White Zombie*'s production, for example, Krellberg began the Principal Film Exchange, his own distribution firm.

A colorful figure, Krellberg was the son of Louis Krellberg, who operated a nickelodeon on New York's Lower East Side in the early 20th century. He began his career as an attorney, though his father convinced him to try the motion picture industry. Krellberg, along with Sam Warner, invested in the 1919 film *My Four Years in Germany*. A hit, the film's success paved the way for Krellberg's lifetime interest in the cinema. By the time of *White Zombie*'s production, he was known, as *Variety* once said, to "greet his distributor customers with the caveat that they'd better pay his terms, as someone was just in the next office inquiring about playing the film in question."[146] Like Phil Goldstone, Krellberg was a shrewd businessman; the involvement of both in *White Zombie* would impact the search for a distributor.

Finding a Distributor

Distribution problems plagued *White Zombie* from the start. On May 3, 1932, *Variety* claimed that Columbia Studios would release the film. Movie mogul Harry Cohn had allegedly offered the Halperins a production cost advance and a percentage of the profits.[147] News by the end of that month shifted from Columbia to Universal, but not for a distribution deal. Universal attached the *White Zombie* negative for some $8,607 in 60 day notes owed by the Halperins.[148] Problems like these may have terminated Columbia's interest, as no more was said of any dealmaking by them for *White Zombie*.

Instead, the brothers Halperin quickly entered into discussions with Educational Pictures, and sometime during the second week of June contracts were signed. Almost immediately, however, *Variety* reported a deal gone bad. Phil Goldstone refused to okay release of the film and called for "$100,000 cash and $100,000 in notes plus a percentage at the brothers' end."[149] He told the trade that, after the Halperins signed the contracts, Educational "wanted to reduce the amount of cash and increase the notes."

At that moment, Goldstone had far more than the Halperins and *White Zombie* on his mind. In early June, he demanded a union settlement regarding wage disputes for independent film productions, threatening to stop backing independent films if he didn't get his way.[150] He even stopped funding two films in production.[151] A few days later, he admitted that unions were less of a concern than his overall feeling that indie films were becoming too hazardous an investment.[152] But even that must only have been part of the truth; Goldstone was touted in industry trades as the "financial backer" of the fledgling Majestic Picture Company, a national independent.[153] Goldstone even visited Chicago during the second week of June to hold an initial sales conference for Majestic with producer Nat Levine.[154] From there, Goldstone traveled to New York to arrange some overseas distribution deals for other films.[155] For *White Zombie*, it seems he was brought in from the beginning to help finance the project and lend an air of credibility to potential talent like Bellamy. By the time of distribution, he would prove far less than helpful in the Halperins' minds, as well as to Amusement Securities.

Despite their troubles, the Halperin brothers forged ahead with attempts to garner publicity for the film. Though little covered by the press, they held a preview of *White Zombie*'s first cut in New York City on June 16, 1932. In their June 17 article "Audience Gasps at Weird Story," *The Film Daily* proclaimed: "Here is a super-thriller that has the additional virtue of novelty, but hardly for key cities. ... Performances are not all that they might be. Bela Lugosi repeats his 'Dracula' characterization and Madge Bellamy is far better in the silent portions than when she speaks. John Harron is a conventional juvenile and Robert Frazer an equally conventional heavy. Which leaves performance honors solely to Joseph Cawthorn. His is a grand piece of work. ... Victor Halperin does a neat job of direction, coupled with some interesting camera set-ups."

As for the preview itself, the trade described a spoken introduction read over the announcing system by "one of the Halperins" to prepare the audience for the film. The trade related that: "The auditorium was in total darkness and the screen black. If they do it just like this on a sound track, they have their introduction. The audience loved it, and shrieked." Not surprisingly, the Halperins' version of the preview was even more exciting. A brief mention of it appeared in the *White Zombie* pressbook:

> From the opening introduction a tense stillness pervaded the atmosphere. Eyes were riveted on the screen and every now and then the stillness was punctuated by shrieks of horror at some thrilling climax until the final exciting sequence practically lifted them from their seats and left them limp.[156]

While an overly praising description of *White Zombie*'s first appearance on a theater screen, the sheer fact a preview occurred at all must have been a relief to the Halperins, who continued to suffer from distribution troubles.

Only a few days later, *Variety* printed the latest news on the film's saga: "Sam Krellberg to New York with print of *Zombie* for state right release."[157] This deal quickly fell apart as well. Two days later, the trade claimed: "Phil Goldstone has refused to okay the deal between the Halperin Brothers and Sam Krellberg for the latter to distribute their picture, *The White Zombie* [*sic*], on a $40,000 cash plus percentage basis unless Krellberg guarantees the outstanding bills against the picture mounting to around $35,000."[158] Though it apparently did not satiate Goldstone's financial appetite, the Halperins had offered to turn their advance over to the producer to cover the lien. The trade added that, "[Goldstone] felt that as he had guaranteed all bills against the picture Krellberg should assume the guarantee for the protection of the film company, laboratory, and mercantile houses which had extended credit to the producers."[159]

In the midst of such problems, the *New York State Exhibitor* offered a very brief review of *White Zombi* [*sic*], published on June 25, 1932; presumably the critic saw the film at the aforementioned preview. "Novelty with a *Dracula* motif a bit modified," their column "Looking Ahead at the Product" believed. "There is enough of the odd and the bizarre to make for showmanship, with the result favorable."

"Favorable" was hardly the word on Phil Goldstone's lips, however. In early July, he extended $11,000 in cash to settle mounting claims by Universal Studios against the film. At the same time, trades noted that the Halperins had "several deals on for distribution."[160] Other "deals" had soured for lack of upfront finances, but fortunately one studio which had become interested in procuring independently made films made a bid for *White Zombie*.

Even after White Zombie *was edited, the film had no distributor in place.*

"UA Buying Up Outside Films," *Variety* proclaimed that summer, adding that "minimum production and bolstered outside purchasing activities is the trend at United Artists."[161] This was so much the case that they "decided to buy all available indie product" that seemed economically viable. Al Lichtman was behind this strategy at UA; in fact, he was so anxious for product he was examining various European productions for potential release.[162] Though Lichtman and the UA heads, at "final conferences" in February 1932, had voted on 12 productions to release for their 1932–33 program they eventually decided on a number closer to 15.[163]

As of July 8, 1932, United Artists was negotiating to acquire *White Zombie* for distribution, with contracts already being written.[164] By July 12, UA struck a deal with the Halperins which was apparently agreeable to both Goldstone and Krellberg. In fact, one trade claimed that Krellberg signed the contract on behalf of all par-

ties.[165] While UA did not release any figures to the press regarding cash advances, it is safe to assume that—since Goldstone agreed—it was more than $40,000. On July 23, 1932, the film was listed in *Variety* as a "coming feature attraction," but still without a premiere date. At the same time, it is clear that United Artists was already mailing press releases to cities across the U.S., as by July 24 a brief notice appeared in the *Times-Picayune* of New Orleans. The newspaper called *White Zombie* "a romance laid against a background of the 'living dead' of Haiti stories ... the picture will have a Broadway opening in a few weeks."[166]

During the dealmaking with United Artists, Edward and Victor Halperin (as Halperin Productions, Inc.) signed pivotally important contracts on July 15 and July 29, 1932. In the first agreement, they assigned to Amusement Securities Corporation the right to distribute, exploit, and reissue *White Zombie* for a period of ten years in exchange for a percentage of the profits. They also guaranteed to ASC that the film was original and trespassed on the rights of no one else, and that they would not use material from the film in "any other photoplay or photoplays" in the future. The second agreement was signed between the Halperins and their father, Robert L. Halperin. For $5,000, the father bought all rights expressed in the first agreement.[167]

With contracts and deals in place, the film neared a theatrical run, and apparently some aesthetic changes were still occurring. For one, *White Zombie* apparently had a running time of 74 minutes at its preview, several minutes longer than the average length of a film in 1932 or 1933.[168] By the time of its appearance on *Variety*'s "Calendar of Current Releases" (where it stayed throughout the autumn of 1932), the film was clocked at 69 minutes. Pressbooks, perhaps designed in part prior to the changes, still listed the film at 74 minutes. Why the changes? Though no records or files exist to explain them, it is possible that the Halperins and/or UA took the advice of a reviewer who cited the preview print as being too long. The critic claimed, "Cutting, particularly in the earlier sequences, is necessary for the good of what follows."[169]

Also curious is the fact that United Artists (in whose name the copyright was originally listed) did not register the film at the Library of Congress until August 1, 1932, three days after its New York City premiere. The film, listed at eight reels and as being "presented by Amusement Securities Corporation," was recorded as Copyright #LP3357.

Other leftover production concerns remained even after the film finally played on initial theater screens. For example, *Variety* reported at the end of August that *White Zombie* receipts were attached by the Music of America Artists, Inc., the American subsidiary of the British company Campbell-Connell. In 1929, the MAA advanced $7,500 to the Halperins; by 1932, the company was seeking to recover the funds and saw *White Zombie* as its opportunity. A court planned to decide how much of the $7,500, over and above moneys due other claimants, could be paid to the MAA. At the same time, Phil Goldstone was also attempting to make a financial claim of some kind against the Halperins.[170]

In a way, such problems act as a commentary on independent films of the early thirties in general. However unique *White Zombie* would prove to be aesthetically and financially in its box-office returns, it was—like almost all other independent productions of the time—planned and shot quickly with far too little money. Distribution was difficult since the film was a speculative work and all those with the power to deliver it to theaters knew that the Halperins, Goldstone, and Amusement Securities had to make a deal quickly to recoup investments. Leftover bills haunted the film, and the filmmakers would never see the kind of financial return that the financiers and distributors saw.

Regardless, distribution occurred, allowing moviegoers to see *White Zombie* and presumably causing *The Hollywood Reporter* to re-evaluate its initial opinion that the film was "hardly for key cities."[171]

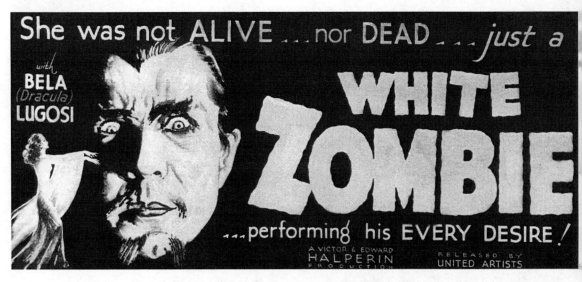

The amazing 24-sheet movie poster for White Zombie, *which was an equally amazing 324 inches × 82 inches in size.*

Chapter Four

Exhibiting the Land of the Living Dead: *White Zombie* on First Release

With a distributor in place, *White Zombie* finally flickered against U.S. theater screens in 1932. After its New York premiere in the summer, the film began appearing at innumerable theaters throughout the fall and winter of the same year. *White Zombie* was a surprise success in many theaters and with some critics, but it was very much a failure in other areas and with other critics; there was certainly a very wide variety of responses. More than most prior horror films and most films in general, *White Zombie* was an anomaly of film spectatorship in its construction of a cinematic subject (as covered in the second section of Chapter One) and in its reception by historically situated viewers.

In film studies, arguments regarding viewers have at times centered on what theorist Judith Mayne identifies as the "homogeneity, of the sociological/mass communications model." In other words, audience analysis in the past tended towards oversimplification. Mayne also believes:

> The very notion of a "response"—not to mention a viewer, or a relationship between a text and a viewer had been postulated in a totally self-evident, unproblematized way. Scholarly responses to the cinema were often indistinguishable from "market research" studies by film studios, and in fact many studies served precisely that purpose.[1]

Some of these studies attempted to chronicle the habits of moviegoers, such as the success of a film genre with audiences of particular ages or genders. More qualitative studies, like the often maligned sociological investigations of the Payne Fund Studies in the 1930s, attempted much the same.[2] Researchers like Herbert Blumer searched for consistent patterns of response in children viewing certain film genres.[3]

In addition to the "sociological/mass communications model" which Mayne describes is the belief that viewers are too complex to analyze and that such analyses thus become vast oversimplifications. For example, film historians Robert C. Allen and Douglas Gomery suggest:

> ...the audience for movies in any sociological or historical sense is really only an abstraction generated by the researcher, since the unstructured group that we refer to as the movie audience is constantly being constituted, dissolved, and reconstituted with each film-going experience.[4]

Their argument must be considered, as diametrically opposed reactions to a film may be experienced by two viewers sitting next to one another in a movie theater. To gauge the vast number of varying responses viewers in a given audience offer to a film is nearly impossible. Mayne notes that:

> ...spectatorship entails much more than individual films or even the individual and collective viewing experiences of audiences. Spectatorship involves the acts of looking and hearing inasmuch as the patterns of everyday life are dramatized, foregrounded, displaced, or otherwise inflected by the cinema.[5]

But the daunting nature of such a task should not prevent studies of audience reactions, as much valuable information can be learned from even an investigation of viewer responses and the various factors that influence them. However much viewers may be affected by or engage in the attempted positioning constructed by a film, they are also real persons. They are situated historically and geographically, and they have experience based on factors like age, gender, ethnicity, and religion.

An 11" × 14" title lobby card for White Zombie's *1932 release.*

Of course, an even wider range of highly individualized factors may also affect a viewer's reception of a film. For example, responses can be altered by the contagious effects of, say, laughter from other viewers. Attention spans might be broken by thinking about personal responsibilities that need to be completed after the film, or even by worrying about a coffee pot that may have been left on at home. A viewer might step outside the theater auditorium during the film for popcorn, a smoke, or a visit to the restroom. An uncomfortable room temperature in a theater auditorium or a whispered conversation of nearby theater patrons might also detract from the viewing experience. Concentration may return to the film soon after such distractions, but they would necessarily alter a viewer's reaction to it.

Given that *White Zombie*'s original release was in 1932, other factors could have impacted the moviegoing experience. Theaters were very popular cultural sites, a pivotal hub of entertainment in the 1930s. They were the remains of vaudeville, and often a place to hear orchestras and music; viewers shifted from watching live entertainment to films (or vice versa) within the course of a few hours or less. Newsreels and short film subjects also affected the viewing environment created for the feature film.

Other events also occurred that shaped feelings about the moviegoing environment; in areas where "Blue Laws" prevented ticket sales on Sunday, some theaters occasionally allowed church services to be performed in their buildings. Occasionally favorite radio shows like *Amos and Andy* would be played on the theater stage before a film screening, and contests like "Dish Night" also altered the viewing experience. Reduced prices and even "penny nights" were ploys of some theaters; others used double (and sporadically even triple) features to lure moviegoers.[6]

Theaters of the 1930s controlled additional practices which affected the screening of the feature film as

This advertisement, printed in the August 6, 1932, Houston Post, illustrates the need for theaters to define zombiism for potential audience members.

well. Whether a theater featured period air conditioning systems or not, or whether its cooling system was too cold could impact patrons, for example. Whether or not a theater allowed refreshments in the theater hall; whether or not a theater was of a luxurious decor or not; whether or not it featured a pronounced motif— say, Art Deco or Egyptian or Asian: these were all factors which might have affected audiences.

Of more critical importance to the viewing process in the 1930s were theaters which censored or changed films themselves or were at the mercy of a local censorship board. Shots, lines of dialogue, and entire scenes could be cut, thus creating a different narrative experience for viewers. For example, when *White Zombie* played in Toronto, theater patrons almost certainly did not see Scene 10, in which Madeline is shown preparing for her wedding in undergarments.[7]

Movie theaters, although cultural sites, could experience major problems or even present danger in the early 1930s. Blue Law infractions by theaters caused fines, legal action, and even court battles that were well known to local moviegoers. Intense debates over double features were also covered in some newspapers. Conflicts between exhibitors and the projectionists' union often led to difficulties as well, including picketing that would have been noticeable to ticket buyers. Theater fires—which often claimed many lives—were common at the time, as were robberies and bombings (both stench and, to a lesser degree, incendiary).[8]

Despite the extreme difficulties in calculating the effects of such concerns and distractions on viewer responses, we can analyze more widespread extratextual factors with greater success. Problems plaguing large groups of people, such as war or widespread economic problems, can easily affect the mood of viewers and how they respond to a given narrative. For example, response among some viewers in the U.S. to *Das Kabinett des Dr. Caligari* (1919) on its original release was impacted by prejudices against Germany, the film's country of origin, due to World War I.

Furthermore, the advertisements and "ballyhoo" heralding a film's screening create preconceptions in a viewer's mind. For example, a movie advertised as a western fosters certain images and generic conventions in the mind of a viewer who has seen prior western films or is familiar with their generic conventions. Allen believes the importance of film genres is that they:

> …specify in advance the content of the narrative. Any given genre of film, such as the western or horror film, draws on themes and images from other texts. … Because the generic intertext already forms a part of the spectator's stock of knowledge, the individual film simply taps into a reservoir of themes and images already possessed by the spectator. … Genre conventions thus minimize the effort required by the spectator to understand a film in its singularity and maximize his [*sic*] capacity to enter the film's narrative world.[9]

White Zombie was a film for which 1932 viewers were somewhat unprepared, as "genre conventions" in horror were not yet fully in place. The 1930s horror cycle was in its infancy, and even if an audience member had seen prior films like *Dracula* (1931), *Frankenstein* (1931), and *Murders in the Rue Morgue* (1932), *White Zombie* worked in a unique way cinematically with a unique topic (zombies) not previously covered in a feature-length film.

The images and text on film advertisements themselves (whether printed in the newspaper or on a movie poster hanging outside a theater) also create viewer expectations that may or may not be met by the film itself. Of these influences on audiences, Mayne suggests:

> The assumption here is that spectatorship is structured not just by the experience of going to the movies and being seduced by the spectacle on the screen, but by the influence of a whole range of texts that seek, in one way or another, to spark interest in films and keep movie theaters full.[10]

Given the localized nature of film advertisements, individual theaters were able to influence the ways viewers received the film by employing various marketing strategies. *White Zombie* would have proved a challenge to viewers who saw its publicity materials in advance of watching the film. Its advertisements would vary from city to city and in descriptions from "horror" to "love story" to "thriller," thus creating at times a generic indeterminacy for the film.

In order for theater exhibitors to construct preconceived notions in the minds of potential audience members, all manner of advertising strategies were employed. United Artists did ship a 32-page pressbook to each theater screening the film, but the sheer variety of materials it included—some emphasizing horror, some emphasizing "thrills," and some emphasizing sexuality—allowed for extreme variations from theater to theater. Moreover, some exhibitors chose to design, or have a local newspaper design, ads for the specific audience being targeted in each city.

In addition to advertisements, many exhibitors constructed elaborate displays or performances outside the theater itself, and extreme disparities between them occurred from theater to theater. But regardless of the nature of the ballyhoo effort, these extratextual devices colored the expectations of audience members, as did local newspaper ads. All of these endeavors impacted the viewing positions of spectators and thus their responses to the film.

Much the same could be said of other publicity techniques, such as biographical stories circulated about the actors in a given film. The kinds of roles associated with a given performer may cause a viewer to reflect during a film on how similar or dissimilar the current characterization is. For example, a viewer might be well aware of the image cultivated by John Wayne and consider it, and prior performances of Wayne, before seeing another film in which he appears. The viewer may also consider how much a given role may or may not be like the "standard" John Wayne role, and hence respond to the film at least in part via comparative analysis. Allen suggests:

> In a manner that complements the effect of genre conventions upon the spectator's perception of narrative film, star persona constitutes a rough character prototype for the character within the film. The spectator need not become acquainted with the character from scratch, but views him [sic] in terms of a familiar set of traits ... Star persona encourages the audience to fuse the role of the character with the real-life body of the actor....[11]

Some 1932 viewers would have been familiar with Bela Lugosi, mainly through his work in films like *Dracula* (1931) and *Murders in the Rue Morgue* (1932). He suggested a terrifying persona to some, a romantic persona to others, and a combination of both qualities to others still. Certainly he was compared in one fan magazines in 1931 to Lon Chaney and was already well associated with the character Dracula.[12] At the time of *White Zombie*'s release in 1932, however, he was not yet irrevocably aligned with the horror cycle. Indeed, as the investigation of the *White Zombie*'s advertising in the present chapter will show, ads often included "Dracula" as a middle name for Lugosi; the result attempted to further his connection with horror, as well as to remind viewers of

his association with a popular film. A viewer's prior knowledge of him likely colored their preconceptions about and response to *White Zombie*.

A major feature of both advertisements, ballyhoo efforts, and other publicity for *White Zombie* drew on one of the public's major visceral associations with Bela Lugosi: his eyes. In both the Broadway stage production of *Dracula* (1927) and the subsequent Hollywood film of the same name released in 1931, Lugosi's eyes had been emphasized in their narratives and advertising. As Chapter Two notes, *White Zombie* utilized Lugosi's eyes to great advantage in terms of the spectatorship constructed by the film. Similarly, the film's promotional efforts emphasized Lugosi's eyes, which gazed out at potential audience members.

Viewer reactions to *White Zombie* varied from the expected responses to a horror film (fright and terror) to fascination, to skepticism, and even to giggles. Reception of *White Zombie* in the 1932 media suggests a greater multiplicity of audience impressions than would be anticipated from a genre-specific film.[13] Rather than the movie having failed to live up to the expectations of the horror cycle by not scaring some of its audiences, such reactions must be partially attributed to the indeterminacy of *White Zombie*'s genre promoted by theaters themselves. Audiences in various cities and sometimes within a given theater responded radically differently from one another. In this way, *White Zombie* evoked a more complex set of receptions than other, prior 1930s horror films.

To examine these issues at length, we need to build a foundation under the ties between horror films and the Great Depression. Against that backdrop we can best consider *White Zombie*'s success as compared to prior movies in the 1930s horror film cycle. To scrutinize potential causes for *White Zombie*'s success or lack thereof, studio publicity materials, variances in theater advertising and publicity, critical responses, and viewer information like age, gender, ethnicity, and religion are explored. In addition, to understand all these issues in the context of geography, a lengthy analysis of key cities in which *White Zombie* played is made from surviving evidence from 1932.

The Great Depression and Horror Cinema

Most U.S. filmgoers of 1932 were victims of the Great Depression, even if some remained empowered economically. The events of that year and the immediately preceding three years colored the reception of all Hollywood films. The stock market crash of 1929 helped

THE *LIVING* DEAD!

The weirdest love story in 2.000 years! —a beautiful girl torn from her lover on her bridal night —rendered lifeless— then soulless—then brought to life again by a fiend and made to perform his every wish!

"WHITE ZOMBIE"

with

Bela (Dracula) Lugosi

Capitol

Features: 12:25, 2:15, 4:05, 5:55, 7:50, 9:40

Published in the September 25, 1932, issue of The Daily Oklahoman, *this advertisement features one of the more eerie images of Murder Legendre.*

pression," with estimates of the unemployed generally over 12 million.[16] A ravaged economy meant that those who held financial power bought and consolidated businesses, forging new monopolies in various industries[17]; such problems widened the gaps between classes, producing what one writer in the 1930s saw as "unbridgeable chasms."[18]

The same year saw specific changes in how the Great Depression was perceived and combated. In February of 1932, President Hoover, who had been unwilling to create social programs for the poor or intervene in any extensive way in the economy, established the Reconstruction Finance Corporation (RFC). Its purpose was not to direct aid to the poor, but rather offer credits to help the railroad companies and release the frozen funds of mortgage corporations and banks.[19] Few outside the upper classes believed the RFC would be much help, and many citizens focused on other problems in the news, like the kidnapping of Charles Lindbergh's baby.[20]

cause a downward spiral of U.S. and world economies, creating the monster of the Great Depression, which hovered over almost every facet of life. By 1930, every fourth factory laborer was no longer employed.[14] Two years later, the total labor income had been reduced by 40 percent, and the total output of goods had been reduced by 37 percent.[15] Historian Frederick Lewis Allen believed that 1932 was the "cruelest [year] of the De-

As the Great Depression deepened, large numbers of U.S. voters blamed President Hoover. In 1932, a presidential election year, there was a tide of popularity for Franklin Delano Roosevelt, governor of New York. According to writer Louis M. Hacker, "Roosevelt's campaign electrified the country. Beginning in the spring [of 1932] he traveled more than 25,000 miles and visited almost every state in the Union."[21] To the masses he appeared a savior who would take direct and immediate action to solve the problems of the middle and lower classes. Roosevelt's victory seemed assured prior to the election, but the poll numbers in his favor far exceeded most predictions.[22] The pendulum had swung to a new leader and new political party. However, public interest in entertainment rivaled public interest in politics.

Though movie studios in 1932 faced economic difficulties, U.S. citizens clung to films as an important luxury, a necessary form of entertainment. Even in the early thirties, movie attendance averaged from 60 to 75 million people every week.[23] Some calculations suggested that 96 percent of the American public during the Depression could be classed as "moviegoers."[24] Despite such impressive figures, movie theaters and studios still suffered financially. For example, the year 1931 was one of the most economically strained in Hollywood studio history; the trend continued the following year. John Alicoate's introduction to *The 1933 Film Daily Yearbook of Motion Pictures* vivified the moviegoing environment of 1932:

> 1932 was a trying year for the industry and its close found the fortunes of the business at their lowest ebb. The year marked the end of the so-called era of extravagance. ... Unless the general economic situation takes a decided change for the better, the industry can hope for little in the way of progress and genuine prosperity.

To achieve such progress, those in the film industry had already begun action of various kinds. For example, many theaters in 1931 cut ticket prices to bolster or even preserve current levels of attendance.[25]

Movie studios also strived for answers to their economic hardship. One was monitoring and then producing successful genres and genre films even more than ever before. Genre films—or "cycle" films as the 1930s movie industry called them—created a unique arrangement between viewer and studio; movie fans responded to a given film of their own choice, but the studios then created subsequent, similar films to capitalize financially on audience interest. As film historian Andrew Bergman notes, "People went to certain kinds of films and cycles began: gangster cycles, 'fallen woman' cycles, 'shyster' cycles, 'backstage' cycles."[26] In 1931, movie audiences regularly began viewing horror films, responding very favorably to *Dracula* (1931) and then being provided a steady diet of them by movie studios.

Prior to *White Zombie*'s release, *Dracula* (1931), *Frankenstein* (1931), *Dr. Jekyll and Mr. Hyde* (1932), and *Murders in the Rue Morgue* (1932)—representative of the first major films in the 1930s horror cycle—had played theater screens across the U.S. The first three films profited strongly at the box office, while the fourth had brought only moderate numbers of viewers to theaters. *White Zombie* would reap financial rewards, but only in certain cities; in other areas, the film would prove to be a financial failure.

The popularity of the horror film cycle during the early years of the Great Depression itself poses an important question. Why would films revolving around gruesome topics prove successful at such a moment of tension and anxiety in U.S. history? At the time and in subsequent years, the most common answer was catharsis, the desire of Depression-era filmgoers to find an outlet for their worries. Richard Watts, Jr., a film critic for the *New York Herald Tribune*, penned an early example of this kind of explanation in 1932:

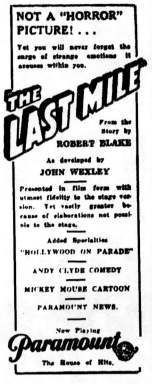

This newspaper ad printed in the September 3, 1932, Amarillo Daily News tried to reassure filmgoers that The Last Mile *would not be another dreaded "horror picture."*

> It is possible, I am sure, to figure out some explanation of the popularity of this type of film, which would tie it up with the national seriousness now overwhelming us as the result of our earnest economic plight. The point could conceivably be defended that picturegoers, finding their own lives filled with commonplace terrors, longed for entertainment which would dramatize their homespun tragedies in fantastic form. An unfortunate citizen, who had just lost his life savings in the stock market, might have found satisfaction, if not pleasure, in watching a screen character who had lost his life's blood in contact with a Draculean vampire, while another unhappy victim of conditions, whose character may conceivably have suffered by his subjection to depression, may have discovered a fairly pleasant surcease in a play wherein a noble and upright Dr. Jekyll has his morale destroyed by his other self, the unspeakable Mr. Hyde.[27]

Then as now, it is easy to read the thirties' horror film as an index of the U.S. dilemma. Most of the cycle's output places American characters in jeopardy in a foreign land, with a foreign villain wreaking havoc on their lives. Such a plot would have externalized the thinking of many middle-aged Americans, who were embittered by having been drawn into European entanglements like World War I and who, by the 1920s, had become suspicious of foreigners. This mentality created attempts to limit both immigration and the internal spread of Communism. Many persons with these beliefs blamed the Great Depression itself on European nations and their failure to repay war debts to the U.S.[28] Above all, though, for Watts, the ability of Americans to enjoy horror films was a healthy process.

The *Herald Tribune* columnist did, however, provide a more complex set of answers than many of his contemporaries or for the horror film's popularity. Watts realized that filmgoers attend films for different reasons and respond differently to them. In addition, and beyond the psychological reasons of audiences, Watts cited the economic situations of movie studios as a factor in horror movie production:

> [The proliferation of cycles suggests] merely that the photoplay magnates are so hopelessly imitative. *Dracula* was a great success in the theater, therefore it was inevitable that a motion picture should be made of it. Then the film turned out to be an economic triumph, and every Hollywood organization determined on a work which would be properly overrun with popular horrors.[29]

His analysis suggests the importance of money to the proliferation of the horror genre, a crucial factor often overlooked in rhetorical or psychological discussions of the horror film cycle's success.

Lastly, Watts considered that an enjoyable escapism was possible for moviegoers to experience when witnessing any quality production. He believed *Dracula*, *Frankenstein*, and *Dr. Jekyll and Mr. Hyde* were "excellent" films, and that the cinema provided an excellent opportunity for "superbly eerie and grotesque atmosphere" given their combination of cinematography, lighting, and set design. "The motion picture," he wrote, "being ideally suited to horror tales by its very nature as a medium, is naturally at its best when given a proper chance to show its potentialities."[30] For him, the horror film was simply another cycle for viewers to enjoy, and one that the cinema from an aesthetic standpoint was particularly adept at constructing.

Regardless of individual perceptions, both film critics and the public generally viewed the horror film cycle as a cinematic movement, a series of films whose production was motivated by prior success. Whatever rea-sons were proffered, most critics connected the popularity of horror in the cinema with the horrors of the Great Depression; and the Depression certainly did act as an important backdrop to Hollywood films of the period, affecting everything from studio production to theater prices and audience attendance.

The Comparative Reception of *White Zombie*

To establish the various responses to *White Zombie* as distinct from responses to similar cinematic texts, the reception of the other, prior films in the thirties' horror film cycle must first be established. As previously stated, four films—*Dracula* (1931), *Frankenstein* (1931), *Dr. Jekyll and Mr. Hyde* (1932), and *Murders in the Rue Morgue* (1932)—constitute the major works in the cycle prior to the release of *White Zombie*. The first three proved generally successful with critics and audiences; the fourth averaged mediocre reactions from the same groups. Exceptions did occur on the films' initial releases, but the four movies represent much more uniform patterns of responses than those which met *White Zombie*.

Even in the early 1930s, critics and audiences viewed these three or four films as a cycle, a cinematic movement. In the January 20, 1932 *Los Angeles Times*, for example, Edwin Schallert's column spoke of the "Heritage of Thrillers." While he referred to such films of the 1920s as *The Phantom of the Opera* (1925) as horror movies, he made clear that "none of these films ever started a cycle, but *Dracula* did, and it is certainly going on into the prescent [*sic*] summer." Others in the press also believed a cycle was occurring. For example, Richard Watts, Jr.'s, review of *Frankenstein* in the *New York Herald Tribune* mentioned that the film was "the second of a series which began with *Dracula* and to be followed by a picturization of Poe's *Murders in the Rue Morgue*."[31]

These comments, as well as others in industry trades and newspaper articles that could be cited, reinforce what has already been suggested about *Dracula*, *Frankenstein*, *Murders in the Rue Morgue*, and *Dr. Jekyll and Mr. Hyde*: they were the first four major horror films of the 1930s cycle prior to *White Zombie*. But a few additions could be made to that list, especially due to attention paid some films in modern horror film histories.

For example, some historians today cite *Svengali*—which starred John Barrymore and was released in May 1931—as a horror film, or its title character as a "forgotten monster" in the words of historian Frank Dello Stritto. While it features some narrative and aesthetic elements which *White Zombie* borrowed (as well as some definite features of German Expressionism), it was not perceived by industry trades or newspaper critics in the early thirties as being a horror film.[32]

Other films included in modern histories of horror include projects like *Murder by the Clock* (1931) and *Murder at Midnight* (1931).[33] However, in industry trade reports, critical reviews, and most advertisements, films like these were touted as "mysteries." For example, *Harrison's Reports* dubbed *Murder by the Clock* (1931) a "fairly good murder melodrama."[34] The same trade called *Murder at Midnight* a "murder mystery melodrama,"[35] while *Motion Picture Herald* announced it as a "murder mystery."[36] In other words, though pre–*White Zombie* films like these two examples and others that could be cited—e.g., *The Phantom* (1931), *Murder at Dawn* (1932), *Sinister Hands* (1932), and *Get That Girl!* (1932)—are now chronicled in books on the horror film, in the 1930s they were generally considered to be mystery films and not part of the burgeoning horror film cycle.[37]

In modern histories of the horror film, *Freaks* (1932) is also catalogued as part of the cycle. While the film was much talked about (and much reviled in some quarters) at the time of its first release, period trade publications and critics often did not speak of it as part of the then current horror film cycle. It is true that some ads for the film used the word "horror," and *Variety* claimed some sections of the film had been reworked with more "horror material" in the aftermath of *Frankenstein*'s success.[38] In addition, when *Freaks* was released, *Motion Picture Daily* connected the film with *Frankenstein*, *Dr. Jekyll and Mr. Hyde*, and *Murders in the Rue Morgue*.[39]

However, most reviews of *Freaks* did not invoke the names of horror movies. *Motion Picture Herald* even went so far as to contrast *Freaks* with the horror cycle, claiming "it deals with and uses the real thing, not playthings."[40] They also said, "It is not necessary, or advisable to present the picture as a gruesome shudder-film. … *Freaks* does not warrant that kind of billing."[41] Some reviews—like the one in *Harrison's Reports*—did not mention the word "horror" at all, and even once called the film a "sex picture."[42]

Following the release of *Freaks*, *The Monster Walks* appeared on a number of theater screens. For *Motion Picture Herald*, the film was a "thrill mystery" that was a "contribution to the group of 'horror' films now holding stage temporarily."[43] But other industry trades like *Motion Picture Daily* saw it as more of a murder mystery film than a member of the horror film cycle.[44] And even if some persons in the 1932 film industry believed *The Monster Walks* was a horror film, its low budget and somewhat limited release kept it from being well discussed or particularly influential.

By summer of 1932, another horror film appeared in the United States. Released on July 17, *Almost Married* hit theater screens less than two weeks before *White Zombie* made its New York premiere. Nearly forgotten today and saddled with a title that belies its inclusion in the horror cycle, *Almost Married* was the story of a homicidal maniac who escapes from an insane asylum and terrorizes his wife, who has committed bigamy by marrying another man. The film was certainly considered part of the cycle by some industry trades, but its limited playdates, box-office appeal, and financial success allow it to be adjudged in the same way as *The Monster Walks*: a horror film that had little impact.

Richard Watts' comment about the horror film cycle consisting of *Dracula*, *Frankenstein*, and *Murders in the Rue Morgue* should now be reconsidered. *Dr. Jekyll and Mr. Hyde*, given that most 1932 critics cited it as a horror film (as did some of its own ads) and given that its box-office success and thus audience viewership were so widespread, is a necessary addition to Watts' list. By contrast, many other films were either too little seen (e.g., *Almost Married* and *The Monster Walks*) to be considered cornerstones of the cycle or were associated with the mystery genre (e.g., *Murder at Midnight* and *Murder by the Clock*). *Freaks* represents a special case, a movie of mixed reputation dubbed a "horror" only by certain members of the 1930s film industry. For these reasons, this study will examine *Dracula*, *Frankenstein*, *Dr. Jekyll and Mr. Hyde*, and *Murders in the Rue Morgue* in comparison to *White Zombie*, and build a picture of the cycle prior to *White Zombie*'s release.

Dracula, the cycle's first film, was highly successful for Universal Studios in 1931, receiving critical praise and strong audience response. Many ads for the vampire film did not use the word "horror," perhaps because it was the first of the cycle and thus no precedent for the word's usage in 1930s cycle films existed. Instead, it was a "vampire thriller" and a story of strange "passion." *The Billboard* believed *Dracula* "has been done splendidly,"[45] and *The Film Daily* admitted that "there is no denying its dramatic power and thrills."[46] No reviewers cited *Dracula* as one of the top aesthetic accomplishments of Hollywood; instead, critics gave only a grudgingly favorable nod to the film. *Time* magazine, for example, called it "exciting," but "not as good as it ought to be,"[47] and the *Chicago Tribune* simply dubbed it a "satisfactory" thriller.[48]

Though *Dracula* was not one of the top ten money-making films of that year, it garnered consistently favorable audience responses. Minor exceptions did of course occur; for example, the Emboyd Theater in Fort Wayne, Indiana noticed only "fair crowds," with those buying tickets more interested in the vaudeville show than *Dracula*.[49] However, horror film historian David J. Skal suggests that *Dracula* "outperformed almost everyone's expectations" and that the film grossed almost double its production cost.[50] The manager of the Palace Theater in Jacksonville, Florida applauded *Dracula*'s "good work" which was "mighty scary," while the manager of Houston's Majestic reported on how "seriously" his viewers took the film.[51] The *Chicago Tribune* noted in March 1931 that an "awed stillness" from movie audiences greeted *Dracula* onscreen.[52] Such "stillness" apparently did not begin until after movie patrons were seated; audiences in many cities scrambled to buy tickets.

The nationwide success of *Dracula* spurred Universal Studios into producing another horror film, an adaptation of Mary Shelley's novel *Frankenstein*. Released near the end of 1931, the film proved more successful critically and financially than its predecessor.[53] Reviewers generally lauded the film, with the December 4, 1931 *Chicago Tribune* believing it to be "compelling" and the December 5, 1931 *New York Herald Tribune* calling it a "superior motion picture."[54]

Audiences also embraced *Frankenstein*, making the film one of the great box-office successes of late 1931 and early 1932. According to the column "About the Showstops" in a November 1931 *Washington Post*, records were "being smashed by the crowds pouring into the theater to have their blood chilled and their nerves shattered!"[55] For approximately a year, it held the record for top grosses at such theaters as the Keith's in Boston, the State Lake in Chicago, the Mayfair in New York City, the Stanley in Philadelphia and the Orpheum in San Francisco.[56] Occasionally audience members did react negatively; for example, two theatergoers wrote to the *Chicago Sunday Tribune* in 1932 complaining about faults in the film.[57] But, as with *Dracula*, these responses were exceptions. On January 3, 1932, six fans included *Frankenstein* when they submitted lists of their favorite films of December to the same newspaper[58]; on the last day of that month, the *Chicago Sunday Tribune* received a letter from a fan claiming that she and her party "liked it immensely."[59]

Director Rouben Mamoulian's *Dr. Jekyll and Mr. Hyde* (1932) proved equally successful. "It is a distinct contribution to the present cycle of 'horror' thrillers which seems to be upon us," *Motion Picture Herald* wrote.[60] At the same time, some of Paramount's national ads for the film called it the "Thriller of All Thrillers!— Plus a great love story... Mystery and horror! Heartwarming Romance and intense drama! Everything! Its Appeal is unlimited."[61] In other words, it seems that Paramount did not shy away from the horror label on the film, but tried to broaden its appeal by claiming the story was more than just that.

Most critical reviews of *Dr. Jekyll and Mr. Hyde* in early 1932 reported favorably on the acting and cinematic style, with the *New York Herald Tribune* believing that the film "results in a brilliant and pleasantly depressing motion picture."[62] In newspapers like the *New York Times* and national magazines such as *The Nation*, critics offered favorable notices on the film.[63] Philip K. Sheuer at the *Los Angeles Times* called the film a "major masterpiece of the screen."[64] *Rob Wagner's Script* believed the film to be "a masterly attempt to picture the impossible."[65] The January 11, 1932 *Los Angeles Times* proclaimed *"Jekyll-Hyde* rivals for unrestrained praise."[66] Actor and star of the film Fredric March won the 1932 Best Actor Oscar for his portrayal, yet another sign of its critical acceptance.[67]

Theater audiences echoed the excitement of critics. It is true that occasionally viewers responded negatively to the film. For example, Frederick C. Botz and Eric O. Kulbartz—two viewers at a Chicago screening of the film—wrote to the *Chicago Tribune*, claiming that they thought the "show was lowsy [*sic*]" and that "Mr. March reminded us so much of [comedian] Harpo Marx."[68] But such responses were extremely rare, and the film's boxoffice success suggests that most audience members enjoyed it. *Dr. Jekyll and Mr. Hyde* appeared on both the *New York Times* and *The Film Daily* "top ten lists" of moneymaking films of 1932.[69]

Thus, *Dracula*, *Frankenstein*, and *Dr. Jekyll and Mr. Hyde* represent a consistent pattern of films that were successful critically and financially. Their box-office appeal helped the horror cycle to continue, making future films of that type feasible investments for studios and independent producers. The popularity of the first major 1930s horror movies also inspired numerous satires, such as a 1933 episode of the short film *Hollywood on Parade* featuring Bela Lugosi as Dracula biting an actress dressed as Betty Boop, or the appearance of comedy team Colonel Stoopnagle and Budd in the short film *Stoopenstein*. In fact, cartoon caricatures of Dracula, Frankenstein's Monster, and Mr. Hyde appear along with other movie celebrities in the 1933 Disney animated cartoon *Mickey's Gala Premiere*.

If the first three films in the 1930s Hollywood horror genre represent consistent patterns of success, however, the fourth—*Murders in the Rue Morgue* (1932)—instead illustrates an example of a different pattern. Even before its release, Universal Studios noticed its aesthetic weaknesses, spending some $21,870 on "retakes" and "added scenes" in an attempt to help elevate the film to the stature of *Frankenstein* and *Dracula*.[70] To *The New Yorker*, the film was "ludicrous" and "inappropriately comic."[71] The *New York Times* believed the film "suffers from an overzealous effort at terrorization, and the cast, inspired by the general hysteria, succumbs to the temptation to overact."[72] The February 12, 1932 *New York Herald Tribune* went even further, with critic Richard Watts, Jr., suggesting that it was in many ways "feeble and foolish."[73] *Variety* proclaimed the film "hokey" and also mentioned that the "third of U[niversal]'s baby-scaring cycle won't have the benefit of shocking them stiff and then making them talk about it."[74] Others like *The Billboard* saw mediocrity at work, suggesting that "for those who go in for thrillers this one will have a certain interest, but not as much as in the two previous U[niversal Studios] horror mysteries, *Frankenstein* and *Dracula*."[75] When critics at newspapers like the *New York Evening Post* found "authentic thrills" in the overall film, they generally cited the already famous Lugosi eyes and eyebrows.[76] Yet others who gave decent reviews, such as the critic writing in the March 1932 issue of *Photoplay*, noted the trite, "time-honored appurtenances" in the film's efforts to scare audiences.

Audience responses were less than enthusiastic as well. One Jeanne B. Price of Bronxville, New York, wrote in a May 1932 *Photoplay* that she was indeed "horrified," but only by "what [producer] Carl Laemmle, Jr., has done to Edgar Allan Poe's classic," adding that parts of the film were "absurd." *Variety* even noted that "a cynical audience hooted at the finale hokum."[77] Audience reactions of course impacted word-of-mouth publicity and the overall financial success of the film. Unlike *Dracula*, *Frankenstein*, and *Dr. Jekyll and Mr. Hyde*, *Murders in the Rue Morgue* performed at many theaters only "moderately" in terms of gross.[78] A quick glance at some theater reports as presented in contemporary trade publications makes this clear. Providence's Albee Theater made some $13,000 in one week, considering the film "good" but attributing its success at least partially to the vaudeville bill booked with the film.[79] In Washington, D.C., it did "okay,"[80] and at Brooklyn's Loew's it generated a modest $22,100.[81] Cities like Detroit, Kansas City, Milwaukee, Philadelphia, and Providence had a respectable amount of success with *Murders in the Rue Morgue*.[82] The Palace Cincinnati, though, had to admit the film's gross was "sad."[83] In Portland, the Orpheum made "only $6,900" in one week with it, as opposed to *Lady with a Past* (1932), which did "fairly for $8,500" the following week.[84] Detroit's Downtown Theater believed it would only "break even" with the film,[85] but at least did better than Newark, which seemed "unable to pull up even with its competitors" showing other films.[86] For the Des Moines Orpheum, *Murders in the Rue Morgue* (which they screened in February 1932) became their lowest grossing presentation since January 1931.[87] As most U.S. critics cited flaws in the film, audiences also generally regarded the production as mediocre.

But *Murders in the Rue Morgue*, like its fellow efforts of the 1930s horror film cycle, resulted in a relatively uniform pattern of financial success. *Dracula* was quite successful, *Frankenstein* and *Dr. Jekyll and Mr. Hyde* even

more so, and *Murders in the Rue Morgue* much less so. However, the same was not at all true of *White Zombie's* fractured reception, or even the varied manner with which it was advertised.

Studio Publicity Materials

If *White Zombie* worked differently on most levels than previous horror films, these differences were reflected in materials printed and disbursed by United Artists, the film's distributor. Advertisements and exhibition strategies shape the initial impressions of viewers toward films, creating perceptions that affect how audience members respond to them. In the case of *White Zombie*, for example, some studio publicity materials suggested

Cover of the 1932 pressbook.

ads that explained what zombies were to potential theatergoers who had no former experience with the word;
a viewer's understanding of what the title meant would
have impacted the level of suspense they experienced before and during the film.

A cornerstone of the United Artists' publicity materials was the film's original pressbook, which the distributor shipped to each U.S. theater screening the film
in 1932.[88] The pressbook, titled *White Zombie: Complete
Exhibitors* [*sic*] *Campaign Book*, was prepared by UA's promotional staff, a group which—according to the studio—
were "showmen who understand advertising, the operation of theaters, and distribution."[89] The staff were split
into ten territories across the U.S. to service and supervise accounts, as well as maintain close contact with exhibitors. Pressbooks were probably shipped to theaters
from the territorial office closest to them.

For the *White Zombie* pressbook, it was Hal Horne,
Director of Advertising and Publicity for United Artists,
who apparently developed many of the marketing
schemes contained therein. The same day on which *Motion Picture Daily* announced that UA would release *White
Zombie*, they also announced that "Hal Horne … is already absorbed in *White Zombie*."[90] Horne was already
well known in the film industry for both his sharp wit and
for reworking UA's publicity force in 1931.[91] Prior to the
Halperin film, one of his major ad campaigns was for
Mickey Mouse cartoons.[92]

Along with various ads available for reprint in local
newspapers, the *Complete Exhibitors* [*sic*] *Campaign Book*
for *White Zombie* published Article 249 of the Penal
Code of the Republic of Haiti on a scroll-like drawing.
Because actor Joseph Cawthorn's character quotes from
Article 249 in the film narrative itself, many ads and promotional ideas erupted from the actual legalities regarding zombies in Haiti. The relevant part of the code, as it
was printed in the pressbook, said:

> Also shall be qualified as attempted murder the employ-
> ment of drugs, hypnosis, or any occult practice which
> produces lethargic coma, or lifeless sleep, and if the per-
> son (Zombie) has been buried it shall be considered mur-
> der no matter what result follows.

The translation seems to come from William B. Seabrook's book *The Magic Island* (Harcourt, 1929), though
the pressbook adds the word "Zombie" to further the
connection to the film's title.

Under the subheading "What Writers Found," the
pressbook also offered what was at the time imperative
information for 1932 movie audiences: a clear definition
of "zombie."[93] The entry was a bastardized quotation
from *The Magic Island*, with citations to the text intentionally vague:

The one-sheet movie poster for White Zombie. *(Courtesy of Bill
Pirola and Kevin Gardner.)*

> Recently several American writers have investigated the
> rumors, and at least one of them has brought back verifi-
> cation, which he arrived at through personal observa-
> tion. This writer, in his book upon Haitian sorcery, de-
> clares that he actually saw zombies at work in sugar cane
> fields. He writes: "A zombie is neither a ghost, nor yet a
> person who has been raised from the dead. It is a soul-
> less human corpse, still dead, but taken from the grave
> and endowed by sorcery with a mechanical semblance of
> life. It is a dead body which is made to walk and eat and
> move as though it were alive."

The pressbook continues its uncredited and slightly altered passage from Seabrook by discussing Haitian sorcerers similar to the character Legendre in *White Zombie*:

> People who have the power to create zombies go to a
> fresh grave, dig up the body before it has had time to rot,

galvanize it into movement, and then make of it a servant or slave. Occasionally for the commission of a crime,
but more often simply as a drudge around the habitation
of the farm, setting it to dull, heavy tasks and beating it
like a dumb beast if it slackens.

To help theater managers attain a quick education about
Haiti's indigenous monsters, the pressbook added:

> The Cult of the Dead, or, as it is called by the natives,
> "Le Cult des Morts," is a limited witchcraft group, most
> of whose members have sinister designs. They are, of
> course, outlawed, and very few white visitors to the is-
> lands ever are permitted to witness any evidences of the
> practice.

Descriptions such as this one comprehended the public
and theater managers' lack of knowledge on issues of
voodoo and zombies to the degree that—even if they are
inaccurate and at times ethnocentric—they use touchstone words like "witchcraft" to be more easily understood.

A 1932 window card for White Zombie; *a large blank space at the
top (not shown here) left room for individual theaters to personal-
ize it. This publicity item is fascinating not only due to its imagery,
but also for the fact that it is not pictured in the film's pressbook.
(Courtesy of Bill Pirola.)*

The need to explain what zombies were did not end
with theater managers either. Many newspaper ads either
described the creatures ("Neither dead nor alive—They're
zombies!") or offered quick definitions for potential ticket
buyers. For example, ads in Baltimore newspapers added
"Meaning Living Dead" to the film's title.[94] After all, although Seabrook's book *The Magic Island* had been a success, most theatergoers would still have been unaware of
its discussion of zombies. Even for those who had read
the book on its successful release, three years had passed.

Though United Artists' press materials did not outwardly mention Seabrook's name and book, *Motion Picture Herald* advised theater managers to make the connection for potential audience members:

> Without looking up the pressbook to see if the tie-up is
> mentioned there, the thought comes to our mind that a
> book called *Magic Island* dealing with the wide variety
> of witchcraft practiced by the natives of Haiti and a big
> seller at the time, was published a few years ago. It ought
> to make a corking bookstore tie-up for this picture.[95]

Despite how many audience members remembered Seabrook's book, some were likely made aware of it thanks
to *White Zombie* publicity of the type the *Herald* suggested.

Along with connections to Seabrook, the film's setting in exotic and distant Haiti followed in the tradition
of foreign settings for American horror films. At the same
time, many publicity materials attempted to American-
ize the phenomenon of zombies, making it seem closer
to home.

For example, newspapers drew on the pressbook's
mention of Robert E. Lee's mother. *The Chicago Herald
and Examiner* published the story as "*White Zombie* Revives Puzzle of Suspended Animation," claiming:

> It is a matter of history that Mrs. Lee had actually been
> buried for seven days in her casket in the mausoleum of
> the Lees, where she lay surrounded by generations of her
> family. On the eighth day, an old sexton, hearing a faint
> cry for help, went to Mrs. Lee's coffin and raising the
> glass lid covering her face, observed that her lips were
> quivering and her eyelids struggling to open. The Lee
> family had the coffin removed to the manor house, and
> in a surprisingly short time Mrs. Lee was restored to per-
> fect health. Fifteen months afterwards Robert E. Lee
> was born to her.[96]

All of these cases—Article 249, allusions to an investigator and "his book," and the Ann Carter Lee story—indicate a consistent pattern. Beyond simply having to
overcome the average moviegoer's question of what a
zombie even is, all these other efforts offer credibility to
the film's fantastic qualities. "Can such things be?" an

A 1932 scene lobby card for White Zombie. *(Courtesy of Leonard J. Kohl.)*

advertisement in 1932 Baltimore papers asked. The ad's answer: "History says yes."[97]

Also, in order to help heighten the mystery of actor Lugosi's persona already created by the fan press, the article "Bela Lugosi a Hermit and Mystic; Spends Time in Mountain Retreat" appears for use in the pressbook. The article attributes exotic qualities to the actor:

> He remains in his inaccessible retreat in the Hollywood mountains, and his constant companion is a half-wild malamute dog which howls at night just as if it were more wolf than domestic pet. ... The star unintentionally put all of his philosophy into one paragraph one day recently, when an interviewer managed to catch him at his home. Lugosi had been looking off into space toward the Pacific Ocean, when he suddenly swerved around and said: "People—thousands of them—chained by monotony, afraid to think, slinging [sic] always to uncertainties and terrified by the unknown. They live like ants.

I want to get away from people. I must get away somewhere where I can be free. And I can do it soon too. Not many more years and I will have enough of this world's goods to pursue my own course and to pay for whatever research I desire to make. I'm going into the mountains, completely away from people, to study." ... "I have lived too completely, I think," he said on a subsequent occasion. "I have known every human emotion. Fear, hate, hope, love, rage, despair, ambition—all are old acquaintances, but they have ... nothing to offer me. Only study and reflection remain. I must know what I have learned. I must analyze all my theories and be alone to think."

Though far less than accurate, such quotations furthered the eerie and occasionally Garboesque perception of Lugosi that many fan magazines gave moviegoers. These materials, of course, did not simply remain in the pressbook; for example, the above article appeared as "Lugosi

Mysticism Awes Hollywood" in the August 21, 1932, New Orleans *Times-Picayune*.

The pressbook also suggested catchlines to theater managers hinting at necrophilia, including: "What does a man want in a woman? Is it her body or is it her soul?"; "Would you know a zombie if you saw one?"; "She became a ZOMBIE—Neither Living nor dead—Walking, doing his every bidding without a soul. Was this what he wanted?" These tags indicate less a horror film than a love story, even if it was quite a unique and provocative one.

Variations in White Zombie *Advertisements*

Advertising the film in 1932 became a much more convoluted process than any pressbook can indicate. It is true that some theater managers took advice and suggestions from the pressbook, as well as images from a quickly printed and separate supplement that presented a collection of ads from the New York City premiere.[98] However, it became necessary for individual exhibitors to choose between marketing the film as a horror movie, a "thrill picture," or a love story—unlike, say, some ads for *Dr. Jekyll and Mr. Hyde* (1932) which incorporated all of those ideas. The *White Zombie* pressbook did not help theater managers to understand or answer this problem. As *Motion Picture Herald* suggested to exhibitors in 1932, "Use your own judgment" when planning local ad campaigns.[99]

Reactions to the horror film cycle in 1932 yield some helpful indications as to why this was an issue at all. If the box-office success of *Dracula* (1931), *Frankenstein* (1931), and *Dr. Jekyll and Mr. Hyde* (1932) was clear, so was their connection to horror. On February 21, 1932, however, A. L. Woodbridge's New York newspaper column noted a potential swing away from such films:

> The time is ripe for a cycle of motion pictures loaded with laughs. The country is surfeited with horror pictures, gangster pictures, and murder pictures until theater patrons have reached the point where they want to cry out in their sleep. ... Some believe gangster and horror pictures have had their day and reaction to them already has set in.[100]

Despite the fact that this prediction proved untrue, studio heads watched for the same signals Woodbridge examined. As a result, the March 15, 1932, *Variety* noted:

> Stories previously placed in the horror class by Universal [Studios] are now being defined as "weird mysteries"

Newspaper ad promoting the "strange" aspects of White Zombie.

by this studio, which for a while was wild about horror yarns. *Cagliostro*, once spoken of as a "horror story to end horror stories," is now tamed down to just a mystery.

Variety also noted that Universal began to consider *The Invisible Man*, *Suicide Club*, and *The Empty Chair* (the last two of which did not even go into production) as mysteries rather than horror films.

The same month, *The Film Daily* of March 28, 1932, printed the results of a Hays poll regarding the public's preferences for movie topics. "Thrill films lead," the headline read, with the article itself adding, "the almost universal preference for entertainment that thrills, expressed by banker and butcher, by artist and housewife, by poet and merchant alike, [is] evidenced in the decided choice of adventure and mystery themes."[101]

Theater promotions for *White Zombie* often drifted from strictly horror to the idea of "thrills." Newspaper ads occasionally featured those very themes (e.g., "the weirdest of all thrillers"), with the "weirdest love story in 2000 years" being another repeatedly used tag.[102] The latter was similar to *Dracula's* publicity as the "Strangest of All Love Stories." Moreover, when ads and theater promotions borrowed from UA's bag of suggestions, they often used descriptions like those in the aforementioned trade ad. Along with words like "unusual," the ads repeatedly

This ad, published in the August 27, 1932, Chicago Tribune, eschews the term "horror" in favor of "thrill-drama."

spoke of the "fiend" that made a beautiful girl into a "slave" to his passion. Such promotion was more reminiscent of a *Svengali* (1931) than a "monster" movie like *Frankenstein* (1931).

United Artists itself claimed in a large, two-page trade advertisement: "Give the public a *Frankenstein*, a *Dracula*, a *Scarface*, a *Bring 'Em Back Alive*, and out they come ... the paying thousands ... packing your house ... breaking your records ... EVEN IN THESE TIMES!" While touting *White Zombie*, UA managed to skirt its placement in the horror genre. More than just offering titles like *Scarface* as having comparative qualities, many of the studio's trade ads featured such plot descriptions as the following: "...a glamorous love-tale told on the borderland of life and death ... the story of a fiend who placed a beautiful woman under his strange spell, rendering her soulless, lifeless ... yet performing his every desire."[103]

The August 6, 1932, *Motion Picture Herald* advised theater managers to play up these "unusual" and "mysterious" aspects of *White Zombie*:

A thrill picture with a somewhat different theme, this independently produced effort offers the exhibitor numerous opportunities for unusual show-selling. At the outset it is emphatically suggested that the "horror" implication be avoided. There are other angles to be utilized to good effect, without the necessity of splashing "horror" and "monster" all over the campaign. Doing so would probably frighten away a goodly portion of the potential audience.[104]

Given the success of campaigns for *Frankenstein* which generally heightened the "horror" and "monster" content, *Motion Picture Herald* must have genuinely believed that the horror cycle was either dead or confined to too small an audience to target.

Just as the words "thrills" and "thriller" were popular tags, so was the adjective "unusual." Many of United Artists' press materials for the film proclaimed, "Unusual Times Demand Unusual Pictures." The idea of identifying a film as "unusual," however, did not begin with *White Zombie*; trades in August 1932 carried full page ads

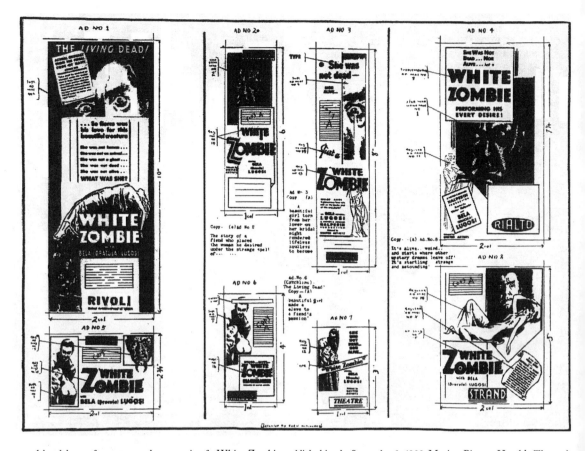

A breakdown of newspaper ad construction for White Zombie *published in the September 3, 1932,* Motion Picture Herald. *These ads were designed by Eddie Hitchcock, who worked under Hal Horne at United Artists' publicity department.*

for Unusual Pictures of New York City, whose own promotional materials asked, "What does the box office need? What does the exhibitor want? What will the public ALWAYS buy?" The answer to each question was of course, "Unusual Pictures."[105] As with "thriller," such terms were sometimes viewed as making movies more salable to the public than terms like "horror." In June 1932, *Motion Picture Herald* even announced "Horror has run its course."[106]

However, by August—only two months later—trade publications realized that the horror film cycle was in fact moving forward. *The Film Daily* of August 1, 1932, mentioned that the "cycle of so-called 'horror' pictures will continue through the new season," speaking of such upcoming projects as Paramount's "*Isle of Lost Souls*," and RKO's "*Kong*." The article also mentioned three horror films in "current release … *Zombie*, [a] United Artists picture; *Almost Married*, Fox; and *Most Dangerous Game*, from RKO."[107]

The *Los Angeles Times* of August 31, 1932, noted, in "Cinema Horror Cycle Resumed," that:

> New pictures seem to be portraying phases of the warped mind. This follows quite naturally on the heels of the horror cycle films, which are not over, although some of the projected horrors, widely publicized, have not been made as yet.

Whether or not theater managers were aware of such articles, they were acutely sensitive to what sold tickets, and, as the United Artists' trade ads noted, such concerns were heightened by the Great Depression.

Many theaters used press materials to design their own ads accentuating *White Zombie*'s "horror" elements. For example, in a few distinctive New York ads, the Rivoli promised, "This is a picture for strong hearts!"[108] The Loew's Midland of Kansas City echoed that phrase repeatedly in their own ads. In *White Zombie*'s Dallas run, the Old Mill Theater promised "IT WILL MAKE

Ads like this one (from the Pittsburgh Post-Gazette *of September 9, 1932) tried to create curiosity out of the public's general lack of knowledge.*

YOUR BLOOD RUN COLD."[109] St. Louis saw the same kind of ads when the Loew's State proclaimed, "The Love-Madness of *Dracula* Pales, The Fiendish *Frankenstein* Is an Angel—Compared to the Greedy, Horrifying Cult of the Zombies." [110] In San Francisco, it was even touted as "the latest in the blood-curdling cycle of horror films."

The June 25, 1932, *New York State Exhibitor* predicted *White Zombie* was a "trick picture" whose success "depends upon the exploitation."[111] For most key theaters, such ballyhoo extended beyond the choice of pressbook materials. All kinds of gimmicks were employed by major theaters to cause passersby to stop and buy tickets; many played up horror elements by using skeletons, live actors as "zombies," coffins, so on. "Maybe you'd like to test the squeamishness of the citizens of your community?" the *Motion Picture Herald* asked with regard to how horrifying promotions for *White Zombie* should be.[112]

In a move that visually mixed eroticism and violence, some ad schemes emphasized the aspects of sexual greed within the horror tale. For *White Zombie*'s Los Angeles debut, newspaper advertisements centered on such traits. The film failed miserably at the box office in that city, and—though it's impossible to attribute that failure to the theaters' promotion alone—the repeated use of nude, female caricatures in sexually charged ads may have played a role.

At any rate, the decision on what publicity angle to pursue rested with theater managers. As a 1932 *Motion Picture Herald* said of advertising:

> If you were to accumulate several hundred theatre ads clipped from newspapers from all over the country on the same picture, you would get the surprise of your life to see how many totally opposite slants are injected to sell the same picture in the different localities.[113]

With *White Zombie*, the seeming lack of genre specificity—heightened in some cities due to the particular kinds of ads run in the newspapers—would have caused at least a few audience members problems in knowing

An ad showing artwork of zombie Chauvin (Frederick Peters) holding a woman who is far more sexualized in appearance than the character Madeline is in the film. Published in the Los Angeles Times *of November 18, 1932.*

what to expect. For example, when the Loew's 7th Avenue theater ran a small ad in the *New York Amsterdam-News* on August 31, 1932, the tag line read, "Shudders! Chills! Creeps!" Yet, the brief film synopsis on the same page—presumably supplied to the paper by the theater itself—spoke only of a "burning glamorous love-tale told on the border land of life and death."

The Eyes of Bela Lugosi

The *White Zombie* pressbook claimed, "Lugosi's very name has become synonymous with strange, secret powers, and this is not altogether due to Dracula and his other eerie portrayals. There is something of a mysterious, hypnotic quality about the man himself, particularly about his deep-set eyes...." A major aspect of ballyhoo efforts, newspaper advertisements, and movie posters was artistic and photographic representations of actor Bela

The original caption for this artwork—which was printed in the July 31, 1932, New York Herald Tribune*—reads "Bela Lugosi Gives You the Hypnotic Eye."*

Lugosi's eyes, an aspect of the actor's anatomy which had already gained notoriety through his previous films. As indicated in Section II of Chapter One, *White Zombie* utilized Lugosi's eyes to help construct the "spectator-as-character"; historically, his eyes invited possible audience members to purchase theater tickets to the film.[114]

Given Lugosi's success and his connection with the role of *Dracula* on stage and screen, it is quite logical that—in the same way studio publicity materials, newspaper ads, and theater ballyhoos often mentioned *White Zombie*'s lead as "Bela 'Dracula' Lugosi"—the use of Lugosi's eyes became prominent not just in the film *White Zombie* but in various promotional materials for it. In terms of the pressbook, advertisements and movie posters prominently feature Lugosi's eyes, either looking directly at the viewer or at artwork of a female heroine; some even feature beams of light emanating from his eyes.

Beyond movie posters and print advertisements, individual exhibitors often chose to incorporate Lugosi's eyes into their ballyhoo efforts. For example, an issue of *Motion Picture Herald* in September 1932 described what

viewers of Canton, Ohio experienced in the days before *White Zombie* hit the local Loew's Theater: "For two weeks in advance he [Theater manager A. H. Buehrig] used teaser trailers on the screen and paved

Theater ballyhoo at Loew's Theatre in Canton, Ohio. Manager A. H. Buehrig is seen in front of the theater.

the way for a unique lobby display of a head of Lugosi with flashing green eyes."[115]

It is not difficult to see the use of Lugosi's eyes in the film and in publicity materials as one cause of the reactions the film would eventually receive in 1932. The use of Lugosi's eyes in *The Silent Command* (1923) inspired the *New York Times* to consider them an antiquated and less than threatening sign of his character's villainy; a similar reaction would occur with *White Zombie*. Some critics and audience members alike would find the film's use of his eyes more laughable than horrifying.[116] As one 1932 critic wrote, "innumerable closeups of [Lugosi's] eyes either glittering or dilated are tiresome and faintly comic."[117] By contrast, some viewers responded as the filmmaker's intended: Lugosi's eyes, whether in or outside the filmic text, could cause fright and horror.

Critical Reception

If the use and creation of ad materials and exploitation gimmicks played a role in bringing patrons to the theater (or causing them to stay home or see another film), *White Zombie*'s critical reception may also have had an effect.[118] Many of the printed histories about the film refer to the overwhelmingly bad notices the film received upon release.[119] Under scrutiny, however, the 1932 critical reception reveals more complexities than have generally been discussed.

An argument can easily be mounted against much film history for failing to represent accurately the original readers of critical reviews. It is not difficult for even the nonhistorian to realize that the everyday moviegoer did not examine trades and trade reviews. If what *Variety*, *Motion Picture Herald*, *The Film Daily*, and the *Hollywood Reporter* said in their notices had any direct impact in the 1930s, it was not on potential theater patrons, but on theater managers contemplating whether or not to book a particular film or pondering how well it would perform when it arrived via block booking. Even then such reviews would probably have held little sway against box-office reports from other cities which had already shown the film. For example, it was immediately following *White Zombie*'s simultaneous box-office success and critical failure in New York that bookings were secured in Philadelphia and Salt Lake City.

In terms of the *New York Times*, a newspaper commonly cited in film history texts and essays, it is important to note that most moviegoers outside New York would not necessarily have read the *Times* or sought out a review of a particular film in it. Moreover, the timespan between a New York review and a film playing elsewhere in the country could have been weeks or months; thus, even the *Times*' readers outside New York may have been hardly persuaded by reviews that were published weeks before the film was on a local screen. While this is not to undermine the importance of sources like the *Times* to film history, their contemporary readership must be considered by film historians employing them in their research.

As far as everyday theatergoers were concerned, many—including of course children—would not have read any reviews at all. Those who did most likely would have seen notices that appeared either in national magazines or in their local newspapers. In addition, given that a film like *White Zombie* received attention in major publications in August, but did not appear in many cities and towns until later in the autumn or in the winter, the impact of those reviews may well have been as minimal as the *New York Times*'. As a result, local newspaper critiques probably affected theatergoers to a much greater degree.

The influence of any critical review is of course in question. During the early thirties, *The Film Daily* addressed this very issue, claiming:

> Most folks don't care to have their films dissected for them, any more than they would ask a bartender for a recipe with his cocktails. ... Critics do not influence fans materially, as proven by the failure of films which were showered with praise, and the success of many that were slammed.[120]

In keeping with the same idea, *Variety* reported of *White Zombie* and other films playing Pittsburgh in mid–Sep-

An August 9, 1932, industry trade ad that depicts not only the disparity between critical and audience reactions, but also the brief United Artists ad campaign that erupted as a result.

tember 1932 that there was "[p]lenty of indication around here this week that the film public or the critics are screwy. Customers are pooh-poohing films lauded to the skies by the cricks and buying those spanked by the press."[121]

More recently, film theorist Judith Mayne has also noted the disconnect between printed critiques and audiences, reminding us that "film reviews are 'texts,' and as such they cannot be defined as more immediately reflective of the real conditions of spectatorship [than the textual or psychoanalytic analysis of film]."[122]

In the case of *White Zombie*, the critical responses suggest a particularly complex situation. For one, more complimentary reviews appeared than have generally been acknowledged, such as those in the New Orleans *Times-Picayune* and *The Film Daily*, which called the film "cleverly handled" and believed it rated "with the best of this type of film."[123] *Motion Picture Daily* wrote that "[o]ther pictures that fit into the same category [horror] have had considerably more production value, but not the gripping tenseness of this film."[124]

The national media coverage basically shrugged its shoulders at the film; indeed, after *Dracula, Frankenstein,* and *Dr. Jekyll and Mr. Hyde,* fewer reviews of the horror films appeared in national magazines. Those that did generally were less than kind, reflecting the horror film cycle's growing lack of critical acceptance.

For example, *Time* magazine believed that Bela Lugosi in *White Zombie* looked "like a comic imbecile," and that the "acting of everybody in *White Zombie* suggests that there may be some grounds for believing in zombies."[125] *The Commonweal* suggested that "*White Zombie* is interesting only in the measure of its complete failure."[126] And in evaluating the entire year's Hollywood output, *Vanity Fair* even nominated the film for "Worst Movie" of the year.[127]

Fan magazines, yet another source of movie information and film reviews, were easily accessible to viewers in the early 1930s. While it has been established that 65 to 70 million people went to the movies each week during that era, only some five million purchased fan magazines each month.[128] *Photoplay*, apparently the only fan magazine to print reviews of *White Zombie*, sold over half a million copies every 30 days.[129] The September 1932 issue believed, "If you're just a fiend for horror pictures, you'll take [*White Zombie*] and like it."[130]

While that comment reads like an endorsement, albeit a cycle-specific one, the following month the same magazine wittily critiqued the film in a brief review as "utterly fantastic ... and you don't need to bother seeing it." Even if a *Photoplay* reader placed faith in its reviews, such contradictions from issue to issue would have proved confusing.

Yet, crowds—which grew not just due to ads and ballyhoo but also by word of mouth—remained large in some cities. As the *Variety* column on Minneapolis's theater grosses claimed: "Sensational and skillful advertising also is bringing customers for *White Zombie* at the Lyric and is delivering by sending the customers away talking about it."[131]

The disparity between critics' and spectators' responses did not go unnoticed at the time either. "In the case of *White Zombie* at the [New York] Rivoli, the local critics almost without exception gave it a weak rating ... and what happened?" *The Film Daily* of July 30, 1932 asked. It answered its own question by saying:

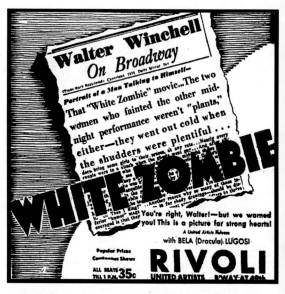

To help heighten the horror element—as well as to highlight positive audience responses since there were generally negative critical reviews in New York City—this August 4, 1932, New York World-Telegram *ad features an excerpt from Walter Winchell's "On Broadway" column.*

They are piling 'em in at every performance. ...and that's what the average newspaper critic so often misses. He is so busy with his own hardboiled, critical mental processes that often he entirely overlooks the reaction of the folks around him ... the folks who make it possible for him to hold his job. And, in this case, we are willing to lay a bet ... that *White Zombie* on the b.o. [box-office] gross will prove certain reviews don't mean a thing.[132]

Others in 1932 believed the critics did have an effect, but in a different manner than would commonly be expected.

For example, *The Hollywood Reporter* of August 1, 1932, ran the column "Pans Make Business for *White Zombie*," which believed "The production has provoked considerable discussion in the press and most of the reviewers have sneered at the theme. However, box-office reaction has been remarkably good and it is felt that this type of criticism actually makes for better patronage."[133] The following month, that hypothesis was believed truthful; *Motion Picture Herald* claimed the film "has served to upset accepted precepts concerning newspaper reviews."[134]

The idea that criticisms spurred audiences to see *White Zombie* even ignited some advertising efforts. At the Crescent Theater in Little Rock, Arkansas, the theater manager—having read disparaging remarks about the film before booking it—ran an ad in the city with the text: "Should we or should we not show *White Zombie*

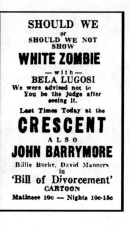

Ad printed in Little Rock's Arkansas Democrat on March 21, 1933.

with Bela Lugosi? We were advised not to. You be the judge after seeing it." His response to the ad "drew well," convincing him it was a "good picture of its kind."[135]

Yet, critical response to *White Zombie* was diverse, with no clear patterns emerging from either geography or venue (e.g., newspapers and trade publications). The reviews ranged from positive to moderate to extremely negative; their effect, however, is unclear. The degree to which audience members were swayed by reviews, saw the film to spite reviewers, or even read them at all is questionable. Nonetheless, no matter how tenuous their impact, the notices were an important backdrop to the film's screenings.

Audience Responses

Observations regarding contemporary spectatorship can be substantiated further by examining particular audiences, critics, and theaters in particular cities, and attempting to understand the interactions between them. For example, *Variety* included reports from the Warner theater in Pittsburgh: "Despite critical panning, horror film packing them, with ballyhoo methods given most of credit."[136]

Yet, several key questions remain. How successful was *White Zombie* at the box office? What impact or effect did it have on viewers? And, can any single response adequately describe overall audience reaction on the film's first release?

The film was indeed more successful than the Halperins could have hoped, but it is also dangerous to assume that hordes of theatergoers swarmed into theaters playing *White Zombie* in *every* city. For instance, the film bombed at the Loew's State in Providence. As one trade publication wrote, "Unless there is a sudden sprint this one looks as though it will catch the booby prize. This, in spite of one of the most remarkable campaigns the town has seen in many a moon."[137] The Krieghbaum Theatre in Rochester, Indiana, also had disastrous results on screening *White Zombie*, and claimed that the film "will hurt your theatre if you run it."[138] After its run had ended at most theaters, industry trade *Harrison's Reports*

dubbed *White Zombie's* overall U.S. box-office results as "Good to Fair."[139]

It is also easy to claim that theater audiences were "scared" by *White Zombie*. After all, this was the "golden age" of the horror film; these movies were new, and thus they held the power to frighten audiences. Yet, close scrutiny of sources of the period reveals a multiplicity of responses in theatergoers beyond mere fright, suggesting something very different than the homogeneous reception attributed by some historians and theorists to the horror film.[140] Reactions to *White Zombie* range from goosebumps to giggles, with no clear patterns—say, geographical or economic—arising from available materials. If anything, such responses show the extreme diversity of the moviegoing public in 1932.

Religion, Gender, Age, and Ethnicity

Audiences of *White Zombie*, as with any film, were not structured or solidified groups. They were random assemblages of persons, fragmentary and temporary coalitions with each member convinced by unique reasons to purchase a theater ticket. It would be incorrect, therefore, to posit assumptions or generalizations about such a group without breaking down the audience into categories. It is necessary then to examine religion, gender, age, and ethnicity in order to further analyze *White Zombie's* viewership, as well as to answer questions raised by film trade publications in 1932.

Religion is one lens through which many in 1932 would, at least partially, have viewed *White Zombie*, though it seems not to have affected them in any major way. On one level, voodoo was certainly a religion in which most viewers in the U.S. would not have participated. Many of them, thanks to the intellectual history discussed in Chapter Two, would have had negative feelings towards voodoo and would probably have viewed it less as a religion than a cult. But that distinction is less important for this analysis since *White Zombie* made little overt exploration of voodooism and even little use of the term "voodoo." Viewers may have even read the story more as one of a Christian (Dr. Bruner) battling the forces of evil (Legendre).

Another somewhat religious aspect of the narrative, the idea of the dead coming back from the grave (a concept not far removed from the resurrection of Jesus Christ in a Christian tradition), held the potential for controversy in some quarters, though it seemingly did not occur. In 1936, the *New York Times* noted the Halperins were tempted to push the envelope of zombies to include religious figures, a notion they knew could cross the line of acceptability. Journalist John T. McManus claimed: "They have their eye on another zombie picture, based on Eugene O'Neill's *Lazarus Laughs*. Lazarus, the brothers insist, was a zombie—a contention that may invoke some ecclesiastical censure."[141]

White Zombie saw no such censure on its original release, though the trade publication *Harrison's Reports* of August 6, 1932 did suggest it might be an insult to Christianity and screening it on Sundays may cause disruptions.[142] Other reviewers did discuss the film's cemetery setting. As the *New York Daily Mirror* noticed, "*White Zombie* approaches the graveyard with no reticence."[143] The *Pittsburgh Post Gazette* said, "Walking cadavers aren't exactly pleasant specimens, but the idea isn't at all bad for this type of film."[144] The reasons why religion proved less important probably stems partially from audiences' religious sensibilities being deadened by both *Dracula* (1931)—certainly a creature resurrected from the grave—and *Murder by the Clock* (1931)—a mystery film in which a dead character is brought back to life. In addition, cemeteries aside, it was more of a catatonic state in which Madge Bellamy's character rested in her grave; she really did not return from the dead.[145] Ultimately, other situational factors, such as gender, had a much greater impact on how audience members reacted to *White Zombie*.

Unfortunately, few exhibitors or critics commented on the ratio of men to women in the audience. Females did go to see the film, as evidenced by Walter Winchell and *The Film Daily*'s comments regarding young women enthralled by screenings of *White Zombie*.[146] Given contemporary studies by the Payne Fund on gender preferences for film genres, however, it would seem safe to say that males outnumbered females in many audiences.

Though no archival materials make clear the age distribution of *White Zombie*'s audiences, certain assumptions can be safely made. For one, the moviegoing public in the early thirties spanned all age groups, including children. The ages of *White Zombie* patrons most likely echoed those of film spectators in general. Critics and reporters used for this study specifically mention adult audience members watching *White Zombie*, and at least one venue—San Francisco's United Artists Theater—screened the film to "adults only" crowds.[147] On August 6, 1932, *Harrison's Reports* made clear that the film was "not suitable for children.[148]

Despite such warnings or prohibitions, the findings of the Payne Fund Studies help prove "youngsters" in the 1930s did often attend movies viewed as dangerous. They determined that many children, particularly males, favored horror and mystery films[149]; in fact, at times some children were definitely not scared by the horror films of the early 1930s. For example, Grace Kingsley wrote in a

January 1932 issue of the *Los Angeles Times* that, when a group of children went to view a "supposedly spine-tingling picture," they "yawned languidly through it all, and didn't see anything so very thrilling in it."[150] One of the few recorded responses of a child to *White Zombie* appeared in a tongue-in-cheek column in *Variety*: "Appearing with [*White Zombie*, during its New York premiere run] is an Olsen and Johnson [comedy film] short, so we took our little nephew. He laughed at *Zombie* but Olsen and Johnson frightened him."[151]

Some adult filmgoers even believed "adults only" shows to be an affront to the moviegoing public. An anonymous "movie fan" wrote in the March 29, 1931, *Chicago Sunday Tribune*, stating that films not being "suitable or fit for children [meant that they are thus] not fit for respectable adults and they [should] stay away from them."[152] At any rate, *White Zombie*, being a horror picture, would have been a popular viewing choice for youngsters, and one that—except for a few cities like San Francisco—was not barred to them.

More than gender and age, however, archival materials suggest that ethnicity played a role in *White Zombie*'s success. In August 1932, *Variety* ran a short blurb indicating that "*Zombie* is drawing strong colored trade at the Rivoli, New York. So much so that a general notice has gone out from United Artists that when the picture plays the south attaches should make a special drive for Negro patronage." The alleged reason? "Among colored people there is a reported superstition about Zombies [*sic*]."[153] Their feeble analysis fails on many levels. For one, it overlooks the fact that other ethnic groups were buying tickets to the Rivoli in equally large or larger numbers.[154] Moreover, while African-Americans in regions like New Orleans may well have been aware of the voodoo religion, the film concentrates on zombies, a creature known in Haitian voodoo cults but apparently not those in the United States of 1932. As Chapter Two noted, the word "Zombi" in the U.S. voodoo tradition referred to a snake god.

It is highly possible that the interest some African-Americans had in *White Zombie* stemmed from one of its cast members, Clarence Muse. Though his part as the carriage driver in the film is a minor one, it does allow Muse, an African-American, to appear in a credible role, instead of having to portray, say, an ignorant laborer or servant. Indeed, it is he who conveys to the viewer important knowledge about zombiism. The very name of Clarence Muse may have drawn many African-American patrons to theaters, as he was by 1932 a well-known and respected actor and songwriter.

While seeing *White Zombie*, many African-Americans would have viewed the film with a different set of background beliefs regarding Haiti than those of white America.[155] While the U.S. press as a whole generally painted a picture of Haitians that evoked little sympathy from readers, the black press of the 1920s did just the opposite. For example, *The Black Dispatch*, an African-American newspaper, printed such articles in the 1920s as "Haitians Great People, Cultured, Want Exploitation to Cease" and "Charge Americans Commit Grave Offenses in Haiti, A.M.E. Minister Returned From Long Stay, Tells of Deplorable Conditions in Negro State." The proliferation of such articles in publications aimed at African-Americans in the decade prior to *White Zombie*'s release would have likely instilled in them a far more sympathetic and understanding view of Haitians than that which white America held in 1932.[156]

If the motivations and viewing experiences of African-Americans regarding *White Zombie* differed from those of other ethnic groups, it becomes important to consider how much their ticket-buying power helped augment the film's success. Despite *Variety*'s mention that UA would encourage exhibitors to elicit African-American patronage, no evidence suggests any theaters did. For example, though the Rivoli Theater of New York City reported strong attendance from blacks, when the film played at a black theater in New York, the Loew's 7th Avenue, ads in the August 31, 1932, *New York Amsterdam News* mentioned only that the film featured "Shudders! Chills! Creeps!" The exhibitor made no apparent attempt at pursuing a campaign slanted towards African-Americans.

Thus, a question remains regarding the extent to which blacks contributed to the success of *White Zombie*, in the South particularly. Unfortunately, though, it is very difficult to determine now how many tickets they purchased. It is just as difficult to hazard a guess as to the number, even by an examination of theaters in areas with substantial African-American populations. Not all theaters allowed African-Americans to purchase tickets, and even when it can be determined which did, segregation of seating meant that an indeterminate limit would have

been imposed on how many blacks could have attended a given showing. Alternatively, certain theaters might have devoted specific screenings to African-American audiences; others may only have allowed black attendance in segregated audiences on particular days of the week.[157]

Given these problems, it is not surprising that blacks-only theaters proved popular with African-Americans, and in 1932 some 445 existed in the United States.[158] Though this number was hardly comparable to the ratio of white theaters to white citizens, the black theaters did provide more comfortable social conditions for African-Americans to enjoy the cinema; this was especially true in the South, where the largest number of black theaters was concentrated.[159] Though black newspapers (where they existed) and promotions like movie window cards in store windows helped promote films at such theaters, white newspapers rarely took advertisements for them. As a result, it is difficult even to establish which black theaters in given cities may have exhibited *White Zombie*, and in cases where a theater did screen the film, it is difficult to ascertain how many tickets were sold.[160] Indeed, for many cities it is far from easy to determine 1932 black population statistics, let alone the number of seats a black theater offered or, more specifically, the number of African-Americans attending a theater in a given week.[161]

A case in point is the Broadway theater in Washington, D.C. Ads appeared for *White Zombie* in *The Afro-American* newspaper, but no reviews of the film were published and no box-office reports were sent to industry trade publications.[162] It is thus impossible to know whether or not the film proved successful. *White Zombie* did not rate a holdover, but the initial ads for its two-day engagement listed the upcoming three films of the same week; the lack of a more lengthy stay does not then suggest failure. The screening of

Ad printed in the Afro-American *newspaper on October 1, 1932.*

the film in early October—prior to many first-run houses on the West Coast booking the film, but still two months after a white theater in the same city showed it—seems difficult to explain. Perhaps the fact that ads proclaimed the Broadway to be a Lichtman theater—bearing as it did the same last name as Al Lichtman, in charge of bookings at United Artists—had some effect. Regardless, the Broadway screening is an example of the difficulties in charting the success of 1930s Hollywood films among black audiences.

It is almost impossible then to know how many tickets to *White Zombie* were purchased by African-Americans, whether at racially mixed venues or blacks-only theaters. Archivally, nothing substantive seems to exist beyond the aforementioned blurb in *Variety* which touted viewer interest among African-Americans. At any rate, little more than speculation can contribute to this discussion further.

If categories associated with *White Zombie* viewers like gender, age, and ethnicity offer a modicum of insight into its spectatorship, this analysis does not suggest generalities regarding, say, children who saw the film, or how African-Americans responded to the film and why. While being a member of one of these categories may have helped frame the lens through which a viewer saw *White Zombie*, it does not mean that, say, all women reacted to *White Zombie* in the same way. If anything, examining these categories of viewers reiterates the diversity of responses to the film, and makes clear that a reaction to a film does not occur as a result of a single factor. A wide variety of factors may help sculpt a viewer's reception of a film, including current events and geography.

Investigation of Key Cities

To better understand the various ways theatergoers responded to *White Zombie*, an investigation of key cities in which it was screened becomes important. Local critiques in the newspaper, the mode and tone of advertising, publicity schemes at the theater itself, and audience reactions—as well as any important local events occurring during *White Zombie*'s run—all of this data helps build an idea of how the film was received in a given city. Examining numerous cities then allows a more thorough picture to develop, displaying many different responses to the film and the lack of a uniform pattern of geographical reception. At the same time, this investigation does offer insight into localized influences that may have affected spectatorship in a given city.

Cities and theaters at which *White Zombie* played during its first release followed the general policies set forth by Al Lichtman, key strategist of United Artists'

distribution plan. His belief was that first-run films should play only one, and only occasionally more than one, "first-class" theater in any major city. Advertisements for such films should indicate that the film would not be shown again subsequently in the same city for less than a first-run admission price. Lichtman believed this would help both distributors and theater owners in a financial sense, including smaller theater owners, who could choose films not already, in his words, "run to death."[163]

This strategy did evoke strong criticism from some quarters, however. For example, *Harrison's Reports* suggested that if "United Artists were to use their mental energies toward producing entertaining pictures it would not be necessary for them to seek an increase of revenue by exotic selling schemes."[164] At any rate, while prices would of course vary in different cities, *White Zombie*—like many UA-distributed films of the time—would appear at only one theater in many large, major cities at first-run ticket costs. Despite Lichtman's plan, though, at times *White Zombie* quickly made its way to second-run theaters in those same cities at reduced prices.

Most theaters in cities, whether screening *White Zombie* on a first-run basis or not, employed outlandish publicity techniques to attract attention to the film. The financial gain aside, the efforts themselves varied from city to city, again showing little or no uniformity along geographical lines. The often creative efforts of theater managers meant that these extratextual devices—experienced by audiences prior to seeing the film and thus shaping their initial perceptions of the narrative—could differ from viewer to viewer and certainly city to city.

For example, manager Wally Caldwell of the Loew's Theater in Toledo concocted two major stunts, chronicled in an August 1932 *Motion Picture Herald*.[165] One was a drawing contest built around Lugosi, which was tied in with a local newspaper. According to the *Herald*, "Hundreds of replies were received by the stunt editor for the paper and broke all time records." Caldwell's second major scheme was a "mysterious photographer" idea. A photographer snapped shots of unknowing citizens, with the pictures then appearing in the town newspaper "with the offer of a guest ticket to [the] picture if they would call at the newspaper office."

Motion Picture Herald also listed the more standard aspects of Caldwell's campaign, which included:

> ...the placarding of 26 parking lots, garages and parking zones with "Park Here" half-sheets, the distribution of 5,000 9 × 12 heralds [small promotional posters] in selected residential neighborhoods, stuffing of 1,000 heralds in customer's packages at a large market, wrapping of 500 heralds in laundry bundles, the pinning of several hundred heralds to packages in dry cleaners' establishments, the posting of 15 special one-sheets in selected

The first published White Zombie *ad of any note, printed in* Variety *on July 26, 1932.*

empty stores, posting of 200 heralds at prominent corners....[166]

As with his promotions for other films, Caldwell also pursued a vigorous campaign of newspaper advertisements.

For theater managers of houses owned by Harry Arthur in New Haven, Hartford, Bridgeport, Springfield, and Worcester, Hal Horne, director of UA's exploitation department, outlined special promotional plans similar to those used for the New York City premiere.[167] The September 6, 1932 *Variety* detailed these ideas, which included "zombies" again walking the streets. They wore no signs or advertisements, but merely attempted to draw crowds to the theater.[168]

On October 4, *Variety* detailed another scheme, one used by manager Edgar Hart of Spokane's Orpheum Theater. Carrying a police permit, a "blonde girl" with no explanatory placard wandered the streets aimlessly. She attracted a tremendous amount of attention, with

local newspapers printing the explanation for curious readers.[169] Her walk and blank stare had imitated the character Madeline from *White Zombie*.

The exterior of a Cincinnati United Artists theater received such a great *White Zombie* makeover that its manager gave one look and told its designers, "My God, that thing will scare everybody away from the theater!" Along with the decor ballyhoo, one stunt included a casket, skeleton, and some electrical devices. A loudspeaker was placed in the coffin, with its wire taken through a hole in the floor and into the cellar. Designers also attached an "invisible" string to the skeleton's jaw. A young woman in the cellar gave the bony publicity machine a voice by speaking into the loudspeaker's microphone and pulling the string to make its mouth move.[170]

The skeleton at the Cincinnati theater wasn't a fake; it was on loan from a local doctor. The skull featured three bullet holes inflicted by a firing squad in World War I. A man planted by the theater told passersby of the skeleton's real-life execution. When a good-sized crowd

Coffin exploitation outside a 1932 theater, probably the Warner Brothers' Appleton in Appleton, Wisconsin.

had gathered, the woman in the cellar interrupted with the following whispered words (a slight variation on a suggested "catchline" in the pressbook): "Look around you, do your friends act queerly—strangely? They may be zombies—living, breathing, walking under the spell of the master of the living dead." The speech ended with a scream and an announcement of the film. "Unusual Times demand unusual pictures," she concluded. "See this live, weird, strangest of all love stories."[171]

Yet, the *Motion Picture Herald* of November 5, 1932, detailed perhaps the most intriguing free publicity garnered by any theater. The Warners Theater of Pittsburgh landed front-page attention in city newspapers by another use of a coffin. This time, however, the box in question bounced out of the back of a truck on Penn Avenue. The result brought police, who rushed it to station No. 6 in order to avoid the forming crowd. In it, they dis-

covered a "corpse" that later moved; it was actually a man named Bill Sloan. After he informed cops it was a press agent stunt for *White Zombie*, they quickly arrested him. As the trade mentioned, "…even though this coffin gag has been described as gruesome exploitation by many in our unusual business, both public and newspapers appear to regard the stunt with interest, morbid or otherwise."[172]

With regard to U.S. theaters that played *White Zombie* in 1932, it is important to remember that other events outside the theater's home city may also have colored the perceptions of theatergoers. For example, *White Zombie's* popularity quickly spawned at least one cultural offspring. Encountering apparently no copyright trouble, band leader Joel Shaw and His Orchestra (featuring Mike Kardos and Mike Doty) recorded the instrumental song "White Zombie" for Crown Records in New York City in October, 1932. The big band tune was a well-arranged novelty, featuring a scary laugh at both its beginning and end.[173] The 78 rpm record may well have been available to potential moviegoers by the time *White Zombie* screenings occurred in major cities like San Francisco.

Walter Futter recorded ten topics from his *Curiosities* short film series onto 15-minute electrical transcriptions, for broadcast over a national radio hookup. *Motion Picture Daily* announced the series on July 19, 1932.[174] Given the fact that two of Futter's *Curiosities* film shorts of 1931 dealt with zombies and that *White Zombie* was such a hit in New York City at its premiere only days later, it is highly likely that the radio series spoke about zombies.[175] It would have aided at least some listeners in learning what a zombie was, and perhaps peppered them with impressions on the subject before they saw *White Zombie* at a theater.

The general backdrop of the Great Depression must also be remembered when investigating cities where the film appeared on theater screens. Indeed, the timeline of 1932 suggests that current events too could directly impact the viewing process of *White Zombie*. For example, in August 1932, viewers in Washington, D.C., watched the film as a group of unhappy veterans in the Bonus Army were marching on the U.S. Capitol Building. Similarly, on a given November 1932 evening, a viewer in Seattle would have heard presidential election returns on a theater radio the same evening as they saw the film.

In a more direct sense, viewers in Los Angeles who saw the film in November may not have read the trade reviews or newspapers of other cities, but some most likely read the *Los Angeles Times*. The *Times* had printed poor reviews of *White Zombie* weeks before it opened in Los Angeles, as well as when it finally did. Factors like repeatedly poor newspaper notices were present in the minds of at least some viewers in their respective cities. As a result, the investigation of specific cities that follows appears chronologically, beginning with the city of the film's premiere. Subsequent cities appear with regard to the screening dates of the film, with some cities grouped under a single heading when screening dates coincided.

The choice of cities in this study results from several considerations. For one, cities reflect various geographical regions of the United States. Major cities in those regions were selected, over perhaps smaller or more rural towns, because only they could provide the data that this study hoped to find. In addition, small town newspapers often did not print critical reviews, which both eliminates the possibility of finding a contemporary critique and of discovering audience responses recorded in such reviews. Although *Motion Picture Herald* published small town theater manager quotations about how their audiences reacted to given films, the column—entitled "What the Picture Did For Me"—did not begin until mid–December 1932. As a result, the *Herald* published only three small town reports on *White Zombie*.[176]

Metropolitan cities were thus necessary for the following study; the choice of specific cities occurred due to the availability of information on *White Zombie*'s screenings. Preference was given to those cities whose newspapers printed reviews, and even more to those newspaper reviews which remarked not only on the aesthetic qualities of the film, but also on local audience reactions. Some not only fulfilled the desire for these data, but were also augmented with information from theater reports published in industry trades like *Motion Picture Herald* and *Variety*.

When possible, theater grosses for *White Zombie* and its thirties' horror cycle predecessors—*Dracula, Frankenstein, Dr. Jekyll and Mr. Hyde*, and *Murders in the Rue Morgue*—are provided for given cities in this analysis. It is important to consider these amounts only to build a picture of the film's run in a given city, for comparative purposes. In other words, even if a theater gross for *Dracula* in a city was larger than the gross for *White Zombie* in the same city, that really means little. *Dracula* could have been a higher-priced rental for the theater in question, or that theater may have seated more persons at different prices than the venue screening *White Zombie*. What this could mean is that in this example *White Zombie* netted more profit than *Dracula*, even if its theater gross was less.

Another area which needs to be considered is the ownership of theaters. From the cities investigated in this chapter—as well as many others examined in lesser detail in Appendix H—two major points emerge. One is the importance of chain theaters to *White Zombie*'s distribution; specifically, these were Loew's, Publix, and United Artists. Secondly, independent exhibitors played a less

critical but still important role in screening *White Zombie* in the U.S., especially in smaller towns.

As mentioned previously, the chosen cities in this chapter's analysis are presented in the chronological order of their 1932 playdates, with some cities grouped because of screenings on the same (or approximately the same) date. Part of the discussion of timelines mentions whether *White Zombie* had a one-week run at a given theater or rated a holdover of two or more weeks. As a final point of consideration, it's important to remember that holdovers were more rare in the 1930s than later in the 20th century; a one-week run did not necessarily signal a film's lack of success at a given theater.

New York City

Though initially scheduled for August 4, 1932, at New York City's Rialto Theater, *White Zombie*'s premiere came one week earlier at 9:30 A.M. on July 28 at the nearby Rivoli Theater.[177] The date was announced only two days prior in industry trades.[178] Publix, the chain

An ad promoting the film's premiere, published in the New York World-Telegram *of July 27, 1932.*

that owned the Rivoli, had planned on closing the theater in mid–July due to what *Motion Picture Daily* called
a "declared product shortage."[179] They changed their
minds, and screened *Aren't We All* and then *Igloo* for the
second half of the month. The demand for more films
then helped create a need for *White Zombie*. Ticket prices
at the 2,200-seat theater ranged from 40 cents to $1.10.[180]

New York City critics ravaged the film immediately
after its opening. The *New York Times* review dismissed
the movie entirely, joking that "[t]he screen, shuddering
slightly, can go on; it can forget, it can be a Zombie [*sic*],
too."[181] For the *New York Herald Tribune*, "...the new
melodrama is clumsily wrought and unhappily acted."[182]
The New York *Daily Mirror* wrote, "[t]he acting of the
principal players is uniformly terrible."[183] The *New York
World-Telegram* was even harsher, announcing that
"[t]here have been worse pictures shown in this town
than *White Zombie* at the Rivoli. Yet at the moment I can
think of few films so nicely compounded of tedium and
banality in equal parts."[184] For the *New York Evening
Post*, "...it overreaches the mark all along the line and resolves into an unintentional and often hilarious comedy."[185] Even Irene Thirer in the New York *Daily News*,
who seemingly tried to be somewhat kind to the film,
claimed, "[m]any fantastic and eerie scenes are evolved,
but most of them border on the ludicrous."[186]

Nonetheless, critics were not foremost in the Rivoli
Theater's box-office strategy. In an effort to bolster public interest, the theater employed—apparently with the
help of United Artists' Hal Horne—a tremendous exploitation campaign, including an elaborate theater front
and a sidewalk show.[187] "The fun outside the theatre almost equals the fun within," the *Daily Mirror* wrote on
July 29.[188] As reported in an August 1, 1932 issue of *The
Film Daily*, the outdoor exploitation featured:

> ...three mechanical men in full dress [who] work out
> front almost continuously. They go through slow mo-
> tion with their wax features and mechanical movements,
> getting over the theme of "suspended animation" of the
> story. As they disappear slowly inside the lobby one after
> another, the crowds automatically are lured right to the
> cashier's window. At periodic intervals, the "big show" is
> put on. A narrow stage has been built above the marquee.
> Nine figures slowly troop out, exact replicas of the prin-
> cipal characters in *White Zombie*. ... They go through
> several short scenes from the picture, while mobs liter-
> ally jam Broadway. In addition to all this there is a "magic
> illusion" on the side of the theater, done with mirrors, that
> has the sidewalk blocked from morn till night.[189]

The Rivoli's "big show" for *White Zombie* surpassed even
its exploitation for *Dr. Jekyll and Mr. Hyde*, which reigned
supreme for five weeks at the Rivoli during January and
February 1932.

An ad from White Zombie's *first week in New York City, published
in the* New York World-Telegram *on August 1, 1932.*

In *The 1933 Film Daily Yearbook of Motion Pictures*,
Hal Horne added even further detail to the tales of the
White Zombie ballyhoo effort in New York City:

> The past history of some of the members of the [outdoor
> Rivoli] cast hit a real story of heart-break since several
> of them were actors and actresses out-of-work who had
> seen better days, and in fact the actor impersonating Bela
> Lugosi was formerly a leading man in his own right on
> Broadway. The doll-like figures of the girls were dressed
> in white flowing robes and the men looked just as if they
> had been dug up from the ground with wooden splints
> on their legs and battered facial expressions that drew the
> interested gaze of many bystanders. Crowds gathered all
> day, lured there not only by the drama enacted above the
> theater front but by the *White Zombie* sound effect record
> which included the screeches of vultures, the grinding of
> the sugar mill and beating of the tom-toms, and other
> nerve-wracking sounds.[190]

Later, the New Orleans *Times-Picayune* recounted other
information about the film's New York premiere in an
article titled "Gris-Gris and *Abie's Irish Rose*":

> [The day after *White Zombie* opened] critics of every
> paper in town panned it unmercifully, going out of their
> way to say mean things about the film and going to their
> dictionaries to dig up unpleasant adjectives about Bela

Tremendous two-page ad, published in the August 1, 1932, Motion Picture Daily. *Due to the deterioration of the original, much reconstruction has been performed on the lettering of this image.*

Lugosi, Victor Halperin, the director, Madge Bellamy, the undead girl who couldn't fool an old *Dracula* fan, and even Pete Clark, recording engineer, although we can't remember what it was one of them said concerning Pete other than that it was not a Rotarian sentiment. The manager of the theater decided to fire the staff, shut up shop, and beat it, but suddenly the staff got so busy it couldn't be fired. What's more, it kept busy. The box office cash register began ringing so fast it burned out its bearings and the ticket girls worked their makeup off.[191]

Their article attributed *White Zombie*'s success to the fact that "somebody had gone out and told somebody else how the shivers ran down his spine, and the word circulated around until, almost overnight, a flop had become a big hit...." The Rivoli theater manager himself had to admit *White Zombie*'s success had "been a surprise."[192]

Phil M. Daly's article in *The Film Daily* offered even another version of the film's New York premiere, describing the morning of July 29, 1932 as follows:

At nine o'clock there was a line formed at the Rivoli ... we kept checking every two hours throughout the day ... they were piling 'em in. We queried ten patrons right after they bought their tickets as to what induced them to buy ... three had been influenced by the supernatural in the front billing ... one by Bela Lugosi's name ... two by the magic illusion ballyhoo out front ... two by newspaper advertisement ... two by word of mouth ... and the pix had only opened the day before! Here were ten cash customers picked at random ... who evidently didn't read newspaper reviews, or if they did, were not influenced adversely by them. [All ellipses exist in the author's original.][193]

In his trade column, Daly also described an audience reaction of two young women on opening day:

When we caught the picture ... two girls sat alongside us ... they were intelligent girls as their whispered remarks proved ... "What a macabre situation" ... "But it's intriguing" ... said the other ... "It's enthralling" replied the first ... now, girls who talk like that are not dumb ... they know what they like ... and so these two sat bent forward with taut nerves ... and when it was all over ... they relaxed with sighs of complete satisfaction ... they had been thoroughly entertained.[194]

Daly's example illustrates then that *White Zombie* not only had the power to scare some audience members, but that its scares could translate into entertainment and enjoyment.

The film's Broadway success even attracted the attention of Walter Winchell, who discussed other audience responses in his New York *Daily Mirror* column of August 3, 1932:

That *White Zombie* movie is too spooky ... the two women who fainted at the other midnight performance weren't "plants" either—they went out cold when the shudders were plentiful.... This type of flicker does bring some girls to their senses, at any rate.... Nearly every couple were in a clinch when the ghosts went gay.... And, after all, most of the lads who take their dolls to the midnight shows do not always go just to see the picture.

His notice confirms Phil M. Daly's; some 1932 viewers were genuinely frightened by the film, while others used the film as a backdrop for petting.

Playing off the film's success and the names of successful Broadway producers George White and Earl Carroll, journalist Jack Osterman kidded "Now that White has a zombie, we suppose Carroll will put one in his show."[195] Additionally, he joked that "there are enough half dead people walking up and down Broadway without going to see *White Zombie*."[196]

The film's triumph with ticket sales continued. Hal Horne claimed that "By actual clocking during one noon hour, more than 14,608 people stopped to witness the playlet being put on for their benefit."[197] Among those high numbers on at least one afternoon were Victor and Edward Halperin. The success of the premiere meant

A photograph taken during the film's first few days at the Rivoli Theater in New York City.

that they were staying in New York City for a short time that August before rushing to Hollywood.[198]

Unfortunately, high numbers of ticket buyers didn't last during the film's entire run. *White Zombie* found unexpected success during its first week at the Rivoli (grossing $25,500; considerably more than the theater had grossed in weeks), and credible success in its second week (grossing $15,000); however, business dropped off considerably by the third.[199] The Rivoli theater manager even referred to grosses of $8,000 for *White Zombie*'s final days at the venue as "sickly."[200] It is difficult to account for the immense dropoff; *Dr. X*, which had premiered during *White Zombie*'s second week and grossed $42,000 over seven days, may have acted as competition for moviegoers seeking horror.[201]

Those numbers for *White Zombie*'s three weeks can

be placed in better perspective by comparing them to other horror film openings in New York. For example, in one week at the Roxy *Dracula* grossed $112,000, though that figure was gained in part because of Broadway-priced movie tickets.[202] Months later at the Mayfair, *Frankenstein* took $53,800 its first week, $42,500 its second, and $28,000 its third.[203] And *Dr. Jekyll and Mr. Hyde* played an amazing five weeks at the Rivoli at ticket prices essentially the same as those for *White Zombie*; its overall gross was an astounding $167,800, with $67,100 of that amount coming in the first seven days.[204]

After limited ticket sales in week three, *White Zombie* was replaced at the Rivoli by *Love Me Tonight*. The nearby Palace Theater then screened *White Zombie* for one week along with a stage show featuring Arthur Tracy. Ticket prices at the Palace ranged from 30 cents to a dollar as compared to the Rivoli's 40 cents to $1.10. Initial reports to trades were that the show wasn't "drawing much," and that only a "deprecating" $12,800 gross was expected.[205] By the week's end on August 26, the film had grossed a fair $18,000, perhaps aided by the publicity stir generated by the earlier screenings at the Rivoli.[206]

In the weeks immediately following *White Zombie*'s premiere, United Artists remembered the Rivoli Theater in particular. On August 30, *Motion Picture Daily* announced UA's intentions to buy the theater from Publix. Takeover was planned on September 15, 1932.[207] UA had started a theater chain expansion program in February 1932[208]; however, it seems more than coincidental that they honed in on the Rivoli right after *White Zombie*'s premiere. Perhaps the successful ballyhoo of the film helped in part to convince them to acquire the theater.

Theater purchases aside, *White Zombie* was a hit in New York City in three major ways. For one, its first two weeks at the Rivoli were financially quite successful. Secondly, the film received more press than the average independent film on its opening. Thirdly and most importantly, given that expectations for *White Zombie*'s box-office appeal were initially low, its surprise success and well-discussed publicity schemes helped secure future theatrical bookings, particularly with independent exhibitors across the U.S.

Washington, D.C., Baltimore, and Kansas City

While New York City acted as the site of *White Zombie*'s premiere on July 28, 1932, the film opened in at least three other U.S. cities the same weekend: Washington, D.C., Baltimore, and Kansas City. *White Zombie*'s screening in the U.S. capital was quite successful, though its first week was far more successful than weeks two and three. Theaters in Baltimore and Kansas City showed *White Zombie* only for a single week each, but both made credible ticket sales.

Newspaper ads during the film's Washington, D.C., run asked, "What does a Man want in a Woman ... IS IT HER BODY OR HER SOUL?"[209] A particularly interesting joint promotion of the Loew's Fox and *Washington Post* offered free pairs of tickets for *White Zombie*. Readers of the paper July 26–29, 1932, could answer ten questions about the *Post*'s advertisers, ranging from

After White Zombie's *New York premiere, United Artists quickly seized the moment and promoted the film's box-office success to those in the film industry. Ad printed in the August 2, 1932, issue of* Variety.

"Where is the Arizona Hotel?" and "Who offers Plymouth 1932 sedan[s] for $525?" to even "Who offers [a] complete funeral for $75?" Along with mailing in their answers, readers had to "write not more than 25 words telling WHY YOU PREFER *Post* Want-Ads either as a reader or a user." The "best 15 complete answers each day" won two "Guest Tickets" for the Loew's Fox, which seated 3,434 at ticket prices of 15 to 60 cents.[210]

On July 29, 1932, the last day of the *Post* free ticket contest, a brief radio version of *White Zombie* was heard over the local airwaves. At 8:30 P.M. EST, the Northern Dramatic Company presented a 15-minute audio

FIND THE ANSWER**S**
To Win
a Pair of Guest Tickets to

Loew's FOX Theater

ZOMBIISM...Living Death
...A Superstition of Haiti...
Robs the Grave! Makes Liv-
ing Soulless Slaves of the
Dead!

**A PICTURE FOR
STRONG HEARTS!**

"WHITE ZOMBIE"

BELA *(Dracula)* LUGOSI   THE STAGE—"CHAINS"
                              LOEW VAUDEVILLE REVUE

HOW TO WIN THE TICKETS

Listed below will be found ten questions—the answers of
which will be found in The Post Want-Ads in these pages.
A simple, profitable way to read the Want-Ads, and at the
same time possibly earn a pair of guest tickets to see "White
Zombie" at Loew's Fox beginning next Friday.

All you have to do is to find the advertisements which answer the
questions. Easy, isn't it? List your solutions on one side of the paper,
then write not more than 25 words telling WHY YOU PREFER Post
Want-Ads either as a reader or a user. Mail or bring to The Post
Theater Contest Manager, Want Ad Department. Best 15 complete
answers each day will receive one pair of Guest Tickets to Loew's Fox
Theater. Watch this space tomorrow for more questions.

THE 10 QUESTIONS:

1—Who advertises a modern home for $3,750 on convenient terms?
2—What apartment house bears the name of a famous U. S. Government
    Hospital?
3—What does F. M. Doyle advertise?
4—What is Atlantic 4939 offering?
5—What was lost in taxi Sunday?
6—Where is experienced rug salesman needed?
7—Where can you buy 2½-karat "perfect" diamond for $450?
8—What is color of lost police dog?
9—Where can you buy 1931 Ford delivery truck in best of condition for $345
    on easy terms?
10—Where is beautifully furnished private home for lease?

It Will Be Impossible to Answer Personal or Telephone Calls
About This Contest. All Necessary Information Is Plainly Printed.

TICKETS WILL BE MAILED THE WINNERS

THE WASHINGTON POST
"CLASSIFIED ADS BRING RESULTS"

Published in the Washington Post *on July 26, 1932, this ad offered
free pairs of tickets to newspaper readers who answered a ten-ques-
tion quiz.*

dramatization of the film over Washington station
WOL. Charles C. Gillman portrayed Murder, and "Miss
Fritz Fiery" played Madeline. Ronald Dawson directed
the short production, whose dialogue continuity came

directly from the film.[211] That same day, *White Zombie*
opened in Washington, D.C., appearing with a "Loew
Vaudeville Revue" featuring Gold and Raye, Paul Mall,
"Sun Kissed Beauties," and others.

Along with the radio show and an impressive array
of ads for the film, Washington newspapers reviewed the
film in detail. In the July 30, 1932, *Washington Post*, critic
Nelson B. Bell believed that it would "strike many as
being more grotesque than gripping.[212] Moreover, he
spoke of the film's effect on the opening day's audience:
"If your hair is not turning gray rapidly enough as it is,
your sleeping hours are not sufficiently harassed by nightmares and gooseflesh is a luxury to which you are not ac-
customed, this is the sort of thing you will like."

The Washington *Evening Star* of July 30, 1932, preferred the accompanying stage show, calling *White Zombie* "a confused, naive little sketch of what seems to be
Haiti's favorite parlor game, this is not the sort of thing
advised by this department—and which therefore the
public will probably flock to." For its critic, the film was
"a gruesome fable, blessed with dozens of Frankensteins
on the loose, this may be one of the sadder film recre-
ations of the year. A second-rate cast, indulging in second and third rate acting, includes Bela 'Dracula' Lugosi,
who does little toward lightening the proceedings—and
you are apt to agree with one of the characters, who says
half way through it, 'This is all very confusing—I don't
know what it is all about.'"[213]

The film managed to stay three weeks in the city,
with its first week grossing $17,500; over a year before,
Dracula grossed $18,000 in its week at Washington's Ri-
alto Theater.[214] The Fox theater manager later claimed
that *White Zombie* "started okay" but its box-office quickly
"eased off plenty."[215] While that may have been the case,
it does not seem that local problems were to blame. The
Bonus Army of some 15,000 World War I veterans in-
vaded the city that May demanding immediate payments
of a financial "bonus" not due to them until 1945. The
group camped out in the nation's capital throughout the
summer, but the government still did not grant their
wishes. On July 28, 1932, the situation culminated in
President Hoover ordering General Douglas MacArthur
to break up their camp; infantry, cavalry, tanks, and tear
gas helped bring a turbulent end to the Bonus Army.[216]
The conclusion had come just as *White Zombie* opened in
the city, which created what *Variety* called an "[e]xcite-
ment incident" that even brought many sightseers to
town."[217] Many theaters had problems with attendance
during those days, but the Fox did not believe they
suffered any on *White Zombie* from the Bonus Army situation.[218]

Business for *White Zombie* in nearby Baltimore, which
began on July 29, 1932, was apparently not hindered by

Advertisement from the July 1, 1932, Baltimore Sun.

ings to problems with the projectionists' union. Most notably, screenings of *Frankenstein* in December 1931 ran into major problems with local censors, which eventuated in the governor of Kansas firing the head of the state's film censor board.[223]

Promotional advertisements in the July 28, 1932, *Kansas City Star* used leftover artwork of Lugosi from ads for *Murders in the Rue Morgue* (1932), and offered quotations like "Beware of the Zombies!" Film announcements in the newspaper told readers that "Bela Lugosi once more does his vampire act."[224] By the next day, ads were using art from the *White Zombie* pressbook and including definitions of zombiism.

As for describing *White Zombie* ballyhoo efforts, the Loew's Midland sent little information to industry trades. *Motion Picture Daily* did report that theater manager John McManus was "distributing 'faint checks'" to terrified theatergoers, which apparently were vouchers for refunds or a new ticket for those who admitted they were scared. "None of the checks has been cashed, however, says McManus, for the few frightened folks who have dashed from the theater thinking the zombies were after them have kept on running."[225] Interest in faint checks almost certainly didn't match the events sponsored by two competing theaters that same week. Three goats were milked on stage for prizes at one theater, while another featured a male bathing beauty contest.[226]

The *Kansas City Star* review uses puns and jokes to convey its point about the *White Zombie*:

> Here is a picture that should knock you for a ghoul. ... The dialogue does no credit even to dead men and the ending suggests that the scenario writer had joined the dear departed before he had put his world affairs, including this script, in good order. ... In about half this picture [Victor Halperin] employs his old silent technique most effectively. However, what the picture gains by reviving silent directorial methods it loses by resurrecting silent actors who long since have gone to their rewards.[227]

The critic ended his review with the line, "[y]ou need more than a makeup kit to produce a *Frankenstein*." Many moviegoers in Kansas City may well have agreed, as the

Bonus Army problems either. The film played one week in the city; though holdovers were rare, both *Frankenstein* and *Dr. Jekyll and Mr. Hyde* had both played two-week runs there.[219] The Loew's Stanley booked *White Zombie* with a ZaSu Pitts–Thelma Todd comedy and a Mickey Mouse cartoon. Publicity in the July 31, 1932, *Baltimore Sun* claimed: "As natives of various localities believe in putting 'spells' on their enemies, the jungle peasants of Haiti and the West Indies pray to the Green Serpent to protect them from zombies. It is around this Voodoo clan that the story of *White Zombie* ... is written."[220] The next day, newspaper ads claimed, "NOW Baltimore Is Gasping—At the Weird Daring of This Strange Romance."[221]

White Zombie also opened in Kansas City on July 29, 1932, playing at the Loew's Midland with the comedy short *Wild Babies*, a Mickey Mouse cartoon, and a Metrotonews newsreel. The theater seated 4,000 moviegoers at ticket prices of 25, 35, and 40 cents. The same week, bandleader Ted Lewis and his orchestra were garnering much more attention at the Mainstreet Theater, appearing onstage with the film *Molly Louvain*.[222]

Though there is no indication *White Zombie* was directly harmed, various controversies about film exhibition did arise in Kansas City throughout 1932, ranging from theater violations of Blue Laws barring Sunday show-

film garnered only a "fair $14,000."[228] Earlier, *Dracula* grossed $21,000 at Kansas City's Mainstreet Theater, *Frankenstein* made $22,500 at the Mainstreet , and *Murders in the Rue Morgue* took $18,000 at the same theater.[229] *Dr. Jekyll and Mr. Hyde* had made a little less at

Left: *An ad from the July 28, 1932,* Kansas City Star *promoting* White Zombie'*s appearance at the Loew's Midland. Bizarre is the fact that the artwork of actor Bela Lugosi is not from* White Zombie, *but from Universal Studios'* Murders in the Rue Morgue *(1932), which had played in Kansas City earlier in 1932.* Above: *Ad promoting* White Zombie'*s first day at the Loew's State in St. Louis, published in the* St. Louis Post-Dispatch *of August 5, 1932.*

the Newman Theater, grossing $16,250 for a one-week run.[230] Perhaps many ticket buyers during the week of *White Zombie*'s run were lured to the city's Fox Midwest, which had created much interest by adding vaudeville to its program in late July.[231]

ST. LOUIS, HOUSTON, ROCHESTER AND BOSTON

On August 5, 1932, seven days after *White Zombie*'s New York premiere, the film opened in St. Louis at the Loew's State theater, which seated 3,000 at ticket prices of 25 to 55 cents.[232] Ads described the film as: "A bride—stolen from the grave. This fiend wanted love—but found only a soulless spectre!"[233] A picture of *White Zombie* character Chauvin accompanied the simple definition, "'Zombies' are *Living Dead!*" For opening day, newspaper ads featured a picture of Lugosi with an artist's arrow pointed to his hands; text inside the arrow read, "Beware the sign of the zombie!"[234]

The theater did not report particular ballyhoo efforts to the trade, perhaps because they seemingly caused an odd set of events in the city. In the August 27, 1932, *Motion Picture Daily*, the trade did speak about a ban on live burials: "Following a conference between City Health Commissioner Max C. Starkloff and Chief of Police Joseph A. Gark, it was announced that police would not permit any more persons to be 'buried alive' for exhibition purposes."[235] The reason was presumably *White Zombie.*

Despite the theater's publicity schemes, the *St. Louis Post-Dispatch* was less than impressed with *White Zombie*. Their review on August 7, 1932, asked:

> Have you got a little Zowie in your home? Pretty handy things to have around, these zowies, although they can be a trifle dangerous at times, and, always, rather ghost-like as you can see by visiting Loew's [State] this week where *White Zowie*—or maybe its *White Zombie*—is on display. This is a horror fillum [sic] which raises the Dracula-Frankenstein-Mr. Hyde trio into a quartette.... The play is replete with busted coffins but the story is as full of holes as the yarning [sic] graveyards which dot every few feet of film.

The film played one week at St. Louis' State theater, whose theater manager described its $10,000

box-office return as "only [a] fair summer draw."[236] Most of the city's business went instead to *Miss Pinkerton* at the city's Ambassador Theater and *Passport to Hell* at the Fox Theater.[237]

White Zombie also started in Houston on the same day, playing one week at the Loew's "cool house of hits"; the comedy short *Boy Friend* was also on the same bill. The August 4, 1932, *Houston Post* featured one major still from the film, oddly choosing a relaxed, production shot of Lugosi lighting a cigar as representative of the "weird feature," with its caption promising a "story as colorful and fantastic as any Poe ever dreamed." Ads claimed, "He'll scare you, but it will be a pleasant scare. The love-maddened *Dracula* and the fiendish *Frankenstein* are angels compared to this weird being."[238]

To help draw crowds, the theater hired a horse-drawn carriage similar to the one seen in the first reel of *White Zombie*. The carriage driver was dressed like Clarence Muse's character, with two former stock players in the carriage itself; a sign on the side of the carriage read "*Not Dead—Not Alive*—WHITE ZOMBIES [sic] at LOEW'S." The stunt took place at night, with green rays from a battery lamp hitting the driver and passengers. To complete the eerie effect, the cab's windows were covered with scrims.[239]

The *Houston Post* newspaper critic expressed praise for the two leads in the August 7, 1932, issue, mentioning that "Miss Bellamy ... plays a convincing role. The part calls for a maximum of tense dramatic aloofness which the star handles to perfection. Lugosi ... plays the part of the arch villain, and his expressive eyes, flashing during the Zombie [sic] ritual, causes one to shiver and maybe call for the lights."[240]

Also on August 5, 1932, *White Zombie* opened at the Loew's in Rochester, New York, and in its ads the theater

A theater ballyhoo outside the Loew's State in Houston, Texas. The stunt, which attempted to echo the carriage scene in White Zombie, *was used at night with green lights from a battery lamp aimed at the occupants. For additional effect, the carriage windows were covered with scrims. Published in the October 1, 1932,* Motion Picture Herald.

Published in the August 4, 1932, Houston Post, *this ad invited potential theatergoers to* White Zombie *at the Loew's Theater.*

deemed the film to be "Stranger Than Your Wildest Dreams!" It played on the same bill as a comedy short called *Wild Babies,* a "Traveltalk" short called *Home, Sweet, Home,* and a Mickey Mouse cartoon. The theater drew attention by persuading the city's *Democrat and Chronicle* newspaper to hold a contest for the best essays on the topic of "My Most Horrifying Experience." The theater provided 50 tickets as prizes, with the best submissions appearing in print. To maintain the serious tone of the film, preference was given to the more "unusual" efforts, rather than the numerous comedic entries that arrived.[241]

The local newspaper review gave little insight into local audience reactions, instead offering a comparison to prior horror films and a brief critique:

> ...while possessing plenty of spooky excitement for those craving a spinal chill, [it] does not measure up to *Dracula* or *Frankenstein.* It shows definite lack of craftsmanship, particularly in the way in which its story has been sent off on a wild, impossible course which tends to weaken strong situations and create much nonsense. So much of the present film must be discarded as fairy tale fiction and trash.... A director with tried success could have produced something immensely effective with this

weird theme. [There is] one scene of this production which is an artistic highlight and tremendously gripping in its weirdness—the scene in which the zombies, or resurrected dead, are shown operating an ancient, creaking treadmill.... Sound is used perfectly here, and there is a Poe-esque quality.... Perhaps we should mention also the opening scene of a native funeral, in which the monotonous chanting of the negroes has been mingled with the sounds of the night insects in excellent style. But elsewhere there is much pseudo-art in the form of over-elaborate settings and the actors, most of them good, are made to do so many ridiculous things that they lose a good many opportunities."[242]

The review, quoted here only in part, would be one of the most in-depth and specific the film would receive in 1932, even if it did make the minor faux pas of claiming a female zombie leads Beaumont to Legendre in the sugar mill scene. Rochester may or may not have agreed that the "present film should be discarded"; either way, it was not held over for a second week.

"A Bride—*Stolen* from the Grave!" ads proclaimed when *White Zombie* played Boston starting on August 5, 1932. The Loew's State, a 3,700-seater, grossed approximately $21,500 from tickets priced 30 to 60 cents.[243] On the same bill was the short *Boy Friends* and a "Flip the Frog" cartoon. The film opened in Boston only one week after the horror film *Almost Married* played there. *White Zombie*'s box-office success in the city was anticipated by a review in *The Boston Globe*:

> Many folks of all ages take delight in horror stories. For that reason, a picture like *White Zombie* ... will have tremendous appeal to local film-goers [*sic*], even if the actors in the cast are not stars of the first magnitude. ... The picture is a trifle modernistic in parts, with one scene fading into another, and two or even three scenes on the same frame."[244]

The *Globe*'s remark about the "modernistic" aspects of *White Zombie* were insightful, but also a departure from the many critical reviews elsewhere that centered on the film's perceived outmoded directing and acting styles.

For the third week of the month, the film moved to the Loew's Orpheum in Boston, a 2,000-seater, where the film grossed $20,000 over seven days from ticket buyers paying 25 to 60 cents each. An average gross for the

LAST TIMES TODAY
"SKY SCRAPER SOULS"
with
Warren William

TO-MORROW

ZOMBIE! THE MOST SHOCKING THRILL IN SCREEN HISTORY!

The Wildest, Weirdest Imaginings of the Human Mind!

HEARTLESS! SOULLESS! MINDLESS! BREATHLESS! DEAD BUT NOT DEAD!

A White Girl Caught in the Zombie Spell—Slave to the Evil Will of the Master Zombie!

"WHITE ZOMBIE"
STARRING
BELA (DRACULA) LUGOSI

ZOMBIE

at **LOEW'S** ROCHESTER 25¢ TO P. M. 35¢ EVENINGS

Newspaper ad promoting the opening of White Zombie *in Rochester, New York. Published in the Rochester* Democrat and Chronicle *on August 4, 1932.*

Orpheum was $18,000. Ads for the screening made the film's importance far subordinate to a vaudeville show that included Bernice Claire, Joe Frisco, Billy Wells and the Four Fays, and Kikutas, a group of Asian acrobats.[245] That same week, competition in Boston included *Horse Feathers*, *American Madness* (with vaudeville provided by the Hilton Siamese Twins), *Speak Easily*, *Hold 'Em Jail*, and *Dr. X*, a film which grossed $35,000—$3,000 more than the theater's average—at the city's Metropolitan Theater.[246]

SALT LAKE CITY, PHILADELPHIA, AND NEW ORLEANS

One week later, on August 12, *White Zombie* initiated the Paramount Theater's "Greatest Show Season" in Salt Lake City. It appeared on the same bill as the Rudy Vallee short *Musical Doctor*, a Henry Gribbon comedy called *Hata Mari*, and a Terry Toon. The film played a single week, beginning just after the Panther Woman contest semifinalists for Paramount's horror film *Island of Lost Souls* (1932) appeared live on-stage in the city.[247] Its booking had been made some ten days before, one of the first cities to schedule the film after its success in New York City was secured.[248]

The August 14, 1932, *Salt Lake Tribune* praised the film, admitting that "After *Dracula*, *Dr. Jekyll and Mr. Hyde*, and *Frankenstein*, one might be inclined to believe that the ultimate in shock thrillers had been reached. But *White Zombie* ... will shatter that theory after five minutes have passed." Two days later, the same newspaper mentioned, "Bela Lugosi ... carries the main burden in the picture and no more sinister character portrayal can be imagined. He is ably assisted by [the rest of the] cast."[249]

On August 13, 1932, the Stanton at Philadelphia also screened the film, pairing it with the ZaSu Pitts and Thelma Todd comedy short *Red Noses*. Small, text-only ads prior to its opening cautioned moviegoers of its arrival with the words: "WARNING! Watch out for *White Zombie*."[250] For the evening of

Ad promoting a midnight screening of White Zombie *at Philadelphia's Stanton Theater. Published in the* Philadelphia Inquirer *of August 14, 1932.*

August 14, "Philadelphia's Thrill-Packed Sensation" played a special midnight show.[251] A description in the same day's *Philadelphia Inquirer* announced, "Movie fans will now be able to see for themselves the occult practices in Haiti...." Of course, such "practices" could only be viewed for a short time. By August 19, an *Inquirer* ad exclaimed, "LAST DAY! Hurry! We Can't Hold It Any Longer!"

The film played a single week at the 1,700-seat Stanton, grossing $8,500 for six days of screening. That amount was $500 less than the theater's average, leaving *Motion Picture Daily* to say that "*White Zombie* failed to show much strength" in Philadelphia.[252] In fact, the Stanton quickly canceled their initial plans for holding the film over for a second week.

For its opening in New Orleans on August 18, 1932, the Saenger Theater paired *White Zombie* with a Betty Boop cartoon and screen tests of the city's three "Panther Women." The tests featured Becky Williams, Lorraine Charbonnet, and Soma Bassova, the three top New Orleans winners in the Paramount Studio's contest to find the appropriate woman for an important role in their upcoming film *Island of Lost Souls*.[253]

As for *White Zombie* itself, the New Orleans *Times-Picayune* of August 18 assured readers that "*White Zombie* was produced in Hollywood, strictly as entertainment, and makes no effort to educate." Most cities, however, made much of the "real-life" qualities of zombies and the film's look at a "true" subject. Such a comment in New Orleans may have been the Saenger's effort to remind patrons not to scrutinize the film's treatment of voodoo too harshly.[254]

Not only did many citizens in the U.S. perceive New Orleans as the country's capital of voodoo, the local newspapers themselves made allusions to the locally brewed voodoo while *White Zombie* was on the screen. On August 21, 1932, Charles P. Jones' column "Postview" in the *Times-Picayune* cited comparisons made in New York between the film's success on Broadway and the long-running Broadway play *Abie's Irish Rose*. Jones drew on voodoo terminology saying, "[this] as

every New Orleanian can understand, was sheer 'gris-gris.'"

In relation to *White Zombie*, Jones' article went on to speak of local voodoo activity:

> Hereabouts, we probably wouldn't have been so quick to romp on a drama of voodooism, since all of us believe in it, one way or another. You'll find references to it by nearly all the early New Orleans writers, and old newspaper files are filled with little police station items about conjure victims and such. ... It was the voodoo uprising in [Santo Domingo] that drove to New Orleans, in 1791, the city's first professional theatrical troupe, headed by Louis Tabary.

Curiously, though, neither Jones nor other 1932 writers drew a comparison of terminology between Haitian zombies and the Zombi snake god of New Orleans voodoo.

The film—which at least one newspaper ad announced simply as *Zombie*—remained at the Saenger for only one week. Reviews, however, were strong; on August 19, 1932 the *Times-Picayune* column "Asbestos" decided:

> *White Zombie* is a film with as many shudders as *Dracula*, and more easily understood by Southern audiences. It is [about] the ultimate horror of voodooism ... [which] came over from Africa with the first cargoes of slaves brought to the New World. Settings and atmosphere are superb. The producers have neglected nothing in their efforts to outdo all the horror dramas that have gone before, and some of the shots showing the undead ... are as spooky as any vampire scene imaginable. The views of ... these unearthly creatures send so many shivers up one's spine that it seems hardly necessary to run the theater's cooling system.

The "Asbestos" column is interesting in that, rather than drawing comparisons between the brutish zombies and the Frankenstein monster as some critics in New York and elsewhere would do, the reviewer linked the film's "living dead" more closely to the vampires of *Dracula*. Perhaps the impetus for the comparison stemmed from Lugosi's appearance in both films.

CHICAGO AND MILWAUKEE

"Today at 9:00 AM: An entirely new and original story," ads read on August 25, 1932, for *White Zombie's* opening in the Windy City.[255] News of the film had already caught the attention of the *Chicago Daily News* readers the week before. On August 18, a large still of actress Madge Bellamy in a swimming suit turned up in the paper with the heading: "To relight the United Artists." The city's Publix-Balaban and Katz United Artists theater had been closed throughout the summer, with *White Zombie* acting as the headliner for its reopening.[256]

Business at most first-run Chicago theaters had been slow during August, and several other local theaters were reopening after having been closed for the summer. As a result, much money was being poured into ballyhoo and advertisement efforts that month. Extensive talk of repealing double features was making most exhibitors in the city happy, as was the rapid success of films like *Horse Feathers*, *Hold 'Em Jail*, and *Bird of Paradise*, a film which appeared at the city's Palace Theater with Jack Dempsey live onstage.

To help compete for ticket buyers, advance newspaper advertisements for *White Zombie* promised that "Chicago will see the most startling picture ever made!"[257] Local reviewers, however, generally did not agree with that statement. On August 26, 1932, Mae Tinée of the *Chicago Tribune* believed it to be, "Not as terrifying as

Ad promoting White Zombie's *opening in Chicago, published in the* Chicago Tribune *of August 25, 1932.*

Frankenstein and more blood-curdling than *Dracula*." She went on to claim, "…in this picture, you behold a small and hideous horde of [zombies] calculated to make your hair stand on end. It's because this calculation is always so apparent that *White Zombie* fails in its intention. 'Boo! Boo!' cried the Boogey Man, 'I bet I scared you then! Now I'm going to make another face and scare you over again!'" Tinée added a reference to the two major audience responses, claiming "If you don't laugh, *White Zombie* will probably give you a mild case of the willies. Leave the children at home."[258]

Clark Rodenbach of *The Chicago Daily News* was somewhat kinder in his "Spooks Scamper Over the Screen at United Artists" review. He immediately praised the "Comfortable and cozy cinema…. But just how much comfort the folk will get with the picture that crashes open the house is a cow of another color. The attraction that opens the pleasant playhouse is not one of the comforting kind." Rodenbach concluded, "It's highly probable that you will like *White Zombie*. … it won't bore you for a minute."[259]

That same day brought Genevieve Harris's "Ghastly Adventures in the West Indies" notice in the *Chicago Evening Post*. Given that the Halperin brothers made the film independently, her condemnation of it appearing too "studio-made" is particularly interesting:

> If you like ghost stories, you'll probably thrill to this. Every effort has been made to give you a good case of gooseflesh. Strange backgrounds, the cries of vultures, the corpselike appearance of the "zombies" who wander through some of the scenes, not to mention Bela Lugosi's macabre make-up, are all designed to make you shudder. The film, however, lacks the touch of fantasy which gave power to *Dracula* and *Frankenstein*. It looks a little too definitely studio-made to be entirely convincing. Perhaps that's just as well!

Harris would have been surprised to know that *White Zombie* was not a studio-financed project, although it did use sets from major studio films like *Dracula*.

On August 30, 1932, *Variety* spoke of the promotional scheme in Chicago, which "used several stooges on the marquee in an animated goosepimple tableau to halt passers-by. This exploitation was most unusual for the house, and accumulated a sidewalk audience at the busy Randolph-Dearborn corner."[260] Additionally, newspapers ran more photos and information about the film. For example, Betty Peterman's column in the August 27, 1932, *Chicago Daily News* said that:

> Bela Lugosi is scaring 'em silly. Br-r-r-r, they can turn off their air-cooling system any time and the patrons will never miss it. Mr. Lugosi, who started digging up the dead in *Dracula*, is back at his old profession again….

The Hollywood p.a.'s (pest agents) say that Lugosi is scared of himself from too much draculating.[261]

In addition to hyping *White Zombie*, *The Chicago Daily News* interviewed a Haitian jumper named Sylvio Cator. Rather than inquire about Cator's adventures, the *Daily News* asked him about zombies. His response: "nothing more than a figment of the white travel writer's imagination."

In the end, though, zombies were not as much on the minds of Chicagoans as the city's 1,700 seat United Artists theater had hoped. Grossing $10,000 from tickets that ranged from 35 to 75 cents, the theater was disappointed. They had believed that $16,000 should have been possible, and passed judgment that *White Zombie* had "failed to bring results."[262] The theater manager may have had too high expectations for the horror film given both its successes elsewhere and his own need for a strong showing after being closed all summer.

Prior horror films had done relatively well in the city. *Dracula* grossed $39,800 in the first of its two weeks at the city's State-Lake Theater[263]; *Frankenstein* had taken $44,000 in just one week at the same theater in December 1931.[264] During January 1932, *Dr. Jekyll and Mr. Hyde* made $25,000 in its first week at the McVickers Theater, and $18,000 in its second.[265] Then, *Murders in the Rue Morgue* made $21,000 for a week at the State-Lake in February 1932.[266]

Instead, the "feeling" in Chicago was that "the horror cycle is over and that more bookings of that kind only invite deficits." At the same time, the theater admitted that "a stage version of the same piece was a legit flop locally last season and that didn't help the going on Randolph Street."[267] The reference was to Kenneth Webb's play *Zombie*, which was not the "same piece," but was apparently easy for some in Chicago to conflate with the new film given their mutual focus on zombies.

Milwaukee's Warner Theater also opened *White Zombie* on August 25, 1932, screening it with the comedy short *Neighbor Trouble* and featuring it with local favorite Al Gullickson at the organ. *White Zombie* replaced the film *Crooner* with David Manners. Matinee tickets before 1 P.M. were 25 cents, and before 5 P.M. were still only 35 cents.

By August 26, the day after *White Zombie*'s local opening, a critical review in the *Milwaukee Sentinel* exclaimed:

> [m]ovie extra! The eerie black magic of mystic Haiti, replete with sepulchral thrills and tense horror has come to town…. *White Zombie* is another variant of the popular *Dracula* theme, with Bela Lugosi again heading his grotesque hordes of Undead through a fascinating nightmare.[268]

If the critic had forgotten Lugosi's connection to Dracula, the Warner newspaper ads acted as a reminder with tags like "Star of DRACULA," as did the pressbook with its use of "Bela (DRACULA) Lugosi."[269]

Unfortunately, the Warner Theater seems not to have reported theater grosses to any movie industry trades. The level of *White Zombie*'s box-office success and its ability to keep up with competition from local films like *Horse Feathers*, *Bird of Paradise*, and a live Charlie Foy vaudeville act are thus unknown. However, children—one important block of audience members—were actively encouraged to attend *White Zombie* in Milwaukee. In fact, kids that clipped a "Lucky Buck" coupon out of the *Milwaukee Sentinel*'s Sunday comic page during the week of August 29 could get to see it for free.[270]

Ad from the August 26, 1932, Milwaukee Sentinel *promoting free tickets for boys and girls to the local* White Zombie *screenings.*

DALLAS, PITTSBURGH, OKLAHOMA CITY, AND ATLANTA

Texas theatergoers caught the film in Dallas when it opened at the Old Mill Theater on September 4, 1932, for a "Big Labor Day Program." Ads promised theatergoers, "It's to HORROR pictures what Scarface was to gangster films … Its WEIRD … ALIVE!"[271] The Old Mill screened the film just after closing sexologist Guy Edward Hudson's stage show "Secrets of Love Lives."[272] As part of the *White Zombie* bill, the Old Mill also presented Burns and Allen in the comedy short *Patents Pending*.

The *Dallas Morning News*, however, refused to be thoroughly convinced by the film. Their reviewer believed:

> Whataman Hudson's sex show was succeeded Sunday by something relatively clean and pure called *White Zombie*,

which has to do only with reanimated corpses working in the mills and fields of Haiti. The story has grisly potentialities which it doesn't realize altogether. There is some confusion in the narrative and also the direction. At best, *White Zombie* is [a] somewhat hackneyed terror very inadequately done.[273]

Some theatergoers in Dallas may well have agreed. The theater had been set to close for the season on September 15, 1932, and by *White Zombie*'s first few days the employees had received their two-week's notices. However, the *Dallas Morning News* of September 6 claimed a "sharp pick-up in local show patronage downtown has sent Publix officials scouting for new releases."[274] Owners thus hoped to keep the theater open during the autumn, but—since *White Zombie* stayed for just under one week—the "pick-up" in ticket sales was probably caused more by the "Secrets of Love Lives" stage show.

The film then opened in Pittsburgh on September 16, 1932, staying for a one week run. All during the prior week ads appeared in the *Pittsburgh Post-Gazette*, serving not just to promote the film but to offer questions like, "What is a Zombie?" and definitions of zombiism. By opening day, ads accidentally claimed it was a Universal Studios production, in which "she obeyed every lustful wish of this madman." Additionally, readers were assured "This picture will scare you ... but it will be a pleasant scare!"[275] During the weekend, new ads added that she—an unnamed character shown in provocative artwork—was "The Toy of a Fiend!" Furthermore, the Warner Theater promised "Frankenstein is an angel compared to the fiendish zombies!"[276]

Reviewers seemed less than convinced of the Warner's claims. For example, the *Post-Gazette* critic suggested:

> When Mr. Bela Lugosi, who acts like Buddy Rogers made up to resemble Mephistopheles, twitches his fingers and strains his veins—that means another redskin has bit the dust—you're supposed to squirm around in your seat and look particularly frightened. However, the whole effect is so hammy ... that laughing out loud seems like a better idea. *White Zombie* is billed as a melodrama, but if it's comedy you're looking for, you could do much worse, much worse indeed.[277]

The review added that Bellamy's inactivity on the screen for some time prior to *White Zombie* was actually "quite a break" for the public, given her less-than-effective acting skills. They even joked, as many would in years to come, that it was difficult to know when her character was entranced and when not.

Left: *Though this ad claims audiences will be scared, it reassures them by suggesting it will be a "pleasant scare." Published in the* Pittsburgh Post-Gazette *on September 16, 1932.*

This ad, published in the Daily Oklahoman *on September 23, 1932, tried to tie audience interest to the State Fair of Oklahoma.*

Poor critical notices were once again accompanied by box-office gains, however, as *Variety* proclaimed "Ballyhoo Overcomes Cricks on *Zombie*." The trade added that:

> *White Zombie* is the big noise at present at the Warner. Horror film got the ha-ha generally, but some circusy and gruesome ballyhoo in the lobby, with living corpses walking in and out of a papier mache tomb is stopping the street crowds and bringing plenty of 'em in.[278]

Initial estimates claimed that crowds would purchase approximately $9,000 in tickets, which *Variety* believed was "very much okay."[279] By the time final tabulations had been made, *Variety* touted the film as a "clean up" at $11,500.[280] However, *Dracula* had grossed $35,500 at the city's Stanley Theater the year before.[281]

"Watch out for *White Zombie*," newspaper ads in Oklahoma City warned readers. The film opened for a one week stay on September 23, 1932, with much of the ballyhoo tied to potential out-of-town business. "A visit to the state fair will not be complete without visiting [the Capitol Theater]. You asked for a thrill!" a *Daily Oklahoman* ad read on opening day. "A picture that will shake your spine! ... blast your notions of the supernatural—and you'll LOVE IT!"[282] The theater asked that patrons see the film from the start, adding that no one would be seated during the last reel.

The Fox Theater of Atlanta opened *White Zombie* as "Another Great Show!" on September 30. First day newspaper ads featured artwork of hearts instead of zombies; to enhance patronage, the theater had coupled *White Zombie* with an elaborate stage presentation called "Land of Romance." Vaudeville acts like The Five Lelands and Jack Rand's 24 Dancing Darlings were also on the bill, as was the Fox Grand Orchestra.[283]

A few days later, theater ads in the October 3, 1932, Atlanta *Constitution* featured the following text:

> We apologize ... we never realized what a stupendous breath-taking screen drama we had in *White Zombie*. We never believed that such an unusual white-heat drama could be procured. Although unbelievable, it is based upon actual practices and facts.

Along with reprinting Article 249 of the Haitian Penal Code, the ad included a quotation from *The Sphinx, an Independent Magazine for Magicians*. In it, editor John Mulholland wrote:

> Not alone in Haiti but in many sections of our own country there is widespread belief in Zombiism and enormous power is attributed to the priest craft of this cult. As a magician I am, of course, entirely skeptical, but I cannot disregard the fact that millions of people base

White Zombie *followed* Land of Romance *into the Fox Theater in Atlanta. This ad was published in* The Constitution *on September 26, 1932.*

their actions on the Zombie beliefs and that their destinies are thereby largely controlled.[284]

The text itself borrows from the film's pressbook, which suggested using *The Sphinx* article to attract audience interest.

In addition to a newspaper article that defined the term "zombie," there was Lewis Hawkins' October 3, 1932, review which detailed the theater's attraction.[285] His notice claimed:

> *White Zombie* brings the living dead into the parade of horror pictures that has been beating a macabre tattoo across the screen for the past several months, and if you liked its predecessors you probably will find a new and better thrill at the Fox this week.

The word "week," singular, is important in recounting the fate of *White Zombie* in Atlanta: the film did stay just one week at the Fox Theater.

SEATTLE AND LOS ANGELES

By November, *White Zombie* finally played Seattle and Los Angeles. For its run in Seattle, the film appeared at the Music Box Theater, an independent theater which seated 900 persons at 25 to 35 cents each. Owner and manager John Hamrick worked to see that *White Zombie* received as much publicity as possible. Ads for its opening day in the November 4, 1932 *Seattle Times* warned "Only the BRAVE dare see it."[286] The Music Box drew good crowds on the evening of November 8, but probably less as a result of "brave" horror fans than the theater's promise to announce U.S. presidential election returns.

By November 5, 1932, the *Seattle Times* was offering a favorable review of *White Zombie*:

> ...the picture has all the elements of the horrible, the bizarre and the weird that is [sic] required by the most rabid thrill seeker. ... Photography and settings are extremely well done to play up the horror element. Mysterious shadow effects and drab, macabre surroundings aid greatly in creating a graveyard atmosphere. ...*White Zombie* will entertain you if you like to be scared and can for the moment believe in black magic. Its explanations are convincing enough if taken in the right spirit.[287]

Whether audiences possessed "the right spirit" for *White Zombie*'s one week run is unknown. John Hamrick claimed its showing was "fair" but "slowed up" to $3,000 after a good start, despite being given "both

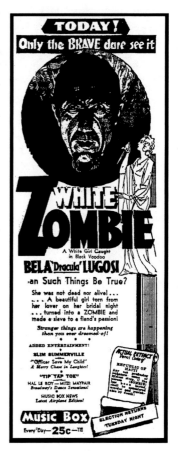

One of the ads which translated the film's title into racist slogans. Published in the November 4, 1932, Seattle Times.

barrels of exploitation."[288] Local competition from popular films like *Red Dust* apparently had an effect. The
year before, *Dracula* had made roughly $16,000 in Seat-
tle in late February–early March 1931, and *Frankenstein*
had grossed $15,000 there in December 1931.[289] One
month later, in January 1932, *Dr. Jekyll and Mr. Hyde* took
$13,000 at the Fifth Avenue Theater.[290]

Also on the west coast, Los Angeles' Fox Criterion
reopened for business with *White Zombie* as its first attraction on November 17, 1932. The theater seated 1,600
at ticket prices of 25 to 55 cents. Inclement weather at
that time meant that other local theaters screening films
like *Faithless* and *You Said a Mouthful* did only fair business.

Readers of the *Los Angeles Times* had long been
aware of *White Zombie*'s reputation, as the paper had
printed columnist Norbert Lusk's description of the film's
premiere in New York on August 7, 1932.[291] The journalist wrote that *White Zombie* "is not considered as impressive as it might have been either as a spectacle or as
an exhibit of acting. Hasty preparation and quick direction are evident throughout while the acting is more
often overwrought than authoritative."

When John Scott's review of the film's Los Angeles run appeared a few months later in the November 19,
1932, *Los Angeles Times*, the sentiment had not changed:
"The production appears to have been hastily assembled
and the direction is nothing to get excited about." Of the
lead, Scott added, "Lugosi does no exceptional acting and
his voice is held to a singsong chant most of the time."[292]

The moviegoers of Los Angeles must have generally
agreed with such views; *White Zombie* played a disappointing six days at the Fox Criterion, making only a
"poor" $3,000.[293] Explanations as to why were nothing
more than sheer speculation, with the exhibitor saying
that "customers [are] just not curious" and trades suggesting that bad weather hurt all local film screenings
that week.[294] Certainly there was not a lack of promotion
or advertisement for the Criterion screenings.

It is possible that by the summer of 1932 horror no
longer generated much interest in the city. *Dracula* had
made a successful two week run at the city's Orpheum,
with its first week taking $21,000.[295] *Frankenstein* had
stayed an amazing five weeks at the same theater in January and February 1932, grossing $34,000 in its first week
alone.[296] *Dr. Jekyll and Mr. Hyde* came close behind with
its first week's gross at $32,000.[297] But when *Dr. X* played
LA in late August 1932, it grossed only $4,800; the av-
erage weekly take of the theater that screened it was almost three times that amount—$13,000.[298] *The Old Dark
House*, which played at the city's RKO the same week
that *White Zombie* appeared at the Criterion grossed
$8,100, which was under the theater's $10,000 average.[299]

Perhaps the most provocative White Zombie *newspaper ad, which
appeared in the November 16, 1932,* Los Angeles Times.

Another reason may well have played the greatest
role in *White Zombie*'s Los Angeles failure. More so than
in many other key cities, the newspaper ads tended to play
up the sexual connotations of the film. "HE MADE
HER HIS SLAVE," one proclaimed, while visually
showing artwork of Lugosi's eyes beaming at the genitalia of a nude woman that looked nothing like actress
Madge Bellamy.[300] Another prominently displayed ad
showed a shapely, scantily clad woman in zombie Chauvin's arms.[301] Moreover, the "weirdest love story" tags
were used generously. It is feasible that, along with the
less enthusiastic critical notices, the overtly sexual ads
and tag lines proved offensive to some potential patrons,
thus harming the film's box-office appeal. Highly sexualized ads had reputations of being detrimental to business at many 1930s theaters, including some in California.[302]

SAN FRANCISCO

For *White Zombie*'s San Francisco appearance, the
United Artists theater, which had been closed for six
weeks during the late summer, touted its exclusive showing in the Golden Gate city and nearby vicinity. The film

opened on Monday, November 28, 1932, staying through December 15. A one-week holdover was decided upon after a rush during the film's first weekend in which *The San Francisco Examiner* claimed "...movie fans want more zombiism." Large crowds meant that *White Zombie* eventually stayed a third week.[303] On the same bill was a Mickey Mouse cartoon, and short subjects featuring Morton Downey and Vincent Lopez.[304]

Both the *San Francisco Chronicle* and *Examiner* ran multiple stories about the film, with the latter printing such tales as "Picture Recalls Haitian Monster":

> The last public record of such an occurrence [as voodoo "blood sacrifices"] is that of Cadeus Bellegarde, a papaloi or head man of Haiti, who turned criminal and proved a pathological monster comparable to Gilles de Rais, the original "Bluebeard," to Landru, the wholesale murderer of France, and to the "Hamburg Butcher." Bellegarde was feared, bitterly hated and finally denounced by the fervent Voodooists themselves. The U.S. Marine Corps investigated and witnessed his sacrifices, testifying against him when the case subsequently was turned over to the Haitian courts. Bellegarde paid a bloodless penalty. He was hanged.[305]

The text itself stems from the United Artists' pressbook, which included information on Bellegarde presumably because he bore a few villainous similarities to the *White Zombie* character Legendre.

Another of the short narratives in the San Francisco press included *White Zombie* director Victor Halperin's assertion that:

> Zombiism at present is being practiced in this country as well as in superstitious Haiti. The swamp lands of the Carolinas, he says, still ring on moonlit nights with the chants of the Devil Worshippers, while in the bayous of Louisiana frequently are heard the incantations of the doctors, or voodoo sorcerers who owe allegiance only to Satan. Only recently, just outside of Charleston, a great gathering of Devil Worshippers was held, although it was not announced as such and the words "Black Mass" were whispered. Despite the fact that the police kept an eye on the ceremonies, it is understood that the sacrifice of the Red Rooster occurred.[306]

The "Red Rooster" sacrifice is not described in the article, which does not borrow its text from the *White Zombie* pressbook.

San Francisco's screening of the film utilized a sophisticated ad campaign with art-deco designs, all of which made clear the theater's policy against admitting

Right: *For* White Zombie*'s run in San Francisco, the city's United Artist theater bypassed the pressbook and designed a variety of fascinating ads. This one was published in the* San Francisco Examiner *of December 2, 1932.*

UNITED ARTISTS
THEATRE Market at 7 TH

**ONLY ADULTS
CAN SEE IT!**
Weird, Voodoo Practices in a Land of Mystery! A Haitian Fiend Bringing the Dead Back to Life, Slavery! A Burning Love Story Screeching its Drama out of the Grave!

WHITE ZOMBIE

With
BELA LUGOSI
FORMER STAR of "DRACULA"
•
EXCLUSIVE
Showing in San Francisco!
Will NEVER be seen in any other theatre of this City and County!
•
Extra Added Attractions:
**MORTON DOWNEY
VINCENT LOPEZ
MICKEY MOUSE**

Coming Soon!...The Film Version of the Broadway Drama that Rocked a Nation!
"THE LAST MILE"

children. "For Adults Only!" the publicity roared, resulting in large ticket sales over an 18-day run. At least one critic agreed with the strong audience reaction:

> Mr. Bela Lugosi does a great deal of sneering and smirking and looking sinister in *White Zombie* … and the audience gets its money's worth of certified, gilt-edged goose flesh. For *White Zombie*, even following, as it does, a long chain of horror films, still manages to create a nightmaric atmosphere that tells upon its audience. Some of the photography is the most artistic and most moving I have seen in a horror opera. Particularly the shot of the castle rising out of the sea and reaching to the heavens like a peak on the cliff it adorns. Many other scenes, too, are excellent, and the more or less "abstract" photography, which expresses moods, is very artfully contrived. There is little for Miss Bellamy to do except look beauteous, or for Mr. Lugosi but to look snaky and menacing. Both do their jobs with efficiency and skill. Long lines were forming at the box office when I emerged from the theater.[307]

Long lines kept forming for days subsequent to the critic's visit to the United Artists theater. *White Zombie*'s success resulted in three weeks at the theater, though by its final week the film's estimated gross was only $8,000–$2,000 less than the theater's average.[308] Months earlier, in December 1931, *Frankenstein* stayed for a three-week run at the nearby Orpheum.[309]

White Zombie theater screenings were clearly advertised as "exclusive" showings, meaning that no other theater in the city would be showing the film, at least not for a long period of time. By October 1932, Al Lichtman of United Artists had announced a policy of "exclusive" showings of their films at United Artists and Loew's Theaters in 18 key U.S. cities at a sustained admission scale averaging some 50 cents a ticket. Immediately, there were negative responses to the idea in industry trades, and United Artists soon withdrew it.[310] However, the idea was at work behind the strategy of *White Zombie*'s San Francisco screening, and it certainly did not prove a detriment to the film's box-office success in that city.

Analysis of Key Cities and White Zombie's Reception

However subjective the choice of key cities and however lacking the quantitative information about *White Zombie*'s screenings in them, the investigation of those cities establishes one certainty: *White Zombie* generated a multiplicity of responses from newspaper critics and theater patrons.

The same statement can be applied when taking into account the variables of age, ethnicity, gender, and geography. The sheer variety of responses was astonishing. Beyond a theater patron or movie critic stating "I liked it" or "I did not like it," the reactions to *White Zombie* drift from fright or thrills to laughter or disbelief, from excitement to simple boredom. As the *Chicago Daily News* claimed in its critical review, "You may laugh at it or you may shiver at it."[311] Even a cursory comparison of these cities suggests wide variations in the reaction *White Zombie* received. In addition to noting differences from city to city, this study does acknowledge that very diverse reactions could have occurred on a single row of seats in the same screening, the same theater, the same city.

The investigation of key cities, as well as this chapter as a whole, also suggests major variations in the presentation of and advertisements for *White Zombie*. The film's pressbook may well have been a guide to theater managers, but that would have been coupled with the changing climate of attitudes towards horror films, as well as differences in the reception of horror films in given regions.

The reception of *White Zombie* in 1932 does illustrate the diversity of audiences in general and their reactions to almost any film in particular, meaning that viewers do not necessarily respond to a cycle or genre film in the way the filmmakers or distributors may desire. For example, a film labeled as a comedy does not necessarily induce laughs in viewers; similarly, a horror film may not instill fright or fear in them. In addition, the reception of *White Zombie* suggests the variety of factors that allow viewers to form reactions to a filmic text. Whether it is the current national or local news, the advertisements and ballyhoo of a given theater, or individual traits like gender, age, and ethnicity, a complex and sometimes unknowable multiplicity of factors affect the manner in which an audience member views a film. Most importantly, however, the case of *White Zombie* indicates that the film represents something of an anomaly.

The reception of *White Zombie* by American audiences shows *extreme* diversity on every level, making the film unique among the burgeoning numbers of horror films of the 1930s.

Chapter Five

Continuing the Tradition: More Voodoo, More Zombies

The financial success of *White Zombie* drew public and industry attention throughout the autumn and winter of 1932, but its audience appeal spawned far-reaching effects. Echoes of *White Zombie* reverberate throughout the 1930s. The film itself illuminated theater screens in several reissues, though its reception received less and less respect as the decade reached twilight. However, *White Zombie* had achieved enough success in 1932 to significantly impact the evolution of the horror film cycle. It had also brandished such an iconic image in Legendre that the character sporadically surfaced in the subsequent career of actor Bela Lugosi.

Basking in the initial glow of *White Zombie*'s fame far more than Bela Lugosi were the brothers Halperin. Though that glow would soon wisp into mere embers for the duo, its initial flame fanned into a studio contract. The two were rapidly lured into an agreement with Paramount to produce another horror film. *Supernatural*, their new cinematic brainchild, proved unsuccessful both aesthetically and financially. Failing to live up to its predecessor, the film helped escort the Halperins back into the very natural world of independent film production.

Their lack of success in subsequent indie film projects—as well as a sustained popular interest in voodoo and zombies—prompted the Halperins to produce a semisequel to *White Zombie* in the mid-thirties; the result ignited a firestorm between the brothers and Amusement Securities Corporation (ASC), their former financiers. Conflict revolved around who held the legal right to even use the word "zombie." Zombies meant money, which in turn meant that an entity like ASC would fight to protect its sole use of the term.

Other filmmakers and studios in the early 1930s quickly began work on voodoo-related themes, presumably hoping to duplicate the original zombie film's financial success. Some of these would even appropriate specific narrative or thematic devices from the Halperins' film, causing filaments of *White Zombie* to illuminate on the screen once again. A large number of books and magazine essays appeared on voodoo and zombies throughout the 1930s as well. Though they seldom drew on *White Zombie* as a source of information, these texts did find larger audiences as a result of a growing public interest in such subjects—a partial result of the Halperins' cinematic success.

But while some wished to duplicate *White Zombie*'s success with zombies and voodoo, others wished to decry its merits. For example, esteemed African-American writer Zora Neale Hurston wrote in 1935 that "...these voodoo ritualistic orgies of Broadway and popular fiction are so laughable." Despite her criticism of fictionalized voodoo texts, it was indeed the "popular fiction" of *White Zombie* which had engendered a mass understanding of zombies. Even the name of the Zombie cocktail—the recipe first published in 1935—can be traced back to the film's popularization of the term.[1] *White Zombie*'s influence cast a long shadow over the 1930s, with voodoo and zombies becoming permanent inclusions in the pool of images and ideas that make up U.S. culture.

White Zombie's Resuscitations in the 1930s

White Zombie's first release essentially ended in the U.S. as the year 1932 closed, with its financial success much talked about but rarely pinpointed in precise dollar amounts. In the 1950s, Bela Lugosi told writer and producer Alex Gordon that *White Zombie* grossed $8 million, but his account can be dismissed in part due to the actor's bitterness over the limited salary the Halperins paid him; overstating the film's gross would have heightened its contrast with the minimal amount of money Lugosi himself made from *White Zombie*. Moreover, Lugosi had no financial investment in the film and seemingly had little subsequent contact with the Halperins, ASC, or United Artists; thus, it seems unlikely that he would have heard detailed financial information which didn't pertain to him. Most importantly, evidence from the 1930s clearly suggests a far different gross amount than $8 million.[2] Disputes over how much money the film made were indeed raised by Amusement Securities, the Halperins, and others in the 1930s, but probably the information admitted as evidence in a 1936 court case is the most accurate at $1,750,000. The Halperins themselves made approximately $80,000, far from the millions Lugosi believed them to have earned.[3]

A comparison of the $1,750,000 *White Zombie* gross as of 1936 with the respective grosses of *Dracula* (1931) and *Frankenstein* (1932) suggests that the Halperins' film likely produced a higher net profit than its major predecessors in the 1930s horror cycle. By June 1932, *Dracula* had grossed $1.2 million worldwide, having cost $341,191.20 to produce. *Frankenstein*, which cost $291,129.13 to produce, had grossed $1.4 million worldwide by June 1932.[4] Though accounts vary, *White Zombie* certainly cost less than $100,000 to make, and—though the grosses of *Dracula* and *Frankenstein* would have increased by 1936—the aforementioned figures illustrate *White Zombie*'s competitive box-office appeal in the 1930s horror cycle.

If its overall financial returns were almost astonishing for an independently made production, *White Zombie* had even managed to break some records at individual theaters. For example, when the film opened at the Loew's Stillman in Cleveland during mid–August 1932, record crowds gathered to buy tickets. At that one theater, 16,728 people saw the film in its first weekend. *The Hollywood Reporter* claimed that it had been over a year and a half since the Stillman had seen anything close to the number of ticket buyers for *White Zombie*.[5]

Box-office success did not end at the geographic borders of the United States, however. *White Zombie* also received well-planned publicity and large crowds in various other countries. For example, theater manager Tom Cleary transformed the front of Montreal's Princess Theater into a "House of the Living Dead." He built a castle turret on the marquee, which was illuminated at night by blue lights. The rest of the building design was made to resemble block masonry. Echoing the New York City Rivoli premiere, seven live zombies walked on the platform "top" of the Princess marquee.[6]

The film received an even greater welcome in Lon-

An advertisement for the London trade show of White Zombie, *published in England's* To-Day's Cinema *on September 13, 1932.*

don, where the trade publication *The Daily Film Renter* claimed it to be:

> ...produced with lavishness and the sinister note stressed with skill in every possible way. ... It may prove too strong for the nerves—and with some audiences the risibilities—of patrons. It is so deftly and imaginatively directed, however, that it avoids the ludicrous, and is effectively weird.[7]

Similarly, *Kinematograph Weekly* believed *White Zombie* was "quite well acted, and has good atmosphere." But it did note the film was "not for the squeamish or the highly intelligent." The more intelligent viewer, the trade believed, would find the film "ludicrous." Instead, it possessed "popular thrills."[8]

A less favorable review appeared in the British trade *The Cinema News and Property Gazette.* Their reviewer, "A.F.," noted that the character of Murder was "vampirish" and that his appearance was "[r]eminiscent in makeup of a previous [Lugosi] role." He also thought that the:

> Exaggerated treatment of subject achieves reverse effect to thrill or conviction. Eerie element accentuated by fanciful direction and over-emphasized portrayal. ... this unusual narrative does not stand on its narrative merits alone, but is lavishly dressed up in a gruesome garb of macabre incident and ghoulish atmosphere.[9]

Like *Kinematograph Weekly,* A.F. also believed *White Zombie* was best suited for "the less sophisticated," who wanted thrills.

For a run at London's Dominion Theatre, *White Zombie* met the creative mind of manager Robb Lawson, who definitely sought popular audiences for the film's popular thrills. His theater campaign included five zombies that acted out a scene in front of the theater and a 40-foot tall display re-creating the film's "House of the Living Dead." At least one trade correlated the theater's promotion with *White Zombie*'s success in the city; the film broke all the Dominion's records for the prior six month period.[10]

Its first release at an end, *White Zombie* continued to play some small town, second-run theaters, and additional foreign countries during 1933, 1934, and 1935. In most cases, little publicity occurred for what was apparently seen as an old film. An example is Lincoln, Nebraska, where the film played the Capitol Theater at the bottom of a double bill. For three days— May 28 to May 30, 1934—one could watch both *Hold That Girl* (1934) with James Dunn and Claire Trevor and *White Zombie* for only a dime. Generally, admission would have been 15 cents, but a highly competitive price war was underway in Lincoln; it forced Capitol manager Bob Livingston to drop ticket costs by a nickel in mid–May, 1934. As for the *Hold That Girl/*

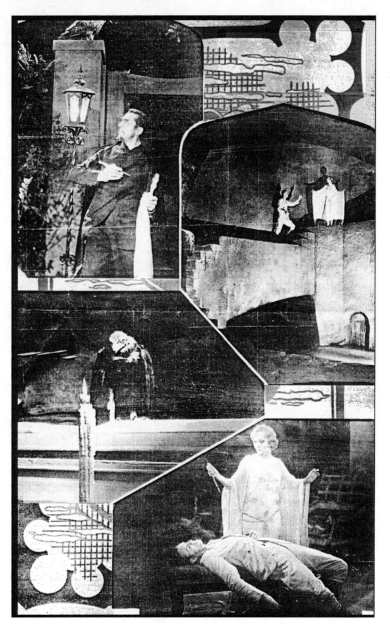

A montage of images from White Zombie *published in England's* The Cinema News and Property Gazette *of September 21, 1932. (Courtesy of Frank J. Dello Stritto.)*

White Zombie screenings, the house gross was rated by Livingston as "okay" at $600, but the next double bill slated for the second half of the same week made almost twice as much at $1,100.[11]

By mid–1936, Sam Krellberg planned even more reissues of *White Zombie,* purchasing the distribution

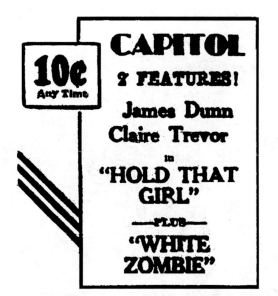

Advertisement for White Zombie *on a reissue double bill, published in the October 21, 1938,* Chicago Tribune.

White Zombie had proved it could rise from the cinematic dead, but on each occasion in the 1930s its resuscitations inflicted less and less terror (and more and more amusement) on audience members. Horror had indeed changed, but only after *White Zombie* had helped its transformation in the early 1930s.

Newspaper ad in Lincoln, Nebraska, for screenings of Hold That Girl *and* White Zombie *that occurred May 28–30, 1934.*

rights back from United Artists.[12] One of these reissues came in 1938, shortly after a *Dracula* and *Frankenstein* double bill that summer spurred a renewed popularity in horror films. *White Zombie* was illuminated on far fewer screens with far less regularity than those two films, but returned from its cinematic grave nonetheless. For example, it played on a double bill with *The Bat Whispers* (1931) at Chicago's Pantheon on October 20, 1938; the next day, Chicago's Maryland Theater paired it with *The Case of the Black Cat* (1936).

As Chapter Six will detail, *White Zombie's* appearances at theaters did not end with the close of the 1930s, but that decade alone shows a profound shift in the film's reception. While *White Zombie* returned repeatedly to theater screens during those years, audience responses shifted from the widely mixed views of its original release to more uniform cries of incredulity and ridiculousness. As film historian George E. Turner indicates in the foreword to the present text, a screening of *White Zombie* in 1938 elicited:

> …howls and hoots from the rowdier members of the audience. Before long they were repeating Lugosi's lines loudly, exaggerating his Hungarian accent. … A later trip to the [theater] proved futile; the same rubes were back, but by this time they had memorized Lugosi's lines and were reciting them in synch with the actor! The same thing happened the following year when *White Zombie* returned with Columbia's *The Black Room* and *Behind the Mask*."

White Zombie *and the 1930s Horror Film Cycle*

Even before any theatrical reissue, *White Zombie* caused a profound effect on the horror film cycle of the early thirties. As shown in Chapter Four, the spring and summer of 1932 saw an important debate in film trade publications as to whether the cycle should continue and whether its films should be advertised as being horror movies, mysteries, or thrillers. *White Zombie's* tremendous success in New York City and across much of the country flew in the face of disparaging remarks from some critics. However much various ad campaigns for different theaters heightened the love story or "thrills" of *White Zombie*, most critics and audiences after viewing the film connected it and star Lugosi with the horror cycle of *Dracula*, *Frankenstein*, and *Murders in the Rue Morgue*.

White Zombie's much talked about 1932 successes in the press and especially trade publications seemingly brought a temporary close to debates on whether studios should continue producing similar films and whether to advertise them with adjectives like "horror." As such discussions halted to whispers and then silence, horror films released in the latter part of 1932—*The Mummy, The Old Dark House, Island of Lost Souls*—appeared with advertisements which generally made clear their inclusion in the horror cycle. Production on other horror films remained steady until 1936, with most readily proclaiming their horrific elements in their ad campaigns.

The argument here is not that *White Zombie* created or prompted the 1930s horror cycle, nor is the argument that its advertising campaign necessarily shaped the visual or textual style of the horror film ad campaigns that followed. Certainly *White* Zombie's aesthetic qualities and cinematic techniques were rarely copied. Rather, the film's box-office triumphs came at an important moment in the industry debate regarding the continued proliferation of horror films and how to advertise them. The timing of its financial victories and its ability to sustain and further its box-office appeal despite critical lambastings meant that it greatly helped move the horror film cycle to its next stage, one in which more horror films than before were produced and one in which most of them openly advertised their content as horror-related.

Bela Lugosi and the Aftermath of White Zombie

If *White Zombie* had played an important role in the 1930s horror cycle, the film also had an important impact on the career of its lead actor, Bela Lugosi. Certainly in retrospect his cinematic interpretation of *Dracula* (1931) and his overall reputation as a horror film star far outweigh the gravity of his appearance in *White Zombie*. And during Lugosi's lifetime and in the ensuing years, it *has* been his association with Dracula, Legendre, Ygor (in 1939's *Son of Frankenstein* and 1942's *Ghost of Frankenstein*), and the mad scientist (in a large number of B-horror films) which generated and have maintained his mystique and popularity. Although Legendre was certainly not the touchstone of Lugosi's career or fame, it was a role and image that resurfaced repeatedly during the actor's lifetime.

Through his success on Broadway and in the Universal film as Dracula, Lugosi had already established a reputation for horror in 1931. His brief brush with *Frankenstein* (1931) in turning down the role of the Monster and his appearance in *Murders in the Rue Morgue* furthered the reputation. However, at the time of *Rue Morgue*'s mediocre reception at the box office, it may well have still been possible for Lugosi to launch another image in different kinds of films.

White Zombie became the final nail in the coffin of his typecasting. Its immediate identification (some advertising variations notwithstanding) with the horror film cycle, its particularly evil and striking role for Lugosi, and its tremendous financial success all factor into the completed construction of the actor's association with horror.

In other words, however much *Dracula* was certainly a horror tale, it represented Lugosi's connection with a single role, not with a genre; indeed, at the time of *Dracula*'s release in 1931 a U.S. horror film genre had not even fully formed. The connection was strong, but many ac-

An ad for Bowery at Midnight *(1942) starring Bela Lugosi. Though the photograph in the lower right is from the film, the artwork at the top of the ad shows a strong influence from* White Zombie. *(Courtesy of Lynn Naron.)*

tors in Hollywood and on Broadway developed popular relationships with single roles and still managed to move on to other kinds of stories.

Lugosi was unique among 1930s horror stars in that his Dracula required little makeup, in contrast to Boris Karloff's interpretation of the Frankenstein Monster. But just because Lugosi and Dracula bore the same face should not alone suggest that he could not have moved into other categories of film. After all, most actors associated with given roles were not buried under makeup, but still managed to escape typecasting. It was the burning triumvirate of *Dracula*, *Murders in the Rue Morgue*, and *White Zombie* that together coalesced to make Lugosi so solidly a horror film star.

As his career progressed and his life went on during subsequent decades, *White Zombie* quietly hovered near Lugosi. In the spring of 1932, Universal Studios' publicity for *Murders in the Rue Morgue* drew links between Lugosi's name and his portrayal of Dracula. "Dracula himself," the film's one-sheet movie poster called Lugosi. Nonetheless it was *White Zombie*'s publicity campaign that in every way possible tried to solidify the connection between Lugosi's name and Dracula's. By repeating to such degree and in such frequency the phrase "Bela (Dracula) Lugosi," *White Zombie*'s publicity helped blaze the path many subsequent ad campaigns would follow: *Night of Terror* (1933), *The Black Cat* (1934), *The Raven* (1935) are examples.

Lugosi's role in *White Zombie* may have also had an impact on his career afterward. The Mephistophelean image of Legendre probably helped theater director Max Reinhardt to envision Lugosi as the heavy in a planned 1936 film version of Goethe's *Faust*.[13] That same Satanic edge to Legendre may also have been the reason that Walt Disney hired Lugosi as a model for the Mephistopheles character in the 1940 animated film *Fantasia*.[14]

It is clear that others in the entertainment industry also remembered Lugosi's work in *White Zombie* in subsequent years. For example, newspaper ads for his 1941 *One Night of Horror* stage show in Chicago pictured him not as Dracula or in an *Invisible Ghost* pose (the 1941 film screened with the show), but instead as Legendre—even though the show had nothing to do with *White Zombie* and he did not appear onstage in makeup similar to that used for the Legendre character. Later, at least one ad for *Bowery at Midnight* (1942), a low-budget Monogram Studios thriller starring Lugosi, used a Legendre pen-and-ink drawing in tandem with a still from the new film. Though in part of the film he did sport a beard, the advertisement in question definitely mimics Legendre and not his *Bowery at Midnight* role.

In 1944, Lugosi appeared on the theater screens in another Monogram Studios B-horror film, *Voodoo Man*. Along with the sheer invocation of voodoo and voodoo drumming, the film mimicked *White Zombie*'s Legendre makeup to a degree for the new Lugosi character, Dr. Marlowe. Though not as understated as in the Halperin film, Dr. Marlowe's beard and eyebrows seem very evocative of Legendre. Even his character's ability to exert mental control from afar over women is reminiscent of the earlier film.[15]

White Zombie itself reappeared in theaters of the 1940s and 1950s, including overseas. Perhaps the most intriguing account of a reissue stems from Basil Bonner, who remembered seeing the film at a South London theater over a period of several weeks. To the best of his memory, he viewed the film over such a lengthy time period because the theater had serialized it into many chapters, playing a new one every few days.[16]

White Zombie also helped establish Lugosi's image in the medium of television. Along with several of the actor's 1930s and 1940s Monogram films and serials, *White Zombie* was an early Lugosi film to hit the airwaves. If he had desired, Lugosi himself could have watched the film on any number of L.A.–area broadcasts. For instance, as early as April 7, 1951, *White Zombie* played KLAC; in 1953, it played Channel 11 on March 1 and KNBH on March 29. The following year, KABC broadcast a midnight screening of it on April 24.[17]

Most television stations in the 1950s would have obtained prints of *White Zombie* from Motion Pictures for Television, an organization that (according to *The Bill board* of March 21, 1953) claimed to own it and over four hundred other features. Companies such as this, as well as TV stations themselves, were probably responsible for many of the shortened prints of *White Zombie* that have circulated throughout the years; clipping several minutes would have allowed a television station to place it more easily in a specific time slot.

On at least one occasion, Lugosi did view *White Zombie* on television with his teenage admirer and close friend Richard Sheffield. Given the time frame of their friendship, this screening would have occurred sometime between 1954 and 1956. The elder actor would complain of the little money he was paid for the film, wrongly claiming that it made the Halperins into millionaires. In practically the same breath, however, he remarked on how atmospheric he believed *White Zombie* to be, ranking it among his favorite film appearances. Lugosi sincerely believed he had created a memorable portrayal as Murder Legendre.

Sheffield cherished watching Lugosi films like *White Zombie* on television with the actor himself, even if Lugosi sometimes complained about not receiving royalties from their broadcasts. He recalled that:

> Bela would gaze at himself on the little TV screen, remembering his past glory. A smile would come over his face, and—even though he really didn't like to watch TV or films, even his own films—he would say, "Godammit! What a good looking bastard I was![18]

Lugosi's feelings toward *White Zombie* ranged from artistic appreciation and personal pride to bitterness over his financial remuneration. He did usually include *White Zombie* in printed filmographies he released to the press; in 1952, he even told a reporter that he might act in a sequel to be titled *Return of the White Zombie*.[19] No corroborating evidence exists of any such plans, and he had apparently not been contacted by Victor Halperin. Perhaps his own zeal for a comeback made him mention a film title he believed others would still recognize. At any rate, presumably some newspaper readers did remember the film, as it was one often named in his obituaries in August 1956.[20]

To a small degree, Bela Lugosi's career forever remained under the shadow of White Zombie.

Though this May 1, 1941, Chicago Tribune *ad promoted a live Lugosi appearance and his film* The Invisible Ghost (1941), *the artwork is far more evocative of* Murder Legendre *and* White Zombie.

Supernatural

Just as it was throughout Bela Lugosi's career, *White Zombie* was definitely discussed in the press in 1932, as were Victor and Edward Halperin. Grace Kingsley's "Hobnobbing in Hollywood" column announced in December 1932, "There is such an opportunity for trick photography, weird lighting and other effects of the sort onscreen that it is a wonder more pictures along the line of the so-called and pseudo-supernatural [*sic*] are not made. Those busy Halperin brothers, Victor and Edward are throwing away no such bet. Having cleaned up with *White Zombie*, they are to make another one along spooky lines."[21]

The follow-up, titled *Supernatural*, reunited the Halperins with author Garnett Weston. Edward again produced, and Victor again directed; Weston's original story for the film was translated into script form by Harvey Thew and Brian Marlow. To help re-create the team which brought forth *White Zombie*, Arthur Martinelli was hired as cinematographer. The Halperin brothers even hired Sir Oliver Lodge, a famous British spiritualist, as a technical director.[22]

According to Kingsley's column, the film was to "contain all the spine tickling and blood curdling incidents imaginable. The Halperins will indeed use hypnotism, spiritualism, and all the other eeric isms in its making."[23] Unfortunately, the result bore little of the unique qualities that channeled *White Zombie* into an aesthetic success.

Madge Bellamy comments in her autobiography, "[The Halperins] tried to get Paramount to employ me for the lead, but the studios insisted on signing that girl I had known at Fox Studio as Jane Peters—her name now was Carole Lombard."[24] Victor Halperin himself once recalled that Bellamy, "would have fit that part very, very well." But Lombard it was, with Randolph Scott, Vivienne Osborne, and Allan Dinehart taking the other top three spots; Beryl Mercer of *Outward Bound* (1930) also played an important supporting role. Even though Bellamy was out, the Halperins did sign former silent cinema names H. B. Warner and William Farnum.

As for leading actress Carole Lombard, Madge Bellamy remembered, "She resented the part, after she got it. Her forte was comedy."[25] Her forte might indeed have been comedy, but Lombard had been slated in December 1932 to appear in *The Dead Reckoning* at Paramount. According to the *Los Angeles Examiner*, the tale—which was an original story by Robert Presnell—was "a murder yarn and concerns a palatial yacht, rich people, and much bloodshed." Sari Maritza and Ricardo Cortez were to appear as well, with Erle C. Kenton directing.[26] The project was never made, though, perhaps because of a surface similarity to the upcoming *Supernatural*. It is also possible that elements of *The Dead Reckoning* were included in *Supernatural*, despite the credit for a completely original story for the latter going to Weston.

Regardless, Carole Lombard's resentment toward the project regularly surfaced on the set, channeled into anger at her director. Writer Sidney Salkow once wrote:

> I worked with her [on *Supernatural*]. She read the script, met ... Victor Halperin, and then promptly threatened to kill herself, Halperin, and everyone in Paramount's front office to avoid the assignment. Finally, worn out by her agent and Paramount's attempts to suspend her, Carole acquiesced. I was thrown in at Carole's request to serve as a minor mediator.[27]

Unfortunately, Salkow had only a limited effect on the contentious situation between the Lombard and Halperin. He remembered that Lombard "bridled" at every suggestion Halperin gave her, and that as shooting progressed her "profanities came more regularly and her appeals for help wracked [*sic*] the stage walls."

Dubbing Victor a "sweet mild-mannered gentleman," Salkow also remembered the director's unintentional habit of placing Lombard on the wrong side of the camera, revealing a scar she preferred hidden from view. "Poor Victor," he recalled, "subject to Carole's pithy and never-ending assaults from morn till night, [he] seemingly could no longer tell her right side from her left. Each time he bumbled, Carole would erupt."[28]

Special effects in the film also caused problems for the emerging Paramount star. Lombard had to remain motionless on camera for lengthy periods of time while makeup and stop-frame photography caused her face to appear more like Vivienne Osborne's, whose spirit enters her body. Salkow remembered that, "For Carole, whose internal combustion machinery was never at rest, this was the final indignity. She came down hard on Victor. 'God, this bastard's trying to paralyze me. Victor, God'll punish you for this...,' she moaned."[29]

Perhaps Salkow's most vivid memory of Lombard's clashes with Halperin is of the March 10, 1933, earthquake, which took 52 lives in the Los Angeles area and shook the ground at Paramount Studios. That afternoon, the earth rumbled and the set shuddered. The *Supernatural* crew "ran shrieking from the set in wild flight," Salkow remembered.[30] Nearby, Bela Lugosi, W. C. Fields, and cohorts were themselves disrupted on the set of Paramount's comedy *International House*. The entire studio was in disarray, except perhaps Lombard. She approached Halperin, who had fled the sound stage, waved her finger at him, and said: "Victor—*that* was only a warning!"[31]

Lombard herself made the newspapers immediately after the earthquake, having lost a $5,000 ring somewhere between the studio—while at work on *Supernatural*—and her home. Only one week after its loss to the police, Lombard "rejoiced" in its recovery. An 80 karat stone, it was found in the gutter in front of a garage near Paramount Studios. Its finder, one Harry Modisette immediately returned the ring to Lombard.[32] Her reception of Modisette was far kinder than that which she regularly gave to Victor Halperin on studio sets.

While her anger at Halperin is hardly excusable, *Supernatural*'s plot is very much unlike any of the other films in which Lombard appeared. In it, a vile murderess named Ruth Rogen (Vivienne Osborne) is sentenced to death for strangling several lovers. Dr. Houston (H. B. Warner) convinces her to let him experiment on her dead body, believing the evil spirit within criminals can live on after death. Meanwhile, the young Roma (Lombard) spends time in mourning, as her brother has recently died. A bogus medium named Paul Bavian (Allan Dinehart)—who was himself associated with the murderess— holds a séance so Roma can speak to her brother. In a bizarre twist, the spirit of Rogen enters Roma as the séance occurs; eventually, she almost succeeds in strangling Bavian. Her fiancé and the doctor help restore normalcy, with a happy ending for Roma. Bavian, however, is brutally hung from the anchor ropes of a yacht while attempting to escape Rogen's spirit.

High drama occurs in even the earliest moments of the film. *Supernatural*'s optically printed title blazes onto the screen in a lightning-bolt style font, followed by a series of quotations in similar lettering printed against a city skyline and aurally accompanied by a dramatic vocal chorus. The proverb "Treat all supernatural beings with respect, but keep aloof from them!" is featured and is attributed to Confucius; it is followed by Mohammed's "We will bring forth the dead from their graves!" The group of quotations is completed with Matthew 10:1 from the Holy Bible: "And He gave his twelve disciples [power] against unclean spirits to cast them out."

In terms of its content, *Supernatural* is punctuated with visual imagery that, while less atmospheric than that in *White Zombie*, is still skillfully executed. A montage of newspaper clippings with the Rogen murders and extreme closeups of her eyes and hands, superimpositions of the deceased character John Courtney, and lengthy segments devoid of any dialogue, all present an effective mise-en-scène that attempts to build on *White Zombie* with the aid of stronger production values.

Cinematographer Martinelli, veteran of *White Zombie*, provides a variety of tracking shots which seem even more smoothly executed than those in the prior Halperin film; one—in an apparent attempt at comedy—even tracks back from Beryl Mercer's buttocks to reveal the entire room in which she stands. Particularly impressive is a camera movement which starts after a dissolve from a car in the rain. The camera moves up the side of a highrise apartment building to its penthouse. The building is a model, but a very believable one. The shot dissolves into a shot of actual windows in the rain, through which Dr. Houston (H. B. Warner) can be seen.

While possessing such visual acumen and drawing on fascinating subject material, *Supernatural* fails aesthetically for some of the same reasons that provided strength to *White Zombie*. Whereas the latter film benefits from the often overacted performances insomuch as it becomes more surreal and dreamlike as a result, *Supernatural* presents very stagy acting from its principals which tends to disable the attempted mood. Osborne seems quite unbelievable as the ruthless killer, and H. B. Warner employs an overstated style of acting as the good doctor. But most devastating to the film overall is Lombard, who fails to provide the magnetic level of personality needed for the film. Unconvincing in the transformation from Roma to Rogen, Lombard—perhaps because of her lack of interest in the film and her lack of audience association with horror—exudes none of the powerful, villainous charisma of a Bela Lugosi.

Secondarily, the visual style of the Halperin-Martinelli team lacks the mystical background and settings of *White Zombie*'s Haiti. Their use of some quite dramatic background music and some extreme closeups, while interesting in the particular, seem at times ill-suited to the generally ordinary sets and characters. However unusual the story, its execution seems rather normal save for these infrequent visual motifs. While *White Zombie* translated the absurd into a coherent atmosphere, *Supernatural* remains far more interesting for some of its individual parts than for its whole.

The film opened at the New York Paramount on April 21, 1933, with ads heralding it as the story of "A Female Jekyll-Hyde."[33] The theater called the program "Broadway's Biggest Show Value!" but promoted the live stage show of radio stars Jane Froman and James Melton with as much space as *Supernatural* in opening day advertisements.

Public response in New York, and indeed across the country, was minimal in comparison to *White Zombie*'s. For example, the New York Paramount's gross for one week of *Supernatural* was only $23,300; their box-office grosses for screenings of other films since January of 1931 had reached as high as $85,900.[34] *Supernatural* appeared in New York City again in July 1933 at the RKO Roxy for a disappointing three-day booking; elsewhere in the U.S., the film often played lesser theaters and even at the bottom of some double feature bills.[35] The manager of a theater in Kansas wrote that another manager would "be supernatural if [they] can get any dough on this one."[36]

Film reviewers in New York City were generally far kinder to *Supernatural* than the Kansas theater manager; they certainly used a gentler tone than they used against *White Zombie*. Big Apple critics were apparently still reeling from so underestimating the 1932 Halperin film. For example, the April 22, 1933, *New York Times* said, "Notwithstanding the incredibility of many of its main incidents, *Supernatural* ... succeeds in awakening no little interest in its spooky doings. ... Mr. Dinehart does very well by his role. Miss Lombard's portrayal also is praiseworthy."

The same day's *New York Herald Tribune* claimed,

Theater artwork designed by Robert Ewing, artist for the Luna Theatre in Lafayette, Indiana. Printed in the September 23, 1933, Motion Picture Herald.

"*Supernatural*, as I hope you have guessed, doesn't make a bit of sense, but it does supply a lot of unwitting fun." The newspaper critic not only referred to *White Zombie* as a prior Halperin movie, but even went so far as to describe Lombard's possessed character as a "platinum Zombie."

Reviewers elsewhere in the U.S. also readily remembered the Halperins' connection with *White Zombie*, though *Newsweek* incorrectly wrote "Brian Marlow and Harvey Thew, who wrote *Supernatural*, Victor Halperin, the director, and Carole Lombard, the star, were all involved in *The White Zombie* [*sic*], another recent challenge to credulity." Of that group, only Halperin had worked on the prior film. *Newsweek* also instructed its national readers that "Those able to take on faith these ["spooks"] and other spirit manifestations should be entertained by *Supernatural*. It has good pace and directors and authors have the sense to present all the supernatural happenings as though they were matters of course and not subject to question."[37]

Industry trades like the *Motion Picture Herald* were less impressed and less kind. Its critic wrote that:

> If the so-called supernatural were made rather less inconceivable, less obviously a machination than a manifestation of something beyond ordinary ken, it doubtless would have more entertainment value. Such comment may well be registered with respect to *Supernatural*. A too-obvious effort to appear mystical, mysterious, and weird causes it at times to descend of its own weight to something approaching absurdity.[38]

The Film Daily added that: "…it was not developed in a manner that makes for good entertainment. … The story never really grips, either in a dramatic way or in the matter of sympathy for any of the characters."[39] *Motion Picture Daily* believed "[s]ome fine acting talent is wasted."[40] *Harrison's Reports* thought that the film was "wholly unconvincing."[41]

Variety was even more harsh, calling *Supernatural* "a sixty-five minute ghost story that dies after the first half hour. Carole Lombard, featured, is pitted against a role that needs more expert handling in acting and direction than it receives." Most critical of all, *The Billboard* of April 29, 1933, wrote that: "it's hard to figure out whether it's meant to be a burlesque or designed for straight consumption. One can only hope the former; it's the only way it could possibly get by."

Suggested ballyhoo efforts certainly requested "straight consumption" by audiences. These included a trade belief that theaters should "Play up the names of Miss Lombard, Miss Osborne, and Scott for whatever marquee worth they may have in the individual community. … The idea of soul or spirit transmission from one body to another—transubstantiation—is not new, but this theory of evil emanations, in search of vengeance, finding new instruments for wreaking that vengeance, is at least novel. The most should be made of it. This is, rather obviously, adult material"[42]

Such adult material probably seemed to the Halperins a vast improvement over *White Zombie*. The glow of their prior success, major studio backing, the lack of distribution problems—all of these would also have excited the former independent filmmakers. It is difficult to determine whether the more comfortable studio environment hurt the film; perhaps it was the choice of actors, or the translation of Weston's story into script form. It could well have been a combination of these difficulties that kept *Supernatural* from duplicating *White Zombie*'s aesthetic or financial success.

For better or worse, when they considered the Halperin brothers after 1933, major studios remembered *Supernatural*'s failures more readily than *White Zombie*'s victories.

Revolt of the Zombies

The Halperins' lack of success with projects like *Supernatural* and their return to independent filmmaking must have made the idea of a follow-up film to *White Zombie* seem quite appealing.[43] By the mid-thirties, the Halperins would also have noticed the success garnered by one horror film sequel, *The Bride of Frankenstein* (1935), and perhaps as a result were even more inspired to make another zombie film. Their only problem was that they had relinquished certain rights in their 1932 contract; even the use of the word "zombie" had been sacrificed to Amusement Securities Corporation. Regardless, the Halperins moved forward. Zombies were still popular, and as a result they were worth a legal fight.

In late November 1935, trades announced Victor Halperin would direct the "sequel" to *White Zombie*, which would be produced by Academy Pictures and scripted by Howard Higgin.[44] The "start" was set for early January, but that deadline quickly came and went. By mid–January 1936, the script was still unfinished, even though the Halperins planned to shoot at the Talisman studio lot in early February.[45] Further, as *The Hollywood Reporter* claimed, "A camera and technical crew will sail from San Francisco [the first week of February] to film background shots for the Halperin Brothers' *Revolt of the Zombies* at Angkor, Indo-China. The crew will be in charge of Harry Pritzker, former Chicago prosecuting attorney."[46]

Others were added to the payroll in February, specifically Lee Smith, an archaeologist signed as technical advisor, and George Savidge of the Chicago Art Institute, who was to assist with art direction. Both had exhaustively researched the lost city of Angkor, the setting of the film. As *The Hollywood Reporter* was quick to mention, the idea for Angkor was not new; Douglas Fairbanks, among others, had once planned to use the city as the focal point of an unmade film.[47]

Though Bela Lugosi was a consideration for the role of lead villain Armand Louque, the Halperins eventually cast Dean Jagger in the part. The decision may have been motivated by budgetary constraints, but it is also possible that the Hungarian was unavailable. In 1936, his Universal Studios contract still demanded one film from him, and that obligation was met with *Postal Inspector*, Lugosi's only film of 1936. Though its shooting schedule would seemingly not have interfered with the Halperin film, perhaps Lugosi's Universal contract would not have allowed signing.

Even without Lugosi, though, the Halperins forged ahead. According to a March 6, 1936, issue of *The Hollywood Reporter*, "Dorothy Stone has been engaged by Halperin Bros. for a lead in *Revolt of the Zombies*. This is the first film part of importance for the dancing daughter of Fred Stone [the vaudevillian who appeared as the Scarecrow in the original 1903 Broadway production of *The Wizard of Oz*]. Shooting starts tomorrow with the script revamped to include songs and sequences to take advantage of Stone's musical talent."[48]

Once again, however, a delay occurred. The Halperins finally began production on March 9, 1936, with the shoot being finished later that same month.[49] Editing on the film was finished in California on or about April 20, 1936, at which time the negative was immediately shipped to New York for positive prints to be struck. Distribution, however, would prove far more difficult than it had been with *White Zombie*.

Legal problems erupted, with the *New York Times* announcing on May 26, 1936, that: "Amusement Securities Corporation ... obtained an order from Supreme Court Justice John F. Carew requiring the producers, distributors, and prospective exhibitors of a new film called *Revolt of the Zombies* to show cause why they should not be enjoined from using the word 'zombie' in their picture. Defendants in the action, which is returnable in Supreme Court tomorrow, are Academy Pictures Distributing Company, Edward J. and Victor Halperin of the Midtown Theatre Corporation, operators of the Rialto Theatre, Producers Laboratories, Inc., Melbert Pictures, Inc., RKO Film Booking Corporation, and Ameranglo Corporation. ... *Revolt of the Zombies* was scheduled to open this week at the Rialto."[50] More simply, *The Hollywood Reporter* announced that "war broke out among zombies in New York...."[51]

All defendants were notified of the plaintiffs' intentions through attorney communications even prior to Justice Carew's order, hoping to stop the exhibition and distribution of *Revolt of the Zombies*. Amusement Securities sent warning letters to Midtown theaters and the Rialto Theatre on May 14, 1936, as the premiere was scheduled at the latter for May 28. Prints had even been shipped to England in April, though at the time of the ASC letters they had yet to be screened.

Just as the May 28 premiere approached, Judge Wasservogel of the New York State Supreme Court announced his decision to refuse a temporary injunction against the Halperins' film, allowing it to be screened until a judgment in the case was reached.[52] Such screenings were also allowed to keep the original film title intact, even though the plaintiffs would press for it to be changed.[53] By June 1, 1936, the court—quickly weary of the problem—appointed attorney Herman Hoffman as referee in the case. His job was to hold hearings and report back to the court with a decision.[54]

Prior to the beginning of hearings, the film was shown June 4–10, 1936 at the Rialto in New York City

under the title *Revolt of the Zombies*. And *The Hollywood Reporter* claimed "Eddie Halperin is not worrying [about the lawsuit] but is on his way back to the [west] coast to resume production," presumably on another project.[55] *Motion Picture Herald*'s description spoke of the premiere of "...a lobby ballyhoo [which] attracted crowds that impeded pedestrian traffic and filled the theater to capacity. Audience reaction noncommittal."[56] Meanwhile, the reaction of Sam Krellberg of ASC was far more intense than that of the Rialto's audience. He quickly petitioned to have his representative investigate *Revolt*'s proceeds, particularly revenue from its run at the Rialto in New York. Supreme Court Justice Velente declined, and—in the words of *The Hollywood Reporter*—the "battle of the zombies [would] have to be settled in the trenches of a court trial."[57]

The case of *Amusement Securities Corporation v. Academy Pictures Distribution Corporation* soon took place in the Supreme Court of New York, at which time referee Hoffman examined various contracts and documents and heard from numerous witnesses.[58] In addition to the Halperins, the other defendants were all involved in either production, distribution, or exhibition of the film. For example, Producers Laboratories had an agreement to manufacture 35mm positive prints of the film, the Midtown Theater Corporation was to exhibit the film through an agreement with Melbert Pictures, and the Ameranglo Corporation was to distribute the film overseas.[59] All were on trial with Academy Pictures Distributing Corporation, of which the Halperins were the principal officers, directors, and stockholders.

The plaintiffs made their accusations against the aforementioned with grim determination. In addition to citing unfair competition, Amusement Securities offered their

Artwork from the Revolt of the Zombies *pressbook.*

July 15, 1932 contract with the Halperins as evidence. In exchange for monetary compensation, the brothers had signed the contract, specifically agreeing to waive their rights to *White Zombie*:

> …including but not limited to all negative and positive prints and films of every kind and all sound tracks, as well as musical recordations and all additions and improvements in and to the said motion picture photoplay, together with the title and story thereof, as well as the motion picture, stage, radio, television, literary and other rights therein and thereto, including but not limited to any and all copyright taken out or which may be taken out in the United States or elsewhere in and to said motion picture photoplay and/or the title and story thereof, or any claims or claim that has been made relative to the right or title to the aforementioned.

Such an all-encompassing relinquishment of rights would not bode well for the beleaguered Halperins and Academy Pictures.

Other contracts surfaced during the trial as well. For example, on approximately February 10, 1934, a conference occurred between Edward, Victor, their father Robert L. Halperin, and a single representative of Amusement Securities Corporation. The meeting resulted in ASC paying Robert Halperin $5,000 for all rights he possessed in *White Zombie*, including "the title and story thereof," in accordance with the agreement by his sons to give up their rights in the film in the July 15, 1932, contract. Why this occurred in 1934 rather than 1932 is a mystery, as is the fee which the Halperins' father was paid.

Prior to the start of Amusement Securities' legal action, the most recent discussions between the Halperins and ASC occurred in October 1935. The two brothers submitted eight tentatively titled screenplays, including *The Thrill of a Century* (later produced and released by the Halperins in 1936 as *I Conquer the Sea*) and *Revolt of the Zombies*. Their negotiations were carried out by Benjamin Solomon, who attempted to elicit financing from ASC for all of the planned films. ASC proposed a contract to option seven of the projects and to provide funding for the eighth: *The Thrill of a Century*. The Halperins declined, sending word in November 1935 that they had made financial arrangements with other investors. But to Amusement Securities' way of thinking, others did not have the right to use the word "zombie."

In his final opinion, referee Herman Hoffman wrote: "It seems that the term 'zombie,' though the term be considered descriptive, is subject to exclusive appropriation as a trade name. A word which is not in common use and is unintelligible and nondescriptive to the general public, though it may be known to linguists and scientists, may be properly regarded as arbitrary and fan-

ciful and capable of being used as a trademark or trade name."

He continued by proclaiming: "The word 'zombie' has acquired a secondary meaning, suggestive of the photoplay *White Zombie*, by association of that term with the title *White Zombie*, in the minds of the public as a result of the widespread and successful showing of *White Zombie*, and the publicity given thereto, which entitles the owner of that photoplay to injunctive relief against the manufacture, exhibition, etc. of the photoplay *Revolt of the Zombies*."

Much of the Halperins' defense to Hoffman was predicated on the historical fact that others had used the term "zombie" prior to their 1932 film. They introduced as evidence both the unproduced 1929 play *Zombi*, and Kenneth Webb's similarly titled Broadway flop *Zombie*. The Halperins' legal defense also made clear that the word "zombie" had by 1936 appeared in dictionaries as well. For example, both the 1935 edition of *Webster's New International Dictionary* and the 1935 *Funk and Wagnall's Dictionary* included comprehensive definitions of the term. Indeed, the former included one definition ("a soulless human corpse, still dead, but taken from the grave and endowed by sorcery with a mechanical semblance of life,—it is a dead body which is made to walk and act and move as if it were alive.") contributed by William B. Seabrook, author of *The Magic Island* (Harcourt, Brace, and Co., 1929).

Hoffman discounted such arguments, however, and noted that—in addition to the fact that "zombie" had never been used in the title of a film prior to *White Zombie*—the word was unknown to the general populace until the Halperins' successful 1932 movie. Even a defense witness under oath admitted that the word "had no general meaning in the English language and that not one person in a hundred knew what it meant" before *White Zombie*. The "Court," as referee Hoffman would describe himself in his decision, had little difficulty in offering numerous examples of descriptive words which had been trademarked in the past, and in finding that *White Zombie* "…has other than reissue rights. It is still being exploited by United Artists on behalf of plaintiff in foreign countries, where it has apparently not yet exhausted itself as a first issue, and there is the possibility of the plaintiff's developing a sequel under the same or a similar name as was done in the case of *The Gold Diggers*."

Amusement Securities had themselves been quick to argue that *Revolt* could harm reissues of *White Zombie* by confusing theatergoers if the two appeared during a similar period in the same locality. Secondly, the plaintiffs alleged that the two films would even compete for the same theaters, making the perhaps overreaching argument that a reissue of *White Zombie* would "likely be played in no less than 3,000 of the 10,000 available theaters, that is, those of the 15,000 in the United States in which it has not yet been played."

Hoffman agreed, believing that the defendants, "under a colorful imitation of plaintiff's title, will appropriate the good will inherent in that name." Indeed, the court acknowledged the fact that "one newspaper commentator actually referred to [the 1936] defendants' picture as *White Zombie*." As for potential profits from reissues of the 1932 film, the court also agreed money was still to be made. Even defense witnesses acknowledged that "Bela Lugosi, who took the principal part in *White Zombie*, and one Karloff are the two outstanding stars now playing the principal parts in horror pictures going to voodooism and other primitive superstitions for their source material and themes, and that Bela Lugosi ... has a great appeal to that part of the public which likes plays of that character."[60] As a result, the Court believed *White Zombie* constituted "a valuable property right" because of the "popularity and renown of a particular member of the cast," meaning Bela Lugosi.

Hoffman also considered that, "in most of the posters [for *Revolt of the Zombies*], the words *White Zombie* appear in heavy or otherwise prominent type calculated to catch the unwary eye which looks only at headlines and nothing else." Similar artwork was also noted, as was the use of a quotation from Article 249 of the Haitian Penal Code that was so important in the ads for *White Zombie*. The Court also saw ads speaking of a "recreated [*sic*] role of Murder" in the "sequel" to *White Zombie*, even though Hoffman came to realize that *Revolt* featured no such character and did not even fit the definition of sequel. To him, the Halperins' offense came in their "studied simulation of a business name ... as a means of decoying some of the good will which *White Zombie* has. The guise is too much the same." That the Halperins had been compensated previously for these attributes of *White Zombie* made the referee believe their conduct all the more unfair.

At the same time, Hoffman did not believe the Halperins had legally offended by their ads announcing *Revolt* was made by the same organization that had produced *White Zombie*. The plaintiffs had introduced evidence of advertisements that included statements like, "Pre-sold to the public through their remembrances of *White Zombie*; pre-sold to the exhibitor through the never-to-be-for-gotten [*sic*] profits of *White Zombie*" and "Following in the million dollar profit tracks laid down by *White Zombie*." These examples apparently did not bother Hoffman's sensibilities either.

More than anything, Hoffman *was* bothered by two key acts committed by the defendants: breach of contract and unfair competition. He did not pursue the former, as it was not part of the ASC's written complaint. But the latter charge was, and as a result Hoffman ruled in favor of the plaintiffs, in his final opinion released on June 27, 1936. Amusement Securities received damages fixed at $7,500 plus $4,000 in legal costs, far less than the $60,000 they had sought.[61] ASC was also granted an accounting of profits from *Revolt*, with permission to seek additional damages in the future.

In addition, Hoffman forever prohibited the defendants from using or exhibiting posters or other advertising "containing cuts, slogans, headlines or other similar material taken from *White Zombie* or tending to identify *Revolt of the Zombies* with it or stating that *Revolt of the Zombies* is a sequel to *White Zombie*." While harsh in the Halperins' eyes, the judgment did allow them to keep their film's original title, even if not all its proceeds.

Long after Hoffman's judgment was released, litigation continued. On August 13, 1936, *The Hollywood Reporter* announced that New York Supreme Court Justice Pecora heard a motion made by the brothers Halperin to be excluded from what had finally become a $10,878 judgment against them, the Midtown Theater Corporation, Producers Laboratory, and the Ameranglo Corporation. The Halperins' belated complaint was that they "were not served, were not residents of California, and were never represented by attorneys in the matter."[62] Pecora was unconvinced and quickly dismissed their request.

By the autumn of 1936, the Halperins attempted yet another legal maneuver to avoid paying ASC; they petitioned a higher court to reconsider Hoffman's decision. Amusement Securities quickly and successfully persuaded the appellate division in New York to dismiss the request for an appeal, and the original judgment stood.[63] Money would finally change hands, and ASC, for better or worse, would legally own the word zombie in the 1930s, at least in the world of cinema.

As Hoffman suggested and as this chapter has argued, *White Zombie* popularized the word and very concept of a zombie for U.S. audiences of the 1930s. It is bizarre, however, that in his decision Hoffman equated the popularization of a concept with the trademarking of a name. However much the Halperins unfairly claimed *Revolt* to be a sequel, they hardly infringed on a trademark. Despite Hoffman's attempts to rely on precedents of cases involving film and entertainment, the ruling seems less than fair in view of the use of the word and concept of zombies in films like *Ouanga*, books like *Damballa Calls*, and articles in magazines like *Country Life*. Blame might go to the Halperins' legal representation, but if the brothers themselves should have been accused of anything, it was creating a film vastly inferior to *White Zombie*.

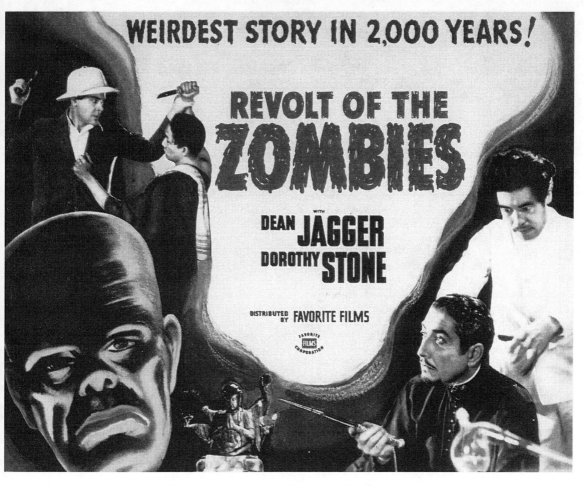

A 1936 11" × 14" title lobby card for Revolt of the Zombies.

"Many strange events were recorded in the secret archives of the fighting natives during World War I. But none stranger than that which occurred when a regiment of French Cambodians from the vicinity of the Lost City of Angkor arrived on the Franco-Austrian front." These dramatic words appear at the beginning of *Revolt of the Zombies* to introduce viewers to its story and setting.

Little can be said of the film itself; aesthetically, it was not worth the sound and fury provoked by the trial. Though a fascinating and original idea for a story, it is conveyed through poorly written dialogue. Drab sets and a generally nonatmospheric style of lighting provide the backdrop to uninspired acting. Sequences without dialogue lack the strength of similarly silent moments in *White Zombie*. Unwisely chosen music also harms the film's mood; even the theme running under the opening credits seems far too lighthearted for the film's attempt

at horror. More disappointingly, Arthur Martinelli's cinematography proves far less inventive than in *White Zombie*; with the exception of a few well-executed tracking shots, the film offers a simplistic, nondescript style of camerawork almost indistinguishable from almost any other "B" film of the thirties.

Only a few visually interesting moments occur. For example, a closeup of Armand Louque (Dean Jagger) dissolves into a well-matched closeup of a bronze idol's face. In general, however, an air of incredulity pervades the film. Shots of the same bronze, multilimbed idol are highly ineffective thanks to their lighting, composition, and repeated use. Much the same could be said of the set's secret panels, a tired cliché thanks to endless gothic novels and old dark house films and plays. The fanning of zombie dust into the eyes of victims appears almost silly in contrast to the subtleties of *White Zombie*. Even the zombies themselves are far more disappointing than in the earlier film; rather than corpselike characters with individual stories and compelling makeup and costumes, they are instead military automatons who suffer without even benefit of moody lighting.

The major similarity to *White Zombie* comes in the extreme closeups shown of eyes.[64] In fact, the eyes in *Revolt of the Zombies* themselves belong to Bela Lugosi—lifted from the earlier film, apparently without Amusement Securities' consent or knowledge; no mention is made in the credits of permission, and no charge of copyright infringement was made in the legal proceedings. The closeups appear in *Revolt* some seven times, in each case superimposed over either static shots of people in danger of zombification or over pans of the automatonlike soldiers. Such visual echoes mark the disparity in quality between the Halperins' first and second zombie films.

Attempts to draw on *White Zombie's* success would not end with Lugosi's eyes. Ideas for theater exploitation for *Revolt* also mimicked those used for the earlier film. "Exploitation possibilities reside chiefly in capitalization of the supernatural or superstitious phenomena associated with the creation of these indestructable [*sic*] men of occult origin," *Motion Picture Herald* told theater managers.[65] *Motion Picture Daily* spoke in similar terms of "…a wealth of exploitation material in this film."[66] Nonetheless, only a small number of audiences would rush to see the film.

Revolt of the Zombies' pressbook had offered theater managers numerous ways to sway uncommitted crowds, suggesting such catchlines as "500,000 people, soulless but alive, piling mighty blocks of granite to build a city which passed away two thousand years ago!" and "Mighty Angkor! Ancient land of mystery … Place of Zombies … Not dead … Not alive … but touched by the finger of death." Along with the more overt appropriations from the *White Zombie* campaign, the *Revolt* pressbook borrowed more general ideas from its predecessor's exploitation. Several catchlines refer to the film as a "passionate romance" with horror as the background, and despite the Halperins' legal claims of the word "zombie" being readily known to U.S. theatergoers, the pressbook does feel compelled to offer a definition.[67]

However exciting exploitation materials claimed the film to be, critics were unimpressed. The June 10, 1936 *Variety* believed *Revolt of the Zombies* had:

> …hardly strength enough to move alone and will need good support to send [audiences] out happy. … There is so little to the real story that the action stalls terribly at times to gain footage. … The photography is seldom good and the direction is futile. … There is never the thrill and suspense that might well have been created from the material.

Harrison's Reports echoed this by calling the film "Mediocre!" and mentioning that the "plot is thin … at times it is ludicrous."[68] *The Billboard* of June 13, 1936 went further, calling *Revolt* "the bottom," adding that "even bonafide zombies, if any, should resent it." Of Victor Halperin, the review said "he must have worked very hard to get such a peak in puerility." Of 11 monitored trade notices, *The Billboard* counted seven unfavorable, four "no comments," and no favorable reviews.[69]

Only *Motion Picture Daily* noticed any redeeming value in the film, suggesting the "story has weird angles and situations in good proportion to the drama. It builds dramatically to an exciting conclusion."[70] It is difficult to believe the reviewer watched the film, as the ringing chorus of complaint from other critics—quite unlike some of their 1932 counterparts who reviewed *White Zombie*—were fair in saddling the film with poor critiques. As mentioned earlier, *Revolt of the Zombies* has little redeeming value aesthetically.

Few reviews turned up in the national media or the daily newspapers, though Frank S. Nugent at the *New York Times* did respond to *Revolt* on June 5, 1936. "It is only in the beginning that the Halperin brothers' new treatise achieves any real degree of horror," he believed. Curiously, the review was much less harsh than the same paper's examination of *White Zombie* four years earlier. Perhaps Nugent remembered how handily the earlier film had conquered the Rivoli, and its tremendous success which flew in the face of the *Times'* review.

Marguerite Talezaar at the *New York Herald Tribune* also reviewed the film on June 5, 1936, claiming "[t]he entertainment, while goofy, proved diverting, holding yesterday's audience rapt if not hypnotized." But most audiences which saw *Revolt of the Zombies* in the subsequent days and weeks of that summer were apparently not as hypnotized, as the film found little success in U.S. theaters.

The movie fared much better at the hands of critics in Great Britain, where *The Cinema News and Property Gazette* heralded it as a "*White Zombie* sequel" and remembered that the earlier 1932 film had broken "records in countless instances in cinemas all over [England]."[71] *Kinematograph Weekly* went so far as to call *Revolt of the Zombies* a "[s]pectacular, romantic drama, a sensational essay in the supernatural, curbed in its serial-like conception to safe industrial dimensions by the painstaking and sincere acting of a sound cast and colourful stagecraft."[72] By comparison to the U.S. reviews, *Kinematograph Weekly* seems almost to have screened a different film.

Overall, *Revolt of the Zombies* is an unfortunate derivation of the aesthetic expertise that created *White Zombie*.[73] Perhaps partial blame for this should go to the limited budget that, unlike in the earlier effort, did not or could not stretch to afford the utilization of preexisting Hollywood sets; possibly the Halperins believed the Angkor setting alone to be fascinating enough to captivate audiences. The absence of author Garnett Weston from the artistic team may also have hurt the film's chances. In addition, as with *Supernatural*, the Halperins did not anchor the story with a strong enough personality in the choice of a lead actor. Attempting as they were to do a series of films within a short amount of time, the brothers may have all too readily believed that an automatic success could be achieved with zombies. They had found themselves in the shadow of their 1932 film, but unable to reproduce its aesthetic or financial success.

More Voodoo in the Cinema and Theatre

In addition to the Halperin brothers, other producers readily saw continued potential with the subjects addressed in *White Zombie*. For example, the theater felt the drums of voodoo in such productions as *Ouanga: Music Drama*, a 1932 libretto by John Frederick Mathews and Clarence Cameron White. Stage or cinema works of this kind often incorporated aspects of *White Zombie*—whether it was the use of voodoo drums and zombies or the inclusion of themes like race relations and labor problems—into their plots. Beyond its narrative and thematic influences, *White Zombie* proved the box-office viability of voodoo and zombies. While it was a link in the historical chain of texts on these subjects, its public consumption greatly exceeded even William B. Seabrook's 1929 book *The Magic Island*.[74] As a result, the film spurred interest among producers in repeating its financial success.[75]

Only days after *White Zombie*'s first preview, *Variety* ran the short article "Negro Voodoo Film," announcing that "Pat Carlisle, former leader of the local Voodoo orchestra, has turned independent film producer. He is headed for the north woods with a band of 20 Negroes for a film based on Voodooism."[76] What became of this film is unknown; most likely given the lack of follow-up articles and reviews in industry trades, the film was never even finished. Carlisle nonetheless had become the first to follow the Halperins' juggernaut.

Other works which went into production after *White Zombie*'s release also bore the mark of its influence. For example, as the Halperin film solidified its success in many U.S. theaters, *The Film Daily* wrote in late August of Faustin Wirkus, a retired U.S. marine, who had previously been "crowned White King of the Black Isle" in Haiti. At that moment, he was traveling through Haiti once again, this time with a film crew. "Because of his power over the natives," the trade claimed, "Wirkus is said to be the only white man who could obtain shots of these [voodoo] ceremonials." The purpose: inclusion in a movie called *Voodoo*, which was to be released through Sol Lesser's Principal Releasing Corporation.[77] Movement on the Wirkus project probably occurred directly because of *White Zombie*'s success.

"You can take any view you wish of this extraordinary religion," Wirkus explained in a *Harper's Monthly Magazine*. "It has combined the ancestor-spirit and snake worship of Ardra and Whydah; the poison art, spells, hypnotism, ventriloquism, and hysterical ecstasy of the witch-doctor; blood sacrifice and approach to the mystery by partaking of blood and flesh; the Christian story of the Crucifixion; some Catholic saints naively felt to correspond to Dembala and Legba—and has mixed this into a striking pattern of its own. But whatever one's feeling about it, no one can deny that its worshippers really believe. Hence its living power over their mind and acts."[78] Like William Seabrook before him, Wirkus offered fantastic tales of voodoo to mass literary audiences.

Voodoo, Wirkus's finished film, was copyrighted on March 31, 1933, and distributed by independent film producer Sol Lesser's Principal Films. After playing New York City, *Voodoo* hit Los Angeles' RKO Hillside Theater later in the spring of 1933, then moved in the summer to such other theaters as the Warner's in Santa Barbara. The film immediately found problems in obtaining bookings; at 36 minutes, it was too long to be considered a short and not long enough to stand alone as a feature.[79]

In terms of its content, *Voodoo* apparently mimicked the style of prior travelogues released by Principal. Marrying both nonfiction sequences and staged scenes, the film attempted to show the synthesis of voodooism with all aspects of Haitians' lives. *Motion Picture Daily* wrote that, "...the picture would have been considerably more effective if [Wirkus] had eliminated the fake dramatics for a straight recounting of life among the voodoo believers."[80] *Motion Picture Herald*'s review added, "Interesting is the pictorial record of the frenzied ritual of the blacks, but when the planned sacrifice of a girl is frustrated by the efforts of Wirkus, the picture smacks too much of the posed melodramatic to be highly effective."[81] At least in some ways, Wirkus followed the path of Seabrook's *The Magic Island*: adding melodramatic touches to nonfiction.

In August 1932, as *White Zombie*'s New York City success was being well covered in industry trades, Columbia Studios purchased Clements Ripley's voodoo short story *Black Moon* with the intention of rapidly

A rare ad promoting the film Voodoo, *published in the June 6, 1933,* Santa Barbara Morning Press.

adapting it to the screen.[82] The studio recounted the tale in press releases: "Beginning in New York's topmost social circles, the story sweeps to the mysterious black nation of Haiti ... and there the fascinating blond woman who had shone so brilliantly in Manhattan society is revealed to be the white priestess of a weird voodoo cult."[83] *The Afro-American* newspaper, expecting *Black Moon* to be a part of the continuing 1930s horror cycle, soon wrote that "it should be even more of an entertaining novelty to movie audiences than *Frankenstein* and *Dracula* and the recent *White Zombie*."[84]

Despite initial plans for expeditious production, *Black Moon* remained in limbo until early 1934. In late February of that year, Jack Holt was signed as the star.[85] By early April, Columbia chose Fay Wray as the female lead and Roy William Neill as the director.[86] The studio also hired dance director Max Schenk to direct some 500 African-American dancers in an elaborate "ritual number" for the film.[87] Schenk, along with Columbia musical director Lou Silvers, also wrote music to accompany the dance sequence.[88]

Black Moon materialized into an interesting film, though its 1934 production meant it borrowed far less from *White Zombie* than it may have had it been made two years earlier. At the same time, *Harrison's Reports* did say that the film "...is something on the order of *White Zombie*."[89] Also, two members of the *White Zombie* cast, Clarence Muse and Robert Frazer, do appear in minor roles. Curiously, even Edna Tichenor—*Black Moon*'s stand-in for actress Dorothy Burgess—held an important place in horror film history; she had been the bat girl in Tod Browning's *London After Midnight* (1927).

However historically interesting *Black Moon* remains, reviewers for industry trades in 1934 were none too

kind about it. For example, *The Film Daily* believed it was "somewhat far-fetched in idea and not always plausible in development,"[90] and *Harrison's Reports* dubbed it "Terrible!"[91] Unfavorable notices and apparently bad word of mouth caused the film to do poorly at the box office. It was quickly forgotten, making little impact on 1934 audiences.

Despite the disappointing financial return of *Black Moon*, other voodoo films continued to surface during the thirties. *Drums O'Voodoo* (1934), directed by Arthur Hoerl and adapted from J. August Smith's play *Louisiana*, centered on the cult practices within that southern U.S. state. The story, transferred to film from the stage version with few changes even in its dialogue, concerns Thomas Catt, owner of a "juke" joint, and his lust for a young woman named Myrtle. Unless Myrtle is given to him, Catt threatens to reveal that the grandfather of a preacher named Amos, Myrtle's fiancé, once killed a man. Amos ignores the threat, and the mysterious Aunt Hagar prepares a voodoo spell. When Catt attempts to tell Amos's congregation the secret he holds, a bolt of lightning resulting from Hagar's hex kills him. Catt is then smothered in quicksand, leaving Amos and Myrtle free from his blackmail.

The play, staged on Broadway by the Negro Theater Guild, closed after only eight performances, perhaps due to a very poor review in the *New York Times*.[92] Though Smith never commented publicly on the origin of his idea, it is highly possible that—given the fact *Louisiana* was written during the Fall of 1932—*White Zombie* may have prompted him to develop a voodoo tale. Even though the Halperins' film did not impact *Drums O'Voodoo*'s story, its box-office success may well have helped Smith gain financing for his first attempt at Broadway. Though the play failed, Smith did manage to raise the needed budget to transfer the story to the screen.

Produced by International Stageplay Pictures, Inc., the film *Drums o' Voodoo* was distributed on a States Rights basis. Playwright Smith appeared as Amos, and many of the other cast members had appeared in the stage version. Voodoo drums, heard effectively in *White Zombie*, are played on most of the *Drums o' Voodoo* soundtrack. Shot at New York's Atlas Soundfilm Recording Studios in March 1933, the film was completed by the end of the same month. Substantial footage was cut prior to release, with *Variety* claiming, "there are snatches of jungle worship dancing, but all clean. Only spicy shot is a girl's snakehips dance in a brief brothel scene."[93] By February, *Drums o' Voodoo* was appearing at four theaters owned by Louis Bernheimer in Washington, D.C., with female star Laura Bowman making personal appearances to help promote the movie.[94] Then a preview occurred at the Capitol Theater in Bayside, California.[95]

Drums o' Voodoo officially premiered in New York City on May 11, 1934, though it would be seen at some subsequent theaters under the title *Louisiana*. *The Hollywood Reporter* spoke none too flatteringly of the "stage technique" seen in the film,[96] though *The Film Daily* claimed it was "well-acted and possessing good dramatic interest."[97] *Variety* was perhaps the most harsh critic, though, claiming it was "cheaply produced and looking it: also badly acted. Fails to rate either as a film laboratory experiment in racial traits or as an entertainment...."[98] Though probably due more to an erratic distribution than to poor trade reviews, *Drums o' Voodoo* saw little in the way of financial return.

The same year, *Chloe: Love Is Calling You*—shot in Kennedy City, Florida—also circulated to theaters via a States Rights release, though it apparently played even fewer theaters than *Drums o' Voodoo*. Marshall Neilan, whose reputation was made in the silent era, directed, while Olive Borden—also best known for work prior to the talkies—starred in the title role. Her character is the half-white daughter of Mandy (Georgette Harvey), a practicing voodoo nursemaid. Mandy takes Chloe and her other children from the everglade swamps to the north, where she intends to exact revenge on the white Colonel Gordon (Frank Joyner) who had brutally lynched her husband. She uses voodoo and a drum-beating ceremony to plot against the colonel. At the same time, Chloe becomes confused when she simultaneously receives romantic attention from Wade (a white man) and Jim (a black man). Eventually, the vengeful Mandy is arrested, while Chloe is rescued from an alligator attack. She is even discovered to be white rather than black, and is thus able to pursue Wade without fear of interracial problems. As is obvious, racism abounds in the film's narrative, a trait not generally found in *White Zombie*'s storyline.

The "Romance of the Southland," as advertisements dubbed *Chloe*, attempted in its publicity to suggest the film was both a love story and a mystery/horror tale, an advertising and promotion tack which had proved successful for *White Zombie*.[99] To help instill more public interest in the film, the sheet music to the song "Chloe" was reprinted by Villa Moret and sold at the time of the film's release.[100] Despite these efforts, *Chloe* proved unsuccessful at the limited number of theaters it played.

While films following the voodoo path of *White Zombie* were proving generally unsuccessful at the box office, other attempts continued to be made. For example, returning to an idea discussed in Seabrook's *The Magic Island*, *Ouanga* (1935) tells the story of Clelie (Fredi Washington) who is given an *ouanga* charm during a voodoo ceremony.[101] By night, Clelie is involved with a voodoo cult; by day, she is a respectable planta-

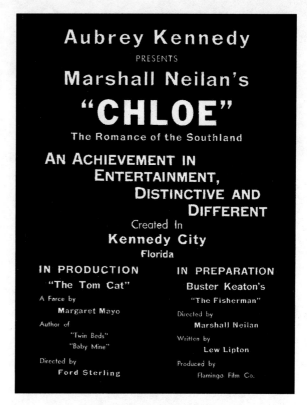

Trade advertisement for Chloe *published in a June 28, 1933, issue of* The Film Daily.

tion owner in love with neighbor Adam Maynard (Philip Brandon). He spurns her affections and plans to marry Eve (Marie Paxton) instead. In retaliation, Clelie secretly passes a death *ouanga* to Eve, who faints during an elaborate party. Despite the curse placed on her, however, Eve mysteriously recovers. With a witch doctor's help, Clelie then raises two zombies from the dead, commanding them to capture Eve. But Lestrange (Sheldon Leonard), Adam's overseer, makes a valiant attempt to rescue his boss's fiancée; Clelie shoots him, but it is not a fatal shot. In fact, Lestrange even manages to steal her personal *ouanga*. Unaware of the theft, Clelie proceeds with plans to sacrifice Eve at a ceremony accompanied by the beat of voodoo drums. Adam rescues Eve however, as Clelie is distracted by Lestrange, who reveals he has stolen her *ouanga*. Deep in the jungle, Lestrange kills Clelie before finally succumbing to his earlier wound. Eve is saved, and goodness prevails.

George Terwilliger, a former scenarist for D. W. Griffith and director of such films as *Daughters Who Pay* (1925, costarring Bela Lugosi), produced, directed, and wrote *Ouanga*. In addition to portraying male lead Adam

Maynard, actor Philip Brandon doubled as assistant director. Female lead Fredi Washington had achieved fame in *Imitation of Life* (1933), and costar Sheldon Leonard would later prove successful as a character actor and then a television producer. Behind the camera was cinematographer Carl Berger, who had earlier shot Frank Buck's popular film *Bring 'Em Back Alive* (1933).

Yet even these experienced crew members and cast could not overcome some of the production troubles which beset *Ouanga*. Originally preparing to shoot in Haiti, Terwilliger befriended the head of a cult and his voodoo followers. When asked to perform in front of the cameras, however, the group became angry. Terwilliger soon found an *ouanga* in his car, as well encountering a punctured tire and a tree deliberately placed in the road. Warnings came of more evil to follow, and Terwilliger quickly decided to move the cast and crew to Jamaica. The morning he was to sail, however, his dancers had disappeared and the drummers and some extras had been arrested. Undaunted, the director began shooting again after settling in Jamaica, only to have a rainstorm drown two Jamaicans working on the film; in addition, sickness killed a crew member, and a cyclone destroyed the sets. After two months, an exhausted Terwilliger returned to the U.S. with footage in hand. Though seen in England as early as 1934, *Ouanga*—for unknown reasons—did not play U.S. theaters until 1936.[102]

More than any other of the post–*White Zombie* voodoo films of the 1930s, *Ouanga* shows the Halperin influence. It's true that the idea of an *ouanga* charm and the film's emphasis on voodoo drums (which occur in quite effective montages) can be traced back to *The Magic Island* and even earlier voodoo texts; the character Clelie's very name is an apparent variation on Célie, a voodoo priestess discussed in the Seabrook text. More importantly, however, the economic viability of a voodoo film would have been buttressed by *White Zombie*'s success, rather than anything to do with Seabrook. In addition, some of *Ouanga*'s plot devices and cinematic techniques also seem influenced by the Halperin film. For example, the use of ethnicity as a source of conflict—treated in such a subtle manner in *White Zombie*—becomes a key aspect of *Ouanga*'s plot. Also, Terwilliger's use of many wipe transitions between shots—seldom employed in 1930s horror films—strongly recalls their earlier and much more artful use in *White Zombie*.

However, *Ouanga*'s use of zombie characters is the most direct appropriation from the Halperins' film. The film does suggest the supernatural as responsible for the dead bodies coming to life, rather than the voodoo powder seen in *White Zombie*, but the zombies' blank stares and overall appearance visually echo their 1932 counterparts. Their ability to be controlled by hand motions also

borrows heavily from *White Zombie*. Shots of Fredi Washington's quite theatrical use of her hands—certainly more overt than Lugosi's use of clasped palms—invoke the spectator-as-character as described in Chapter One. Framed in a low-angle shot that places the spectator's vantage point almost inside the open graves, Washington gazes into the camera as she attempts to raise the corpses from the dead: The result here is reminiscent of *White Zombie*'s use of the spectator-as-character.

Perhaps not directly *White Zombie*–inspired but still voodoo related was the poorly distributed *Obeah!*, made by Arcturus Pictures and distributed in 1935 on a States Rights basis. F. Herrick Herrick directed and scripted the tale, which belongs more in the adventure genre than in horror. An advertisement in the 1935 *Film Daily Yearbook* alleged that filming occurred on a round-the-world cruise that lasted 11 months and stopped in 20 countries, including Haiti and Jamaica. Trade reports claimed the shoot actually lasted only four months, with additional time spent on some last-minute underwater sequences shot off the coast of Panama.[103] The ship's crew, as well as denizens of other countries met on the voyage, helped supplement the cast. Of the performers, Alice Wesslar received the spotlight in some of the limited publicity; at the time of the film's release, she was a dancer at the Paradise night club on Broadway.

Obeah!'s storyline features an adventurer (played by Phillips H. Lord) searching for a lost explorer and eventually finding him on a South Seas island. Similar to Madeline in *White Zombie*, the explorer is mentally under the control of another person. Islanders have him under the spell of obeah, the effects of which are not dissimilar to those of zombiism in the Halperins' film. The adventurer saves the explorer by interrupting a death ritual and breaking the obeah spell. As the two escape, a voodoo curse pursues them.[104] *Obeah*'s surface similarities to *White Zombie* were almost certainly not the result of any direct influence, but its very production was another link in the cinematic chain begun by the Halperins.

To varying degrees, then, and in different ways, the Halperins' 1932 film influenced the other films chronicled in this section.[105] Though its wrong to suggest that no other voodoo-related films would have been produced during the 1930s had it not been for *White Zombie*, the production of such movies was spurred in large part by the Halperins' 1932 financial success. *White Zombie*'s effect also extended to certain narrative elements of these films, such as the use of settings like Haiti and the repetitive use of voodoo drums. Equally striking of course are the ways in which these films did not borrow from the Halperins. After all, however much they embraced the topic of voodoo, only *Ouanga* incorporated zombies into its narrative. Perhaps this was partially due to worries of infringement, a fear realized in the 1936 court case discussed earlier in this chapter. It may also have been due at times to the speed at which some studios bought already written voodoo tales like *Black Moon*. Regardless, *White Zombie* cast its shadow over other areas of 1930s culture, some of which—including several essays and books—readily employed the word "zombie."

Zombies and Voodoo Cults in Print

Various publications on voodoo and zombies appeared in the 1930s subsequent to *White Zombie*'s release, all apparently published in the shadow of the film's enormous success. Some were academic texts, and some were popular-audience studies printed in mainstream magazines and by mainstream presses. Neither category would have drawn from the Halperin film as a research source, but both tackled the subject matter at least in part because of the heightened public interest it had caused. Readers, especially those of mainstream 1930s publications, desired more information on voodoo and zombies than they had had prior to *White Zombie*'s release.

The first post–*White Zombie* book on voodoo was Joseph J. Williams' *Voodoos and Obeahs: Phases of West India Witchcraft*. First published by the Dial Press in December 1932, the book examines snake worship, African ophiolatry, and the history of Haitian voodoo. The last discussion covers pantheism, human sacrifice, and various rituals. Not too surprisingly, *The Magic Island* was one of Williams' major sources of information, but at the same time he viewed Seabrook's tales with an open skepticism.[106]

By the mid-thirties, both Zora Neale Hurston's *Mules and Men* (Lippincott, 1935) and Richard A. Loederer's *Voodoo Fire in Haiti* (Literary Guild, 1935) had shed light on voodoo for a more mass audience than Williams' book had. *Mules and Men*—written by one of the most esteemed African-American authors of the century—speaks of "Hoodoo" in the United States,[107] while *Voodoo Fire in Haiti* explores cults and ceremonies in Haiti. For example, Loederer offers these quotations from a Haitian he encountered:

> Voodoo is strong; stronger even than death. The Papaloi can raise the dead. He breathes life into corpses, who get up and behave like living men. These creatures are bound forever to their master's will. They are called "Zombies." ... Haven't you noticed how even the poorest natives bury their dead under a heavy stone? That's a very necessary precaution, for it stops the bodies from leaving their graves. ... Don't you realize, monsieur, that many of the workers on the sugar fields are mere soulless carcasses brought back to life by magic and now slaving for their masters? ... Voodoo is a devilish cult ... dangerous and devilish.[108]

Presumably Loederer actually heard these words, but even so, their topicality seems reminiscent of *The Magic Island* and their inclusion motivated perhaps by popular

An illustration by Miguel Covarrubias that appeared in Zora Neale Hurston's 1935 book Mules and Men.

interest in such subjects since the success of *White Zombie*.

Other texts of the same period offered examinations of the voodoo culture and zombies of countries outside the purview of the United States and Haiti. Gordon Sinclair's *Loose Among Devils* (Farrar and Rinehart, 1935) describes the "voodoo" of Africa,[109] while F. G. Carnochan and Hans Christian Adamson's *The Empire of the Snakes* (Stokes, 1935) offers a look at the cults in the country of Tanganyika. They write of the drug "kingo" (an abbreviation of "kingoliolo"), which "is supposed to have been used in the past by unscrupulous chiefs and medicine-men to gain power over those whom they would destroy."[110]

The authors were spellbound by the effects of the drug: "Our known narcotics kill slowly, but kingo turns men into robots by robbing them of all their power to think and act for themselves. ... Later I was to see men, in the clutch of this vicious drug, run until they dropped from exhaustion; or poor wretches, who might be called the Living Dead, sit absolutely motionless for hours on end, staring with unseeing eyes, answering no questions and taking no food."[111]

Magazines also co-opted the world of voodoo. For example, during the mid-thirties two articles appeared in *Hygeia*, a popular medical magazine. John Lee Maddox's "Modern Voodooism," published over two issues in February and March 1934, examined the rituals and cures of medicine men in voodoo cults. Though he devalues their religious actualities, Maddox certainly agrees voodoo rites are practiced in many areas of the world, including New York's own Harlem. He notes finally that, "...these superstitions are passing. They will soon be done away with or changed into beliefs and practices far better and far more noble. It is thus that the human race progresses."[112]

Elizabeth Blaine Jenkins' tale "Voodoo Land," printed in May of the following year, relates her personal experiences with voodooism as a narrative:

> The shadows grew deep, and Bob whispered carefully, "Maybe we shall see the zombies, those men that Nebo says are dragged from their graves and made to work in the cane fields!"
> Barbara whispered back to him, "Nebo says that zombies are not permitted to eat meat because if they do, then they know that they are dead and go off to find their graves in the mountain."
> "Maybe we shall see one at Ti-Meme's hut. She says they sit like people asleep, and yet their eyes are open. They have no souls like ours!"[113]

Jenkins' account of zombies seems quite similar to Seabrook's, and may well have borrowed its description of them from *The Magic Island*. Regardless of Jenkins' source, though, *White Zombie*'s popularity may have at least partially been the impetus for the publication of Jenkins' story.

Author Rosita Forbes also discussed zombies in her 1935 *Country Life* article on Haitian voodoo. She claimed such passages as the following to be "...an exact description of the voodoo ceremonies I saw...," which prompts the question of how many outsiders were allowed to view such rituals and how genuine were such accounts. After quoting Article 249 of the Haitian Penal Code, she described zombies as:

> Corpses, raped from their graves before they have time to rot ... those terrible tranced figures with dead eyes which can occasionally be seen working in lonely places. But the Negroes bury their dead within reach, or in a public place and under as much masonry as possible, to protect them from sorcerers who would steal the bodies, imbue them with a mechanical simulation of life, feed them on substances containing neither salt, meat, nor seasoning, and force them to work under their direction.[114]

Descriptions of this kind seem to draw from *The Magic Island* and *White Zombie* even more heavily than Elizabeth Blaine Jenkins' article.

The following year, Hans Possendorf's *Damballa Calls: A Love Story of Haiti* (Hutchinson, 1936) detailed—in what he called a "partly fictitious" manner—his 1925 visit to the country. The discussion ends with his chapter "The Zombie," which includes the following description of one: "...every attempt to penetrate the blank wall of his mind or to extract a word from him failed. His eyes had a horrible expression of lifelessness. He moved his limbs in stiff jerks like a marionette."[115] Such words might be just as accurate in describing the zombies of Victor Halperin as those of Haiti.

Given the continued salability of voodoo and zombies, even more texts appeared in the second half of the 1930s. Seabrook's *The Magic Island* reappeared in 1936 thanks to a Harcourt, Brace, and Company reprint, while a few years later Harold Courlander's *Haiti Singing* (Univ. of North Carolina, 1939) was published.

Along with an extensive examination of numerous kinds of Haitian music, instruments, chants, and lyrics, Courlander offered the results of his own research on zombiism:

> When [those never possessed by a *loa* spirit] die and are buried, there remains, however, a tiny essence called *zombie*, a kind of negative afterimage of the man. It has no special will, and can affect the world of the living only when it has somehow fallen into the power of one who

"serves with two hands," a malefactor. This is not the *zombie* of popular literature, [but] of the song: "Nan Légane, Yo marré *zombie* nans paille *fig-banane*! Abobo *loyo*!" ... Somehow the spirit, the negative afterimage, has refused to be separated from the flesh, which is dead. Together they walk the mountain trails, or, more commonly, work in the fields of one who "serves with two hands."[116]

In addition to the lengthy description, Courlander suggested another, more abstract definition of zombiism, claiming it "equally means the spark which is left when the man dies."[117]

Perhaps the most intriguing of these post–Seabrook works, however, is Zora Neale Hurston's *Tell My Horse* (Turtle Island, 1939). An insightful and engrossing work of anthropology, the book investigates voodoo in Jamaica and Haiti; it is a logical extension of her work with American "Hoodoo" in *Mules and Men*.

In addition to chapters on topics like voodoo gods, *Tell My Horse* offers an entire section on zombiism. It became probably the most lengthy and credible study of zombies to that date, with Hurston offering a vivid account of her own contact with such a creature:

> We found the Zombie in the hospital yard. They just set her dinner before her but she was not eating. ... She seemed to hear nothing. ... And the sight was dreadful. That blank face with the dead eyes. ... There was nothing you could say to her or get from her except by looking at her, and the sight of this wreckage was too much to endure for long.[118]

In addition to descriptions like these, Hurston offered visual proof of her findings. Rather than the grotesque caricatures printed in *The Magic Island*, *Tell My Horse* includes a still photograph of a woman identified as a zombie. Her appearance features the blank stare so common in prior descriptions of zombies.

Zora Neale Hurston's text shows no influence from *White Zombie*, but her interest in dispelling false notions about voodoo and zombies apparently shows an attempt to actively discredit such fictitious texts. *White Zombie*'s major effect on the literature of the 1930s then was not dissimilar to its impact on the cinema and theater. Some of the chronicled works may have borrowed in their descriptions from the film and Seabrook, but the bulk probably did not. Rather, they are indicative of a propensity on the part of some writers and thinkers—a propensity at times academically motivated, at times financially—to offer readers information on voodoo and zombies. Interest had grown thanks to *White Zombie*, something which the Halperins themselves carefully watched but could never capitalize on again.

Conclusion

More than the film's impact on the subsequent careers of its cast and crew or the 1930s horror cycle in general, *White Zombie* induced a widespread interest in voodoo and zombies throughout U.S. culture.[119] Perhaps the best evidence of this popular influence is the degree to which some writers attempted to reclaim the topics of *White Zombie* as their own intellectual territory, much as ASC attempted to do in the 1936 court case. For example, Zora Neale Hurston asserted in her 1942 autobiography: "Of my research in the British West Indies and Haiti, my greatest thrill was coming face to face with a Zombie and photographing her. This act had never happened before in the history of man."[120] Not in the "history of man" perhaps (unless Seabrook is to be believed), but certainly in 1932 movie theaters thanks to Victor and Edward Halperin.

William B. Seabrook, in an attempt to reinstate his name as the popularizer of the term "zombie," wrote in 1942: "The one thing in the Haitian book which seems pretty sure to live whether it stands up as a whole or not, is the zombie. ... I didn't invent the word zombie, nor the concept or the zombies. But I brought the word and concept to America from Haiti and gave it in print to the American public—for the first time. The word is now a part of the American language. It flames in neon lights for names of bars, and drinks, is applied to starved surrendering soldiers, replaces robot, and runs the pulps ragged for new plots in which the principal zombie instead of being a black man is a white girl—preferably blond. The word had never appeared in English print before I wrote *The Magic Island*."[121]

It was not print and Seabrook which truly introduced the word to U.S. culture, however; it was the cinema and *White Zombie*. In addition, not only did the Halperins' film make clear the economic viability of topics like zombies and voodoo, it offered numerous images and themes that later works often appropriated. A few films even had actual clips of *White Zombie* included in them. The extremely low budget roadshow film *Dr. Terror's House of Horrors* (1943) compiled by Max Rosenbloom is an example; *Lock Up Your Daughters*—a compilation of Lugosi clips released in Britain in 1959—allegedly features a few moments of *White Zombie* as well. Lastly, though it bore no resemblance to the Halperin film in terms of plot, an episode of the radio show *Nightbeat* with Frank Lovejoy was entitled "White Zombie."

While Chapter Five has attempted to paint a portrait of *White Zombie*'s influence in the years following its initial release, the film's influence—either direct or indirect—can also be seen in films of later decades. *The Ghost Breakers* (1940) with Bob Hope, *King of the Zombies* (1941) with Henry Victor, *I Walked with a Zombie* (1943) with Tom Conway, *Revenge of the Zombies* (1943) with John Carradine, *Voodoo Man* (1944) with Bela Lugosi, *Zombies on Broadway* (1945) with Bela Lugosi, *Zombies of Mora Tau* (1957), and *The Plague of the Zombies* (1966) all show elements first advertised (e.g., staring eyes in movie posters), seen (e.g., blank-eyed zombies), heard (e.g., voodoo drums), or plotted (e.g., zombies performing manual labor) in *White Zombie*.

The film's efficacy in impacting future films extended well beyond the 1930s, fermenting into often repeated narrative themes and devices. And similar to its own zombies, the Halperin film itself would live again in subsequent years.

Chapter Six

Creeping Back from the Grave:
White Zombie's Modern Cultural Impact

Even though it is a film that has been both praised and lambasted by late 20th-century critics, *White Zombie* possesses the unique ability to captivate new viewers and to be echoed, even if in a relatively quiet manner, by certain sectors of US culture. Movement in this direction began in the 1960s and has continued slowly but steadily ever since. Along with television airplay, *White Zombie* returned to theaters of the 1960s and 1970s thanks to Joseph Brenner reissues, often appearing on a double bill with MGM's film *Freaks* (1932). During those same decades, magazines like *Famous Monsters of Filmland* and several books on the horror film also drew attention to *White Zombie*, engendering in many movie fans a curiosity and at times a respect for the film. Video releases of *White Zombie* during the 1980s and the growing cult of Bela Lugosi in the 1990s also increased interest in the film.

These realities should not suggest, though, that the film has maintained a consistent influence over movie fans or US culture in even a minor degree since its 1932 release. However much Chapter Five attempts to show the film's impact on the 1930s cinema, *White Zombie*'s near-disappearance between the 1940s and the 1960s meant that its influence during those decades dissipated essentially into nothingness. The 1960s helped breathe new life into the film. The revival of the zombie in director George Romero's 1968 film *Night of the Living Dead*, in its sequels, and in its many imitators in the 1970s and 1980s shows a conscious desire to reinvent that subgenre of horror. Corpses walked, but they ate flesh and reveled in gore; voodoo was no longer present. The zombie cinema had departed radically from the path of the Halperin Brothers' film. *White Zombie* had returned in the 1960s, but only in the marginalized way it still did in the latter years of the 20th century.

Even if only pockets of modern US culture recognize the film, however, artists, writers, and filmmakers do and references and tributes to it are occasionally made in their work. Some of these are subtle, such as a popular band who appropriated the film title as its name. Others are overt tributes, such as products based upon the film and marketed to horror movie fans. Finally, some are merely textual references inside larger works, such as literature or films which make brief allusions to the film. Though hardly monumental in number, these examples do show *White Zombie*'s grip on the imagination of some viewers.

The key question regarding *White Zombie*'s revival must concern the meaning the film holds for its modern viewers. Why, in recent years, has *White Zombie* resonated so strongly with certain people, sometimes spurring them to perform tributes to it? The answer will of course vary given the context in which the homage occurs, but must invoke the secondary concern of creator intentionality versus audience consumption. Whatever significance the film holds for those who choose to memorialize it, the audience for such memorials may vary in their level of understanding or appreciation. The audience might be narrow and specific enough to horror film history to receive the reference with an equally strong appreciation of *White Zombie*, the audience might more generally see such a reference as one more generally to Bela Lugosi or "old" horror films, or the audience may be completely unaware that an allusion is being made at all.

One of the earliest references to the film during its modern revivification came in the form of literature. Esteemed novelist Thomas Pynchon, author of such books as *The Crying of Lot 49*, was apparently so intrigued by Lugosi and *White Zombie* that mention of both turn up in his *Gravity's Rainbow* (Publisher, 1973). For

One-sheet movie poster from a French reissue of White Zombie, *probably in the 1960s or 1970s. (Courtesy of Dennis Payne.)*

example, one of the central characters shares the following thoughts:

> "Of course, of course," sez Osbie, with a fluid passage of fingers and wrist based on the way Bela Lugosi handed a certain glass of doped wine to some fool of a juvenile lead in *White Zombie*, the first movie Osbie ever saw and in a sense the last, ranking on his All-Time List along with *Son of Frankenstein, Freaks, Flying Down to Rio*, and perhaps *Dumbo*....

Pynchon's difficult yet compelling novel shows admiration for *White Zombie* in its brief reference, even if the description is askew; in the film, Lugosi never hands a glass of wine to the "fool of a juvenile lead," but instead to the middle-aged actor Robert Frazer, hardly the film's male lead.

As the film's reputation grew, its accessibility also increased thanks to modern video technology. Renewed interest allowed fans of *White Zombie* to infuse references to it into their own work. For example, the rock band "The Manimals" recorded the tune "White Zombie" on

their 1985 EP record *Blood is the Harvest* (House of Pain Records, HP301). Band members included "Dark," "The Wraith," and "Larry the Wolf"; the last two contributed lyrics for the "White Zombie" piece, which show a deep understanding of the film.

> Walking in our sleep
> through fields of Haitian cane
> We've got no worries—
> We've got needles in our brains
>
> Reanimated corpses don't mind
> working over time.

Other lyrics recall *White Zombie*'s Faustian theme, as well as its implicit discussion of racial relations in phrases like the following:

> Black men chanting
> they say, "Listen to the Lambs"
> There's nothing they fear more than a
> white man with voodoo in his hands.

Following those lines, the song ends by focusing on Lugosi: "Murder is his name."

When reminiscing about composing the song and writing lyrics, band member Larry the Wolf spoke of his fascination with *White Zombie* the film:

> The song was written back when it was a truly obscure film. It preceded the days of being able to find a public-domain copy in nearly every video store and was ultra rare to catch on TV. When I finally viewed the film it had a profound effect on me. ... My intent was not to give a musical synopsis of the film, but rather to write lyrics that were inspired by it and perhaps provide the listener with a small mystery to untangle. It's my way of paying homage to, and cryptically recruiting others to seek out and view, one of my very favorite Lugosi performances.[1]

Regrettably, *Blood is the Harvest* received little distribution and has never been reissued on compact disc. Indeed, it would be 13 years before the Manimals would issue another album, which would again draw on 1930s horror films and Bela Lugosi for inspiration.[2]

Further tributes soon appeared in other media, including those in *The Prowler* comic books. Timothy Truman, John K. Snyder, III, Graham Nolan, and Michael H. Price created the comic-book character during 1986–87, intending to use him to convey their "rather jaundiced view of the comix industry's super-hero genre."[3] Price and Truman wrote the stories; Snyder illustrated Truman's modern-day Prowler tales, while Nolan illustrated Price's Depression-era and wartime period pieces. Occasionally, Price and Truman contributed artwork as well.

The tales covered the exploits of fictitious New Yorker Leo Kragg, who had become a masked vigilante in approximately 1929. As the "Prowler," he fought crime

For decades after its original release, White Zombie *and Murder Legendre continued to creep back from their cinematic grave.*

An image of Murder Legendre used to promote a 1996 Los Angeles music concert.

until 1940, finally receiving plaudits from the US government for his efforts. His recurring enemy in those early years was Murder Legendre, who—according to the Price narratives—made periodic forays into the U.S. to peddle his zombie-making formulas to American industry.

In the modern-day *Prowler* stories, Leo Kragg is retired, but remains passionately concerned about freelance crimefighting. He conscripts a young martial-arts enthusiast to become the new Prowler, and the first villain they encounter is a decrepit Murder Legendre, who—according to the comic version—survived his fall at the climax of *White Zombie*, but has maintained a low profile ever since.

Author Michael H. Price recalled: "The Lugosi character was the series' inaugural villain (*Prowler* Nos. 1–4, Eclipse Comics, 1987), gracing the modern-day yarns for four issues. I used Legendre more extensively in my period yarns, notably the 'origin story'; later, in an adaptation of *The Vampire Bat* with a guest appearance by Legendre; in a special crossover issue called *Airboy Meets the Prowler*, with Legendre appearing in transitional flashbacks; and at length in the miniseries *Revenge of the Prowler* and a special one-shot finale book, *The Prowler in White Zombie*."[4]

While wholly original, the Prowler character offered an aura of nostalgia due to the era in which Leo Kragg first donned his mask, as well as the deep understanding his writers had of 1930s and '40s detective comics and movies. Just as some detective films of that era incorporated a sense of horror thanks to the choice of personalities like Bela Lugosi and Boris Karloff to portray their heavies, so did *The Prowler* series with its use of stories like *The Vampire Bat*, originally a 1933 film with Lionel Atwill and Fay Wray. Most especially, though, the connection to horror came thanks to the affectionate and artistic appropriation of *White Zombie*'s villain.

As for the repeated use of references to the film, Michael Price explained that: "Legendre hovered about the series like some catastrophic annoyance to the Prowler, whom the Legendre character considered no great shakes as an enemy. The Prowler seemed forever on the verge of squaring off against Legendre, who always managed to duck out the back way before the Prowler could get his act together. Finally, when the Prowler journeyed to

Haiti for an intended showdown, Legendre treated him with the same mock-hospitality one might show an unwelcome visiting relative. And it's not the Prowler who finally takes Legendre down at the end of the *White Zombie* comic. Yes, the Prowler is pretty self-serious and ultimately inept as a crimefighter, which is my argument entirely in counterpoint to the un-conflicted fun-and-games of most comic-book superheroics."[5]

Even though *White Zombie*'s reputation had grown considerably by the mid– to late 1980s, it was difficult to channel the comic books to those film fans whose would have held an appreciation for them. Price remembered that, "Eclipse Comics scarcely knew what to do with the books, which vanished with scarcely a trace even while brand-spanking new. Those scattered readers who got hold of them, seem to have made up in enthusiasm for the series what was missing in sheer volume of distribution."[6] Regardless of limited readership, the comics stand as a testament to *White Zombie*'s ability to capture the imagination of some viewers; few films of the 1930s have erupted into the comic book marketplace five decades later.

White Zombie as a film met the modern world shortly after *The Prowler* quietly ceased publication, thanks to the controversial technology of colorization. In 1991, Hal Roach Studios unveiled their VHS release of *White Zombie* in color. Along with using a cut print which ran 59 minutes in length, the result transformed the film into pastel mess. More than just a poor job of colorization, the result desecrates *White Zombie*'s artful use of lighting and black-and-white film.[7]

The colorization of *White Zombie* is an example of what causes such desecrations: a film's public domain legal status. In more recent decades, *White Zombie*'s copyright lapsed due to the proper forms not being filed with the Library of Congress in Washington, D.C. *White Zombie* is thus the property of everyone in the world, which might allow for circulation of more copies than if

Artwork from Eclipse's comic book The Prowler in White Zombie. *Gerald Forton and Graham Nolan illustrated, and Michael H. Price scripted.*

it was controlled, but it also means that the film can be used for whatever purposes one might want. The reverence and laws which guide the use of most public property are not at play, so *White Zombie* can be ravaged at will. Those colorizing may do so without anyone's permission or knowledge, just as film clips from it may be duplicated for any reason, whether reverential or financial.

As a partial result of *White Zombie*'s lapsed copyright, the film has also wedged its way into several modern films, perhaps most notably in director Curtis Hanson's *The Hand That Rocks the Cradle* (1992). In it, the demented Peyton (actress Rebecca De Mornay) screens *White Zombie* for the young and innocent character Madeline in an attempt to extend her cultural vernacular. A quick clip of *White Zombie* then appeared in writer-director Willard Carroll's *The Runestone* (1992), which covers the exploits of a monster in Manhattan against the backdrop of two young archaeologists who are inspecting a recently discovered, sixth century Nordic runestone. The *White Zombie* footage is seen briefly on one of the character's televisions.

Even later, facial shots of Lugosi as Legendre surface in director Michael Almereyda's art-house vampire film *Nadja* (1994). The clips actually represent Count Dracula, the deceased father of Nadja (actress Elina Löwensohn). The film manages to intercut such close-ups with grainy, black-and-white scenes of the cloaked Dracula (actor Peter Fonda) on a hillside. The same year, Martin Landau portrayed Bela Lugosi in director Tim Burton's film *Ed Wood* (1994). In it, characters Lugosi and director Ed Wood (actor Johnny Depp) watch clips of *White Zombie* on television. In doing so, both characters mimic the hand motions of Murder Legendre. Similar clips of Legendre's hand clasps also appear in the film *Idle Hands* (1998).

Clips from *White Zombie* have also turned up in numerous nonfiction films on horror movies, with particular attention given to it in the 1970s PBS documentary *The Horror of It All*, the 1986 documentary *Lugosi: The Forgotten King*, the 1994 documentary film *Majestic Dreams: The Coleman Theatre Beautiful*, the 1998 Lugosi episode of the E! Channel documentary series *Mysteries and Scandals*, and the 1998 documentary *Lugosi: Hollywood's Dracula*. The last includes not just clips of *White Zombie* from the 1994 Roan Group restoration, but also sound bites from interviews with film historian George E. Turner and Lugosi friend Richard Sheffield who discuss the film.

Along with the revival of the film in clips, the narrative of *White Zombie* was once resurrected as a live stage play. From September 18 to October 31, 1998, the play *White Zombie* ran at the Stage Left Theatre in Chicago. The Black Cat Productions produced the show on the heels of their summer 1998 stage show based on the horror film *Mad Love* (1935). Colleen Couillard, cofounder of The Black Cat Productions with husband Patrick, wrote the *White Zombie* adaptation as part of an idea to

> ...put on true tributes to the classic horror films, which are not really camp. The humor comes naturally and in a seemingly unintentional way through the melodrama and the otherworldly situations the characters find themselves in. No one else [in Chicago] seemed to be focusing on that particular era and genre, so I thought it would be the perfect venue for us to explore.[8]

Colleen Couillard also headlined as Murder Legendre, playing the character as a kind of "asexual villain." Though she emulated Lugosi's Hungarian accent and dressed in a similar costume, Couillard believed her gender gave the role a "bit of a different spin."[9] Others in cast included Patrick Couillard as Beaumont, Peggy Queener as Madeline, and Cullen Mansfield Sprague as Neil.[10]

Though the play retains much of the spirit of *White Zombie*, it also builds on the film's narrative. Much of the dialogue is the same, though at times it is altered for laughs. For example, the character Beaumont tells Madeline: "I couldn't do half the things I wanted to do to you— I mean, for you." Other additions are both completely new to the story and yet historically insightful. Rather than carve a voodoo doll of Madeline, Legendre breaks out into the lyrics of "Hot Voodoo," first sung by Marlene Dietrich in the film *Blonde Venus* (1932).[11] Overall, the play pays colorful, amusing, and worthwhile homage.

Advertisements for the "voodoo production" borrowed from the film's slogan which said that "She was not alive ... nor dead ... Just a *White Zombie*." The ads helped ensure a successful run. Couillard's *White Zombie* played to several sold houses and enjoyed favorable word-of-mouth publicity, spurring talk of a Los Angeles revival in 2001.[12]

Better known to mass audiences than documentary films and stage plays is the heavy metal band that appropriated the movie's title for the name of their group. As *Rolling Stone* magazine told readers, "Squishy, life-size rubber bats. Shrunken heads. Blow-up dolls (bearing the sign INFLATABLE PEOPLE DON'T HAVE GENITALS. DON'T OPEN PACKAGES). It's a natural environment for White Zombie, who were named after a Bela Lugosi movie."[13]

The band—vocalist Rob Zombie, drummer John Tempesta, and bassist Sean Yseult—burst onto New York's post–punk music scene in 1985, and by 1992 had released their major label debut on Geffen. *La Sexorcisto: Devil Music Volume One* went double platinum. Their 1995 follow-up, *Astro-Creep 2000: Songs of Love, and Other Synthetic Delusions of the Electric Head*, also scored

Footage from White Zombie *has turned up in many film documentaries as well as numerous fictional movies.*

double-platinum sales. A third Geffen release, *Supersexy Swingin' Sounds*, went gold in 1996.[14]

When asked about the group's name in a 1997 interview, vocalist Rob Zombie spoke of his interest in horror films in general and *White Zombie* in particular. "[It's] a great film that not a lot of people know about," he explained to *Monsterscene* magazine. "It amazes me that a film that is so readily available can be so 'lost.'"[15]

Whether or not many of their audience knew the origin of the band's name, White Zombie was highly successful in sales, on innumerable tours, and in the awards arena. The songs "Thunder Kiss '65" and "More Human Than Human" both earned Grammy nominations for Best Hard Rock Performance, and readers of *Rolling Stone* magazine voted White Zombie the Best Metal Band in 1996.

Despite their successes, in September 1998, the band came to an end. "After thirteen years, White Zombie has accomplished everything we set out to do, and we all felt

it was time to move on," a collective band statement claimed. Exactly what they "set out to do" was left unexplained, but White Zombie the band certainly had become the film's ultimate tribute, through music.[16]

As the band drifted closer to dissolution, the Janus Company of Houston, Texas, was preparing a *White Zombie* tribute in a very different mold: a resin model kit diorama of Murder Legendre released in late 1997. The result is an exquisite, museum quality sculpture. The first such *White Zombie* product, its likeness of Lugosi far exceeds the many sculpture, model, and toy tributes to the actor as Dracula which have been produced en masse over the decades since the actor's death. Janus President John Ulakovic described their desire to produce the kit with such strong attention to detail:

We gambled (correctly) that fans would want a non–Dracula collectible. Much credit for the kit's success must be passed on to the sculptor, Thomas Kuntz. Besides

Actors Patrick Couillard and Colleen Couillard in a scene from a live version of White Zombie *staged in Chicago in 1998. (Courtesy of Colleen Couillard.)*

being a world class sculptor, Thomas is also one of Lugosi's biggest fans and his interest is reflected in the exacting detail of his sculpture.

If you watch the *White Zombie*, you'll see we had to cheat a bit in the design of the model kit. In the scene where Lugosi is standing in the courtyard carving the likeness of Madge Bellamy from a wax candle, you'll notice that he is standing in front of a gate. We felt the wooden gate in the film looked too much like Mr. Ed's barn door from the old TV series. We had a problem! We wanted to remain faithful to the film yet make the kit visually appealing. Fortunately, we watched the film closely and found a better alternative. If you review the film, you'll see we used the iron gate pattern from Legendre's sugar mill for the courtyard gate depicted in the sculpture! I think most people would agree we made the right decision.[17]

Their kit, produced with such dedication to excellence, places it in the forefront of all *White Zombie* and Bela Lugosi tributes. It will certainly not be the last, however. Other tributes are in the works, including a more widespread issue of a newly recorded version of the 1932 Joel Shaw tune *White Zombie*. Performed by Michael Aitch Price and His Musical Miscreants at Cremo Studios in 1998, the tune's arrangement was updated by Price.

Whether they are as model kits or in the work of heavy metal bands, some conclusions can now be drawn about modern *White Zombie* tributes and references. Certainly some of the uses of the film discussed in this chapter, including the use of clips in *Nadja*, are more than anything else indications of *White Zombie*'s lapsed copyright. Cinematic appropriations, like the colorization of the film, result from a combination of the aforementioned legal status and the yen among some audiences for all things Bela Lugosi.

Most tributes, however, reveal a genuine admiration for the film, whether they are made in a comic book which spurred little in the way of profit or by a band which garnered millions of dollars and fans. These supporters of *White Zombie* often speak of its position as the first zombie film, its unique dreamlike and fairy

The spectacular Janus Company model kit of Murder Legendre from White Zombie. *(Courtesy of John Ulakovic.)*

Others, like the Manimals, see qualities in the film which can be channeled in new directions, such as into the lyrics of their heavy metal songs. *White Zombie's* marginalized status—first in the 1930s as a low-budget, independent horror film which promoted transgressive themes and won at the box office despite the outcries of some critics, and then in the 1960s as a movie treated both as an exploitation spectacle in reissues with *Freaks* (1932) and as a re-emerged, nearly lost classic of sorts in grainy, gritty prints—is perhaps the goblet from which the band White Zombie drank in searching for their name. After all, given the film's various travails, its revival has in a way become an amazing story.

Consumers who devour these efforts can also be broken into different groups. One would be unaware that a reference to *White Zombie* is being made at all; indeed, they would be oblivious to the existence of the 1932 film while still experiencing its effect on more modern texts. These would include many fans of the band White Zombie, as well as ticket buyers to movies like *The Hand That Rocks the Cradle.* Even highly literate readers of *Gravity's Rainbow* may not be acquainted with *White Zombie* or the scene from the film that Thomas Pynchon invokes.

On the other hand, purchasers of a museum-quality model kit or a comic book often share the same enthusiasm and veneration for the film as their product's creators. In those cases, audience and creator mutually share in the ritualistic adoration of *White*

tale qualities, and especially its tour de force performance by Lugosi. More than merely acknowledging *White Zombie*, designers of projects like the Janus model kit wish to offer reverence to a favored work of art.

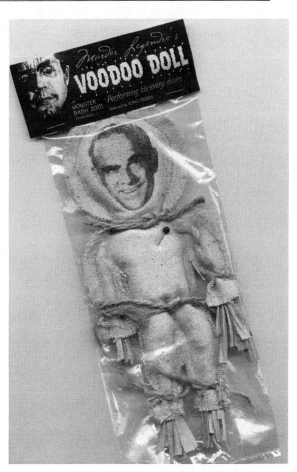

One-sheet movie poster from a reissue of White Zombie *with director Tod Browning's* Freaks *(1932).*

Zombie, reliving whatever they enjoy about the film in an essentially noncinematic exercise. For some of the more obsessive members in this category, it even provides a kind of false nostalgia for a period in which they did not live, a conduit to a person (namely Lugosi) and a past (specifically the horror cycle of the 1930s) extrinsic to their personal experiences.

With *White Zombie's* stone cast into the cultural waters of the US during the 1960s and 1970s, the video revolution of the 1980s has kept the ensuing ripples moving outwardly in larger circles to larger audiences. The result is that a devoted coterie of fans of *White Zombie* has imbued it with new life through sculptures, songs, and sketches. While receiving no response from those consumers unaware of *White Zombie,* they move the film into extrafilmic environments, inviting other, more informed audiences to join in an appreciation or, at the least, an ac-

knowledgment of the film. References to *White Zombie*—even those made purely due to its public domain status—also play their part in forcing recognition of the movie from new audiences and reappraisals of it from old.

Top: *Designed by Joe "Sorko" Schovitz for limited fan distribution at the 2001 Monster Bash convention, "Murder Legendre's Voodoo Doll" features the face of actor Bela Lugosi's horror film rival and sometimes costar Boris Karloff and comes complete with black pin through the heart.*

Bottom: *Sideshow Toys doll of Bela Lugosi as Murder Legendre, released in 2001, features multiple points of articulation and such extras as a knife, a wax voodoo doll, and Madeline's scarf.*

• *Chapter Seven* •

Preserving the History:
The Restoration of *White Zombie*

As much as Chapter Four attempts to offer an index of the responses given to *White Zombie* by 1932 audiences, it neglects one concern that has affected viewers of any era: the varying quality and length of extant film prints. Chapter Three notes that the copy screened at a June 1932 preview ran 74 minutes, but distribution prints seemingly ran 69 minutes. The film's pressbook never reflected the change, which—along with the possible cuts made by local censorship boards or theaters themselves while splicing together the film's eight reels—makes it difficult to know how much of *White Zombie* any 1932 audience saw. Even more impossible to determine are the lengths of all of the release prints of the subsequent reissues of *White Zombie* during the 1930s.

Television revivals of the film in the 1950s often meant even further cuts, with running times sometimes truncated to as brief as 55 minutes. Early TV prints also meant a proliferation of 16mm copies. *White Zombie*'s public domain status, which allowed anyone to copy and sell it without the need to obtain rights, meant that by the 1970s the film was duplicated repeatedly on formats like 16mm and 8mm. New copies were generally made from previously duped 16mm copies, causing a further deterioration of the quality of detail and definition and adding to the plethora of film running times.

The rise of the home video industry in the 1980s only compounded these problems, as a multitude of distributors began selling *White Zombie* on formats like Beta and VHS.[1] Their copies generally came from poor quality 16mm dupes, each with its own maddening array of scratches, hairs, popping splices, and soundtrack troubles. In general, the motives of such video companies were purely profit oriented. In addition to using whatever available prints there were, they made no efforts to clean them or make careful film-to-video transfers; on top of

that, the quality of the videotape stock itself was often poor. Even the video speed at which the film was duplicated was often chosen to use the most minimal amount of tape. New troubles for viewing the film arose, including the video dropping out lines, video noise, and other videotape-related sound problems. As film historian William K. Everson once wrote in reference to *White Zombie* videocassettes, "Buy all the tapes and you can see the movie slowly vanishing before your eyes."[2]

Of course it's the very opaque and cloudy prints that most modern viewers have witnessed, the scratches and murkiness almost seeming to add more years to *White Zombie*'s age. To some horror film fans, these problems also actually added another dimension to the viewing experience; *White Zombie* seemed even more ethereal and mythical through dupey grays and faded detail. Most historians and viewers would differ with the latter opinion. If not the worst of the 16mm dupes on videotape, however, what version should one see to view *White Zombie* properly? And how would a restoration of the film reconstitute that experience?

In his groundbreaking and highly influential essay "The Work of Art in the Age of Mechanical Reproduction," theorist Walter Benjamin considers the differences of artistic merit in older, nonreproduced art forms and in more modern media which can be easily replicated, such as photography and the motion picture. At one point, he considers that: "From a photographic negative, for example, one can make any number of prints; to ask for the 'authentic' print makes no sense."[3] One might at first suggest the same of film prints being struck from a 35mm negative, but this reflects that changes are sometimes made in negatives (as well as positives) and that copies can be made of copies, thus reducing the quality through mechanical reproduction.

Theorist Walter Benjamin's essay "The Work of Art in the Age of Mechanical Reproduction" helps frame important questions regarding which film print or prints should be considered the "authentic" version of White Zombie.

The answer to the question of which version to view to experience the authentic *White Zombie* as one should, rests on the meaning of the words "authentic" and "should." Presumably Victor Halperin intended what was seen at the June 1932 preview, but it's impossible to know now whether he was particularly pleased with that version. Perhaps he even appreciated the version cut by approximately five minutes which was the version seen by audiences during *White Zombie*'s 1932 release. Again, no evidence guides the historian to an answer. Any attempts at an answer could be faulty, as they place the director's vision over all else. For example, if one knew that Victor Halperin preferred the 74-minute version, but that most every audience member in 1932 saw a 69-minute film, would it not be most historically appropriate to champion the latter as the authentic relic to be viewed? Or should that concern be damned and consideration given only to modern audiences, with a nod to the fact that the relatively few who seek out *White Zombie* would want to consume as much footage as possible, especially if they have seen the prior version before? Yet, unless the word

is used completely without meaning, to "restore" a film should mean considering history above modern desire.

Running times are of course only one worry of many. Given the presumption that 1932 audiences, at least those in first-run theaters, saw relatively pristine prints of the 69-minute version, the best path might be to restore a print to make it as close as possible to those seen by 1932 viewers at better venues. At first such a goal seems a simple one to pursue, even if the cost is high and the labor tedious: to strive to make the film look and sound as clean as possible. But with older films that carry the troubles of *White Zombie* prints, often digital means must be employed; these automatically cause changes to the film's appearance, as even technology of the late 20th century causes at times digital artifacting, however slight and often unnoticed it may be. In other words, by eliminating scratches and similar problems to "restore" the film, alterations—however minute—simultaneously occur. No easy answers can be offered, but one would presume the word "restore" would guide the thinking preservationist to realize the limitations of the craft while still pursuing whatever is closest to the way a film would have originally appeared; presumably digital artifacting would be a lesser evil if the film overall is dramatically closer to its original in splendor.

It is easy to build yet a further list of qualifications to experience *White Zombie* as audiences once did, not the least of which is to see a 35mm print in a movie theater setting with an audience. As Chapter Four showed, though, even that setting was a very different environment from theater to theater. Such differences in viewing circumstances must be considered in addition to the immense gulf between all of the experiences a 1932 viewer brought to the film and those of a later era did in their time. Indeed, the experiences and perceptions of any two viewers sitting side by side at the same theater in the same epoch can be radically different.

Differences in viewing environments were a definite concern in the early 1930s. For example, projectionists of the time often debated problems of distortion and warped perspectives occurring when a viewer sat at a certain angle to the screen in a theater, or when the projector itself illuminated images on the screen at a slight angle to it.[4] Similar concerns were voiced over the variations in screen sizes and projectors available at different theaters, irregularities in the style and placement of film reel changeover marks on the film frames, and the possibility of dirt, lint and hairs in the projector or on the film print which would be noticeable when projected on-screen.[5] Trade publications during the era also admonished projectionists about more serious film damage which would impair the viewing experience.[6]

The issue of film reproduction also raised the ire of many in the 1930s. Though high standards in the quality and uniformity of film prints struck in Hollywood existed, occasional problems resulted. Also, at times prints were struck elsewhere in the US or the world, which exacerbated reproduction inconsistencies. A report of the Research Council of the Academy of Motion Picture Arts and Sciences in 1933 (of which L. E. Clark, sound engineer on *White Zombie*, was chairman of the board overseeing the quality of release prints) announced that, "measuring instruments of the various laboratories are not calibrated to any common standard, and specifications for optimum quality prints are difficult to set and enforce."[7] The report thus suggested that some film prints would have been slightly lighter or darker than others, and some would have possessed greater sharpness and clarity of image than others.

Presumably, then, limitations must be placed on the extent to which a viewer decades later could ever experience *White Zombie* in an "authentic" manner; indeed, given variations in the viewing process, perhaps an "authentic" experience could not even be defined. A late 20th

century medium like laser disc or DVD as displayed on a television screen is an alternative experience to seeing the film in a theater. Even a projected 16mm print constructs a different setting than would a 35mm copy. With these realities in mind, one wishing to restore *White Zombie* would apparently attempt a visual-aural reconstruction or a thoughtful addition or deletion of footage to achieve a preferred running time and visual appearance. However impossible Benjamin's word "authentic" becomes for *White Zombie*, however much an idyllic *White Zombie* cannot exist, the emphasis should still be on a thoughtful and careful execution of the meaning of the word "restore."

Apparently the first person to attempt a film restoration of *White Zombie* was Frank Storace, who had purchased an original nitrate negative from Krellberg, Inc. for use in film duplication; his retail prints were handled by Reel Images. Storace's sales consisted exclusively of 16mm copies during the late 1970s. By that time, videotapes had already begun eroding overall film sales, and Storace was reluctant to run a magnetic track and print *White Zombie* down to Super 8mm. His version's quality was the best available to consumers in the 1970s, though multiple other companies purchased Storace's copy specifically to dupe and resell to their customers. Niles Cinema, for example, duped his 16mm version and then struck further 16mm's from it. Thunderbird Films was apparently another such company to utilize Storace's print, releasing both 16mm and Super 8mm versions of the film.

The print Storace himself obtained was approximately 70 minutes in length.[8] As he claimed in 1981, "the original nitrates on *WZ* [*sic*] had been edited—all of the outtakes are the nitrate negs. It all seems crazy, but that's the way it is."[9] His hope was to obtain and restore those film outtakes—which consisted of useable, edited footage, rather than, say, bloopers or alternative takes—to the 16mm copy he was already selling, and release on 16mm the most complete version of *White Zombie* possible. An "authentic" version to him apparently meant one that *all* possible footage.

The film collector press had of course initially rejoiced at the possibilities. John McGee, in his "Reel Reviewer" column of *Classic Film Collector* issue #60 (Fall 1978), wrote:

> …Frank Storace of Storace Films stepped forward and asked to buy the rights to this film with the agreement that he be furnished with the original negatives to copy so that he could sell legally to film collectors original prints. Such an agreement was reached, at no small expense to Storace Films, and those of you interested will be getting better prints than have ever been available or seen on TV, not only from the original negative, but with

re-recorded sound from the 1932 Westrex sound track the owner had retained.

The outtakes, however, seemingly held priority for Storace even over sought-after improvements in audio and visual quality.

Storace once wrote, "the extra footage was on partly decomposed nitrate and we opted for the shorter [approximately 70 minute] version until such time that the footage could be restored and added to our negative."[10] He was apparently told that the outtakes would add approximately four minutes to the 70 in the negative he had already purchased. Storace claimed the scenes themselves consisted of "zombies lurking about and scenes of them working the fields, etc."[11]

However, Krellberg's death in 1979 came before the outtakes changed hands, immediately causing problems. While Storace had paid for the footage, the estate was far less than helpful to him in fulfilling Krellberg's obligations. Attorneys either questioned Storace's claims or believed they could stall transferring the materials, and with each day that passed the amount of decomposition to the nitrate outtakes slowly increased. Storace's frustrations and battles with the estate can be seen in excerpts from letters written by him to film historian and *White Zombie* fan Leonard J. Kohl:

> We have just begun legal proceedings with the Krellberg attorneys and I hope that we can get the extra footage. An extra on our side is that the suit will have to be answered in Arizona courts which may be a possible deterrent to their attempting to counter what little I am asking [November 30, 1979].

> As for *White Zombie*, the case is still in limbo and my attorney doesn't think that it will be worth it to keep going since the costs are even beginning to outweigh whatever I may get in film stock. I have heard from the lab that the nitrate negative is decomposing and there will be a lot of work to get a really acceptable 74 minute nitrate print. Since I am not backed by anyone, I will have to leave the restoring to the [American Film Institute]. I understand that they cannot even get a 74 minute print of the title, so that says something in itself [August 17, 1980].

> Thank you for the letter and your interest in my getting the missing footage to the film *White Zombie*. It has come to pass, however, that I will probably never get it. I pursued the thing through my attorneys and it would have cost a heck of a lot more to get to the footage (assuming that would, indeed, be the end result) than I could afford. The initial "ballyhoo" of the superior quality film has blown over and the additional footage would be of no real commercial value in a business sense, but would be of great value to libraries and schools and, of course, to people like yourself. I really do not feel that people like Krellberg/United Artists or his estate gave a damn about

the footage and the preservation of the title. The only thing they were ever interested in was the money that they could get from any number of people and hang the title. Even with all of the prints sold, I have not made back my investment in full, but—at all times—I was more interested in preserving the film in its entirety or I would never have gone through the trouble for a film which was Public Domain and had been around for many years in inferior prints... [February 27, 1981].

> The negs from the Krellberg estate were sold to a millionaire investor many months ago and the lawsuit would have been beyond my means. The guy doesn't even care about the film—it's simply another of his myriad of investments [April 3, 1981].

As Storace's final letter to Kohl indicates, the restoration was not to be. He never secured the desired footage from the "millionaire investor," and hopes for augmenting *White Zombie*'s running time dissipated. His valiant fight ended, with the footage itself the central casualty. Given the passing years, it is almost a certainty that any outtakes or cut footage from 1932 has turned to dust in the hands of those who purchased the Krellberg collection. Dust without even an urn to honor the lost moments of *White Zombie*'s art.

It was not until the 1990s that another film collector made an attempt at a restoration. Cary Roan—president of the Roan Group, which began to work on *White Zombie* in 1994—had by then already achieved a high level of prestige within the film industry for often amazing efforts at restoring films. His work has been lauded by film historians and even filmmakers like the late Ida Lupino. Roan wisely spends his time with classic films that for various reasons have fallen into the public domain and thus into the world of poor quality dupes. Timeless movies like Orson Welles' *The Trial* (1962) and *Suddenly* (1959) with Frank Sinatra return very close to their original splendor under Roan's careful scrutiny and tireless efforts. *White Zombie* would become one of the films which attracted Roan's attention.

"I wanted to work on a film that would have a strong market," Roan mentioned, "and in the process I asked Greg Luce, president of Sinister Cinema, what were his best selling films. He listed the four or five top ones; *White Zombie* was one of those. I told him I might be able to do something really special if good work materials could be found. Luce told me he had some print material on it, and, when he sent me the prints, I knew I could really do wonders with this wonderful film."[12]

In the end, Roan culled footage from two separate 35mms and one 16mm print. The 35mm prints were of different cuts; though their running times were comparable, each possessed moments or even entire scenes not present in the other print. No one knows the exact origins of these prints, and—given the various companies that rereleased the film in years subsequent to the 1930s—he speculates a third or even fourth cut could have been shipped to some theaters. The sum total of Roan's collected footage would amount to approximately 68 minutes, almost identical to the running time of release prints in 1932.

In a film lab in Pittsburgh, Roan transferred the film materials to digital formats. Both digital and liquid wet gates were used to clean the prints. Engineers removed the bulk of all the lines, scratches, and flaws on the images. Roan also spent much time "shadowing" the film, turning grainy and grey fades into the dark fade-to-blacks much closer to the filmmakers' intentions. In fact, Roan spent much time ensuring that black shades throughout really were black, rather than the muddied grays seen in more recent, duped copies. He also concentrated on curing various problems inherent in all *White Zombie* film prints. For example, the original 1932 marriage prints were apparently lit slightly wrongly during the optical-printing phase, the result being an F-stop exposure or two off in the printer. As a result, very brief flashes occurred near dissolves and transitional effects like wipes. Roan's restoration transformed *White Zombie*'s visuals into an even greater delight than any prints screened in 1932 theaters, his vision apparently preferring aesthetics over history.

He also wisely chose to matte the film. After an initial transfer, he took a VHS screener and played it on a television he knew would crop more than almost any other. That process acted as a gauge for the size of the matte, which later proved successful in keeping the film's visual composition from being cropped by TV sets. The 35mm prints from which he worked also featured full 35mm frames in the tradition of silent film apertures, and Roan determined that the film had been shot with a silent camera using separate RCA sound equipment. As a result, the frames, originally being some 1.2 times larger than those on a 35mm sound-on-film negative, touched one another and splices could readily be seen in the video transfer. The matte at the top of the screen helped conceal all such problems, while preserving the integrity of the original composition. "You'll see the entire picture when you see a Roan Group picture," the company's president promised.

Sound became another crucial consideration. The restoration eliminated as many audio "pops" and as much hiss as possible. The entire soundtrack was removed, restored by engineers, and then synched back to the film. The process involved transferring the audio (much of which came from the 16mm print) to 35mm full coat mag, then transferring it to the digital D2 format. Roan used 35mm to get the most digitally processed sound.

During the process and much to his surprise, Roan found a few moments of dead audio track within the original prints, brief sequences that the original audio technicians had neglected. Roan carefully dropped in background ambient sound in these areas, creating a stronger and more complete audio track than the film possessed even in 1932.

After seeing the initial video screenings of the restoration, the meticulous Roan was displeased with a few minor details. Though weeks and weeks of work were already behind him, he spent yet another day in the lab to correct even more of the film's problems. In the final analysis, the sum total of Roan's hours of effort are evident on the screen; his restoration is a remarkable achievement. Indeed, by comparison to earlier prints, it's astounding that he achieved such a level of visual and aural quality. To complement the film, the Roan Group packaged the film in a laser disc jacket featuring rare 1932 artwork of Lugosi; customers also received a reproduction of the rerelease pressbook and an essay on the film by Gary D. Rhodes.

The result was the best *White Zombie* had looked since 1932. That's not to say that problems of old prints do not linger. In addition to some minor audio problems, a few visual glitches remain. For example, several frames are damaged within Shot 255.[13] At the beginning of Shots 258 and 260, numerous frames are also marred. In addition, a single frame of Shot 259 is damaged as well. Major scratches and missing frames occur in Shot 309, frame damage can be seen in Shot 350, and a black spot is noticeable on the left side of all frames of Shot 404.[14]

Furthermore, the digital forum which so helped the appearance of the film caused some minor changes to it as well. Roan admits that once or twice he had to briefly freeze a frame to extend the length of the dialogue taken from another print. Additionally, a minimal amount of digital artifacting occurs at moments of high-speed action. For example, at Shots 272–273 in Scene 17 when Beaumont throws down his wine glass after realizing Legendre has drugged him, the motion of his arm movement bears this problem, which visually causes a "ghosting" effect.[15] In general, however, chronicling such problems heightens them far beyond their minimal nature. The Roan Group restoration is an almost unbelievable accomplishment, removing the decades of neglect and deterioration suffered by the film.

White Zombie (1932) proved to be the most popular Roan Group laser disc release. "For a classic film of the thirties," Roan believes, "I'd say it's one of the most successful released on laser disc. Response was really superb; one of the nicest things was that Bela Lugosi, Jr., responded very favorably."

In the national media, reviews were particularly

For his elaborate reconstruction of White Zombie, *Cary Roan synthesized footage from two different 35mm prints and one 16mm print.*

strong. *USA Today* believed, "The Haiti-based horror staple, usually seen in wretched prints, probably hasn't looked this good since its original release, thanks to a full scale video restoration that's accompanied by Gary Don Rhodes' elaborate program notes."[16] *TV Guide* echoed those comments, mentioning "For years, only its faded, hard-to-watch versions have been available, but a new Roan Group laserdisc changes all that."[17] Giving the film an "A" rating, *Entertainment Weekly* advised readers that "For its laserdisc premiere … the film has been spliced together from two good 35mm prints and then digitally restored. Very Impressive."[18]

Film journals and magazines also lauded the restoration, with *Films in Review* proclaiming, "The quality of this disc is amazing…." To the July-August 1995 *Filmfax*, it provided "a cleaner, crisper image than we've seen is decades."[19] *Cult Movies* deemed it "undeniably superb,"[20] while *Video Watchdog* called it "definitive."[21] Moreover, *Filmfax* noticed that "close inspection will re-

veal a slight pixelation of the image—digital artifacts caused by the clean up process—but this is usually unobtrusive unless there is rapid motion in the shot.[22] Its reviewer also noticed that some of the footage displaying the most wear and audio noise (such as the extended conversation between Beaumont and his butler at frame #179B6) occurs during segments which are *missing* from some VHS tape versions. In light of Roan's tremendous job, however, such reviewers generally forgave these minor shortcomings.

This is not to say, though, the restoration went without more substantial criticism. For example, *Filmfax* admitted, "There are a few hairline scratches here and there, and one or two instances wherein dialogue is cut short (or completely out) by an errant splice…." Perhaps the most stinging criticism came from one Rich Wannen of Fairway, Kansas. His letter in *The Laser Disc Newsletter* struck at what he viewed as major problems.[23] The publication's review had earlier noted "an occasional jump-cut splice

Not content with his highly praised laser disc of White Zombie, *Cary Roan continued to work on the film for a DVD issue in 1999.*

and the image fluctuates ... [and the] sound is also weak, with dialog lacking an upper range." Wannen believed that such comments were:

> ...almost laughable understatements. Well, there's not much problem with jumping splices. ... Every camera pan or rapid movement by a character elicits trailing or ghosting. Dimension is lost, so that most of the interior settings, especially in medium or closeup shots, look like painted backdrops. ... And the sound doesn't just crap out in the upper ranges of the dialog: I have to turn my volume up 4/5 to maximum just to hear the exciting music of the climax.[24]

These comments seem to overstate by far the minimal drawbacks to a major and highly admirable enterprise that Roan spearheaded. Indeed, the remark about the interior settings is probably a testament to the restored luster and detail Roan achieved. The painted glass shots are less apparent in other prints because of their muddy,

faded, and generally opaque appearance—certainly a far cry from what appeared on the 35mm negatives that Harold McLernon edited in 1932.

Not content with his work on the laser disc restoration, Cary Roan decided to use the emerging DVD home video format as a vehicle to improve upon his first effort. He remastered the laser disc version, digitally flattening the grain to help eliminate the artifacting caused at moments of fast motion by the earlier digital restoration. In the DVD version, artifacting is still noticeable in Shot 246, Shots 272–273, and Shot 484; however, even those shots show less artifacting than did the laser disc restoration. Roan also boosted and reprocessed the audio track, making moments like the last line of Dr. Bruner's dialogue in Scene 16—which in all prior versions had been exceedingly difficult to hear—much more audible. Overall, the DVD presents an improvement over the laser disc restoration, though only in the minor, aforementioned respects.[25]

The Storace and Roan efforts, one a valorous attempt and the other a lasting achievement, represent what film historian and preservationist Paolo Cherchi Usai has called "the fruit of individual tenacity (or obsession)."[26] Even considering their drive for profit, they embody the best of intentions brought to bear within the world of film history.

Usai's praise would most likely be followed, however, with his aesthetic admonition that Storace and Roan worked without benefit of assistance from the original artistic team of *White Zombie* or from a set of detailed notes and script materials to guide them. As a result, Usai might well and quite rightly suggest that these are reconstructions (specifically Roan's, which was fashioned in a Frankensteinian mode from three film prints), not reproductions of the exact form in which *White Zombie* was presented to 1932 audiences, whether at the June preview, the July premiere, or any given theater during its original release. The fact that Roan in a small way reworked his laser disc restoration for the DVD issue reinforces their status as reconstructions. Nonetheless, the Roan efforts (and probably the Storace, had it been finished) are certainly a carefully executed attempt to *restore*, a thoughtful striving towards the impossible "authentic" in an age of cinematic reproduction and repercussion.

Chapter Eight

Re-examining the Reputation: *White Zombie* Under Modern Critical Scrutiny

Thanks to the varying opinions of late 20th century film reviewers and historians who have written about the film, *White Zombie* has led a tumultuous life from a critical standpoint even in more recent years. If its 1932 release provoked mixed views from national and local reviewers as well as moviegoers, the film caused, in the latter 30 years of the 20th century, a cacophony of extremist voices. Some—such as film historians William K. Everson, George Turner, Calvin T. Beck, and Carlos Clarens—praised *White Zombie* highly, while others—like *Films in Review* editor Roy Frumkes—audibly aired their discontent with the film. At the same time, film theorists and academicians have generally ignored the film.

However, among more popular-audience movie critics and historians *White Zombie*'s acceptance has generally grown to something akin to a "classic." This is not to suggest that many of its ardent supporters have not readily acknowledged its weaknesses. For example, William K. Everson once claimed that:

> Although it tried a little too hard to outhorrify its predecessors and was in danger of being silly at times, its gruesome quality is a model of restraint and decorum by contemporary standards. ... It's a movie that garners, and justifiably so, far more respect today than it did a half-century ago. Somehow many of the movies' crudities translate into a raw poetry....[1]

Everson's reputation in 1960s and 1970s film scholarship helped propel *White Zombie* to a level of acceptance it had never previously enjoyed. The reputations of Clarens, Beck and Turner, coupled with their comments, did the very same.

If some viewers like Everson can weigh *White Zombie*'s strong and weak qualities in their initial analyses, others in the latter days of the 20th century seemed willing to do so only over time, perhaps persuaded by growing respect for the film. For example, horror film critic John Stanley wrote of *White Zombie* in his book *The Creature Features Movie Guide* (Warner, 1984):

> By today's standards, a creaky, awful film, only occasionally enhanced by some of the symbolic imaginery [*sic*] injected by producers Victor and Edward Halperin. Bela Lugosi is in severe need of restraint as he overplays Legendre, a sweetless sugar plantation owner n the West Indies who holds sway over an army of zombies. Heavy handed, turgid viewing, recommended only to die-hard buffs or historians wishing to study the decrepit films of yesteryear.

Ten years later, Stanley's updated edition—*Creature Features Movie Guide Strikes Again* (Creatures at Large, 1994)—apparently felt compelled to give in at least in part to the rising critical favor towards *White Zombie*. His new entry on the film ended with an amended critique: "Heavy-handed, turgid viewing, yes, but it's a wonderful glimpse into Hollywood's schlocky past." In general, this example suggests the fluid and indeed political aspect of film criticism, adjusting its sail to the prevalent winds of an era; while *White Zombie* as a film has changed in minor ways due to duplications, editing, and erosion, some of its critics are far more malleable than its celluloid.

The quotations gathered in this chapter represent both a collection of previously printed commentary from publications and books of the modern era, as well as some capsule reviews by horror film historians written especially for this volume. Together they offer widely varying evaluations of *White Zombie*, but they also reveal a majority of voices favorable to the film. In part this result may well be due to a degree of bias in the study's choice of horror film critics and historians to contribute commentary. This chapter is certainly not a quantitative analysis, but rather a qualitative collection. At the same time, the overall lack of academic voices in this chapter illustrates the continued marginalization of *White Zombie* among university-based thinkers and scholarly publications. But even with all these qualifiers in mind, though, Chapter Eight still highlights *White Zombie's* growth in popular acceptance during the latter decades of the 20th century.

* * * * * *

1. "My earliest memories of *White Zombie* were in a local third run 'grindhouse' in Brooklyn. *White Zombie*, like *Freaks* (1932, made the same year), seemed to be a favorite of distributors who reissued them twice a year to small independent exhibitors during the late forties and early fifties. The film was also a staple of early television, but prints were ruthlessly edited for commercials.

"It was years later at a local film society that I finally had an opportunity to see a complete 16mm original print (many dupes were made due to its public domain status) ... [and] I had a chance to reevaluate it. The film has flaws, and its slow place becomes more obvious when compared to today's unsubtle, fast-moving thrillers and horror films. The film has an old-fashioned look to it, as if it was made during the silent period, but this seems to work to the film's advantage. Lugosi's characterization, aided by riveting closeups of his eyes, clearly dominates the film, even when he is off-camera. An example of this is when closeups are used at the beginning to establish the mood of the film. The substitution of visuals to advance the plot are skillfully done, reducing the dialogue considerably, making Lugosi's delivery doubly effective.

"The players are well cast, especially Madge Bellamy and Robert Frazer; the latter is probably in the best role of his career and is very moving in a scene where he falls under Lugosi's spell. The settings, especially the cavernous interior of Lugosi's castle, add a grim, pictorial beauty. Not the least of the film's assets is the musical score, though primitive as it sounds on a first screening, nonetheless adds a genuine poetic and dreamlike quality to the film.

"*White Zombie* has all the trappings of the 'voodoo' film, making it the definitive in the genre. It's a pity the Halperin brothers never made a sequel to *White Zombie* with Lugosi repeating his role. The near-final scene of

the camera lingering on Lugosi's lifeless body, sprawled on the rocks like a broken doll before being washed out to sea, lingered long in my memory"—Richard Bojarski, author of *The Films of Bela Lugosi* (Citadel, 1980).

2. "As usual, [Lugosi] pulled out all the acting stops, but in this particular film, with its fairy-tale atmosphere, his unique style fitted in quite well"—John Brosnan in *The Horror People* (St. Martin's, 1976).

3. "[*White Zombie* is] an excellent example of the genre. The movie invariably fails when it tries hardest to horrify ... but these mistakes are outbalanced by true poetic detail. Whatever period feeling *White Zombie* possessed at the time of release has been erased by the intervening third of a century, making the images more faded, the period more remote, and the picture itself more completely mysterious"—Carlos Clarens in *An Illustrated History of the Horror Film* (Putnam, 1967).

4. "Filmed for $62,500 that obviously wasn't spent on the acting, this creepy cheapie about the limitations of physical beauty is full of nocturnal mood"—Mike Clark in the March 17, 1995, *USA Today*.

5. "*White Zombie* ... remains the definitive zombie film in the eyes of most horror movie buffs"—*Classic Images*, Issue #91, 1983.

6. "Made on a shoestring budget, the cult classic *White Zombie* nevertheless has a marvelously gothic look that compares favorably to [that of] the Universal horror films of its day. ... you can really savor the imaginative work of cinematographer Arthur Martinelli, and director Victor Halperin's ahead-of-its-time use of sound effects to create a feeling of dread"—*Entertainment Weekly*, April 14, 1995.

7. "...in its mood and effect, *White Zombie* is one of the most satisfying films of its period, as well as being the 'definitive' voodoo film—not that there have been more than a handful of films in that category. ... The pictorial values are outstanding throughout, and are backed by solid looking sets, an imaginative use of light and shadows, and a sustained use of music. ... the voodoo necromancer provides Lugosi with his most sinister role, reveling in evil for its own sake, and without even the token sympathy one sometimes felt for the vampire"—William K. Everson in *Classics of the Horror Film* (Citadel, 1974).

8. "The film has an eerie quality about it, as much due to the primitive technical qualities as any inherent Gothic atmosphere. It is now very much a cult movie, not entirely deserved since reviewing reveals a confused plot and indifferent performances apart from an interesting one from Lugosi"—Alan Frank in *The Horror Film Handbook* (Barnes and Noble, 1982).

9. "Feelings vary widely [regarding the merits of *White Zombie*], and I'm in the negative camp. Despite some impressive dramatic moments from Bela Lugosi

and occasionally beautiful cinematography, I find the direction of the actors endlessly stilted"—Roy Frumkes in the September-October 1995 issue of *Films in Review*.

10. "Seeing the picture now, its dated technique gives it an eerie quality and a horrific effectiveness that may have escaped some of the critics at the time. The deliberate pacing and the scenes between Lugosi and Frazier [*sic*] have a hypnotic quality, and the shots of the zombies are unnerving indeed and effective in a more powerful way than much of the blood and gore [and] ... spilling guts [shown] all over the wide screens in vivid color today"—Alex Gordon in "The Pit and the Pen of Alex Gordon" in *Fangoria* 16 (December 1981).

11. "This is one of the underground classics of horror. Made on a shoestring budget and atrociously acted, the film nonetheless emerges as a strangely poetic fairy-tale about a beastly zombie master and the beauty he lures to his lair and functions in a dislocated, dreamlike manner reminiscent of Carl Dreyer's *Vampyr*"—Phil Hardy in his book *The Overlook Film Encyclopedia: Horror* (Overlook Press, 1995).

12. "When discussion turns to *White Zombie*, people inevitably recount (with ripe enthusiasm), the sequence in which one of Legendre's zombies falls into the works of a creaking mill, his body noisily crushed as his undead comrades continue silently with their work. It's a great moment, no argument, but my favorite is more subtle, and comes early in the film, when Legendre approaches Madeline's coach. The sorcerer stands in the foreground of the frame, while behind him—arrayed on a hillside in the moonlight—stands a group of his zombies, waiting with eternal patience for their master's next command. It's a tableaux from hell, and one of the most unsettling of all horror film images.

"*White Zombie* director Victor Halperin created and sustained an overpowering mood, a feat that eluded Tod Browning, whose *Dracula* (1931)—the other truly great Lugosi vehicle—stumbles badly after a marvelous opening reel.

"*White Zombie* will never carry the cultural weight of *Dracula*—Legendre, after all, has neither the literary origin or the fascinating allure of Stoker's vampire count—but in many ways the film is superior to Browning's. It takes full advantage of exteriors as well as interiors; it has an unnerving sexual subtext that is considerably more pointed than that of *Dracula*; and where Browning's film goes suddenly, deadeningly silent for long stretches, *White Zombie* exploits silence to heighten drama.

"On the debit side, I'm completely unimpressed with romantic leads Madge Bellamy and John Harron; she with her wide child's eyes and bee-stung lips; he with his boyish physique and faintly prissy demeanor. And Lu-

gosi, just one year removed from *Dracula*, was already in professional decline. It's ironic and unbearably sad that *White Zombie*, although a splendid film by any standard, marked the beginning of the actor's long association with low budget independent pictures, an association that would quickly kill his aspirations to professional respectability"—David H. Hogan, author of *Dark Romance: Sexuality in the Horror Film* (McFarland, 1986).

13. "This was one of the first zombie films and is still one of the most potent after 60 years. ... All in all, the film is a remarkable accomplishment given its brief shooting schedule and piddling budget"—Wesley G. Holt in the July-August 1995 *Filmfax*.

14. "Of all the Zombie films, I must admit my favourite is a little-seen one by Victor Halperin, called *White Zombie*, which starred Bela Lugosi as a kind of madman ... despite its over-the-top celebration of the macabre, this film worked with a peculiar intensity near to poetry"—Tom Hutchinson in *Horror and Fantasy in the Movies* (Crescent, 1974).

15. "...what was previously seen as mere staginess now has the appeal of an opera without arias, an interpretation that makes the film's worst, most overplayed performances seem more appropriate to the overall tenor of production. After all, if performed on a more realistic keel, the supporting performances might have made Lugosi's own mesmerizing performance seem out-of-register"—Tim Lucas in *Video Watchdog* #29 (1995).

16. "*White Zombie* is one of my personal five favorite films made by my father—and it was one of his. I like the film because of the quality of his performance, the direction, and the memorable scenes. One of the strongest scenes from the film [is] Murder Legendre casting a spell over the voodoo doll of Madge Bellamy..."—Bela G. Lugosi in "Remembrance of My Father" in the *Bela Lugosi/White Zombie: Instructions for Assembling and Painting* pamphlet which accompanied the Janus Company's 1997 *White Zombie* resin model kit.

17. "*White Zombie* remains one of the most hotly debated artifacts of the Golden Age of Horror Films. It offers an atmosphere of palpable gothic horror and a surreal, dreamlike quality, but these same qualities nearly conspire to destroy it. Like dreams, *White Zombie* seems shapeless and overly languid, and, like dreams, it is sometimes best appreciated while asleep.

"Many of the visuals at the graveyards and in and around Lugosi's castle seem to carry the essence of Poe. Slower and less 'fun' than most horror classics, *White Zombie* has the same macabre beauty as some of the finest silent horror films. It is a masterpiece of design, if not construction, with interiors more atmospheric and resonant than those in *Dracula* and *Frankenstein*. At times, *White Zombie* plays like some weird anticipation of the

Film historian Bob Madison writes that "White Zombie remains one of the most hotly debated artifacts of the Golden Age of Horror Films. It offers an atmosphere of palpable gothic horror and a surreal, dreamlike quality, but these same qualities nearly conspire to destroy it."

1960s: a Vincent Price movie paired with a bad acid trip.

"What ensures the film's classic stature, however, is Bela Lugosi's performance. Many of his most memorable movie scenes can be found in this modest shocker. *White Zombie* also does much to distill the Lugosi persona: his Legendre is a monster of lust, egotism, and pride. Lugosi wants power, deference, and sex. It is not that Lugosi breaks the law; rather, he is above the law. When we admire Lugosi, we admire the strong, dark part of ourselves"—Bob Madison, editor of *Dracula: The First Hundred Years* (Midnight Marquee, 1997).

18. "While there's much I admire about *White Zombie*, I can't write that it's in my Top Ten List of Horror Films. I seriously doubt if it will crash my Top Twenty.

"Yes, I applaud Bela Lugosi's magnificently evil Murder Legendre; the fairy tale ambiance; the cinematography of Arthur Martinelli; the effective musical score; and the creativity that the Halperin brothers achieved with such limited resources. But also in *White Zombie*, there is (for me, anyway) a nasty sense of exploitation—so that watching this venerable film becomes a painful experience rather than an enjoyable one.

"Why?

"Well, first of all, there's that woeful emoting of the romantic lead, John Harron. This actor is so bad that one wishes the Academy Awards in 1996 would bring 96-year old David Manners down from Santa Barbara and give him a six-decades-late Oscar for his comparatively brilliant work in *Dracula*, *The Mummy*, and *The Black Cat*.

"Then there's Madge Bellamy, whose performance as the *White Zombie* makes even the incredibly coy Sidney Fox of *Murders in the Rue Morgue* look like a dramatic powerhouse.

"There are some stiff, silly scenes, and my space

allows noting only one: the death scene of Brandon Hurst, as the Butler. Tossed by the zombies into the water, this old warhorse character actor—as all *White Zombie* aficionados surely know—*holds his nose* as he splashes down. A responsible producer or director would have demanded a retake (or hired a double); instead, Hurst's comic (or desperate!) touch sinks the scene.

"But what perhaps bothers me most about *White Zombie* is Lugosi's late-in-life lament that he was only paid about $800 to $900 for his classic acting in the film. Considering that Bela looks for much of *White Zombie* like a professional actor somehow drafted into performing with junior high school students; that he gave it his total dramatic energy, despite being reportedly ill all through the shooting; that his portrayal is the only reason (despite the film's various clever assets) that makes the film worthy of revival today; and that, later in 1932, Bela declared bankruptcy while *White Zombie*'s producers made a fortune—all these thoughts nag at me throughout a viewing of *White Zombie*.

"Perhaps I shouldn't allow such prosaic realizations to embitter me against *White Zombie*. They apparently didn't embitter Bela Lugosi, who, according to the late William K. Everson, had greatly respected the 'speed and efficiency' with which the film had been produced.

"Still, a reeking sense of hokey, sideshow exploitation, mostly at the expense of Bela Lugosi, seems to attach itself to *White Zombie*.

"And, alas, that's the most frightening thing I find about the movie"—Gregory Mank, author of *Hollywood Cauldron: Thirteen Horror Films from the Genre's Golden Age* (McFarland, 1994) and *Karloff and Lugosi: The Story of a Haunting Collaboration* (McFarland, 1990).

19. "The pace of *White Zombie* is as slow as its creaky grindstones in the sugar cane mill—as it should be. This is, after all, a movie about zombies, the undead, sluggish slaves with no will of their own. In our age of short attention spans and expectations for immediate gratification, *White Zombie* is a refreshing throwback to a time when a film was allowed to luxuriate in stagnant, nightmarish atmosphere. *White Zombie* is a slow but deliberate ride in a horse-drawn hearse, not a quick-thrill fix on a roller coaster. Viewers do not so much watch the film as they do soak in it—a wash of obscene horror.

"Forgive the occasional self-indulgent arty shot and the somewhat flawed narrative structure and, instead, applaud them as the filmmakers' ambitious, fascinating misfires. The Halperin brothers achieved more in this low budget horror movie than did any other independent outfit of the 1930s.

"Dismiss some of the florid performances. Revel instead in the personality who is at the heart of this picture and gives the filmic dirge its monstrous beat: Bela Lugosi. That the actor was Hungarian does not fully account for his odd, indefinable manner and exoticism. He possesses a "foreignness" in this film that suggests he has traveled Stygian waters and tutored Hades over cyanide cocktails. Lugosi's exquisite portrayal of evil incarnate, as Murder Legendre, transcends pure evil into a realm of poetic depravity that is wickedly, slyly sexual and heartlessly manipulative.

"Lugosi was an original. No actor before or since him could have contributed the memorable brand of endurance he accorded *White Zombie*. The revelatory madness he was able to give lines like "For you, my friend, they are the angels of death," as his brand of zombies approach his intended victim, are unsurpassed in the annals of horror cinema"—Mark A. Miller, author of *Christopher Lee and Peter Cushing and Horror Cinema: A Filmography of Their 22 Collaborations* (McFarland, 1994).

20. "...eerie, unique, low budget chiller"—Leonard Maltin in his book *Movie and Video Guide* (Signet, 1994).

21. "Though some of it is intentionally comic, the film deserved a better fate. It was a wholly original work, imaginatively done and not soon forgotten by the viewer"—*Motion Picture Guide* (Cinebooks, Inc., 1987).

22. "This is Lugosi's film all the way. Everything else is secondary. ... It's satisfying to know that *White Zombie* has gained respect throughout the years and continued to do so. Although the acting and technical aspects seem quite primitive by today's standards and it's obvious that *White Zombie* was made on a limited budget, it has done nothing but add to the overall effectiveness of this remarkable film"—Mark D. Neel in "*White Zombie*: An Analysis of the Film Which Turned Bela Lugosi from Rising Star to B-Movie Boogeyman Overnight!" in *Monsterscene* 3 (Fall 1994).

23. "For those absolutely dedicated to gothic silliness"—*New Yorker*, 1977.

24. "...*White Zombie* will remain [to me] forever unforgotten. ... The whole added up to an encounter with deep-seated fears from which I felt I emerged with credit; I remember the experience with gratitude as a liberating and exhilarating one..."—S. S. Prawer in *Caligari's Children: The Film as Tale of Terror* (Da Capo, 1980).

25. "*White Zombie*, for all its legendary horror status, is in reality a fully realized romance triangle, albeit a rather creepy one. What separates *WZ* is that here the triangle concerns the heroine and the two lead villains.

"Neil, the hero of the piece, is mostly ineffectual. Before the film is half over, he twice loses the object of his desire, first looking on helplessly as Madeline literally dies in his arms at their postnuptial meal; he later drunkenly arrives too late to prevent his wife's body from being carted off from her tomb, thus 'losing' her a second time. Still later, he becomes limply ill as he rides to her rescue, and then swoons or stumbles about [during] much of the film's climax in a fever or stupor (this guy makes David Manners look like Errol Flynn), leaving Murder and Beaumont to struggle for Madeline's fate.

"Indeed, the scenes shared by Murder and Beaumont are the most effective in the film, particularly where Beaumont slips deeper and deeper under the effect of Murder's zombifying drug. Lugosi's playing here is superb, regarding his victim in turn with curiosity, arrogance, and some strange sort of sympathy, at one point tenderly patting Beaumont's hand with a very fatherly understanding. It is significant to note that it is Beaumont, not Neil, who tosses the bellowing, loosely stuffed figure of Murder onto the watery rocks at the film's finale. Though Beaumont perishes as well, he emerges as the true hero of the film. Neil may get the girl, but Beaumont gets our respect.

"Madeline sums up the film with her simple, eloquent line, "I dreamed." *WZ* is a dark dream, a Brothers Grimm fable out of Caligari's cabinet, and one of Lugosi's finest hours"—Jeffrey Roberts, film historian and collector.

26. "Generally revered as an atmospheric triumph from the Golden Age of Horror and equally treasured as one of Bela Lugosi's finest hours (and nine minutes), *White Zombie* stands as a prime example of mood over money. Though not a perfect film (thanks to some painfully creaky histrionics), *White Zombie* manages to rise above an inadequate budget to create a brooding, otherworldly atmosphere all its own. In addition, though it did nothing for the actor's career (and little for his wallet), *White Zombie* sports a quintessential Lugosi performance to be savored with each repeated viewing. In short, *White Zombie* rightfully deserves that oft-misused appellative honor, "classic"—Bryan Senn, author of *Golden Horrors: An Illustrated Critical Filmography of Terror Cinema, 1931–1939* (McFarland, 1996).

27. "Frederick James Smith was a young critic of the teens, twenties, and thirties with whom I am usually in agreement. Of *White Zombie*, he wrote in *Liberty* magazine (September 10, 1932), 'If you do not get a shock out of the thriller, you will get one out of the acting. It would worry even a zombie.' I am inclined to agree with his opinion of the supporting players here, but at the same time, there is a fascination in watching former silent performers Madge Bellamy and John Harron destroy whatever last vestiges of their careers that existed. Here, Madge Bellamy seems set on the course that was to find her at the end of her life closely resembling Louise Dresser in *The Goose Woman*; and the tragedy of John Harron's acting in *White Zombie* is matched by the sorrow of his big family life, with a brother, Robert, who died of a self-inflicted gunshot wound and a father killed in a robbery.

"Is it because the remainder of the cast is so bad that Bela Lugosi appears so good? I think not. For all its faults, *White Zombie* provides Lugosi with one of his finest screen roles. He is mesmeric as Legendre, and how brilliant of the director to introduce the actor with a close-up of his eyes. The body and voice of the actor may dominate the scenes, but it is the eyes that haunt the viewer, transforming *White Zombie* from what might have been nothing more than a grade 'B' thriller into a classic gothic horror. Val Lewton's *I Walked with a Zombie* may have higher production values and better supporting performances, but for all its ragged edges—and sometimes ragged middle—*White Zombie* is the better entertainment value"—Anthony Slide, author of *Nitrate Won't Wait: A History of Film Preservation in the United States* (McFarland, 1992) and editor of *They Also Wrote for the Fan Magazines: Film Articles by Literary Giants from E. E. Cummings to Eleanor Roosevelt, 1920–1939* (McFarland, 1992).

28. "The film ... manages some delightfully creative moments, particularly in the use of shadows which play over the carriage as the young lovers first meet Lugosi and his living dead. The hero, after realizing that his wife is dead, becomes drunk and despondent as he watches the shadows of dancing couples on the wall. Suddenly, visions of his dead wife appear on the wall and he stumbles about trying to grasp at her. Only in Dreyer's *Vampyr* have shadows been used as creatively"—David Soren in his book *The Rise and Fall of the Horror Film* (Midnight Marquee, 1995).

29. "While Lugosi's best performance remains Ygor in *Son of Frankenstein* (1939), his role here comes a close second. ... *White Zombie* is Lugosi's film all the way. The rest of the cast is, at best, competent, and, at worst, uninteresting. And while director Halperin does manage some haunting images, such as the arrival of Bellamy by coach during a funeral procession, his latter efforts—*Supernatural* (1933) and *Revolt of the Zombies* (1936)—proved disappointing. As a result, one is left with the feeling that maybe he used all his good ideas in this one film. Furthermore, one wonders, if Lugosi were not in the film at all, if *White Zombie* would have retained the same power it still holds today"—John Stell in *Monsters from the Vault* (Summer 1995).

30. "It's a hard picture to classify—short on shocks, to be sure, but positively steeped in creepy atmosphere. ... *Zombie* really is the stuff nightmares are made of"—*TV Guide*, April 8, 1995.

31. "Regardless of narrative difficulties, the zombie scenes of men and women with blank, unseeing eyes, wind-up doll movements, utterly emotionless affect, yet still strangely human behavior are some of the most concussive images in all moviedom"—James Twitchell in his

"Bela, in one of his best horror roles, deserved much better support," suggests film historian Tom Weaver.

book *Dreadful Pleasures: An Anatomy of Modern Horror* (Oxford, 1985).

31. "It goes without saying that there are dozens of ways to enjoy, and to judge, and to remember a movie, but every time I'm offered an opportunity to watch *White Zombie*, I have the same involuntary reaction: The one and only thing that instantly springs to my mind is the acting ... the marvelous, Mephistophelean performance of Lugosi, and the just-plain-awful acting of his co-stars. *White Zombie* features one of my favorite Lugosi characterizations, but any time I'm faced with the prospect of a *WZ* screening, I have to guesstimate whether my enjoyment of Lugosi will be greater than my frustration with Madge Bellamy, John Harron and Joseph Cawthorn.

"Cawthorn's Dr. Bruner, the Borscht Belt's answer to Prof. Van Helsing, disrupts the movie's macabre mood, but he has a few good "moments" and is generally inoffensive. It's the bizarre non-acting of Bellamy and Harron

that sets me on edge, sometimes to the point where *White Zombie* teeters at the brink of falling into the category of 'negative entertainment.' Apologists sometimes try to pass off their performances as being in the 'silent film style,' but I'm not buying it; their acting is too unreal even for this sort of grotesque, operatic fairy tale. Like Mina in *Dracula* (1931), who is bland and bloodless *before* Lugosi puts the bite on her, Bellamy seems zombified right from her first scene. And Harron, the poor man's Dick York, is worse, making funny faces and doing bizarre line readings; next to Harron, Universal's foppish, inane 'horror hero' David Manners looks like a Hong Kong action star. Even in scenes where *other* people are talking and doing all the acting while Bellamy and Harron are just off on the sidelines, their facial expressions and reactions are sometimes weirdly unsuited to the situations; so even if *White Zombie had* been a silent, these same performances would have detracted from it.

"Yes, *White Zombie* has wonderful atmosphere, some

great musical cues, standout horror scenes and several other attractions, all of them examined in loving detail elsewhere in this book. I've got a copy—but I seldom watch it. And when friends offer to screen it at *their* homes, my reaction, sad to say, is always the same. My mind's eye automatically fills with a mental image of Bellamy and Harron, one or both of whom are in practically every scene ... and the first words out of my mouth are generally, 'What *else* you got?'

"Bela, in one of his best horror roles, deserved much better support"—Tom Weaver, author of *Poverty Row HORRORS! Monogram, PRC, and Republic Horror Films of the Forties* (McFarland, 1993) and coauthor with John and Michael Brunas of *Universal Horrors: The Studio's Classic Horror Films 1931–1946* (McFarland, 1990).

33. "...a unique, ancient-looking but fascinating low-budget horror movie. ... In addition to great sets, and lots of the living dead, there's weird music..."—Michael Weldon in *The Psychotronic Encyclopedia of Film* (Ballantine, 1983).

34. "*White Zombie* is by turns imaginative and embarrassing, exhilarating and campy—a horror film fan's delight and despair. ... At [Lugosi's] worst here, however, he's still hokily enjoyable. At his *best*, he wittily underplays his menace and is rather magnificent. The other actors succumb to a kind of slow-motion stylization that's closer to catalepsy than to acting"—Donald C. Willis in *Horror and Science Fiction Films II* (Scarecrow Press, 1982).

Chapter Nine

Reviewing the Literature:
White Zombie in Print

Despite the vastly discordant views on *White Zombie* and its growing popularity during the 1980s and 1990s, only a limited amount of the written literature on the film becomes necessary reading. Most of the available writing echoes the whole of horror film historiography written for popular audiences: derivation, repetition, and empirical inaccuracies. As noted in Chapter Eight, the sheer omission of *White Zombie* from nonhorror centered texts on film history is a sign of its marginalization in more academic discourse. Despite its economic success and importance as an independent film, *White Zombie* has been largely ignored by discussions of 1930s cinema.

However, a few historians and theorists have not ignored *White Zombie*. The annotated bibliography which follows includes essays and books which shed unique historical or theoretical light on the subject, as well as four that were instrumental in bringing about a more widespread critical investigation, if not exclusively an acceptance, of the film. While these texts have weaknesses as well as strengths, their merits transform them into important works on *White Zombie*.

1. Beck, Calvin T. *Heroes of the Horrors.* **New York: Macmillan and Co., 1975.**

Aimed at a popular audience, Beck's biographical survey of horror film actors includes a lengthy chapter on Bela Lugosi. Far more than any other single Lugosi film, Beck discusses *White Zombie* in terms of its narrative and its artistic merits (e.g., its mood, atmosphere, Lugosi's performance). While the chapter's value in subsequent years as an important source on the film has waned given its brevity, Beck's work is important to consider historically as a force in placing emphasis on the film; the result both expanded and improved the film's reputation among horror movie fans.

2. Benshoff, Harry M. *Monsters in the Closet: Ho-*

mosexuality and the Horror Film. **Manchester: Manchester University Press, 1997.**

Benshoff's study takes an in-depth look at homosexual undercurrents in the history of the horror film. He includes readings of Lugosi's films with Boris Karloff (e.g., *The Black Cat*), as well as a brief section entitled "De-repressing the homosocial triangle in *White Zombie*." In that section, Benshoff interprets the relationship between Legendre and Beaumont as sadomasochistic and homosexual in nature, a situation all the more complex due to the two being triangulated with Madeline through lust for her. To Benshoff, the film's recurrent vulture serves as a signifier of male-male desire, appearing as it does at moments that Benshoff views as homosexual. Supported by investigations of numerous scenes and examples, Benshoff's argument regarding *White Zombie* becomes one of the most important on the film, examining it in a valid but different perspective than prior interpretations.

3. Clarens, Carlos. *An Illustrated History of the Horror Film.* **New York: Capricorn Books, 1967.**

Clarens' text remains one of the more widely read on the horror film genre at large, with its intelligent discussion of *White Zombie* causing many during the late 1960s to re-examine the film's merits. His comments on the film span only a few pages, with a good part devoted to plot summary and a rudimentary production history. But Clarens' endorsements of *White Zombie* remain important considerations in that they helped force a re-evaluation of the film in the late 1960s and early 1970s.

4. Everson, William K. *Classics of the Horror Film.* **Secaucus, NJ: Citadel Press, 1974.**

While Everson's groundbreaking *Classics of the Horror Film* does not include individual sections on such well-known Bela Lugosi films as *Dracula* (1931) and *The Raven* (1935), the book does offer a four-page chapter on

Film historians like George E. Turner, William K. Everson, and Calvin T. Beck helped bring about a more positive re-evaluation of White Zombie.

White Zombie. Along with Calvin T. Beck and Carlos Clarens, Everson became an important element in the select group of film historians and critics who sought to elevate the film critically and historically.

His *Classics of the Horror Film* chapter on *White Zombie* offers no unique historical information, but his critical insight—much of which has been appropriated by subsequent writers—remains fascinating. For example, Everson speaks of the Halperins' "morbid preoccupation with the ritual of death" in their films, the sparse but key use of dialogue in *White Zombie,* and the film's occasional similarity to the work of director Carl Dreyer. As with Clarens' *An Illustrated History of the Horror Film,* Everson's book should be read as much or more for its help in raising *White Zombie's* status among critics in the 1970s as for its critical discussion.

5. Glassy, Mark. *The Biology of Science Fiction Cinema.* **Jefferson, NC: McFarland, 2001.**

In his chaper entitled "Pharmacology," Glassy engages with *White Zombie* in a brief but distinctive analysis by examining the film's depiction of drugs. For example, he addresses the use of Legendre's voodoo/zombie powder being put into a "glass of wine," as the character himself suggests; Glassy explains that in reality alcohol would likely act as a "catalyst and enhance the absorption of the drug...," thus offering somewhat of a scientific basis for Legendre's suggestion. In terms of the powder's effect, he determines that it seemingly disrupts the neuromuscular junctions between nerve endings and muscle cells within the person who ingests it. In conclusion, Glassy—following on the work of anthropologist Wade Davis—believes there are real-world roots to the overall zombie lore in the film.

6. Gordon, Alex. "The Pit and the Pen." *Fangoria* **Issue 16 (December 1981): 25–27.**

Lugosi friend and film writer Alex Gordon tackled *White Zombie* in his regular *Fangoria* column after an encounter with Teresa A. Taylor, a high school teacher from Wilson, North Carolina. Taylor, an avid Lugosi buff, had never seen the 1932 classic until Gordon screened it for her. The first part of his article becomes a series of quotations from Taylor's response to the film. Gordon then offers an account of the film's production history and a brief mention of the zombie films that followed. He also makes comments about the degree to which Lugosi could have "directed" sections of *White Zombie.* He does not dismiss the possibility, but probably bases his belief on actor Clarence Muse's quotations to that effect in Robert Cremer's *Lugosi: The Man Behind the Cape* (Henry Regnery, 1976).[1]

7. Lennig, Arthur. "*White Zombie.***"** *Classics of the Film.* **Editor, Arthur Lennig. Madison, WI: Wisconsin Film Society Press, 1965 (pp. 218–230).**

In addition to editing this volume of film essays, Lennig included his own treatise on *White Zombie.* Though *Classics of the Film* saw far less distribution than the books of Beck, Clarens, and Everson chronicled elsewhere in this bibliography, Lennig's examination of *White Zombie* is far more in-depth than those of his colleagues.

On top of a good deal of plot summary, the essay provides a discussion of romanticism and fairy tales as they relate to the film. Lennig also explores reasons why horror films in general are often disliked by critics who view them. There is little doubt that he expected critical eyebrows to raise at his inclusion of *White Zombie* in the book. Some of the essay's content became absorbed into Lennig's book *The Count: The Life and Films of Bela "Dracula" Lugosi* (Putnam, 1974).

8. Lowry, Edward and Richard deCordova. "Enunciation and the Production of Horror in *White Zombie.***"** *Planks of Reason: Essays on the Horror Film.* **Editor, Barry Keith Grant. Metuchen, NJ: Scarecrow Press, 1984 (pp. 346–389).**

Lowry and deCordova's essay is a unique, insightful, and thought-provoking work on *White Zombie,* using theoretical perspectives on cinematic spectatorship to examine the film. Their analysis specifically looks at *White Zombie's* "enunciative" techniques, meaning the specific "filmic and narrative devices by which the classical film attempts to produce horror." In *White Zombie,* these devices include dissolves, split screens, superimpositions, intercutting, and other cinematic artifices.

For Lowry and deCordova, the "production of fear in the viewer depends on the text's success in situating the viewer ... in a disturbing relationship to the enunciation of desire and the system within which it operates." Lowry and deCordova believe *White Zombie* worked somewhat differently from other horror films of the 1930s due to the "kind of experimentation characteristic of the early films with a generic cycle," as well as the historical fact of its independent production. Their analysis, however, proves far different than that presented in Chapter One of the present work.

Much of their essay focuses instead on the film's "exemplary ... production of two different types of space: one, the so-called transparent, realistic, sutured space; the other, a 'fantastic' space in which the marks of punctuation are foregrounded." Essentially, their argument points out the more normal shots and scenes in which characters speak and act. The scene of Neil and Madeline's first meeting with Beaumont, as well as Neil and Dr. Bruner's meeting at Bruner's office, would serve as two examples. With regard to the "fantastic space," Lowry and deCordova seek to point out the less-traditional zone in which some action or images occur, such as the extreme closeups of Lugosi's eyes seen against blackness, or his severed eyes floating by Neil and Madeline's carriage. The spectator is not meant to believe that a large pair of real eyes are genuinely hovering in the air; instead, the eyes are part of the fantastic space. Lowry and deCordova also examine how the two spaces work in tandem, explore at length Scene 12, and deem Legendre to be in "control over the enunciation in *White Zombie*."

On the whole, however, Lowry and deCordova's theoretical investigation is weakened by an apparent lack of interest in historiography. In their talk of spectatorship and the "production of horror," no attention is given to the reality beyond the imaginary spectatorial position created for the viewer by the film. In other words, however much the film attempts to situate the spectator, viewers may choose to situate themselves in a different way, especially in different epochs of time. Thus, whatever the film attempts to produce (e.g., the "production of horror") may be a far cry from how a viewer actually responds; moreover, this raises the question of how successful *White Zombie* is at the production of horror.

This criticism should not undermine the fact that "Enunciation and the Production of Horror in *White Zombie*" is a work of major importance, offering a valuable and extended discussion of *White Zombie*. Lowry and deCordova present a worthwhile and highly original perspective on the film, creating one of the more in-depth and intelligent essays ever written on a 1930s horror film. It should be viewed as necessary reading on the subject.

9. Ludlam, Harry. *My Quest for Bram Stoker.* **New York: Dracula Press, 2000.**

In his chapter entitled "I Meet Bela Lugosi," Ludlam describes his first encounter with a Bela Lugosi film. At fourteen years old, he viewed *White Zombie* at an (approximately) 1939 British screening. Ludlam daringly bought a ticket and made his way into the theater despite his being too young to view an "H" ("Horror") certificate film. Of Lugosi and the character Legendre, he recalls:

> [t]hat haughty presence, that richly sepulchral voice, those deep, penetrating eyes and the horrid suggestion of it all. It was too much; I couldn't take it. I got out of the row of seats as fast as I was able, blushing madly I'm sure and wildly hoping that no one had noticed me and was wondering why the hell that strange young fellow was suddenly vacating his seat.

While Ludlam's discussion is brief and built only on a personal anecdote, it is worthy of consideration simply because it is the major audience member memory of a 1930s screening of *White Zombie* in England, and one of the relatively small number from any country outside the U.S.

10. Price, Michael H. and George E. Turner. "The Black Art of *White Zombie*." *The Cinema of Adventure, Romance, & Terror.* **Editor, George E. Turner. Hollywood: ASC, 1989 (pp. 146–155).**

Price and Turner first covered *White Zombie* in their groundbreaking book on poverty-row horror films, *Forgotten Horrors* (A.S. Barnes, 1979). Later, they expanded their work into the article "*White Zombie*: Today's Unlikely Classic" for the February 1988 *American Cinematographer*.

The importance of the aforementioned essays wane only by comparison to their most recent version of the same essay *The Cinema of Adventure, Romance, & Terror*. The essay features a plot summary and brief mention of the film's many proponents and detractors, but more than anything it is particularly satisfying as a trip into the film's production history. Well written and impeccably researched, the piece adds a personal dimension to *White Zombie*'s creation thanks to quotations from assistant cameraman Enzo Martinelli and Howard A. Anderson, son of Howard Anderson. Still photographs of the film, which include rare pictures of Martinelli at the camera, complement the essay. Overall, "The Black Art of *White Zombie*" becomes the best empirical study of the film to date.

11. Sevastakis, Michael. "*White Zombie*: Death and Love Together Mated." *Songs of Love and Death: The Classical American Horror Film of the 1930s.* **Westport, CT: Greenwood Press, 1993 (pp. 41–56).**

In his collection of essays on the 1930s horror films, Sevastakis examines what he calls the "symbiotic relationship of love and death" in *White Zombie*, believing the film centers on necrophilia and "the power of the necromancer, Murder Legendre." To explore the "romantic as necrophile," Sevastakis selects for analysis five sequences of the film: Neil and Madeline's carriage ride to Beaumont's home, the wedding banquet that is intercut with Legendre, Neil's delusions in the tavern, the cemetery where Madeline's body is stolen, and Neil's subsequent search for her.

In his essay, Sevastakis makes numerous analyses, often using pre–1932 literature as source material. For example, his interpretation of Legendre's eyes is that: "In sexual terms, Legendre's piercing glance may be taken quite literally as an effective way of displacing the phallic sign." Sevastakis then provides numerous examples of the same use of eyes in Gothic literature—including quotations from Radcliffe's *Manfrone* and Maturin's *Melmoth the Wanderer*. At times such references have only weak links to the given scene or theme in *White Zombie*, but in general they constitute an informative albeit brief intellectual history.

Perhaps most important is Sevastakis' inclusion of references from gothic literature to necrophilia, "morbid emotions," and repeated quests for heroines, and his

Film theorist Tony Williams analyzes White Zombie *as an allegory of U.S.–Haitian relations in his fascinating essay* "White Zombie: Haitian Horror."

comparison of these with scenes in *White Zombie*. For example, doors which open by themselves in J. Sheridan LeFanu's *Uncle Silas* are compared with those that do the same in *White Zombie*. Similarly, Sevastakis cites a series of quotations from 18th and 19th century literature in which brides not unlike Madeline experience blends of weddings and funerals. It is these connections between *White Zombie* and literature that makes Sevastakis' piece important reading.

12. Williams, Tony. "*White Zombie*: Haitian Horror." *Jump Cut* 28 (1993): 18–20.

Tony Williams' essay offers a unique examination of *White Zombie*, viewing it as an "important example of the disguised and suppressed radical critique the horror genre can often manifest." In particular, he sees the film as a reflection of America's 20th century relations with Haiti.

Using Hans Schmidt's 1971 book *The American Occupation of Haiti*, Williams' history of U.S.–Haitian relations provides the background information on which the analysis is built. In particular, he discusses the American occupation of Haiti, beginning with the 1915 invasion by the U.S. Marines and their subsequent proclamation of martial law. Williams briefly covers the occupation to its end in 1934.

As he readily admits, *White Zombie* makes no overt references to any of these historical facts. Nonetheless, he views Beaumont's "British pretensions" as indicative of the American imperialist desire to copy England's occupation of Egypt with military intervention in Haiti. Also, while Williams admits Neil and Madeline's outward positions as victims, he sees the two as implicitly taking part in the "U.S. corruption of Haitian life." After all, Neil is an American working in Port-au-Prince and even hopes to become Beaumont's agent.

For Williams, "Black zombie slavery in the film ... represents a macabre version of the forced labor system which the U.S. inflicted on the Haitian population in 1918," and "Legendre represents a distorted embodiment of U.S. guilt feelings concerning the occupation." Lastly, he views Dr. Bruner as having "remarkable links with Legendre," for—in Williams' eyes—he is a "cog in the imperialist machine...."

Williams does make a few factual errors concerning the film, such as his claim that Legendre's maids and zombies are African-Americans, when many are white actors or white actors in makeup. However, such minor quibbles do not detract from a wholly original and satisfying exploration of the film's political dimension.

Chapter Ten

Reconstructing a Director:
The Life and Career
of Victor Hugo Halperin

In his 1969 column "On Film," *Take One* journalist Clive Denton critiqued Andrew Sarris' book *The American Cinema: Directors and Directions*.[1] More than just a review, Denton's commentary expressed a disappointment that Sarris' text had neglected "one fascinating director, perhaps the last undiscovered 'auteur' from Hollywood's gloriously murky past." Denton suggested that:

> Everyone else has neglected this man too: his name is Victor Halperin. To be accurate, in some of the credits the name elongates and becomes, indeed, Victor Hugo Halperin! A touchingly apposite name, that longer one, for a colourful artist of outsize imagination. It was Hollywood's peculiar revenge on an independent-minded aristocrat to confine him, mostly, to the dungeon's of low-budget mayhem. No matter; Halperin walked tall, even in the lower depths of poverty row.[2]

Some years before he reached poverty row, a 1924 newspaper article at the dawn of Victor's film career emphasized the phrase "Watch Victor Halperin."[3] Over four decades later, it was Clive Denton who realized that only a small number of persons in the film industry had ever heeded the newspaper's advice. That situation has changed little in the past two decades. At the beginning of the 21st century, obscurity embraces Victor Halperin; it consumes him.

Though he is best known as the director of *White Zombie*, Victor was a key figure in independent film production throughout the 1920s and 1930s. Whether or not he was an "auteur" is a question to be answered, but Victor Halperin is an important person in cinema history.

His story deserves to be told, though telling it is an increasingly difficult task.

Few film archives keep files on Victor Halperin, few university film courses mention him, few film historians even know his name. Even Victor's widow—Venita Halperin—possesses only a limited number of her husband's papers. "I had several hundreds of them," she said, "and all of them burned in a house fire after he died."[4] What time alone couldn't erase, smoldering flames did.

Very little information about Victor survives. As of 1999, the number of living actors of even minor status who worked with him on feature films had apparently dwindled to less than eight. They remember little of him. Victor's widow is, at this writing, in her nineties, carefully revealing only the memories she chooses to share. As Clive Denton suggested, Victor remains "undiscovered", or—at the least—a director with no biography. His life story is far more shadowy than the "gloriously murky" history of Hollywood which Denton describes. Even Victor's death has been a mystery to film historians of the past, with no obituary appearing in any publication either at the time of his death or in the ensuing years.

Tawny newspaper articles and movie trade clippings, a small number of personal effects and letters, a few remaining files at his university alma mater, a spate of memories from his widow and his granddaughter—these are the few dusty fragments which exist. But they are only pieces in a puzzle which will be forever incomplete. Too much is lost to history.

Victor's own words represent the greatest conundrum. Most of his surviving quotations feature inaccuracies. Whether he had a faulty memory, an intentional desire to skew facts, or both, is unknown. But his stories were clearly capable of embellishment, which makes it difficult to know when and in what quantities he peppered them with extra flavor.

As a result of all these problems, a clear picture of his life and career cannot develop for us like a photographic image in a darkroom. Instead, Victor Halperin's biography at this point evokes a more bleak metaphor, that of a blurry light in a sea of fog. The fog of time grows thicker with each passing year, engulfing those few remaining persons who know his story. That blurry, evanescent light shines only bright enough to help us reconstruct a partial outline of his life, as well as cast a few rays on the remains of his work.

A Biography

What do we know about him? Victor Hugo Halperin was born in Chicago on August 24, 1895, to parents Robert and Rose Halperin. His striking black hair and brown eyes attracted attention at a young age, as did his violin playing. When he was a young boy, Victor once even appeared onstage in a Chicago vaudeville show playing classical music; his innate talent for appealing to an audience was well noticed at the time.

His brother Edward, who would later play an important role in Victor's film career, was born in Chicago on May 12, 1898. He attended McKinley High School in Chicago, then went to Northwestern University. His major was Business Administration and Commerce, for which he received a Bachelor of Science degree.

Victor instead chose the University of Chicago, though he may have first briefly attended the University of Illinois campus in Chicago. While enrolled, Victor

performed in the University of Chicago orchestra (most likely playing violin) and sang first bass in the Men's Glee Club.[5] His 1915-16 school year at the university's Hitchcock Hall became what the school yearbook called a "sober" one, with sober meaning "just what it means, of course." Despite that rather moral claim, many "dances, smokers, 'high teas,' and other parties ('other' is very significant) [sic] served to conserve the midnight oil."[6]

That school year, Victor worked on the finance committee for the "Washington Promenade," at which a "record-breaking crowd" of 156 couples enjoyed supper and a dance in the university gym until two in the morning. The promenade also featured one show with a "grand march" that climaxed in a rendition of the school's alma mater.[7]

Perhaps Victor's most oft-repeated stories of his college days mentioned his work in drama. Curiously, he was not a member of the Dramatics Club, and the university archives do not include mention of his having directed any plays. However, Victor was very instrumental in an annual show produced by the Blackfriars, a popular men's club on campus. The Blackfriar mantra was always recited at their events:

> Jovial Friars full of glee,
> Troop forth from dull monastery
> And, doffing cowl and gown, essay
> To be the clowns in sportive play
>
> From novice Friar to Abbot sage,
> Each monk appears upon the stage.
> The curtain's up, the sports begun;
> Gay laughter tells of mirth and fun![8]

For their 1916 dramatic production, writer Walter S. Pogue contributed a play which won the unanimous support of the Blackfriar judges, *A Night of Knights*. Victor acted in it in a major role, though no surviving reviews shed any light on the quality of his performance.[9] Though he didn't direct the play, Victor's acting must have later provided a modicum of insight into working with actors on film sets.

Victor claimed that while in Chicago he began a career in professional writing. He acted as a ghost writer for a famed author of the period, remembering in later years that:

> ...as a young writer I received an early literary training as a "ghost writer" for Elbert Hubbard,

The 1915 Men's Glee Club at the University of Chicago. Victor is seen in the front row, second from the right.

Members of the University of Chicago's Tiger's Head group in 1915-16. Victor is on the right end of the middle row.

renowned editor, publisher, and modern philosopher. Hubbard was the one who said, "If you're going to have wrinkles, let them be joy lines." I got joy lines fulfilling assignments to write articles in the distinct Hubbard style. Later on, in April 1912, Elbert Hubbard and Alice, his wife, met a tragic end when the *Titanic* went down with all on board.[10]

But Victor's story is only partially incorrect. Though the well-known author Hubbard *wrote* about the *Titanic* tragedy, he and his wife were not passengers on the ill-fated vessel. Oddly, after Hubbard had written with particular affection and admiration about the *Titanic* deaths of Isidor Strauss and his wife, who died in each other's arms aboard the sinking ocean liner, Mr. and Mrs. Hubbard died in each others' arms at sea when German torpedoes sank the *Lusitania* in 1915.[11] Victor's account here is one of many in which his version of a story doesn't concur with the historical record.

As another example, Victor once mentioned that he wrote for *The Philistine* during the same time period.[12] Surveying the magazine during the mid- and late teens does not reveal his name, making his participation as difficult to confirm. *The Philistine* generally did not publish bylines on most of their essays, which further complicates judging the verisimilitude of Victor's claim.

After graduating from the University of Chicago in 1916, Victor shifted to the University of Wisconsin's School of Journalism. The chosen area of emphasis was advertising, but it is unclear whether he actually obtained a degree from Wisconsin. His resume seemed carefully worded on this point, claiming only that he "attended" the program. However his study there ended, Victor's skills at advertising proved important throughout his career.

One reason that he may not have completed his second degree was World War I. He volunteered for service and entered training sometime in 1918, but never actually made it to a war zone. Victor's second wife Venita remembered, "He was very disappointed. The very day he was supposed to leave [for overseas], he got word that it was over."[13]

After an honorable discharge from the military, Victor landed work at the General Fireproofing Company of Youngstown, Ohio. Following his tenure there as an assistant advertising manager, he moved to a large advertising agency, the George Batten Company, planning national ad campaigns for various building materials.[14] Later, he worked as an advertising manager for the Vityfix Company in Chicago, again creating national campaigns for building materials.[15]

At one point in the mid- to late teens, he established his own advertising agency in Chicago, calling it "The Advertising Engineers." After arriving in Los Angeles with his brother Edward, Victor started a West Coast branch of the firm. Though Victor sold his interest in the company after joining the film industry, the Advertising Engineers stayed operational into the 1950s. Before considering a life in the movies, Edward had also been the manager of an ad agency. Their work in targeting national audiences with ad campaigns for retail companies no doubt helped them later sculpt successful exploitation materials for their films.

The Hollywood Reporter in 1937 harrowingly recounted the brothers' entry into filmmaking, claiming they were "unprepared for any particular profession," and "it was a question of 'sink or swim.'"[16] Though that version of the story is untrue given their relative success in

Victor Halperin's signature on a membership card for an alumni association at his alma mater.

advertising, the Halperins did believe filmmaking could lead to fortunes, especially with prudent production methods. *The Hollywood Reporter* quoted them both as asking:

> [W]hy couldn't a picture be produced with the same sense of security and responsibility that a man opens a clothing store? Although a motion picture property might not be as materialistic as a store stocked with merchandise, the same identical methods of safe and sane operation could well be practiced.[17]

It was that ideology, as well as what *The Hollywood Reporter* called a "small nest egg," that led the Halperins into the movie industry.

At least that ideology *possibly* led them into the movie industry. In yet another interview, Victor claimed that his boss at the General Fireproofing Company said, "Pack your trunk, you're going to Hollywood to organize sales for your company." The story had him completing some sales work in California, then making trips to the studios in search of writing jobs.[18] Edward wasn't even mentioned in this anecdote.

Whichever story is true—if *either* of them is—Victor did find work writing for the Westerns. The producing company was Cactus Features, Inc.; even as early as a 1924 retrospective, a newspaper asked readers skeptically, "Ever hear of 'em?" Victor started as a scenario writer at the tiny company, receiving $50 for each story they accepted.[19] The low-budget nature of the films caused him to take on further responsibilities, and he quickly developed skills in other areas,. Decades later, Victor would remember the following anecdote from one Cactus film shoot:

> ...I will illustrate what silent subtitles once did for me. We were making a western thriller, featuring Bob Graves, around an abandoned ranch house just outside of Hollywood. Marty Martinelli, my cameraman, late in the day anxiously advised me that we had better prepare to quit shooting. The sun would begin to lose the photo graphic value of the actinic rays on the film emulsion. We would soon be getting only shadows and bare outlines on the film. But this spelled disaster to me, operating on a short budget. Another day's shooting would be impossible. We simply had to finish the picture that day....
>
> So, I revised the story then and there. I had the characters go through the broad action only—chase each other, fight, run in and out of the ranch house, jump off the roof, run in and out of the doors and windows, demolish a barn, stampede horses, set fire to an old cabin, etc. Marty, the cameraman, finally threw up his hands and moaned, "That's it. All we've got now is a lot of ghosts having fun in a graveyard. The film won't show a thing!"...
>
> Well, next morning we saw the dailies, the film developed by the laboratory overnight. With out revised story and new subtitles, I renamed the picture, *Phantom*

of the Hills. It proved to be the best-selling and most popular of the eighteen western series.[20]

Little is known of *Phantom of the Hills* and his other early westerns; they don't appear in any *American Film Institute Catalogs*.[21] Very likely—given Halperin's own choice of the term "western actions" to describe them—they were short subjects, two or three reel westerns.

Cactus Films itself remains a mysterious entity. Whatever it was, Victor said in 1924 that, "Somehow or other I fooled them. They Okey'ed [*sic*] every one of my western thrillers and in nine months I owned the company. Then my troubles began. I was office manager, production chief, casting director, actor and office boy for a many long months."[22] Though Victor's takeover of Cactus may have been a more involved enterprise than his tale suggests, he quickly renamed the company "Halperin Productions."

Though ego may have played a role in Victor's recrowning of Cactus Productions, other reasons were probably in play as well. *Moving Picture World* wrote in mid-1922 that "[a] director's name means much to an independent picture. In fact, the question usually hurled at a distributor by buyer and exhibitor is: Who directed the picture?"[23] To build his own name value, Victor chose to use his middle name on credits, with the "Victor Hugo Halperin" drawing on the name value of novelist Victor Hugo. To help further instill the name "Halperin" in the minds of picturegoers and exhibitors, Victor may have renamed the company in hopes that repetition would work.

But the film company's title wasn't the only name that changed to "Halperin" during Victor's early days in Hollywood. Sometime during (approximately) 1919, he met twenty-year-old Irene McDaniel, originally of Dallas, Texas. She was a dancer and pianist, and the duo shared many happy hours with her at the keyboard and him at the violin. Happiness abounded such that Victor and Irene married within some two years of their first date. By 1924, a daughter named Elaine was born. Five years later, they had Joan, their second daughter.

The young family moved to New York City during the mid-1920s, with Irene even appearing onscreen in one (or perhaps more) of Victor's films as a dancer. As his production interests turned westward, Victor and family moved to Beverly Hills in December 1927. The couple became particularly popular among Hollywood's social set, often throwing parties in their home and projecting films in their private screening room. In phone conversations and emails with the author during the summer of 2001, Victor's granddaughter Linda Ortiz mentioned Victor and Irene's relationship was very passionate and romantic. Their life together during the 1920s was a happy one.

By contrast, the late 1921, early 1922 film release season had been, in the words of *Moving Picture World*, "one of the most disastrous in the history of the business."[24] For the 1922-23 release season, many exhibitors eagerly looked toward independents to reverse that trend. The *World* wrote "[t]hat independent exchanges with good pictures will have no trouble getting proper exhibition dates … [contact with representative theater circuits] point promisingly to the greatest and most prosperous season in the history of the field of independent endeavor."[25] Charles C. Burr, President of Affiliated Distributors, went so far as to announce in 1922, "The Independent [*sic*] market has arrived."[26] It was into that favorable milieu that *Danger Point*, the first film of the fledgling Halperin Productions, was released in December 1922.

Danger Point featured Carmel Myers and William P. Carleton in a story Victor had written; on-screen directing credit, however, went to Lloyd Ingraham. But even as early as a 1924 interview, Victor claimed that he himself directed the film, after convincing the principals involved to "trust" his "directorial abilities."[27] If Victor in fact directed any of the film at all, he didn't take credit in 1922. The two versions of who directed the film are contradictory, and represent yet another fissure in the accuracy of Victor's biography. At any rate, Victor had entered feature filmmaking with a small company under his own control.

A mixture of comedy and drama, *Danger Point* features a young city woman named Alice moving to a small town after marrying an oil magnate named James. Quickly disenchanted with both oil wells and rural life, she writes a farewell note and leaves him. While en route to the train depot, she runs into an old suitor named Duncan; he boards Alice's train and soon tries to rape her. In the midst of these troubles, the train wrecks and all victims are taken back to the small town which they had just left. After reading Alice's note, James suspects she has been unfaithful, but the dying Duncan tells him otherwise. At the story's conclusion, the young married couple are reunited.

Danger Point was noted by critics at the time for its effective use of cross-cutting, which juxtaposes Alice fending off Duncan's advances with shots of James fighting an oil fire. Some reviews also praised its special effects, which were best featured in dramatic scenes of the disastrous oil fire and the train wreck. As for its narrative, *Harrison's Reports* told exhibitors "the story is the kind that has been put in pictures repeatedly; it has become too familiar."[28] Clichéd melodrama and sentimentality ruled the story's plot.

Regardless of any one reviewer's qualms, the film emboldened its writer, who valued economic concerns far more than critical commentary. "I had my troubles with distributors, but finally marketed the product," Victor would say of *Danger Point* in 1924: "It made me some money. I was encouraged and happy. Then and there I decided I'd produce a picture I had tried to sell [to] every scenario editor in Hollywood."[29]

That picture, produced by the recrowned "Victor H. Halperin Productions," was released in 1923 as *Tea—with a Kick!* Among many other performers, the cast sported silent screen notables ZaSu Pitts and Chester Conklin. In particular, *Exhibitors Herald* gave attention to the signing of Creighton Hale as the lead male actor.[30] Victor penned the comedy-drama, leaving the directing responsibilities to Erle C. Kenton. Perhaps he chose this path to help learn more about directing by watching the talents of another.

In any event, the film's rather simple story finds the young Bonnie opening a tearoom and cabaret show to help raise funds for her father, who has been unfairly jailed. Passing over another suitor, Bonnie marries a young lawyer who helps get her father released. The father's happy

Grauman's Million Dollar Theatre in Los Angeles the day of a preview screening for Tea—with a Kick!

Publicity artwork for Tea—with a Kick! *in the September 8, 1923,* Exhibitors *[sic]* Herald.

return occurs at the height of the tea room's success. The tea, of course, had a "kick" thanks to a violation of the 18th Amendment.

"Intoxicating with Laughter; Bubbling over with Mirth," ads for the film proclaimed. Tag lines promised, "*Tea—with a Kick!* is up to the minute, in a delightful, unbiased manner. It holds up to the American public the humorous side of the 18th Amendment. It is reported that by actual count there are in *Tea—with a Kick!* 1 continuous roar, 3 yells, 4 screams, 30 laughs, and 231 chuckles."

Despite the name actors and its popular appeal, *Tea—with a Kick!* didn't draw much attention among New York City newspapers. Victor was undaunted. "I made a picture costing very little so far as productions go," he said, "but it was a financial success to both me and the distributor."[31] His comment is borne out by industry trades of the period, one of which claimed in July 1924 that "...exhibitors are realizing the unusual value of the Associated Exhibitors' jazzy girl picture [*Tea—with a Kick*] ... as a hot weather attraction, as bookings have increased at an astonishing rate for July and August."[32]

Audience reactions to those *Tea—with a Kick!* screenings were varied. The film "pleased all who came in" to a theater in Dover, Ohio,[33] and it was particularly successful at the Capitol in Oklahoma City. The theater manager there wrote that the film was "up to the minute," and "delightful."[34] But in Silver City, New Mexico "[a]ttendance fair when it started; nothing when it finished. They all left."[35] A manager in McComb, Mississippi added that "We didn't see any tea and box office got no kick."[36]

The most stinging criticism came from the Pontiac Theatre Beautiful in Saranac Lake, New York. Their the-ater manager groaned that *Tea—with a Kick!* was the "worst 'mess of drivel' I have ever showed [sic] in this theatre. They walked out on it, demanded money back, said it was 'the bunk,' and other 'pleasing?' epithets. [The film is an] unfunny, impossible, badly directed, garbled attempt at screen entertainment. ... it may damage you with your patrons."[37]

As always, though, Victor was undeterred by negativity. His financial success with *Tea—with a Kick!* was buttressed by the ever-growing possibilities of independent feature filmmaking. In the summer of 1923, *Exhibitors Herald* wrote:

> The rise of the heretofore little-considered independent film company during the past twelve months has been little short of spectacular and that there is a consistent market for the product turned out by the independent is evidenced by the fact that local banking interests are taking a hand in the financing of such ventures—an unprecedented thing.[38]

By the following year, the same trade publication announced progress, claiming that "[t]he independent is striving to do his best, both with his product, the material that is in it, and its status from the standpoint of quality, and with the fullest cooperation with all concerned in mind."[39]

Victor's third film of the decade, *When a Girl Loves*, inexplicably returned to the "Halperin Productions" name. Released in March 1924, the romantic drama featured Percy Marmont and Agnes Ayres in the lead roles. One of the few published trade reviews appeared in *Exhibitors Herald*, which proclaimed "[t]he story contains a number of improbabilities which at times are apt to tax the credulity of an audience."[40] Another was printed in *Moving Picture World*, which believed the film sported an "...all star cast which is really all star, with a list of real box office pullers which will delight every exhibitor. No use in remarking that the acting is exceptionally good, for with these players, it could not be anything else."[41]

Despite the *World*'s promise, exhibitors were not necessarily delighted, even if they did acknowledge the film's strong points. "It will please those who see it," the manager of one Helena, Montana theater claimed, "but the title hurts its drawing power."[42] Another manager called the film "[a] good little picture without much drawing power. Even with exceptionally good cast this picture is little out of program class."[43]

The narrative features Sasha and Count Michael, a couple in love during the Russian Revolution. Sasha moves to America with her family, where she marries Dr. Godfrey Luke. When Count Michael comes for Sasha, a fight ensues in which both Sasha and the Count are wounded. Dr. Luke saves Sasha, and—according to the

An Associated Exhibitors ad promoting When a Girl Loves *to theater exhibitors, printed in the May 10, 1924,* Moving Picture World.

Moving Picture World review—"Grisha, a dwarf who has invented a radio cure, comes and brings Michael back to life" after he has died.[44] The outrageous plot resonates with importance not only because it was written by Victor, but also because it was directed by him. *When a Girl Loves* foreshadows the rather bizarre storylines that Victor and Edward embraced in the 1930s.

The relatively impressive box-office returns on *Tea—with a Kick!* and *When a Girl Loves*—as well as greater industry optimism towards independent filmmakers in general—meant Halperin Productions could forge ahead with even greater vigor.[45] In June 1924, Edward rapidly tried to find new story material and sign acting talent to contracts in New York while Victor managed their Hollywood office. Edward then toured the country and visited key cities to speak with various theatrical exhibitors. *Moving Picture World* wrote that:

> It is a policy of the Halperins to cooperate fully with exhibitors on every production before the actual camera work commences. Tie-ups with national subjects will be

arranged and every possible exploitation angle will be covered so as to insure every possible advertising aid beneficial to the exhibitor.[46]

Through comments like these, it seems apparent that money and success rather than artistry governed the Halperins' minds. That emphasis may have been why Victor considered *Danger Point* and *Tea—with a Kick!* his own films even though he didn't receive directorial credit.

Though Victor would write and direct *The Unknown Lover* (1925, with Elsie Fergusson and Mildred Harris),[47] his 1924 film *Greater Than Marriage* marked the beginning of a long-term shift in his cinematic emphasis. Made for Romance Pictures rather than his own production company, Halperin directed the film. Though he also contributed the screenplay, the story was not one of his own invention; it was based on Louis Joseph Vance's 1913 novel *Joan Thursday*. *Greater Than Marriage* was a relatively simplistic drama about a woman who eventually chooses love over a stage career. The film, which starred Marjorie Daw, Lou Tellegen, and Tyrone Power, Sr., began Halperin's accent on directing over writing.

Shortly before the film's release, Vitagraph (Halperin's chosen distributor) ran ads to spur excitement among exhibitors. "What is *Greater Than Marriage*?" the ads asked, encouraging answers of ten words or less to be mailed to their Brooklyn offices. One hundred dollars was offered for the best answer. Given his background in advertising, Victor may well have contributed the idea to Vitagraph.

When they finally screened *Greater Than Marriage*, theater managers gave mixed opinions. "A very satisfactory picture and pleased generally," one Illinois manager told *Moving Picture World*.[48] A New Hampshire exhibitor was more excited, claiming the film was "very good" and "pleased the ladies."[49] But a manager in Kansas contradicted his colleagues, complaining that the film had "nothing to it" but "rotten audience appeal."[50]

Victor would later speak fondly of *Greater Than Marriage*, claiming "I got a great deal of pleasure out of directing Lou Tellegen. He is a fine actor, an educated man who assimilates things. He feels his part and then puts that feeling into action that fairly radiates on the screen."[51] Tellegen, an actor known for both his films and his stage work with Sarah Bernhardt, gained a rather morbid level of lasting fame for committing suicide by thrusting a pair of scissors into his chest.[52]

More than on Tellegen or any actors, though, Victor's directorial focus would generally center on narrative concerns, which harked back to his days as a writer. He also attributed his interest in narrative to telling bedtime stories to his two daughters, Elaine and Joan. "They provided a great audience on which to try out suspense, drama, and humor, he would later remember. "Trust a child to react delightfully to one's impossible story concoctions."[53]

In many ways, the mid-twenties were Victor's happiest and most productive era. Independent filmmaking was viewed more and more favorably by industry trades and exhibitors, allowing Victor to move rapidly from one film project to the next. "[E]very exhibitor owes it to himself to do his share toward keeping alive and encouraging independence in picture production," *Moving Picture World* told exhibitors in January 1925.[54] One distributor claimed that the independent market for 1925 and beyond seemed to be "constantly improving," a situation due in part to exhibitor's anger at major studios attempting to force block booking of films.[55] Industry prophecies correctly proclaimed that over 200 independent films would be made in the U.S. during 1925.[56] Victor contributed to that pool of independent talent, palpably enjoying his freedom from the major studios.

The next story he filmed also came from an authorial source other than his own pen: Leonard Merrick's 1907 novel, *The House of the Lynch*. Retitled *School for Wives* and made by "Victor Hugo Halperin Productions," the film starred Conway Tearle and Sigrid Holmquist in the lead roles, with the entire female chorus of Earl Carroll's *Vanities* (the annual Broadway revue of the 1920s and 1930s) appearing in a dance number.

School for Wives may now be best remembered for featuring actor Brian Donlevy in a supporting role. In later years, Victor spoke of having discovered Donlevy, whose then unknown name was even misspelled in many *School for Wives* reviews as "Dunlevy." But Victor's claim was more of a boast; Donlevy had already achieved a level of notoriety in the original 1924 Broadway production of *What Price Glory?* and his screen success would only come after numerous other films.[57] Victor's film had neither discovered an unknown Donlevy nor created a new screen star.

Along with directing, Victor prepared the scenario and wrote the title cards for *School for Wives*. Vitagraph distributed the film, which they called "[t]he very best in a long line of big photoplays produced by Victor Hugo Halperin." The response of Vitagraph's officials and executives was unanimously enthusiastic after first screening the film in early February 1925.[58] By the end of the month, Vitagraph was publishing ads in trade magazines, inviting readers to "Make your application now!" to the *School for Wives*.

As a work of cinema, *School for Wives* yielded mixed reviews among contemporary critics, with film industry trade *Variety* claiming:

> Halperin, hitherto an unimportant director, has treated all of his subject matter with such unfailing showmanship and intelligence he is now someone to notice. Only in spots does he get maudlin and, although his casting [is not] all that it should be, and the sets are plainly of that type used in cheaper productions, the general impression is that the story, backed by good scenario and direction, has made [it] a good film. ... Heaven knows it has most of the Vitagraph output beaten by a mile.[59]

Ad for School for Wives *in the February 28, 1925,* Moving Picture World.

A relaxed portrait of Victor Halperin from the 1920s.

as we may, we fail to find anything in *School for Wives* that would please any one older than ten years.[63]

Regardless of praise or scorn, *School for Wives* was the first Halperin film reviewed by either *Variety* or the *New York Times*. Even if not in a positive light, Victor's name was being mentioned in perhaps the most respected industry trade and U.S. newspaper.

Victor's name recognition was growing, and he quickly rushed into production on another film, this time for Welcome Pictures. Based on Leroy Scott's short story "In Borrowed Plumes," the film—which kept the title—tells the story of a young, impoverished girl who pretends to be a countess. She falls in love with a member of a prominent family, but is exposed as her true self when the real countess finally arrives. However, the countess becomes enchanted by the impostor and is the first to suggest that the double marry her sweetheart.

Victor directed the film, but apparently did not involve himself in the screenplay adaptation or even the writing of intertitles. *In Borrowed Plumes*, released in 1926, starred Marjorie Daw and Niles Welch. *Moving Picture World* believed its:

> ...story is rather implausible and much of the development follows along familiar melodramatic lines. The plot advances at a good pace and although there is little suspense as to the outcome, it holds the interest and offers fairly pleasing entertainment for the average patron.[64]

Though causing much less of a box-office or critical impact than *School for Wives*, *In Borrowed Plumes* does give insight into a growing aspect of Victor's direction. The film costarred Dagmar Godowsky and Wheeler Oakman; Godowsky, along with Marjorie Daw, had already appeared in *Greater Than Marriage*, while Oakman would later appear in the 1939 Halperin film *Torture Ship*. These represent early examples of Victor's predilection for working repeatedly with the same talent when possible.

During his silent film years, Victor particularly enjoyed working with stage stars from New York. One reason, beyond whatever talent which those actors possessed, may have been Victor's general love of New York City. He especially appreciated stage stars' lack of familiarity with the cinematic process. One of his favorite anecdotes of the period concerns a stage actor who was posing for a publicity still photograph for a Halperin film. The actor asked, "say, do I move for a still picture?" The comment immediately broke the film crew into laughs. A good-natured kind of joking ensued, Halperin remembered.[65]

For his next foray into cinema, Victor coproduced *Convoy* (1927, starring Lowell Sherman, Dorothy Mackaill, William Collier, Jr., and Ian Keith) with his brother Edward for Robert Kane Productions. For years, Kane

By contrast, fellow film trade *Moving Picture World* believed the film was "old school melodrama" with "little to recommend it to the discriminating patron."[60]

Among popular-audience newspapers, the *New York Times* was unimpressed, chiding the story and its intertitles; the newspaper review ended on the phrase "We imagine that no further comment is needed on this Victor Hugo Halperin effort."[61] Apparently reviewer Mordaunt Hall had believed the whole of his review had already included more than enough insults.

The *New York Herald Tribune* initially announced *School for Wives'* release as the "long-awaited picturization of Leonard Merrick's novel." Their column noted that, "Halperin ... is noted for his sincerely impressive treatment of dramatic situations, and in *School for Wives* is said to have created one of his most faithful adaptations."[62] However, once Harriette Underhill, the *Herald Tribune*'s film critic, saw the film, a new judgment appeared in the newspaper:

> It is too naive and too young. It seems to say, "Here I am, a poor, feeble thing. Strike me and I perish." But the wonder of it is—how did it ever get in the Rialto? ... try

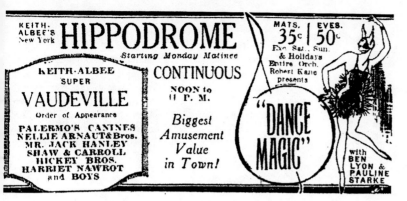

An ad promoting Dance Magic *published in the* New York Herald Tribune *on July 10, 1927.*

had been general manager of production at Famous Players-Lasky; by 1925, he had begun independent film production.[66] In *Convoy*, a German spy is captured by a society girl working under cover for the U.S. government. Industry trade *Harrison's Reports* claimed, "None of this material is new or convincing and some of it is just foolish."[67] While that may be true of its story, *Convoy's* special effects feature some impressive naval battles and ships sinking into the depths.[68]

Next came *Dance Magic*, which Victor also made for Robert Kane Productions. Released in July of 1927, *Dance Magic* was based on Clarence Budington Kelland's novel of the same name. A young country girl comes to New York City to become a star. She meets two men, both of whom wish to help her career. One is morally upright and falls in love with her; the other has far less dignified intentions. For at least one exhibitor who screened the film, the story was definitely "not one for the whole family."[69]

The *New York Times* believed "sufficient momentum" existed "to carry [*Dance Magic*] through [to] its melodramatic conclusion."[70] The *New York Herald Tribune* pinpointed more serious problems, though, mentioning that while *Dance Magic* "starts off rather amusingly, ... it dwindles alarmingly." After noting that some of the narrative was "a little too much even for one who was viewing the proceedings with a lenient eye," its critic suggested the problem stemmed partly from melodramatic, almost "burlesque" intertitles.[71]

Harrison's Reports was particularly critical, claiming there was "nothing to it!" and that it was "sentimentally ridiculous ... artificial ... and frequently absurd."[72] *Variety* was far more harsh, beginning its review of *Dance Magic* with the one word exclamation "Hopeless!" Not content to end that quickly, its critic, Sime, added:

> Here's a bad picture, a really slovenly written story, and the entire fault is in that story. ... It seems unnatural

that amongst a First National experienced crowd, such a mess as this could have been turned out and how. ... Nothing here for the official censors to object to, unless they don't care for amateur pictures running up to $85,000 or more. ... For blah stuff this is a pip. Of course everything kept step with that story, from direction to acting to camering [*sic*].[73]

The all-encompassing critique of "blah stuff" extended of course to the film's stars, Ben Lyon and Pauline Starke. Starke would later surface again in connection with Victor's film *White Zombie*.

Undaunted by harsh critical reviews, Victor seemed always to look to the future, with hopes that success waited around every corner. To help in his goal, he decided that better stories and better actors were necessary components of making highly successful films. He believed geography was key to obtaining both elements. In 1924, he claimed:

> I've produced in California, in Arizona, in small towns and larger cities, but New York has everything all these others had and more. New York is life. No matter what my script may call for I can find it here. There is every type, every character known to motion pictures in this city. All one needs to do is to find them. Within a short time I expect to have two, possibly three units at work turning out Halperin productions. Such is my faith in New York.[74]

The additional units of Halperin Productions never materialized, but Victor and Edward continued to obtain financing and produce films in New York whenever possible. Indeed, the mid-twenties saw a boom in independent production in New York.[75]

Despite his geographical strategy for making films, Victor's hopes for success in the cinema were certainly not helped by his marital problems.

According to his granddaughter Linda Ortiz, Victor's mounting debts led to his abandoning his family in early 1933, leaving Irene to fend for herself and the two daughters. In order to survive financially, Irene and the girls moved to Texas, the state where Irene had been born. During 1934, Victor attempted to reconcile and the couple again lived together in the Los Angeles area. But prior difficulties must have resurfaced or new ones formed, as they divorced in 1936.

Venita Halperin's sole comments on the subject suggest that Victor's first wife was:

*This low-contrast, almost ghostly picture of Victor Halperin dates
from the late 1920s or early 1930s.*

...crazy about Mischa Auer. When [Victor] was making
movies in New York, he sent for her to come and she
wouldn't do it. She had the doors locked and the keys
changed; she talked to [Victor] through the door and
told him he was no longer welcome.[76]

It should be added, however, that Victor's daughters and
granddaughters vigorously argue against the idea that any
infidelity occurred on Irene's part. Their concern about
the validity of this story is understandable not only because they are Irene's relatives, but also because of their
historical knowledge. For example, it is certain that Irene
moved to Texas following the couple's 1934 breakup; if
she had been having an affair with anyone and had locked
Victor out of his house, why would she then immediately
move out of California and thus *away* from any alleged
lover? Furthermore, given that Victor didn't marry again
until years later, his second wife has no firsthand knowledge of this era; Venita Halperin's memories about Victor in the 1930s rest solely on the stories she heard from
him years later. And yet, even if Victor's mounting debts
had indeed caused him to leave the family in 1933, was
it indeed the same problem that caused the 1936 divorce?
Is it possible there are many other important details not

known to survivors? We are left with something of a biographical puzzle.

Regardless of the cause, however, the marriage was
over. The happy days of married social life in Hollywood
were behind Victor. The couple's popular Tinseltown
parties were at an end.[77] And so was Victor's contact with
Joan and Elaine; Irene worked hard to raise both daughters herself against the backdrop of the Great Depression.

Despite their lack of contact, Victor remained proud
of both of his daughters, claiming in his later years that:

> Elaine and Joan grew up into strikingly attractive young
> ladies. In fact, if you will please excuse a parent, I will say
> Elaine was truly beautiful. She became executive secre-
> tary for MGM's legal department, in charge of contracts.
> Among her good friends and admirers, she attracted
> many Hollywood celebrities, such as Clark Gable, Cary
> Grant, Robert Taylor, Gregory Peck, and John Wayne.
> Clark Gable was her frequent escort to parties and
> dances. Elaine was indeed the envy of most all of the
> country's young women (including a few older ones).[78]

Halperin's comments about daughter Elaine were apparently no boast, as the *Los Angeles Examiner* of March 5,
1949, featured a photograph of her dancing with Clark
Gable. She is as attractive as he claimed.

While Victor was certainly proud of his daughters,
he was growing equally proud of his film career by the
late 1920s. Immediately after *Convoy* (1927), films like
Dance Magic and subsequent efforts carried a different
credit for the director. Rather than relying on his middle
name—which of course invoked Victor Hugo of literary
fame—he instead scaled back his on-screen credit to
"Victor Halperin." The credit illuminated on motion picture screens was finally *his* name, not the adoption or appropriation of a famed author's. Victor himself was no
longer an author so much as a director, and with his growing importance and recognition as a filmmaker came the
opportunity for a particularly prestigious project in the
cinema.

In 1929, the brothers Halperin jointly produced a
film called *She Goes to War*; it would forever remain one
of Victor's favorites. In 1978, he recalled:

> We made an arrangement to coproduce it with Inspira-
> tion Pictures, Inc. ... Exploitation value in mind, I got
> Rupert Hughes, popular novelist then contributing to
> *Red Book* and *Cosmopolitan* magazines, to novelize my
> story so that it could be published in book form. I vis-
> ited Hughes one night during his nightly work hours. He
> drank about three pots of cold, black coffee, thick as mo-
> lasses, and complained about the coffee taste. After read-
> ing his completed novel script, I figured Rupert hadn't yet
> found the right brand of coffee. Had this happened today
> I presume the $10,000 he received would just about have
> paid his coffee costs.[79]

The novelization was actually just a short story, published in Hughes' collection called *She Goes to War, and Other Stories*. Victor's comment about Hughes novelizing "my story" suggests he was involved in the tale's origin; however, all available contemporary information on *She Goes to War* suggests that the tale was solely from Hughes' mind and pen.

The $10,000 for Hughes was only a portion of the money the Halperins received for the sale of the story. They set a record in getting $50,000 for *She Goes to War*, the most money ever paid at that time for a story not submitted through an agent.[80]

Hughes' narrative chronicled the tale of Joan Morant, a young rich girl who decides to be of help to the U.S. efforts in the Great War. Though she loves the wealthy Reggie, she trifles with the affections of Tom, a garage owner. Joan's path crosses those of both men in France when she arrives to begin her assistance to the army. Tom rejects her advances, having been transformed by his war experiences. Reggie, on the other hand, works as a supply sergeant and cowardly manages to avoid combat. Rather than follow Reggie's lead, Joan becomes involved in combat, almost getting killed during one attack but managing to save the entire army outfit.

In many ways, the story and the film of *She Goes to War* recognized the plight of women in U.S. society during the teens in a sympathetic and understanding manner. The following excerpt from Hughes' story is an example:

> There were numberless men in America who were of the Kaiser's opinion and ridiculed the high ideals of womankind. Tom Pike had mouthed the hateful phrase that locked the door on women's hopes: "A woman's place is the home."[81]

More than simply identifying the problems women faced in the U.S., Hughes' *She Goes to War* also uses World War I as a vehicle to suggest both the possibility of and the need for change:

> Women were at large for the first time after untold centuries of seclusion and suppression. There were new things ahead of them, and experiences more wonderful than could ever fall to any man, for, after all, these soldiers were going to do what men had always done. These women were going to do what had never been dreamed before.[82]

Ads for the film drew on an understanding of Hughes' themes, claiming "The first great GIRL EPIC of the Great War! WOMEN This is YOUR Picture."[83]

The cast of *She Goes to War*, headed by Eleanor Boardman as Joan and John Holland as Tom, also included Edmund Burns, Alma Rubens, and Al St. John. Behind the camera, the famed Henry King was director, with art direction provided by Al D'Agostino and cinematography handled in part by John Fulton. Harry Akst composed the music, which included the songs "Joan" and "There Is a Happy Land." For the Akst score, the Halperins made special plans. Victor later remarked that:

> ...we convinced the great Los Angeles Symphony Orchestra to try [recording the soundtrack music], their first picture score. And overwhelmingly thrilling and awesome it was! When they boomed out a climax you knew you had been somewhere![84]

> We contracted with United Artists to distribute the picture when completed. President Joe Schenck ... insisted that we not make it a talkie. He regarded sound track dialogue as only a temporary fad. Finally, he conceded that we might insert only one talking sequence, the rest to be silent, according to the then-present custom. United Artists, the elite selling organization, mainly owned by Charlie Chaplin, Mary Pickford, and Doug Fairbanks, would then not bear the stigma of selling a hundred percent talking picture.[85]

By the time of the film's release, however, UA aggressively tried to promote *She Goes to War* as a talkie. Though not using common phrases like "All-Dialogue," their advertisements certainly gave that impression.[86] The film was a "Song and Sound Miracle," "a document ...HEARD and SEEN on the screen," and a "Song, Sound, and Dialogue Revelation."[87]

Despite such promotional boasts, the critics and public quickly learned what Victor already knew: only one scene features dialogue, and the principal players do not speak at all.[88] The *Los Angeles Times* wrote that "*She Goes to War* has only a very few lines of dialogue."[89] The *New York Herald Tribune* went even further, claiming that the one talking sequence:

> ...lent bewilderment to the spectator, who, following most of it as a silent picture, was startled by the swift

Joan (Eleanor Boardman) and Tom (John Holland) embrace in a scene from She Goes to War *(1929).*

adjustment necessary when words were heard, only to be equally confused when without warning they ceased but the lips kept on moving.[90]

Years later, Victor claimed that "The lack of a complete dialogue soundtrack cost the picture an estimated one million dollars in gross revenue from sales. Yes, talkies were here to stay!"[91]

While his comment about talkies was true, it is not clear that it was the lack of dialogue that destroyed the film's chances of financial success. Mixed reviews certainly didn't help, but they generally stemmed more from story problems than from the obfuscation generated by one talkie sequence. The *Los Angeles Times* called the film "an interesting one,"[92] but other newspaper critics were less kind. The *Chicago Tribune* suggested that "seldom does a movie put such a strain on one's credulity."[93] The *New York Herald Tribune* believed that: "if it carries along your interest, wrings tears from you, it does it in the way that popular pot-boilers do, leaving you at the end empty, so far as any real emotion is concerned."[94]

Nonetheless, *She Goes to War* was initially greeted in the film community with immense respect, perhaps due to the eyebrows raised by the $10,000 fee paid to Hughes for the story. Among the accolades *She Goes to War* received were Cecil B. DeMille's statement that it was "a magnificent piece of work" and King Vidor's remark that the "picture" is "superbly directed, story beautifully told and execution of battle scenes nothing short of amazing."[95]

Most of Hollywood paid attention to *She Goes to War*, at least early in the film's theatrical release. Opening night in Los Angeles, for example, brought out not only most of the cast and crew of the film, but also such Hollywood luminaries as William Collier, Jr., Lupe Velez, Gary Cooper, Lewis Milestone, and Ben Lyon. The *Los Angeles Times* claimed that "*She Goes to War* is proving of particular interest to members of the film colony … as it is the first women's war epic, showing the work of women in the conflict, and following the adventures of a girl who goes to the front to save her fiancé's honor."[96]

In the last days of May 1929 as *She Goes to War* was readied for its New York premiere, the Halperin brothers spoke to the press about their forthcoming production plans. Their confidence level was high enough for them to announce a series of films, which they hoped Hollywood would watch as eagerly as they had *She Goes to War*. Edward would produce; Victor would direct. The films would be based on Shakespearean plays and photographed in color. However, plans for the series apparently dissipated as quickly as they appeared in industry trades.[97]

For his next realized cinematic effort, Victor returned to the director's chair for a Victory Pictures' adaptation of Edwin Balmer's 1927 novel *Dangerous Business*. Retitled *Whoopee Girl* and finally *Party Girl*, the film starred Douglas Fairbanks, Jr., and Jeanette Loff, with the rest of the cast including such silent screen notables as Marie Prevost and Lucien Prival.

Another interesting face in the film is actress Judith Barrie's, who had been born in Sacramento and educated at Berkeley.[98] Edward Halperin met Barrie in artist James Montgomery Flagg's studio and convinced her to make a career change from modeling to acting. *Party Girl* marked her first film appearance; shortly thereafter, she posed as the model for a life-size bronze used to symbolize California's welcome to those attending the Olympics of 1932.[99] Barrie, who trades announced would star in the next Halperin film, soon became Mrs. Edward Halperin.[100]

More than a provider of a new sister-in-law, *Party Girl* was important in Victor's career as his first "All-Talking" picture.[101] Seizing on the opportunity of sound, he employed both dialogue and a number of songs.[102] Many in the film industry had believed the transition to the talkie era had sounded a death knell to independent producers who couldn't afford or understand the required technology[103]; certainly *Motion Picture Daily* dubbed 1928 and the year or two that followed the "lowest ebb in the history [of independent productions]."[104]

Indie producers recovered in 1930 and 1931 as smaller town theaters wired for sound, but Victor cleverly stayed busy even during the tougher period by dabbling in sound with *She Goes to War*, even though it meant letting another person direct, and then forging ahead by helming *Party Girl*.

Victor also appreciated talkies from an artistic standpoint, claiming they were more suited for "realism and [a] greater opportunity to express human emotions." However, financial concerns trumped those feelings in his mind. "…with silents we could produce good entertainment for less money," he moaned. "By use of intertitles and the subtle art of suggestion, we could save on sets, costumes, and cast costs; also, on production time. Plus widen the scope of our story backgrounds."[105] At any rate, Victor never returned to silent filmmaking following *Party Girl*'s completion.

After *Party Girl*'s premiere rang in the New Year of 1930, the film stayed for an amazing five-week run at New York City's Gaiety Theatre. The film's "Foreword," which was signed "The Producers," explains its ostensibly moral purpose:

> Sex in business—the "Party Girl" racket—threatens to corrupt the morals of thousands of young girls who seek to earn their living decently. The shameful effects of the practice would be brought home to you more forcibly if your own daughter, sister, or sweetheart were involved.

Theater crowds visiting Party Girl; *note the signs which incorrectly spell Douglas Fairbanks, Jr.'s, name. Printed in the January 31, 1930, issue of* The Film Daily.

This may happen! It is our sincerest hope that this film may arouse you and other public-spirited citizens to forcibly eliminate the vicious "Party Girl" system.

Expecting many potential viewers would need a definition of what "Party Girl" actually was, Marguerite Talezaar of the *New York Herald Tribune* defined her as:

> ...one who is hired to entertain out of town and local business men so that they will throw their trade in certain directions. She is employed by a bureau and is expected to please the customers at any cost. We see this

bureau operating in all its secretive vulgarity and, subsequently, are shown the parties at which intoxicated patrons paw the girls, one of whom is forced publicly to bathe in a perfume bath.[106]

Talezaar also suggested that, despite *Party Girl*'s "Foreword" and narrative conclusion, the film had a definite and "juicy desire to scandalize but manages, rather, to be merely dull."[107]

"One thing's for certain; it's not a revivalist meeting," one character in *Party Girl* enthuses about a depicted illicit gathering. Two men carry one woman into a back room, after which several others rush in to watch; she giggles heartily in her offscreen encounter, heavily suggestive of sexual contact.

More than the effort at exploitation, however, Victor weaves into the story several cinematic elements that would mark his future films. Music is used to convey dramatic action in a relatively sophisticated manner, especially for an early talkie. Montage is also employed at length. Jeanette (Ellen Powell), the girlfriend of Jay Roundtree (Fairbanks Jr.), reflects on their happy times through an assemblage of superimposed pictorial memories: the two frolicking in a park, canoeing, dancing, cavorting near polo horses, and enjoying night clubs.

Party Girl includes other fascinating moments as well. A lengthy song at a frat party may well hark back to Victor's own fraternity days in Chicago. In addition, a special effects shot of one character falling out of a building to her death is particularly well done, prefiguring in some respects the visual appearance of actor Norman Lloyd's death scene at the climax of Alfred Hitchcock's *Saboteur* (1942).

Nonetheless, for the *New York Times*, *Party Girl*'s "indelicate" humor and shock value were not the making of a good film. Of the story, reviewer Mordaunt Hall believed that:

Victor Halperin, seen here in the late 1920s or early 1930s.

> Although Victor Halperin has performed part of his task with a certain skill, queer ideas are flaunted in the course of this story. Mr. Halperin goes to great pains to shock his audiences by the spectacle of a girl committing suicide by jumping from the fire-escape on the top floor of a high building. It hardly seems possible that this sinful young creature could recover consciousness after the fall, but she does.[108]

Hall was little impressed with *Party Girl*, as he would prove to be with all of Victor's films.

For *Variety*, *Party Girl* "goes pretty hot pretty often, especially when the parties are being held. ... a good picture for the moral lesson it tells without teaching."[109] Though *Variety* was correct to cite a "moral lesson" at the film's conclusion, edification seems less like the film's goal than a cautious narrative excuse for the rather provocative party scenes that dominate the film. After all, *Variety* itself had mentioned that Prevost appeared as a "pip party eyeful of joy," and that the film shows "enough of herself to let you know she has a lot" in scenes that "the censors went near-sighted over." Elements of exploitation were an important consideration.

Victor's next film enterprise again teamed him with his brother Edward, but this time in the joint roles for which they would eventually become a famous pair in Hollywood. Victor directed, and Edward produced.[110] Given their previous work in Hollywood, they were already known to publications like the *Los Angeles Times* as the "Halperin Brothers," joint partners in the cinematic enterprise.[111]

To garner funding for their next film, Edward and Victor helped create Liberty Productions in 1930, using funds from the wealthy Gumbiner brothers of Chicago's General Fiber Company to get productions off the ground.[112] Along with Edward, M. H. Hoffman acted as producer. The Edward L. Klein Corporation was brought in to handle distribution on the East Coast and overseas.[113] The idea was to keep the independence which Halperin Productions possessed, and add a far greater financial base and with Hoffman's 20 years of experience and contacts.[114]

The plan was to produce 20 films a year, some on 35mm and some on wide screen, a format which fascinated the Halperins even while Victor was still working on *Party Girl*.[115] Their plans at one point even considered methods by which exhibitors could lease projector lenses for "Giant Screen" films at $100 a year. Color films and programs for television (then a hot topic in industry trades) were also considerations. Hoffman also announced a five-year franchise distribution plan, as well as intentions for Liberty to handle all film advertising and exploitation itself.[116]

Though his name does not appear on their credits, Victor would later claim credit for involvement on *Mother's Millions* (1931) and *The Mad Parade* (1931), two of the first films made under the Liberty banner.[117] Given his financial interest in Liberty in 1930, it is easy to believe Victor did have some association with the two productions, even if it was minor or indirect.

Mother's Millions was a simple comedy-drama about a wealthy Wall Street mother raising her children with a hardened demeanor, hoping that it will best prepare them for inheriting their fortune. May Robson starred, and James Flood directed. Liberty sold the film (which would also be released under the title *The She-Wolf*) to Universal Studios shortly after completing it in 1931.[118]

Given Victor's excitement over *She Goes to War*, he presumably had a stronger personal interest in *The Mad Parade* than *Mother's Millions*. *The Mad Parade*, according to *Variety*, was a "story entirely told by women, with women thrown into the quagmire of life that [the Great War] brought about, [and] it is an innovation for the screen."[119] The film starred Evelyn Brent, Irene Rich, Louise Fazenda, and Lilyan Tashman. William Beaudine directed, and M. H. Hoffman took credit as producer.

You'll Thrill To Its Drama!

EX-FLAME

A Modernized Version Of "EAST LYNNE"
With

NEIL HAMILTON
MARIAN NIXON

A flaming human docu ment revealing the pow of true love over hat and jealousy. It runs the entire gamut of huma emotions.

Beg. Saturday

Special Jubilee Week Feature
"STOLEN JOOLS"
55 Stars In One Big Comedy

Last Times Today
RICHARD ARLEN
FAY WRAY
"The Conquering Horde"

—MARY—
ANDERSON

Advertisement for Ex-Flame *printed in the April 3, 1931,* Louisville Times.

Simply being financially involved with films was never enough for Victor, who felt his role should be an artistic one. Trying his hand at writing once more, he penned the script for *Ex-Flame*, which he based on Mrs. Henry Wood's 1861 book and stage play *East Lynn*. The tale, which covers the affairs and divorces of English aristocrats, was updated to a modern setting. Actors Neil Hamilton and Marian Nixon took the lead roles, with the supporting cast including Norman Kerry, Snub Pollard, and cameos by Louis Armstrong and His Orchestra. Judith Barrie appeared in the film as well, but didn't star as had originally been planned.

More than any actor, Victor received the press attention regarding *Ex-Flame*. "Directorial Device Used in New Film," the press announced about Victor's work on the film. The device—called by Halperin a "radio technique"—introduced characters or suggested action by voice or sound only, aurally identifying them by employing offscreen space. The newspapers, drawing on studio publicity, quoted the director:

Over the radio, action and personalities create mental vision entirely. Why not add suspense and interest to

talking pictures by letting dialogue hold the attention of audiences for short periods.[120]

Examples of the technique in *Ex-Flame* include shots of the hood of an automobile driving towards its destination. Heard but not seen are the characters that Neil Hamilton and Marian Nixon portray. Their conversation occurs for some time before their faces are shown.

Despite Halperin's new "device," critics were generally less receptive toward the film itself than they had been toward *Party Girl* and *She Goes to War*. The *Los Angeles Times* believed *Ex-Flame* was "pretty awful."[121] Industry trades were equally unimpressed, with *Variety* dubbing it "old fashioned mush"[122] that "might have been a better talker with better acting."[123] *The Film Daily* spoke of "unconvincing situations," caused by "either poor story writing or directing."[124] *Harrison's Reports* mentioned that, while it was a "fairly appealing picture ... the theme, however, is not presented from a novel angle."[125] *Motion Picture Daily* claimed that the film "...is likely to inspire raucous jeers."[126] Perhaps due to numerous poor reviews, *Ex-Flame* was actor Norman Kerry's only Halperin film; trades prior to *Ex-Flame*'s release had claimed it would be his first of four projects for the Halperins.[127]

Though critical and box-office response to *Ex-Flame* was not overly strong, the brothers Halperin were quickly gaining greater fame and prestige as independent filmmakers among the Hollywood establishment.[128] Given that most of Victor's silent films of the twenties had been shot in New York, it was only by the dawn of the 1930s that he was a more recognizable figure on the West Coast. Society pages of the stars even mentioned his name on occasion. The *Los Angeles Times*—whose reporter Grace Kingsley kept readers abreast of Hollywood parties—mention Victor and Edward on numerous occasions in the society news in 1930 and 1931. For example, on December 14, 1930, the brothers (accompanied by their wives) appeared at a gathering held by comedian Harry Langdon. Among the others in attendance were Lucien Littlefield, Glenn Tryon, and Hungarian violinist Duci de Kerekjarto, who was a close friend of actor Bela Lugosi's.

Beyond socializing, the Halperins also became members of various West Coast cinema organizations in the early 1930s. Both were members of the Academy of Motion Picture Arts and Sciences, for example, with Victor a member in the Director's Branch and Edward an associate member of the Producer's Branch. Edward pursued his interests in swimming and horseback riding; he was also a member of Sigma Nu, the Masonic Lodge, the Shriners, the Rye Country Club, the Rancho Golf Club, and the New York–based Motion Picture Club.[129]

Their Halperin Productions was growing in stature

White Zombie *became Victor Halperin's masterpiece, or at least the closest any of his work would come to "classic" status.*

as well. Victor was president, and Edward was secretary and treasurer. In November 1930, shortly before the release of *Ex-Flame*, they sold their interest in Liberty Productions to M. H. Hoffman and H. M. Gumbiner, announcing that their own Halperin Productions would soon produce four films.[130] Whether the cause of the brothers' divestment was financial, artistic, or personal remains unknown.[131]

At any rate, together the two Halperins forged ahead.[132] When speaking of the growing numbers of independent films, *Motion Picture Daily* wrote that indie producers would shoot as many as 300 movies and 900 shorts for the 1931-32 production season.[133] *Motion Picture Herald* mentioned that the "Halperin Brothers, with a long record behind them, are … in the field."[134]

Victor had tackled talkies with a vengeance, but yearned for unusual stories. The dawn of the horror film cycle with *Dracula* (1931) and *Frankenstein* (1931) excited his interests. At that stage in his life, he enjoyed fantasy and the fantastic, and the horror film provided a perfect playground for such narrative concerns. His time for a major box-office hit had arrived.

In 1932, the Halperins' film *White Zombie* became the pivot in their careers. It was, as their films generally were, an independently produced project; unlike their prior movies, however, *White Zombie* became a huge success with national audiences in 1932. Edward once attributed its box-office appeal to:

> …a scientific formula, a chart so to speak. Before we begin a picture we write down a list of questions—questions that might be asked everyone concerned in the film's making and seeing, the distributor, exhibitor, audience, director, etc. When, and only when, our story measures up to every one of the established qualifications, we start

laying the foundation of production. In such cases where our contemplated picture misses out on a point, we then go about the task of rectifying it.[135]

White Zombie certainly did not miss a "point." It built on the success of the emerging horror film cycle, but also blazed a new cinematic trail with its choice of zombies as a subject for a feature film. It borrowed from the *mise en scène* of prior horror films even to the degree of using leftover sets from movies like *Dracula*, but it created a haunting and elegiac visual texture very distinct from its predecessors'.[136] *White Zombie* became Victor's masterpiece, or at least the closest any of his work would come to a "classic" status. From its inception to its final cut, *White Zombie*'s aesthetic success can be linked in part to the freedom the Halperins and their production team enjoyed. It seems he heavily valued artistic independence, but generally not at the sacrifice of money in hand.

Interesting too is that even with his greatest commercial success, Victor felt the need to color his version of the film's spectacular Broadway premiere with facts that cannot be substantiated. "Voodoo chants from loud speakers, heard for blocks, helped along [in getting publicity]," he said in 1978. "The theatre manager achieved his ambition of being arrested for disturbing the peace. This made the front pages of the New York papers, which was translated into ticket-buying jams at the box-office."[137] A thorough search of newspapers during the film's entire 1932 run at the Rivoli Theatre in New York City proves that Victor was wrong on this point.

Despite Victor's incorrect anecdote, *White Zombie* had been a tremendous financial success. He and Edward were now major players in Hollywood. Among other advancements, they rented both offices and stage space at RKO-Pathé Studios' lot in Culver City in October 1932.[138]

As Victor and Edward moved ahead with their new offices, *White Zombie* moved forward in its box office triumphs. Throughout 1933 and 1934, the film continued to score in many small American towns, in major venues in England, and even in Germany. Under the title *Flucht*

von der Teufelsinsel (*Curse of the Devil's Island*), *White Zombie* numbers among the few U.S. horror films to be released during the Nazi regime. The film had truly become a phenomenal hit, especially considering its independent roots.

White Zombie's box-office success also landed Victor a Paramount studio contract to produce a series of films with a production unit capacity similar to that which B. P. Schulberg had with the studio.[139] *Supernatural*, his film project for the studio, allowed him to work again with his brother Edward, as well as other favored colleagues like cinematographer Arthur Martinelli. While intriguing in many ways, *Supernatural* (1933) fails to live up to the artistic expectations created by *White Zombie*. However one might judge Victor's talents as a filmmaker, they did work to a greater degree of success outside the rigors of a movie studio. *Supernatural*'s box-office failure helped end earlier talks of a series of Paramount films, quickly delivering Victor back to the independence of independents.[140]

Indeed, Victor must have felt a level of ease reading the April 19, 1933, issue of *Motion Picture Daily*, which claimed:

Advertisement published in the New York Times *on April 21, 1933.*

Much important talent here [on the West Coast] is strong for independent production. This is particularly true among directors who complain about being shackled to big studios with little or no chance for selection of stories or casts or of sharing in developing story treatments.[141]

The trade claimed that the cure for these complaints regarding individual expression was for such directors to go into business producing their own films.

To help generate such funds for their next productions, the Halperin Brothers decided to sell a story to a studio for others to produce and direct. By late February 1934, RKO purchased their original tale *The Great American Harem*. Ginger Rogers and William Gargan were slated to star in the film, but when cameras finally rolled in May 1934, Rochelle Hudson and Stuart Erwin portrayed the lead roles.[142]

The comedy begins with character William Watts, who loses his job in the city marriage bureau. Watts starts his own matrimonial business by advertising in the newspaper, and soon the company becomes quite prosperous. Its success causes a crooked businessman named Barney Nolan to attempt to buy William out. When William refuses to sell, Nolan has the local district attorney begin an investigation of the matrimonial business. Chaos results when various men and women attempt to find mates. William finally agrees to sell out to Nolan, but thanks to a police raid the business has become worthless. Nonetheless, Nolan has already paid William $25,000. William then marries Cynthia, a woman who has loved him during the course of the entire story.

Retitled *Bachelor Bait*, the film was released by RKO in late July 1934. Pandro S. Berman produced, and George Stevens directed. The Halperins' story had been adapted into a screenplay by Glenn Tryon. Victor and Edward's opinion of the final product is unknown, but—during

the same summer of *Bachelor Bait*'s release—they left the major studios forever behind them.

Their future strategies were covered by the June 2, 1934, *Motion Picture Herald*, which wrote that:

> Victor and Edward Halperin are re-entering independent production with plans for eight features from stories by such authors as Rex Beach, Vicki Baum, Garnett Weston, George Waters, and Albert Payson Terhune. Among the players with whom the Halperins are negotiating are Elissa Landi, Bebe Daniels, Edmund Lowe, Gregory Ratoff, and John Boles.

An even more positive interpretation of their move back into indie filmmaking appeared in one article which said that "they decided to bring their experience in producing for the majors into the Independent [*sic*] market."[143] How did the Halperins decide to hone that experience? The same writer claimed that:

> Their first step was an eight thousand mile trip around the country, during which they personally contacted distributors and exhibitors alike. Their trip resulted in the formation of plans to produce what is anticipated to evolve into a series of eight ... features yearly.[144]

But the eight-film production schedule never materialized.

A January 18, 1936, ad in the New Bedford Standard Times *promoting the premiere of* I Conquer the Sea's *world premiere.*

Another plan for the Halperin Brothers' independent films was reported in the September 7, 1935, *Motion Picture Herald*. The trade announced that "The newly-formed Academy Pictures has leased space at Mascot Studios in Hollywood and is closing deals for release of a maximum of 12 pictures in the current season." Victor was named as president, and Edward as vice-president and general manager. The trade also claimed that "Eight films have been announced, the first, *Storm in Their Hearts*, starting September 9, and the list may be expanded by four pictures." Despite the announcement, however, the whaling epic underwent a couple of title changes to become the first Academy Pictures release.

The new film began with the working title *The Thrill of a Century*. Shot in Newfoundland and Laguna Beach, California, the picture was retitled *I Conquer the Sea*. Victor and Edward hoped it would be an epic love story juxtaposed with the rocky waters of the whaling business.

Stanley Morner, later to achieve fame under the name Dennis Morgan, appeared in the film courtesy of MGM. Just as he alleged that he had discovered Brian Donlevy, Victor would claim that he made Morgan a star. Other performers in major roles were Steffi Duna and Douglas Walton; Frederick Peters of *White Zombie* played a small part.

Along with hiring Abe Meyer as music supervisor, the Halperins employed Arthur Kay as music director. As he so often did, Arthur Martinelli acted as Victor's cinematographer. And dialogue director George Cleveland doubled his workload to portray the character, Caleb.

Psalms 104:26, "There is that Leviathan"; Psalms 89:9, "Thou stillest the waves"; Jonah 2:10, "Jonah upon the dry land." These three Biblical quotations introduce the film, creating a textual prologue similar to that used in *Supernatural*. An on-screen foreword also claims that the film is dedicated to "the last of the heroic whalers of Newfoundland, Canada—where the action of this story is laid—and to our intrepid staff and crew who spent one long hazardous year 'ahunting whales' to complete this production."

I Conquer the Sea concerns the two sons of a whaler. Tommy (Dennis Morgan) is a harpooner on a whaling boat, and his brother Leonard (Douglas Walton) is a local doctor. As Tommy makes plans to marry Rosita, Leonard shows his reservations. Rosita is Portuguese, and Leonard fears for Tommy's happiness in an ostensibly mixed marriage. However, Tommy's happiness is soon shattered by a whaling accident that causes the loss of his arm. At the same time, Leonard and Rosita are falling in love, encountering one another as Leonard helps Rosita's crippled brother to walk. A second whaling accident occurs when Tommy learns that Rosita really loves Leonard. Tommy lets himself fall into the oncoming tides and drowns.

The film premiered at the Empire Theater in New Bedford, Massachusetts, on January 18, 1936. A notice in *The Hollywood Reporter* implied that Edward would appear at the theater in person.[145] Whether he did or not is unknown, but surprisingly the screening made almost no splash in the local newspapers; the *New Bedford Morning Mercury* didn't even bother to print a review.[146] The film then opened in New York City at the Fox Brooklyn on January 23, 1936.[147]

One 1936 critic believed that "the director makes the most of the movie's big moments,"[148] and *Harrison's Reports* deemed it "pretty good entertainment" with "thrilling" scenes of whaling.[149] But perhaps *I Conquer the Sea*'s strongest review came from *The Hollywood Reporter*. The publication called it "a simple and moving folk-tale" whose scenes "bear every evidence of genuineness." Along with praising the acting and Arthur Martinelli's "distinguished" cinematography, the *Reporter* claimed "Victor Halperin's sympathetic directing does much for this wholesome sea saga...."[150]

By contrast, *Variety* saw problems with both *I Conquer the Sea*'s aesthetic execution and its audience marketability. According to their critic, the film's "effort ... is not aided particularly here either by the writing, acting, or direction. ... In more capable hands it might have meant something." Moreover, the film had "extremely limited appeal" due to "the title and running time," as well as the "absence of [star] names."[151] The public must have come to a similar conclusion to *Variety*; *I Conquer the Sea* was certainly not a major financial success.

Though a terse melodrama, *I Conquer the Sea* does not quite possess the epic feeling for which Victor hoped. Incredibly exciting shots of whaling remain stunning, yet their effect is tempered by a few unconvincing shots of the characters on a set-bound boat matted against real ocean waters. Cinematically, though, the overall film is visually impressive. Its cinematography and editing are the most superb of any Halperin film after *White Zombie*. A particularly effective montage occurs at the film's climax when character Tommy is dying. Superimposed scenes of himself with Rosita on different occasions blend into a memorable chiaroscuro with shots of the love amulet which she presented to Leonard, his rival for her affections.

The acting in *I Conquer the Sea* is among the best of any in Victor's talkies. Dennis Morgan, Douglas Walton, and Steffi Dunna give very credible performances, and the supporting players are certainly adequate. The story itself works well on many levels. It unfolds in a circular pattern, beginning and ending at a church service. It features a subtle use of metaphors as well, most poignantly with Tommy's loss of an arm a sign of his decreasing potency. "I guess this [arm] will be strong enough to hold

Victor Halperin's on-screen credit from I Conquer the Sea.

you," he says to Rosita, whose expression immediately suggests otherwise. Leonard cures Rosita's brother Pedro of his crippled legs (a reason for Rosita's shifting affections), but cannot cure his own brother's disability. Certainly Tommy's last whaling voyage itself suggests his frustration at Rosita and Leonard's love. After learning of their bond, Tommy tries not only to keep his harpooned whale but to harpoon the whale's mate as well. His anger leads to his downfall.

Despite *I Conquer the Sea*'s lack of major success at the box office, the film made news over a decade after its initial release. In 1951, *Variety* wrote that writer Richard Carroll was suing Favorite Films, Inc. (a firm that was releasing the film worldwide in 35mm prints), Nu-Art Films (which was distributing the film on 16mm to TV stations), and Joan of Arch Pictures (which were also releasing 16mm prints), and was asking for an injunction to restrain all three from distributing the film. He contended that he wrote the script based upon his own 1935 short story "Storm in their Hearts," and that his contract with Academy Pictures (which distributed the film for Halperin Productions) guaranteed all rights to the tale

would revert to him in ten years. Producers Laboratories, named as a party defendant in the suit, claimed to hold all rights to *I Conquer the Sea*, as it had held a lien on the film after advancing production money to Academy years before. Producers Laboratories had no knowledge of Carroll's alleged agreement with Academy.[152] The outcome of the suit is unknown, as it was not mentioned in the trade publications again. The dispute may well have been settled out of court.

However *I Conquer the Sea* ended its 1951 legal voyage, the Halperins were uninvolved, having made their money on the film years before and quickly left it behind them. They next set sail back to a cinematic topic where they had earlier found a hit: zombies. They had continued to delight in their initial success with *White Zombie*, with Edward once saying "You can't kill [zombies], you see, because they're already dead. Capital system, what?"[153] He might just as well have been speaking about zombie films, given that the brothers went into production on a *White Zombie* sequel. Despite the enormous legal debacle that ensued with those persons who had bought the rights to *White Zombie*, *Revolt of the Zombies* played theater screens in the U.S. during the summer and fall of 1936.[154] If their first zombie effort remains Victor's greatest aesthetic success, their second became the director's worst.

Of his horror films in general, Victor would later confess a growing distaste. "I don't believe in fear, violence, and horror, so why traffic in them," he told an interviewer in 1978. "The time arrived in my experience when I refused to supply the inordinate demand for that kind of entertainment."[155] Victor said much the same to his second wife. "Vic was sorry he made those horror films," Venita Halperin remembered. "He said, 'If I had known then what I do now, I wouldn't have made a single one.' When he got older, he realized that it was all wrong to produce them [due to their content]."[156]

Immediately prior to *Revolt of the Zombie*'s release, the Halperins planned production of at least two other films. One was to be called *Slave of the Sheik*, a modernized *Uncle Tom's Cabin* with a sheik taking the place of Simon Legree. Another would have been based on Eugene O'Neill's *Lazarus Laughs*.[157] Though Edward enthused about both projects to the newspapers, neither film moved beyond the planning stage.

Instead, *Nation Aflame*, the Halperins' next project (with Victor again directing and Edward producing), was an entirely different story from any of those announced. But *Nation Aflame*'s origin is somewhat unclear. *The Hollywood Reporter* announced originally in June 1936 that "Leon D' Usseau has sold an original, 'Avenging Angels,' to Maurice Cohn."[158] Cohn's connection to the Halperins is unknown; presumably he was involved with Treasure Pictures Corporation, which financed *Nation Aflame*.

When *Nation Aflame* finally appeared on *Hollywood Reporter*'s production schedule in November, the story was listed as an original by "Oliver Drake, Thomas Dixon, and Rex Hale."[159] Another production discrepancy remains unsolved as well: Ethel Jackson is listed as a cast member in *Hollywood Reporter*'s production charts, but it is difficult to spot her appearance in existing prints. Regardless, the film—which began shooting on approximately November 15, 1936—completed its production phase around the beginning of December.

An article written in the February 20, 1937, issue of *The Hollywood Reporter* claimed:

> *Aflame* has already received recognition from the Hays office, women's organizations, and is being sponsored by the American Legion. A cast of comparatively fresh faces has been used in this picture and the Halperins expect to use them as the nucleus of their future productions, eventually bringing them together as contract players.[160]

Of course many in the cast were *not* fresh faces; Lila Lee had earlier been a popular silent screen actress, and Snub Pollard was a well-known actor to comedy film fans and viewers of Victor's film *Ex-Flame* (1931).

Nation Aflame's narrative concerns a band of conmen led by Adams (Harry Holman) and Sandino (Noel Madison), who descend on a town where Adams was once mayor. After raising sufficient funds from his daughter Wynne (Norma Trelvar) and others, they begin an organization called the "Avenging Angels." Its alleged purpose is to fight for the rights and jobs of "real" Americans over "foreigners." The organization quickly grows in membership and power, but Sandino's corrupt plans lead to his downfall. At the time of the film's production, parallels were often drawn between the fictional Avenging Angels and the Ku Klux Klan. While the film acts as a strong commentary against such organizations as the KKK, it seems that the inspiration for the Avenging Angels actually came from another secret society, the Black Legion.

Critic Barn at *Variety* suggested that the overall print quality of *Nation Aflame* appeared crisper and cleaner than that of many low-budget films, but at the same time:

> ...so many mob scene files were used, the audience will expect to see Mussolini anytime. One laugh comes with Holyman's address to the relief people, there being no indication of a last year's suit or a pair of overalls in the whole mob.[161]

Barn was correct; no tattered clothes are noticeable among those demanding a relief bill. However, the use of stock footage is not nearly as grating as his Mussolini comment suggests.

The Film Daily, who adjudged Halperin's direction "poor" and Martinelli's cinematography "fair," claimed that *Nation Aflame* was a "poor attempt to use recent anti–Klan publicity; picture moves slowly."[162] *The Hollywood Reporter* even still announced it as a "KKK Film Premiere."[163] Of the film's premiere at New York's Criterion, *Motion Picture Herald* claimed, "[a] scattered audience followed the picture closely but gave no hint of approval or disapproval."[164]

Again Victor chose to begin his film with a quotation, selecting a speaker immediately associated with anti-racist beliefs and actions. Abraham Lincoln's words appear in written form: "This nation under God shall have a new birth of freedom, that government of the people, by the people, for the people, shall not perish from the earth."

Unlike Lincoln's quotation, *Nation Aflame*'s sets and lighting appear flat and lack depth, its moving camerawork is at times unsteady, and its music has the repetitive and melodramatic flavor typical of mid-thirties B-movies. The film's dialogue is rather stilted, and—though

Noel Madison, Norma Trelvar, Lila Lee, and especially Harry Holman give quite credible performances—the acting is generally uninspired. Some crucial moments in the plot suffer heavily under the weight of such problems. For example, when a newspaper editor unfriendly to the Avenging Angels (actor Alan Cavan) is set up, he speaks to the character who has betrayed him. What should be a dramatic scene falls apart under unconvincing lighting and acting, as well as dialogue in which the editor rather calmly and stiffly says "Judas got thirty pieces of silver for his double cross...." to the traitor who helps kill him.

However, a few segments in the film do possess significant power. For instance, Sandino has his partner Adams killed when Adams decides to sign a relief bill into law. After he is shot, Adams' familiar walking stick falls to the ground. Its handle—a sculpture of a clown's head—is broken in two. The scene creates an effective, understated use of emotion.

Throughout the film, Victor relies heavily on edited montages to show the passage of time. Some feature newspaper headlines to convey action in a manner none too different from that employed by most B-films of the period. However, others draw on Victor's strength as a silent film director. Set to music and sound effects, one shows the gossip about a love affair between Sandino and Wynne Adams. Extreme closeups of objectified mouths and ears talking and listening are revealed in quick cuts which signify the rapidity of the spread of the rumor. It is one of the highlights of Victor's sound films.

The Halperins intended to start production on two movies as *Nation Aflame* neared its national release. *Merrily We Go to Jail*, written by Damon Runyon and to star 14 comedians, was first on their agenda. The next was to be called *Court for Girls*.[165] Neither was produced, probably due to a lack of funds.

In 1938, perhaps because of an inability to get new productions in the works, the brothers looked for employment elsewhere. Victor joined the Walter Kane agency to handle stories and what *Hollywood Reporter* vaguely called "special material." Earlier the same year, Edward had taken a job with the Sam Berkowitz unit at Grand National to produce a Fine Arts film.[166]

Though the Berkowitz–Fine Arts production apparently fell through, it did initiate a period of Edward working apart from Victor.[167] Edward penned both an original story and screenplay that became *Code of the Cactus* (1939), a western starring Tim McCoy. He then wrote the screenplay to *Yukon Flight* (1939), which was part of the "Renfrew of the Royal Mounted" film series. The next year, Edward received on-screen credit for two more "Renfrew" scripts. The first was *Danger Ahead*, released in January 1940; the second, *Sky Bandits* (1940), was produced by *White Zombie*'s Phil Goldstone. The brothers

seemingly did not work together in independent productions again.

In 1938, Victor then may have begun work on the film *Racing Blood* (1938) with producer Maurice Cohn, who had earlier been involved in *Nation Aflame*. The film starred Frankie Darro and Kane Richmond; it was directed by Rex Hale. Victor's name does not appear in the credits, but he mentioned the film in one of his resumes; however, Victor did not state his role in the production.[168] Given his previous association with Cohn and *Racing Blood*'s minimal importance, it is highly possible he did play a role in the film's production, even if a minor or indirect one.

The project *Torture Ship* was to "inaugurate [Producer's Distributing Corporation's] series of thrill-action melodramas."[169] By the end of the first week in August 1939, George Sayre and Harvey Huntley had completed their screenplay, which was suggested by Jack London's story "A Thousand Deaths"; the tale was scheduled to go before cameras on August 14. Time passed, and the production got further behind.

As of late August, Rex Hale had been signed to direct what would be the first film in Producer's Distributing Corporation's 1939-40 season. *Torture Ship* was rescheduled to go before cameras the last week of August, even though no cast had been assembled as of August 22.[170] Days passed, and still no shooting. Only by August 31 had the producers leased space on the Grand National lot, but no cast was announced until September.[171]

By the time *Torture Ship* finally went into production, Victor Halperin had replaced Hale as director, though trade publications don't indicate why. The Call Bureau Cast Service originally listed John Miller to play the role of Jesse, though Skelton Knaggs appeared in the role in the finished film. Harvey Huntley, for whatever reason, received no on-screen credit for his script participation with Sayre.

The screenplay concerns a Dr. Herbert Stander (actor Irving Pichel), who helps criminals escape the authorities in exchange for testing his theory that glandular dysfunctions cause people to commit crimes. Lt. Bob Bennett (actor Lyle Talbot) runs the yacht on which a number of criminals and his uncle, Dr. Stander, travel. The criminals, with Ritter (actor Wheeler Oakman) as their guide, avoid undergoing Stander's operations and end up murdering the good doctor. Bennett outwits the criminals, helping also to prove one of them, Joan Martel (actress Jacqueline Wells), innocent. He and Martel begin a romantic fling.

Decades later, Jacqueline Wells (née Julie Bishop) told author-historian Gary D. Rhodes that:

> The film [*Torture Ship*] is one that I scarcely remember. Given its low-budget nature, I just didn't pay that much

Lieutenant Bob Bennett (Lyle Talbot) lifts a chair against Dr. Herbert Stander (Irving Pichel) and his crew in Victor Halperin's film Torture Ship *(1939). (Courtesy of Lynn Naron.)*

attention to it. I tried to do well in my role of course, but received little direction from Victor Halperin. He apparently wasn't an "actor's director."[172]

Her comments about Halperin are consistent with most people's memories of his limited interaction with actors and his greater emphasis on a film's *mise en scène*. Her unenthusiastic comments about the film itself are not dissimilar to those voiced by critics in 1939.

For *Variety*, *Torture Ship* was a "quickie action thriller that misses fire [*sic*] all the way on its possibilities." Though their critic, Herb, believed that "there can be no quarrel with the acting of the principals," he claimed that the "yarn has so many unreasonable and unexplainable points that it will annoy even the most jueve-minded [*sic*]."[173] *The Film Daily*, which also praised the film's acting, dubbed Victor's direction "O.K." and announced the film "has enough punch and drama to satisfy the nabe trade."[174]

Torture Ship's narrative remains an intriguing fusion of the horror and crime genres, though the limited budget minimizes the film's dramatic success. Though the opening sequences of Dr. Stander speaking with several criminals feature rather effective high-contrast lighting, the lighting is rather flat throughout. Only a few visually memorable moments occur. In particular, a newspaper picture of machine gunner Jesse (actor Skelton Knaggs) dissolves into a closeup of Jessie smiling. The shadowy lighting creates the effect of a face mask on Jesse's head. The result is one of the most striking images in Victor's films.

However, the image of Jesse is an exception in the film as a whole. Cheap sets and uninspired cinematography combine with lengthy action scenes which feature no dialogue or music to make a far less than exciting film. Unlike *Nation Aflame*, *Torture Ship*'s use of montage is solely an economical one, explaining important narrative action through newspaper headlines. While some of the acting—specifically that of Lyle Talbot, Irving Pichel, and Jacqueline Wells—is very credible, the drama suffers from (among other things) the fact that the very rough waters seen in shots on the boat's deck, seemingly have no effect on the rock-steady action in the boat's interior.

After finishing *Torture Ship*, Victor quickly moved into production on his next film, *Buried Alive*.[175] He shot the movie during the first half of October 1939 for Producer's Pictures Corporation; Edward was not involved in the film at all.[176] Actor Clem Wilenchick was scheduled to play the character Manning, but by the time of shooting he had been replaced by Wheeler Oakman. Similarly, the Call Bureau Cast Service initially mentioned that Archie Twitchell would portray the role of Carson, though he was eventually replaced by Dave O'Brien.

The film's plot is a rather simplistic one. Johnny Martin (actor Robert Wilcox) is a young man in prison who is nearing an almost certain chance for parole. However, while driving state executioner Ernie (actor George Pembroke) around town, he becomes involved in a barroom fight. Several press reporters brawl with Ernie, and Johnny believes he has to help. However, reporter Manning (Wheeler Oakman) uses the event as a headline against the state government, which thus refuses Johnny's parole. His anger is intensified by his wishes to pursue a romance with prison worker Joan Wright (actress Beverly Roberts) upon his release.

Problems mount even further when Johnny's cellmate, Big Billy (actor Don Rowan) kills two police guards. Johnny leaves his cell to help one of the guards, but is later accused and convicted of murder. Other guards kill Big Billy, who is unable to help proclaim Johnny's innocence. The only one who can exonerate him is a prisoner who dislikes Johnny and thus lies at his trial.

Johnny is sentenced to die in the electric chair, but is saved thanks to a ruse concocted by the warden and the executioner. They fool the prisoner who has lied into telling the truth, which saves Johnny at the last minute. He is then pardoned and can pursue his relationship with Joan.

The acting in *Buried Alive* is generally less credible than it is in most of Victor's films. In particular, the Big Billy character—which borrows heavily from Lennie in Steinbeck's *Of Mice and Men*—is very ineffectively portrayed by actor Don Rowan. However, the weakest link throughout is the dialogue. For example, Ernie—who pulls the switch for electrocutions—is affected negatively by his job. At one point, he speaks in a very stilted fashion of his pain and nightmares as an "accusing phantasmagoria."

At the same time, the character Ernie helps promote what is the major theme of the film: *Buried Alive* in many ways is an anticapital punishment text. Whatever the flaws in execution of dialogue, acting, and otherwise, the film raises questions about the state's right to kill a human being and about the moral difference (if any) between the state which employs capital punishment and a murderer on death row.

Most memorable cinematically is an electrocution scene which features a sophisticated use of pacing, editing, and sound effects. A closeup of a voltmeter, shots of onlookers and then a doctor with a stethoscope—this fascinating montage appears without the body being shown. Equally as important as the visuals here is the impact of sound: electricity at a high volume overcoming all other noise. The sequence helps enliven what is visually and cinematically one of Victor's least interesting films.

The Film Daily believed that *Buried Alive* "falls short of being a convincing drama. It will probably be okay as program material in the small nabe houses." Its critic rated Halperin's direction as "O.K."[177] *Variety* was less kind, calling the film "inferior all the way, particularly in its direction and playing, outside of Beverly Roberts. ... Most obstinate factor in this film's chances is the trite yarn, chief reason for the cast's failure to do better."[178] The *New York Post* critic claimed "it's so bad it seems almost like a new experience. Judging from the quality of most of the acting and direction, I should guess that it was a quickie film originally scheduled for six days' shooting but shortened to four. ... *Buried Alive* heads the January mustn't list."[179]

Buried Alive was quickly laid to rest in film vaults. By the 1940s, Halperin depended on whatever fame *White Zombie* still held, not on B-prison dramas. One of his own press notices mentioned that he had "written and produced [*White Zombie*] in collaboration, that it had "broken all summer attendance records in theatres thruout [*sic*] the country; also, it holds the industry long-distance playing record—having played for the past ten years to date—and still going strong." As was so often the case, Victor's story here is not entirely true; though *White Zombie* was one of the box-office successes of the summer and fall of 1932, absolutely no evidence supports his claim about the "long-distance playing record."

Nonetheless, by the beginning of the 1940s, *White Zombie* was too far in the past to bring much attention to Victor. His final film credit as a director was *Girl's Town*, a low-budget film produced by Lou Brock and Jack Schwarz at PRC. Once again, Edward was not involved. Shooting began on December 15, 1941.[180]

Girl's Town was perhaps his most conventional film narrative since the silent era. The story is of an aging actress called "Mother" who runs a boarding house for aspiring actresses. Among them is Myra, who will do anything to get into films, including walking all over her sister or the other actresses at the boarding house.

Despite the fact that among the cast are former silent screen stars Alice White and Anna Q. Nilsson, *Variety*'s review claimed the film was "lacking names." Their critic also believed *Girl's Town* overall was a: "[f]eatherweight yarn, directed in halting fashion ... [which] shapes up as a minor programmer, suited mostly for lesser theaters. ... Film in many ways constitutes an awkward screen test for many comparative newcomers."[181] Unmerciful in its critique, *Variety* proclaimed that the "[d]irection, production and scripting are mediocre even for such an inexpensive programmer. Tipoff on story's quality is the fact no author or scripter is credited."

The Film Daily was more kind, calling Edith Fellows acting "outstandingly good," and the rest of the cast's performances "nice." The story was "not unusual but capable of holding interest." Perhaps the review's most negative comment was that "Victor Halperin ... could have more with a little imagination thrown in."[182]

Though Victor's career of directing feature films essentially ended with that comment of *The Film Daily*'s, he did sell one final original story that others transformed into a feature. A low-budget western. Ironically, after a fascinating, long-term, and often successful career as a independent filmmaker and director, Victor was essentially back where he had first started in the film business with Cactus Features: selling stories for the westerns.

Lone Star Trail, which Victor sold to Universal Studios, was the last teaming of cowboy film stars Johnny Mack Brown and Tex Ritter. Also in the cast was the Jimmy Wakely Trio, popular western music stars. Elmer Clifton directed the film, which began production in September 1942.

Victor's story features a rancher named Blaze Parker (portrayed by Johnny Mack Brown) who spends two years in jail after being framed for a stagecoach robbery. The unscrupulous businessmen who set him up, try to kill him on his release, but he survives with the help of Fargo Steele (played by Tex Ritter). The businessmen then frame both Blaze and Fargo for another crime, but Blaze escapes after their arrest and proves their innocence. Fargo, a U.S. marshal, then recommends a full pardon for Blaze, who then marries his girlfriend.

Variety said the film "gives Johnny Mack Brown and Tex Ritter ample opportunity to please the western fans and they do it up in expert style."[183] *The Film Daily* was more excited, claiming "[o]n the score of action this Johnny Mack Brown western is away above par. The film is a biff-bang exhibition that will have the kids jumping up and down in their seats."[184] And *The Hollywood Reporter* began its review by claiming the film "[packs] a

story ... [made] considerably more suspenseful ... than most Western scripts...."[185]

By the time of the *1944–45 International Motion Picture Almanac*, Victor's biography had dwindled to only a few lines.[186] At some point during World War II, he became vice-president in charge of production at the Pictures Corporation of America, a company based out of New York City,[187] but his position there was apparently short-lived. He spent most of the war era away from the film industry, helping to manufacture military supplies for the U.S. Army.[188]

In the two years immediately following World War II, Victor worked as a special sales representative for the Harvey Machine Company in Los Angeles, then in 1947 began work in a nearby public relations office. Advertising, marketing, and promotion: Victor had come full circle to before the dawn of his film career.[189] Much like his early attempts to enter filmmaking, he faced tough odds to obtain backing for his new projects. According to *The Hollywood Reporter* of September 27, 1948:

> Victor Hugo Halperin, producer-director for 18 years prior to 1942, is returning to pictures. His first production will be *Overthrow*, a high-budgeter of international intrigue. Halperin ... is completing arrangements for a series of pictures he plans to produce during the next 18 months.

The needed funds must never have materialized; neither *Overthrow* nor the "series of pictures" did either. Halperin's years of directing films were over.

In the 1951 *Motion Picture Production Encyclopedia*, Victor was listed as president of Personality Pictures on Las Palmas Avenue in Hollywood. His brother Edward was not mentioned as having any role in the short-lived company. Subsequent editions of the encyclopedia do not mention Personality Pictures at all.[190]

In 1978, Victor remembered that his problems in raising funds for independent films in the fifties were caused by television. "Most of us independent producers lost our shirts, became virtually bankrupt," he said. "So our principal market vanished along with our investments." Nevertheless, Victor did seek out television as a new forum for his talents.

In a resume from the 1950s, Victor claimed that he had been writer and director for television's "Charlie Chan series," though it is difficult to confirm his involvement with that program.[191] Exhaustive searches through contemporary and more recent sources have not yield his name in connection with any TV incarnations of Charlie Chan.

In addition to plans for a TV program called *Terror Theater*, Victor teamed up with James Burkett for a true-life adventure program. He would direct the series, as well as coproduce it with Burkett. *The Hollywood Reporter* detailed their plans:

> Veteran film producers Victor Halperin and James S. Burkett have started preparations for a series of TV films to be made under the general title of Soldiers of Fortune, dealing with the true-life exploits of individual members of the Adventurers Clubs in Los Angeles, New York, Chicago, and Copenhagen, and the Savage Club of London. Stories have been prepared for the first 26 half-hour shows of the series.... The explorers contacted have made available some 200,000 feet of film taken on their travels.[192]

The same column mentioned that Halperin and Burkett had made arrangements with cinematographers in various other countries in an effort to procure needed footage. The duo also had plans to make "Tex" Stone—a big-game hunter who lived outside of Laredo, Texas—a part of the series. As a final strategy to elicit interest from TV stations, Halperin and Burkett planned to have well-known actors portray the adventurers in brief re-creations of their exploits.

The first episode premiered on L.A.–area television station KHJ on Friday, September 14, 1956. By that time, the show had been retitled *Strange Lands and Seven Seas*, with Chuck Niles acting as host. Leon Paddock, who had for five years traveled the world in search of adventure, shared his experiences and film footage for the program. One sequence highlighted Paddock's underwater footage, while another offered a re-enactment of the mutiny aboard pirate Henry Morgan's ship. Impressed with *Strange Lands*, *The Hollywood Reporter* believed the "opener came off as a high-level travelogue that, if subsequent shows duplicate, will certainly gather a large share of adventure-loving viewers."[193]

TV TRUE ADVENTURE THRILLS TONIGHT!

"STRANGE LANDS and 7 SEAS"   7:00

TONIGHT:

"FIGHTING BULLS"

the story of the men who train them and the matadors who meet them in the arenas.

Advertisement for Victor Halperin's major foray into television; printed in the November 28, 1956, Los Angeles Times.

In a typed handout given to potential sponsors entitled "Why This Show Is a Proven Attraction for All Ages of Viewers," Victor wrote:

> We have here high adventure—action—some of our subjects costing as much as a feature picture—but having the value of being true. Our format includes a host-narrator who introduces the adventurer and then either adventurer or host delivers an exciting narration of the picture action, building dramatically to a thrill climax... AND THIS BUILDS AUDIENCES FOR YOUR PRODUCT OR SERVICE THAT TRANSLATE [*sic*] INTO SALES AND DOLLARS...[194]

As *The Hollywood Reporter* mentioned, "no sponsor was evidenced on the opener, but on the strength of this initialer, that problem should be solved soon."[195]

Halperin and Burkett, who headquartered at Eagle-Lion Studios, did solve that problem, but for reasons unknown moved *Strange Lands and Seven Seas* to another L.A.-based station, KTLA. In a July 11, 1957, rating, the show captured 7.1 percent of the Los Angeles television audience. By the time of a four-week study made during September and October, it had gained slightly and took 7.5 percent of the L.A.-area viewers.[196] Topics ranged from racing drivers and bullfighters to an Alaskan prospector lost on a glacier.[197]

Augmenting what appeared to be a burgeoning career in television was Victor's personal life in the mid–1950s. During 1955, he met a woman named Venita. Decades later, she remembered:

> We met in church. A friend introduced me to him, and a few weeks later he called me for a dinner date. I still didn't know what his occupation was. After a month or so, I mentioned that I remembered that when I was young and watching films in St. Louis, the name Victor Hugo Halperin would appear in big letters on the screen. I asked if he was any relation, and he said "You're pulling my leg." Later when I asked a friend of his, the friend said, "Vic *is* Victor Hugo Halperin." Well, I nearly fell out of my seat.[198]

Victor and Venita married in 1957. It was his second wedding and her first. The couple would have no children. They remained together until the time of Victor's death.

Though he was very happy in his personal life, Victor's TV career ended more abruptly than expected. By December 1957, *Strange Lands and Seven Seas* was off the air, replaced by a program entitled *High Road to Danger*. Movie work was available, but Venita recalled that producers only wanted him to make "girlie pictures." She also believed that her husband "thought Hollywood was [a] degrading atmosphere," especially by the 1950s.[199]

Victor was uninterested in exploitation films of the

Victor Halperin in the 1970s.

era, just as he was apparently uninterested in capitalizing on the growing independent film market of drive-ins. Venita recalled that:

It was strange. He retired from producing, quit completely. He retired for four years. During that time, he took a course in real estate. He sold new tracts in orange groves. They were marvelous when they were in blossom. He sold expensive houses too. Vic once sold 26 in one day, somewhere near Claremont. People were eager to get out of L.A. proper, and Vic did well financially.[200]

Geographically, he was miles from Hollywood, but while working on real estate deals he regularly drove past the home of Madge Bellamy, the lead actress in *White Zombie*, a concrete reminder that memories of years gone by wouldn't easily fade. Even though his production career had ceased, Victor did spend time on film library sales, funneling his old movies to television.[201]

Another reminder of Victor's years in the movies

Victor and Venita Halperin's home in Sulphur Springs, Arkansas.

was his brother Edward. For at least part of the 1950s, the brothers still remained in touch. Unfortunately, their contact eventually came to an almost complete halt. Venita recalled why their relationship crumbled:

[Edward] and his wife were both alcoholics. Victor tried to help. When he was involved in real estate, Vic even gave him a home in Pasadena. We invited Edward and his wife both out to dinner, but they would just want to drink until late into the evening. After trying so hard, Vic gave up on them. It was all in vain.[202]

But Victor's first family doubts stories of Edward's alcoholism, even though they had lost touch with him after the 1930s. Regardless, in 1978, Victor mentioned that his brother was "retired" and living "out on the desert somewhere." When Edward died is unknown. *Variety* and other film trades ignored his death in their obituaries, and Victor's wife Venita was never informed of the details. Exhaustive searches made for this text have yielded no information on the date of his death, or whether or not Judith Barrie, Edward's wife, is deceased. What is clear is that the falling out between Victor and Edward had extended even into death. They spoke little before Victor's demise.

Health problems soon added to Victor's list of troubles. Sometime in the early 1960s, he suffered a relatively mild stroke. To help him recover, Venita suggested that they move to Arkansas. Her parents at one time had lived in Bentonville, and she thought it would be a nice place to go on a two-year sabbatical. Victor didn't want to move at first, quickly revealing his dislike for small towns. Eventually, however, the couple not only bought a home in Sulphur Springs, Arkansas, but stayed in it until Victor's death.[203]

At that Arkansas home, Victor loved to spin stories about his beliefs on life. For example, at age 84, he offered one of his favorite maxims to interviewer Raymond J. Nielsen: "I still feel that I must actively support whatever good cause that presents itself. Folks will always be folks, and folks will always need love and understanding."[204]

Arkansas days were halcyon days. Victor devoted much of his time to playing the violin, having kept stacks and stacks of sheet music from prior decades. He had no interest in jazz or popular music, and focused his talents on classical music and sacred tunes like "The Holy City."[205] He also spent much time reading, having a strong interest in Dickens and other canonical literature.

As Venita once recalled, "Victor and I rarely watched films together. He didn't enjoy watching films. [But] he was very partial to Randolph Scott. He enjoyed watching Jimmy Stewart. He also liked Clark Gable, whom Victor's daughter Elaine dated." His few favorite films from his own past were *Supernatural, She Goes to War,* and *Tea—with a Kick!*.[206]

Victor did realize that most film buffs preferred *White Zombie* over his own personal favorites. In his only return to the cinematic limelight, he and Madge Bellamy participated in a joint telephone interview with Arkansas PBS station AETN moderator Raymond H. Nielsen, which was later broadcast on October 28, 1978, the same evening as a TV screening of *White Zombie.* Venita Halperin recalled the genesis of his appearance. "[After moving to Arkansas,] Victor had never mentioned to anyone that he was once a producer and director in the movies. [Following the broadcast with Nielsen] Victor's secret was out! Sulphur Springs had a celebrity."[207]

Bellamy wrote to Victor after the broadcast, speaking affectionately of his directing talents and of *White Zombie:*

> Talking to you was so clear it was as if you were beside me, also your voice brought the past into the present as if I were on the set of *White Zombi* [sic]. We were fortunate, you to make, I to be in, such a classic as *White Zombi* [sic]. I think, beside the fine direction, it was because of the wonderful story. The allegory of the uselessness of possession without returned love. The symbolism of the exploited worker. The power of the myth on the human mind. I will always be grateful to you.[208]

Always a Halperin fan, Bellamy signed the letter "Yours Admiring, Madge Bellamy." She seems to have been the only film star with whom he had contact in the 1970s.

No more attention came to Victor during his twilight years. In August 1978, Ray Nielsen of AETN tried to sell a story about Victor to *Modern Maturity,* but the magazine showed no interest. A doctoral candidate at the University of Arkansas planned a dissertation on Halperin's career, but the college cannot confirm whether it was finished. Obscurity had engulfed Victor almost completely while he was still alive.

Far worse in Victor's mind than a lack of publicity was the lack of attention from his two daughters. "They didn't come see him before he passed on," Venita remembered; "...it was very sad. The mother had turned them completely against him."[209] But except for one brief phone call during a visit he and Venita made to Southern California, Victor had apparently kept out of touch with Irene and his daughters since the 1936 divorce. Victor's granddaughter Linda Ortiz commented to the author in a June 2001 interview that Irene and the daughters never even knew where he was all those many years. His complete absence from their lives had perhaps been self-imposed, and so of course Joan and Elaine didn't ever phone or write him: How could they when they had no idea of where he was?

After a year of rapidly declining health, Victor Halperin died on May 17, 1983. Of her late husband, Venita Halperin said, "He was so tender-hearted. I miss him so."[210] Actress Madge Bellamy was one of the few in the film industry who acknowledged his passing. She would write: "How sorrowful it makes me to know Victor is gone. It seems the best and kindest are gone. He was certainly one of them and the finest of film directors. How sad I am."[211]

Sulphur Springs, Arkansas, has no newspaper. The nearby Gravette, Arkansas, newspaper printed no obituary;[212] nor did film trades like *Variety.* Even thorough film texts like Ephraim Katz's *The Film Encyclopedia* (HarperCollins, 1998) confess a lack of information regarding Victor's date of death. He had died in complete but undeserved anonymity.

A Critique

Far more important than the specific date of Victor Halperin's death is his life, his career in films, the legacy he left. Was Madge Bellamy correct when she called him one of the "finest of film directors"? Is he, as book reviewer Clive Denton suggested, an "undiscovered 'auteur' from Hollywood's gloriously murky past"? The answers, if they can be unlocked at all, require us to invoke the history of authorship studies in film theory.[213]

Denton's use of the term "auteur" in his review of Andrew Sarris's book is readily understandable. Sarris used the term auteur in describing the individual styles of great Hollywood directors, in describing the romanticized idea of the director as the "author" of their film.[214] Though the present text believes that the debate on Victor Halperin's merits as a filmmaker necessarily invokes questions of auteurism and authorship, this section of Chapter Ten does not pretend to engage with those questions in any way other than to use them as a very basic source of discussion. While merely touching the surface, it is hoped that by addressing issues of authorship and auteurism—even if in brief—a better understanding of Victor Halperin the director will emerge.

Of course, the orthodoxy of auteurism has been negatively critiqued for years due to its overly simplistic transplantation of romantic ideas about artists onto filmmakers and the filmmaking process. Even under minimal scrutiny, the belief of the director (or at least those highly artistic and unique directors, the "auteurs") being in control of all aspects of their work, is problematic. After all, many persons other than the director work behind the scenes and in front of the camera, and many concerns other than aesthetics are always at play in a film's creation (e.g., budgetary matters and technological limitations).

These issues immediately cause questions—if not problems—for auteurism.

However, in popular film magazines and reviews the notion of the director as auteur has for decades remained a very dominant viewpoint. Part of the reason for this is the fact that—though Sarris's book clearly articulated what the auteur is and lobbied for the usage of the term—the basic idea of director as primary author-artist has surfaced with great regularity since the early days of the cinema. In 1923, for example, director Maurice Tourneur proclaimed that "[t]he director is to the motion picture what the artist is to the painting."[215] Throughout the 20th century, popular film reviews and sometimes studio publicity generally held up the director as the creator, the artist, the auteur.

For some modern theorists, any questions regarding authors of films and literature are now uninteresting and even unnecessary. Drawing on Sassure's theory of signification, theorist Roland Barthes pronounced the "death of the author" and thus the "birth of the reader." By these words, he meant that it "is language which speaks, not the author," and that meaning does not originate in the mind of the author. For Barthes, language "ceaselessly calls into question all origins," including authors'.[216] Theorists such as Stephen Heath have applied Barthes' ideas to film theory, thus casting doubt on the merits of auteurism by emphasizing a film's impact on audiences. However, despite the importance and attention paid elsewhere in this text to the "readers" of his films—the subject, the viewer, the emergent spectator—the "death of the author" too easily dismisses the important commonalities present in the various works of Victor Halperin.

Even if we eschew the particular term auteur, we must consider Denton's question regarding Victor Halperin in terms of his particular contributions to the films he directed. Was he responsible for certain repeated stylistic motifs in his films? Whether or not that answer is an affirmative, we must also consider whether there is indeed a "Halperin style," even if Victor Halperin may have not been consciously responsible for it.

In the 1960s and 1970s, structuralism—a mode of criticism developed from structural linguistics that analyzes language and literature—allowed a theoretical framework for scholars like Peter Wollen to examine the repeated motifs within the works of specific filmmakers. For example, differences between the revisions of Wollen's important text *Signs and Meaning in the Cinema* show his emphasis changing from the conscious creation of director to "the unconscious, unintended meaning [which] can be decoded in the film, usually to the surprise of the individual involved."[217] Repeated codes and conventions within a filmmaker's body of work can then be pinpointed. Rather than Victor Halperin, the conscious creator is "Victor Halperin"—a structure traceable within a group of films, of which the man Victor Halperin may be unaware. A "Victor Halperin" film style thus emerges. That structure—whatever its origins and however it resulted—is the object of study.

Certainly the structuralist perspective removes the need to exact details of who thought of what on a film set. For instance, author Bryan Senn writes at length about *White Zombie* in his book *Drums of Terror: Voodoo in the Cinema*. Without any historical evidence, he suggests that Arthur Martinelli's cinematography "undoubtedly" led Victor Halperin's "visual acumen."[218] In an apparent contradiction of this claim, he mentions that Halperin actively "places" Martinelli's camera in a certain position for an early scene in the film. Later in his text, he suggests yet a third possibility for the film's artistry: the placement of the camera could have been made by *both* the cinematographer and director.[219] He sums up the discussion by mentioning that Martinelli's visual output remains stronger than Halperin's. That conclusion is tenuous at best, because it comes from both an apparently limited knowledge of Halperin's other work and a lack of appreciation of the visual plainness of many Martinelli-lensed films.[220]

However, structuralism would have us not worry about the concerns that Senn raises or concerns we might raise ourselves, such as the input of Victor's brother Edward. Structuralism would have us concentrate instead on the sheer emergence of repeated motifs that could be dubbed the work of the structure "Victor Halperin," even if a cameraman like Arthur Martinelli occasionally made some suggestions to the man Victor Halperin on a film set. In Chapter One we examine at length the use of the spectator-as-character. We could now do so through the lens of structuralism; in other words, we can trace what is clearly happening in the film without the need to worry about whether the actual man Victor Halperin was consciously the decision maker and innovator of it. The reality is that the spectator-as-character is constructed by the filmic text. It exists as a function of *White Zombie*, even if Victor Halperin was unaware of it.

We could say the same of the thematic structures that emerge in Victor's work. For example, many of his films are politically charged with liberalism and humanism. *In Borrowed Plumes* makes a case against rigid class structures, and *She Goes to War* advocates gender equality. *I Conquer the Sea* promotes antiracism; similarly, *Nation Aflame* is a veiled statement against the Ku Klux Klan. *Revolt of the Zombies* is almost Marxist in its critique of a power-hungry individual exploiting masses of people for their labor. *Torture Ship* addresses the need for the rehabilitation of criminals in the U.S., and the character Ernie in *Buried Alive* advances a clear argument against capital punishment. Victor's films are often far more progressive thematically than many others of the 1920s and 1930s. It is impossible to know how much credit for these themes should be given to the writers of such stories and films, and to Victor. Nevertheless, these are traceable structures in his works.

Perhaps the greatest narrative thread between films in the Halperin canon is the use of irony. That quality is apparent in his early works like *Danger Point, In Borrowed Plumes, School for Wives*, and *She Goes to War*. Irony becomes even more developed in Victor's major sound films, in which improbable characters are so often in quest of the impossible: Beaumont in *White Zombie*, Roland Adams in *Nation Aflame*, and Dr. Stander in *Torture Ship*. Perhaps the best example is the spiritualist and fakir, Paul Bavian, in *Supernatural*. He attempts to fool the young and wealthy Roma into giving him money and affection through his alleged ability to contact her dead brother; however, the disembodied spirit of Paul's old flame, murderess Ruth Rogen, is able to enter Roma's body and cause Paul's death. Again, how aware Victor the man was of qualities like irony in his work—let alone how responsible he was for their origins—is unknown; structuralism would allow us to simply recognize them as part of the qualities that are the work of the "Victor Halperin."

However, limitations still exist for us in examining Victor's work. We need to penetrate his work beyond pinpointing emergent motifs. In many ways, these limitations are founded on an inherent problem in the use structuralism for understanding film: ahistoricalness. Structuralism allows the luxury of forgetting history and the importance of it to the creation of a cinematic text. Yet that luxury limits the depth of such studies, becoming in fact a major liability. As a result, much of film theory shifted to historical materialism in the 1970s and 1980s to better investigate questions of authorship.

Theorist John Ellis became a key figure in the historical materialist movement through his important study on the comedy films produced by England's Ealing Studios in the late 1940s and early 1950s. His work is interested in three determinants that produce a filmic text: 1) the technology of the cinema, both as it exists at the moment of the production's creation and the history of cinema prior to it (inclusive not only of production, but also distribution and exhibition); 2) the production's organization from start to finish (including the control of various persons over the stages of production, distribution, and exhibition); and 3) the beliefs, aesthetic or otherwise, of those persons controlling the production.[221]

Ellis ties these three determinants into a rather complex dialectical relationship of agency and structure, in which all filmmakers have to make choices regarding their films based on technology, economics, and ideology. The results of certain decisions create a situation by which subsequent decisions are made. Using the Ellis model, we can further investigate Victor Halperin's body of films and the era and manner in which they were produced.

In his review of the Andrew Sarris text, Clive Denton proclaimed that "[i]t was Hollywood's peculiar revenge on an independent-minded aristocrat to confine [Victor Halperin], mostly, to the dungeon's of low-budget mayhem." An interesting observation, but one that should be mediated with historical realities, including the fact that the entity of Hollywood or its film industry did not consciously and intentionally force Halperin into the low-budget world of B-movies. Indeed, it seems as if Victor enjoyed certain aspects of independent filmmaking.

True, Victor was tied to investors and the rigors of rapid shooting schedules, perhaps more so than many studio directors. However, it was his independence that allowed him to combat the *Zeitgeist* of typical Hollywood narratives and conventions. Though he clearly did not produce a body of work equal in artistic merit to that of an Ingmar Bergman or Carl Dreyer, Victor did share some aspects of their freedom. He was generally in control of what stories he chose to make into films and the manner in which to make them; these were freedoms not always accorded studio-based Hollywood directors. Yet, economic concerns were always present in preproduction, production, and postproduction phases of a given Victor Halperin film.

More questions then arise. Would a story choice Victor liked be salable to distributors and moviegoers in the U.S. during the 1920s or 1930s? Could he rent or build the sets required to convey the story in the way he wished? Would he be granted the luxury of time to create more intricate kinds of shots, such as those employing mobile cameras? How much input did others have on his work? Did he view the cinema as a forum for his ideological views? These are just a few of the questions that Ellis' model allows us to invoke. Unfortunately, the lack of thorough production information and firsthand accounts alone prohibit us developing a deep enough investigation of Victor Halperin's work to adequately answer those questions. We can use his films as a guide, though, as well as their relationship to other films of the same time period.

When film theorists Bordwell, Staiger, and Thompson examined studio-produced Hollywood films from 1917 to 1960 in their text *The Classical Hollywood Cinema*, they determined the main features of those works to be narrative unity, realism, and invisible narration.[222] Their explanation for the emergence of what they called the "classical style" centered on economics, ideology, and technology. In particular, Bordwell et al. cite stylistic factors as being of key importance in establishing the specificity of narrative; they suggest "[a] mode of film practice then consists of a set of widely held stylistic norms sustained by and sustaining an integral mode of film production."[223] Considering their views in tandem with those of Ellis allows us to expand further upon Victor's work and particularly its similarities and differences to the work of other U.S. filmmakers of his era.

Victor's movies, in his words, feature stories of "topical awareness."[224] His brother Edward once elaborated on this idea by suggesting: "We have always tried to be unique. In lining up our stories, we strive to obtain material that differs from the run-of-the-mill offerings of Hollywood studios."[225] The progression of Halperin film narratives generally shows greater and greater conscious striving towards originality, whether offering the first zombie story ever told in a feature-length film in *White Zombie* or crossing elements of the horror and gangster genres in *Torture Ship*.

Even during his formative period as a film director, Victor chose topically aware narratives like *When a Girl Loves*, a tale of unrequited passion; the film features an outlandish and completely unexpected conclusion in which a man is brought back to life. When economic factors would dictate a story choice like *Revolt of the Zombies*, Victor attempted a completely new slant on the horror tale of zombies, rather than draw more closely on the groundwork established by *White Zombie*. Original and unique, almost all of Victor's films were, as one advertising tag line for *White Zombie* claimed, "unusual pictures for unusual times."

Some of Victor's "unusual pictures" began with written forewords, text that helped frame their given stories. Chapter Four addressed the impact that movie publicity, theater ballyhoo, and critical reviews can have on the spectator's mindset about a particular film before the projector ever begins; in the same way, forewords to films can also sculpt audience opinion about an overall film narrative in the film's first few moments of flickering on a screen. Victor used forewords as a motif, but they were certainly used at times in many other Hollywood films, including some produced at major studios.

In *Revolt of the Zombies*, the opening printed words on the screen attempt to give information and create a mood for the film's setting, the Lost City of Angkor. Three quotations begin *Supernatural*, all of which speak to the idea of life after death; one from Confucius, one from Mohammed, and one from the Holy Bible. The choice of sources implicitly suggests the film's tolerance of all religions and viewpoints, as well as the belief that the dead know no bounds, whether geographical or ide-

ological. The very words themselves bolt onto the screen in a font similar in style to lightning, reinforcing their meanings with a large degree of vigor.

The three Biblical quotations which open *I Conquer the Sea* invoke not only the story of Jonah and the whale, but they also foreshadow character Tommy's arrogance in his whaling abilities and the problems he suffers as a result. Lastly, given that all of the opening quotations draw on a Christian religious tradition, they offer insight into a major bulwark of the character's lives: the importance of the church. Thus, the opening foreword allows Victor to frame audience impressions of his story before the film's on-screen action begins.

Narratives in his films, whether or not they begin with a foreword, often show traces of a kind of melodramatic sentimentality which Victor loved in the early silent films he saw, as well as the 19th century Anglo-Saxon literature and stage plays with which he was familiar. Anchoring many of his stories with such sentimentality causes some to appear more dated than they actually are. Conclusions of films like *Danger Point*, *In Borrowed Plumes*, *Greater Than Marriage*, and even the reunion of Madeline and Neil in *White Zombie* possess a simplistic and at times naive quality. Even reviewers of Halperin's era criticized this quality of his work.[226]

At the same time, Victor was seemingly not averse to enunciating sexualized moments in his films to appease whatever some audiences of the period may have desired; whether these scenes resulted from his initiative or someone else's and whether Victor included them more for artistic or economic reasons is unknown. Regardless, a number of his films were peppered with such moments.

Party Girl is the best example of an extended use of sexual suggestiveness, as scantily clad women are seen in numerous provocative situations. Other films bear the same use of exploitation, even if in more brief manifestations. Madeline is shown in her undergarments preparing for her wedding in *White Zombie*. Similarly, the spiritualist Bavian places his hand on Roma's breast in *Supernatural*. While these examples are not *non sequiturs* in relation to their plots, they hardly advance the plots or even need to occur narratively; instead, some of Victor's films provide almost unnecessary moments of rather overt sexuality and sexualized images of females. Apparently these devices are an attempt to please or titillate the audience, and thus represent a striving towards economic success; whether they were Victor's idea or not is unknown.

The character Roma in *Supernatural*, along with being one of those sexualized women, also provides insight into Victor's work ethic. Actress Carole Lombard played the role, and it seems that Victor's suggestions to her were limited and that those he did make she did not consider taking.[227] The few occasions on which actors have discussed his methods indicate that he was not an actor's director, that he gave only minimal advice on character portrayals. Victor's conscious concerns seem to have been more with choice and execution of narrative, cinematic technique, and—at least at times—the pictorial imagery and design of his film's *mise en scène*.

The result of Victor's lack of intensive interaction with actors has wrongly led at times to a marginalization of his directorial talent. Often these critiques draw on actor Clarence Muse's comments that Bela Lugosi directed *White Zombie*, a suggestion which is strongly argued against in Chapter Three. To devalue Victor as a film director just because of his level of interaction with actors, would clearly be unfair. For example, we do know that Victor was very interested in blocking out scenes to the degree of placing actors where he wanted them in given shots.[228] Furthermore, famed directors like John Huston and Alfred Hitchcock also concentrated less on advice to actors during film shoots than on other cinematic concerns.

While of course Victor's films are clearly not in an artistic class with Hitchcock's, the comparison yields another insight into his work ethic: like Hitchcock, he drew on the same coworkers repeatedly, apparently trusting in their own talents. As this chapter's biography of Victor has already noted, he often directed the same actors (e.g., Marjorie Daw, Dagmar Godowsky, Wheeler Oakman) repeatedly; others like Madge Bellamy and Bela Lugosi we know he desired to work with a second time, even if repeated collaborations with them did not occur. Presumably, the repetition of on-screen talent further allowed Victor to trust in his actors and their ability to craft suitable characterizations.

That attitude may have worked against him at times, of course. Victor's choice of certain on-screen talent for his early talkies—made often as a result of budget limitations which determined whom he could afford to hire—still incites the negative criticism that talking films like *White Zombie* feature elements of silent film acting styles. This flaw, combined with Victor's aforementioned affinity for sentimentality, hinders his films and makes them appear more dated than the work of some of his contemporaries.

The desire to work repeatedly with the same colleagues also extended to those working behind the scenes. For example, Victor often hired Abe Meyer for help with film music. At Victor's request, Arthur Martinelli photographed a great number of his films. Last, but certainly not least, Victor worked closely, through the majority of his career, with his brother Edward. Each drew on the other's strengths in striving for the ultimate goal of continuous independent film production.

Relying on the same talent may have helped create Victor's characteristic cinematic style, but it was—for better or worse, aesthetically—a style generally sustained in films made without those regular coworkers. We have already discussed the confusion which Arthur Martinelli's cinematography caused for one film historian examining *White Zombie*. At this point, we can look at the whole of Victor's work and the degree to which Martinelli did contribute. For example, Arthur Martinelli did not photograph *Party Girl*, *Torture Ship*, or *Buried Alive*, but all three films bear marked similarities to Victor's films which he did shoot. Furthermore, Martinelli was presumably not responsible for both repetitive narrative motifs in Victor's work that we have already addressed, nor was he presumably responsible for various aspects of Victor's cinematic technique.

That cinematic technique—the Victor Halperin film style—is one in which the artifices of cinema are often apparent, artifices which draw attention to the narration rather than always sustaining the "invisible narration" of which Bordwell et al. speak. We know we are watching a film, as his films themselves regularly remind us. For example, some of Victor's films consciously strive for audience involvement. The most developed attempt comes in *White Zombie*, in which the viewers become the *spectator-as-character* described in Chapter One. But several of Victor's other films feature brief breakdowns of that barrier between cinematic text and audience, even if the spectator is not invited to become an extended character. In *Supernatural*, character Ruth Rogen's eyes (and Roma's while she is possessed by Rogen) stare directly into the camera, directly at the audience; actor Bela Lugosi's eyes are used in *Revolt of the Zombies* for a similar purpose. In *Nation Aflame*, character Roland Adams even speaks directly into the camera at one point, suggesting to the audience members, "you can join" the Avenging Angels organization.

Rather than allowing the audience to be lost within a seamless kind of cinematic storytelling, Victor's films employ other techniques that call attention to filmic experience. Montages became one way for his films to convey sections of their stories economically, artistically cutting a series of shots together with superimpositions and artistic wipes. Like the use of printed forewords at the beginnings of Victor's films, montages were widely in use among Hollywood filmmakers; however, we can suggest that Victor was particularly adept at their usage. He was far more creative and audacious in constructing montages than many of his contemporaries in the U.S. film industry.

Examples of montages occur in all of the major sound films that Victor directed: *White Zombie* (Neil and Bruner's trip to Legendre's castle), *Supernatural* (Rogen's murders and imprisonment), *Torture Ship* (lawbreakers committing crimes and running from the authorities), *Revolt of the Zombies* (Louque's growing control of hundreds of zombies), *Nation Aflame* (the Avenging Angels' increasing membership rolls and rise to power), and *I Conquer the Sea* (Tommy's dying visions of Rosita and himself).

Though they rarely comment on his use of the montage, some historians and critics have complained that Halperin's cinematic style is irrevocably tied to the silent film era, that he couldn't forge ahead into more modern, talking picture styles. While true in some ways (like many B-movies, some of his films do feature very static-ridden moments with background music and little dialogue), at times his work was more advanced than that of many of his contemporaries. Victor's use of music and sound effects is one way in which his talkies are sometimes particularly sophisticated. Though *White Zombie* features little dialogue, it uses music to extreme advantage and in far greater quantities than other U.S. horror films of the era. One of Halperin's few recorded comments on filmmaking indicates his belief: "[m]otion picture entertainment must be a heartfelt collaboration between actors and musicians."[229]

Even more innovative is his films' use of sound effects. The sugar mill sequence of *White Zombie* is certainly one of the most sophisticated marriages of image and sound filmed in Hollywood's early talkie era. The lack of dialogue may have its roots in Victor's silent film experience, but the sounds—the grinding of that millstone, for instance—synthesized with images of the sugar mill remain powerful and inventive, and represent a step forward into talkies, not a step backwards into silents. Much the same occurs in *Buried Alive*, in which the sound of electricity heightens the tension and action prior to electrocutions.

The whole of Victor's work suggests even more specific uses of cinematic techniques that, in the aggregate, form a particularized style. Closeups of characters often cut directly to similarly composed closeups of other characters. Rather than creating a "jump," the result yields narrative insight into the relationships between the characters in question. For example, the growing closeness of the relationship between Bavian and Roma in *Supernatural* is twice suggested by such cuts.

Shifting relationships in *I Conquer the Sea* are conveyed repeatedly through closeup-to-closeup cuts: the closeness of Tommy and Rosita, the closeness of Tommy and his father, and the closeness of Tommy and his brother. As the latter relationship grows more strained, it is depicted by cuts of more oppositional composition (e.g., one brother shown in closeup cut to the other brother in a medium shot).

Many closeup-to-closeup cuts also occur in *Revolt of the Zombies* when the zombies reawaken, all sharing the same sense of anger at Louque. Closeups occur repeatedly in *Nation Aflame* when Sandino thinks of starting the Avenging Angels; the closeups show all those with whom he is in league. Much the same occurs between shots of the criminals dining aboard the vessel in *Torture Ship* when they hear that they will have a "fifty-fifty" chance of survival following the doctor's experiments.

To conclude the present discussion of Victor's films, we should acknowledge the unique aspects of his work, whether or not those aspects were of his conscious making and whether or not they were heavily impacted by other persons, finances, or technology. Of his films, we can say that sometimes obsolescent acting styles are tethered to a visual tableaux that builds on—among other devices—relational closeups, montage, sound effects, and mobile camerawork. Audience involvement occasionally occurs through the spectator-as-character, particularly in *White Zombie*.

The cinematic playground for all of these qualities is a string of unique stories. These elements all represent ways in which Victor's films—for whatever reasons of economics, technology, and control (aesthetic or otherwise)—seem to differ from the predominant filmmaking norms of the period. Yet at the same time—also for reasons of economics, technology, and control—the bulk of his films' content is representative of the classical Hollywood style.

By again considering Clive Denton's column "On Film," we can see an important point that helps pinpoint the allure of Victor Halperin's body of work. "...each film," Denton suggests, "is a minor epic of grandeur, at least in fiery conception and sustained hot-house atmosphere."[230] Victor Hugo Halperin was not a great filmmaker, and his body of work on the whole is not what we might call great. Yet Clive Denton knew years ago what we might now repeat: Victor was innovative to a degree, but still enough of a conformist for audiences of the period to understand and at times appreciate his work. He remains a unique figure, a standout among independent filmmakers of his time, and the figurehead of a fascinating group of films.

As Denton's column said of Victor Halperin, "Equations like soldiers as zombies would never be popular in usually conformist Hollywood. So its hardly surprising that V.H.H. never got to direct Garbo. But we don't need to forget him, do we? Who's for a screening of *Supernatural* or *Torture Ship*?"[231]

Reviews of *The Magic Island*

The following represent relevant excerpts from New York newspaper and national media critiques of William B. Seabrook's book *The Magic Island* (Harcourt, Brace, and Co., 1929). The choice of excerpts, however subjective, results from the criterion of the periodical's reputation, and—in some cases—the review's mention of topics (like voodooism) which would become relevant to *White Zombie*.

Bela Lugosi as Murder Legendre in White Zombie, *a film heavily influenced by William B. Seabrook's* The Magic Island.

Critiques in New York Newspapers

P. Montague in the "Books" section of the January 6, 1929, *New York Herald Tribune*: "Here in its own field is the book of the year."

R. L. Duffus in the January 6, 1929, *New York Times*: "It can be said of many travelers that they have traveled widely. Of Mr. Seabrook, a much finer thing may be said—he has traveled deeply. It is apparent that he has penetrated as few white men have done, perhaps as no white man has done in so short a time, to the soul of Haiti."

F. Van de Water in the January 12, 1929, *New York Evening Post*: "*The Magic Island* seems to us the best and most thrilling book of exploration that we have ever read. Mr. Seabrook has investigated Voodooism, not with the rigid superiority of the average white man delving into native lore, but humbly, respectfully, as an initiate himself.... He has done a successful, vivid, and, we believe, an immensely important book."

Notices in the National Media

Robert Redfield in the March 29, 1929, *Booklist*: "Mr. Seabrook's book is a series of excellent stories, about one of the most interesting corners of the American world, told by a keen and sensitive person who knows how to write."

Lyle Saxon in the February 1929 *Bookman*: "It is not a twice told tale, but a vivid record of things seen; it is no ladylike book, but a man's story written for adult minds."

Herschel Brickell in the February 1929 *North American Review*: "A fascinating first-hand study, made by a traveler of wide experience.... By all odds one of the most interesting books of recent months."

The March 2, 1929, *New Statesman*: "Although Mr. Seabrook has seen a great deal more than the average white man sees in the island, he has become so excited about it all that he cannot hope to be taken as an altogether credible witness. In the chapters on Voodoo, particularly, he mixes quite valuable material with a lot of hearsay, legend, and speculation, which are merely sensational."

"Speaking of Books" in the *Outlook and Independent* of January 9, 1929: "In *The Magic Island*, a courageous, imaginative and skillfull [*sic*] man has investigated the soul of Haiti, [and] reports upon it, brilliantly. The same success which attended the Seabrook book on Arabia should fall to *The Magic Island*. It is a prize among books."

Zombie Program Information

The following photographs are from the Biltmore Theatre program for *Zombie*, published by the New York Theatre Program Corporation in February 1932.

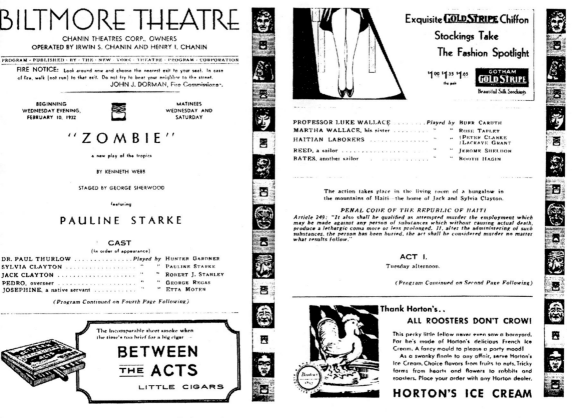

Left to right: *Key pages of the Biltmore Program.*

ACT II.
Friday evening.

ACT III.
A few minutes later.

Setting designed and painted by Anthony W. Street. Constructed by Charles Auburn. Miss Starke's gowns by Jay Thorpe, Inc. Antiques by Julia E. Kuttner. Artificial flowers by Filippelli General Flower Decorating Co. Electrical equipment and lighting effects by Century Lighting Equipment Co.

EXECUTIVE STAFF

Lawrence Wood	Business Manager
Allan C. Dalrell	Press Representative
Booth Hagin	Stage Manager

STAFF FOR BILTMORE THEATRE

Business Manager	William A. Connor
Treasurer	William Ridgway
Chief of Staff	Geoffrey Davis
Master Mechanic	John Shearing
Master of Properties	Max Landsman
Master Electrician	Joseph Saltman

This Theatre Designed by Herbert J. Krapp

Left to right: *Key pages of the Biltmore Program.*

Reviews of *Zombie*

The following represent relevant excerpts from reviews of Kenneth Webb's 1932 play *Zombie*, including from New York City-area newspapers, national publications, industry trades, and Chicago newspapers. The criteria for chosen excerpts were: overall evaluations of *Zombie*, contextualization of *Zombi* [*Zombie*] as a horror story, and specific comments on zombie characters.

Critiques in the New York Newspapers

J. Brooks Atkinson in "The Play: Raising the Dead" in the February 11, 1932, *New York Times*: "It is a bully idea for the cold sweat school of drama. Part of the hilarity that greeted it last evening was probably inverted nervousness. Although Kenneth Webb has not turned the zombie's swan song into a work of art, the walking dead are not to be despised in the drama. When the zombies moved silently and rigidly against a darkened stage last evening, this department paid strict attention to business.... As a matter of practical fact, Mr. Webb's play is pretty loosely knocked together."

"Voodoo Cult: Zombie Shows How the Dead Walk in Haiti" in the *Brooklyn Eagle* of February 11, 1932: "Search for another *Dracula* goes merrily on.... There is every opportunity for strong drama. Many of the scenes are good, but many others are not. Altogether the theme is one worthy of better treatment than it has received, but it is good entertainment nevertheless."

John Mason Brown in the *New York Evening Post* of February 11, 1932: "From the beginning to end, Mr. Webb shows no real skill making use of his materials. Often his dialogue is so stereotyped and feeble that it invites titters in the wrong places. And in general his touch is maladroit. But even Mr. Webb, as aided and abetted by his distressingly negative actors and his uncertain gifts as dramatist, cannot quite succeed in smothering the thrills which belong to his material, or in completely obscuring its Black Magic.... The pity is that *Zombie* is in most respects so many leagues from what it might have been. But I suppose what really matters is not its obvious shortcomings but the fact that even in its present inexpert condition, it provides those who are not too squeamish with a more than sufficient number of thrills. As hokum pure and simple—sometimes very simple—*Zombie* unquestionably has its moments. Believe me they are shuddery moments too."

Gilbert Gabriel in "Dead Pans: *Zombie*, in Which the Corpses Come Alive All Around the Hinterland of Haiti" in the *New York American* of February 11, 1932: "As soon as you finished William Seabrook's *The Magic Island*, I'll bet my bottom shilling-shocker, and had read all about the 'zombies,' those strange and empty-eyed cadavers hauled out of fresh graves to slave as silent workers in the fields, you swore you'd sit down and write a play forthwith about the Haitians, there Voodoos, and there Zombies [*sic*]. I wish you had. You'd probably have written a more imaginative and effective one that [*sic*] Kenneth Webb has.... Mr. Webb used to do musical shows. They were smart and cheery musical shows and I am sorry he ever stopped.... For Mr. Webb has made a domestic squabble out of one of the most horror-drenched and memorable legends in the history of the world's wilds. He has reduced a magnificently picturesque superstition to almost kittenish plot and patient platitudes. A grand idea for a mystery is sunk in squeaks and chuckles."

Arthur Ruhl in "*Zombie*: Melodrama by Kenneth Webb Presented at the Biltmore" in the *New York Herald Tribune* of February 10, 1932: "Hayti, that 'doux petit pays,' has had to endure a lot from foreign writings, of which Kenneth Webb's *Zombie* ... is one of the worst.... Mr. Webb's piece had got so lurid ... the audience wasn't quite sure whether or not it was intended to be taken in the light spirit which conventionally greets the mystery thriller. A good many decided that it was so intended and laughed accordingly."

William Boehnel in the *New York World-Telegram* **of February 11, 1932:** "…by the end of the play there have been more reasons for laughs than spinal chills. And this in spite of the fact that the zombies are always coming. Surely the prospect of an approaching army of Frankensteins, Draculas, and Whoopoos, under the spell of an enraged Pedro, should chill the hearts of even a first night audience. But last night's premiere hounds walked from the Biltmore on their own power, smiles on their faces, zombieology flippantly on their lips. This state of lightheartedness would have been praiseworthy had author, director-producer, actors, and stagehands realized that *Zombie* has the makings of a devastating comedy."

Notices in the National Media

Time **of February 22, 1932:** "Mr. William Seabrook's romantic fibs about far-off places do no one any harm, have certainly not harmed *Zombie*, whose playwright seems to have read Author Seabrook's *The Magic Island*…. For the most part wretchedly overacted … and beset with deplorably written dialog, *Zombie* has at least four authentic shudders for your spine, to wit: 1) When the shrouded grave-folk first appear, 2) When one of them is released from half-life to total death by spell and incantation, 3) When Actress Starke discovers that her husband has become a zombie, 4) When the zombies grope their way toward their master, who is in peril."

John Carb in *Vogue* **of April 15, 1932:** "On a board outside the Biltmore Theatre, one may now read: '*Zombie*, A Drama of Startling Revelations.' The locale of the play inside is Haiti, where, it seems, soulless bodies can be raised from the grave and made to labour. In them, Kenneth Webb has found a startling—and provocative—basis for a drama, but his dramaturgy is not equal to the task of exploiting it. *Zombie* skims the surface, more often a sketch than a portrait."

Reviews in the Industry Trades

Eugene Burr in the February 20, 1932, issue of *The Billboard*: "To paraphrase the grand lead that Jack Chapman used in his review of *Heat Wave* last spring, Kenneth Webb's *Zombie* has its plot laid in Haiti, down where natives beat the tom-tom and dramatic critics beat their breasts. Mr. Webb, starting with an idea of ghoulish horror, or grim and freezing intensity, builds around it a play

that is hackneyed, trite, and feeble; a play which manages to turn all of its chances for blood-curdling terror into heeby-jeebies of the *House of Doom* school. *Zombie*, in other words, is a grand idea gone woefully to waste.

Variety **of February 16, 1932:** "Boo! and plenty of it in this mystery play, or rather thriller, of the tropics. *Zombie* at times will put the chill on the spines even of first nighters. That's something…. *Zombie* is creepy enough, but it's no [commercial success]—unless the cut rates underwrite it."

Reviews in the Chicago Newspapers

Charles Collins in the *Chicago Tribune* **of March 14, 1932:** "*Zombie*, which came to the Adelphi Theatre last night, is a voodoo play—so prepare for a few agreeable shudders…. The play passes through a slow, plodding phase in its first act, as it laboriously instructs its audience in the zombie cult, telling how Negroes who have died and are buried are often found, in this weird land of Haiti, toiling in the fields like human cattle—corpses that move and walk and drudge. But then its thrills begin to function, with a certain degree of effectiveness. The zombie business gets hot and the audience becomes pleasantly bothered. The play, in spite of its cast of second rate actors, clicks in a stirring manner when the zombies begin to drift across the stage in their mortuary manner…."

An advertisement heralding the opening of Zombie *at Chicago's Tivoli Theatre. Published in the* Chicago Tribune *on March 13, 1932.*

• *Appendix D* •

White Zombie Cast and Credits

Cast: Bela Lugosi (Murder Legendre), Madge Bellamy (Madeline Short), Joseph Cawthorn (Dr. Bruner), John Harron (Neil Harron), Robert Frazer (Charles Beaumont), Clarence Muse (Driver), Brandon Hurst (Silver), Dan Crimmins (Pierre), Frederick Peters (Chauvin), George Burr McAnnan (Von Gelder), John T. Prince (Latour), Claude Morgan (Zombie), John Fergusson (Zombie), Velma Gresham (Maid), Annette Stone (Maid).

Credits: Edward Halperin (Producer), Victor Halperin (Director), William Cody (Assistant Director), Garnett Weston (Story and Dialogue), Arthur Martinelli (Director of Photography), Harold McLernon (Editor), Abe Meyer (Music Director), Carco (RCA Photophone Noiseless Recording), Ralph Berger (Art Director), Jack Pierce and Carl Axcelle (Make-up), Herbert Glazer (Second Assistant Director), Herbert Farjeon (Dialogue Director), Conrad Tritschler (Art Effects), Howard Anderson (Special Effects), L.E. ["Pete"] Clark (Sound Engineer), Enzo Martinelli (Assistant Cameraman), Charles Bohny (Assistant Cameraman), J. Arthur Feindel (Operative Cameraman), Guy Bevier Williams (Original Music), Xavier Cugat (Original Music), R. Nathaniel Dett (Additional Music), Gaston Borch (Additional Music), Hugo Riesenfeld (Additional Music), Leo Kempenski (Additional Music), Hen Herkan (Additional Music), H. Maurice Jaquet (Additional Music).

Halperin Productions, distributed by United Artists. Released on July 28, 1932. Copyrighted on August 1, 1932 as LP3357 at eight reels (73 minutes).

Left to right: Bela Lugosi, Brandon Hurst, and Frederick Peters in White Zombie.

White Zombie Pressbook Information

White Zombie's 1932 pressbook—officially titled *Complete Exhibitors Campaign Book*—was designed by the New York City Department of Advertising and Publicity of the United Artists Corporation. Its length—18 folded, front and back pages—included numerous articles, ads, and suggestions for theater managers to succeed in promoting *White Zombie*. In addition, it acted as a catalogue for the purchase of posters, handbills, and other advertising materials. To preserve the pressbook's contents and present them to readers of the present study, major clippings from the document are reproduced under three convenient categories.

Articles

From the 1932 pressbook.

Ballyhoo Suggestions

Street Ballyhoo

Make Theatre Display of Enlargement of Penal Code

Pin Point Novelty

The most dramatic sequence in the picture is where Bela Lugosi ensnares his victims by means of a powerful drug which requires "Only the top of a pin-point" to make it effective on the victim.

A clever novelty has been devised. A card carrying a pin with its point dipped in red, and reading—"Just a pin-point, and she became a WHITE ZOMBIE."

On the reverse side of the card you explain how this powerful drug, administered by a fiend, transformed a woman into one of the Living Dead and, of course, your theatre imprint and playdate is also on the reverse side.

These cards are priced at:

500—$4.00	3,000—$5.50 per M
1,000— 6.00	5,000— 5.00 per M

Order them direct from Economy Novelty and Printing Company, 239 West 39th Street, New York City.

From the 1932 pressbook.

PUBLICITY SECTION "WHITE ZOMBIE"

Taxi Tie-up

Arrange with the largest cab company in your city for a parade of cabs to the front of your theatre. These cabs all to bear signs stating, "Yellow Cabs will see you safely home from WHITE ZOMBIE if you're afraid to go home alone."

Plan to have them park these cabs right in front of your theatre, hinting that the weird sequences of WHITE ZOMBIE will scare so many people that rather than go through the streets of the city alone, they prefer to ride home safely in the cabs of the company with which you tie-up.

TELL THEM WITH TRAILERS

To permit you to take full advantage of the advertising possibilities of your screen, a punchy trailer, complete with interest-arousing scenes and strong sales copy, has been prepared for your use.

Trailers enable you to reach the people who make up the backbone of your audience and afford you an opportunity of striking home the salient points of "White Zombie" in terms of entertainment.

National Screen Service has prepared a trailer which not only gets its message home in very brief time, but also, through its mounting and artistic finish, conveys to the patron the production values that are to be found in "White Zombie."

Write for special contract arrangement

NATIONAL SCREEN SERVICE, Inc.

126 West 46th St., N. Y. C.   810 So. Wabash Ave., Chicago, Ill.

1922 So. Vt. Ave., Los Angeles, Calif.

300½ So. Harwood Ave., Dallas, Tex.

THEATRE BALLYHOOS

Herewith are shown various exploitation ideas that directly apply to the operation of your theatre. These are not suggestions but actual stunts that have been worked successfully and greatly benefited the theatres' receipts. If you can't use them all, select the ones that will create the most attention value for your theatre and put them over in strong circus fashion.

Negro Tom Toms

Hire several negroes to sit in front of your theatre and beat a steady tattoo on tom-toms.

Magician Props

Arrange a display of magician props in your lobby.

Sound Effect Records Will Draw the Crowds

A regular ten-inch Victor Record has been made which reproduces the exciting sounds heard in WHITE ZOMBIE.

Shadow Box

Vulture on Marquee

From the 1932 pressbook.

Items Available for Order

Cut-out Head of 24-Sheet Creates SMASH MARQUEE DISPLAY

The head and eyes of Bela Lugosi are weirdly portrayed as a center illustration on your pictorial 24-sheet.

There is a mysterious, almost hypnotic glint to the hateful eyes. Cut this head out of your 24-sheet, mount it on compo board and cut out the eyes putting a green filter near them with a flasher light behind so that these green eyes will go on and off in ominous fashion.

Also several theatres have built a bread-mill affixed to their marquee, whereby a procession of ZOMBIES made of wax figures, move along in steady plodding fashion following the girl in her white flowing robes. To add to the realistic appearance, an electric fan should be placed behind the girl so that the white gauzy dress should blow in the breeze.

As a sound effect, a vulture should be mounted on the marquee and the sound effects of hideous shrieks can be broadcast from a record which reproduces the cries of the vulture as actually heard in the film. (See page 6.) The greenish glare of a spotlight should be thrown over this display at night so as to give it a mysterious appearance.

Put three or four of these cut-out heads on the front of your marquee. For example, you can put one on each end so as to be visible on either approach to the theatre. Have these cut-out heads made up long in advance and placed in strategic spots in your theatre such as on loccinos and exits facing people as they come out of the theatre. That will start them talking about "White Zombie."

Haunting Eyes Make Thrilling Display

The one-sheet on WHITE ZOMBIE has as a background several pairs of glaring, mysterious eyes. Cut these eyes out of the one-sheet and display them all over your lobby. Wherever anyone looks, there will be a pair of eyes staring out at them; brooding eyes that lend a mysterious tinge to your lobby.

Some of the eyes should be mounted in front of a green light so that they will be visible against a black background.

Window Display of Thriller Books

Arrange with your book dealer for a display of all books on the thriller angle, such as Dracula, Frankenstein and The Gold Bug. Also books involving Haiti, such as Black Majesty, Black Magic, etc. Provide the dealer with stills mounted on compo board, mentioning the name of your theatre and playdate.

In addition, have the book dealer advertise these books during the week of the showing of the picture at your theatre and to reciprocate you could provide for a display of this type of books in the lobby of your theatre.

Famous Eyes Contest

Arrange with your newspaper for them to run a "Famous Eyes Contest." Here's sample wording for the opening day announcement.

"The Daily ...., in connection with the showing of White Zombie at the .... Theatre, opening next ...., begins today the publication of cut-out photographs showing the eyes of twelve world famous personalities whose pictures are before you almost daily and whose eyes are easily recognized. Eyes play an important role in "White Zombie." See if you can recognize these personalities by their eyes. The contest starts today with the following prizes. . . ."

Then each day the newspaper will publish eyes belonging to Lindbergh, Hoover, Eddie Cantor, Mussolini, etc. Descriptive matter to go with the twelve pair of eyes can be obtained by writing to the Exploitation Department, United Artists Corp., 729 Seventh Avenue, N. Y.

"WHITE ZOMBIE" Order Blank

(Their Prices Prevail for United States Only)	Price	How Many	Amount
POSTERS (Lithographed)			
One Sheet	$0.15		
Three Sheet	.45		
Six Sheet	.90		
Twenty-four Sheet	2.40		
WINDOW CARD (Lithographed)	.07		
BLACK AND WHITE SQUEEGEE PHOTOS, 8 x 10			
All purpose (30 in set, including newspaper, lobby star heads)	3.00		
Special First Run Stills (20 in set)	2.00		
Single Copies, each	.10		
LOBBY DISPLAY CARDS:			
Hand colored, 22 x 28, each	.40		
Hand colored, 11 x 14, set of eight	.75		
INSERT CARD, Hand Colored, 14 x 36, each	.25		
SLIDES, COLORED	.15		
HERALDS, per 1,000	3.50		
	Mat	Cut	
1—Two Col. Star Scene Head	.10	.50	
2—One Col. Star Scene Head	.05	.30	
3—Two Col. Scene	.10	.50	
4—One Col. Scene Head (Lugosi)	.05	.30	
5—One Col. (Boy and Girl)	.05	.30	
6—One Col. Scene (Two Men)	.05	.30	
7—Four Col. Ad	.30	1.50	
8—Three Col. Ad	.20	.75	
9—Three Col. Ad	.20	.75	
10—Two Col. Ad	.10	.50	
11—Two Col. Ad	.10	.50	
12—Two Col. Ad	.10	.50	
13—One Col. Ad	.05	.30	
14—One Col. Ad	.05	.30	
15—Two Col. Ad Slug	.10	.50	
16—One Col. Ad Slug	.05	.30	
17—Two Col. Ad	.10	.50	
Complete Set "WHITE ZOMBIE" Mats....$1.25			
Complete Set "WHITE ZOMBIE" Cuts...$8.10			
TOTAL			

Apply at your nearest United Artists Exchange for CUTS and MATS

From the 1932 pressbook.

Telegraph Pole Teaser

Put tack cards on telegraph poles along the main roads leading to your theatre.

These teaser cards should go at least a week in advance of the showing of WHITE ZOMBIE at your theatre and will tend to arouse the curiosity of people. Use this teaser copy:

"Beware or WHITE ZOMBIE will get you."

Your Slide

Tie Up With Department Stores on the White Zombie Angle

On the right is reproduced a three-column newspaper ad which recently appeared in the Los Angeles Times. The expression ZOMBIE has acquired a tremendous word of mouth usage due to the fact that WHITE ZOMBIE was being filmed on location in the vicinity of Los Angeles. Bullock's cleverly wove this ad about the fashion angle realizing that the strange word ZOMBIE in itself, was a sure-fire eye-catcher that would give the headline a dollar and cents value. Bullock's is one of the largest department stores in the west.

Work Similar Stunt With Local Merchants

Dealers in your city are anxious to get a new advertising slant that will lift their ads from the usual rut and make them pop right out of the page, attracting the reader's attention. There's no limit to the types of merchandise that can be tied in with the term ZOMBIE. Style goods can be handled similar to the Bullock ad. For example, a men's wear ad would read as follows:

"Do you dress like a ZOMBIE, or are you wearing the up-to-the-minute styles displayed in Fickey-Heeman Clothes?" Dealer advertisements will help make your city WHITE ZOMBIE conscious.

Free Serialization That Newspapers Will Grab

The story of WHITE ZOMBIE is an original written especially for the screen and based on the legend of the Living Dead of Haiti.

Here is a newspaper circulation builder if there ever was one. It makes all mystery stories look like tame affairs as compared to the thrilling exploits depicted in WHITE ZOMBIE.

This serialization is made up in six installments and contains 10,000 words. At the head of each chapter are old numbers taken from the regular sets of 20's and 30's, illustrating scenes from that portion of the story.

Get the best newspaper in town to run this serialization, starting at least a week in advance or your showing so that you will create an air of mystery about ZOMBIES and create interest on the part of the readers to see the film when it plays at your theatre.

You can obtain Free copies of this serialization at your nearest United Artists Exchange.

Throwaway That Will Attract Attention

The Penal Code of the Republic of Haiti, Article 249, plays an important part in the motivation of WHITE ZOMBIE.

On Page 3, you will see the actual wording of this article, which places the death penalty upon the crime of transforming a person into a ZOMBIE.

A teaser herald measuring 5 x 7 is available and bears this phrase on its cover—"Do you know where the body is buried?". Inside is a reproduction of Article 249, with a short resume of the theme of WHITE ZOMBIE. On the back cover, of course, is your theatre playdate and imprint.

They are priced:

500—$3.00	3,000—$4.50 per M
1,000— 5.00	5,000— 4.00 per M

Order direct from Economy Novelty and Printing Company, 239 West 39th Street, New York City.

Window Display of Thriller Books

Arrange with your book dealer for a display of all books on the thriller angle, such as Dracula, Frankenstein and The Gold Bug. Also books involving Haiti, such as Black Majesty, Black Magic, etc. Provide the dealer with stills mounted on compo board, mentioning the name of your theatre and playdate.

In addition, have the book dealer advertise these books during the week of the showing of the picture at your theatre and to reciprocate you could provide for a display of this type of books in the lobby of your theatre.

From the 1932 pressbook.

Additional *White Zombie* Ballyhoo

It is important to realize how key exploitation techniques were used in building *White Zombie*'s business the specific cities *White Zombie* played in 1932 as explored in Chapter Four. Though elaborate publicity schemes did not ensure strong business, most exhibitors realized that they certainly helped in the attempt. These extratextual aspects of the theatergoing experience must have shaped (or at least in a small way affected) the manner in which spectators viewed the film.

For example, manager Wally Caldwell of the Loew's Theater in Toledo concocted two major stunts, chronicled in the August 20, 1932, *Motion Picture Herald*. One was an artwork contest built around Bela Lugosi, which was tied in with a local newspaper. According to the same publication, "Hundreds of replies were received by the stunt editor for the paper and broke all time records." Caldwell's second major scheme was a "mysterious photographer" idea. A cameraman snapped shots of unknowing citizens, with the pictures then appearing in the town newspaper "with the offer of a guest ticket to [the] picture if they would call at the newspaper office."

Motion Picture Herald also listed the more standard aspects of Caldwell's campaign, which included: "the placarding of 26 parking lots, garages and parking zones with 'Park Here' half-sheets, the distribution of 5,000 9 × 12 heralds in selected residential neighborhoods, stuffing of 1,000 heralds in customer's packages at a large market, wrapping of 500 heralds in laundry bundles, the pinning of several hundred heralds to packages in dry cleaner's establishments, the posting of 15 special one-sheets in selected empty stores, posting of 200 heralds at prominent corners, and the usual comprehensive newspaper ad and story campaign."

The Loew's of Rochester, New York also garnered publicity by tie-ins with the local newspaper; the theater persuaded the *Democrat and Chronicle* to hold a contest in which readers submitted essays on the topic "My Most Horrifying Experience." The theater provided 50 tickets as prizes, with the best submissions appearing in print. In keeping with *White Zombie*'s serious tone, preference was given to the more "unusual" efforts, rather than the numerous comedic entries that arrived.

For theater managers of houses owned by Harry Arthur in New Haven, Hartford, Bridgeport, Springfield, and Worcester, United Artists ad chief Hal Horne outlined special, promotional plans. The September 6, 1932, *Variety* detailed these efforts, which included "zombies" again walking the streets. They wore no signs or advertisements, but merely attempted to draw crowds to the theater.

Variety also mentioned Horne's idea for a "perambulated coffin-like box placarded with the statement that the Zombie contained therein would be delivered to the theatre at a certain time." When that time came, a truck delivered the box to the theater and the lid removed by unscrewing bolts. The trade added, "The greater part of the time there was no one in the coffin, the impersonator taking his place shortly before the box was delivered. Unscrewing the lid not only added to the effect, but it gave time for a mob to collect, which was the payoff." When the lid was removed, the "zombie" popped out and lumbered into the theater, with crowds following right behind.

Elsewhere, it was actor Bela Lugosi's image which drew crowds. The *Motion Picture Herald* of September 24, 1932, described what viewers of Canton, Ohio experienced in the days prior to *White Zombie* hitting the local Loew's Theater: "For two weeks in advance [Manager A. H. Buehrig] used teaser trailers on the screen and paved the way for a unique lobby display of a head of Lugosi with flashing green eyes. The entire theater front was decorated especially for the occasion, featured by large white cutout letters of the title." He also put together six special window displays and played the sound record (prepared by United Artists and described in the pressbook) through an amplifier on the marquee.

When *White Zombie* arrived at the Loew's for its run, Buehrig planned multiple other gimmicks. For instance, during the film's run, he paid for an ambulance to sit at the curb by the theater's front entrance—its purpose: to assist with "those unable to stand the horror and thrills of the picture." As at some theaters before him, Buehrig had a "white zombie" in person roaming the sidewalk near the theater. Additionally, he printed and distributed "novelty pin throwaways" promoting the film, as well as giving out heralds from house to house. At least one local market even tucked heralds into customer's packages.

For a screening in Greenville, South Carolina, Edwin C. Hough illuminated a *White Zombie* theater front at the Rivoli with four flood lights borrowed from a local airport. Beaming at the Rivoli from across the street, the floods lit up the theater name in blue and the words "*White Zombie*" in white and green. Hough shrouded the top and sides of the theater in black cloth drapery. The finishing touch was a cutout of Bela Lugosi's head from the *White Zombie* 24-sheet.[1]

On October 4, 1932, *Variety* detailed yet another theater scheme, one used by manager Edgar Hart of Spokane's Orpheum Theater. Carrying a police permit, a "blonde girl" with no explanatory placard wandered the streets aimlessly. She attracted a tremendous amount of attention, with local newspapers printing the explanation for curious readers. Once again, a live show external not just to the filmic text but also to the theater building helped attract interest.

The exterior of a Cincinnati United Artists theater received such a great *White Zombie* makeover that its manager gave allegedly one look and told its designers, "My God, that thing will scare everybody away from the theater!" Along with the decor ballyhoo, one stunt included a casket, skeleton, and some electrical devices. A loudspeaker was placed in the coffin, with its wire taken through a hole in the floor and into the cellar. Designers also attached an "invisible" string to the skeleton's jaw. A young woman hidden in the cellar gave the boney publicity machine a voice by speaking into the loudspeaker's microphone and pulling the string to make its mouth move.

The skeleton itself wasn't a fake; it was on loan from a local doctor. The skull featured three bullet holes inflicted by a firing squad in World War I. A man planted by the theater told passersby of the skeleton's real-life execution. When a good-sized crowd had gathered, the woman in the cellar interrupted with the following whispered words (a slight variation on a suggested "catchline" in the pressbook): "Look around you, do your friends act queerly—strangely? They may be zombies—living, breathing, walking under the spell of the master of the living dead."

The speech ended with a scream and an announcement of the film. "Unusual Times demand unusual pictures," she concluded. "See this live, weird, strangest of all love stories."

The *Motion Picture Herald* of November 5, 1932, detailed perhaps the most bizarre of any free publicity garnered by a U.S. theater screening *White Zombie*. The Warners Theater of Pittsburgh landed front-page attention in city newspapers due to another use of a coffin. This time, however, the box in question bounced out of the back of a truck on Penn Avenue, near Point Breeze. The result brought police, who rushed it to station No. 6 in order to avoid the forming crowd. In it, they discovered a "corpse" that later moved; it was actually a man named Bill Sloan. After he informed the police that it was a press agent stunt for *White Zombie*, they quickly arrested him. As the *Herald* mentioned, "...even though this coffin gag has been described as gruesome exploitation by many in our unusual business, both public and newspapers appear to regard the stunt with interest, morbid or otherwise."

Only one other lengthy description of a U.S. ballyhoo for *White Zombie* appeared in the 1932 trade publications. Though not offering the name of the location itself, the November 22, 1932, *Variety* spoke of a successful, "talking ghost standing to one side of the box office" in a small, unnamed U.S. town. The theater made the ghost from a dress frame, with a skeleton mask added to give a face. A loud speaker fit inside the "body," which was covered by a light, shroud-like fabric. Wires for the speaker were run inside to the box office, where a young employee spoke through a mike to give the ghost a "voice." The trade article mentioned the ghost's robe gave the voice a hollow, eerie timbre. The ghost drew crowds, and it informed them about *White Zombie* and his own "lamentable condition."

Wherever that city was, it serves as a typical example of the ballyhoo efforts theater managers undertook. As discussed in Chapter Four, these exploitation devices not only prepared ticket holders for the kind of drama *White Zombie* constituted, but they also helped sculpt audience preconceptions of the film, becoming an important part of the moviegoing experience.

Reviews of *White Zombie*

Similar to the presentation of reviews in Appendix A and Appendix C, the following *White Zombie* reviews are divided into categories which reflect their audiences: New York City citizens during the time of the film's premiere, those in the film industry, those readers of film fan magazines, and those readers of mainstream, national publications. Chosen excerpts were made to reveal overall impressions of *White Zombie*, to illustrate how the film was contextualized in the emerging 1930s horror cycle, and to record comments on the direction and acting in the film.

Critical Response in New York City

William Boehnel in the July 29, 1932, *New York World-Telegram*: "*White Zombie* is such a potpourri of Zombies, frightened natives, witch doctors, leering villains, sinister shadows, painted sets, and banal conversation … that the actors of necessity just move along. There are, however, moments when they get a chance to act. But the less said about that the better." On August 2 in the same newspaper, Boehnel added: "There have been worse pictures shown in this town than *White Zombie* at the Rivoli. Yet at the moment I can think of few films so nicely compounded of tedium and banality in equal parts. The plot … is really ridiculous, but not more startlingly so than the acting."

Thornton Delehaney in the July 29, 1932, *New York Evening Post*: "The unsuspected terrors of life among the vo-de-voo-doos of Haiti are dragged forth in a curiously unmoving tale…. Obviously designed to titillate the spinal column, the story strains and struggles to out–*Frankenstein Frankenstein*, and so earnest is it in its attempts to be thrilling that it overreaches the mark all along the line and resolves into an unintentional and often hilarious comedy. After all, when a story which is meant to scare the wits out of you misses its mark, the chances are it will fill you with uncontrollable glee, and even comedy of the unintentional kind is not to be disparaged these days. Therefore, if it is laughter you are bent on finding, go by all means to see *White Zombie*…. Its idiocies, moreover, are emphasized by a brand of acting that might have been understandable twenty years ago but which hardly fits into the melodramatic style of today."

Bland Johaneson in "*Frankenstein* Has a Rival" in the July 29, 1932, *New York Daily Mirror*: "*White Zombie* approaches the graveyard with no reticence. *Frankenstein* and *Dracula* are dainty compared to it. And the stunning sound accompaniment is punctuated by the merry howls of vultures. The acting of the principal players is uniformly terrible. But that doesn't matter. For you aren't expected to believe in their bizarre adventures. You merely are to be thrilled and appalled by them."

L.N. in "Beyond the Pale" in the July 29, 1932, *New York Times*: "…Nor was there, to be candid, much reason for *White Zombie*. The screen, shuddering slightly, can go on; it can forget, it can be a Zombie, too…. All the actors have strange lines to say, but appear to enjoy saying them. Those given to Mr. Harron seem, on retrospection, to be me the most fantastic—if a superlative of any sort is allowable in a discussion of *White Zombie*. 'Not that,' he says at one point. 'Better death than that.' Yes indeed, much better."

Irene Thirer in the July 29, 1932, New York *Daily News*: "A super spine-chiller which fails in its purpose by going too far. Many fantastic and eerie scenes are evolved, but most of them border on the ludicrous…. It would be difficult to imagine a more fantastic story, and it would be absurd to expect a credible picture. But the players have done their best to emphasize the lurid horrors of the thing, and indulgent filmgoers may get a spurious thrill or two out of it."

Most New York critics in 1932 gave negative critiques of White Zombie.

Richard Watts, Jr., in the July 29, 1932, *New York Herald Tribune*: "It occurred to the producers of *White Zombie* that if one Frankenstein monster would make cinema audiences collapse in the aisles, several dozen of them would bring about heights in mass hysteria. Unfortunately the evidence supplied at the Rivoli ... suggests that these screen terrors work out in reverse ratio. Where the lone monster succeeded in providing reasonable amounts of public shivering, the score or so of Zombies [*sic*] proves to be at least many times less frightening. Perhaps, however, this decreasing scale is not the result of a mathematical rule. It may be caused by the fact that the new melodrama is clumsily wrought and unhappily acted.... Bela Lugosi, as the amiable Mr. Murder, proves that a good makeup cannot conceal a bad actor and the rest of the playing isn't altogether what it should be. Or maybe it is, considering the production."

Industry Trade Reviews

The Film Daily of July 29, 1932: "Another variant on the 'Dracula' theme, and with the work of Bela Lugosi it has the same quality of spooky thrills and weirdness. The atmospheric stuff has been cleverly handled. It rates with the best of this type of film.... Bela Lugosi is very impressive and makes the picture worthwhile."

Motion Picture Daily of July 29, 1932: "Produced with no fuss and sold to United Artists the same way, *White Zombie* yesterday began to make up for lost noise with an opening smash at the Rivoli such as Broadway hasn't seen since *Bring 'Em Back Alive* made traffic by the Mayfair a police problem.... The creaky, mysterious atmosphere surrounding [the] story will put *White Zombie* into the money division. Other pictures that fit into the same category have had considerably more production value but not the gripping tenseness of this film.... If Vic

Halperin, who directed the picture, can lift the gag out of the film [Lugosi's character controlling others by clinching his hands] and make it apply to faltering grosses and tottering amusement issues the business would be glad to erect a monument to his miracle. We're willing to subscribe to any fund right now."

Variety of August 2, 1932: "Victor Halperin goes to Hayti, hotbed of obi, for the latest addition to the blood curdling cycle, and with good results.... Now and then a tendency to overplay jars slightly, but in the main the atmosphere of horror is well sustained and sensitive picturegoers will get a full quota of thrills. The macabre atmosphere is evenly maintained and heightened by the action and the settings, though one seashore set is too palpably scenic to be convincing and would better be cut to a flash merely to establish the locale. Events are ordered in a nice progression with mounting suspense, and the few attempts at comedy relief through the priest are not interruptive. The story is fairly steeped in gloomy mystery.... The entire cast is well selected and the acting is of an even texture, which is not always the case in a practically one man story." A "Miniature Review" in the same edition of the trade added, "Excellent example of the supreme horror story."

Harrison's Reports of August 6, 1932: "This is certainly not up to *Dracula* or *Frankenstein*, but the type of audiences that go in for horror pictures will enjoy it, for it has many situations that will send chills through one. As for other types, it is too gruesome to be entertaining for them.... The picture has been produced extremely well.... Not suitable for children or for Sunday showing."

Motion Picture Herald of August 6, 1932: "A thrill picture with a somewhat different theme, this independently produced effort offers the exhibitor numerous opportunities for unusual show-selling."

Welford Beaton in the *Hollywood Spectator*, **circa late 1932 or early 1933:** "Victor directed [*White Zombie*] with consummate skill. When I read in an English paper that it had broken the attendance records at the Dominion Theatre, in London, England, I thought it was high time I look it up.... It was an outstanding success in this country.... If you have not seen *White Zombie*, you have missed something very worthwhile."

Reviews in Movie Fan Magazines

Photoplay of September 1932: "If you're a fiend for horror pictures you'll take this and like it, but if weird screams and tom-toms don't make your blood curdle any more, you'll find this just a little funny."

Photoplay of October 1932: "An utterly fantastic tale about the half-dead, known as zombies.... And you

needn't bother seeing it." [This review, unlike that of September 1932, was a more capsule critique. Its less kind tone is difficult to explain in comparison to the terror of the September notice, except that perhaps there were two different reviewers.]

Critiques in the National Media

Time magazine of August 8, 1932: "*White Zombie* is the latest jitter and gooseflesh cinema. *Dracula* was the first of the current witches' sabbath, followed by *Frankenstein*, *Murders in the Rue Morgue*, and *Freaks*. All have been box office successes.... The acting of everybody in *White Zombie* suggests that there may be some grounds for believing in zombies."

The *New Yorker* of August 6, 1932: "Whether *Rebecca of Sunnybrook Farm* or *White Zombie* is the more gruesome movie I cannot say with any exactitude. In fact, at times one seems very much like the other. There is certainly a good deal of zombie in Rebecca, and Bela Lugosi often suggests Louise Closser Hale in one of her more irate moods. I need hardly add that no such similarity was the purpose of the producers of these two films. One was to be the embodiment of sweetness and light, the other the essence of the horrors. Nothing in the zombie picture, however, was as creepy to me as the 'sunniness' of that Rebecca as she runs about adopting stray infants, bringing them right into the house, reconciling married couples, softening the temper of that rich aunt of hers, whose acerbity has been obviously the one triumph of her career. On the other hand, the mooniness of Mr. Lugosi commands at times a welcome, refreshing titter."

The Commonweal of August 17, 1932: "The superstitions of Haiti should offer magnificent material for the play of keen imagination and unearthly horror on the screen. But the effort of United Artists to produce a play of the *Dracula* variety in Haitian surroundings fails to achieve much beyond gruesome implications and an almost farcical improbability.... There is no ... artistry in the writing or filming of *White Zombie*—no more than in the clap-trap play of *Dracula* which also dwelt on the theme of the undead.... Details of the plot become unmanageable.... Apparently Hollywood does not trust its audiences enough. It is obsessed with the idea of the 'twelve-year old mentality'—forgetting that with the twelve-year-old mind go an imagination and an instinctive response to artistry as deeply rooted as the life of humanity itself. *White Zombie* is interesting only in the measure of its complete failure."

Frederic Smith in the **September 10, 1932,** *Liberty* magazine: "[The] sorcerer seizes upon the pretty sweetheart of an American. The frantic attempts to save the girl are revealed before a background of ghastly lock-stepping zombies. If you do not get a shock out of the thriller, you will get one out of the acting. It would worry even a Zombie."

Pare Lorentz in the January 1933 *Vanity Fair*: In his category for "Worst Movie" of 1932, Lorentz cites a "Terrific deadlock with *Blonde Venus* holding a slight lead over *White Zombie, Bring 'Em Back Alive*, and *Murders in the Rue Morgue*."

White Zombie Theater Grosses

The information in this section offers theater grosses for *White Zombie*'s 1932 screenings in various cities, which are (when possible) compared to grosses garnered by *Dracula, Frankenstein, Dr. Jekyll and Mr. Hyde*, and *Murders in the Rue Morgue* in the same cities. The cities are examined in the chronological order of their respective screenings, and are chosen for this study because they were the cities which reported *White Zombie* grosses to the industry trade publications.

Any surviving words or descriptions from trade publications or theater managers themselves are printed to best gauge what the gross means. In other words, just because *White Zombie* grossed less in a given city than, say, *Dracula*, that does not mean it made less net profit. Rental prices on films differed greatly, as did ticket prices. Both of these factors *could* result in a high gross with little net profit. These realities should be considered while examining this data. In its totality, the following discussion can supplement the information found in Chapter Four.

Providence, Rhode Island, was one of the first U.S. cities to see *White Zombie*. The film opened at the Loew's State, a 3,700–seater owned by United Artists, on July 29, 1932. Even at ticket prices of 15–75 cents, those in the city seemed to have little interest. *Variety* initially wrote that its gross looked like $7,000, which was "about 50% off."[1] The trade also believed the film would probably catch a "booby prize," as its poor grosses were in light of "one of the most remarkable build-up campaigns the town has seen in many a moon" and a wave of "fairly cool weather" that seemed to be helping most theater grosses.[2] The final tally of *White Zombie*'s gross was $9,900 for its one-week stay.[3] Months earlier, *Frankenstein* had taken $10,000 at the city's RKO Albee, in December 1931[4]; *Murders in the Rue Morgue* had then made $13,000 for a week's run in Providence during February 1932.[5]

Another city which screened *White Zombie* during the week of July 29, 1932 was Indianapolis. The Loew's Palace, a 2,800-seater owned exclusively by the Loew's chain, charged moviegoers 25–35 cents per ticket to see the film, which grossed approximately $5,000 for its one-week run. That was comparable to their take on the prior week's screening of *Blonde Captive*, but even still it ranked among their lowest grosses of the year.[6] *Motion Picture Daily* wrote that the "Palace wasn't any too happy about *White Zombie*, but what audiences saw it were pleased enough."[7] Much of the city's theatergoers preferred seeing *Roar of the Dragon* at the Circle Theater, which was paired with a live stage show of the Mills Brothers. Several months earlier, *Frankenstein* had taken $6,500 in one week at the city's Apollo, in December 1931.[8] *Dr. Jekyll and Mr. Hyde* had grossed $8,250 for a week at the nearby Circle Theater, in January 1932.[9] *Murders in the Rue Morgue* had made $4,000 in one week at that same theater, in February 1932.[10]

Screenings for *White Zombie* also came during the week of July 29 in Louisville, Kentucky, whose Loew's Theater seated 3,252 at ticket prices ranging from 15 to 40 cents. The film at first looked like a "good" gross of $8,000; that prediction was partially based on the fact that the city had gained ticket sales at evening shows at all theaters thanks to heat-relieving rains.[11] By the time the week ended, though, the box-office pull was only a "so-so" $7,500.[12]

For the week of August 3, 1932, Montreal's Princess Theater ran *White Zombie* and *Aren't We All*. The theater seated 1,600 at prices ranging from 35 to 60 cents. Initial predictions were for an "above average" $8,000.[13] Once the week ended, however, the total gross was only $6,500, which was roughly the same that the Princess made with *Roar of the Dragon* and *Roadhouse Murder* the week before.[14] In March 1931, *Dracula* had grossed $14,000 at the Palace Theater.[15]

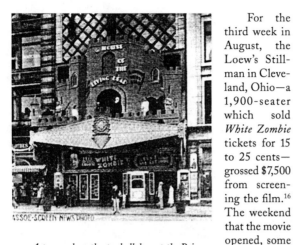

A tremendous theater ballyhoo at the Princess Theatre in Montreal, Canada, designed by Tom Cleary of Consolidated Theatres, Limited. Photograph published November 12, 1932.

For the third week in August, the Loew's Stillman in Cleveland, Ohio—a 1,900-seater which sold *White Zombie* tickets for 15 to 25 cents—grossed $7,500 from screening the film.[16] The weekend that the movie opened, some 16,728 people bought tickets, breaking records at the Stillman. In fact, the theater manager reported that "it was the first time in a year and a half that [we] have had anything like that to gloat over."[17]

On August 21, St. Paul's Riviera Theater reported its *White Zombie* gross to *Motion Picture Daily*. The theater, which seated 1,300 at 25 to 55 cents, made $5,500 from seven days of playing the film. That gross was $1,000 above average for the theater; the Paramount and the Tower, the other two major theaters in the city, also had above average grosses that same week.[18]

Curious stunt designed by M. A. Malaney that allegedly helped draw attention to the Loew's Stillman in Cleveland, Ohio. The zombie was driven around Cleveland for hours, maintaining a rigid posture and blank expression. Photo published in the September 10, 1932 Motion Picture Herald.

The Fox-Poli Theater, New Haven, Connecticut, booked *White Zombie* for a one-week run with another film, *Speak Easily*. The theater seated 3,640 at 35–55 cents, with matinee seats going for a quarter each. The show, which ran the last full week in August, did best at those lower-cost af-ternoon matinees, offsetting evenings that "[took] it on the chin," due in part to local competition screening *Horse Feathers*.[19] The screenings looked initially like they would bring a "fair" $4,500, but by August 27, the last day for the two films, the Fox-Poli ended up with a $5,000 gross.[20] In February 1931, *Dracula* had grossed $9,000 at the nearby College Theater.[21]

Columbus, Ohio's, Broad Theater, owned jointly by Loew's and United Artists and seating 2,500 at prices ranging from 15 to 40 cents, screened the film for the week of August 25. The film did so well by midweek that *Variety* reported it was "[j]ust too bad the price scale is so low here, but even at that this film will top $8,000, which is plenty heavy."[22] That was well over the "fair enough" $3,500 the same theater had grossed the prior week with the horror film *Almost Married*. Its success may have been partially due to what *Variety* called "some unknown reason" causing:

> ...this burg [to] suddenly [go] picture crazy. After a plenty slack summer, up to now, ... [i]t certainly looks as though there is plenty of sugar waiting to be spent and plenty people now ready to do just that.... It amounts to a run on the theaters, and if the state fair visitors should join the local folk in this run even the heavy expectations will be topped.[23]

Against competition that week from films like *Bird of Paradise*, *Downstairs*, and *Hollywood Speaks*, *White Zombie* "also had 'em waiting" to buy tickets. The year before, *Dracula* had grossed $16,000 at the city's Palace Theater.[24]

White Zombie then grossed a "fair" $7,200 for the week ending September 3, 1932, at Minneapolis' Lyric Theater, a Publix-owned house that seated 1,238 at 25 to 40 cents a ticket. Their *White Zombie* take was $300 more than the prior week's screening at the same theater. During the film's run, *Variety* claimed that "[s]ensational and skillful advertising also is bringing customers in for *White Zombie* at the Lyric and is delivering by sending customers away talking about it."[25] Initial expectations of a "big" $8,000 gross for *White Zombie* did not come true. The year before, *Dracula* had made $17,000 at the Minneapolis RKO Orpheum, in February 1931.[26] *Dr. Jekyll and Mr. Hyde* had taken $13,000 for one week at Minneapolis' Minnesota Theater in January 1932.[27] *Murders in the Rue Morgue* had grossed $12,000 at the city's RKO Orpheum, in February 1932.[28]

White Zombie then played at Detroit's United Artists Theater, which seated 2,070 at ticket prices ranging from 25 to 75 cents. For the week ending September 8, the theater grossed $10,000 on the film, only making half of its $20,000 average. Despite what *Motion Picture Daily* described as "cool weather and the labor day week-end

White Zombie *received a mixed box-office reaction at theaters in the United States in 1932.*

[*sic*]," business at all Detroit theaters that week was bad.[29] Despite the poor returns, the United Artists screened *White Zombie* the following week as well, grossing $9,000 against an average take that was $15,000—$5,000 less than the prior week's because of *White Zombie*'s poor ticket sales then.[30]

For the week ending September 17, the Loew's State of Newark, New Jersey, screened *White Zombie* in its 2,780-seat theater at ticket prices ranging from 15 to 65 cents. The gross of $7,000 was "not so strong" for the six-day run; *Blondie*, the film that replaced it, garnered a much higher gross at (approximately) a "sweet $11,000."[31] The year before, *Dracula* had grossed $23,000 at the city's RKO Proctor's Theater.[32]

During the third week of September 1932, the Warner Theater in Pittsburgh, a 2,000-seater owned by Warner Brothers, screened *White Zombie* at ticket prices of 25–50 cents. In the face of critical panning in city newspapers, ballyhoo efforts were given credit for moderately high ticket sales.[33] *Variety* wrote that there were "[p]lenty of indications around here this week that the film public or the critics are screwy. Customers are pooh-poohing films lauded to the skies by the cricks and buying those spanked by the press."[34] Though initial predictions were for a $9,000 gross (which would have been "very much okay"), the one-week run became "a clean up for $11,500."[35] For a net profit, it was the best in Pittsburgh that week. Over one year before, *Dracula* had grossed $35,500 at the city's Stanley, in February 1931.[36]

For the first week of October, the Publix-owned Orpheum Theater in Lincoln, Nebraska, screened *White Zombie* to satisfactory results. The theater, which seated 1,200 at ticket prices of 10 to 30 cents, took a gross of approximately $1,200. While that rated an "okay" from the theater, it was better than the $1,150 from the prior week's showing of *Big City Blues*.[37]

That same week, *White Zombie* played the Hippodrome in Buffalo, New York. The theater was a 2,100-seater that charged 25 to 35 cents per ticket to the zombie opus. Its gross over a seven-day run was estimated at $11,000, far more than the theater's $6,500 average. *White Zombie*'s showing was so strong that *Motion Picture Daily* called it one of the "surprises" of the week.[38]

The Oriental Theater, a John Hamrick-owned, 2,500-seater in Portland, opened *White Zombie* during the third week of October 1932. Ticket prices were a modest 25–35 cents. During its run, the theater reported that it was "in line for a moderate $3,500," which would be $500 lower than their prior week's screening. After its week-long stay ended, *Variety* told readers that the film "answered to exploitation and connected for $3,600." The theater reported a gross of $4,200 on *White Zombie* to the *Motion Picture Herald*, though that amount was an early and optimistic estimate.[39] The year before, *Dracula* had played at the RKO Orpheum in February 1931, and grossed $13,000.[40] *Frankenstein* had taken $15,300 in December 1931 at the same theater.[41]

In Denver, *White Zombie* played the city's Paramount Theater, a 2,000-seater owned by Publix. At ticket prices of 25–40 cents, the film grossed $6,000 for the week ending October 24, 1932 after "good bally"; the result—which was $400 higher than the prior week's screening—was deemed "oke," especially in light of a blizzard that had hit the city.[42] The year before, *Dracula* in Denver at the Huffman's Tabor had almost set a record, grossing $14,000 in March 1931.[43] *Frankenstein* in Denver had grossed a little less at the same theater at the end of 1931, taking $12,000.[44] *Dr. Jekyll and Mr. Hyde*'s appearance at the Denver Theater had then grossed $14,000 in February 1932.[45]

For a one-week run during the second week of November 1932, *White Zombie* grossed $2,100 at the Blue Mouse theater in Tacoma. The theater, which was owned by John Hamrick, offered only 650 seats at 25 cents each. *White Zombie*'s take was considered "pretty nice."[46] In 1931, *Dracula* had grossed $5,200 at the city's Orpheum.[47]

Unfortunately, the bulk of specific theater grosses for *White Zombie* are lost to time. Most exhibitors did not send their weekly grosses to industry trades; those who did may have missed publication deadlines or had their material cut by an editor for reasons of space, or they may not have had their numbers included because their theaters or cities were deemed unimportant.

In particular, small town theater grosses are under-catalogued in the trades of the early 1930s and—as a direct result—are underrepresented in Chapter Four and in this appendix. At the same time, those random city grosses which have survived yield further insight into the varied audience responses detailed at length in Chapter Four.

White Zombie British Pressbook Information

Some months after Hal Horne prepared the *Complete Exhibitors Campaign Book* (United Artists' initial United States pressbook for *White Zombie*), the pressbook for the film's major theatrical run in England was compiled. It is unknown whether Horne worked on the British pressbook, but its contents do make clear that it was published even afer the film's London premiere. Indeed, it's the images and materials unique like those of the London premiere that make the inclusion of materials from the British pressbook crucial to the current text. And in this case we owe a debt of gratitude to Buddy Barnett, publisher of *Cult Movies* magazine and a well-known Bela Lugosi collector and film connoisseur, for offering use of what is one of likely only a few existing copies of the materials seen here.

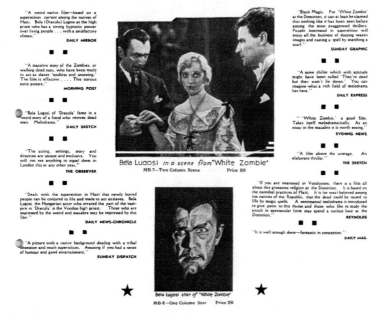

273

DOUBLE CROWNS

THESE ATTRACTIVE POSTERS IN <u>THREE COLOURS</u>

Complete with your Theatre Overprinting and Supporting Bill, for

12/6 per 100

As used at the

DOMINION THEATRE

LONDON

Where the publicity given to this film created a Box Office record for the Theatre.

Free Serialization
That Newspapers Will Grab

The story of "WHITE ZOMBIE" is an original written especially for the screen and based on the legend of the Living Dead of Haiti.

Here is a newspaper circulation builder if there ever was one. It makes all mystery stories look like tame affairs as compared to the thrilling exploits depicted in "WHITE ZOMBIE."

This serialization is made up in six instalments and contains 10,000 words. Illustrate each chapter with a still from the set of 10, illustrating scenes from that portion of the story.

Get the best newspaper in town to run this serialization, starting at least a week in advance of your showing so that you will create an air of mystery about Zombies and create interest on the part of the readers to see the film when it plays at your theatre.

You can obtain **Free** copies of this serialization from UNITED ARTISTS PUBLICITY DEPT.

Bela Lugosi *in a scene from* "White Zombie"

MB-3—One Col. Star   Price 3/6

Street Parade of Zombies
Will Cause Sensation

A street parade of ZOMBIES is certain to cause a lot of talk in your town.

In London the parading of the Zombies (as illustrated) played a big part in the wonderful success of the film at the premier presentation at the Dominion.

These Zombies were supplied by the Nuway Publicity Service, Coventry House, Coventry Street, W.1., and exhibitors in the London area can obtain from this company any number of Zombies, complete with costumes and make-up, at a reasonable exclusive charge.

Write direct to the Nuway Publicity Service for prices and full particulars.

Here's a ballyhoo that will actually bring pounds into your box-office. Arrange for a parade of Zombies through the main streets of your city, the man following a girl in white. The faces should be stolid, staring, gaping with empty eyes. They should walk with a mechanical, deathlike precision, looking neither to the right nor the left and not returning the gazes of the interested onlookers. The men to be dressed in sombre black.

Their backs should bear cards reading, "I'm a Zombie." Then in large letters on the back of the woman is imprinted "White Zombie" with emphasis on the word White. The girl to be dressed in flowing robes similar to the heroine in the picture and if possible, in connection with the men, get a series of death masks which will give them an ominous, mysterious appearance.

Tip off newspaper offices that "Black Magic" is being practised on the streets of your city so that when this weird appearing troupe of Zombies heads toward your theatre the local paper will play it up as a news story.

TWO ESSENTIAL ACCESSORIES

A CURIOSITY AROUSER

The illustration at left shows an unique teaser throwaway which is bound to fasten attention on your showing of "White Zombie" and bring new patrons to your theatre. Each side of the strip is shown and also what it looks like when it is folded up. The first words which are read are: "Are you a Zombie?"

Order them from:

Messrs. WILLSONS,
Gloucester Mansions,
CAMBRIDGE CIRCUS,
LONDON, W.C.2.

Price—**12/6** per 1,000, including overprinting.

A CHALLENGE

Who will View this Film ALONE?

CHALLENGE
WHITE ZOMBIE
The Weirdest Love Story in 2,000 Years
THE GREATEST THRILLER OF ALL
Will be screened at Midnight
(DATE   )
TO AN AUDIENCE OF
**ONE
LADY**
WHO WILL BE THE ONE?
The —— Cinema will give £5 to the lady who will view this picture—ALONE!
FOR CONDITIONS PLEASE SEE OVER

Inside of Bill

Here is a stunt that has actually been worked with great success on this film. The idea is to throw out a challenge to all the ladies of your district. Flood the town with handbills reading something like the one shown at right and left here. Print your own conditions and state that in the event of more than one lady accepting the challenge the names will be pooled and the one drawn for on your stage.

Your local newspaper will boost this one for you.

CONDITIONS | CINEMA — TOWN | White Zombie — Commencing Date | EERIE CREEPY SUPERNATURAL

Outside of Bill

"WHITE ZOMBIE" A LONDON SUCCESS

SIX MONTHS RECORDS BROKEN AT DOMINION THEATRE!

Negro Tom Toms

Hire several negroes to sit in front of your theatre and beat a steady tattoo on tom-toms. Attire them in tropical garments and every once in a while have them cut loose with a couple of blood-curdling yells. Be sure they simulate the negro rhythm as heard in the first reel of the picture. (During the burial in the road scene.)

White Zombies practising their macabre arts on the marquee of the Dominion, where the U.S. horror production, "White Zombie," has done unusual business. Striking exploitation, of which the above is a specimen, has marked the presentation.

From the "CINEMA"

EXPLOITING "WHITE ZOMBIE"

Midnight Audience of One

RESOURCE OF DOUGLAS SHOWMAN

An unusual stunt was put over by Mr. George Jordan, manager of the Picture House, Douglas, in support of his booking of "White Zombie."

The stunt consisted of an invitation to the ladies of Douglas for one of them to see a private showing of the film at midnight. There were over 400 entries, and when the selected applicant entered the theatre at 11.45 p.m., huge crowds attended and even waited for her re-appearance after the performance.

Naturally, the stunt was given wide publicity, and Mr. Jordan reports "House Full" boards for the entire week of the booking.

"WHITE ZOMBIE"

U. A.'s Exploitation Breaks Dominion Records.

Six Months' Figures Shattered.

Zombies Stage Macabre Act on Theatre Marquee.

Others Walk West End.

All records for the last six months were, it is claimed, broken last Monday, when United Artists' "White Zombie" was given its London premiere.

The queues lined up at midday opening and at the evening shows other queues had to wait nearly an hour before they could get in.

"White Zombie" was ushered in by an unusual campaign which created a sensation in Tottenham Court Road. A 40 ft. high display depicting "The House of the Living Dead" was erected on the facia of the theatre and in front of this an 18 ft. high Zombie blinked his green eyes forebodingly.

On a runaway over the marquee top, five Zombies, characters in the story, enacted a scene, a new sensation which had the effect of drawing thousands of people to the front of the theatre, and called for police action to control the crowd.

During the past week a number of Zombies have been parading the West End streets and posters have been appearing round the immediate district of Dominion Theatre bearing the slogans: "What is a Zombie?" and "Beware the Spell of Zombie."

The above is a reproduction from the "CINEMA"

Shadow Box.

Construct a shadow box with the aid of the illustration on the Quad. Mask in the sides with black cloth. Then attach a skidoo plug to two green lights which will flash on and off behind the eyes of Bela Lugosi.

AND HERE'S YOUR LOBBY MATERIAL!

LINEN BANNER   :   EYELETTED   :   10ft. x 3ft.   :   Price 9/-

FRONT OF HOUSE DISPLAY CUT-OUT, 10ft. x 8ft.   Price £4 10s.
This Display can be made any size.   ::   Price on application.

:: EASEL QUAD DISPLAY BOARD ::
Price 10/6 : Also 5ft. x 3ft. at £1 1s.

Process Cut-Out, Price 7/6

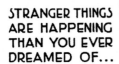

STRANGER THINGS ARE HAPPENING THAN YOU EVER DREAMED OF...

Look at the people near you! They may be living, walking, breathing, under the spell of

"WHITE ZOMBIE"

with BELA DRACULA LUGOSI

MB-11—Two Column Ad   Price 6/-

Stranger things are happening than you ever dreamed of

"WHITE ZOMBIE"

Theatre Next Monday

MB-13—One Column Ad.   Price 2/6

"WHITE ZOMBIE"

with BELA (Dracula) LUGOSI

Stranger things are happening than you ever dreamed of

MB-15— One Col. Ad Price 3/6

Stranger things are happening than you ever dreamed of...

?"WHITE ZOMBIE"

NEXT MONDAY

MB-16 — One Col. Ad Price 2/6

STRANGER THINGS ARE HAPPENING THAN YOU EVER DREAMED. *Wierd' Alive! A glamorous love tale told on the borderland of life and death*

"WHITE ZOMBIE"

with BELA (DRACULA) LUGOSI

MB-12 - One Column Ad   Price 3/-

STRANGER THINGS ARE HAPPENING THAN YOU EVER DREAMED OF

Beware! THE SPELL OF

"WHITE ZOMBIE"

with BELA (DRACULA) LUGOSI

MB-14—Three Column Ad   Price 4/6

STARTLE THEM INTO YOUR THEATRE

Do You Believe in ZOMBIES?

MB-1 One Col.
Vulture Price 2/6

As soon as your publicity starts breaking there will be a tremendous amount of curiosity aroused concerning the term ZOMBIE.

Many people will soon become familiar with the sound of the word, but will not know its derivation or actual meaning.

Here's a chance for your newspaper to arrange a contest which undoubtedly will prove a circulation builder and evoke a storm of comment as well as many hundreds of letters.

The prize-winning entrant can be given a guest ticket to see "WHITE ZOMBIE" at your theatre, or some other suitable prize.

Due to the fact that there have been many volumes written on this subject and a great deal of discussion as to the actual existence of ZOMBIES, you have a topic of real publicity value at your theatre.

Cut-out Poster Heads

Put three or four of these cut-out heads on the front of your marquee. For example, you can put one on each end so as to be visible on either approach to the theatre. Have these cut-out heads made up long in advance and placed in strategic spots in your theatre such as on landings and exits facing people as they come out of the theatre. That will start them talking about "WHITE ZOMBIE."

Drug Store Tie-up

"WHITE ZOMBIE" is the most thrilling film yet produced and will test the nerves of most cinema-goers.

Here then is a natural tie-up with Drug Stores and Chemists, etc. Arrange with them to fill their windows with special displays of nerve tonics and have large cards exhibited tying up with your showing.

Have the cards read something like this :—

STRENGTHEN YOUR NERVES
for the
THRILLS
that await you in
"WHITE ZOMBIE"
at the . . . . Theatre

"WHITE ZOMBIE" is a

Showman's Picture . . .

Exploit it to the Limit

MYSTERY POST-CARD

Here is a little messenger to arouse curiosity among your distant patrons.

JUST HAND THIS BLOCK TO YOUR PRINTER TOGETHER WITH YOUR MAILING LIST AND AWAIT RESULTS.

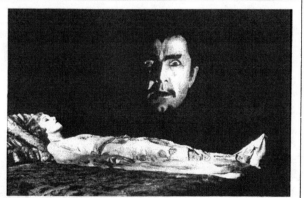

BELA LUGOSI and MADGE BELLAMY in "WHITE ZOMBIE"
The weirdest love story in 2,000 years. Coming to............Theatre next Monday.

MB-2—Postcard   Price 4/6

Make Theatre Display of Enlargement of Penal Code

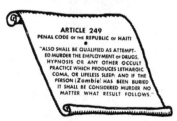

ARTICLE 249
PENAL CODE of the REPUBLIC of HAITI

"ALSO SHALL BE QUALIFIED AS ATTEMPTED MURDER THE EMPLOYMENT of DRUGS, HYPNOSIS OR ANY OTHER OCCULT PRACTICE WHICH PRODUCES LETHARGIC COMA, OR LIFELESS SLEEP; AND IF THE PERSON (Zombie) HAS BEEN BURIED IT SHALL BE CONSIDERED MURDER NO MATTER WHAT RESULT FOLLOWS."

The Penal Code of the Republic of Haiti definitely recognises the existence of ZOMBIES, and places a death penalty on this type of necromancy.

An enlargement of the above scroll built into your theatre front or displayed in your lobby will stop passers-by and attract crowds of people, eager to read this novel display.

Here's something, while terrifying, still has a showmanship quality that will create tremendous interest in the picture at your theatre.

White Zombie Videocassette Releases

Few horror films have ever received the sheer number of video releases as *White Zombie*. The reason can be attributed to the combination of the film's public domain status and the cult attention given to Bela Lugosi. Financial success—however meager—often results, and each year seems to bring forth new *White Zombie* videocassettes. The print quality on most is abominable, as they are usually drawn from inferior 16mm prints.

Running times as listed on their packaging are generally incorrect, usually claiming more footage than appears on the cassette; some perhaps adopt information from reference books which have often used the film's 1932 pressbook as a guide for running times. Such packaging often makes numerous other errors, the most egregious being the 1986 Hal Roach video release which claimed the film's director was "Edgar O. Ulmer." In

Because of both cult attention and public domain status, White Zombie *has been released on VHS by many different video companies.*

addition to wrongly omitting Victor Halperin's name, the reference to Edgar G. Ulmer incorrectly identifies his middle initial.

Packaging aside, the overwhelmingly poor quality of nearly all of these releases has made the present study rely on the Roan Group's 1994 laser disc restoration, chronicled at length in Chapter Seven. Two different video companies offer the Roan restoration on VHS videocassettes: Sinister Cinema of Medford, Oregon, and Englewood Entertainment of Kansas City, Missouri, the latter of which features perhaps the most attractive packaging of any *White Zombie* video release.

The following list offers the names of the companies which have released *White Zombie*, their location, the year of their *White Zombie* video, and the running time they attribute to the print. Unless otherwise noted, these versions all represent NTSC VHS video cassettes. The sheer proliferation of small video companies means that this may well not be a complete list:

TV Cassette Corporation of America: New Canaan, NH, 1979—73 minutes

Crown Video: New York, 1980—73 minutes

Foothill Video: Lancaster, CA, 1980—62 minutes[1]

Hollywood Home Theater: Hollywood, 1980—73 minutes

Murray Hill Video: New York, 1980—73 minutes

Silver Screen Video: Ocean, NJ, 1980—74 minutes

Kartes Video Communications: Indianapolis, 1984—65 minutes

Prism Entertainment: Los Angeles, 1985—73 minutes

United American Video Corporation: Nashville, 1985—74 minutes[2]

Video Classics: Burbank, 1985—78 minutes

Vintage Video: Rahway, NJ, 1985—73 minutes

Crown Video: New York, 1986—73 minutes

Hal Roach Studios Film Classics: [No city listed on packaging], 1986—62 minutes

Trans-Atlantic Video: S. Plainfield, NJ: 1987—74 minutes

Sinister Cinema: Medford, OR: 1988—68 minutes[3]

Video Signature: Sunnyvale, CA: 1988—64 minutes

Silver Screen Video: Ocean, NJ, 1989—74 minutes

Dodd Files: Denton, TX, 1991—63 minutes

Republic Pictures Home Video: Los Angeles, 1991—59 minutes[4]

Madacy Music Group: Quebec, 1993—66 minutes

Hollywood Select Video/Timeless Video: North Hollywood, 1994—66 minutes

Timeless Video: North Hollywood, 1994—72 minutes

Liberty/VCI Home Video: Tulsa, 1995—69 minutes

Alpha Video Distributors: Piscataway, NJ, 1997—73 minutes

Englewood Entertainment: Kansas City, 1998—68 minutes

Subsequent Careers of *White Zombie*'s Cast, Crew, and Auxiliaries

To varying degrees, the cast and crew of *White Zombie* have become remembered as much or more for their participation in the film than for any of their other work. For example, however many earlier silent films had starred Madge Bellamy in the 1920s or however many books and scripts Garnett Weston would write in the 1930s, *White Zombie* has certainly become the most examined work of both. Much the same could be said of the Halperins, cinematographer Arthur Martinelli, and the various other talent involved. The numerous essays and critiques of *White Zombie* in recent years have also meant it is the major conduit through which generally forgotten writers like William B. Seabrook and plays like *Zombie* are discussed. In fact, for most everyone involved, *White Zombie* would prove their greatest—or at least best remembered—contribution to the cinema.

Bela Lugosi's life and career after *White Zombie* oscillated from success to failure. Typecasting meant that, when the British imposed a ban in 1938 on importing and screening Hollywood horror films, Lugosi found himself without work. As the spectre of financial doom leaped from out of the shadows, the actor returned in *Son of Frankenstein* (1939) as Ygor, the demented and broken-necked friend of the Monster. Universal Studios produced the film on the heels of a wildly (and certainly unexpectedly) successful reissue of *Dracula* (1931) and *Frankenstein* (1931) in 1938. His career rebounded, even though the bulk of his work during World War II came in B-movies at lesser studios.

As Lugosi's financial troubles lifted, personal ones mounted. He and fourth wife Lillian separated in 1944. They reunited, but she divorced him in 1953. By that time—indeed, ever since the war's end—his work had dwindled to a small number of meager films, summer stock and live appearances, and a handful of television programs.

With his career in the doldrums, Lugosi placed his hopes in producer-director Edward D. Wood, Jr., who launched the actor into Z-grade films like *Glen or Glenda* (1953) and *Bride of the Monster* (1955). For the latter, the director even deliberately attempted to duplicate the extreme closeups of Lugosi's eyes as used in *White Zombie*. The actor, however, had greater problems on his mind than nostalgia for the 1930s; his addiction to morphine and related drugs led to a public confession and three months in a California state hospital for a cure. Despite hopes of a comeback after leaving the hospital, Lugosi died on August 16, 1956, at age 72.[1]

Aside from Bela Lugosi, Joseph Cawthorn and Clarence Muse probably fared the best among *White Zombie*'s cast in the years immediately subsequent to the film's 1932 release. As the film was about to premiere in New York City, Muse found it nearly impossible to take the European vacation he desired. Instead, other film roles were offered, and more contracts appeared for his popular lectures. In August 1932, he even opened in a special revue at Harlem's Lafayette Theater.[2] While *White Zombie* was in its first release, Muse's fame was at an all-time high. During the fall of 1932, he appeared in stage versions of *Green Pastures* and *Forgotten Men*, as well as acting in Universal's film *Laughter in Hell*. He appeared at various live events that year as well, including one in mid–August that illustrates the esteem much of the U.S. held for him.

Muse, Richard Dix, and members of the KNX radio "Gang" (of which Muse was the star) were slated to appear at the Tenth International Olympic Games for the benefit of athletes. However, Norman Manning, Chairman of the Entertainment Committee, quickly rescinded the invitation to Muse, claiming that no African-Americans would be allowed in the Olympic Village. Muse reacted calmly with his impeccable dignity intact. He would not appear, and would not cause a stir. Out of respect for their colleague, Dix and the other white performers refused to appear, and the entire incident received much publicity. "Race prejudice reared its ugly head," one account read, blaming Manning for his inexcusable action. By garnering publicity, a racist helped reveal the respect and admiration much of white America had for the actor.[3]

Such respect followed Muse for the rest of his career. From the thirties through the fifties, he continued to appear regularly in major Hollywood films. His subsequent credits would include: *Cabin in the Cotton* (1932), *Flying Down to Rio* (1933), *The Count of Monte Christo* (1934), *Show Boat* (1936), *Way Down South* (1939), *The Flame of New Orleans* (1941), *Tales of Manhattan* (1942), *Shadow of a Doubt* (1943), *Heaven Can Wait* (1943), *Watch on the Rhine* (1943), *Night and Day* (1946), and *Porgy and Bess* (1959). During those same years, he continued to sing, lecture, write, compose, and act on the stage and radio.

In the 1970s, Muse's career received further recognition when he was among the first honored in the Black Filmmakers Hall of Fame. During the same decade, he appeared on theater screens in such films as *Car Wash* (1976) and *The Black Stallion* (1979). Shortly after working on the latter film, he died, on October 13, 1979, at age 89, leaving behind him an important legacy of films, stage performances, and music.[4]

Actress Madge Bellamy, who would outlive Muse, did not possess his ability to stay in front of the camera; her desired comeback would never materialize, even though she costarred in a number of subsequent films. In 1933, she appeared in both *Riot Squad* and *Gigolettes of Paris*, as well as in the Buck Jones serial *Gordon of Ghost City*. The following years brought only a small number of minor roles: *Charlie Chan in London* (1934), *The Great Hotel Murder* (1935), *The Daring Young Man* (1935), and *Under Your Spell* (1936).

More than through any film appearance, however, Bellamy gained publicity through her tumultuous private life. In 1943, she raised a pistol and fired at lumber magnate and her then paramour A. Stanford Murphy. In her subsequent trial, the judge found her guilty of carrying a concealed gun without a license, and gave her a six-month suspended sentence. In an odd twist, she then sued Murphy for divorce, claiming that—while they had not obtained a marriage license—the two had married in Nevada, where a license was not then a requirement. After months of debate, attorneys for both parties crafted an agreement in which Bellamy obtained $100,000 from Murphy, the very man at whom she had earlier fired a gun.[5]

Her private life caused headlines throughout the Murphy debacles, generating far more publicity than her remaining career would. Bellamy appeared in only one more film after her legal troubles, *Northwest Trail* (1945) with Bob Steele, but she continued to work on the stage, appearing in such plays as *Holiday Lady* (1946). Most of the rest of her years were spent battling financial problems and writing an autobiography. Though *A Darling of the Twenties* would be published with the help of film historian Kevin Brownlow, it did not reach print until after her death in 1990.[6]

The careers of both Robert Frazer and John Harron also declined after *White Zombie*'s release. The former appeared in numerous other B-movies, notably *The Vampire Bat* (1933), but spent most of his remaining years as a character actor in movie serials: *The Three Musketeers* (1933), *The Miracle Rider* (1935), *The Clutching Hand* (1936), *The Black Coin* (1936), *Dick Tracy vs. Crime Inc.* (1941), *Captain America* (1944), and others. Frazer died in 1944 after a lingering illness; he was 50 years old, but still decades past the starring roles he once enjoyed.[7]

John Harron's remaining days were even more unfortunate. Only a handful of B-movies appear on his list of credits during the 1930s, including: *Murder in the Private Car* (1934), *Symphony of Living* (1935), *Missing Witness* (1937), *Invisible Menace* (1938), *Torchy Gets Her Man* (1938), *Secret Service of the Air* (1939), and *Indianapolis Speedway* (1939). He died in 1939 at age 36, virtually forgotten by a public who had never considered him to be a major star.[8]

By contrast, Brandon Hurst maintained a consistent level of fame as a character actor in subsequent films, appearing in *Sherlock Holmes* (1932), *The Lost Patrol* (1934), *The Charge of the Light Brigade* (1936), *Suez* (1938), *Jane Eyre* (1942), *Road to Utopia* (1945), and *My Favorite Brunette* (1947). A recognizable face to movie fans, he died in 1947 at age 81.[9] Unlike most of his *White Zombie* cohorts, Hurst's career continued at a similar level of success for the rest of his life after that 1932 film.

The same could not be said of *White Zombie*'s more minor character actors; for example, Claude Morgan, John Fergusson, and Annette Stone apparently did not appear in any other films of the 1930s. Velma Gresham, who received very minimal parts in the early to midthirties, gave up hopes of a film career, married, and settled in California.[10] Others, like Dan Crimmins and Frederick Peters, also lingered in obscurity even as their careers continued; for example, the former appeared in minor roles in *Vagabond Lady* (1935) and *George White Scandals of 1936* (1935), while the latter appeared to little notice in the Halperins' *I Conquer the Sea* (1936). George Burr MacAnnan scored memorable roles in *Supernatural* (1933), *The Black Room* (1935) and *Sherlock Holmes and the*

Neil (John Harron, on the left) and Beaumont (Robert Frazer, on the right): Neither fared well in the years after White Zombie. *(Courtesy of Venita Halperin.)*

his planned projects for that year were *Service*, *House of Trujillo*, and *Mutiny of the Dead*. Mentioned once in a trade and never produced, *Mutiny* may itself have even been a zombie tale.[15] Equally intriguing is Goldstone's unrealized vision of an elaborate version of *20,000 Leagues Under the Sea*. He announced the idea in mid–1934, even before signing a contract at MGM.[16] Trade publications claimed the studio would finance the film in 1935, but his desire for a lengthy vacation meant that he anticipated that one more year would pass prior to production. The vacation resulted in a permanent one from MGM.

Goldstone's contract expired on October 21, 1935, at which time he expressed no interest in a renewal. He completed his production supervision of *Last of the*

Secret Weapon (1943), but he never achieved any level of fame.[11]

On the other hand, those behind the camera of *White Zombie* generally fared better in the ensuing years. For example, the men responsible for the financing of *White Zombie*—Sherman S. "Sam" Krellberg and Phil Goldstone—continued to be major players in the film industry for years to come. In addition to heading Amusement Securities Corporation, Krellberg produced serials like *The Lost City*.[12] Between 1934 and 1939, he operated the Regal Distributing Corporation and produced films like *When Lightning Strikes* (1934) and *Thunderbolt* (1936).[13] From the 1940s to the 1960s, he also produced Broadway shows, including *The Pink Jungle* with Ginger Rogers and *Josephine Baker*, which returned its title star back to the New York stage. But Krellberg's major interest, especially in his later years, was in his Principal Film Exchange, through which he distributed reissues of films and feature versions of movie serials. He died in 1979 at age 87.[14]

Phil Goldstone's activity in the cinema also continued with success for some years after *White Zombie*'s release. By 1935, he became a producer at MGM. Among

Actor John T. Prince as Latour, the witch doctor who has become a zombie at the hands of Murder Legendre. (Courtesy of Venita Halperin.)

Pagans (1936), then left MGM for good. *The Hollywood Reporter* claimed Goldstone was "angling for a contract to produce independently for one of the majors."[17] His heart, it seems, was in the kind of independent production which had turned *White Zombie* from idea into reality. That choice, however, meant that Goldstone's beloved *20,000 Leagues* project would never be produced, perhaps because an indie budget would not have supported his extravagant plans.

Regardless, Goldstone continued to work as a producer and as a supporter of the film industry in other areas; among other activities, he was one of the founders of both the Motion Picture Relief Fund and the Motion Picture Academy of Arts and Sciences. On June 19, 1963, the industry mourned his death from cancer; Goldstone was 70 years old. He had remained involved in independent production even during his last years.[18]

Cinematographer Arthur Martinelli's career continued through the thirties and forties, but rarely would his camerawork be as artful as in *White Zombie*. Some of his later films like *The Devil Bat* (1941)—also starring Bela Lugosi—are shot in such a visually plain manner that it is almost difficult to accept that he was also responsible for the cinematography of *White Zombie*. At any rate, Martinelli shot several other Halperin films, including *Supernatural* (1933), *I Conquer the Sea* (1936), *Revolt of the Zombies* (1936), and *Nation Aflame* (1937). In the 1940s, he shot such films as *Criminals Within*, *Double Cross*, *The Miracle Kid* (1941), *Inside the Law*, *The Power of God* (1942), *Cinderella Swings It*, *Here Comes Kelly* (1943), *Black Magic*, *Call of the Jungle*, *Swing Out the Blues* (1944), *In Old New Mexico*, *Youth for the Kingdom* (1945), and *The Story of Life* (1948). After being relatively inactive in his later years, Martinelli died in 1967 at the age of 85.[19]

As with Martinelli, musical director Abe Meyer became entrenched in independent and low-budget filmmaking during the thirties and forties. Among the many films that utilized his company's services were *A Shriek in the Night* (1933), *The Vampire Bat* (1933), and *Mysterious Mr. Wong* (1935). By 1938, his success had led to a major post at MCA handling conductors, composers, arrangers, and musicians; concurrently, the Meyer Synchronizing Service continued to provide music for B-movies.[20] Eventually, Meyer would even become head of the MCA music department, a position he held until his retirement in 1959. Ten years later, the Composers and Lyricists of America gave him a special award for his pioneering contributions to music in motion pictures. He died on May 14, 1969, of a heart attack, only a couple of weeks after the ceremony.[21]

Makeup man Jack Pierce also continued in the film industry during the 1930s and 1940s. He became one of the masters of his field, creating makeup for such horror

Actor George Burr MacAnnan as Von Gelder, a zombie whom Legendre calls a "swine." (Courtesy of Venita Halperin.)

films as *The Werewolf of London* (1935), *Bride of Frankenstein* (1935), *Son of Frankenstein* (1939), *The Wolf Man* (1941), *The Ghost of Frankenstein* (1942), and many others. To return the favor of his contributed talents, his employer, Universal Studios, terminated him at the end of the 1940s. His later years were spent on a handful of low-budget efforts like *Beyond the Time Barrier* (1960) and *The Creation of the Humanoids* (1962). Outside of horror movie magazines like *Famous Monsters of Filmland*, Pierce was largely forgotten when he died at age 79 in 1968.[22]

Like Pierce, art director Ralph Berger was also quite active in the thirties and forties, working on several films in each year of that decade. These included numerous westerns, a number of Spanish-language films, and such films as *Tarzan's Desert Mystery* (1943), *Mystery Man* (1944), *Back to Bataan*, *Dick Tracy* (1945), *Genius at Work* (1946), *The Boy with Green Hair*, *If You Knew Susie*, *The Miracle of the Bells* (1948), and *The White Tower* (1950). Harold McLernon also stayed perennially busy, editing *The Kennel Murder Case* (1933), *Dames* (1934), *Torchy Gets Her Man* (1938), *A Shot in the Dark* (1941), *Lady Gangster* (1942), *The Last Ride* (1944), and many others. Other crew members, like dialogue director Herbert Farjeon and sound engineer L.E. Clark, also worked on numerous other films of the period. Clark's name, for example, appears on *The Ghost Walks* (1934), *Peck's Bad Boy* (1934), and *Symphony of Living* (1935).

Others on the set of *White Zombie* fared far less well in the cinema. For example, makeup man Carl Axcelle's only other film credits of the thirties were *Stingaree* (1934), *Chasing Yesterday* (1935), and *Suez* (1938). Assistant to the Producer Sidney Marcus, Assistant Director William Cody,[23] and Second Assistant Director Herbert Glazer[24] also quickly drifted into obscurity. The names of all in this category surface only in discussions of *White Zombie*, and even then only as appended names in a lengthy list of credits.

Screenwriter Garnett Weston, on the other hand, enjoyed an admirable level of prosperity in both the cinema and the literary world during the 1930s; *White Zombie*'s success opened the door for him into both forums. Immediately prior to the film's release, Weston's career was already forging ahead. On June 8, 1932, *The Hollywood Reporter* announced Paramount had signed him to write a screenplay, the topic of which was not mentioned.[25] Later that month, on June 24, the same publication claimed Fox had hired Weston as part of a writing staff for *Robber's Roost*, a George O'Brien western.[26] By Halloween day of 1932, some three months into *White Zombie*'s theatrical release, *Variety* mentioned that Weston had signed with RKO to write an original "Orien-

An ad for Garnett Weston's novel Murder on Shadow Island, *published in the April 20, 1933,* New York Herald Tribune.

tal yarn" to be directed by Ernest Schoedsack and produced by Merian C. Cooper.[27]

The Schoedsack-Cooper project never materialized, but Weston's career as a prolific screenwriter soon did. Along with contributing to the script treatments for *It's a Gift* (1934) with W.C. Fields and *Ruggles of Red Gap* (1935) with Charles Laughton, Weston cowrote scripts for *The Old Fashioned Way* (1934), *Nevada* (1935), *Daughter of Shanghai* (1938), *The Crooked Road* (1940), *Emergency Squad* (1940), and *Opened by Mistake* (1940). After cowriting 1941's *The Great Train Robbery*, Weston's name seems to disappear from movie credits as a screenwriter.

However, Weston's writing career continued in other ways. At least two of his short stories would be made into movies without his involvement in their respective screenplays. The first, *The Preview Murder Mystery* (1936), starred Frances Drake and Reginald Denny and met with relatively kind reviews. Another, *The Pony Soldier* (1952), starred Tyrone Power and Cameron Mitchell.

Weston's greatest fame in the cinema after *White Zombie* came through mystery and detective films. He wrote *Bulldog Drummond in Africa* (1938), *Bulldog Drummond's Secret Police* (1939), and—working with Stuart Palmer—cowrote *Bulldog Drummond's Bride* (1939). While hardly classic scripts, the Drummond series allowed Weston's vivid imagination to appear on-screen. As the *New York Times* once said, "It is generally accepted that a grain of salt must be initially applied to almost any picture which has to do with international spies. But this morning's recommendation is that any one [*sic*] going to see *Bulldog Drummond in Africa*, now showing at the Criterion—if at all of a precise turn of mind—should take a whole box and keep shaking it throughout the entire picture. In that way the full and wholesome flavor of a fabulous but exciting film may be enjoyed."[28]

Weston's penchant for unusual mystery and detective stories also found expression in a series of novels. His first—or at least first published—book was titled *Murder on Shadow Island* (Farrar, 1933). The *New York Times* would call the novel "farfetched," but it certainly paved the way for a series of equally or more bizarre novels.[29] The book, Weston's major literary project after *White Zombie* and *Supernatural*, illustrates an ability to sculpt fascinating descriptions even while pushing the envelope of material coherence:

> Bending to his oars, Bert made the light skiff leap across the still water. Momentarily Shadow Island drew nearer, its tall forest walls rising darker and more mysterious. Kim noticed the brooding light in the girl's eyes. He glanced ahead. For the first time since morning, he remembered the feeling of uneasiness which had assailed him when last he had seen the island. It had suggested danger, to his sensitive mind, even in the bright sunlight.

Now, with the dark shadows gathering like cowled forms, there was something sinister about the place.[30]

Descriptions like these are peppered with qualities with which he had imbued *White Zombie*, specifically, in this excerpt, an innocent young man—Bert in the novel, Neil in the film—surrounded by danger and menaced by shadows.

Detectives were popular characters in the fiction of the 1930s and appeared and reappeared in novel after novel. Weston fully understood this popularity and, to further establish himself as a mystery novelist, he created his own detective. In *Murder in Haste* (Stokes, 1935), he introduced the character Highway, who unravels the mystery at the novel's climax. One critic believed the story put "quite a strain on the credulity of the reader"[31] while still packing "more incident and excitement"[32] than most literature of its kind. The book sold well enough that Highway returned in *Dead Men Are Dangerous* (Stokes, 1937), which was called by one reviewer "excellent,"[33] while others still questioned the outlandishness of Weston's characters.[34] However outlandish, though, the character of Highway was a road Weston never travelled again.

However, subsequent books like *Man with the Monocle* (Doubleday, 1943)—a spy thriller about an archaeologist searching for a journalist in the clutches of the Nazis—preserved Weston's often outrageous style of storytelling. The *New Yorker* called it "one of the wildest goose chases in recent spy fiction. Makes you wonder at times if some limits shouldn't be set on improbabilities of international intrigue."[35]

Most bizarre of all, however, is perhaps his book *Poldrate Street* (Messner, 1944), in which a conspiracy between a doctor and an undertaker results in numerous murders. At its climax, the current group of victims are saved with only moments to spare by a mysterious tramp who spends his time on a sidestreet in Los Angeles where the killings occur. A bewildered critic at *Book Week* called it "a book not to read ... it is a basic script for some super horror movie that would provide fat parts for the Wolf Man, the Walking Dead, and Frankenstein's Monster, with all its sisters and its cousins and its aunts."[36]

Though he didn't rely on Frankensteins or wolf men, Weston would again employ themes like crime, intrigue, mystery, and murder in the novel *The Hidden Portal* (Crime Club, 1946) and *Legacy of Fear* (M.S. Mill, 1950). But by the 1950s, however, Weston's urge to write must have faded, as no novels surfaced under his name again. Years later, Weston would publish one final book, *Death Is a Lonely Business*; a collection of poetry—much of which he had written during World War I. The publisher was a rather minor press in British Columbia,

and—given its poor distribution—*Death Is a Lonely Business* became a lonely, generally unread book.

His eventual death would go almost completely unnoticed as well. His earlier novels were soon forgotten; his contribution to cinema was overlooked. Occasionally texts on the detective film mention his work on the Bulldog Drummond series, but it is only for *White Zombie* that his name finds much discussion or praise. As he had written in 1970, "to be alive is absurd—but to be dead is utterly ridiculous."[37]

Those in the outer currents of *White Zombie's* maelstrom were often plagued with problems of their own; their deaths often solidified anonymity. For example, Kenneth Webb, author and director of the 1932 play *Zombie*, joined the BBD&O's radio department and directed shows like *Cavalcade of America* and *Armstrong Theatre of Today*. He died on March 5, 1966 in Hollywood[38]; whether he commented on *White Zombie* or not during his later years is unknown.

Actress Pauline Starke never achieved the comeback she desired during the 1930s. Her remaining years were spent in relative obscurity in Santa Monica; she died on February 9, 1977 after spending some three months in St. John's Hospital.[39] Her husband, George Sherwood, was sporadically involved in Los Angeles–area theater, but in later years the two devoted much of their time to hobbies like sailing. Even with decades of glamour behind them, they never forgot their bitterness over *White Zombie*.

The man responsible for *The Magic Island* perhaps suffered most of all. William B. Seabrook's life during the thirties and forties proved exciting, fantastic, tumultuous, devastating, and—more than anything else—sad. He certainly achieved more publicity than actors like Robert Frazer, actresses like Pauline Starke or and Madge Bellamy, cameramen like Arthur Martinelli, and playwrights like Kenneth Webb, but much of the writing about him chronicled an enormous amount of pain.

Seabrook's first book after *The Magic Island* was *Jungle Ways* (Harcourt, Brace, and Co., 1930), which related his wild experiences in tropical Africa, including participation in devil worship and eating human flesh. He calmly described the latter as a "meat that tasted like good, fully-developed veal."[40] *The Commonweal* believed it had "significance, as a news event of a singular and repulsive kind...."[41] Then came *Air Adventure* (Harcourt, Brace, and Co., 1931), Seabrook's history of his flight with a French flying ace across the Sahara Desert, travelling to Timbuktoo and back. Seabrook's mission was to interview Père Yakouba, a monk he had previously discussed in *Jungle Ways*.

That same year, in July 1931, the magazine *Hearst's International Cosmopolitan* printed Seabrook's essay "I

Artwork by Erté that accompanied William Seabrook's essay "I Saw a Woman Turn Into a Wolf" in its original July 1931 publication.

Saw a Woman Turn Into a Wolf." The story described his 1926 encounters with a Russian refugee named "Mara Orloff." Seabrook's friend Bannister believed he witnessed Mara's transformation into a werewolf, swearing "Look, look, her face is growing black—the fur!" Seabrook, however, believed Mara was merely a woman with an animal inside her. Despite the essay's fanciful title and the beautiful but bizarre Erté artwork which accompanied it, the tale is a rare example of Seabrook denying an opportunity to proclaim the supernatural's existence.

Despite his steady pace of writing and travels, Seabrook battled various personal problems, including a serious case of alcoholism. By 1934, he was drinking an average of a quart and a half of whiskey each day. Eventually, he faced his troubles by committing himself to the New York State hospital:

> ...I was locked up where I couldn't run away, either by boat or bottle. I had to stay with myself and look at myself and it wasn't pleasant. I saw, for one thing, that I had nothing to blame on whiskey, nor even on intoxication, which may sometimes be divine. Whiskey was a gift of the gods—dangerous, like fire and all gifts from heaven—to be used by the strong man with pleasure for joy, to solace and stimulate the imagination, to clothe reality in rosy light, evoke elusive happiness. I had misused it as a stupefying poison, to deaden consciousness—as an escape.[42]

Asylum (Harcourt, Brace, and Co., 1935), Seabrook's reflections on his seven months in the hospital, became a bestselling book. Despite initial pronouncements of a cure, he continued to have major problems with alcohol.

Seabrook's private life was also plagued by ill-fated relationships. His first wife, Katherine Pauline Edmondson, divorced him in 1934 after some 22 years of marriage. Seabrook then married novelist Marjorie Washington, keeping the wedding secret for some seven months; the reason may have had something to do with the fact that Seabrook's former wife had married Washington's former husband.[43]

Only five years passed before Washington herself wanted a divorce. Her reason? Seabrook had met a redhead in the Woodstock art colony, found her attractive, and invited her to move in with him and Washington. Finding himself single for a brief moment, Seabrook then married the new girlfriend, a woman named Constance Kuhr. She remained with Seabrook until his death, and also bore his only child.[44] However, even his son William was a disappointment; Seabrook had wanted a daughter. "I am the seventh William Seabrook," he claimed, "and there's been too damned many of US."[45]

Personal problems like these, rather than impeding his writing career, seemed to inject it with a fervent energy. For example, *These Foreigners* (Harcourt, Brace, and Co., 1938), one of his major works of the latter thirties, examined tales of five immigrant groups in the U.S.: Scandinavian, German, Polish, Russian, and Italian. His findings hailed immigrants as assets contributing to the good of the country.

Yet another of his later books is *Witchcraft: Its Power in the World Today* (Harcourt, Brace, and Co., 1940), a collection of tales and anecdotes about his own experiences with black and white magic in Africa, Europe, and the U.S. Some critics attacked its lack of a coherent narrative, while others found in it a terrifying set of first-person encounters with witchcraft. The *Springfield Republican*, for example, called it, "one of the eeriest evenings of reading since *Dracula* descended on a horror-stricken world."[46]

Soon Seabrook's pen turned inward for an equally, if not more engrossing story. In 1942, Lippincott published his sometimes bizarre, generally disheartening autobiography, *No Hiding Place*. The book covers the exploits of a life in which he believed he had no place to hide "from the cradle to the grave where my bones will lie peacefully pickled in alcohol when my wild wandering in the vale of tears is ended."[47]

Of the book, *The New Yorker* wrote: "It is hard not to want to mother a chap who has gone so far, under such unpleasant conditions, in search of an escape from something so confused and tangled that he himself is not sure what it is."[48] *Newsweek* believed it the "Harrowing confession of a tortured soul,"[49] while *Time* dubbed it "the year's weirdest autobiography...."[50]

Even if the "weirdest" autobiography was published, however, Seabrook continued to carve details into his life fit for inclusion in any of his more dramatic books. For example, as his alcoholism continued, wife Constance plunged his arms into boiling water—hoping that scalded elbows would hurt to bend and would thus raise fewer glasses of liquor to his mouth.[51]

His final story was perhaps the most surprising of all. Despite the many periods of turmoil through which he had lived, Seabrook took his own life on September 20, 1945.

One publication wrote this of his intentional drug overdose:

> The coroner says Bill Seabrook committed suicide. But his friends have a different explanation of what happened. They say he only was making another more drastic attempt to accomplish what he had tried, vainly, all his life to—to get away from himself. Thus ends the strange career of one of the strangest personalities of the era, an enigma even to himself. The career moved to staccato rhythm up and down the world, into and out of civilization. Sometimes it blazed with color. Often it was darkened by the shadow of forbidden things. But it never was commonplace.[52]

Zombies and voodoo in mass media, though, they had become commonplace, largely due to Seabrook's *The Magic Island* and its effect on *White Zombie*. More than any literary prowess or high adventures, he is best remembered now for his indirect ties to the Halperins' film. Even shortly before his death, the origins of Seabrook's legacy were in place. A 1942 episode of the horror radio show *Dark Fantasy* offered a fictional tale of voodoo, with the explanation of its Haitian background given by a character appropriately named "Dr. Seabrook."[53]

Revolt of the Zombies
Pressbook Information

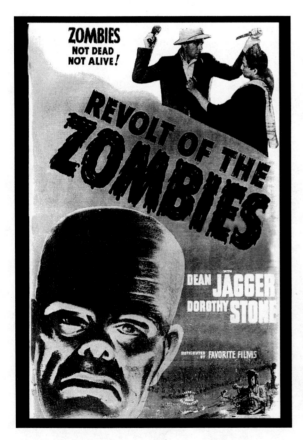

Left: *Artwork from the* Revolt of the Zombies *1936 pressbook*. Right: *Poster choices from the* Revolt of the Zombies *1936 pressbook*.

Victor Halperin
Family Scrapbook Photographs

The following photographs represent moments from Victor Halperin's first marriage, ranging from pictures of his wife and children to his Beverly Hills home. These images are now part of the collection of Linda Ortiz, Victor's granddaughter. She has kindly allowed them to be represented herein.

Irene Halperin, circa 1927, perhaps posed in a costume she wore in one of Victor Halperin's films.

Irene Halperin, circa 1927.

The exterior of Victor and Irene Halperin's beautiful home at 514 N. Beverly Drive in Beverly Hills, circa late 1920s.

The living room of Victor and Irene Halperin's 514 N. Beverly Drive home in Beverly Hills, circa late 1920s.

The master bedroom at Victor and Irene Halperin's home, 1929.

Top: *Elaine (left) and baby Joan Halperin at Victor and Irene Halperin's home, 1929*. Bottom: *Victor and Irene Halperin play violin and piano as daughter Elaine dances, circa 1929. Regrettably, their two friends on the left side of the photograph are unidentified.*

Irene Halperin during a portrait shoot, perhaps for a small role in one of Victor's films. Victor can be seen holding the ladder at the bottom of the photograph.

Cast and Credits for Other Victor Halperin Films

The following listing offers cast and credit information for all films in which Victor Halperin made credited contributions, except for *White Zombie* (for which see Appendix D).

Two Liberty films of 1931, *Mother's Millions* and *The Mad Parade*, are excluded; Victor claimed involvement with the two productions, though he received no on-screen credit. Any association he did have with those two films was probably the result of his financial interest in Liberty.

In addition, this appendix omits *Racing Blood* and *When East Meets West*, two films listed on one of Halperin's personal resumes; extensive research has not been able to confirm his participation with any movies bearing those titles.

The films are listed chronologically. Cast listings offer actors' names, followed by their respective characters' names in parentheses. Credits offer the contributors' names, followed by their job titles in parentheses.

An attempt has been made to mimic the precise title used on-screen or in original pressbook materials; additional information on the same point is added in brackets. In the case of Halperin himself, an effort has been made to give his name exactly as it appeared on a given film (e.g., "Victor Halperin," or "Victor Hugo Halperin").

The Danger Point

Cast: Carmel Myers (Alice Torrance), William P. Carleton (James Benton), Vernon Steel (Duncan Phelps), Joseph J. Dowling (Benjamin), Harry Todd (Sam Biggs), Margaret Joslin (Elvira Hubbard).

Credits: Lloyd Ingraham (Director), Adelaide Heilbron (Titles), Victor Hugo Halperin (Story), Ross Fisher (Photographer), Albert Rogell (Technical Director).

Halperin Productions, distributed by American Releasing Corporation. Released December 24, 1922. Copyrighted November 11, 1922 as LP18624 at six reels (5,807 feet). [*Film Year Book* offers a conflicting release date, claiming it was November 3, 1922.]

Tea—With a Kick!

Cast: Doris May (Bonnie Day), Creighton Hale (Art Binger), Ralph Lewis (Jim Day), Rosemary Theby (Aunt Pearl), Stuart Holmes (Napoleon Dobbings), ZaSu Pitts ("Brainy" Jones), Irene D'Annelle (Irene), Gale Henry (Hesperis McGowan), Dot Farley (Mrs. Juniper), Louise Fazenda (Birdie Puddleford), Dale Fuller (Kittie Wiggle), Edward Jopson (Octavius Jiniper), Spike Rankin (Mrs. Bump), Harry Lorraine (Reverend Harry White), Sidney D'Albrook (Pietro), Tiny Ward (King Kick), Earl Montgomery (Convict Dooley), Hazel Keener (Hazel), Julanne Johnston (Gwen Van Peebles), William De Vaull (Napoleon), Hank Mann (Sam Spindle), Chester Conklin (Jiggs), Snitz Edwards (Oscar Puddleford), William Dyer (a businessman), Harry Todd (Chris Kringle), Billy Franey (Convict Hooney), Victor Potel (Bellboy 13).

Credits: Victor Hugo Halperin (General Supervisor, Story), Director (Erle C. Kenton), William Marshall (Photography), Philip Rand (Photography).

Victor H. Halperin Productions, distributed by Associated Exhibitors. Released August 26, 1923. Copyrighted August 11, 1923 as LP19296 at six reels (5, 950 feet).

When a Girl Loves

Cast: Agnes Ayres (Sasha Boroff), Percy Marmont (Count Michael), Robert McKim (Dr. Godfrey Luke), Kathlyn Williams (Helen), John George (Grishka), Mary Alden (The Czarina), George Seigmann (Rogojin), Ynez Seabury (Fania), William Orlamond (Alexis), Rosa Rosanova (Ferdova), Leo White (Yussoff), Otto Lederer (Peter).

Credits: Victor Hugo Halperin (Director-Writer), Alvin Wyckoff (Photography).

Halperin Productions, distributed by Associated Exhibitors. Released April 20, 1924. Copyrighted March 20, 1924, as LP20010 at six reels (5, 876 feet).

Greater Than Marriage

Cast: Marjorie Daw (Joan Thursday), Lou Tellegen (John Masters), Peggy Kelly (Maizie de Noovan), Tyrone Power [Sr.] (Father), Mary Thurman (Venetia), Dagmar Godowsky (Nella Gardrow), Raymond Bloomer (Vincent Marbridge), Effie Shannon (Mother), Florence Billings (Aunt Helena), William Ricciardi (Sam Goldman), Ed Roseman (Charlie Quan).

Credits: Victor Hugo Halperin (Direction and Scenario), Victor Hugo Halperin (Titles), Edward Paul (Photography), Carl Vanderbroch (Photography). Based on Louis Joseph Vance's 1913 novel *Joan Thursday*.

Romance Pictures, distributed by The Vitagraph Company of America. Released November 16, 1924. Copyrighted October 20, 1924, as LP20682 at seven reels (6,821 feet).

School for Wives

Cast: Conway Tearle (Richard Keith), Sigrid Holmquist (Betty Lynch), Peggy Kelly (Lady Atherton), Arthur Donaldson (Jordan B. Lynch), Allan Simpson (Howard Lynch), Brian Donlevy (Ralph), Dick Lee (Tomlinson), Dorothy Allen (Muggins), Gerald Oliver Smith (Ronald Van Stuyvesant), Emily Chichester (Kitty Dawson), Alyce Mills (Mary Wilson), Orlando Daly (Harold Waldehast), Jill Lynn (Dardy Waldehast).

Credits: Victor Hugo Halperin (Direction and Scenario), Joseph Ruttenberg (Photography), Jack Zanderbrock (Photography), Tec-Arts Studios (Sets). Based on Leonard Merrick's 1907 novel *The House of Lynch*.

Victory Pictures, distributed by the Vitagraph Company of America. Released April 5, 1925. Copyrighted February 14, 1925, as LP21155 at seven reels (6,782 feet).

Ad for School for Wives *published in the May 29, 1925,* New York Herald Tribune.

The Unknown Lover

Cast: Frank Mayo (Kenneth Billings), Elsie Ferguson (Elaine Kent), Mildred Harris (Gale Norman), Peggy Kelly (Gladys), Leslie Austin (Fred Wagner).

Credits: Victor Hugo Halperin (Director-Writer). Victory Pictures, distributed by the Vitagraph Company of America. Released on October 30, 1925. Copyrighted on July 11, 1925, as LP21647 at seven reels (6,895 feet).

In Borrowed Plumes

Cast: Marjorie Daw (Mildren Grantley/Countess D'Autreval), Niles Welch (Philip Dean), Arnold Daly (Sam Wassup), Louise Carter (Clara Raymond), Peggy Kelly (Mrs. Harrison), Wheeler Oakman (Jack Raymond), Dagmar Godowsky (Clarice).

Credits: Victor Hugo Halperin (Director). Based on Leroy Scott's shot story of the same title, first published in the magazine *Smart Set*.

Welcome Pictures, distributed by Arrow Pictures. Released on February 10, 1926. Copyrighted on February 16, 1926, as LP22403 at six reeles (5, 719 feet).

Convoy

Cast: Lowell Sherman (Ernest Drake), Dorothy Mackaill (Sylvia Dodge), William Collier, Jr. (John Dodge), Lawrence Gray (Eugene Weyeth), Ian Keith (Smith), Gail Kane (Mrs. Weyeth), Vincent Serrano (Mr. Dodge), Donald Reed (Smith's Assistant), Eddie Gribbon (Eddie), Jack Ackroyd (Jack), Ione Holmes (Ione).

Credits: Robert Kane (Presented by), Victor Hugo Halperin and Edward R. Halperin (Associate Producers), Joseph C. Boyle (Director), Willis Goldbeck (Scenario), Ernest Haller (Photographer), Leland Hayward (Production Manager). Based on John Taintor Foote's 1923 novel *The Song of the Dragon*.

Robert Kane Productions, distributed by First National Pictures. Released on April 24, 1927. Copyrighted April 11, 1927, as LP23841 at eight reels (7, 724 feet).

Dance Magic

Cast: Pauline Starke (Jahala Chandler), Ben Lyon (Leach Norcutt), Louis John Bartels (Jed Brophy), Isabel Elson (Selma Bundy), Harlan Knight (Jahala's Father), Judith Vosselli (Jahala's Mother).

Credits: Robert Kane (Presented by), Victor Halperin (Director), Adelaide Heilbron and Earle Roebuck (Scenario), Ernest Haller (Photography), Leland Hayward (Production Manager). Based on Clarence Budington Kelland's 1927 novel *Dance Magic*.

Robert Kane Productions, distributed by First National Pictures. Released on June 12, 1927. Copyrighted on June 11, 1927, as LP24068 at seven reels (6, 588 feet).

She Goes to War

Cast: Eleanor Boardman (Joan), John Holland (Tom Pike), Edmund Burns (Reggie), Alma Rubens (Rosie), Al St. John (Bill), Glen Walters (Katie), Margaret Seddon (Tom's Mother), Yola D'Avril (Yvette), Evelyn Hall (Joan's Aunt), Augustino Borgato (Major), Dina Smirnova (Joan's maid), Yvonne Starke (Major's Wife), Eulalie Jensen (Matron of Canteen), Captain H. M. Zier (Major [diff. character than Borgato's]), Edward Chandler (Top Sergeant), Ann Warrington (Lady Hostess), Gretchen Hartman and Florence Wix (Knitting Ladies).

Credits: Victor Halperin and Edward R. Halperin (Associate Producers), Henry King (Director), Howard Estabrook (Scenario), John Monk Saunders (Dialogue and Titles), Mme. Fred De Gresac (Adaptation), John Fulton and Tony Gaudio (Photography), Al D'Agostino and Robert M. Haas (Art Direction), Lloyd Nosler (Film Editor), Harry Akst (composer of the songs "Joan" and "There is a Happy Land"). Based on the short story "She Goes to War" by Robert Hughes.

Advertisement from the New York Herald Tribune *of June 9, 1929.*

Inspiration Pictures, distributed by United Artists. Released July 13, 1929 [following a special New York premiere on June 8, 1929]. Copyrighted June 10, 1929, as LP453 at ten reels (9,500 feet). [The film includes sound effects, a music score, and some talking sequences by Movietone. While partially silent, the film acted as Victor Halperin's entrance into talking pictures; all of his subsequent films would be sound.]

Party Girl

Cast: Douglas Fairbanks, Jr. (Jay Roundtree), Jeanette Loff (Ellen Powell), Judith Barrie (Leeda Cather), Marie Prevost (Diana Hoster), John St. Polis (John Roundtree), Sammy Blum (Sam Metten), Harry Northrup (Robert Lowry), Almeda Fowler (Maude Lindsay), Hal Price (Lew Albans), Charles Giblyn (Lawrence Doyle), Sidney D'Albrook (Investigator), Lucien Prival (Paul Newcast), Florence Dudley (Miss Manning).

Credits: Victor Halperin (Director), Monte Kat-

Newspaper ad promoting Party Girl, *published in the December 31, 1929* New York Herald Tribune.

terjohn, George Draney, and Victor Halperin (Scenario and Dialogue), Henry Cronjager and Robert Newhard (Photography), Russell Schoengarth (Film Editor), Harry Stoddard and Marcy Klauber (Songs: "Farewell" and "Oh, How I Adore You"), R.S. Clayton, William R. Fox, Alfred M. Granich, and Ben Harper (Recording Engineers). Based on Edwin Balmer's 1927 novel *Dangerous Business*.

Victory Pictures, distributed by Tiffany Productions. Released on Jan 25, 1930 [following a New York premiere on January 1, 1930]. Copyrighted on January 17, 1930, as LP1001 at nine reels (7,401 feet). [Though a talkie, *Party Girl* was released in a 6,750 foot silent version as well. It was also originally reviewed under the title *Dangerous Business*.]

Ex-Flame

Cast: Neil Hamilton (Sir Carlisle Austin), Marian Nixon (Lady Catherine), Judith Barrie (Barbara Lacey), Norman Kerry (Beaumont Winthrop), Snub Pollard (Boggins), Roland Drew (Umberto), José Bohr (Argentinean), Joan Standing (Kilmer), Cornelius Keefe (Keith), May Beatty (Lady Harriett), Lorimer Johnson (Colonel Lacey), Joseph North (Wilkins), Charles Crockett (Parson), Billy Hagerty (Master Stuart Austin), Louis Armstrong and His Band (as themselves).

Credits: M. H. Hoffman and Edward R. Halperin (Supervision), Victor Halperin (Director, Story by), Herbert Farjeon (Dialogue Director), George Draney (Adaption and Dialogue), Ernest Miller (Photography), Charles Cadwallader (Art Director), Donn Hayes (Film Editor), Harold Hobson (Recording Engineer), Gordon Cooper (Assistant Director), George Bertholon (Production Manager).

Liberty Productions. Released on November 19, 1930, with a New York State license granted. Eight reels, with prints reviewed at both 6, 480 feet and 6, 698 feet.

Supernatural

Cast: Carole Lombard (Roma Courtney), Allan Dinehart (Paul Bavian), Vivienne Osborne (Ruth Rogen), Randolph Scott (Grant Wilson), H.B. Warner (Dr. [Carl] Houston), Beryl Mercer (Landlady [Madame Gourjan]), William Farnum ([Nick] Hammond), Willard Robertson (Warden), George Burr MacAnnan (Max), Lyman Williams (John Courtney).

Credits: Edward R. Halperin (Producer), Victor Halperin (Director), Harvey Thew and Brian Marlow (Screenplay), Sidney Salkow (Dialogue Director), Garnett

Weston (Story and Adaptation), Arthur Martinelli (Photography), [Second cameramen: Jockey Feindel and Roy Eslick. Assistant Cameramen: Eddie Adams and Al Smalley].

Paramount Productions, Inc., distributed by the same. A Victor and Edward Halperin Production. Sound by Western Electric Noiseless Recording. Released May 12, 1933 [following a New York opening during the week of April 21, 1933]. Copyrighted on May 4, 1933, as LP3857 at seven reels (65 minutes). PCA certificate number 1409-R.

Bachelor Bait

Cast: Stuart Erwin (William Watts), Rochelle Hudson (Cynthia Douglas), Pert Kelton (Allie Summers), "Skeets" Gallagher (Bramwell Van Dusen), Burton Churchill ("Big" Barney Nolan), Grady Sutton (Don Beldon, alias Diker), Clarence H. Wilson (District Attorney Clem), [also in cast: William Augustin and Hazel Forbes].

Credits: Pandro S. Berman (Executive Producer), Lou Brock (Associate Producer), George Stevens (Director), [Assistant Directors: Doran Cox and Jean Yarbrough], Glenn Tryon (Screenplay), Edward Halperin and Victor Halperin (Story), David Abel (Photography), [Camera operator: Harry Wild], Van Nest Polglase and Carroll Clark (Art Directors), James B. Morley (Editor), Walter Plunkett (Costumes), Max Steiner (Music Director), Clem Portman (Sound Recording), Fred Hendrickson (Still Photographs).

RKO Radio Pictures, Inc., distributed by the same. Sound by RCA Victor Systems. Released July 27, 1934. Copyrighted on July 27 as LP4874 at eight reels (75 minutes). PCA certificate number 52. [The working title of this film was *The Great American Harem*.]

I Conquer the Sea

Cast: Steffi Duna (Rosita Gonzales), Stanley Morner [Dennis Morgan] (Tommy), Douglas Walton (Leonard), George Cleveland (Caleb), Johnnie Pirrone, Jr. (Pedro Gonzales), Fred Warren (Sebastian), Anna De Linsky (Mrs. Gonzales), Charles McMurphy (Zack), Frederick Peters (Stubby), Tiny Skelton (Flukes), Olin Francis (Gabe), Albert Russell (Josh), Dorothy Kildaire (Gabe's Wife), Renee Daniels (Stubby's Wife), James Hertz (Tiny), Elaine Deane, Joan Deane, [also in cast: Margaret Woodburn (Widow Penecoste)].

Crew: Edward Halperin (Producer), Victor Halperin (Director), George Cleveland (Dialogue Director),

Leander de Cordova (Assistant Director), John Hicks (Production Director), Richard Carroll (Story and Adaptation), Rollo Lloyd and Howard Higgin (Dialogue), Arthur Martinelli (Photography), F. Paul Sylos (Art Director), Douglas Briggs (Editor), Arthur Kay (Music Director), Abe Meyer (Music Supervisor), G.P. Costello (Sound), Leigh Smith (Technical Director).

Halperin Productions, distributed by State Rights and Academy Pictures Distributing Corporation. Released January 24, 1936 [following a premiere in New Bedford, Massachussetts, on January 16, 1936, and a New York opening on January 23, 1936]. Copyrighted on January 7, 1936, as LP6061 at seven reels (68 minutes). PCA certificate number 1623.

Revolt of the Zombies

Cast: Dorothy Stone (Claire Duval), Dean Jagger (Armand Louque), Roy D'Arcy (General Mazovia), Robert Noland (Clifford Grayson), George Cleveland (General Duval), E. Alyn "Fred" Warren (Dr. Trevissant), Carl Stockdale ([Ignacio] MacDonald), William Crowell (Priest Tsiang), Teru Shimada (Buna), Adolph Millard (Schelling).

Credits: Edward Halperin (Producer), Leon d'Usseau (Studio Executive), Victor Halperin (Director), Howard Higgin, Rollo Lloyd, and Victor Halperin (Story), Arthur Martinelli (Director of Photography), J. Arthur Feindel (Operative Cameraman), Leigh Smith (Technical Director), Douglas Biggs (Editor), Abe Meyer (Music Director), G. P. Costello (Sound Technician), Phillip Scheer (Coiffures), John Hicks (Production Manager), [Harry Pritzker (Supervisor, location shooting), Ray Mercer (Special Effects)].

Halperin Pictures, distributed by Academy Pictures Distributing Corporation. Released on May 20, 1936. Copyrighted on April 22, 1936, as LP6289 at eight reels (62 minutes). PCA certificate number 2161

Nation Aflame

Cast: Noel Madison (Frank Sandino, Sands), Norma Trelvar (Wynne Adams), Lila Lee (Mona Burtis), Douglas Walton (Tommy Franklin), Harry Holman (Roland Adams), Arthur Singley (Bob Sherman), Snub Pollard (Wolfe), Earl Hodgins (Wilson), Si Wills (Walker), Roger Williams (Dave Burtis), Alan Cavan (Harry Warren), Dorothy Kildaire (Toots), Elaine Deane, Lee Phelps, Carl Stockdale, C. Montague Shaw (President of the United States), [also in cast: Lee Shumway (Campbell)].

Credits: Edward Halperin (Producer), Victor Halperin (Director), Charles Gerson (Dialogue Director), Paul Hughes (Assistant Director), Oliver Drake (Screenplay), Thomas Cixon, Oliver Drake, Leon D'Usseau, and Rex Hale (Story), William Lively (Additional Dialogue), Arthur Martinelli (Photography), H.C. Ramsay (Operating Cameraman), Leigh Smith (Art Director), Holbrook Todd and Frank Bayes (Film Editors), Dr. Edward Kilenyi (Music Director), J. S. Westmoreland (Recording Engineer), F. Herrick Herrick (Production Manager). [Some sources of the period credit the tale's origin as a Thomas Dixon short story.]

Treasure Pictures Corporation, distributed by Television Pictures and Treasure Pictures Corporation. A Victor and Edward Halperin Production. Released on October 16, 1937. Running time, eight reels (76 minutes). No copyright form filed with the Library of Congress. PCA certificate number 2964.

Torture Ship

Cast: Lyle Talbot (Lieutenant Bob Bennett), Irving Pichel (Dr. Herbert Stander), Jacqueline Wells (Joan Martel), Sheila Bromley (Mary Slavish), Anthony Averill (Dirk), Russell Hopton (Harry), Julian Madison (Paul), Eddie Holden (Ole Olson), Wheeler Oakman (Ritter), Stanley Blystone (Briggs), Leander de Cordova (Ezra), Dmitri Alexis (Murano), Skelton Knaggs (Jesse), [Adia Kuznetzoff (Krantz), William Chapman (Bill), Fred Walton (Fred)].

Credits: Sigmund Neufeld (Associate Producer), Victor Halperin (Director), George Sayre (Screenplay), Jack Greenhalgh (Director of Photography), Fred Preble (Art Director), Holbrook Todd (Editor), David Chudnow (Music Director), Hans Weeren (Sound Engineer). Based on Jack London's story "A Thousand Deaths."

Producers Distributing Corporation, distributed by the same. Released on October 22, 1939. No copyright form filed with the Library of Congress. Running time, 62 minutes. PCA certificate number 5714.

Buried Alive

Cast: Beverly Roberts (Joan Wright), Robert Wilcox (Johnny Martin), George Pembroke (Ernie Mathews), Ted Osborne (Ira Hanes), Paul McVey (Jim Henderson), Alden Chase (Dr. Robert Lee), Don Rowan (Big Billy), Peter Lynn (Gus Barth), Norman Budd (The Kid), Bob McKenzie (Al Garrity), Wheeler Oakman (Manning), Ben Alexander (Riley), Boyd Irwin (Rutledge), Edward Earle (Charlie Blake), Dave O'Brien (Carson),

[Gerald Storm (Robert Fiske), Mike Gurney (Joe McGuinn), Jack C. Smith (Mort Jarvis), Bob Sherwood (Holmes), Joe Caits (Rizinski), James H. McNamara (Wegley)].

Credits: Ben Judell (Producer), Sigmund Neufeld (Associate Producer), Victor Halperin (Director), George Bricker (Screenplay), William A. Ullman, Jr. (Story), Jack Greenhalgh (Photography), Fred Preble (Art Director), Holbrook N. Todd (Film Editor), Dave Chudnow (Music Director), Hans Weeren (Sound).

Producers Pictures Corporation, distributed by the same. Running time, 62 minutes. Released on November 6, 1939. No copyright form filed with the Library of Congress. PCA certificate number 5817.

Girl's Town

Cast: Edith Fellows (Sue Norman), June Storey (Myra Norman), Kenneth Howell (Kenny Lane), Alice White (Nicky), Anna Q. Nilsson ("Mother" Lorraine), Warren Hymer (Joe), Vince Barnett (Dimitri), Paul Dubov (Lionel Fontaine), Peggy Ryan (Penny), Dolores Diane (Sally), Helen McCloud (Mayor), Bernice Kay (Ethyl), Charlie Williams (Coffer).

Credits: Lou Brock (Producer), Jack Schwarz (Producer), Victor Halperin (Director), Gene Kerr (Screenplay), Victor McLeod (Screenplay), Arthur Reed (Photography), Lee Zahler (Music Director), Martin G. Cohn (Film Editor), [Eddie Saeta (Assistant Director), Harry Reif (Set Dressing), Arthur Hammond (Production Manager)].

A Preference Picture. Distributed by Producer's Releasing Corporation. Released on April 7, 1942. Copyrighted on January 25, 1942, as LP11136 at seven reels (66 minutes).

The Lone Star Trail

Cast: Johnny Mack Brown (Blaze Barker), Tex Ritter (Fargo Steele), Fuzzy Knight (Angus McAngus), Jennifer Holt (Joan Winters), George Eldredge (Doug Ransom), Michael Vallon (Jonathan Bently), Harry Strang (Sheriff Waddell), Earle Hodgkins (Cyrus Jenkins), Jack Ingram (Dan Jason), Bob Mitchum (Ben Slocum), Ethan Laidlaw (Steve Bannister), The Jimmy Wakely Trio (as themselves, Jimmy Wakely, Cyrus Bond, and Scott Harrell), Henry Roquemore (Tax Collector), Eddie Parker (Henchman), [also in cast: Reed Howes, Fred Graham, William Desmond, Denver Dixon, Billy Engle, Carl Mathews, Bob Reeves, Tom Steele, and Art Mix].

Credits: Oliver Drake (Associate Producer), Ray

Taylor (Director), Oliver Drake (Screenplay), Victor Halperin (Original Story), William Sickner (Director of Photography), Jack Otterson (Art Director), Ralph M. DeLacy (Associate Art Director), Ray Snyder (Film Editor), Milton Rosen and Everett Carter (Song: "Welcome Home"), Oliver Drake (Song: "Adios Vaquero"), Jimmy Wakely, Dick Reinhart, and Frank Reneau (Song: "I Got to See Texas"), Milton Rosen, Oliver Drake, and Jimmy Wakely (Song: "Trail Dreamin'"), R. A. Gausman (Set Decorations), A. J. Gilmore (Associate Set Decorator), H. J. Salter (Music Director), Bernard B. Brown (Sound Director), Jess Moulin (Sound Technician), [Assistant Director (Melville Shyer)] .

A Universal Pictures Company film, distributed by the same. Released on August 6, 1943. Copyrighted on November 16, 1942, as LP11692 at six reels (57 minutes). PCA certificate number 8918.

Strange Lands and Seven Seas

The following list represents an episode log for Victor Halperin's television program, *Strange Lands and Seven Seas*, when it appeared on the Los Angeles–based station KHJ. All quotations regarding episodes stem from the *Los Angeles Times*' TV listings for the same date as the show.

September 7, 1956
Debut show on KHJ; episode offered "films of skin divers off the coast of Florida."

September 14, 1956
"[A]rchery on the Guatemala-Mexican border."

September 21, 1956
"[F]ilm from the Mexican stock car road race finds Ack Miller demonstrating how his homemade hot rod placed him high on the list of drivers."

September 28, 1956
"*Fighting Bulls*, the story of the men who train them and the matadors who meet them in the arenas."

October 5, 1956
"*Lion Sentenced to Hang*."

October 12, 1956
"*Battle with a Boa*."

October 19, 1956
"The Caribbean's treacherous Andros Reef is the subject tonight."

October 26, 1956
"A safari through dangerous African territory to find a rare species of giraffe is scheduled."

November 2, 1956
"*Combat with a Killer*."

November 9, 1956
"*Captors of the Huanaco*."

November 16, 1956
"Actor Wayne Morris steps in as narrator tonight when veteran driver Sam Hanks presents his racing film *Land of the Daredevils*."

November 23, 1956
"Professional adventurer Bob Herts travels in Peru tonight."

November 30, 1956
"A filmed search over treacherous mountain crags to find the almost extinct condor is tonight's adventure."

December 7, 1956
"How Amazon head hunters shrink their war trophies is shown in tonight's film."

December 14, 1956
"Communist-inspired guerillas fight against colonials in *Red Terror of Malaya*."

December 21, 1956
"Wayne Morris narrates a trip to New Guinea."

December 28, 1956
"A filmed hunt for a *Rogue Rhino* follows two sportsmen to Africa."

January 4, 1957
"*Blind Adventure*. Wayne Morris explains how photographers film birds of prey in their natural habitat."

January 11, 1957
"Reveals mystic cults in *Superstitious India*."

January 18, 1957
"*Struggle for Survival*."

January 25, 1957
"*Africa Awakes*, an account of witch doctor rituals and supernatural secrets."

February 1, 1957
"*Zulu Wedding Drums*."

February 8, 1957
"A filmed tour of Borneo's untamed wilds is narrated by missionary guest, Dr. Louis T. Talbot."

February 15, 1957

"*Heart of the Zulu* covers Africa's death laws, rituals."

February 22, 1957

"*Arrow for a Jaguar* follows archer Andy Vail to Mexico to hunt wild game."

March 1, 1957

"*Brave Nomad* covers the Sudanese Arabs' endless search for water on [the] Central African desert."

March 8, 1957

"Danger stalks the jungles of Malaya as hunting party captures a female Orangutan and her baby when they are attacked by the beast's mate."

March 15, 1957

"Ande Dail demonstrates the art of shooting a bull's-eye with a bow and arrow while hanging upside-down from a hovering helicopter."

March 22, 1957

"Explorer Tex Stone faces danger when he enters the Malaya jungle to capture male and female tigers."

March 29, 1957

"Sonny Tuffs spotlights [*signals*] made by an explorer marooned in the Arctic waste."

The following list represents an episode log for Victor Halperin's television program, *Strange Lands and Seven Seas*, when it appeared on the Los Angeles–based station KTLA. All quotations regarding episodes stem from the *Los Angeles Times*' TV listings for the same date as the show.

June 7, 1957

"New channel and time for this adventure series. A headhunter battling a 25-foot boa constrictor should get things off to a lively start."

June 14, 1957

The *Los Angeles Times* listed the show as being broadcast on this date, but it offered no program description.

June 21, 1957

"Ed Harrison presents an exciting study on one of California's most interesting natives, the condor."

June 28, 1957

"Film of [an] African safari showing Margaret and Leetate Smith as they shoot down [a] man-eating lion and stop [a] rhinoceros charge. Bill Guyman hosts."

July 5, 1957

"*Sail to El Salvador*. Trip with the Pugsley family by boat across Pacific."

July 12, 1957

"*Capture of the Rare Guanaco*. Films taken 16,000 feet high in the Andes will be shown."

July 19, 1957

"*Land of the Headhunter*."

The list that follows describes in Victor Halperin's own words the plot synopses of several episodes in the television series *Strange Lands and Seven Seas*. Halperin sent the descriptions to Dick Robbins at KTLA in the summer of 1957. He entitled the following text—which herein duplicates his writing, spelling, and punctuation—as "Coming Subjects....*Strange Lands & 7 Seas.*"

July 26....."BLIND ADVENTURE"

Ed Harrison, famed adventurer and member of the Board of Governors of the L.A. County Museum, takes us into the "Strange Land of Flying Mouse-traps".... where the magnificent kite-hawk hold sway...where a skyscraper blind—built to film the life-cycle of the kite-topples to the ground....where no small living thing has a chance when a kite's babies are hungry.....

Aug. 2....."ADVENTURE IS MY BUSINESS"

We go with Bob Herts, professional trouble-shooter for anyone with troubles in the wilds of South America, on several of his missions—to capture rare animals and find missing persons.....What a life!

Aug. 9....."LAND OF THE DAREDEVILS"

"A famous racing driver shows us how daredevils who are never happy unless their lives hang by a thread are made....How, by stages, thru drag strips, motor-cycle contests and road races he himself became a speed maniac......A thrill-fest."

Aug. 16....."RACE OF DEATH"

Most exciting auto race on earth—the Pan-American Road Race—2,000 miles from Mexico's border to border...With Los Angeles own entry, Ack Miller—who builds his own car at home and finishes on top...

Aug. 23....."LOST ON A GLACIER"

An adventurer prospector in Alaska gets lost with his two pet bear clubs in the crevaces of a roaring glacier—and how he is rescued from death by parties in plane and dog-sled....A spectacular!

Aug. 30....."FIGHTING BULL"

Inside scenes showing little-known facts about bull-fighting in Peru....Howbulls are raised, and se le cted for the kill by matadors who study their individual characters before the fight....and then the thrilling test of blood and courage—bull versus matador!

The following list continues the episode log of *Strange Lands and Seven Seas*' run on KTLA, picking up with the show immediately following the last description in the above materials of Victor Halperin.

September 6, 1957

"Tex Stone, champion archer, depicts [the] prowess of Ande Vail, target artist with the flaming arrow."

September 13, 1957

"*Assignment Ocean Bottom.* Two-man submarine used by Italians to destroy Allied shipping is converted for sports use."

September 20, 1957

"*Orangutan.* Tex Stone, famous collector who for many years brought wild animals back alive for zoos, [shows] how a family of huge orangutans is captured."

September 27, 1957

"*Attack of the Walrus.* White hunters are surrounded on ice floe by army of walrus."

October 4, 1957

"Tex Stone shows how a criminal killer is tracked down in *The Lion That Was Sentenced to Hang.*"

October 11, 1957

"Tex Stone shows how a criminal killer lion is tracked down by pro hunters and a pack of dogs."

October 18, 1957

"*Search for the Reticulated Giraffe.* Naturalist Ed Harrison goes safari-ing for a rare African specimen."

October 25, 1957

"*Brave Nomad.* Story of Arab tribe of the Sudan and its flight for survival."

November 1, 1957

"*Malaya Tiger Hunt.*"

November 8, 1957

"A whale hunt off the coast of South Africa."

November 15, 1957

"*Footsteps of Henry Morgan.* Leo Paddock and crew retrace the course of a notorious Spanish Main pirate."

November 22, 1957

"Underwater battles with sharks and moray eels are featured by host Leon Paddack, noted skin diver and photographer." [Note: The *Los Angeles Times* spelled Leon Paddock's name differently, and in both cases wrongly, in the November 15 and November 22, 1957 television program listings.]

November 29, 1957

"Adventure into the Mayan sacrificial wells of [the] Yucatan."

White Zombie Shot List

The following shot list has been compiled for ease of following some of the more detailed discussions of *White Zombie*. Given the various cuts of the film that have circulated, this shot list should be viewed as accurate only for the 1994 laser disc restoration by the Roan Group and the subsequent 1999 Roan Group DVD—the versions from which these data were transcribed and the versions which the present text adopts as the finest available.[1] In addition to describing each shot, this list identifies visual transitions between shots like dissolves and wipes. Where no such transitions are identified, straight cuts between shots occur. The list also breaks down the film into its 23 scenes, but these are simply to assist in dissecting the narrative. Unless a specific transition is noted, movements from scene to scene are visually made by straight cuts.

Scene 1: Burial in the Road

1. Long shot of burial scene appears under opening credits.
2. Long shot of carriage.
3. Medium two shot of Neil and Madeline.
4. Long shot of burial in road.
5. Medium close up of carriage driver.
6. Medium two shot of Neil and Madeline.
7. Long shot of carriage and burial.
8. Closeup of Madeline through carriage window.
9. Medium closeup of carriage driver.
10. Close up of Madeline through carriage window.
11. Medium closeup of carriage driver.
12. Closeup of Madeline through carriage window.
13. Medium shot of Neil and Madeline.
14. Long shot of burial scene; camera pans to right to show carriage, then pans left to follow the carriage's movements.
15. Medium shot of Neil and Madeline.
16. Long shot of burial scene; camera pans slightly to the right.

Scene 2: Introduction of Legendre

17. Long shot of carriage approaching camera; extreme close up of Legendre's eyes, fixed on the spectator, are superimposed over the image. The camera tracks back to make superimposed eyes smaller. The long shot of the carriage fades to black.
18. Legendre's eyes remain onscreen, drifting to the upper left corner of the composition and dissolving away. The shot fades up to Legendre standing in long shot as carriage approaches him and stops.
19. Medium closeup of carriage driver asking a question of offscreen Legendre.
20. Long shot of Legendre approaching carriage window.
21. Medium closeup of driver.
22. Long shot of Legendre approaching carriage.
23. Medium shot of Legendre from inside carriage window and over the shoulder of Madeline.
24. Extreme closeup of Legendre's face, looking directly at the camera.
25. Medium shot of Neil and Madeline, who puts her nervous hand to her mouth.
26. Closeup of Legendre's hand on Madeline's scarf, which is partially resting on the window seal.
27. Medium shot of Neil and Madeline.
28. Medium long shot of zombies on hill walking toward the camera.
29. Medium shot of Neil and Madeline, whose hand is touching her mouth in fear.
30. Medium closeup of driver.
31. Medium shot of Neil and Madeline.
32. Long shot of carriage; Legendre pulls scarf from Madeline; camera pans to right slightly as carriage leaves left side of frame, leaving Legendre standing alone.
33. Medium shot of Neil and Madeline, who clutches her throat.
34. Long shot of carriage moving through grave-

In Scene 1, Neil (John Harron) and Madeline (Madge Bellamy) travel to Beaumont's home by carriage. (Courtesy of Leonard J. Kohl.)

yard; camera pans to left slightly to follow its movement; carriage turns toward camera and leaves frame on left side of screen.

35. Medium shot of Legendre on hillside with zombies clustered behind him; camera tilts down slightly; Legendre walks out of frame on right side after placing scarf in his vest. While placing scarf in his vest, Legendre can be seen staring into camera lens on several frames.

36. Long shot of carriage moving down the road.

37. Medium shot of Neil and Madeline.

38. Medium long shot of carriage moving down road; camera tilts down and pans slightly to end in closeup of carriage's wheels before carriage leaves frame.

39. Medium shot of Neil and Madeline, who is clutching at her throat.

40. Medium long shot of zombies walking down hill and leaving frame on the right side of screen.

dissolve to:

Scene 3: Arrival at Beaumont's Home and Description of Zombiism by Carriage Driver

41. Establishing long shot of Beaumont's house w/carriage pulling up to door.

42. Medium long shot of driver hopping off carriage and opening carriage door.

43. Medium closeup of driver.

44. Medium shot of back of driver and fronts of Neil and Madeline.

45. Medium closeup of driver.

46. Medium shot of the back of the driver and fronts of Neil and Madeline.

47. Medium closeup of driver.

48. Medium two shot of Neil and Madeline holding one another.

49. Medium closeup of driver.

50. Medium long shot of driver getting back on carriage, with Neil and Madeline standing nearby.

51. Extreme long shot of zombies on hill.

52. Medium closeup of driver's back; he turns toward camera.

53. Extreme long shot of zombies on hill.

54. Long shot of carriage driving off as Neil and Madeline are left standing.

55. Long shot of Neil and Madeline standing in front of Beaumont's home.

56. Medium shot of Neil and Madeline embracing.

57. Long shot of Dr. Bruner approaching Neil and Madeline out of the shadows.

58. Medium shot of Neil and Madeline embracing.

59. Long shot of Dr. Bruner continuing to approach Neil and Madeline out of the shadows.

60. Medium long shot of Neil and Madeline embracing as Dr. Bruner walks up.

61. Medium shot of Neil and Madeline.

62. Closeup of Dr. Bruner.

63. Medium shot of Neil and Madeline.

64. Closeup of Dr. Bruner.

65. Medium long shot; door opens and Silver, the butler, is revealed.

66. Three shot of Dr, Bruner, Neil, and Madeline, who turn and walk towards the door.

67. Medium long shot of Silver at door, as Madeline, Neil, and Bruner walk into house.

Scene 4: Waiting Inside Beaumont's House

68. Medium long shot of Dr. Bruner and Neil standing; Madeline is seated.

69. Closeup of Dr. Bruner.

70. Medium long shot of Dr. Bruner and Neil standing; Madeline is seated. Silver approaches them.

71. Medium shot of Silver.

72. Medium long shot of Silver, Dr. Bruner and Neil standing; Madeline is seated.

73. Medium shot of Silver.

74. Medium long shot of Silver and Dr. Bruner standing; Madeline is seated. Neil sits down. Silver leaves, and Bruner sits.

75. Medium shot of Bruner seated.

76. Medium shot of Silver eavesdropping on others.

77. Medium shot of Bruner seated.

78. Medium long shot of Bruner, Neil, and Madeline seated.

79. Medium shot of Silver eavesdropping on others.

80. Medium long shot of Bruner, Neil, and Madeline seated; Bruner stands.

Scene 5: Beaumont and Silver's Conversation

81. Long shot of Silver and Beaumont.

82. Medium shot of Beaumont, seen over Silver's shoulder.

83. Long shot of Silver and Beaumont.

84. Medium shot of Silver and Beaumont.

85. Closeup of Beaumont.

86. Medium shot of Silver and Beaumont.

87. Long shot of Silver and Beaumont.

Scene 6: Meeting Beaumont

88. Long shot of Bruner, Neil, and Madeline standing; Beaumont enters the room.

89. Medium shot of Neil.

90. Long shot of Bruner, Beaumont, Madeline, and Neil.

91. Medium shot of Neil.

92. Long shot of Bruner, Beaumont, Madeline, and Neil; Silver enters room.

93. High angle long shot of zombie carriage driver.

94. Long shot of Silver, Madeline, Neil, Beaumont, and Bruner.

95. Medium shot of Silver on stairs.

96. Medium shot of Beaumont at the bottom of the staircase.

dissolve to:
Scene 7: Beaumont Leaves to Meet Legendre

97. Pan Longshot of Neil in bedroom; he walks outside onto the terrace.

98. Medium shot of Neil on terrace.

99. High angle long shot of Beaumont getting onto zombie carriage.

100. Closeup of Beaumont.

101. Closeup of zombie's hands holding reins to horse.

102. Closeup of Beaumont, pans to closeup of zombie carriage driver, then pans back to initial closeup of Beaumont.

103. High angle long shot of Beaumont and carriage driver leaving in carriage.

104. Medium shot of Neil on terrace, looking to off-camera space of carriage leaving.

fade to black/fade up to:
Scene 8: Beaumont's Arrival at Legendre's Sugar Mill

105. Establishing long shot of sugar mill interior; numerous zombies are working.

106. Long shot of zombie carriage driver and Beaumont approaching door from exterior of mill.

107. Long shot of interior of mill.

108. Long shot of railing on second floor of mill and three windows inside mill; faces of zombie carriage driver and Beaumont seen walking through the windows.

109. Long shot of zombie carriage driver and Beaumont coming through door on second floor of mill; legs of zombie workers seen walking in foreground. Shot occurs at knee level.

110. Medium shot of Beaumont at doorway.

111. Long shot of zombie workers walking and carrying baskets on their heads.

112. Medium shot of blades grinding sugar cane.

113. Medium long shot of zombie walking, who falls in the mill; camera tilts down to long shot of workers below.

114. Medium shot of zombie workers grinding the sugar.

115. Medium two shot of carriage driver and Beaumont; camera pans to follow them as they walk down a flight of stairs.

116. Long shot of the carriage driver and Beaumont coming down a flight of stairs.

117. Medium shot of zombie workers grinding sugar; Beaumont walks into background.

118. Medium long shot of Beaumont walking toward camera; camera tracks back to reveal iron patterns in a door through which Beaumont passes. Camera track speeds up as Beaumont approaches door.

Scene 9: Meeting with Legendre

119. Medium long shot of Beaumont, zombie, and Legendre's hand that enters from offscreen space.

120. Closeup of Legendre's hand clutching.

121. Closeup of Legendre's face.

122. Medium long shot of Beaumont and Legendre framed through a shelf containing various bottles.

123. Medium two shot of Beaumont and Legendre seated.

124. Medium shot of Legendre seated.

125. Medium shot of Beaumont seated.

126. Medium shot of Legendre seated.

127. Medium two shot of Beaumont and Legendre seated.

128. Medium shot of Beaumont seated.

129. Medium shot of Legendre seated.

130. Medium shot of Beaumont seated.

131. Medium shot of Legendre seated.

132. Medium shot of Beaumont seated.

133. Medium shot of Legendre seated.

134. Medium shot of Beaumont seated.

135. Medium shot of Legendre seated.

136. Medium shot of Beaumont seated.

137. Medium shot of Legendre seated.

138. Medium shot of Beaumont seated.

139. Medium two shot of Beaumont and Legendre seated; Legendre stands as camera tilts up. Then Beaumont stands.

140. Closeup tilt from feet of zombie up to face (Beaumont POV).

141. Medium shot of Beaumont, with Legendre entering frame to whisper in his ear.

142. Medium long shot of Beaumont and Legendre.

143. Closeup of Legendre's hand holding zombie powder.

144. Closeup of Legendre's face and hand.

145. Medium shot of Beaumont.

146. Medium two shot of Beaumont and Legendre.

147. Medium shot of Beaumont.

148. Closeup of Legendre.

149. Medium shot of Beaumont.

150. Closeup of Legendre.

151. Medium shot of Beaumont.

152. Medium two shot of Beaumont and Legendre; Beaumont walks off and camera tilts up slightly, then down again as Legendre is left by himself in frame.

153. Long shot of Beaumont at door.

154. Medium long shot of Legendre.

fade to black/fade up to:
Scene 10: Preparation for the Wedding

155. Long shot of Madeline and maid in bedroom.

156. Medium shot of maid opening terrace door.

157. Medium shot of Madeline preparing hair; camera pans slightly to follow her steps toward the terrace door.

158. Medium shot of maid at terrace door.

159. Medium shot of Madeline looking at offscreen maid and terrace door.

160. Medium shot of maid closing terrace door.

161. Long shot of maid bringing dress to Madeline.

dissolve to:
Scene 11: The Wedding

162. Medium long shot of organist playing organ.

163. Medium shot of Silver placing flower from bouquet on silver tray.

164. Medium long shot of Madeline and Beaumont descending staircase; camera pans left and tilts down to follow them.

165. Medium long shot of the two turning corner of staircase; camera begins motionless, then tracks backward and tilts down to follow their movements. Camera then stops movement when Madeline and Beaumont do; Beaumont walks out of camera frame.

166. Medium shot of Beaumont taking flower from silver tray.

In Scene 9, Beaumont (Robert Frazer, left) meets with Murder Legendre (Bela Lugosi, right) at the latter's sugar mill.

167. Medium shot of Beaumont presenting flower to Madeline.

168. Medium shot of Silver watching an offscreen Madeline and Beaumont.

169. Long shot of wedding ceremony.

170. Medium closeup of hand clasp between Madeline and Neil.

171. Medium long shot of wedding ceremony.

172. Medium shot of Beaumont.

173. Medium long shot of wedding ceremony.

dissolve to:

Scene 12: The Wedding Reception and Zombification of Madeline

174. Long shot of the back of Legendre (in front of Beaumont's house).

175. Long shot of the front of Legendre.

176. Medium long shot of Legendre blowing out candle in lamp and preparing to carve voodoo doll. Le-

gendre noticeably and purposefully looks directly into camera.

177. Medium closeup of Legendre's hands wrapping scarf around candle. Camera tilts upward to show Legendre's face.

178. Long shot of Beaumont's house.

179. Medium closeup of Legendre and lamp; camera tilts upward to reveal vulture perched on stone column.

180. Closeup of Legendre's face, looking up at offscreen vulture.

181. Closeup of vulture's face.

182. Closeup of Legendre's face, his glance moving from offscreen vulture (above frame line) to his offscreen hands (below frame line).

183. Closeup of Legendre's hands carving voodoo doll.

dissolve to:

184. Long shot of Legendre carving an almost

finished voodoo doll; he moves across frame and as he does he noticeably and purposefully looks directly into camera.

185. Long shot of wedding reception.

186. Medium shot of Beaumont; camera tilts upward as he stands up from his chair; camera then pans right to reveal medium shot of Neil; camera then pans left past Beaumont to reveal medium shot of Madeline.

187. Medium long shot of all three at reception table.

188. Medium shot of Madeline looking into glass of wine.

189. Extreme closeup of wine glass from top view; Legendre's face appears on the surface of the wine.

190. Medium shot of Madeline.

191. Long shot of all three at reception table.

192. Medium two shot of Neil and Madeline.

193. Medium long shot of Legendre, standing by lamp at exterior of house and burning voodoo doll in its flame.

194. Closeup of hand holding voodoo doll in flame of lamp.

195. Medium two shot of Madeline and Neil; Madeline faints into the arms of Neil and then the camera pans right to frame only Beaumont.

196. Medium shot of Neil holding Madeline in his arms.

197. Medium closeup of Legendre (in profile) holding voodoo doll in flame of lamp.

198. Closeup of hand holding voodoo doll in flame of lamp.

199. Medium two shot of Madeline and Neil.

200. Extreme closeup of Legendre's eyes looking directly into camera. He is still located geographically outside the house.

201. Closeup of Madeline; her eyes close as she dies.

202. Medium shot of Legendre looking directly into camera; he walks toward lens with his face filling the screen, and quickly covering the screen in black.

fade up to:
Scene 13: Madeline's Funeral
203. Closeup of floral arrangement.

204. Medium longshot of pallbearers carrying coffin toward tomb inside mausoleum, with Neil and Beaumont watching from a distance. Camera track back to reveal outline of tomb, with screen almost filled in black as coffin is pushed toward camera.

fade to black/fade up to:
Scene 14: Haunted by the Memory of Madeline
205. Medium long shot of Neil drinking in Haitian bar, with shadows dancing on the wall behind him.

206. Closeup of table top, with transparent image of Madeline appearing in lower right corner of screen.

207. Medium long shot of Neil grasping at the image of Madeline.

208. Medium closeup of woman's shadow; translucent image of Madeline appears over it.

209. Medium long shot of Neil moving toward the image of Madeline.

210. Medium shot of image of Madeline over woman's silhouette; Neil steps into frame to grasp at image of Madeline. He turns facing camera; camera visibly moves back slightly to reveal more of the wall around him.

Scene 15: Taking Madeline from the Graveyard
211. Long shot of Legendre and Beaumont; Beaumont points to offscreen zombies and camera pans right to reveal them on hillside of graveyard.

212. Long shot of Legendre and Beaumont approaching zombies.

213. Closeup of one zombie; camera pans left to reveal another zombie in close up.

214. Long shot of Legendre and Beaumont standing by zombies.

215. Closeup of one zombie; camera tilts down and pans left to reveal another zombie closeup.

216. Medium two shot of Beaumont and Legendre; camera pans slightly to the right as Legendre moves to center of frame and looks directly into camera.

217. Extreme close up of Legendre's hands.

218. Long shot of Legendre, Beaumont, and zombies as they enter mausoleum.

219. Long shot of Beaumont, Legendre, and zombies entering crypt as seen through the viewpoint of behind Madeline's coffin (which is in extreme foreground). Camera shot remains through the outline of the tomb even after Madeline's coffin is removed.

220. Medium long shot of zombies resting Madeline's coffin on stairs of crypt interior as Beaumont and Legendre watch.

221. Closeup of Madeline's face.

222. Medium closeup of Legendre's profile looking down at offscreen Madeline.

223. Closeup of Beaumont's profile looking down at offscreen Madeline.

224. Medium long shot of Beaumont and Legendre flanking coffin with zombies standing nearby.

225. Long shot of Neil approaching exterior of crypt.

226. Medium closeup of Legendre.

227. Closeup of Beaumont.

228. Medium long shot of Beaumont and Legendre leaving crypt as zombies carry Madeline's coffin and

In Scene 15, Murder Legendre (Bela Lugosi, right) and Beaumont (Robert Frazer, left) arrive at the cemetery where Madeline is buried. (Courtesy of Venita Halperin.)

follow; camera tilts down slightly as zombies walk up stairs of crypt.

dissolve to:
229. Extreme long shot of zombies on hillside carrying coffin.
230. Medium long shot, from high angle, of Legendre, Beaumont, and zombies walking under eye of camera.
231. Extreme long shot of zombies on hill carrying coffin.
232. Long shot of Neil; camera pans slightly to the right as he walks through graveyard.
233. Long shot of crypt door.
234. Long shot of Neil walking across graveyard; camera pans to right to follow him.
235. Long shot of Neil arriving at door of crypt and entering.

fade to black/fade up to:
Scene 16: Neil's Meeting with Dr. Bruner

236. Extreme closeup of Neil's back; his back moves to the right to reveal Dr. Bruner through the arch made by Neil's arm leaning on a desk; camera tracks back to reveal both at a desk in a medium long shot; camera pans slightly to catch their movement, then tracks in as they speak behind desk. Camera then pans to the right to keep Dr. Bruner in frame as he sits at the desk briefly. Next, camera pans right to follow Dr. Bruner as he makes his way to a bookcase, then camera pans left as he returns to the desk and sits. Camera tracks back and pans left as Bruner moves to the front of desk and sits on its corner. Camera then pans right and tracks in as Bruner returns to seat behind his desk. Camera pans right again to match earlier composition of Bruner shown through the arch made by Neil's arm resting on the desk; camera pans further right for Neil's back to fill screen with black.

fade to black/fade up to:
Scene 17: The House of the Living Dead
237. Extreme long shot of castle and the crashing waves of the ocean below.

dissolve to:
238. Long shot of exterior patio of castle.

dissolve to:
239. Long shot of castle interior.

dissolve to:
240. Medium long shot of Beaumont seated; shot begins on a track from the right of Beaumont and chair and ends by moving right to the chair at a 45° angle to the left side of the screen.
241. Closeup of Beaumont.
242. Medium shot of Beaumont; camera tilts upward as he stands, and pans right to follow his movements, becoming a medium long shot as Beaumont reaches his destination, a jewelry box. The camera then moves away from Beaumont, panning right to a long shot of Madeline playing a piano. The camera then tracks in to become a medium shot of Madeline shown through the arch of the piano top and the stand that keeps it up.

dissolve to:
243. Closeup of Madeline.
244. Medium long shot of Beaumont approaching and sitting by Madeline on piano bench.
245. Medium two shot of Beaumont and Madeline.
246. Medium long shot of Madeline standing from piano bench; camera tilts diagonally upward to the left to show a medium long shot of Legendre on a staircase.
247. Medium long shot of Beaumont and Made-

line; camera pans slightly to right when Beaumont stands up from piano bench.

248. Medium long shot of Legendre on staircase.

249. Medium shot of Legendre.

250. Medium long shot of Beaumont and Madeline.

251. Long shot of Legendre walking down stairs; framed through a flower-shaped opening in the staircase's architecture.

252. Long shot of Beaumont and Madeline standing.

253. Long shot of Legendre; camera pans slightly to the right to follow him.

254. Long shot of Beaumont and Madeline standing.

255. Medium long shot of Legendre; Madeline walks into composition, followed by Beaumont.

256. Medium shot of Beaumont.

257. Medium two shot of Legendre and Madeline.

258. Medium shot of Beaumont.

259. Medium two shot of Legendre and Madeline.

260. Medium shot of Beaumont.

261. Medium two shot of Legendre and Madeline.

262. Long shot of Legendre and Beaumont, with Madeline walking out of frame. Camera pans slightly to left to follow Beaumont's movement, as Madeline appears back in frame and walks up staircase.

263. Medium closeup of Beaumont.

264. Long shot of Beaumont and Legendre, with Madeline is seen finishing her ascent of the staircase.

265. Medium long shot of door opening and butler walking through it.

266. Closeup of Legendre looking directly into camera.

267. Medium long shot of butler bringing wine glasses to Legendre; camera pans left to follow Legendre and reveal Beaumont.

268. Medium closeup of Beaumont drinking.

269. Medium closeup of Legendre holding glass.

270. Medium closeup of Beaumont smelling wine.

271. Medium closeup of Legendre holding wine glass.

272. Medium closeup of Beaumont looking at wine glass, which he begins to throw down.

273. Medium two shot of Beaumont and Legendre; Beaumont throws down wine and backs out of frame.

274. Medium long shot of Beaumont.

275. Medium closeup of Legendre.

276. Medium long shot of Beaumont.

277. Medium closeup of Legendre.

278. Long shot of Beaumont, Legendre, and butler.

279. Medium shot of Silver clasping silver tray.

280. Closeup of Legendre turning to look directly into camera.

281. Medium shot of Silver clasping silver tray.

282. Closeup of Legendre looking directly into camera; focus blurs.

283. Medium shot of Silver.

284. Medium long shot of door opening and zombies entering.

285. Medium long shot of zombie coming around corner.

286. Medium shot of zombie walking toward camera; camera tilts up slightly as he moves closer to the camera; shot ends as closeup of zombie.

287. Medium shot of butler, with zombie approaching from behind

288. Medium shot of Beaumont.

289. Long shot of Beaumont, Legendre, zombies, and butler; camera pans left slightly as zombies carry butler.

290. Medium long shot of Beaumont and Legendre; zombies still seen on staircase.

291. Long shot of zombies entering frame from behind right side of camera.

292. High angle long shot of zombies carrying butler; camera tilts down to reveal river into which butler is thrown; camera tilts upward to long shot of zombies.

293. Medium long shot of Beaumont and Legendre; camera pans to right to follow Beaumont's movement.

294. Closeup of vulture at window.

295. Medium long shot of Beaumont and Legendre; camera pans to the right to follow Beaumont's movement.

296. Medium closeup of vulture at window.

297. Medium long shot of Beaumont and Legendre.

298. Medium shot of Legendre and Beaumont.

fade to black/fade up to:
Scene 18: Journey to the Land of the Living Dead

299. Long shot of Dr. Bruner and Neil on horseback; composition changes as they ride closer and past the camera.

"V"-shaped wipe to:

300. Long shot of native and wagon coming into screen from left and continuing deeper into composition, as Neil, Dr. Bruner, and Pierre ride into view from center of screen.

301. Medium long shot of Dr. Bruner and Pierre on horseback; one native standing.

302. Medium two shot of Pierre and native.

303. Medium two shot of Neil and Dr. Bruner.

304. Medium two shot of Pierre and native.

305. Long shot of Dr. Bruner, Neil, Pierre on horseback, and native walking off on foot.

306. Medium shot of Neil and Dr. Bruner.

307. Medium shot of Pierre.

308. Medium long shot of all three; camera pans slightly left to capture all in frame.

309. Medium shot of Pierre and Dr. Bruner.

Diagonal wipe beginning in lower right and moving to upper left of screen to:
Scene 19: Arrival at the House of the Living Dead

310. Extreme long shot of Dr. Bruner and castle.

311. Long shot of Dr. Bruner approaching Neil at a makeshift campsite.

312. Medium closeup of vulture.

313. Long shot of Neil and Dr. Bruner, who throws rock at offscreen vulture.

314. Medium closeup of vulture; rock hits limb.

315. Long shot of Dr. Bruner and Neil.

316. Medium shot of Neil sitting up; Dr. Bruner crouches into frame.

317. Long shot of Dr. Bruner and Neil.

318. Extreme long shot of Dr. Bruner and castle.

319. Long shot of terrace; Madeline enters through terrace doors.

320. Medium long shot of two maids looking at offscreen Madeline.

321. Extreme long shot of castle.

322. Diagonal wipe (beginning in upper left and moving to about one-third of the screen downward) reveals long shot of Madeline on terrace, leaving castle shot. Diagonal wipe up from lower right to upper left—meeting with the shot of Madeline—reveals Neil. (Castle shot remains transparent behind both images).

Horizontal wipe, from bottom of screen to top, to:

323. Medium shot of Neil.

Curtain wipe, from bottom of screen to top, to:

324. Long shot of Madeline on terrace.

Diagonal wipe, from lower right to upper left, to:

325. Long shot of Neil.

326. Long shot of Madeline on terrace; she turns to walk back inside the castle.

327. Extreme long shot of Neil and castle.

Scene 20: Madeline in Bedroom and Neil's Entrance to Castle

328. Long shot of Madeline in bedroom with maids.

329. Medium long shot of Madeline seated and maids about to brush her hair.

330. Long shot of Neil coming up stairs of castle.

331. Long shot of Madeline and maids in bedroom.

332. Long shot of Neil walking in lower level of castle.

333. Medium shot of river.

334. Long shot of Neil walking, looking down at river, and continuing to walk; camera pans slightly right to follow his movement.

335. Long shot of Madeline walking back onto terrace. [This may actually be part of Shot 319 used a second time.]

Scene 21: Legendre and Beaumont

336. Extreme long shot of castle interior; Legendre and Beaumont in distance at table.

337. Medium shot of Beaumont.

338. Medium two shot of Legendre and Beaumont at table.

339. Medium shot of Beaumont.

340. Medium two shot of Legendre and Beaumont at table.

341. Medium shot of Beaumont.

342. Medium shot of Legendre carving doll; camera pans right to become medium shot of Legendre and Beaumont.

343. Medium two shot of Legendre and Beaumont at table.

344. Medium long shot of Neil entering frame from behind camera on left side; he approaches and enters through a door.

345. Medium long shot of Neil on other side of door; camera pans left slightly to follow him; camera tilts down to reveal river; camera tilts up to return to Neil; camera pans left slightly to follow him.

346. Long shot of Neil walking along stairway around river; camera tilts down to follow his movements; he walks past and to the right of the camera.

347. Extreme long shot of castle interior; Legendre and Beaumont at table, and Neil enters from staircase entrance.

348. Medium closeup of Legendre.

349. Medium shot of Neil.

350. Medium closeup of Legendre.

351. Medium shot of Neil, who falls onto a piece of furniture.

352. Medium shot of Legendre and Beaumont at table; Legendre stands up.

353. Extreme closeup of castle interior; Legendre walks across castle floor.

354. Medium long shot of Legendre approaching Neil.

355. Closeup of Neil.

356. Medium shot of Legendre looking directly at camera and smiling.

In Scene 21, Legendre (Bela Lugosi, left) explains to Beaumont (Robert Frazer, right) that the latter is becoming a zombie.

357. Closeup of Legendre's hands.

358. Medium closeup of Legendre staring into camera; camera tracks in to extreme close up of his face.

dissolve to:

Scene 22: Madeline's Attempt to Murder Neil

359. Medium long shot of Madeline on bed.

360. Medium long shot of Madeline getting off bed.

361. Medium long shot of Madeline walking across room and leaving through door; camera pans from right to left to follow her movements.

362. Long shot of Legendre and Beaumont in castle interior.

363. Medium long shot of Madeline walking through one door, down a hallway, and through another door.

364. Medium long shot of Madeline walking through door.

365. Long shot of Madeline walking down the stairs by the river.

366. Extreme long shot of Legendre and Beaumont in main room of castle interior.

367. Medium long shot of Madeline entering main room of castle interior.

368. Long shot of Madeline walking down stairs, framed through a flower-like part of the stairway's architecture.

369. Medium long shot of Legendre (standing) and Beaumont (seated) at table looking at offscreen Madeline; camera pans slightly to the left as Madeline walks into frame.

370. Medium shot of Beaumont seated, looking at offscreen Madeline.

371. Closeup of Madeline, out of focus as seen through the eyes of Beaumont.

372. Medium shot of Beaumont seated, looking at offscreen Madeline.

373. Medium shot of Legendre, looking at offscreen Madeline.

374. Medium long shot of Legendre and Madeline (standing) and Beaumont (seated).

375. Medium shot of Beaumont seated.

376. Medium shot of Legendre, his head turning to look at offscreen Beaumont.

377. Medium long shot of Legendre and Madeline (standing) and Beaumont (seated).

378. Medium shot of Legendre looking at offscreen Madeline.

379. Medium long shot of an unconscious Neil.

380. Extreme long shot of castle interior, with Madeline leaving table with knife. Legendre (standing) and Beaumont (seated) remain at table.

381. Medium shot of Beaumont (seated) looking at offscreen Legendre.

382. Medium shot of Legendre looking at offscreen Beaumont.

383. Medium closeup of Beaumont (seated) looking at offscreen Legendre.

384. Medium long shot of Madeline with knife approaching unconscious Neil.

385. Extreme closeup of Neil's face; camera tilts down for an extreme closeup of his neck.

386. Medium closeup of Legendre looking at camera.

387. Closeup of Legendre's hands clasping.

388. Medium shot of Madeline raising knife.

389. Medium shot of Beaumont seated.

390. Medium shot of Madeline raising knife.

391. Extreme closeup of Legendre's eyes looking directly into camera.

392. Medium shot of Madeline with knife lowered, then raising it a second time.

393. Extreme closeup of Neil's neck.

394. Medium long shot of Neil (unconscious) and Madeline with knife raised. A hand from behind a curtain grabs her wrist, causing the knife to drop.

395. Closeup of Legendre's hands clasped.

396. Closeup of Madeline.

397. Closeup of Legendre's hands clasped.

398. Medium long shot of Madeline fleeing from Neil's unconscious body.

399. Closeup of Legendre's hands clasped.

400. Long shot of Madeline descending stairs.

401. Medium shot of Beaumont seated.

402. Medium long shot of Neil awaking.

403. Medium shot of Legendre turning his head to look at Neil.

404. Medium long shot of Neil sitting.

405. Extreme long shot of castle interior, with Neil on stairs and Madeline running toward Legendre and Beaumont at table.

406. Medium long shot of Neil at top of stairs.

407. Medium long shot of Madeline running past Legendre and Beaumont.

408. Extreme long shot of Neil descending stairs, with Legendre and Beaumont still at table.

Scene 23: Climax

409. Extreme long shot of Madeline descending stairs onto outdoor patio of castle.

410. Long shot of Madeline reaching the bottom of stairs and walking toward camera into a medium shot.

411. Medium, high angle over-the-shoulder shot of Madeline looking at crashing ocean waters below. She moves and turns, making the shot a medium long shot of her.

412. Medium long shot of Madeline at the ledge of patio, with Neil rushing down stairs.

413. Medium long shot of Madeline, her back to camera as she looks out over the ledge of the patio.

414. Medium long shot of Neil looking at Madeline, pulling her back from the ledge. Legendre descends stairs as Neil embraces Madeline; the couple walk out of the left side of the frame with her.

415. Medium long shot of Madeline and Neil sitting on bench.

416. Medium two shot of Neil looking at Madeline.

417. Medium shot of Legendre looking at offscreen Neil and Madeline, clasping his hands to control Madeline.

418. Long shot of Madeline and Neil on bench, Legendre standing at bottom of stairs, and group of zombies descending stairs. Neil walks toward Legendre.

419. Medium two shot of Legendre and Neil.

420. Long shot of Madeline on bench, with Neil standing beside Legendre. Zombies are approaching Neil.

421. Medium shot of Legendre and Neil.

422. Long shot of Neil stepping back from Legendre and the advancing zombies.

423. Medium shot of Neil pulling his gun.

424. Medium shot of zombie; camera tilts down towards his chest, which becomes a medium closeup as the zombie approaches camera.

425. Medium closeup of Neil firing gun at offscreen zombie.

426. Closeup of zombie's chest with bullet hole; camera tracks back to reveal medium shot of zombie's upper torso.

427. Medium shot of Neil looking at zombies.

428. Medium shot of Neil's legs and feet, standing as they are right on the patio ledge.

429. Long shot of Neil firing on advancing zombies.

Ballyhoo for Bela Lugosi as Murder Legendre in White Zombie.
(Courtesy of Fritz Frising/Vampir Unlimited.)

430. Long shot of shadow on wall.

431. Long shot of Dr. Bruner in disguise walking up behind Legendre.

432. Medium shot of Legendre, who is hit on the neck by Dr. Bruner's club.

433. Medium long shot of various zombies closing in on Neil.

434. Medium shot of Neil's legs and feet, standing as they are right on the patio ledge.

435. Long shot of Neil surrounded by zombies.

436. Medium shot of Dr. Bruner, looking at offscreen Neil.

437. Extreme long shot of Madeline, Dr. Bruner, and Neil, who on his hands and knees makes his way through advancing zombies.

438. Long shot of unconscious Legendre on patio ground.

439. Long shot of zombie walking over ledge, and falling off the patio.

440. Medium long shot of other zombies approaching ledge.

441. Medium long shot of front of silhouetted zombie falling off patio.

442. Medium long shot of another zombie walking off patio ledge.

443. Extreme long shot of patio, with more zombies walking off ledge as Neil, Madeline, and Dr. Bruner remain away from cliff.

444. Medium long shot of Dr. Bruner and Neil.

445. Closeup of Madeline.

446. Medium long shot of Dr. Bruner and Neil looking at offscreen Madeline.

447. Medium long shot of Madeline, who sits back down on bench.

448. Medium long shot of Dr. Bruner and Neil; the latter walks out of frame by advancing to left of camera.

449. Medium long shot of Madeline and Neil on bench; Dr. Bruner walks into frame.

450. Closeup of Neil looking at offscreen Madeline; the focus is slightly blurred, suggesting Madeline's point of view.

451. Closeup of Madeline.

452. Closeup of Neil looking at offscreen Madeline; light moves from darker to lighter which sharpens the focus, again suggesting Madeline's point-of-view.

453. Closeup of Madeline beginning to smile.

454. Medium shot of Dr. Bruner looking at offscreen Madeline.

455. Medium two shot of Madeline placing hand on Neil's face.

456. Medium long shot of Legendre lifting himself off ground.

457. Medium long shot of Madeline and Neil (seated) and Dr. Bruner (standing).

458. Medium long shot of Legendre lifting himself off ground.

459. Medium two shot of Madeline and Neil.

460. Medium shot of Dr. Bruner, looking at offscreen Madeline.

461. Medium long shot of Madeline and Neil (seated) and Dr. Bruner (standing).

462. Long shot of Legendre making his way to and up the patio stairs; camera pans right to follow his motions.

463. Medium shot of Neil and Dr. Bruner, who exit screen right.

464. Long shot of Legendre ascending stairs.

465. Medium shot of Legendre.

466. Long shot of Legendre throwing smoke bomb onto stairs as Neil and Dr. Bruner approach him.

467. Medium closeup of ground as smoke from smoke bomb lifts.

468. Medium shot of Neil and Dr. Bruner coughing.

469. Medium shot of Legendre clasping his hands; a shadow can be seen on the wall beside him.

470. Medium shot of Neil and Dr. Bruner coughing.

Bela Lugosi as Murder Legendre toasts the audience in this publicity still for White Zombie.

471. Medium shot of Legendre clasping his hands.
472. Medium shot of vulture.
473. Medium shot of Legendre with Beaumont approaching and ambushing him from behind.
474. Extreme long shot of Beaumont pushing Legendre off patio as Dr. Bruner and Neil look on; Madeline remains seated.
475. Extreme long shot of Legendre's silhouetted body falling by the cliff.
476. Long shot of Legendre's body hitting water and rocks below.
477. Extreme long shot of Beaumont falling from cliff as Neil and Dr. Bruner look on; Madeline is now standing.

478. Long shot of vulture flying off patio.
479. Extreme long shot of Neil approaching Madeline.
480. Medium shot of Neil embracing Madeline.
481. Closeup of Madeline.
482. Closeup of Neil.
483. Closeup of Madeline.
484. Medium two shot of Madeline and Neil in embrace.
485. Medium shot of Dr. Bruner.

fade to black/fade up to:
"The End"

Chapter Notes

Chapter 1

1. Dixon, Wheeler Winston. *It Looks at You: The Returned Gaze of the Cinema.* Albany: State University of New York Press, 1995 (p. 144).

2. Plot summary developed from a print of *White Zombie* restored by Cary Roan for a 1994 laser disc release from The Roan Group (then of Atlanta, Georgia; as of this writing in 2000, they are based out of Hayesville, North Carolina.

3. Shot and scene numbers, such as the reference to "Scene 14," correlate with the complete *White Zombie* shot list as printed in Appendix P.

4. Jung, Carl G. *Man and His Symbols.* London: Aldus Books, 1964.

5. Bettelheim, Bruno. *The Uses of Enchantment.* New York: Knopf, 1977 (p. 25).

6. See Angela Care Evans' excellent *The Sutton Hoo Ship Burial* (British Museum, 1986) for a historical examination of one of the most famous of Anglo-Saxon ship burials.

7. The lack of a firm time period in *White Zombie's* setting may also act as another of the film's dreamlike qualities.

8. Propp, V. *Morphology of the Folktale.* 2nd. Edition. Austin, TX: University of Texas Press, 1968.

9. *Ibid.*, p. 20.

10. *Ibid.*, p. 21.

11. Haughton, Rosemary. *Tales from Eternity: The World of Fairytales and the Spiritual Search.* New York: Seabury, 1973 (p. 78).

12. *The Mummy* (1932), *The Werewolf of London* (1935), and *Dracula's Daughter* (1936) are the major exceptions to this rule. By contrast, the number of nonsupernatural U.S. horror films of the 1930s dwarf the aforementioned; these include, for example, *The Bat Whispers* (1930), *Frankenstein* (1931), *Dr. Jekyll and Mr. Hyde* (1932), *Dr. X* (1932), *Island of Lost Souls* (1932), *The Most Dangerous Game* (1932), *Murders in the Rue Morgue* (1932), *The Old Dark House* (1932), *King Kong* (1933), *Mystery of the Wax Museum* (1933), *The Black Cat* (1934), *The Black Room* (1935), *The Bride of Frankenstein* (1935), *Mad Love* (1935), *Mark of the Vampire* (1935), *The Raven* (1935), and *The Invisible Ray* (1936). This list does not even include the many low-budget horror films of the period that concentrate not on the supernatural, but instead on old dark houses or mad scientists.

13. Much the same could be said of Robert Armstrong in *The Most Dangerous Game* (1932), Maude Eburne in *The Vampire Bat* (1933), Charlie Ruggles in *Murders in the Zoo* (1933), and Ted Healy in *Mad Love* (1935).

14. Borland, Elena. "Manners Stands Apart." *Los Angeles Times,* 16 Nov. 1930.

15. McManus, John T. "Walking Dead in Angkor." *New York Times,* 24 May 1936.

16. For example, similar circumstances can be seen in *The Mummy* (1932), *The Vampire Bat* (1933), *The Black Cat* (1934), and *The Raven* (1935).

17. Subsequent U.S. horror films exemplifying this plot device include: *Murders in the Rue Morgue* (1932), *The Mummy* (1932), *Island of Lost Souls* (1932), *King Kong* (1933), *Murders in the Zoo* (1933), *The Vampire Bat* (1933), *The Raven* (1935), *Dracula's Daughter* (1936), and *Revolt of the Zombies* (1936).

18. Todorov, Tzvetan. *The Fantastic: A Structural Approach to a Literary Genre.* Ithaca, NY: Cornell University Press, 1975 (p. 33).

19. *Ibid.*, p. 25.

20. See Shots 284 and 361.

21. Freud, Sigmund. Qtd. in Sabine Prokhoris' *The Witch's Kitchen: Freud, Faust, and the Transference* Ithaca, NY: Cornell University Press, 1995 (p. 31).

22. Goethe, Johann Wolfgang von. *Faust: A Tragedy.* Translated by Alice Raphael. New York: Jonathan Cape and Harrison Smith, 1930 (p. 139).

23. *Ibid.*, p. 82.

24. *Ibid.*, p. 167.

25. In his text *Goethe's Faust: A Commentary* (St. Louis, MO: Sigma Publishing, 1886), Denton J. Snider claims: "When thou permittest Mephisto to glut thy senses now, thou art in reality his slave in the eternal life at this moment; when he serves the sensual part, he subjects the spiritual; though he be thy slave in the particular, just for that reason thou art his slave in the universal; following the senses simply, thou art with him destructive to the good, to the world order..." (p. 142).

26. Goethe, p. 53.

27. Enright, D.J. *Commentary on Goethe's Faust.* New York: J.J. Little and Ives, 1949.

28. Jung, *Man and His Symbols.* London: Aldus Books, 1964.

29. See Alan P. Cottreel's essay "The Theme of Sacrifice and the Question of Faust's Redemption" in his text *Goethe's Faust: Seven Essays.* Chapel Hill: University of North Carolina Press, 1976.

30. Weston, *Murder on Shadow Island*, p. 45.

31. Du Maurier, George. *Trilby*. New York: Harper and Brothers, 1894 (p. 74).

32. Actor Wilton Lackaye's portrayal of Svengali was well touted. *Photoplay* of December 1917 dubbed the 1917 film a "masterpiece of atmospheric achievement."

33. Du Maurier, p. 69.

34. *Ibid.*, p. 75.

35. *Ibid.*, p. 74.

36. For example, see Du Maurier pp. 316, 317, and 321.

37. In the novel, Gecko describes Svengali's power, which is not solely dependent upon the use of his eyes: "...with one wave of his hand over her—with one look of his eye—with a word—Svengali could turn her into the other Trilby, *his* Trilby—and make her do whatever he liked ... you might have run a red-hot needle into her and she would not have felt it..." (*Ibid.*, p. 458).

38. Björnström. *Hypnotism: Its History and Present Development*. New York: Humboldt Publishing Co., 1889 (p. 229).

39. *Ibid.*, p. 4.

40. *Ibid.*, p. 71.

41. Vincent, Ralph Harry. *The Elements of Hypnotism: The Induction, the Phenomena, and the Physiology of Hypnotism*. London: K. Paul, Trench, Trubner, 1897 (p. 102).

42. Oppenheim, Nathan. *Mental Growth and Control*. New York: MacMillan, 1913 (p. 180).

43. *Ibid.*, p. 217.

44. Park, Roswell. *The Evil Eye Thanatology and Other Essays*. Boston: Gorham Press, 1912 (p. 16).

45. Carleton, William. *The Evil Eye; or, The Black Spectre*. Dublin: James Duffy and Sons, 1880 (first page of unpaginated preface).

46. Schoeck, Helmut. 'The Evil Eye: Forms and Dynamics of a Universal Superstition." *Emory University Quarterly* 11 (1955): 153–161.

47. European films had also used Lugosi's eyes for effect, specifically *Sklaven fremdes Willens* (1919), in which the actor portrayed a hypnotist. For more information on that film, see Gary D. Rhodes' *Lugosi: His Life in Films, on Stage, and in the Hearts of Horror Lovers*. Jefferson, NC: McFarland, 1997.

48. "The Screen: The Panama Canal and Spies." Review of *The Silent Command*. *The New York Times*, 5 Sept. 1932: 15.

49. The articles on Lugosi by fan magazine writer Gladys Hall are representative of this. For example, see "True Hollywood Ghost Stories: The Case of the Man Who Dares Not Fall Asleep" in *Motion Picture* (Aug. 1929), and "The Feminine Love of Horror" in *Motion Picture Classic* (Jan. 1931).

50. While one might suggest the differences in presentation between Lugosi in *Dracula* and *White Zombie* occurred for legal reasons, the Halperins' development of *White Zombie* as detailed in Chapter Three (as well as the whole of their careers, such as the filming of *Revolt of the Zombies* as described in Chapter Five) shows little fear of copyright concerns. Quite possibly the differences between the two films occurred due to *White Zombie*'s attempts at adopting diverse influences for creative reasons.

51. "Asbestos." New Orleans *Time-Picayune*, 19 Aug. 1932.

52. For example, see the article entitled "Zombies Really Do Exist in Haiti; American Investigator Saw Some" in *White Zombie: Complete Exhibitors [sic] Campaign Book*. New York: United Artists Corp, 1932.

53. Seabrook, William B. *The Magic Island*. New York: Literary Guild of America, 1929 (p. 94).

54. The ring actor Lugosi wears is not an idea borrowed from *The Magic Island* or seemingly any other voodoo or zombie reference source. Indeed, it may well have belonged to the actor, as an apparently identical ring can be noticed on Lugosi's finger in the 12-chapter serial *The Return of Chandu* (1934).

55. Seabrook, *The Magic Island*, p. 93. (The quotation was spoken by a Haitian named Polynice, who described zombiism to Seabrook.)

56. *Ibid.*, p. 103.

57. *Ibid.*, p. 103.

58. Chapter Two will explore in detail these other texts predating *White Zombie*.

59. Feldman, Gene (Writer-Director). *The Horror of It All*. Wombat Productions. MPI Home Video, 1991.

60. Snider, Denton J. *Goethe's Faust: A Commentary*. St. Louis, MO: Sigma Publishing, 1886 (p. xx).

61. Many other examples could be given of Mephistophelean/Satanic images similar to the Chaliapin portrayal mentioned in the text. From U.S. culture in the period immediately prior to *White Zombie*'s production, the cinematic short subject *The Devil's Parade* (1930) starred actor Charles Middleton as the Devil; his makeup is almost identical to both Chaliapin's and Legendre's. The same could be said of the cartoon mascot for Peek Frean's Allwheat Crispbread, advertised heavily in U.S. publications during 1931; the devilish figure sported eyebrows and a goatee almost identical to those of Legendre.

62. Whether the Garnett Weston script for *White Zombie* called for a vulture or yet some other bird of prey is unknown, but vultures were readily available to studios on the West Coast. As the Carlisle Jones article "Indolent Eagles and Vultures Exhaust Director's Vocabulary" in the April 28, 1933 *New York Herald Tribune* indicated, vultures were the only bird of prey available in Hollywood to filmmakers of the era.

63. Bruner still wears the black cloak when he knocks Legendre temporarily unconscious in Scene 23.

64. The cinematic analogue to this sequence comes in the ninth chapter (*The Evil Eye*) of a 1921 Kosmik Films serial called *The Hope Diamond Mystery*. Actor Harry Carter's character, "Nang Fu," hypnotizes heroine Mary (actress Grace Darmond) and demands she pick up a knife and kill John Gregge (actor George Chesebro), who sleeps outside her doorway. Just before she completes the task, a hand belonging to the unseen character Dakar (actor Boris Karloff) knocks the knife out of her grasp. The extreme closeups of Nang Fu's eyes, the shots of Mary, the manner in which she holds the knife, and the objectified hand knocking it out of her hand strongly suggest Victor Halperin (or one of his associates) had seen this particular sequence and remembered it.

65. Examples include Shots 217, 397, and 399.

66. "New Films Reviewed." *The Boston Globe*, 6 Aug. 1932.

67. Ulmer, Rivka. *The Evil Eye in the Bible and in Rabbinic Literature*. Hoboken, NJ: KTAV Publishing House, 1994 (p. 21).

68. See Chapter Three for a discussion of the preview and subsequent cuts, as well as Chapter Seven for a description of the cut footage.

69. "Weird Tale Booked At Criterion." *Los Angeles Times*, 17 Nov. 1932.

70. Legendre's name is still invoked in mathematics, with his name attached to certain polynomials and coefficients.

71. Quotations from these New Orleans *Time-Picayune*,

articles of the late 1880s can be found in Robert Tallant's book *Voodoo in New Orleans* (New York: MacMillan, 1946).

72. Baring-Gould, S. *Curiosities of Olden Times*. New York: Whittaker, 1896 (pp. 2–3).

73. Diegetic in this context means music which is a part of the story (and thus heard by characters), rather than background music on the soundtrack not heard by the characters. The other three examples of diegetic music in *White Zombie* are "Chant" at the film's opening in Scene 1, the wedding march in Scene 11, and the Spanish jota in Scene 14.

74. Romanes, George. *Essays*. London: Longman, Green, and Co., 1897 (p. 215).

75. See Du Maurier's description of Trilby in the novel: "And also many a flower, born to blush unseen, would be reclaimed from its desert, and suffered to hold its own, and flaunt away with the best in the inner garden of roses!" (p. 102).

76. Weston, Garnett. *Poldrate Street*. New York: Julian Messner, 1944 (p. 11).

77. Weston, Garnett. *The Man with the Monocle* (p. 245).

78. In his book *Dreadful Pleasures: An Anatomy of the Modern Horror Film* (New York: Oxford, 1985), James B. Twitchell asks on page 265, "Does [Murder] want [Madeline] as a sexual object to violate, or as a way to extend his plantation empire?" His question is bizarre enough to ask if he has seen the film, as nothing in its narrative suggests the latter possibility; indeed, the zombified Madeline never works or is even seen in the sugar mill. Rather than being a worker, she is cared for delicately, even to the degree that two maids care for her. And as the present chapter discussion makes clear, all of Murder Legendre's words and actions suggest a sexual interest in her.

79. Du Maurier, p. 136.

80. Benshoff, Harry M. *Monsters in the Closet: Homosexuality and the Horror Film*. Manchester: Manchester University Press, 1997.

81. Romanes, pp. 217–218.

82. Qtd. in Ralph Harry Vincent's *The Elements of Hypnotism: The Induction, the Phenomena, and the Physiology of Hypnosis*. London: Kegan-Paul, Trench, Trübner, and Co, 1897.

83. It's possible that Weston's research helped him develop the names of others in the cast. For example, zombie Chauvin's name may have stemmed from Chavannes, a volunteer from Saint-Domingue in 1779 who left Haiti to fight alongside George Washington's army during the American Revolution.

84. Nikiforuk, Andrew. *The Fourth Horseman: A Short History of Epidemics, Plagues, Famine, and Other Scourges*. New York: M. Evans and Co., 1991 (p. 146).

85. Hamer, Sir William. *Epidemiology Old and New*. London: Kegan-Paul, Trench, Trübner and Co., 1928 (p. 65).

86. Cashman, Sean Dennis. *America in the Twenties and Thirties: The Olympian Age of Franklin Delano Roosevelt*. New York: New York University, 1989 (p. 231).

87. *Ibid.*, p. 233.

88. An investigation of industry trade publications of 1931 and 1932 yields information on a myriad of strikes and union problems. In the November 12, 1931 issue of *The Film Daily*, for example, the article "Aftermath of Union Controversy Being Felt by Chicago Theaters" recounts an operator strike in the Windy City, while a headline in the same publication speaks of a nationwide strike at Fox Theaters that was called off.

89. Jones, Charles P. "Post-view: Gris-Gris and Abie's Irish Rose." New Orleans *Times-Picayune*, 21 Aug. 1932.

90. Nie. "The Week's New Films." *St. Louis Post*, 7 Aug. 1932.

91. Twitchell, p. 264.

92. See the *White Zombie: Complete Exhibitors* [*sic*] *Campaign Book*. New York: United Artists Corp, 1932. (In a *White Zombie* advertisement published in the July 28, 1932 *Kansas City Star*, the suggested catchline was changed to: "Zombies Stole a White Girl, Then the Fury of Hell BROKE LOOSE.")

93. It is here that I would insert my conclusion to a published debate regarding the merits of Clarence Muse's portrayal in *White Zombie*. In her review of the *White Zombie* laserdisc restored by the Roan Group, printed in *Cult Movies* 15 (1995), Johanne L. Tournier critiqued my liner notes and spoke of my being "over-effusive" towards Muse's appearance in the film; however, Tournier gave absolutely no reason to substantiate her charge. Presumably she means to equate screen time (of which Muse has little in *White Zombie*) with levels of critical praise. Certainly she is also viewing the film through a modern lens, unaware of Muse's renown in 1932, and thus appears to be writing an extensive review without benefit of thorough research. I would invoke Muse's enunciation of the definition of zombiism in *White Zombie*—so key to 1930s audiences—his subtle and believable acting in that regard, his appearance as an African-American in a credible, nondemeaning role, and his inherent credibility from prior works (including famed musical compositions and other highly lauded acting performances; see Chapters Three and Five for further details). All of these points seriously call into question Tournier's complaint, which suggests limiting praise for Muse without apparent reason.

94. Muse, Clarence. *The Dilemma of the Negro Actor*. Los Angeles: [Publisher Unnamed], 1934 (p. 11).

95. Eisner, Lotte H. *The Haunted Screen: Expressionism in the German Cinema and the Influence of Max Reinhardt*. Los Angeles: Univ. of CA, 1990.

96. Again, see Rhodes' *Lugosi*. Jefferson, NC: McFarland, 1997.

97. Optical printing occurs on an optical printer, which is a device combining the features of a camera and projector. It is thus able to rephotograph shots for a film while adding visual effects.

98. In their essay "Enunciation and the Production of Horror in *White Zombie*" (in *Planks of Reason: Essays on the Horror Film*. Metuchen, NJ: Scarecrow Press, 1984), Edward Lowry and Richard deCordova speak at length of the different "spaces," the supernatural and the natural, created by the film through its superimpositions and its closeups of Legendre's eyes.

99. Lowry and deCordova speak of the film's use of wipes and its other enunciative techniques (e.g., dissolves, split screens, superimpositions, and intercutting) as perhaps being "related to a kind of experimentation characteristic of the early films within a generic cycle" (p. 349).

100. By the term "spectator" in this chapter, I mean to encompass both theoretical subject and historical viewer.

101. Mayne, Judith. *Cinema and Spectatorship*. New York: Routledge, 1993 (p. 37).

102. For a thorough overview of the various theoretical perspectives on spectatorship and "subjects," see Harriet E. Margolis' *The Cinema Ideal: An Introduction to Psychoanalytic Studies of the Film Spectator*. New York: Garland, 1988.

103. Allen, Richard. *Projecting Illusion: Film Spectatorship*

and the Impression of Reality. Cambridge: Cambridge University Press, 1995 (p. 3).

104. In this category is Paul Willemen's "Notes on Subjectivity—on Reading 'Subjectivity under Siege,'" *Screen* Volume 19, Issue 1, Spring 1978 (p. 45).

105. Margolis, p. 203. (Theorist Daniel Sallitt shares Margolis' viewpoint in his "Point of View and 'Intrarealism' in Hitchcock," *Wide Angle* Volume 4, Issue 1, 1980.)

106. Bordwell, David. *Narration in the Fiction Film.* Madison: Univ. of Wisconsin, 1985 (p. 29).

107. Branigan, Edward. *Point of View in the Cinema: A Theory of Narration and Subjectivity in Classical Film.* New York: Mouton, 1984 (p. 4).

108. Dixon, p. 43.

109. Mayne, p. 37.

110. *Ibid.*, p. 33.

111. *Ibid.*, p. 37.

112. One of the few comments on the use of Lugosi's eyes in *White Zombie* comes in Bryan Senn's text *Drums of Terror: Voodoo in the Cinema* (Midnight Marquee, 1999). Though in his chapter on *White Zombie* Senn often questions who was in control of the production (e.g., director Halperin, cinematographer Arthur Martinelli, or both), he claims that Lugosi looks directly into the camera "no doubt at Halperin's [mis]direction" (p. 24), rather than wondering at that moment if someone else deserved the artistic credit or blame. Other than mentioning the "theatricality" of the eyes, Senn doesn't comment on why he deems their use misdirection. He does claim that the effect of their use serves "to distance the viewer from the proceedings" (p. 25). That claim is unsubstantiated by any argument or reasoning in his text. Indeed, these comments are particularly confusing since they follow Senn's earlier comment praising the use of Legendre's eyes staring at the viewer in Scene 1. Senn writes: "Via these orbs, Halperin visually evokes the near-omniscient otherworldly power of Murder Legendre—before we've even met him—to generate an uneasy awe at this pivotal introduction" (p. 21). The contradictions leave one unable to reconcile Senn's claims one with another.

113. Browne, Nick. "The Spectator-in-the-Text: The Rhetoric of *Stagecoach.*" *Film Theory and Criticism*, 4th Edition. New York: Oxford University Press, 1992 (p. 210).

114. Certain comedy films prior to *White Zombie* do often address the spectator directly through similar gazes, such as in the work of Buster Keaton and the work of Laurel and Hardy, but they usually do so for the purpose of gaining sympathy from an onlooker as opposed to constructing the spectator-as-character.

115. Some historians would cite *Freaks* (1932) as another film in the 1930s horror cycle prior to *White Zombie*, and others might invoke the names of films like *The Monster Walks* (1932). Chapter Four, in a section titled "The Comparative Reception of *White Zombie*," makes a strong argument for considering *Dracula* (1931), *Frankenstein* (1931), *Dr. Jekyll and Mr. Hyde* (1932), and *Murders in the Rue Morgue* (1932) as the four major horror films in the cycle.

116. Analysis results from viewings of the three sound films in question, as well as the following films which have often been categorized as horror movies or as possessing qualities of the horror film: *Frankenstein* (1910), *Dr. Jekyll and Mr. Hyde* (1911), *Dr. Jekyll and Mr. Hyde* (1913), *The Avenging Conscious* (1914), *Furcht* (1917), *Trilby* (1917), *Das Kabinett des Dr. Caligari* (1919), *Unheimliche Geschicten* (1919), *Der Golem* (1920), *Dr. Jekyll and Mr. Hyde* (1920, both Hollywood versions pro-

duced that year), *Der müde Tod* (1921), *Häxan* (1921), *The Hunchback of Notre Dame* (1923), *Schatten* (1921), *Nosferatu* (1922), *Orlacs Haende* (1924), *Das Wachsfigurenkabinett* (1924), *The Monster* (1925), *The Phantom of the Opera* (1925), *The Bells* (1926), *The Magician* (1926), *Midnight Faces* (1926), *The Cat and the Canary* (1927), *Seven Footprints to Satan*, (1927), *The Unknown* (1927), *The Fall of the House of Usher* (1928, both the French and Hollywood versions), *The Man Who Laughs* (1928), *West of Zanzibar* (1928), *The Last Performance* (1929), *The Last Warning* (1929), and *The Monster Walks* (1932). The major American horror films not viewed for this study include two that are considered lost (*A Blind Bargain* of 1922 and *London After Midnight* of 1927), as well as one that is currently inaccessible (*The Gorilla* of 1927). In addition, this study does not consider *The Terror* (1928), a film often regarded as the first sound horror film; it is currently believed lost. Dates and information on these films appear in *The Overlook Film Encylopedia: Horror.* Ed. Phil Hardy. Overlook: Woodstock, New York, 1995.

117. The shot and scene numbers presented here refer to the Shot List provided in Appendix P.

118. Browne, p. 221.

119. Mayne, p. 27.

120. *Ibid.*, p. 38.

121. Browne, p. 219.

122. See Chapter Four for an extended discussion of the historical reception of *White Zombie.*

123. Similar examples of Legendre gazing into the camera lens can be seen in Shot 24 in Scene 2, as well as in Shots 386 and 391 in Scene 22.

124. Branigan, p. 73.

125. *Ibid.*, p. 83.

126. *Ibid.*, p. 106.

127. Browne, p. 223.

128. Branigan, p. 106. (A similar example of Legendre's stare at the camera without it being linked to another character in the narrative comes in Shot 266 in Scene 17.)

129. In their essay "Enunciation and the Production of Horror in *White Zombie*" in *Planks of Reason,* Lowry and deCordova examine Scene 12 in its use of space and enunciative techniques; the result yields a very different (though not necessarily conflicting) reading of the scene. See Chapter Nine for an examination of their essay.

130. Of course, Legendre's first name—"Murder"—itself suggests the concept of death.

131. Browne, p. 219.

132. *Ibid.*, p. 219.

133. Few, if any, examples of the power brief cuts hold could be offered from the 1920s and 1930s horror film. More modern examples can be seen in Stanley Kubrick's *The Shining* (1979), which uses very brief cuts of Delbert Grady's two daughters juxtaposed against lengthy shots of a hotel hallway to achieve such an effect.

134. These calculations have been prepared for this study by examining the restored print of the film as released by the Roan Group; they must be considered approximate, given the precise projection rate of this print, as well as flaws which impact running time. Indeed, in Shot 177 it seems clear that—given an obvious splice—some 24–48 frames are missing. Thus, the calculation of Legendre's screen time, as it is he shown in that particular shot, may be 1–2 seconds too short. Furthermore, it should be noted that the calculation of Legendre's screen time in general includes all of Shot 179 and also 180. The vul-

ture—his signifier—has thus added some six seconds to his screen time.

135. These arguments, as all others in this chapter, must be made with an understanding that other factors are at work in the mind of a live audience. The mind of one viewer may drift, forgetting momentarily the action on the screen, another might blink at an inopportune moment, and another might kiss or speak to a companion or leave briefly to purchase popcorn. The spectatorship as constructed by a film is indeed present on the celluloid, but the effects on real viewers do not take place in a vacuum.

136. See Castle's autobiography *Step Right Up! I'm Gonna Scare the Pants Off America*. New York: Putnam, 1976 for more in-depth discussions of these and other gimmicks he invented. While—unlike the process of 3-D—these gimmicks were generally external to the projected image on the screen, they were used during the screening, even timed to occur at specific moments in the film narrative.

137. See Carpenter's discussion on p. 187 of Carol J. Clover's *Men, Women, and Chainsaws: Gender in the Modern Horror Film*. Princeton: Princeton University Press, 1992.

138. Mayne, p. 4.

139. Hansen, Miriam. *Babel and Babylon: Spectatorship in American Silent Film*. Cambridge: Harvard University Press, 1991 (p. 6).

Chapter 2

1. Hazard, Samuel. *Santo Domingo, Past and Present, with a Glance at Hayti*. New York: Harper and Brothers, 1873.

2. Lawless, Robert. *Haiti's Bad Press*. Rochester, VT: Schenkman Books, 1992.

3. Schmidt, Hans. *The United States Occupation of Haiti, 1915–1934*. New Brunswick, N.J.: Rutgers, 1971.

4. *Ibid.*, p. 11.

5. Millspaugh, Arthur Chester. *Haiti Under American Control, 1915–1930*. Boston: World Peace Foundation, 1931.

6. Bellegarde-Smith, Patrick. *In the Shadow of Powers*. Atlantic Highlands, NJ: Humanities Press International, 1985. (p. 143).

7. See James Weldon Johnson's "Self-Determining Haiti: I. The American Occupation." *The Nation* 2878 (Aug. 28, 1920): 236–38; "Self-Determining Haiti: II. What the United States Has Accomplished." *The Nation* 2979 (Sept. 4, 1920): 265–67; "Self-Determining Haiti: III. Government of, by, and for the National City Bank." *The Nation* 2880 (Sept. 11, 1920): 295–97; "Self-Determining Haiti: IV. The Haitian People." *The Nation* 2882 (Sept. 25, 1920): 345–47.

8. See Paul H. Douglas' "The American Occupation of Haiti, I." *Political Science Quarterly* 2 (June 1927): 228–58; "The American Occupation of Haiti, II." *Political Science Quarterly* 3 (September 1927): 368–96.

9. *Ibid.*, p. 137.

10. St. John, Sir Spenser. *Hayti, or the Black Republic*. London: Smith, Elder, & Co., 1889.

11. *Ibid.*, p. 188.

12. *Ibid.*, p. 222.

13. *Ibid.*, p. 192.

14. *Ibid.*, p. 222.

15. *Ibid.*, p. 203.

16. Froude, James Anthony. *The English in the West Indies, or, the Bow of Ulysses*. New York: Charles Scribner's Sons,

1888 (p. 344).

17. Articles also appeared in *Century Magazine* in 1886 and *Popular Science Monthly* in 1891.

18. Newell, William W. "Myths of Voodoo Worship and Child Sacrifice in Hayti." *The Journal of American Folk-lore* I: I, April–June 1888: 16–30.

19. Newell, William W. "Reports of Voodoo Worship in Hayti and Louisiana." *The Journal of American Folk-lore* II: IV, January–March 1889: 41–49.

20. Pritchard, H. Hesketh. *Where Blacks Rule Whites: A Journey Across and About Hayti*. Revised Edition. London: Nelson, 1910 (p. 81).

21. *Ibid.*, p. 79.

22. *Ibid.*, p. 74.

23. *Ibid.*, p. 94.

24. Also of note is that Pritchard believes that "vaudoux priests" are "to a certain extent hypnotists" (p. 98) and that Haytians feared the "evil eye" (p. 91). Though the team involved with *White Zombie* likely had not read these specific passages, their film would draw on both ideas, embodying them in the character Legendre.

25. Chester, Colby M. "Haiti: A Degenerating Island." *National Geographic* 19: 200–217.

26. "Haiti and Its Regeneration by the United States." *National Geographic* 38, 1920: 497–512.

27. Arthur C. Holly's preface to *Les Démons du Culte Voudo* (Imprimerie Edmond Chenet, 1918) went much further than Léger, and it became one of the earliest printed defenses of the voodoo religion. The fact it was published at Port-au-Prince and written in French helped to keep it from gaining any widespread readership in America.

28. Parsons, Elsie Clews. "Spirit Cult in Hayti." *Journal de la Société des Américanistes de Paris*, 1928.

29. These include: "Charms, Luck Tokens, and Love Powders Fail to Save Negro Hoodoo Doctor," printed in the November 17, 1914, New Orleans *Times-Picayune*; "Cupid Will Have to Worry Along Without Powders" in the August 27, 1915, *New Orleans American*. However, one can also find similar articles in the mid-19th century. For example, see the articles on voodoo ceremonies as covered in the New Orleans *Times-Picayune* of July 1, 1850, and the New Orleans *True Delta* of June 29 and August 27, 1850.

30. A later press item spoke of a god named "Zombi." Lyle Saxon's essay "Voodoo" was published in a March 1927 issue of *The New Republic*. "There are a great many people who will tell you that Voodoo or snake-worship among American Negroes has ceased to exist," Saxon wrote. "This is not true, for within the last year I have been an eye-witness at a secret Voodoo ceremony." At the height of the rituals he saw, those involved were "swaying, twitching with the drumbeats." The voodoo queen, "eyes glazed, standing alone in the center of the group, screams aloud: 'Zombi!' The dance stops. The drums break off short. Men and women fall face down on the floor, lying prostrate, moaning: 'Zombi! Zombi!'"

31. Moreau de Saint-Méry, Mederic-Louise-Elie. *A Civilization That Perished: The Last Years of White Colonial Rule in Haiti*. Lanham, Maryland: University Press of America, 1985. (English-language reprint of the 1792 French text.)

32. Madiou, Thomas. *Histoire d'Haiti*. 8 vols. Port-au-Prince: J. Courtois, 1847. (Reprinted in 1922 as an E. Chenet imprint.)

33. Dayan, Joan. *Haiti, History, and the Gods*. Berkeley: University of CA Press, 1995 (pp. 36–38). Her discussion on

Zombi draws partially on the earlier work of Hénock Trouillot.

34. Cable, George W. "Creole Slave Songs." *The Century Magazine* XXXL, 6 (April 1886): 807–828.

35. Castellanos, Henry C. *New Orleans As It Was: Episodes of Louisiana Life.* 2nd Edition. L. Graham Co., Ltd.: New Orleans, 1905.

36. Austin, Judge Henry. "The Worship of the Snake Voodooism in Hayti Today." *New England Magazine*, Mar.–Aug. 1912: 170–182.

37. Alfarez, Don Mariano. "Why the Black Cannibals of Hayti Mutilated Our Soldiers." *New York American*, 13 Feb. 1921.

38. Even earlier, Frankétienne's novel *Dézafi; Roman* (Fardin, 1795)—written in Haitian creole and published in Port-au-Prince—covers a sinister revolt in a zombie colony. The "zombie" most likely refers to the person, Jean Zombi.

39. Reid, Captain Mayne. *The Maroon: A Tale of Voodoo and Obeah.* Place of publication unknown: The Dime Library, 1883.

40. An attempt to catalogue in a short space stories and novels of corpses returning to life would prove futile, but they include such famous tales as: Edgar Allan Poe's "Ligeia" (published in *Tales of the Grotesque and Arabesque* by Lea and Blanchard, 1840) and Nathaniel Hawthorne's "Roger Malvin's Burial" (published in *Mosses from an Old Manse* by Wiley and Putnam, 1846), as well as less remembered stories like Gertrude Atherton's "The Dead and the Countess" (published in *The Bell in the Fog, and Other Stories* by Harper in 1905). Many fictional works like these contain revenants, vampires, or ghouls, but lack a connection to voodoo.

41. Downing, Henry Francis. *Voodoo: A Drama in Four Acts.* London: Francis Griffith, 1914.

42. Calland, Annie. *Voodoo.* New York: Harold Vinal, 1926. (In addition to Calland, we should briefly note the 1926 Broadway play *Kongo*, which starred Walter Huston as Flint. Though not a story of voodooism per se, the exotic tale includes a character named "Zoombie.")

43. With regard to use of the "zombi" god—and indeed some of its other qualities—Scott's play recalls the article "Voodoo" in the March 23, 1927, edition of *The New Republic*. In addition to screams and moans of "Zombi," author Lyle Saxon speaks of bubbling cauldrons, incantations meant to bring forth dead spirits, and euphoric dancing; all of these resonate with similar detail in Scott's play.

44. Even earlier, Bert Williams and George Walker's song "The Voo-doo [sic] Man" was published in 1900.

45. Guion, David W. "Voodoo" [Sheet Music]. *Five Imaginary Early Louisiana Songs of Slavery.* New York: G. Schirmer, 1929.

46. Antebellum America feared a slave uprising and revolt similar to that which had occurred in Haiti. After the Civil War, fears continued in a different manner. As a 1904 *National Geographic* warned, "it is well to consider whether we too may not expect some such acts of savagery [as voodooism] to break out in our own country if our own colored people are not educated for better things."

47. As Lawless says in *Haiti's Bad Press*, "the [American Anglo-Saxon] stereotype of the black sexual animal is inextricably tied to the concept of the innate sense of rhythm in blacks."

48. For example, radio station WEEI of Boston, Massachusetts, broadcast "Voodoo Drums at Midnight" in October 1931.

49. Lea, M. S. "Two-head Doctors." *American Mercury*, Oct. 1927: 236–240.

50. Quotes of Seabrook and Smith taken from pages 272–3 of Seabrook's autobiography *No Hiding Place* (New York: Lippincott, 1942).

51. *Ibid.*, p. 273.

52. *Ibid.*, p. 280.

53. *Ibid.*, p. 273.

54. Seabrook, William B. *The Magic Island.* New York: Literary Guild of America, 1929 (p. 46).

55. *Ibid.*, pp. 48–9.

56. *Ibid.*, pp. 86–7.

57. *Ibid.*, pp. 88–9.

58. *Ibid.*, pp. 300–1.

59. *Ibid.*, pp. 93–4.

60. *Ibid.*, pp. 93–4.

61. *Ibid.*, p. 95.

62. *Ibid.*, p. 96.

63. *Ibid.*, pp. 98–9.

64. *Ibid.*, p. 99.

65. *Ibid.*, p. 100.

66. *Ibid.*, pp. 101–2.

67. Seabrook, *No Hiding Place*, p. 281.

68. Seabrook, *The Magic Island*, p. 103.

69. Seabrook, *No Hiding Place*, pp. 274–6.

70. Robbins, Frances Lamont, editor. "Speaking of Books." *Outlook and Independent*, 9 Jan. 1929.

71. Van de Water, F. "*The Magic Island*." *The New York Evening Post*, 12 Jan. 1929.

72. *Yale Review* Autumn 1929: 185; *American Journal of Sociology*, Sept. 1929: 316.

73. Firmin-Didot published the 1932 French edition as *L'Île Magique*.

74. Another period piece on the idea of Zombi as a god or voodoo snake deity is "The Snake Worshippers of Louisiana," an article in the *New Orleans Item* of March 30, 1924.

75. Chapter One of the present volume addresses racial interpretations of the title of *White Zombie*.

76. Bedford-Jones, H. *Drums of Damballa.* New York: Covici-Friede, 1932.

77. *Ibid.*, p. 181.

78. Cunningham, James. "Asides and Interludes." *Motion Picture Herald*, 5 Aug. 1933: 23.

79. Given the date of *The Film Daily*'s synopsis, the *Curiosities* short film on voodoo and zombies was most likely the episode noted as C224, which was copyrighted on August 10, 1931 as MP2738.

80. Wilk, Ralph. "A Little from 'Lots.'" *The Film Daily*, 11 Aug. 1931: 8.

81. "Curiosities." *Motion Picture Daily*, 5 Dec. 1931: 5.

82. According to the *Cleveland Plain Dealer* of December 5, 1931, the original title of Futter's "travelaugh" was *Voo-Doo in Haiti*.

83. Medbury was known to some film fans for his *Cleveland Plain Dealer* newspaper column "Mutter and Mumble."

84. "Reviews of Sound Shorts: *Voodoo Land*." *The Film Daily*, 28 Feb. 1932: 12.

85. "*Song of the Voodoo*." *Motion Picture Daily*, 31 Oct. 1931: 5.

86. "Reviews of Sound Shorts." *The Film Daily*, 25 Oct. 1931: 9.

87. Roy Webb left New York City shortly after the talking picture era began. He quickly became well known as a film

composer and later as a cofounder of ASCAP. He died on December 10, 1982, at the age of 94.

88. "Personalities in the Village." Undated article in Kenneth Webb file at the New York Public Library, Reference Department Theatre Collection. Circa 1920s.

89. "Henderson Enthuses Over Johnny Hines." *Moving Picture World*, 26 Aug. 1922: 687.

90. *Ibid.*

91. "Kenneth Webb Always Knew the Theater." *New York Herald Tribune*, 6 June 1926.

92. "Who's Who in the Cast." *Zombie* [Program] New York City: New York Theatre Program Corporation, 1932.

93. Perhaps the most interesting biographical article on Starke remains Anthony Slide's column in the May 1977 *Films in Review*.

94. Kohl, Leonard J. Interview with Etta Moten Burnett, 26 Apr. 1999.

95. Burr, Eugene. "The New Plays on Broadway: Biltmore/*Zombie*." *The Billboard*, 20 Feb. 1932: 17.

96. *Ibid.*, p. 17.

97. *Ibid.*, p. 17.

98. Kohl, Leonard J. Interview with Etta Moten Burnett, 26 Apr. 1999.

99. "Voodoo Cult: *Zombie* Shows How the Dead Walk in Haiti." *Brooklyn Eagle*, 11 Feb. 1932.

100. Gabriel, Gilbert W. "Dead Pans: *Zombie*, in Which the Corpses Come Alive All Around the Hinterland of Haiti." *New York American*, 11 Feb. 1932.

101. Burr, Eugene. "The New Plays on Broadway: *Zombie*." *The Billboard*, 20 Feb. 1932.

102. "*Zombie* Play of Thrills and Voodoo Rites." *Chicago Daily Tribune*, 14 Mar. 1932.

103. *Ibid.*

104. See the ad for *Zombie* in the March 20, 1932 *Chicago Daily Tribune*.

105. Collins, Charles. "Another *Dracula*." *Chicago Daily Tribune*, 20 Mar. 1932.

106. *Ibid.*

107. Kohl, Leonard J. Interview with Etta Moten Burnett, 26 Apr. 1999.

Chapter 3

1. Weston, Garnett. *Death Is a Private Affair*. Victoria, British Columbia: Morriss Printing, 1970.

2. In addition to the discussion presented in this section of Chapter Three, the biography of Victor Halperin in Chapter Ten includes information on independent U.S. filmmaking in the 1920s and 1930s.

3. "Big Distribs in Market for Good Indie Films." *The Film Daily*, 10 Aug. 1931: 1, 8.

4. Hoffman, M. H. "Independents Facing Their Greatest Opportunity." *The Film Daily*, 23 Aug. 1931: 13. (Two months before, production executive H. D. Edwards had claimed much the same in *The Film Daily* of June 10, 1931.)

5. "Independent Product at Higher Level." *The Film Daily*, 30 Oct. 1931: 1, 4.

6. Hancock, Don. "Independents Geared For Action." *The Film Daily*, 23 Aug. 1931: 10.

7. "Independents Find the Studio Field Ripe." *Motion Picture Herald*, 12 Sept. 1931: 20.

8. Freuler, John R. "Independent Producers Get Break at Last." *The Film Daily*, 28 Dec. 1931: 3.

9. "622 Feature Releases in 1931; 104 Independent, 121 Foreign." *The Film Daily*, 12 Jan. 1931: 1, 8.

10. Alicoate, John. "The Parade ... As We See It." *The Film Daily*, 26 Jan. 1932: 1, 2.

11. "Indie Studios Schedule 200; 16 Under Way." *Motion Picture Daily* 29 Jan. 1932: 1, 6. See also "M. H. Hoffman Launching Five-Year Indie Plan." *The Film Daily* 7 Feb. 1932: 9. (In 1930, Hoffman was involved with the Halperin brothers in Liberty Productions. Chapter Ten describes their business relationship.)

12. "Indie Body to Aid Relief of Studio Labor." *Motion Picture Daily* 23 Jan. 1932: 1, 4. See also "More than 200 Features Already Planned by Smaller Units." *The Film Daily*, 8 Feb. 1932: 1, 7.

13. "Manpower of Independent Ranks Boosted by Upheavals." *The Film Daily*, 26 Feb. 1932: 1, 12.

14. "Will or Must Pictures Go Independent?" *Variety*, 16 Feb. 1932.

15. Darling, W. Scott. "The Independents Are Making Good Pictures." *The Hollywood Reporter*, 15 March 1932: 19.

16. "Will or Must Pictures Go Independent?" *Variety*, 16 Feb. 1932.

17. Hoffman, Jerry. "Little Firms Teach Giants of Moviedom: Hard Times Make Independent Economics Interesting." *Milwaukee Sentinel*, 7 Aug. 1932.

18. Kann. "Independence." *Motion Picture Daily*, 16 May 1931: 1, 14.

19. This section of Chapter Three is meant to complement the vast array of materials in Chapter Two.

20. See Chapter Two for an in-depth examination of Kenneth Webb's 1932 play *Zombie*.

21. Carb, David. "Seen on the Stage." *Vogue*, 15 Apr. 1932.

22. Cunningham, James. "Asides and Interludes." *Motion Picture Herald*, 20 Feb. 1932: 19.

23. "March Production Survey." *Variety*, 12 Apr. 1932: 21.

24. See Chapter Ten for a discussion of the Halperins' financial involvement in Liberty Productions, as well as their departure from it.

25. Pitts, Michael R. *Poverty Row Studios, 1929–1940: An Illustrated History of 53 Independent Film Companies, with a Filmography for Each*. Jefferson, NC: McFarland, 1997 (p. 223).

26. Beall, Harry Hammond. "With the Procession in Los Angeles." *Exhibitors Herald*, 1 Sept. 1923: 63.

27. Ankerich, Michael G. "Madge Bellamy." *Broken Silence: Conversations with 23 Silent Film Stars*. Jefferson, NC: McFarland, 1993.

28. "Independents on Coast Plan New Comeback." *Motion Picture Daily*, 19 Dec. 1931: 1, 4.

29. Though his name appeared on some Tiffany productions released in 1932, *Motion Picture Daily* of February 10, 1931, did announce that he had resigned his position at the company due to "ill health and a desire to make pictures again on his own" (p. 1). But Goldstone was quickly back at Tiffany Studios. On July 20, 1931, *Motion Picture Daily*'s column "Off the Record" asked "Is Phil Goldstone out or in? The veteran Tiffany studio head has been reported in and out probably more times than any other exec. Grant L. Cook in New York the other day stated that Goldstone definitely would stay with the company. Now, on the Coast [*sic*], Goldstone says that's all wet and that he intends to quit August 1. ... Goldstone plans to produce elsewhere, but is mum on his future connection" (p. 2).

30. "RCA Ties with Goldstone for Recording Deal." *Variety*, 15 Mar. 1932.

31. "Cinema Rights to Plays Bring Pretty Prices." *Chicago Tribune*, 10 Apr. 1932.

32. *Hollywood Reporter*, 10 Aug. 1932.

33. Slide, Anthony. "Films on 8 and 16." *Films in Review*, May 1977: 305–306, 310.

34. "Cal York's Monthly Broadcast from Hollywood." *Photoplay*, Apr. 1931.

35. "Miss Starke Wins Order for Alimony." *Los Angeles Times*, 12 May 1931.

36. See *Amusement Securities Corporation v. Academy Pictures Distribution Corporation*. New York County: Supreme Court of New York, 27 June 1936.

37. See Chapter Five for a discussion of *Amusement Securities Corporation v. Academy Pictures Distribution Corporation*.

38. See Chapter One for an in-depth examination of the particular influence of *The Magic Island* on *White Zombie*, and Chapter Two for a biographical look at Seabrook and a historical examination of *The Magic Island*'s importance in the chronology of voodoo and zombie texts.

39. See the article "Zombies Really Do Exist in Haiti; American Investigator Saw Some" in the *White Zombie: Complete Exhibitors [sic] Campaign Book*. New York City: United Artists Corporation, 1932.

40. "Weird Tale Booked at Criterion." *Los Angeles Times*, 17 Nov. 1932.

41. Audiences may have also remembered the film *Black Magic* (1929) with Henry B. Walthall. It was not based on the Bowen novel, but was a relatively recent Fox film at the time of *White Zombie*'s release.

42. Nielsen, Raymond J. Interview with Victor Halperin. AETN-TV, Arkansas. Circa 1978.

43. Weston, Garnett. *Death Is a Lonely Affair: Collected Poems of Garnett Weston*. Victoria, British Columbia: Morriss Printing Co., 1970 (p. 13).

44. "Garnett Weston." *The 1935–36 Motion Picture Almanac*. New York: Quigley, 1936 (p. 698).

45. Weston, p. 105.

46. *Ibid.*, p. 149.

47. *Ibid.*, p. 131.

48. The *1935–36 Motion Picture Almanac* listed Weston's plays by the following names: *Undertow, Lady Descends*, and *The Devil Is a Lady*.

49. "Motion Pictures." *Theatre Guild Magazine*, Aug. 1931.

50. "*The Viking*." *The Film Daily*, 21 June 1931.

51. "Hollywood Now Produces Pictures by Series of Scientific Charts." *White Zombie: Complete Exhibitors [sic] Campaign Book*. New York City: United Artists Corporation, 1932.

52. "*White Zombie* Dialogue Reduced to Minimum." *The San Francisco Examiner*, 5 Dec. 1932: 10.

53. For example, see the Le Roy Stone's article "More Pantomime and Less Talk" in the February 2, 1931, issue of *The Film Daily*. Also, see John Alicoate's column "Just Chatter—on Nothing Much" in *The Film Daily* of March 17, 1931.

54. Sullivan, C. Gardner. "Talkies have too much talk." *The Hollywood Reporter*, 15 Mar. 1932: 43.

55. Many others had complained about the sheer amount of dialogue in talking pictures. For example, J. S. O'Connell (in "Talkers 'Producer's Rattles,' Says Pioneer; 'Sound Is No Improvement.'" *Motion Picture News* 7 June 1930: 117) wrote that "[d]ialogue is being employed by many producers today much as a baby plays with a rattle. Delighted over the discovery that the screen can make a noise, they can't allow it to be silent or simply musical for so much as a second."

56. "Independent Indies Rely on Actors for Anything from Dialog to Props." *Variety*, 29 Mar. 1932: 4.

57. Rhodes, Gary. Interview with Richard Sheffield, 31 Mar. 1996.

58. See Chapter Four for a lengthy investigation of these topics.

59. "Lugosi Broke, with Furniture Main Assett." *Variety*, 25 Oct. 1932.

60. Rhodes, Gary D. *Lugosi: His Life in Film, On Stage, and in the Hearts of Horror Lovers*. Jefferson, NC: McFarland, 1997 (p. 49).

61. Lugosi and the Halperins did have at least one mutual friend: Hungarian violinist Duci de Kerekjarto.

62. Bellamy, Madge. Letter to Richard Bojarski, 3 Nov. 1977.

63. Nielsen, Raymond J. Interview with Madge Bellamy. AETN-TV, Arkansas. Circa 1978.

64. Price, Michael H. and George E. Turner. *The Cinema of Adventure, Romance, & Terror*. Hollywood: ASC Press, 1989 (p. 152).

65. Kingsley, Grace. "Seen on the Boulevard." *Los Angeles Times*, 11 May 1931.

66. Shaffer, Rosalind. "Popularity of Many Film Stars Is Short Lived." *Chicago Tribune*, 1 Mar. 1931.

67. Woodridge, A. L. "Rainbow Fixed in Hollywood Sky for All Who Once Were Stars." *New York Herald Tribune*, 14 Feb. 1932: sec. 7, p. 3.

68. "Madge Bellamy Wins Stardom!" *The Silver Sheet* 1922. (Month of magazine unknown; clipping exists in the Madge Bellamy file at the Margaret Herrick Library in Beverly Hills, CA.)

69. Woodbridge, p. 3.

70. Bellamy, Madge. *A Darling of the Twenties*. New York: Vestal Press, 1989 (p. 117).

71. "Madge Bellamy in Shorts." *The Film Daily*, 3 Feb. 1930: 8.

72. Halperin, Venita. Letter to Gary D. Rhodes, 11 Sept. 1997.

73. Bellamy, p. 121.

74. On the point of United Artists, Bellamy's memory fails her; at the time she was hired, UA was not involved in the film to any degree.

75. Nielsen interview with Madge Bellamy.

76. Bellamy, p. 121.

77. Johaneson, Bland. Untitled. (Follows a paragraph on Greta Garbo entitled "Preserved Mystery.") *The Daily Mirror* (New York), 3 Aug. 1932.

78. Nielsen interview with Victor Halperin.

79. Kingsley, Grace. "Maritza Doubles in Gelatin." *San Francisco Chronicle*, 10 Feb. 1933.

80. "Obituaries: Joseph Cawthorn." *Variety*, 26 Jan. 1949.

81. Kingsley, Grace. "Star's Vehicle Selected." *Los Angeles Times*, 15 Oct. 1930.

82. "Obituaries: Joseph Cawthorn." *Variety*, 26 Jan. 1949.

83. Nye, Myra. "Society of Cinemaland." *Los Angeles Times*, 4 Jan. 1931.

84. Kingsley, Grace. "A Silver Anniversary." *Los Angeles Times*, 5 Oct. 1930.

85. "Obituaries: Robert Frazer." *Variety*, 23 Aug. 1944.

86. "Robert Frazer Has Chief Part in Radio Play." *Los Angeles Times*, 31 Oct. 1929.

87. John Harron's other brother Charles died in an automobile wreck in 1915, and his sister Mary died as a casualty of the 1918 pandemic of influenza.

88. McManus, John T. "Walking Dead in Angkor." *New York Times*, 24 May 1936.

89. "Muse Woos Many Muses." *Los Angeles Times*, 4 Jan. 1931.

90. Sampson, Henry T. *Blacks in Black and White: A Source Book on Black Films*. Metuchen, N.J.: Scarecrow, 1977 (p. 246).

91. "*Porgy* Due Tonight at Music Box." *Los Angeles Times*, 5 Jan. 1931.

92. Wilk, Ralph. "A Little from 'Lots.'" *The Film Daily*, 18 Oct. 1931: 4.

93. Muse, Clarence. *The Dilemma of the Negro Actor*. Los Angeles, 1934.

94. *Ibid.*, p. 21.

95. "Brandon Hurst." *Variety*, 23 July 1947.

96. The pressbook incorrectly lists "John Peters" as portraying Chauvin; this has meant that many filmographies still include *White Zombie* among the credits of actor John Peters (of *The Student Prince*, 1927, and others). This includes *The American Film Institute Catalog of Motion Pictures Produced in the United States: Feature Films, 1931–1940* (Univ. of CA, 1993). In reality, he had nothing to do with the film.

97. "Obituaries: John T. Prince." *Variety*, 12 Jan. 1938.

98. Film historian George E. Turner has suggested that "Claude Morgan" may have actually been actor Clive Morgan.

99. "Dan Crimmins." *Variety*, 18 July 1945. (Though Crimmins' name is spelled correctly on the *White Zombie* film print and its publicity materials, he was incorrectly named "Sam Crimmins" in the October 1932 issue of *Photoplay* magazine.)

100. Cunningham, James. "Asides and Interludes." *Motion Picture Herald*, 5 May 1934: 33.

101. "Obituaries: Arthur Martinelli." *Variety*, 20 Sept. 1967.

102. As of this writing, the Howard Anderson Company is still in business, with its name changed slightly to reflect the name of Anderson's son: the Howard A. Anderson Company. The company reorganized with that name after the senior Anderson's death.

103. Nielsen interview with Victor Halperin.

104. Given that Phil Goldstone sometimes rented space at Universal for productions he helmed, it is possible he facilitated rental of these sets for *White Zombie*.

105. My gratitude for this information goes to my friend, the late film historian George E. Turner.

106. "Farjeon Will Handle Liberty Stage Tryouts." *The Film Daily*, 10 June 1930: 2.

107. "Carl Axzelle." *Standard Casting Directory*. Oct. 1925. (Axcelle's name, as the title of his entry in this casting directory suggests, was at times spelled 'Axzelle.'")

108. Price and Turner, p. 151.

109. Madge Bellamy mentioned the shoot lasted 11 days, in both her autobiography *A Darling of the Twenties*, and in a November 3, 1977, letter to film historian Richard Bojarski.

110. Kingsley, Grace. "Halperins Busy." *Los Angeles Times*, 8 Mar. 1932.

111. Price and Turner, p. 151.

112. Again, I must thank the late George E. Turner for his meticulous research into this area of *White Zombie*'s production history.

113. Cremer, Robert. *Lugosi: The Man Behind the Cape*. Chicago: Henry Regnery, 1976 (pp. 130–131).

114. Cremer, p. 131.

115. Nielsen interview with Madge Bellamy.

116. Cremer, pp. 193–194.

117. Price and Turner, p. 152.

118. Nielsen interview with Victor Halperin.

119. "He Turns Modiste." *White Zombie: Complete Exhibitors [sic] Campaign Book*. New York City: United Artists Corporation, 1932.

120. "Madge Bellamy Needs Auto-biographical Help." *Classic Film Collector* 26 (Winter 1970).

121. Bellamy, Madge. Letter to Richard Bojarski, 3 Nov. 1977.

122. Bellamy, Madge. Letter to Victor Halperin, 18 Oct. 1978.

123. "Madge Bellamy Needs Auto-biographical Help," pagination unknown.

124. "The Box Office Rates the Players of 1931–32." *Motion Picture Herald*, 18 June 1932: 8.

125. Stothart, Herbert. "Timely Topics: The Place of Music in the Motion Picture." *The Film Daily*, 13 July 1933: 23.

126. "Warners Plan More Music as Aid to Action Films." *The Film Daily*, 19 Dec. 1933: 2.

127. It may well be that Goldstone suggested hiring Meyer; Meyer would do much work for Goldstone's Majestic Pictures.

128. "Meyer Suggests Lower Music Scale for Indies." *Variety*, 2 Aug. 1932.

129. "Abe Meyer." *The 1944–45 Motion Picture Almanac*. New York: Quigley, 1945.

130. Karlin, Fred. *Listening to Movies: The Film Lover's Guide to Film Music*. New York: Schirmer, 1994 (p. 8).

131. Marmorstein, Gary. *Hollywood Rhapsody: Movie Music and Its Makers, 1900–1975*. New York: Schirmer, 1997 (pp. 18, 22).

132. "Riesenfeld Scores UA Pictures for Music and Effects." *Exhibitors Herald and Moving Picture World*, 18 Aug. 1928: 13.

133. "Pioneers in Presentations: Hugo Riesenfeld." *Moving Picture World*, 11 Apr. 1925: 568.

134. "Applaud Riesenfeld on Return to B'way." *Motion Picture Daily*, 14 May 1932: 2.

135. In addition to *White Zombie* being unmentioned in Cugat's book *Rumba Is My Life* (Didier, 1948), no mention is made of the film in Luis Gasca's text *Cugat* (Madrid: Alberto Alcocer, 1995).

136. Herkan's *S-O-S* would later be heard in the serials *The Miracle Rider* (1935) with Tom Mix and in Chapter Four of *The Return of Chandu* (1934) with Bela Lugosi.

137. Ray Wilk's column "A Little from 'Lots'" in the May 4, 1931, issue of *The Film Daily* mentioned that Meyer stopped during a cross country drive at the 101 Ranch in Oklahoma to secure a variety of drums for use in making drum effects for film scores. Though the trip occurred long before *White Zombie*'s production, it is very possible the drums heard during *Chant* are in part those obtained from the 101 Ranch.

138. The American Film Institute Catalog of Motion Pictures Produced in the United States: Feature Films, 1931–1940. Berkeley: University of California, 1993.

139. Simpson, Anne Key. *Follow Me: The Life and*

Music of R. Nathaniel Dett. Metuchen, NJ: Scarecrow, 1993 (p. 449).

140. *Ibid.*, p. 449.

141. *Ibid.*, p. 454.

142. As for Dett's fame, he was not only remembered in 1932 for his musical compositions and his prior post as head of the Department of Music at the Hampton Institute, but in 1932 received publicity for his connection with the Eastman School of Music; among his contributions to the latter was training singers for radio station WHAM of Rochester, New York.

143. Harris, Genevieve. "Weird Music in *White Zombie*." *Chicago Evening Post*, 27 Aug. 1932.

144. C.P.J. "Asbestos: *White Zombie*." *The Times-Picayune* (New Orleans), 19 Aug. 1932.

145. "Krellberg Heads Finance Company." *Motion Picture Daily*, 25 May 1932: 6.

146. "Sherman S. Krellberg." *Variety*, 17 Jan. 1979.

147. "Col. Taking Outsider." *Variety*, 3 May 1932: 21.

148. "Universal Grabs *Zombie* Neg." *Variety*, 31 May 1932: 21.

149. "Goldstone Won't Let Ed. Take Halperins' *Zombie*." *Variety*, 14 June 1932: 6.

150. "Goldstone Demands a Settlement." *Motion Picture Herald*, 4 June 1932: 10.

151. "Goldstone Not to Back Independents." *Motion Picture Daily*, 1 June 1932: 1.

152. "Goldstone's Move Blow to Independents." *Motion Picture Daily*, 6 June 1932: 1.

153. "Goldstone Forming New 'First Nat'l.'" *Motion Picture Daily*, 11 June 1932: 1.

154. As Anthony Slide indicates in *The American Film Industry* (University of Wisconsin Press, 1985), Majestic Pictures Corporation was active from 1932 to 1935. Goldstone headed the production unit, and had formed Majestic with Joe Simmonds and Herman Gluckman. On November 18, 1933, *The Film Daily* announced that Majestic would break into two production units—one under Goldstone's supervision, one headed by Louis Sarecky. The new arrangement must have worked out none too well, as on December 16, 1933—less than one month later—*The Film Daily* wrote of Goldstone's resignation.

155. *The Film Daily*, 16 Dec. 1933: 6.

156. "What *Scarface* Meant to Gangster Films *White Zombie* Meant to Thrillers." *White Zombie: Complete Exhibitors* [*sic*] *Campaign Book*. New York City: United Artists Corporation, 1932.

157. "Krellberg Has *Zombie*." *Variety*, 21 June 1932: 29.

158. "Halperins' *Zombie* Deal Held Up By Goldstone." *Variety*, 23 June 1932: 23.

159. *Ibid.*, p. 23.

160. "Goldstone Ties *Zombie*." *Variety*, 5 July 1932: 6.

161. "UA Buying Up Outside Films." *Variety*, 19 July 1932.

162. "United Artists." *Variety*, 9 Aug. 1932.

163. See "UA Heads Confer on 1932–33 Program." (*The Film Daily*, 12 Jan. 1932: 2) and "Schedule Conference on New UA Product" (*Motion Picture Daily*, 16 Feb. 1932: 1) for discussions on UA's original program schedule. See "UA Schedule May Get to Total of 15" (*Motion Picture Daily*, 17 Aug. 1932: 8) for a discussion of the revised release schedule.

164. "UA Negotiating to Buy *White Zombie*." *Motion Picture Daily*, 8 July 1932: 1.

165. "United Artists to Release *White Zombie*; *Scarface* Passed." *Motion Picture Herald*, 16 July 1932. (Also, see "UA Gets *Zombie*." *Motion Picture Daily*, 13 July 1932: 7.)

166. "Lugosi to Be Star of Haitian Picture." *The Times-Picayune* (New Orleans), 24 July 1932.

167. *Amusement Securities Corporation v. Academy Pictures Distribution Corporation*. Supreme Court of New York, New York County. 162 Misc. 608: 294 NYS 279. 27 June 1936.

168. See "72-Min. Average Footage Now Against 67 Minutes a Year Ago" in *The Film Daily* of February 7, 1934 for a discussion of increasing running times of 1930s films.

169. "Audience Gasps at Weird Story." *The Hollywood Reporter*, 17 June 1932: 3.

170. "Among others, MAA Asks $7,500 of *White Zombie*." *Variety*, 30 Aug. 1932.

171. "Audience Gasps at Weird Story," p. 3.

Chapter 4

1. Mayne, Judith. *Cinema and Spectatorship*. New York: Routledge, 1993 (p. 34). (A major example of the kind of audience-based research that Mayne describes is Leo A. Handel's *Hollywood Looks at Its Audience: A Report of Film Audience Research*. [University of Illinois, 1950.])

2. The most extensive modern account of the Payne Fund Studies comes in the work of Garth Jowett, Ian C. Jarvie, and Kathryn H. Fuller. See their text, *Children and the Movies: Media Influence and the Payne Fund Studies*. Cambridge: University of Cambridge, 1996.

3. As an example, see Blumer's *Movies and Conduct*. New York: MacMillan, 1933.

4. Allen, Robert C. and Douglas Gomery. *Film History: Theory and Practice*. New York: McGraw-Hill, 198. (p. 156).

5. Mayne, p. 31.

6. Industry trade publications of the early 1930s like *The Film Daily*, *Motion Picture Daily*, *Variety*, and *Motion Picture Herald* regularly wrote about the impact of *Amos and Andy*, "Dish Night," reduced ticket prices, double features, vaudeville, so on, at movie theaters.

7. The April 11, 1932, *Motion Picture Daily* article "Ban 'Bronx Cheer'" describes the Toronto censorship board edict against "intimate" scenes stressing the "female form."

8. Industry trade publications of the early 1930s like *The Film Daily*, *Motion Picture Daily*, *Variety*, and *Motion Picture Herald* regularly wrote about the many fires, bombings, Blue Law troubles, so on, in their pages.

9. Allen, Richard. *Projecting Illusion: Film Spectatorship and the Impression of Reality*. Cambridge: Cambridge University Press, 1995 (p. 115).

10. Mayne, p. 64.

11. Allen, p. 116.

12. See Gary D. Rhodes' chapter "Image, Icon, and Apparition" in the text *Lugosi: His Life in Film, on Stage, and in the Hearts of Horror Lovers* (Jefferson, NC: McFarland, 1997) for a further examination of Lugosi's image at this stage of his career.

13. The present study realizes that, at least in many ways, a horror film "genre" did not yet exist in the United States; it was being created in the early 1930s immediately prior to, during, and following *White Zombie*'s release. Therefore, the

term "cycle"—much in use by trade publications during 1932—acts as a more accurate substitute in this chapter.

14. Allen, Frederick Lewis. *Since Yesterday: The Nineteen-Thirties in America*. New York: Harper and Brothers, 1940 (p. 31).

15. Hacker, Louis M. *American Problems of Today: A History of the United States Since the World War*. New York: F. S. Crofts, 1938 (p. 178).

16. Allen, Frederick, p. 57.

17. Hacker, p. 180.

18. *Ibid.*, p. 179.

19. *Ibid.*, p. 192.

20. Allen, Frederick, pp. 67–73.

21. Hacker, p. 195.

22. *Ibid.*, p. 196.

23. Bergman, Andrew. *We're in the Money: Depression America and Its Films*. New York: New York University Press, 1971 (p. xi).

24. Gillette, Don Carle. "Moviegoers ... Are They Human Beings?" *The Film Daily*, 2 Jan. 1934: 1.

25. Bergman, p. xx.

26. *Ibid.*, p. xv.

27. Watts, Richard, Jr. "The Era of Screen Terror." *New York Herald Tribune*, 21 Feb. 1932, sec. 7: 3–4.

28. A lengthy analysis of the many problems involved with payment of war debts and reparations appears in Louis Hacker's *American Problems of Today: A History of the United States Since the World War* (New York: F. S. Crofts, 1938).

29. Watts, p. 3.

30. *Ibid.*, p. 3.

31. Watts, Richard, Jr. "On the Screen: *Frankenstein*." *New York Herald Tribune*, 5 Dec. 1931: 13.

32. See Frank J. Dello Stritto's article "*Svengali*: The Forgotten Monster" in *Cult Movies* 24 (1997): 28–37.

33. For example, *Murder by the Clock* is given more space than Tod Browning's *Dracula* in William K. Everson's *Classics of the Horror Film* (Citadel Press, 1974), and a chapter on *Murder at Midnight* appears in George E. Turner and Michael F. Price's *Forgotten Horrors* (A. S. Barnes, 1979).

34. "*Murder by the Clock*." *Harrison's Reports*, 25 July 1931: 118.

35. "*Murder at Midnight*." *Harrison's Reports*, 26 Sept. 1931: 155.

36. "*Murder at Midnight*." *Motion Picture Herald*, 10 Oct. 1931: 48.

37. It is certainly possible that, say, a critical review from the period could be produced on one of these films that does use the word "horror"; however, the bulk of surviving materials from the era suggests that these movies were generally considered mysteries.

38. For *Freaks* publicity mentioning the word "horror," see the ad in the February 8, 1932, *Los Angeles Times*. In terms of changes in the film's content to heighten the horror element, see "Believe Metro May Call in *Freaks*." *Variety*, 15 Mar. 1932.

39. "The Pay Off." *Motion Picture Daily*, 11 Apr. 1932.

40. Meehan, Leo. "*Freaks*." *Motion Picture Herald*, 23 Jan. 1932: 46.

41. "*Freaks*." *Motion Picture Herald*, 23 July 1932: 48.

42. "*Freaks*." *Harrison's Reports*, 16 July 1932. Also, see "Will H. Hays' Misleading Assertions About Block Booking—No. 3" in the May 20, 1933, issue of *Harrison's Reports* for the comment about *Freaks* being a "sex picture."

43. "*The Monster Walks*." *Motion Picture Herald*, 6 Feb. 1932: 38.

44. "*The Monster Walks*." *Motion Picture Daily*, 4 May 1932: 5.

45. Harris, Sidney. "*Dracula*." *The Billboard*, 21 Feb. 1931.

46. "*Dracula*." *The Film Daily*, 15 Feb. 1931.

47. "The New Pictures: *Dracula*." *Time*, 23 Feb. 1931: 62.

48. Tinée, May. "Awed Stillness Greets Movie, About *Dracula*." *Chicago Tribune*, 21 Mar. 1931: 21.

49. Rhodes, Gary D. "*Dracula*: Addenda to the Children of the Night." *Cult Movies* 13 (1995): 35–39.

50. Skal, David J. *Hollywood Gothic: The Tangled Web of Dracula from Novel to Stage to Screen*. New York: W. W. Norton, 1990 (p. 147).

51. Rhodes, p. 36.

52. Tinée, "Awed Stillness," p. 21.

53. See Gregory William Mank's *It's Alive: The Classic Cinema Saga of Frankenstein* (A. S. Barnes, 1981) for a discussion of *Frankenstein*'s success.

54. Watts, "On the Screen: *Frankenstein*," p. 13.

55. Bell, Nelson B. "About the Showstops." *Washington Post*, 26 Nov. 1931: 12.

56. "Theatre Receipts." *Motion Picture Herald*, 10 Dec. 1932: 52–53, 56.

57. "The Voice of the Movie Fan." *Chicago Sunday Tribune*, 10 Jan. 1932, sec. 7: 6.

58. See "Fans Submit December's Six Best." *Chicago Sunday Tribune*, 3 Jan. 1932, sec. 7: 9.

59. Kafka, Ruth C. Letter, "The Monster's Identity." *Chicago Sunday Tribune*, 31 Jan. 1932, sec. 9: 8.

60. Meehan, Leo. "Passing in Review: *Dr. Jekyll and Mr. Hyde*." *Motion Picture Herald*, 26 Dec. 1932: 27.

61. See ads for *Dr. Jekyll and Mr. Hyde* in *The Film Daily* and *Motion Picture Herald* in 1932.

62. Watts, Richard, Jr. "On the Screen: *Dr. Jekyll and Mr. Hyde*." *New York Herald Tribune*, 2 Jan. 1932, sec 4: 6.

63. See H.T.S.'s review "Frederic March in a Splendidly Produced Pictorial Version of *Dr. Jekyll and Mr. Hyde*" in the January 2, 1932, *New York Times* (p. 14), and Margaret Marshan's review "Films: Spectacle vs. Story" in the January 20, 1932, *The Nation* (p. 82).

64. Scheuer, Philip K. "*Dr. Jekyll and Mr. Hyde*." *Los Angeles Times*, 26 Dec. 1931: 5.

65. Wagner, Rob. "*Dr. Jekyll and Mr. Hyde*." *Rob Wagner's Script*, 2 Jan. 1932: 9–10.

66. Lusk, Norbert. "*Jekyll-Hyde* Rivals for Unrestrained Praise." *Los Angeles Times*, 10 Jan. 1932, sec. 3: 13.

67. Mank, Gregory W. *Hollywood Cauldron: Thirteen Horror Films for the Genre's Golden Age*. Jefferson, NC: McFarland, 1994 (p. 21).

68. Botz, Frederick C. and Eric O. Kulbartz. Letter, "The Voice of the Movie Fan." *Chicago Sunday Tribune*, 24 Jan. 1932, sec. 7: 8.

69. Mank, *Hollywood Cauldron*, p. 21.

70. Mank, Gregory W. "Universal's 'Golden Age': Some Facts and Figures." *Midnight Marquee* 13 (Fall 1986): 11–14.

71. J.C.M. "The Current Cinema" *The New Yorker*, 20 Feb. 1932: 62.

72. A.D.S. "After Edgar Allan Poe: *Murders in the Rue Morgue*." *New York Times*, 11 Feb. 1932: 16.

73. Watts, Richard, Jr. "On the Screen: *Murders in the Rue Morgue*." *New York Herald Tribune*, 12 Feb. 1932: 11.

74. Bige. "*Murders in the Rue Morgue*." *Variety*, 16 Feb. 1932: 24.

75. Strauss, H. David. "Motion Picture Reviews: *Murders in the Rue Morgue*." *The Billboard*, 20 Feb. 1932: 18.

76. Delehanty, Thornton. "The New Film: *Murders in the Rue Morgue*. Another of the Horror Pictures Is Shown at the Mayfair." *New York Evening Post*, 12 Feb. 1932: 6.

77. Bige, p. 24.

78. Mank, "Universal's," p. 12.

79. "*Morgue*-Vaude $13,000 in Prov.; Fay's $7,000." *Variety*, 9 Feb. 1932.

80. "*Freaks* Down, *Morgue* $10,000 and Capital Okay." *Variety*, 23 Feb. 1932: 8.

81. "B'klyn Is Slow, but 'Past' a Good $25,000." *Variety*, 23 Feb. 1932: 8.

82. For comparative theater grosses on *Murders in the Rue Morgue* in these cities, see *Motion Picture Herald* of March 19, 1932, February 27, 1932, March 12, 1932, and February 20, 1932.

83. "Cincinnati Improves." *Variety*, 23 Feb. 1932: 8.

84. "P'land Sees Nice Biz; $12,500 for *Pleasure*." *Variety*, 1 Mar. 1932.

85. "Detroit Pepless, but Fireman Looks Bright on $20,000—Fisher." *Variety*, 8 Mar. 1932.

86. "Newark Weak, with $15,000 about Limit." *Variety*, 5 Apr. 1932.

87. "Theatre Receipts." *Motion Picture Herald*, 20 Feb. 1932: 42.

88. *White Zombie: Complete Exhibitors* [*sic*] *Campaign Book*. New York City: United Artists Corporation, 1932. (A copy of this pressbook is available at the Library of the Performing Arts in the Lincoln Center at the New York City Public Library, as well as in the film archive at the University of Madison/Wisconsin. A reproduction of the reissue *White Zombie* pressbook was made available by the Roan Group as an enclosure to their 1994 laser disc restoration of the film.)

89. "UA's Promotion Staff." *Variety*, 22 Apr. 1931.

90. "Purely Personal." *Motion Picture Daily*, 13 July 1932: 2.

91. "Horne Realigns UA Ad, Publicity Force." *Motion Picture Daily*, 23 July 1931: 16.

92. "Purely Personal." *Motion Picture Daily*, 14 Apr. 1932: 2.

93. Despite the previous success of Seabrook's book *The Magic Island* and the appearance of Kenneth Webb's play *Zombie* on Broadway and Chicago stages in 1932, the press at the time would often suggest that the tremendous response of *White Zombie* qualified it to take credit for educating the public about zombiism. The popularization of the word "zombie" did not go unnoticed at the time. For instance, *The Film Daily* of August 10, 1932, wrote that "if nothing else, that picture has contributed a new phase [*sic*] to the English language. They now call those dopey people who wander through the days in a perpetual haze, 'Zombies.'"

94. See the Loew's Stanley ad for *White Zombie* in the July 1, 1932, Baltimore *Sun*.

95. "Unusual Treatment Given Thrill Film by Manager Buerig." *Motion Picture Herald*, 24 Sept. 1932: 62.

96. "*White Zombie* Revives Puzzle of Suspended Animation." *The Chicago Herald and Examiner*, 28 Aug. 1932.

97. See the Loew's Stanley ad for *White Zombie* in the July 1, 1932, Baltimore *Sun*.

98. Whether any copy of the supplement is extant is unknown. Mention of it (by description and not by title) occurs in Eddie Hitchcock's article "Newspaper Ad Construction" in the September 3, 1932, *Motion Picture Herald*.

99. Hitchcock, Eddie. "Newspaper Ad Construction!" *Motion Picture Herald*, 27 Aug. 1932: 67.

100. Woodbridge, A. L. "'Anything for a Laugh' Echoes in Cinema Reaction to Shudders." *New York Herald Tribune*, 21 Feb. 1932, sec. 7: 4.

101. "Thrill Films Lead in Preference, Hays Poll Shows." *The Film Daily*, 28 Mar. 1932: 1, 8.

102. An example of this would be the *St. Louis Post-Dispatch* of August 6, 1932, which published an ad proclaiming *White Zombie* the "MOST UNUSUAL THRILL YOU'VE EVER HAD!" Similarly, the *Chicago Tribune* of August 26, 1932, ran an ad featuring the tag, "SEE IT NOW FOR YOUR MIGHTIEST THRILL!" and the following day published another ad with the tag "The Thrill-Drama you will want to see!" Such theaters as the Loew's in Houston published advertisements announcing the film as "THE WEIRDEST LOVE STORY IN 2000 YEARS!"; one of these ads appeared in the August 5, 1932, *Houston Post*.

103. For example, see the two-page ad in *Variety* of July 26, 1932 (pp. 24–25).

104. "*White Zombie*." *Motion Picture Herald* 6 Aug. 1932: 36.

105. For an example of this advertisement, see *The Film Daily* of August 15, 1932.

106. Meehan, Leo. "Timeliness Is New Studio Motto." *Motion Picture Herald*, 11 June 1932: 16.

107. "Schedules Show Cycle of 'Horror' Pictures Continuing." *The Film Daily*, 1 Aug. 1932: 1, 7.

108. For an example, see the Rivoli's ad for *White Zombie* in the August 4, 1932, *New York Times*.

109. For an example, see the Old Mill's ad for *White Zombie* in the September 4, 1932, *Dallas Morning News*.

110. For an example, see the Loew's State ad for *White Zombie* in the August 4, 1932, *St. Louis Post-Dispatch*.

111. "Looking Ahead at the Product: *White Zombi* [*sic*]." *New York State Exhibitor*, 25 June 1932: 22. (The term "trick" in this context seems to suggest the difficulty in knowing how to promote the film, and that the chosen promotion would lead to box-office success or failure.)

112. "Give 'Em Sensation Says A. B. Ward; Sees End of Compo Fronts." *Motion Picture Herald*, 29 Oct. 1932: 54.

113. Chick. "Individuality in Advertising." *Motion Picture Herald*, 20 Feb. 1932: 53.

114. It is in this discussion of Bela Lugosi/Murder's eyes that we can see a point where the theoretical subject constructed by the text and the historical viewer of 1932 overlap, or—to use theorist Judith Mayne's words—where they "rub" against one another. See Section II of Chapter One for a detailed discussion of *White Zombie*'s constructed spectatorship.

115. "Unusual Treatment," p. 62.

116. A thorough discussion of Lugosi's eyes can be found in Chapter One.

117. Unsourced clipping in the Bela Lugosi file at the Library of the Performing Arts in the Lincoln Center at the New York City Public Library. Though it is not dated, the content of its text clearly proves it is from 1932.

118. See Appendix G for a collection of excerpts from *White Zombie*'s New York City newspaper, national movie fan magazine, and national publication reviews.

119. For example, see: Arthur Lennig's essay "*White Zombie*" in *Classics of the Film* (Madison: Wisconsin Film Society,

1965, p. 220); Carlos Clarens' discussion of the film in his *Horror Movies* (London: Panther, 1968, p. 136); George Turner and Michael H. Price's "The Black Art of *White Zombie* in *The Cinema of Adventure, Romance, and Terror*. (Ed. George E. Turner. Hollywood: ASC, 1989, p. 150).

120. Gillette, Don Carle. "The Reviewers Tell Their Side." *The Film Daily*, 16 June 1933: 1–2.

121. "Ballyhoo Overcomes Cricks on *Zombie*, $9000 Best in Pitt." *Variety*, 20 Sept. 1932.

122. Mayne, Judith. *Cinema and Spectatorship*. New York: Routledge, 1993 (p. 157).

123. "*White Zombie.*" *The Film Daily*, 29 July 1932: 4.

124. "The Pay Off." *Motion Picture Daily*, 29 July 1932: 2.

125. "The New Pictures: *White Zombie.*" *Time*, 8 Aug. 1932: 18.

126. Skinner, Richard Dana. "The Screen: *White Zombie.*" *The Commonweal*, 17 Aug. 1932: 392.

127. Lorentz, Pare. "The Screen." *Vanity Fair*, Jan. 1993: 48, 62.

128. McTaggart, Leonard. "The Inside Story." *Vanity Fair*, July 1933: 41–42.

129. *Ibid.*, p. 41.

130. "The Shadow Stage: *White Zombie.*" *Photoplay*, Sept. 1932.

131. "Mpls. Sizzling with Wow Trade; *Down to Earth*, $15,000; Marcus Show, *Zombie*, Well Bally'd." *Variety*, 30 Aug. 1932: 10.

132. Daly, Phil M. "Along the Rialto." *The Film Daily*, 30 July 1932: 3.

133. "Pans Make Business for *White Zombie.*" *The Hollywood Reporter*, 1 Aug. 1932: 2.

134. Hitchcock, Eddie. "Newspaper Ad Construction." *Motion Picture Herald*, 3 Sept. 1932: 66.

135. "What the Picture Did for Me." *Motion Picture Herald*, 15 Apr. 1933: 47.

136. "Ballyhoo Overcomes Cricks on *Zombie.*"

137. "*Zombie* Kidded, but Paradoxical Prov.-Ups." *Variety*, 2 Aug. 1932.

138. "What the Picture Did For Me." *Motion Picture Herald*, 14 Jan. 1933: 48.

139. "Box-Office Performances of the 1932–33 Pictures." *Harrison's Reports*, 29 July 1933: 120.

140. It has been rare, at least in comparison to other genres, that academics have devoted study to the horror film. Among those that have, some, like William K. Everson in *Classics of the Horror Film* (Secaucus, NJ: Citadel, 1974), generally suggest audience response was either uniform, or—at the most—it broke down along gender lines, with scared females clinging to male companions for whom the horror film was a test of courage. More modern studies, like Rhona J. Berenstein's *Attack of the Leading Ladies: Gender, Sexuality, and Spectatorship in Classic Horror Cinema* (New York: Columbia, 1996), move away from such generalizations and consider spectatorship in a much more specific and detailed manner.

141. McManus, John T. "Walking Dead in Angkor." *New York Times*, 24 May 1936: IX, 3:4.

142. *White Zombie* with Bela Lugosi." *Harrison's Reports*, 6 Aug. 1932: 126.

143. Johaneson, Bland. "*Frankenstein* Has a Rival." *The Daily Mirror* (New York), 29 July 1932.

144. "*White Zombie.*" *Pittsburgh Post-Gazette*, 17 Sept. 1932.

145. See Chapter One for an in-depth examination of Madeline, the character portrayed by Madge Bellamy.

146. See "Walter Winchell on Broadway" in the August 3, 1932, New York *Daily Mirror* and Phil M. Daly's "Along the Rialto" in *The Film Daily* of July 30, 1932.

147. Ads for the United Artist's San Francisco screening of *White Zombie*, as can be seen in the November 26, 1932, *San Francisco Chronicle* (p. 7) make clear its "adults only" policy.

148. "*White Zombie* with Bela Lugosi," p. 126. (Some theaters had already enforced an "adults only" policy for screenings of prior 1930s horror films. For example, an ad in the December 24, 1931, *Chicago Tribune* makes clear that the McVickers Theater would admit no children to see *Dr. Jekyll and Mr. Hyde* (1932). Mae Tinée, the newspaper's film critic, helped explain why in her review of the movie, "Old Shocker Full of Thrills as New Talkie," published in the December 28, 1931, edition of the *Tribune*. "You won't soon forget *Dr. Jekyll and Mr. Hyde*," she told readers, "and the children never would." Other publications suggested much the same. J.C.M.'s review in "The Current Cinema" section of the January 9, 1932, *New Yorker* claims "[*Dr. Jekyll and Mr. Hyde*] … is not for children, unless the tots are making a nursery study of sadism." Similarly, the February 1932 issue of *Photoplay* echoed earlier reports by suggesting, "Too bad this filming … is not good fare for children nor even for adults who are easily unnerved.")

149. While the topic of horror and mystery films is addressed in numerous Payne Fund Studies, the most extensive discussion occurs in Herbert Blumer's *Movies and Conduct* (New York: MacMillan, 1933, pp. 74–94). While the films discussed are generally silent movies produced by 1920s Hollywood, the variety of responses makes clear that some children became very frightened after watching horror films, while others were excited and even incorporated the plots of such films into their playtime habits. In either event, many children in the U.S. definitely attended films of the horror genre.

150. Kingsley, Grace. "New Films to Be Thrillers." *Los Angeles Times*, 25 Jan. 1932: 11.

151. Osterman, Jack. "I'm Telling You." *Variety*, 9 Aug. 1932: 33. (While some children and adults may well have found *White Zombie* unintentionally funny, others that laughed at the film may have done so to release tension. For example, Rhona Berenstein, in her book *Attack of the Leading Ladies*, discusses many cases of the 1930s horror film in which laughter indicated to critics of the period that audiences experienced discomfort due to fright, and thus used laughter as an outlet for relief.)

152. "'Morons Only' Next?" *Chicago Sunday Tribune*, 29 Mar. 1931, sec. 7: 14.

153. "*Zombie*'s Negro Trade." *Variety*, 9 Aug. 1932.

154. Given that African-American patrons were almost certainly segregated from others in all U.S. theaters of the 1930s which allowed admission to all races, whites must have constituted much of the film's audiences. In addition, photos of crowds at New York's Rivoli show predominantly Anglo-Saxon ticket buyers.

155. See Chapter Two for a discussion of how many white U.S. citizens viewed Haiti and Haitians.

156. See "Haitians Great People, Cultured, Want Exploitation to Cease" in the June 18, 1920 issue of *The Black Dispatch* (an Oklahoma City newspaper) and "Charge Americans Commit Grave Offenses in Haiti, A.M.E. Minister Returned from Long Stay, Tells of Deplorable Conditions in Negro State" in the April 20, 1920, issue of *The Black Dispatch*.

157. Gomery, Douglas. *Shared Pleasures: A History of*

Movie Presentation in the United States. Madison, University of Wisconsin Press, 1992 (pp. 157–8).

158. "Colored Theaters." *The 1932 Film Daily Yearbook of Motion Pictures*. Ed. John Alicoate. New York: *The Film Daily*, 1932: 834–835. (A brief article in the December 1, 1930, issue of *The Film Daily* claimed that 455 theaters in the U.S. catered to African-American audiences. The discrepancy in numbers over the two years probably indicates that some ten African-American theaters closed during that time, perhaps due to the economic devastation caused by the Great Depression.)

159. Gomery, p. 160.

160. It is actually quite difficult to determine the number of tickets sold at any theater, even when the number of theater seats is known. For example, some theaters of the time continued to sell tickets even beyond capacity, forcing a standing-room only situation. This was apparently such a common, irritating problem to theater patrons in Washington, D.C., that they felt the need to make a change. The January 21, 1932, *Washington Post* printed the article "Owners of Theaters Agree to Give Notice on Seating"; while theaters in that city still sold tickets beyond capacity, signs in the lobby would inform potential ticket buyers that all seats were taken.

161. For more information on black population statistics and black migration during the Great Depression, see Robert B. Grant's *The Black Man Comes to the City: A Documentary Account from the Great Migration to the Great Depression, 1915-1930* (Chicago: Nelson Hall, 1972). For contemporary accounts of these same topics, see Warren S. Thompson and P. K. Whelpton's *Population Trends in the United States* (New York: McGraw-Hill, 1933, pp. 74–80) and C. Warren Thorthwaite's *Internal Migration in the United States* (Philadelphia: Univ. of Pennsylvania, 1934, pp. 12–14).

162. See the ad for *White Zombie* in the October 1, 1932, *Afro-American* newspaper.

163. "New UA Sales Policy Will Start in August." *The Film Daily*, 11 May 1932.

164. "United Artists the 'Exclusives.'" *Harrison's Reports*, 29 Oct. 1932: 1.

165. "Two Stunts Stood Out in Campaign Made by Caldwell." *Motion Picture Herald*, 20 Aug. 1932: 60.

166. *Ibid.*, p. 60.

167. Horne succeeded Fred Schaefer as head of UA's exploitation and publicity in early May 1931, according to the May 7, 1931, issue of *The Film Daily*.

168. Sargent, Epes W. "Exploitation: Arthur's Zombies." *Variety*, 6 Sept. 1932: 19.

169. "Walked a Zombie." *Variety*, 4 Oct. 1932.

170. "Give 'Em Sensation," p. 54.

171. *Ibid.*, p. 54.

172. "Tyson Crashed the Front Page with a Stunt on Zombie." *Motion Picture Herald*, 5 Nov. 1932: 62.

173. Joel Shaw and His Orchestra recorded the song "White Zombie" for Crown Records in New York City in October, 1932; the tune was catalogued as "1906-2" and released on Crown 3413 along with the song "The Old Man of the Mountain." "White Zombie" was later reissued by Varsity Records under the title "Zombie," with the band renamed "Dick Robertson and His Orchestra." The tune can be heard on the compact disc release *Lugosi: Hollywood's Dracula (Original Movie Soundtrack)*, released by McWhorter-Greenhaw of Mesquite, Texas, in 1997.

174. "Futter to Record His Curiosities." *Motion Picture Daily*, 19 July 1932: 7.

175. See Chapter Two for a discussion on Futter's *Curiosities* film shorts.

176. For example, in the December 24, 1932, *Motion Picture Herald*, C. L. Niles of the Niles Theatre in Anamosa, Iowa, claimed *White Zombie* was "A horror picture that will get some money." In the January 28, 1933, issue of the same publication, R. L. Nowell of the Cherokee Theatre in Monroe, Georgia, claimed his result with *White Zombie* was just the opposite. His one word response to the film and its business at his theater: "terrible."

177. The July 23, 1932, *Motion Picture Herald*, in its column "The Release Chart," listed *White Zombie* but did not yet have a premiere or release date scheduled. The article "*Zombie* Release Ready" (in *Motion Picture Daily*, 15 July 1932: 2) mentions the original premiere plans for the Rialto.

178. "*Zombie* Opens Thursday." *Motion Picture Daily*, 26 July 1932: 3.

179. "New York Rivoli Remaining Open." *Motion Picture Daily*, 15 July 1932: 1.

180. *Variety*, 16 Aug. 1932.

181. L.N. "Beyond the Pale." *New York Times*, 29 July 1932.

182. Watts, Richard, Jr. "*White Zombie*." *New York Herald Tribune*, 29 July 1932.

183. Johaneson. "*Frankenstein* Has a Rival."

184. Boehnel, William. "*White Zombie*." *New York World-Telegram*, 2 Aug. 1932.

185. Delehaney, Thornton. "*White Zombie*." *New York Evening Post*, 29 July 1932.

186. Thirer, Irene. "*White Zombie*." *New York Daily News*, 29 July 1932.

187. The reason the present text believes Hale Horne had possible involvement in the Rivoli's exploitation on July 28, 1932, stems from a comment in the "Purely Personal" column of the *Motion Picture Daily* (29 July 1932: 2).

188. Johaneson. "*Frankenstein* Has a Rival." *The Daily Mirror* (New York), 29 July 1932.

189. "Using Novel Theater Fronts to Ballyhoo Broadway Films." *The Film Daily*, 1 Aug. 1932: 6.

190. Horne, Hal. "United Artists Best Was *White Zombie*." *The 1933 Film Daily Yearbook of Motion Pictures*. Ed. John Alicoate. New York: *The Film Daily*, 1933: 674.

191. Jones, Charles P. "Gris-Gris and *Abie's Irish Rose*." *Times-Picayune* (New Orleans), 21 Aug. 1932.

192. "B'way Bix Booms, 3 Possibly 4 Holdovers; *Madness*, \$15,000; *Souls*, \$52,000; *Dr. X*, \$42,000." *Variety*, 9 Aug. 1932.

193. Daly, Phil M. "Along the Rialto." *The Film Daily*, 30 July 1932: 3.

194. *Ibid.*, p. 3.

195. The reference connects the last name of George White to the word "zombie," thus becoming the name of the film. Producer White was well known for his *Scandals*, a series of Broadway variety shows featuring scantily clad young females; Earl Carroll was famous for a similar series of shows, the *Vanities*. The two men were in a sense competitors.

196. Osterman, p. 33.

197. Horne, p. 674.

198. "Purely Personal." *Motion Picture Daily*, 20 Aug. 1932: 2.

199. *Variety*, 9 Aug. 1932.

200. *Variety*, 16 Aug. 1932. (In the article "Reopened Roxy, Marx Bros.' \$58,000 Highlight Broadway" in the August 23, 1932, *Motion Picture Daily* [p. 8], the Rivoli's third week gross was purported to be \$9,000.)

201. "B'way Biz Booms," p. 9.

202. "Comparative Grosses for February." *Variety*, 19 Mar. 1931.

203. "Theatre Receipts." *Motion Picture Herald*, 2 Jan. 1932: 42.

204. "167,800 Is 5-Week *Jekyll* Rivoli Take." *Motion Picture Daily*, 11 Feb. 1932: 4.

205. *Variety*, 30 Aug. 1932.

206. "Roxy Garners Broadway Top with $65,000." *Motion Picture Daily*, 30 Aug. 1932: 3.

207. "United Artists May Get Rivoli Sept. 15." *Motion Picture Daily*, 30 Aug. 1932: 1, 8.

208. "United Artists Will Continue Chain Plan." *Motion Picture Daily*, 5 Feb. 1932: 1.

209. See the Loew's ad for *White Zombie* in the *Evening Star* (Washington, D.C.) of July 28, 1932.

210. The first two questions are taken from a *Post* ad of July 29, 1932, and the third question is taken from a July 28, 1932, *Post*. The text regarding *Post* want ads and the guest tickets appears in both of the aforementioned ads.

211. Heinl, Robert D. "Radio Dial Flashes." *Washington Post* 29 July 1932.

212. Bell, Nelson B. "*The White Zombie*." *Washington Post*, 30 July 1932: 14.

213. E. de S.M. "From the Front Row: Reviews and News of Washington's Theaters." *The Evening Star* (Washington, D.C.), 30 July 1932.

214. "*Dracula*'s 2 Wks. in Wash. $28,000; *My Past* $23,000." *Variety*, 25 Feb. 1931.

215. "B.E.F. Excitement NSG For Wash; *YR*, $16,000." *Variety*, 2 Aug. 1932.

216. Allen, pp. 83–86.

217. "B.E.F. Excitement NSG for Wash; *YR*, $16,000." *Variety*, 2 Aug. 1932.

218. *Ibid.*

219. "4 Balto Runs Extended." *The Film Daily*, 11 Jan. 1932: 7.

220. "At the Stanley." *The Sunday Sun* [Baltimore], 31 July 1932: 1.

221. See the ad for the Loew's Stanley screening of *White Zombie* in the August 1, 1932, issue of the Baltimore *Sun*.

222. "Ted Lewis Panics K.C., Helps Molly, $21,000." *Variety*, 2 Aug. 1932.

223. "*Frankenstein* Dispute Ousts Kas. Censor." *Motion Picture Daily*, 28 Dec. 1931: 2.

224. *Kansas City Star*, 28 July 1932.

225. "Faint Checks." *Motion Picture Daily*, 5 Aug. 1932: 11.

226. "The Pay Off." *Motion Picture Daily*, 5 Aug. 1932: 2.

227. "*White Zombie*." *Kansas City Star*, 1 Aug. 1932.

228. In the column "Comparative Grosses for August" of the September 20, 1932, *Variety*, the gross for the Loew's Mid-land was listed as "$11,500." And in the August 6, 1932, the Kansas City gross was listed as $13,000.

229. "Mainstreet, K.C., Good for $18,000." [*Dracula* grosses] *Variety*, 18 Mar. 1931; "Theatre Reports." [*Frankenstein* grosses.] *Motion Picture Herald*, 19 Dec. 1931: 39; "Theatre Receipts." [*Murders in the Rue Morgue* grosses.] *Motion Picture Herald*, 27 Feb. 1932: 47.

230. "Theatre Receipts." *Motion Picture Herald*, 16 Jan. 1932: 27.

231. "Fox Midwest Houses Adding Vaudeville." *Motion Picture Daily*, 29 July 1932: 1.

232. "Brent-Young $18,000 on P.A. Lead St. L. Biz." *Variety*, 9 Aug. 1932.

233. See the ad for the Loew's State screening of *White Zombie* in the August 4, 1932, *St. Louis Post-Dispatch*.

234. See the ad for the Loew's State screening of *White Zombie* in the August 5, 1932, *St. Louis Post-Dispatch*.

235. "Ban 'Live' Burials." *Motion Picture Daily*, 27 Aug. 1932: 1.

236. "Brent-Young $18,000 on P.A. Lead St. L. Biz." *Variety*, 9 Aug. 1932.

237. *Ibid.*, p. 10.

238. See the ad for the Loew's screening of *White Zombie* in the August 4, 1932, *Houston Post*.

239. "Publicity Man Becomes 'Zombie!'" *Motion Picture Herald*, 1 Oct. 1932: 64.

240. Scott, Bess Whitehead. "Tipping You Off." *The Houston Post*, 7 Aug. 1932, sec. 2: 4.

241. "*White Zombie* Film Inspires 'Terrifying Experience' Contest." *Rochester Democrat and Chronicle*, 4 Aug. 1932.

242. Chamberlin, Willard. "Rochester Theater." *Rochester Democrat and Chronicle*, 6 Aug. 1932.

243. *Motion Picture Herald*, 13 Aug. 1932.

244. "New Films Reviewed: *White Zombie*." *The Boston Globe*, 6 Aug. 1932.

245. "Orpheum Theatre: Bernice Claire, *White Zombie*." *Boston Globe*, 20 Aug. 1932.

246. "*Hold 'Em* at $22,000 with Boston Show." *Motion Picture Daily*, 31 Aug. 1932: 10.

247. See the ad for *White Zombie* and accompanying short subjects in the August 14, 1932, *Salt Lake Tribune*; see also the ad for the "Panther Woman" finalists in the August 11, 1932, *Salt Lake Tribune*.

248. "*White Zombie* bookings." *The Film Daily*, 3 Aug. 1932.

249. "At Salt Lake Theaters." *The Salt Lake Tribune*, 14 Aug. 1932.

250. See the ad promoting *White Zombie* in the August 11, 1932, *Philadelphia Inquirer*.

251. See the ad for Stanton Theater in the August 14, 1932, *Philadelphia Inquirer*.

252. "*Dollar Legs* Hits $17,000, Philadelphia." *Motion Picture Daily*, 22 Aug. 1932: 8.

253. C.P.J. "Asbestos: Saenger." *The Times-Picayune* (New Orleans), 19 Aug. 1932.

254. "Shivers Promised at Saenger Show." *The Times-Picayune* (New Orleans), 18 Aug. 1932.

255. See the ad for *White Zombie* at the United Artists' theater in the August 25, 1932, *Chicago Tribune* and *The Chicago Daily News*.

256. "B & K Reopening UA on August 26." *Motion Picture Daily* 23 Aug. 1932: 8. (This article claimed the reopening would occur on August 26, 1932; in fact, the date was moved to August 25.)

257. See the ad for *White Zombie* in the August 23, 1932, issue of *The Chicago Daily News*.

258. Tinée, May. "*White Zombie*." *Chicago Tribune*, 26 Aug. 1932: 11.

259. Rodenbach, Clark. "Spooks Scamper Over the Screen at United Artists." *The Chicago Daily News*, 26 Aug. 1932.

260. "*Zombie* at U.A., Chi $16,000; *70,000 Witnesses* $20,000 Fair; Montgomery Billed Over Davies." *Variety*, 30 Aug. 1932: 9.

261. Peterman, Betty. "The Bogey Man." *The Chicago Daily News*, 27 Aug. 1932. (The reviewer's use of the phrase "pest agents" seems to refer to those working in studio publicity departments.)

262. "Too much *Hell* on Chi Marquees; Palace $25,000 with *Paradise*; *Robinson Crusoe* Is Mild, $12,000." *Variety*, 6 Sept. 1932: 9.

263. "Comparative Grosses for March." *Variety*, 15 Apr. 1931: 10.

264. "Theatre Receipts." *Motion Picture Herald*, 19 Dec. 1931: 38.

265. "Theatre Receipts." *Motion Picture Herald*, 16 Jan. 1932: 26.

266. "Theatre Receipts." *Motion Picture Herald*, 20 Feb. 1932: 42.

267. "Too much *Hell* on Chi Marquees," p. 9.

268. O'Dea, Dawn. "Motion Picture Review." *Milwaukee Sentinel*, 26 Aug. 1932.

269. See the newspaper ad mentioning "Star of Dracula" in the August 26, 1932, *Milwaukee Sentinel* and the ad mentioning "Bela (DRACULA) Lugosi" in the August 28, 1932, *Milwaukee Sentinel*.

270. See the ad promoting "Lucky Buck[s]" in the August 26, 1932, *Milwaukee Sentinel*.

271. See the ad for *White Zombie* in the September 5, 1932, *Dallas Morning News*.

272. "Theater Row: Old Mill Stage Show to Close—Fairbanks Jr. and Dvorak, Capitol." *Dallas Morning News*, 3 Sept. 1932.

273. "The Screen: One Dracula and a Chorus of Frankensteins in Mild Horror Film." Rev. of *White Zombie*. *Dallas Morning News*, 5 Sept. 1932.

274. "Old Mill May Remain Open Through Season." *Dallas Morning News*, 6 Sept. 1932.

275. See the ad for *White Zombie* in the September 16, 1932, *Pittsburgh Post-Gazette*.

276. See the ad for *White Zombie* in the September 17, 1932, *Pittsburgh Post-Gazette*.

277. "*White Zombie*." *Pittsburgh Post-Gazette*, 17 Sept. 1932.

278. "Ballyhoo Overcomes Cricks on *Zombie*, $9,000 Best in Pitt." *Variety*, 20 Sept. 1932.

279. *Ibid.*

280. "Pitt Cheery; *Bird* $15,000, *Earth* $4,000." *Variety*, 27 Sept. 1932.

281. "Comparative Grosses for February." *Variety*, 18 Mar. 1931: 27.

282. See the ad for *White Zombie* in the September 23, 1932, *Daily Oklahoman*.

283. See the ad for *White Zombie* in the September 30, 1932, issue of the *Constitution* (Atlanta).

284. See the ad for *White Zombie* in the October 3, 1932, *Constitution* (Atlanta).

285. Hawkins, Lewis. "More Horror Unfolded in Ghoulish Film at Fox." The *Constitution* (Atlanta), 3 Oct. 1932.

286. See the ad for *White Zombie* in the November 4, 1932, *Seattle Times*.

287. "Story of Occult Is Displayed in Music Box Film." *Seattle Times*, 5 Sept. 1932.

288. "Seattle Going Strong, Par, 14G; *Work* 9½G." *Variety*, 15 Nov. 1932.

289. "Theatre Receipts." *Motion Picture Herald*, 12 Dec. 1931: 47. (The *Motion Picture Daily* of November 18, 1932, overestimated and suggested that *White Zombie* would gross $4,000 for one week at the Music Box.)

290. "Theatre Receipts." *Motion Picture Herald*, 13 Feb. 1932: 48.

291. Lusk, Norbert. "Audiences Give Lie to Critics." *Los Angeles Times*, 7 Aug. 1932: sec. 3: 15.

292. Scott, John. "Eerie Yarn Offered at Criterion." *Los Angeles Times*, 19 Nov. 1932, sec. 3: 7.

293. "Holiday Helps L.A., but Quickly Eases Off; *Holmes, Match* in 2 Houses, Weak 17G and 15G; Par 17G." *Variety*, 29 Nov. 1932: 8. (The *Motion Picture Daily* of November 28, 1932, overestimated *White Zombie*'s gross at the Criterion at $4,500.)

294. "An Idea of L.A.'s Biz Is $13,700 for *Mouthful*, Town's Top Gross; *Faithless* in 2 Houses, $18,300." *Variety*, 22 Nov. 1932.

295. "Nothing Special in L.A., Now Tho *Skippy* $25,000 at Par; Hollywood 2d Runs Hold Up." *Variety*, 8 Apr. 1931.

296. "Theatre Receipts." *Motion Picture Herald*, 6 Feb. 1932: 66.

297. "Theatre Receipts." *Motion Picture Herald*, 16 Jan. 1932: 27.

298. "Coast Houses Nose Dive in Torrid Spell." *Motion Picture Daily*, 25 Aug. 1932: 8.

299. "*Mouthful* Is Only Draw in Los Angeles." *Motion Picture Daily*, 25 Nov. 1932.

300. See the ad for *White Zombie* in the November 16, 1932, *Los Angeles Times*.

301. See the ad for *White Zombie* in the November 18, 1932, *Los Angeles Times*.

302. See Harry C. Browne's "Study Local Sales Angles of Each Picture; Then Go Ahead" (in *Motion Picture Herald*, 7 Jan. 1933: 51) for a warning against "sex angles" in advertising campaigns. Additionally, anger towards "indecent shows" even caused a local ban on "hot shows"—girl acts coupled with feature films—at area theaters in mid–1932. See "Los Angeles Moves to Ban 'Hot' Shows" in *Motion Picture Daily*, 29 July 1932: 1.

303. Thompson, Lloyd S. "*Trouble in Paradise* at Warner Friday"; "*White Zombie* Stays at United Artists." *The San Francisco Examiner*, 6 Dec. 1932.

304. See the ad for *White Zombie* in the December 2, 1932, issue of *The San Francisco Examiner*.

305. "Picture Recalls Haitian Monster." *The San Francisco Examiner*, 8 Dec. 1932: C24.

306. "Zombie Voodoo Art Is Practiced in U.S." *The San Francisco Examiner*, 7 Dec. 1932.

307. "*White Zombie* Shiver Drama, at U.A.; *Brief Moment* Due at Curran Monday." *The San Francisco Examiner*, 29 Nov. 1932.

308. "*Flesh* with $16,500 Take Frisco's High." *Motion Picture Daily*, 22 Dec. 22 1932: 7.

309. "Theatre Receipts." *Motion Picture Herald*, 2 Jan. 1932: 45.

310. For example, see "United Artists—The Exclusives" in *Harrison's Reports* (29 Oct. 1932: 1) and "The 'Exclusive' Idea Will Soon Be Dead" in *Harrison's Reports* (5 Nov. 1932: 180).

311. Rodenbach, Clark. "Spooks Scamper Over the Screen at United Artists." *The Chicago Daily News*, 25 Aug. 1932.

Chapter 5

1. Baker, Charles H. *The Gentleman's Companion: An Exotic Drinking Book*. New York: Crown, 1946. (Perhaps the

first connection in print between the drink and the Halperin films came in a May 24, 1936, *New York Times*, in which journalist John T. McManus quoted Edward Halperin as saying, "Now you take a zombie." The author's response: "We would have preferred absinthe, if you'll pardon our lisp, but we ordered jinn, sloe gin, to be on the safe side and still remain more or less in the spirit of things.")

2. Gordon, Alex. "The Pit and the Pen of Alex Gordon." *Fangoria* 16 (1985).

3. *Amusement Securities Corporation v. Academy Pictures Distribution Corporation*. New York County: Supreme Court of New York 27 June 1936.

4. Figures for *Dracula* and *Frankenstein* negative costs and grosses appear in *Cult Movies* 9, as contributed by writer–film fan Karl Thiede.

5. *"White Zombie* Blasts Records!" *The Hollywood Reporter*, 24 Aug. 1932.

6. "Front made by Tom Cleary for *Zombie* Was a Real Stopper." *Motion Picture Herald*, 12 Nov. 1932: 64.

7. *"White Zombie." The Daily Film Renter*, 21 Sept. 1932: 8.

8. *"White Zombie." Kinematograph Weekly*, 22 Sept. 1932: 37.

9. A.F. *"White Zombie." The Cinema News and Property Gazette*, 21 Sept. 1932: 13.

10. *"Zombie* in London." *Motion Picture Herald*, 31 Dec. 1932: 74.

11. "Lincoln's Price War." *Variety*, 29 May 1934.

12. *Hollywood Reporter*, 16 May 1936.

13. Rhodes, *Lugosi*, p. 220. (The film, planned for Warner Brothers, was never produced.)

14. Rhodes, p. 213. (Controversy remains over whether animators actually used the footage they filmed of Lugosi in animating the Mephistophelean character of the *Night on Bald Mountain* sequence; it seems most likely that, while Disney sought out Lugosi's assistance, animators did not draw on his help.)

15. Lugosi also appeared in *Zombies on Broadway*, a 1945 RKO horror-comedy. Though he does control zombies, the film shows little influence from *White Zombie*.

16. Bonner, Basil. Email to Andi Brooks, 24 Feb. 2000.

17. See the "TV Movie Highlights" columns in the *Los Angeles Times* of March 1, 1953, and March 29, 1953, and "Saturday Television/TV Highlights" in the *Los Angeles Times* of April 7, 1951, and April 24, 1954.

18. Rhodes, Gary D. Interview with Richard Sheffield, 9 Oct. 1996.

19. Rhodes, Gary D. Interview with Buddy Barnett, 22 Oct. 1994.

20. Examples include "Lugosi Dies: Plan Burial in 'Dracula' Garb" in the Hollywood *Citizen-News* of August 17, 1956, and "The Cloak of Dracula, Symbol of His Career, Will Shroud Lugosi" in the *New York Post* of August 19, 1956.

21. Kingsley, Grace. "Hobnobbing in Hollywood." *Los Angeles Times*, 19 Dec. 1932.

22. "Plan Spiritualistic Film." *Motion Picture Daily*, 26 Jan. 1933: 8.

23. Kingsley.

24. Bellamy, Madge. *A Darling of the Twenties*. Vestal, NY: Vestal Press, 1989: 121.

25. Nielsen, Raymond J. Interview with Victor Halperin and Madge Bellamy. AETN-TV, Arkansas. Circa 1978.

26. *Los Angeles Examiner*, 22 Dec. 1932.

27. Salkow, Sidney. "Carole Lombard: Blithe Spirit." Close Ups: Intimate Profiles of Movie Stars and Their Costars, Directors, Screenwriters, and Friends. Ed. Danny Peary. New York: Fireside/Simon and Schuster, 1985. (p. 31).

28. *Ibid.*, p. 31.

29. *Ibid.*, p. 31.

30. *Ibid.*, p. 32.

31. *Ibid.*, p. 32.

32. Unsourced clippings, dated 14 Mar. 1933 and 21 Mar. 1933. Carole Lombard clipping file. Microfiche. Margaret Herrick Library. Beverly Hills, CA.

33. *The Film Daily* of April 17, 1933, claimed that the film's Paramount opening would occur on April 20, 1933. However, New York newspaper ads confirm its premiere took place on April 21, 1933.

34. "Theatre Receipts." *Motion Picture Herald*, 6 May 1933: 38.

35. See "Theatre Receipts" in the July 8, 1933, *Motion Picture Herald* for information on *Supernatural*'s booking at the RKO Roxy in New York, as well as its status at the bottom of a double bill at San Francisco's St. Francis Theater. The sheer lack of "Theatre Receipts" for *Supernatural* in other spring and summer 1933 *Motion Picture Herald*s indicate that the film did not play at most of the country's top movie theaters.

36. "What the Picture Did for Me." *Motion Picture Herald*, 8 July 1933: 48.

37. "Spirits: Put on Good Show If Taken at Face Value." *Newsweek*, 29 Apr. 1933.

38. Aaronson. *"Supernatural." Motion Picture Herald*, 29 1933: 30.

39. *"Supernatural." The Film Daily*, 22 Apr. 1933: 4.

40. *"Supernatural." Motion Picture Daily*, 22 Apr. 1933: 3.

41. *"Supernatural." Harrison's Reports*, 29 Apr. 1933: 66.

42. Aaronson, p. 30.

43. See Chapter Ten for an examination of other, non-horror films the Halperins made in the 1930s.

44. "Halperins Have New *Zombie* Next on Sked." *The Hollywood Reporter*, 27 Nov. 1935: 2.

45. *"Zombies* in Two Weeks." *The Hollywood Reporter*, 13 Jan. 1936: 4.

46. "Halperin Crew Sails for Revolt [*sic*] Exteriors." *The Hollywood Reporter*, 25 Jan. 1936: 4.

47. "Delve into Angkor's Past for *Zombies*." *The Hollywood Reporter*, 15 Feb. 1936: 6.

48. *Revolt of the Zombies* may have been an odd choice for dancer Dorothy Stone, but it was not her first film appearance; she starred in the three-reel Vitaphone short *Look for the Silver Lining* in 1934.

49. "Pictures Now Shooting." *The Hollywood Reporter*, 9 Mar. 1936: 31.

50. "Suit Over *Zombie* Film." *New York Times*, 26 May 1936.

51. *The Hollywood Reporter*, 26 May 1936.

52. *The Hollywood Reporter*, 29 May 1936.

53. Some modern sources (including Michael H. Price and George E. Turner in their essay "The Black Art of *White Zombie*, published in *The Cinema of Adventure, Romance, & Terror*. Hollywood: ASC Press, 1989) suggest that the lawsuit forced a retitling of the film to *Revolt of the Demons* until the court case ended. While it is possible this change was mentioned in an industry trade article unfamiliar to the present study, close scrutiny of the film's opening and theatrical screenings in New York City—which occurred after the lawsuit began

and finished before the legalities came to a close—indicate with certainty that the retitling did not actually occur.

54. *The Hollywood Reporter*, 1 June 1936.

55. *Ibid.*

56. *Motion Picture Herald*, 13 June 1936: 68.

57. *The Hollywood Reporter*, 12 June 1936.

58. By that time, the action against one of the defendants—the RKO Film Booking Corporation—had been discontinued, though unfortunately Hoffman's opinion does not explain why.

59. In addition to distributing independent film product overseas, Ameranglo (whose name in film trades was also occasionally spelled "AmerAnglo" and "Amer-Anglo") imported films of other countries into the U.S.

60. Contextually, it seems the use of the word "character" here means "horror."

61. "Film Injunction Recommended." *New York Times*, 30 June 1936.

62. Only two weeks later, Sam Krellberg tried to obtain part of the settlement money from Producers Laboratory. His claim was that they held some $10,000 owed to Academy Pictures; as a result, he asked for the surrender of the *Revolt* negatives, preventing the laboratory from "disposing of the Academy picture property until the end of the bankruptcy action." The latter comment spoke of an involuntary bankruptcy action plaguing Melbert Pictures caused by the Hoffman decision.

63. *The Hollywood Reporter*, 17 Oct. 1936. (On May 10, 1937, *The Hollywood Reporter* wrote that "Producer's Laboratories and Ameranglo have been granted an appeal from a lower court decision which upheld adjudication for Amusement Securities Corporation in the case arising from the use of the name *Revolt of the Zombies*." Apparently, those organizations severed their codefendant status with the Halperins and pursued the earlier judgments on appeal. Attorney Saul Rogers acted as representative for the defendants.")

64. Another similarity occurs, though it is a slight one. The makeup effects of bullets hitting the chest of one zombie are quite reminiscent of those in a similar shot in *White Zombie*.

65. *Motion Picture Herald*, 13 June 1936: 68.

66. *Motion Picture Daily*, 8 June 1936.

67. *Revolt of the Zombies* pressbook of 1936. Courtesy University of Madison–Wisconsin.

68. "*Revolt of the Zombies*." *Harrison's Reports*, 20 June 1920: 98.

69. "Film Consensus." *The Billboard*, 20 June 1936.

70. *Motion Picture Daily*, 8 June 1936: 18.

71. "New Pathé Group; Two British Productions; *White Zombie* Sequel." *The Cinema News and Property Gazette*, 27 May 1936.

72. "Reviews: *Revolt of the Zombies*." *Kinematograph Weekly*, 25 June 1936: 37.

73. Curiously, this disconnect seemed all the more great when Hal Roach Studios released *Revolt of the Zombies* to videocassette in 1986. The box art used a still photograph from *White Zombie*, serving only to heighten the difference in quality between the two separate works. But recent decades in general have not helped the film's reputation either. It made little to no impact when it first began appearing on television in the 1950s, being broadcast mainly due to the cheap rentals offered to television studios. Status as a public domain film has not helped its distribution in the age of home video, with horror film critics of the eighties and nineties perhaps even more harsh

than those of the thirties. Only its connection to *White Zombie* has allowed some historians to fidget in their seats, struggling with boredom to its conclusion.

74. See Chapter Two for an in-depth examination of Seabrook's *The Magic Island*.

75. More than a month after *White Zombie*'s New York premiere, Joseph von Sternberg's *Blonde Venus* was released, in September 1932. Though not a horror or even a voodoo film, *Blonde Venus* includes a dramatic and well-discussed nightclub scene in which actress Marlene Dietrich sings the tune "Hot Voodoo" by Sam Coslow and Ralph Rainer. The sounds of voodoo drums introduce the sequence, which takes place on a jungle set. An ape appears, pawing at the chorus girls and beating its chest. Its hands and arms sway in rhythm to the music before it lifts off its mask. Dietrich is inside the costume, and the nightclub audience applauds heavily. The proximity of release dates should not suggest that *White Zombie* influenced the inclusion or creation of the number; rather, its origin was probably spurred by the same overall backdrop as *White Zombie* as explored in Chapter Two.

76. "Negro Voodoo Film." *Variety*, 12 July 1932.

77. "Making Voodoo Film." *The Film Daily*, 29 Aug. 1932.

78. Wirkus, Faustin E., with Henry Wysham Lanier. "The Black Pope of Voodoo: Part I." *Harper's Monthly Magazine*, Dec. 1933: 38–49. (Part II of the same article appeared in *Harper's*, Jan 1934: 189–98.)

79. Though copyrighted with the unusual spelling *Voodo*, newspaper ads and critics of the period restored its title to the more commonly used *Voodoo*.

80. "*Voodoo*." *Motion Picture Daily*, 25 Mar. 1933: 2.

81. "*Voodoo*." *Motion Picture Herald*, 13 May 1933: 27.

82. "Col. Buys *Black Moon*." *The Hollywood Reporter*, 17 Aug. 1932. (Oddly, trades and newspapers referred to the Clements Ripley story as being published in a 1931 or 1932 *Hearst's International Cosmopolitan* magazine, calling it either "Black Moon" or "Haiti Moon." Though Ripley wrote for the magazine, no voodoo story under his [or anyone else's] byline appeared in the magazine during 1931–2.)

83. "*Black Moon* to Be Made into Columbia Film." *Los Angeles Times*, 31 Aug. 1932.

84. "What the New Movies Are Like." *The Afro-American*, 10 Sept. 1932.

85. Wilk, Ralph. "A 'Little' from Hollywood 'Lots.'" *The Film Daily*, 26 Feb. 1934: 6.

86. Wilk, Ralph. "A 'Little' from Hollywood 'Lots.'" *The Film Daily*, 9 Apr. 1934: 2.

87. Wilk, Ralph. "A 'Little' from Hollywood 'Lots.'" *The Film Daily*, 30 Apr. 1934: 7.

88. Wilk, Ralph. "A 'Little' from Hollywood 'Lots.'" *The Film Daily*, 7 May 1934: 5.

89. "Substitutions, Tenth, and Indecent Pictures—No. 2." *Harrison's Reports*, 23 June 1934: 1.

90. "*Black Moon*." *The Film Daily*, 28 June 1934: 6.

91. "*Black Moon*." *Harrison's Reports*, 7 July 1934: 107.

92. See George E. Turner and Michael F. Price's *Forgotten Horrors* (A.S. Barnes, 1979: 119–120).

93. "*Drums o' Voodoo*." *Variety*, 15 May 1934: 27.

94. "*Drums o' Voodoo* Booked." *The Film Daily*, 2 Feb. 1934: 2.

95. "*Voodoo* Preview Set." *Motion Picture Daily*, 6 Apr. 1933: 7.

96. "*Louisiana*." *The Hollywood Reporter*, 14 June 1934: 3.

97. *"Drums o' Voodoo." The Film Daily*, 5 May 1934: 2.

98. *"Drums o' Voodoo." Variety*, 15 May 1934.

99. Unlike *White Zombie*, *Chloe* presents a very racist narrative.

100. Daly, Phil M. "Along the Rialto." *The Film Daily*, 19 Jan. 1934.

101. See Chapter Two for a discussion of Seabrook and *The Magic Island*.

102. Production history taken from Turner and Price's *Forgotten Horrors* (A.S. Barnes, 1979: 175–176).

103. Alicoate, John. *The Film Daily*, 26 Oct. 1934.

104. Plot summary stems from a review in *The Film Daily* (13 Feb. 1935: 11).

105. One such appearance of voodoo in the thirties was *Beyond the Caribbean* (1936), also known as *Man Hunters of the Caribbean*. Though not a horror story, the film's plot employs voodoo in a minor way. Still, *White Zombie* seems not to have had an impact on its storyline or been of even implicit aid in its financing.

106. Seabrook's *The Magic Island* had even been republished in 1932 by the Albatross Press.

107. "Hoodoo" is a variation of the word "voodoo" and is heard in Louisiana and the southern United States.

108. Loederer, pp. 252–253.

109. The use of the term and spelling "voodoo" with regard to Africa—while certainly ethnocentric and inaccurate in some ways—stems from Sinclair's text.

110. Carnochan and Adamson, p. 77.

111. *Ibid.*, p. 77.

112. Maddox, John Lee. "Modern Voodooism: Part I." *Hygeia* Feb. 1934: 153–156. (Part II was published in Hygeia, Mar. 1934: 252–255.)

113. Jenkins, Elizabeth Blaine. "Voodoo Land." *Hygeia*, May 1935: 456–459.

114. Forbes, Rosita. "The Priestess of the Impossible." *Country Life*, Sept. 1935: 51–52, 74–77.

115. Possendorf, p. 284.

116. Courlander, p. 18.

117. Courlander, p. 18.

118. Hurston, p. 206.

119. Subsequent careers of *White Zombie*'s cast, crew, and auxiliary figures are covered in Appendix K.

120. Hurston, Zora Neale. *Dust Tracks on a Road*. Philadelphia: Lippincott, 1971. (Original text copyright 1942.)

121. Seabrook, William B. *No Hiding Place*. New York: Lippincott, 1942 (pp. 280–281). (See Chapter Two for an investigation of the earliest uses of the term "zombi/zombie," some of which predate the publication of Seabrook's *The Magic Island*.)

Chapter 6

1. Larry the Wolf. E-mail to Gary D. Rhodes, 27 Jan. 1999.

2. The Manimals' second album, written and produced by "Larry the Wolf" was recorded and copyrighted in 1998; as of this writing, it has not yet appeared commercially on CD. It includes another tune which "Larry the Wolf," in a January 27, 1999, e-mail to the author, claims to be "a more complete *WZ* inspired song…. Entitled 'Dead Man's Eyes,' it has a tempo which matches the dreamlike cadence of the film more effectively than the earlier song."

3. Price, Michael H. E-mail to Gary D. Rhodes, 7 Sept. 1998.

4. *Ibid.*

5. *Ibid.*

6. *Ibid.*

7. American Film Technology, Incorporated's colorized *White Zombie*, credited with a publication date of August 29, 1990, was registered with copyright #PA54-617 on April 3, 1991. The reason for the new copyright: the film was a "minor change version."

8. *A Little Background About The Black Cat Productions* [one-page flyer]. Chicago: The Black Cat Productions, 1999.

9. Rhodes, Gary D. Interview with Colleen Couillard, 24 Sept. 1999.

10. The rest of the cast included Betty Madonna (Betina, Legendre's Mother), Eva Wilhelm (Latour, Legendre's Former Friend), Jane Haldiman (Hecco, the Witch Doctor), Phil Selvey (the Guide), Michael Hora (Dr. Bruner), Bob Dawson (Silver), Miss Jezzi Belle (Juanita).

11. See Footnote 75 of Chapter Five for more information on the song "Hot Voodoo."

12. Couillard, Colleen. Letter to Gary D. Rhodes, 29 Sept. 1999.

13. Darzin, Daina. "Dancin' with the Devil: White Zombie Mint Gold from Goth." *Rolling Stone*, 9 Dec. 1993: 13–14.

14. "White Zombie Pulls the Plug Saying It Was Time to Move On." Geffen Records Home Page. Released 23 Sept. 1998. Accessed 24 Nov. 1998. Address: www.geffen.com/planetzombie/

15. "It's True! Zombies Love Munsters!" *Monsterscene* 11 (Winter 1998): 11.

16. Josh Alan's 1994 musical *The Worst!*—which covers the life of director Ed Wood—also makes an allusion to the film *White Zombie*. One scene includes 1950s horror hostess Vampira introducing the film on late night television; her character then sings Alan's composition "Bad Dreams." The reference to the film's incessant closeups of Lugosi's eyes also suggests its repeated performances on 1950's television sets. The lyrics on the Dallas-based Black Cracker Music compact disc release of 1994 are sung by Phoebe Legere; as of 1998, a live production of the entire show had yet to occur.

17. Ulakovic, John. E-mail to Gary D. Rhodes, 7 Oct. 1998.

Chapter 7

1. See Appendix J for a list of video companies which have released *White Zombie*.

2. Everson, William K. "Public Domain." *Video Review*, Sept. 1984.

3. Benjamin, Walter. *Illuminations: Essays and Reflections*. Ed. by Hannah Arendt. New York: Schocken, 1969 (p. 241).

4. As an example of projectionists' concerns regarding optimum viewing conditions, see Clifton Tuttle's article "Distortion in the Projection and viewing of Motion Pictures." *Motion Picture Herald*, 23 Sept. 1933: 17.

5. See "Proper Size of Screen Image." *Motion Picture Herald* 1 July 1933: 32. Also, see "Variations in Borders Protested." *Motion Picture Herald*, 11 Mar. 1933: 22.

6. For an example, see "F. H. Richardson's Comment and Answers to Inquiries." *Motion Picture Herald* [Better Theatres Section], 26 Sept. 1931.

7. "2,000-Foot Reels Are Discussed as Big Economy to the Industry." *Motion Picture Herald*, 7 Jan. 1933: 9.

8. The "approximately seventy minutes" of the negative Storace obtained could well have been almost the exact same print as the approximately 69-minute-long print reviewed by many critics in 1932. In an October 5, 1979, letter to Leonard J. Kohl, he even wrote that "some people time [the print] as 68 minutes, but it is all about the same." Presumably one should take all Storace's mentions of running times as quite approximate.

9. Storace, Frank. Letter to Leonard J. Kohl, 17 July 1981.

10. Storace, Frank. Letter to Leonard J. Kohl, 5 Oct. 1979.

11. Storace, Frank. Letter to Leonard J. Kohl, 17 Aug. 1980.

12. Rhodes, Gary D. Interview with Cary Roan, 3 Nov. 1996.

13. See the shot list in Appendix P for more information on these specific shot numbers.

14. It seems that the spot noticeable on a few frames of Shot 409 is probably not a flaw in the source material, but rather glare recorded by the camera lens during production.

15. Other examples of such artifacting include Shots 246 and 273 during Scene 17.

16. Clark, Mike. "*White Zombie.*" *USA Today*, 17 Mar. 1995: 3D.

17. "Bringing Zombie Back to Life." *TV Guide*, 8 Apr. 1995: 46.

18. "*White Zombie.*" *Entertainment Weekly*, 14 Apr. 1995: 73.

19. Frumkes, Roy. "*White Zombie.*" *Films in Review*, Sept.-Oct. 1995: 37.

20. Tournier, Johanne L. "*White Zombie.*" *Cult Movies*, 15 1995: 14–16.

21. Lucas, Tim. "*White Zombie.*" *Video Watchdog*, 29 1995: 74–75.

22. Holt, Wesley G. "*White Zombie.*" *Filmfax*, 51 July-Aug. 1995: 28, 30.

23. Wannen, Rich. Letter to the Editor. *The Laser Disc Newsletter*, August 1995: 16.

24. Wannen additionally claimed that the Roan Group misspelled my name on the printed liner notes. I defer here to my birth certificate and parents' wisdom; the Roan Group had definitely not erred in this regard.

25. In *Midnight Marquee* (Summer/Fall 1999), Gary J. Svhela called the DVD an "essential disk" for film collectors.

26. Usai, Paolo Cherchi. *Burning Passions: An Introduction to the Study of Silent Cinema.* London: British Film Institute, 1994 (p. 41).

Chapter 8

1. Everson, William K. "Public Domain." *Video Review*, Sept. 1984.

Chapter 9

1. Muse's tale of Lugosi "directing" *White Zombie* is addressed in Chapter Three of this book.

Chapter 10

1. Sarris, Andrew. *The American Cinema: Directors and Directions 1929–1968.* New York: Dutton, 1968.

2. Denton, Clive. "On Film." *Take One* Volume 2, Issue 3 (1969).

3. Bradley, George E. "'Vic' Halperin Once Directed 'Mobs.'" *The Morning Telegraph* (New York), 14 Dec. 1924: 10.

4. Halperin, Venita. Letter to Gary D. Rhodes, 11 Sept. 1997.

5. *Cap and Gown* [University of Chicago Yearbook] Chicago: University of Chicago, 1916 (pp. 214, 217).

6. *Ibid.*, p. 204.

7. *Ibid*, p. 230.

8. "A Night of Knights." [Program of a Blackfriars annual show.] Chicago: The Blackfriars, 1915.

9. According to the *Cap and Gown* for 1916, the play featured the music of L. J. Fuiks, W. H. Weiser, R. B. Whitehead, A. W. Haupt, J. Rhodes, S. Kusel, M. Herzog, and F. F. Gualano. Their songs included "Some Day," "Honolulu," "To the Challenger," and "Hero of Mine."

10. Nielsen, Raymond J. "After 45 Years Victor Hugo Halperin Awarded 'Classic' Honor ... Now Wins Directorial Accolade for 1932 Film *White Zombie*, starring Bela Lugosi." Unpublished essay, 1978 (p. 4).

11. Lynch, Don. *Titanic: An Illustrated History.* Toronto: Madison Press, 1992 (pp. 212, 215).

12. Bradley, p. 10.

13. Halperin, Venita. Letter to Gary D. Rhodes, 11 Sept. 1997.

14. All information in this paragraph stems from one of Halperin's undated resumes, in the possession of his widow, Mrs. Venita Halperin.

15. Information regarding Vityfix appears in Halperin's 1960 resume, in the possession of his widow.

16. Hanna, David J. "Halperins Follow 'Scientific' Formula in Film Production." *Hollywood Reporter*, 20 Feb. 1937.

17. *Ibid.*

18. Bradley, p. 10.

19. *Ibid.*, p. 10.

20. Nielsen, p. 10.

21. Neither *The American Film Institute Catalog of Motion Pictures Produced in the United States: Feature Films, 1911–1920* (Univ. of California, 1988) nor *The American Film Institute Catalog of Motion Pictures Produced in the United States: Feature Films, 1921–1930* (R. R. Bowker Co., 1971) speak about Victor Halperin's western films or Cactus Films.

22. Bradley, p. 10.

23. Lee, Joe. "Independence and Showmanship." *Moving Picture World*, 8 July 1922: 127.

24. Ferri, Roger. "The Passing Week in Review." *Moving Picture World*, 10 June 1922: 565.

25. "Exhibitors Clamor for Independent Films as Future Promises Greatest Season Ever." *Moving Picture World*, 26 Aug. 1922: 686.

26. Burr, Charles C. "Independent Has Arrived, but Acid Test Has Just Begun, Says Charles C. Burr." *Moving Picture World*, 8 July 1922: 158.

27. *Ibid.*, p. 10.

28. "*The Danger Point.*" *Harrison's Reports*, 11 Nov. 1922: 178.

29. Bradley, p. 10.

30. "Hale Is Engaged for New Halperin Picture." *Exhibitors Herald*, 17 Feb. 1923: 76.

31. *Ibid.*, p. 10.

32. "Showmen Everywhere Vote for *Tea—with a Kick.*" *Moving Picture World*, 12 July 1924: 121.

33. Powell, A. Van Buren, editor. "Straight from the Shoulder Reports." *Moving Picture World*, 1 Mar 1924.

34. Powell, A. Van Buren, editor. "Straight from the Shoulder Reports." *Moving Picture World*, 12 Jan. 1924.

35. Powell, A. Van Buren, editor. "Straight from the Shoulder Reports." *Moving Picture World*, 8 Mar 1924.

36. *Ibid.*

37. Powell, A. Van Buren, editor. "Straight from the Shoulder Reports." *Moving Picture World*, 19 Apr. 1924.

38. "Independents." *Exhibitors Herald*, 7 July 1923: 200.

39. Brandt, Joe. "Independent Future Is Brilliant." *Exhibitors Herald*, 31 May 1924: 61.

40. "*When a Girl Loves.*" *Exhibitors Herald*, 17 May 1924: 51.

41. Barrett, Beatrice. "*When a Girl Loves.*" *Moving Picture World*, 3 May 1924: 85, 87.

42. Powell, A. Van Buren, editor. "Straight from the Shoulder Reports." *Moving Picture World*, 1 Nov. 1924.

43. Powell, A. Van Buren, editor. "Straight from the Shoulder Reports." *Moving Picture World*, 18 Oct. 1924.

44. *Ibid.*, p. 87.

45. "Independent Producers Plan Seven Million Dollar Outlay." *Exhibitors Herald*, 7 Apr. 1923: 30.

46. "Halperins Now Planning Their Future Productions." *Moving Picture World*, 14 June 1924: 649.

47. *The Unknown Lover* is a drama about a young woman named Elaine who marries Kenneth, a wealthy man who is disinherited by his parents because of the marriage. Though Kenneth becomes a successful businessman, his health worsens and he neglects his bride. Elaine purposely sets out to ruin his business thanks to help from Fred, a former suitor. Kenneth then leaves the country, returning in good health and with apologies for neglecting Elaine. She forgives him, they reunite, and the business prospers with Fred as a partner.

48. Powell, A. Van Buren, editor. "Straight from the Shoulder Reports." *Moving Picture World*, 11 Apr. 1924.

49. Powell, A. Van Buren, editor. "Straight from the Shoulder Reports." *Moving Picture World*, 25 Apr. 1924.

50. Powell, A. Van Buren, editor. "Straight from the Shoulder Reports." *Moving Picture World*, 18 Apr. 1924.

51. Bradley, p. 10.

52. Katz, Ephraim. *The Film Encyclopedia*. 3rd edition, revised by Fred Klein and Ronald Dean Nolen. New York: HarperCollins, 1998.

53. Nielsen, p. 4.

54. Welsh, Robert E. "Strong Array of Product in the INDEPENDENT MARKET [*sic*]: Special Section of *Moving Picture World.*" *Moving Picture World*, 24 Jan. 1925: 333.

55. "Joe Brandt Discusses 1925 Outlook for Independents." *Moving Picture World*, 3 Jan. 1925: 79.

56. "Independent Films for 1925 to Cost About $15,000,000." *Moving Picture World*, 3 Sept. 1924: 143.

57. For a thorough examination of Donlevy's career, see Gregory William Mank's chapter on him in the book *The Hollywood Hissables*. Metuchen, NJ: Scarecrow, 1989 (pp. 241–298).

58. "Halperin's *School for Wives* Pleases Vitagraph Officials." *Moving Picture World*, 14 Feb. 1925: 717.

59. "*School for Wives.*" *Variety*, 1 Apr. 1925.

60. "*School for Wives.*" *Moving Picture World*, 11 Apr. 1925: 583.

61. Hall, Mordaunt. "The Screen: Love Versus Money." Rev. of *School for Wives*, 1 Apr. 1925.

62. "*School for Wives*, with Peggy Kelly, at Rialto." *New York Herald Tribune*, 29 Mar. 1925.

63. Underhill, Harriette. "On the Screen." *New York Herald Tribune*, 31 Mar. 1925.

64. Sewell, C. S. "*In Borrowed Plumes.*" *Moving Picture World*, 27 Mar. 1926: 286.

65. Bradley, p. 10.

66. "Kane Explains Production Plans and Announces Staff." *Moving Picture World*, 13 June 1925: 803.

67. "Convoy." *Harrison's Reports*, 21 May 1927: 82.

68. *Ibid.*, p. 82. *Harrison's Reports* wrote that "In spots the spectacular appeal is strong, although such thrills, while they awaken interest, are not pleasant. Many of the shots are taken from news reels [*sic*], others from government films. The big naval battle is very exciting and impressive. The sinking of one German ship, with the sailors crawling over its bottom, scores drowning as they leap into the water, is horribly realistic. The sequences of the convoy, escorted by destroyers and cruisers, which attack hostile submarines, and hidden behind a smoke screen, are effectively photographed."

69. "What the Picture Did for Me." *Exhibitor's Herald and Moving Picture World*, 8 Dec. 1928: 67.

70. "Dance Magic." *New York Times*, 13 July 1927.

71. Underhill, Harriette. "*Dance Magic*—Hippodrome." *New York Herald Tribune*, 12 July 1927.

72. "*Dance Magic.*" *Harrison's Reports*, 23 July 1927.

73. Sime. "*Dance Magic.*" *Variety*, 13 July 1927.

74. Bradley, p. 10.

75. "Independent Boom Around New York." *Variety*, 9 June 1926.

76. Halperin, Venita. Letter to Gary D. Rhodes, 11 Sept. 1997.

77. Grace Kingsley's column in the December 14, 1930, *Los Angeles Times* mentions Victor and his wife (who is not named in the article).

78. Nielsen, p. 5.

79. *Ibid.*, unpaginated.

80. McManus, John T. "Walking Dead in Angkor." *New York Times*, 24 May 1936: sec. IX, p. 3.

81. Hughes, Rupert. *She Goes to War and Other Stories.* New York: Grosset and Dunlap, 1929. (p. 27)

82. *Ibid.*, p. 53.

83. Full-page newspaper ad featured in the *Los Angeles Times* of 27 June 1929.

84. Nielsen, p. 6.

85. *Ibid.*, p. 6.

86. Studios in 1928 and 1929 advertised numerous films which were not "All-Dialogue" with phrases and catchlines that misled audiences into believing they were. *Harrison's Reports* of 4 May 1929 ran an editorial titled "Honest Advertising of Sound Pictures" which highlights this problem.

87. Ad for *She Goes to War* in the *Los Angeles Times*, 27 June 1929.

88. *Harrison's Reports* of 15 June 1929 wrote that *She Goes to War* was "...produced in silent form, but an attempt was made to superimpose a few lines of dialogue here and there, unsuccessfully. A song or two are sung, too, supposedly by a woman character, but it is too obvious that the singing was grafted. Almost all of the dialogue consists of a few commands, given by officers to soldiers. It would be a misrepresentation to advertise it as a talking, or even a part-talking, picture."

89. Schallert, Edwin. "Heroine in Battle Is Effective." Rev. of *She Goes to War*. *Los Angeles Times*, 29 June 1929.

90. M.T. "*She Goes to War*—Rivoli." *New York Herald Tribune*, 10 June 1929.

91. Nielsen, p. 6.

92. Schallert, page number unknown.

93. Nangle, Roberta. "One More War Film Is Added to the Hundreds." *Chicago Tribune*, 28 July 1929.

94. M.T. "*She Goes to War*—Rivoli." *New York Herald Tribune*, 10 June 1929.

95. Ad for *She Goes to War*. *Exhibitors Herald-World*, 25 May 1929.

96. "Artists Give Picture Gala Performance." *Los Angeles Times*, 28 June 1929.

97. "Halperins to Produce Shakespearean Plays." *Exhibitors Herald-World*, 8 June 1929: 39.

98. "Barrie, Judith." *The 1935–36 Motion Picture Almanac*. Hollywood: Quigley Publishing Co., 1935.

99. Wilk, Ralph. "A Little from 'Lots.'" *The Film Daily*, 22 May 1930: 8.

100. "Judith Barrie to Be Starred." *The Film Daily*, 4 May 1930: 4.

101. Though Victor's direction of *Party Girl* is confirmed by all sources of the period, reissue prints inexplicably list Rex Hale's name as director on the opening credits.

102. *Harrison's Reports* of 11 Jan. 1930 wrote that *Party Girl*, like so many other early talkies, was available to exhibitors as a silent feature as well.

103. "367 Companies Active in 1929 Against 338 in Previous Year." *The Film Daily*, 3 Feb. 1930: 1.

104. Kann. "Independence." *Motion Picture Daily*, 16 May 1931: 1, 14.

105. Nielsen, p. 10.

106. Talezaar, Marguerite. "On the Screen." Rev. of *Party Girl*. *New York Herald Tribune*, 2 Jan. 1930.

107. Talezaar, p. 16.

108. Hall, Mordaunt. "The Screen: Blackmail." Rev. of *Party Girl*. *New York Times*, 2 Jan. 1930.

109. "*Party Girl*." *Variety*, 8 Jan. 1930.

110. Credits for *Ex-Flame* list Edward Halperin and M. H. Hoffman as having "Supervised" the film; their specific responsibilities, though, were equivalent to that of producers.

111. "*Ex-Flame* Booked at Orpheum." *Los Angeles Times*, 16 Dec. 1930.

112. Churchill, Edward. "Successes of Independent Producers Bringing New Money Into This Field." *Motion Picture Herald*, 14 Mar. 1930: 46. (The Gumbiners were sometimes referred in industry trade articles as the "Gumbin" brothers.)

113. "Standard Width Versions Also Planned by New Company." *The Film Daily*, 22 May 1930: 1.

114. As the *Moving Picture World* explained in its December 4, 1926 article "M. H. Hoffman ... The Tiffany Man"

(p. 333), Hoffman took over management of a theater in Massachusetts in 1910. By 1920, he had founded Tiffany Productions, Inc., which over the next few years filmed many of Mae Murray's popular silent films.

115. "Halperins Set on Wide Film." *The Film Daily*, 13 Mar. 1930: 8.

116. "Liberty Co. May Adopt Five-Year Franchise Plan." *The Film Daily*, 4 June 1930: 1, 4.

117. Undated fact sheet in the possession of Venita Halperin titled "Regarding Victor Halperin."

118. *Mother's Millions* briefly became embroiled in a 1931 lawsuit between Liberty Productions and an overseas distributor named Ameranglo. The latter company would feature in Victor's life five years later when it issued *Revolt of the Zombies* overseas.

119. Char. "*The Mad Parade*." *Variety*, 22 Sept. 1931.

120. "Directorial Device Used in New Film." *Los Angeles Times*, 21 Dec. 1930.

121. M.B. "Throbbing Melodrama Unreeled." Rev. of *Ex-Flame*. *Los Angeles Times*, 19 Dec. 1930.

122. "Miniature Reviews: *Ex-Flame*." *Variety*, 28 Jan. 1931.

123. "*Ex-Flame*." *Variety*, 28 Jan. 1931.

124. "*Ex-Flame*." *The Film Daily*, 25 Jan. 1931.

125. "*Ex-Flame*." *Harrison's Reports*, 31 Jan. 1931: 18.

126. "*Ex-Flame*." *Motion Picture Daily*, 27 Jan. 1931: 8.

127. "Norman Kerry to Halperin." *Los Angeles Times*, 6 Sept. 1930.

128. In terms of *Ex-Flame*'s box-office appeal, *Motion Picture Herald* (of February 7, 1931, January 3, 1931, and February 21, 1931 respectively) noted that the film brought acceptable business to the Woods Theater in Chicago, but that it caused disappointing ticket sales for the Orpheum in Los Angeles. For the Earle Theater in Philadelphia, *Ex-Flame* became the lowest-grossing film it had shown in a year.

129. *1930 Motion Picture News Bluebook*. New York: Motion Picture News Inc., 1930.

130. "Hoffman and Gumbin[er] Buy Halperin Share in Liberty." *The Film Daily*, 13 Nov. 1930: 1.

131. As noted in the February 17, 1931, *Motion Picture Daily*, M. H. Hoffman left Liberty himself to pursue a production deal with Columbia Studios.

132. Hoffman forged ahead with Liberty as well, overseeing numerous other films. In 1935, Liberty briefly merged with Monogram, Mascot, and Supreme to form Republic Pictures. After only a few months, Hoffman withdrew Liberty from the conglomerate and again forged ahead. As Chapter Three describes, in 1932 Hoffman was President of the Independent Motion Picture Producers' Association.

133. "Independents to Produce 300 Features, 900 Shorts." *Motion Picture Daily*, 25 Aug. 1931: 1, 8.

134. Churchill, p. 46.

135. Hanna, page number unknown.

136. For information on *White Zombie*'s production, see Chapter Three; for information on its distribution and audience reception, see Chapter Four.

137. Nielsen, p. 8.

138. "Halperins Rent Stage." *Motion Picture Daily*, 28 Oct. 1932: 10.

139. "Halperins to Para." *Motion Picture Daily*, 16 Dec. 1932: 6.

140. For more information on *Supernatural*, see Chapter Five.

141. "Coast Talent Leans Toward Independents." *Motion Picture Daily*, 19 Apr. 1933: 1.

142. "Brock to Make Halperin Story." *The Film Daily*, 20 Feb. 1934: 2.

143. Hanna, page number unknown.

144. *Ibid.*

145. "New Bedford Premiere for *I Conquer the Sea*." *The Hollywood Reporter*, 9 Jan. 1936: 4.

146. Advance notice of *I Conquer the Sea*'s premiere appeared in the *New Bedford Morning Mercury* on 18 Jan. 1936.

147. "Eight Pix Open in NY This Week." *The Hollywood Reporter*, 22 Jan. 1936: 2.

148. R.C. "*I Conquer the Sea* Story of Whalers." (Unsourced review in the Halperin file at the Theater Collection in the New York Public Library.)

149. "*I Conquer the Sea*." *Harrison's Reports*, 25 Jan. 1936: 14.

150. "Story of Whalers, Well Made, Cast." Rev. of *I Conquer the Sea*. *The Hollywood Reporter*, 17 Jan. 1936: 3.

151. "*I Conquer The Sea*." *Variety*, 29 Jan. 1936.

152. "15-Year-Old Sea Yarn Subject of NY Suit on Ownership by Scribe." *Variety*, 5 Dec. 1951: 20.

153. McManus, p. 3.

154. See Chapter Five for a lengthy discussion of *Revolt of the Zombies*' legal problems.

155. Nielsen, p. 8.

156. Halperin, Venita. Letter to Gary D. Rhodes, 27 Mar. 1998.

157. McManus, p. 3.

158. "D'Usseau Sells Original." *The Hollywood Reporter*, 29 June 1936: 2.

159. "Hollywood Production...." *The Hollywood Reporter*, 30 Nov. 1936: 19.

160. Hanna, page number unknown.

161. Barn. "*Nation Aflame*." *Variety*, 7 Apr. 1937: 15.

162. "*Nation Aflame*." *The Film Daily*, 20 Oct. 1937: 6.

163. "KKK Film Premiere." *The Hollywood Reporter*, 13 Oct. 1937: 3.

164. *Motion Picture Herald*, 23 Oct. 1937: 54.

165. Hanna, page number unknown.

166. "Halperin Joins Agency." *The Hollywood Reporter*, 8 Nov. 1938.

167. "Halperin Joins Fine Arts." *The Hollywood Reporter*, 17 June 1938: 1.

168. All information in this paragraph stems from one of Halperin's undated resumes, in the possession of his widow, Mrs. Venita Halperin.

169. *Motion Picture Herald*, 16 Sept. 1939: 62–63.

170. "Producers Pix Signs Hale for Initial Production." *The Hollywood Reporter*, 22 Aug. 1939: 4.

171. "*Ship* on GN Lot." *The Hollywood Reporter*, 31 Aug. 1939: 3.

172. Rhodes, Gary D. Interview with Jacqueline Wells, Apr. 17, 2000.

173. Herb. "*Torture Ship*." *Variety*, 29 Nov. 1939: 14.

174. "*Torture Ship*." *The Film Daily*, 22 Nov. 1939: 6.

175. *Buried Alive* may have been the project mentioned in the April 20, 1933 *New York Herald Tribune* as a Majestic Pictures' property.

176. "Hollywood Production...." *The Hollywood Reporter*, 7 Oct. 1939: 4.

177. "*Buried Alive*." *The Film Daily*, 23 Jan. 1940: 8.

178. "*Buried Alive*." *Variety*, 17 Jan. 1940: 16.

179. Undated *New York Post* review of *Buried Alive* in the Victor Halperin file at the New York Public Library Theater Collection.

180. "PRC's Exploitation *Town* Eases Up to Cameraman." *The Hollywood Reporter*, 12 Dec. 1941: 6.

181. Wear. "*Girl's Town*." *Variety*, 15 Apr. 1942.

182. "*Girl's Town*." *The Film Daily*, 9 Apr. 1942: 4.

183. "*Lone Star Trail*." *Variety*, 8 Sept. 1943: 16.

184. "Rip Snorting Western Packed With Incidents That Will Draw Enthusiastic Response from Kids." Rev. of *The Lone Star Trail*. *The Film Daily*, 2 Sept. 1943.

185. "*The Lone Star Trail*." *The Hollywood Reporter*, 11 June 1943: 3.

186. Ramsaye, Terry, editor. *1944–45 International Motion Picture Almanac*. New York: Quigley, 1945.

187. Untitled, unsourced clipping in the Victor Halperin file in the New York Public Library Theater Collection.

188. *The Hollywood Reporter*, 27 Sept. 1948.

189. Information taken from Halperin's personal resume of 1960, the original of which is in the possession of his widow, Venita Halperin.

190. Wachner, Audrey Kearns, editor. *Motion Picture Production Encyclopedia*. Hollywood, California: The Hollywood Reporter Press, 1951.

191. Halperin, Victor. Undated resume (circa 1950s), the original of which is in the possession of Venita Halperin.

192. "Halperin-Burkett Launch TV Series." *The Hollywood Reporter*. Undated, in the collection of Venita Halperin.

193. "TV Reviews: *Strange Lands and Seven Seas*." *The Hollywood Reporter*, 13 Sept. 1956.

194. Typing style (e.g., use of hyphens and all caps) precisely mimics Victor's typing from the handout "Why This Show Is a Proven Attraction for All Ages of Viewers," a copy of which is in the possession of his widow, Venita Halperin.

195. *Ibid.*

196. Rating sheets in the collection of Venita Halperin.

197. See Appendix O for a list of surviving program synopses.

198. Halperin, Venita. Letter to Gary D. Rhodes, 11 Sept. 1997.

199. Halperin, Venita. Letter to Gary D. Rhodes, 11 Sept. 1997.

200. *Ibid.*

201. Information taken from Halperin's personal resume of 1960, the original of which is in the possession of his widow, Venita Halperin.

202. *Ibid.*

203. *Ibid.*

204. Nielsen, p. 12.

205. Halperin, Venita. Letter to Gary D. Rhodes, 11 Sept. 1997.

206. Halperin, Venita. Letter to Gary D. Rhodes, 27 Apr. 1998.

207. Halperin, Venita. Letter to Gary D. Rhodes, 20 Aug. 1997.

208. Bellamy, Madge. Letter to Victor Halperin, 18 Oct. 1978.

209. Halperin, Venita. Letter to Gary D. Rhodes, 20 Aug. 1997.

210. *Ibid.*

211. Bellamy, Madge. Letter to Venita Halperin, 19 Dec. 1983.

212. Halperin, Venita. Letter to Gary D. Rhodes, 29 Nov. 1996.

213. By suggesting the need to examine Denton's question through the history of film authorship studies, I still acknowledge that our focus is on Victor Halperin and that space alone will not allow for a full engagement with all or even most aspects of such authorship studies.

214. Sarris, Andrew. *The American Cinema: Directors and Directions 1929–1968*. New York: Dutton, 1968.

215. Tourneur, Maurice. "The Director and His Future." *Exhibitors* [sic] *Herald*, 7 July 1923: 218.

216. Barthes, Roland. *Image-Music-Text*. Translation by Stephen Heath. London: Fontana, 1977 (p. 143).

217. Wollen, Peter. *Signs and Meaning in the Cinema*. 3rd Edition. London: Secker and Warburg in association with the British Film Institute, 1972 (p. 96).

218. Senn, Bryan. *Drums of Terror: Voodoo in the Cinema*. Baltimore: Midnight Marquee, 1998. (p. 19)

219. *Ibid.*, pp. 21–22.

220. Senn's text lacks grounding on a few aspects of *White Zombie*'s history, including the unsubstantiated claim that playwright Kenneth Webb sued the Halperin brothers in March 1932, and the claim that one of Arthur Martinelli's last films was *The Devil Bat* (1940), when in fact Martinelli worked on feature films until 1948 and even later worked on at least one industrial film.

221. Ellis, John. "Made in Ealing." *Screen* Volume 16, Issue 1. Spring 1975.

222. Bordwell, David, Janet Staiger, and Kristin Thompson. *The Classical Hollywood Cinema: Film Style and Mode of Production to 1960*. London: Routledge and Kegan Paul, 1985.

223. *Ibid.*, p. xiv.

224. McManus, p. 3.

225. Hanna, page number unknown.

226. For example, see the quotations printed earlier in this chapter from the July 23, 1927 issue of *Harrison's Reports*.

227. See Chapter Five for a thorough discussion of *Supernatural*'s production.

228. See Chapter Five for a discussion of Halperin actively placing Carole Lombard within the composition of a certain scene.

229. Nielsen, p. 6.

230. Denton, page number unknown.

231. *Ibid.*, page number unknown.

Appendix F

1. "Eddie Hough Busy with His New Job in Greenville, S.C." *Motion Picture Herald*, 8 July 1933: 58.

Appendix H

1. "*Zombie* Kidded, But Paradoxical Prov.-Ups." *Variety*, 2 Aug. 1932.

2. *Ibid.*

3. "Comparative Grosses for August." *Variety*, 20 Sept. 1932.

4. Theatre Receipts." *Motion Picture Herald*, 8 Dec. 1931: 51.

5. "*Tomorrow* $5,000 Above in Providence." *Motion Picture Daily*, 17 Feb. 1932: 22.

6. "Mills-*Dragon*, $7,500, *Guilty*, $8,000, OK, Ind." *Variety*, 9 Aug. 1932.

7. "*Dragon* and Mills Bros. Strong Cards." *Motion Picture Daily*, 15 Aug. 1932: 7.

8. "Theatre Receipts." *Motion Picture Herald*, 19 Dec. 1931: 39.

9. "Theatre Receipts." *Motion Picture Herald*, 16 Jan. 1932: 27.

10. "Theatre Receipts." *Motion Picture Herald*, 27 Feb. 1932: 47.

11. "Louisville Looks Up; *Zombie*, $8,000, Nice." *Variety*, 9 Aug. 1932.

12. "*Downstairs* Is Up in Louisville, Does $9,200." *Variety*, 16 Aug. 1932.

13. "Montreal Up Nicely; *Back Alive*, $13,500." *Variety*, 16 Aug. 1932.

14. "Loew's Repeals Palace's Film and Cap's Stage Draw." *Variety*, 23 Aug. 1932.

15. "Comparative Grosses for March." *Variety*, 15 Apr. 1931.

16. *Motion Picture Herald*, 27 Aug. 1932.

17. "*White Zombie* Blasts Records!" *The Hollywood Reporter*, 24 Aug. 1932: 4.

18. "Twin Cities' Best Draw Is *Devil*, *Deep*." *Motion Picture Daily*, 22 Aug. 1932: 8.

19. "*Horsefeathers* Panics New Haven, $13,000." *Variety*, 23 Aug. 1932.

20. "Comparative Grosses for August." *Variety*, 20 Sept. 1932.

21. "Comparative Grosses for February." *Variety*, 18 Mar. 1931.

22. "Columbus Nuts Over Heavy Trade." *Variety*, 30 Aug. 1932.

23. *Ibid.*, p. 9.

24. "Comparative Grosses for March." *Variety*, 15 Apr. 1931.

25. "Mpls. Sizzling with Wow Trade; *Down to Earth*, Dandy $15,000; Marcus Show, *Zombie*, Well-Bally'd." *Variety* 30 Aug. 1932. (On October 25, 1932, *Variety* reported that the city's Aster Theater made only "light" money.)

26. "Minneapolis Leaping." *Variety*, 25 Feb. 1931.

27. "Theatre Receipts." *Motion Picture Herald*, 16 Jan. 1932: 27.

28. "Theatre Receipts." *Motion Picture Herald*, 27 Feb. 1932: 47.

29. "*Speak* High in Very Dull Detroit Week." *Motion Picture Daily*, 16 Sept. 1932: 6.

30. "*Back Street* Tops Detroit in Hold-over [sic]." *Motion Picture Daily*, 19 Sept. 1932: 9.

31. "*Paradise* Ballyhoo $12,000 in Newark." *Variety*, 20 Sept. 1932.

32. "Comparative Grosses for February," p. 27.

33. "Ballyhoo Overcomes Cricks on *Zombie*, $9,000 Best in Pitt." *Variety*, 20 Sept. 1932.

34. *Ibid.*

35. "Pitt Cheery; *Bird* $15,000, *Earth* $4,000." *Variety*, 27 Sept. 1932.

36. "Comparative Grosses for February," p. 27.

37. "*Venus* Heads Lincoln, But Mild on $3,500." *Variety*, 4 Oct. 1932.

38. "*Zombie* Big Buffalo Draw with $11,000." *Motion Picture Daily*, 8 Oct. 1932: 6.

39. *Motion Picture Herald*, 29 Oct. 1932.
40. "Comparative Grosses for February." *Variety*, 18 Mar. 1932.
41. "Theatre Receipts." *Motion Picture Herald*, 26 Dec. 1931: 44.
42. "Storms Dent Denver." *Variety*, 25 Oct. 1932.
43. "Denver Spotty; *Dracula* $14,000—*Lynne* $10,000." *Variety*, 11 Mar. 1931.
44. "Theatre Receipts." *Motion Picture Herald*, 19 Dec. 1931: 39.
45. "Theatre Receipts." *Motion Picture Herald*, 20 Feb. 1932: 42.
46. "Tacoma Reacts to *Head Hunters* Bally, $4200." *Variety*, 15 Nov. 1932.
47. "Chaplin $5,900—Tacoma." *Variety*, 25 Feb. 1931.

Appendix J

1. Foothill Video has continually upgraded their copies of *White Zombie*, and—as a result—they offer in 1999 a version of the film different than copies sold at earlier dates.
2. United American also released cassettes of the same print of *White Zombie* in 1990 and 1991.
3. The date on this Sinister Cinema release is of a rather clean *White Zombie* print sold with a brief and (until-then) unseen 1955 interview with Bela Lugosi; the company had previously old the film on video as taken from a 16mm print since their inception in the mid–1980s. By 1995, Sinister Cinema had begun selling VHS copies of the Roan Group restoration.
4. This Republic Pictures Home Video release is of the colorized *White Zombie* as discussed at length in Chapter Six.

Appendix K

1. For a further investigation of Lugosi's life, see Robert Cremer's *Lugosi: The Man Behind the Cape* (Henry Regnery, 1976) and Gary D. Rhodes' *Lugosi: His Life in Film, on Stage, and in the Hearts of Horror Lovers* (McFarland, 1997).
2. "Muse Expected Her in August." *The New York Amsterdam News*, 27 July 1932.
3. Arlen, David. "White Actors Stand by Muse." *New York Amsterdam News*, 17 Aug. 1932.
4. "Obituaries: Clarence Muse." *Variety*, 24 Oct. 1979.
5. Bellamy, Madge. *A Darling of the Twenties*. New York: Vestal, 1989 (pp. 149–160).
6. *Ibid.*
7. "Obituaries: Robert W. Frazer." *Variety*, 23 Aug. 1944.
8. "Obituaries: John Harron." *Variety*, 29 Nov. 1939.
9. "Obituaries: Brandon Hurst." *Variety*, 23 July 1947.
10. Gresham's other films include *Play Girl* (1932), *I Give My Love* (1934), *Straight Is the Way* (1934), *Night Life of the Gods* (1935), *A Notorious Gentleman* (1935), *Straight from the Heart* (1935).
11. Crimmins also appeared in: *Six Day Bike Rider* (1934), *Diamond Jim* (1935), *George White's 1935 Scandals* (1935), *Mississippi* (1935), *Vagabond Lady* (1935), and *The Jungle Princess* (1936). MacAnann would later appear in *Supernatural* (1933), *We Live Again* (1934), *The Black Room* (1935), and *He Stayed for Breakfast* (1940).

12. Gordon, Richard. "Re Sherman S. Krellberg." Letter to the Editor. *Variety*, Feb. 1979.
13. Pitts, Michael R. *Poverty Row Studios, 1929–1940: An Illustrated History of 53 Independent Film Companies, with a Filmography for Each*. Jefferson, NC: McFarland, 1997 (p. 302).
14. "Obituaries: Dan Crimmins." *Variety*, 17 Jan. 1979.
15. *Hollywood Reporter*, 5 Aug. 1935.
16. *Hollywood Reporter*, 6 Mar. 1934; *Hollywood Reporter*, 25 Mar. 1934.
17. *Hollywood Reporter*, 10 Oct. 1935.
18. "Obituaries: Phil Goldstone." *Variety*, 26 June 1963.
19. "Obituaries: Arthur Martinelli." *Variety*, 20 Sept. 1967.
20. "Meyer Joins MCA." *The Hollywood Reporter*, 19 Nov. 1938: 2.
21. "Obituaries: Abe Meyer." *Variety*, 28 May 1969.
22. "Obituaries: Jack P. Pierce." *Variety*, 31 July 1968.
23. Though Cody seemingly disappeared from the cinema post–1933 (at least in terms of recorded credit), he did work on *Christopher Strong* (1933) and *Son of Kong* (1933).
24. Glazer's only other recorded film credit of the thirties seems to be *They All Come Out* (1939).
25. "Garnett Weston to Para." *The Hollywood Reporter*, 8 June 1932: 7.
26. "Weston with Fox." *The Hollywood Reporter*, 24 June 1932: 2.
27. "Weston's Oriental Yarn." *Variety*, 1 Nov. 1932.
28. B.C. "At the Criterion." *New York Times*, 25 Aug. 1938: 15.
29. Anderson, Isaac. *New York Times*, 9 Apr. 1933: 12.
30. Weston, Garnett. *Murder on Shadow Island*. New York: Farrar, 1933 (p. 141).
31. *New York Times*, 23 June 1935: 12.
32. *Chicago Daily Tribune*, 22 June 1935: 12.
33. *Saturday Review of Literature*, 13 Mar. 1937.
34. *Books*, 21 Mar. 1937: 14.
35. *New Yorker*, 18 Dec. 1943.
36. Quinn, Peter. *Book Week*. 14 May 1944: 2.
37. Weston, *Death Is a Lonely Business*, p. 25.
38. "Obituaries: Kenneth Webb." *Variety*, 23 Mar. 1966.
39. "Obituaries: Pauline Starke." *Variety*, 9 Feb. 1977.
40. Seabrook, William B. Qtd. in "Ending Career Packed with Melodrama." *Everbody's Weekly* in *The Philadelphia Inquirer*, 21 Oct. 1945: 4.
41. "Convert to Paganism." *The Commonweal*, 15 Apr. 1931: 648.
42. Seabrook, William B. *Asylum*. New York: Harcourt, Brace, and Co., 1935 (p. 254).
43. "Ending Career Packed with Melodrama," p. 4.
44. *Ibid.*, p. 4.
45. *Ibid.*, p. 4.
46. "Witchcraft: Its Power in the World Today." *Springfield Republican*, 5 Sept. 1940: 8.
47. Seabrook, William B. Qtd. in "Books: Seabrook's Hell." *Newsweek*, 2 Nov. 1942: 72.
48. Fadiman, Clifton. "Books: Seabrook the Semi-Sinister—Another Family Saga." *The New Yorker*, 31 Oct. 1942: 78.
49. "Books: Seabrook's Hell." *Newsweek*, 2 Nov. 1942: 72.
50. *"No Hiding Place."* *Time*, 16 Nov. 1942: 104.
51. "Ending Career Packed with Melodrama," p. 4.
52. *Ibid.*, p. 4.
53. The use of Seabrook's name as a character was in the

January 30, 1942 episode of *Dark Fantasy*, written by Scott Bishop and entitled "Death Is a Savage Deity." The program originated from WKY in Oklahoma City, but episodes such as this one were broadcast all over the NBC network.

54. See Chapter Six for an in-depth discussion of the merits of the Roan Group restoration.

Index

Numbers in italics denote illustration.